A Reference Publication in Literature
Ronald Gottesman, *Editor*

SOUTHERN LITERATURE, 1968—1975
A Checklist of Scholarship

Compiled by the
Committee on Bibliography
of the
Society for the Study of Southern Literature

Conflated, edited, and supplemented by
Jerry T. Williams

A continuation of
A Bibliographical Guide to the Study of Southern Literature
ed. Louis D. Rubin, Jr.
conflated from the annual checklists
published in the Spring issues of the
Mississippi Quarterly

G. K. HALL & CO., 70 LINCOLN STREET, BOSTON, MASS.

Library of Congress Cataloging in Publication Data

Society for the Study of Southern Literature. Committee
    on Bibliography.
    Southern literature, 1968-1975.

    "A continuation of A bibliographical guide to the
study of Southern literature, ed. Louis D. Rubin, Jr.,
conflated from the annual checklists published in the
spring issues of The Mississippi quarterly."
    Includes index.
    1. American literature--Southern States--Bibliography.
I. Williams, Jerry T. II. Title.
Z1225.S63   [PS261]   016.81   77-15938
ISBN 0-8161-8051-2

This publication is printed on permanent/durable acid-free paper
MANUFACTURED IN THE UNITED STATES OF AMERICA

Dedicated to
the memory of

WALTER PASCHAL REEVES

1917—1976

Contents

PREFACE vii

JOURNAL ABBREVIATIONS ix

I. COLONIAL (1607-1800)

George Alsop, Robert Beverley, James Blair,
    John Botsford, William Byrd I, William
    Byrd II 1

Ebenezer Cooke, Samuel Davies, Thomas
    Atwood Digges 2

Anthony Gavin, John Hammond, Thomas
    Jefferson 3

Richard Lewis, James Madison. 4

Alexander Martin, William Vans Murray,
    William Parks, George Percy, Eliza Lucas
    Pinckney, James Reid, John Smith,
    George Washington 5

George Whitefield, Miscellaneous. 6

II. ANTEBELLUM (1800-1865)

Washington Allston, Joseph Glover Baldwin,
    Albert Taylor Bledsoe, William Wells
    Brown 9

Edward Caledon Bruce, William Alexander
    Caruthers, Thomas Holley Chivers, Joseph
    B. Cobb, John Esten Cooke, Philip
    Pendleton Cooke, Davy Crockett, George
    Washington Parke Custis 10

Jefferson Davis, Frederick Douglass, John
    G. Drayton, William Elliott 11

Charles N. B. Evans, William Cuthbert
    Falkner, George Washington Harris,
    Caroline Lee Hentz, George Frederick
    Holmes, Johnson Jones Hooper. 12

George Moses Horton, Daniel R. Hundley,
    Joseph Holt Ingraham, John Beauchamp
    Jones, John Pendleton Kennedy, Hugh
    Swinton Legaré, James Mathewes Legaré,
    Henry Clay Lewis, Augustus Baldwin
    Longstreet. 13

Alexander McNutt, Charles Noland, Edgar
    Allan Poe 14

Reuben Potter, Irwin Russell, William
    Gilmore Simms 38

John Taylor, William Tappan Thompson,
    Thomas Bangs Thorpe, George Tucker,
    Nathaniel Beverley Tucker 41

Nat Turner, David Walker, William Wirt,
    Miscellaneous 42

III. POSTBELLUM (1865-1920)

James Lane Allen, Sherwood Bonner, James
    Branch Cabell 49

George Washington Cable 52

Charles Waddell Chesnutt. 54

Kate Chopin 55

Samuel Langhorne Clemens. 57

John Brown Gordon Coogler, Harris Dickson,
    Thomas Dixon, Jr., Sarah Anne Dorsey. . . 78

Harry Stillwell Edwards, John Fox, Jr.,
    Charles Gayarré, Ellen Glasgow. 79

Will Harben 80

Corra Harris, Joel Chandler Harris, Robert
    Hamilton Harris 81

Paul Hamilton Hayne, Lafcadio Hearn, James
    Barron Hope, Richard Malcolm Johnston,
    Grace King. 82

Sidney Lanier 83

Walter Malone, George Marion McClellan,
    Mary Noailles Murfree, Thomas Nelson
    Page. 84

Walter Hines Page, William Sydney Porter,
    Opie Read, Amélie Rives 85

Abram Joseph Ryan, C. Alphonso Smith,
    Charles Henry Smith, John Bannister

Contents

Tabb, Henry Timrod, Albion Winegar
Tourgée, William Orrie Tuggle, Joseph
Addison Turner, Booker T. Washington . . . 86

Albery Allson Whitman. 87

Espy W. H. Williams, Miscellaneous 88

IV. CONTEMPORARY (1920-1975)

Edward Abbey, James Agee 91

Conrad Aiken 93

A. R. Ammons 94

Sherwood Anderson, Maya Angelou, Anne W.
Armstrong, James Aswell, John Barth. . . . 95

Hamilton Basso, Barry Benefield, Hal
Bennett, Wendell Berry, Doris Betts,
John Peale Bishop, Marion Cyrenus
Blackman, Maxwell Bodenheim. 99

Arna Bontemps, Cleanth Brooks, Erskine
Caldwell 100

Truman Capote 101

Wilbur Joseph Cash, Fred Chappell, Alice
Moser Claudel, David Cohn, Hubert
Creekmore, Harry Crews, Henry Dalton,
Donald Davidson. 103

Burke Davis, Borden Deal, James Dickey . . .104

Robert Drake, Charles East, Ralph Ellison. .107

John Faulkner. 112

William Faulkner 113

Zelda Sayre Fitzgerald 147

John Gould Fletcher, Shelby Foote. 148

Jesse Hill Ford, Ernest J. Gaines. 149

Frances Gaither, George Garrett, Nikki
Giovanni, Edwin Godsey, Gail Godwin,
Caroline Gordon. 150

William Goyen, Alice Walworth Graham,
Shirley Ann Grau 151

John Graves, Julian Hartridge Green,
Paul Green, John Howard Griffin,
Julian Harris, William Harrison,
Mildred Haun, Lillian Hellman. 152

Dubose Heyward, Chester Himes. 153

Zora Neale Hurston, Mac Hyman,
Randall Jarrell. 154

James Weldon Johnson 155

Madison Jones, Helen Keller, Edward
Kimbrough, Don Lee, Harper Lee 157

Huey P. Long, Andrew Nelson Lytle. 158

David Madden, William March, Carson
McCullers. 159

Harold Grier McCurdy, Ralph McGill,
Henry Louis Mencken. 162

Sara Haardt Mencken, Vassar Miller,
Edwin Mims, Margaret Mitchell. 165

Marion Montgomery, Merrill Moore, Willie
Morris, Albert Murray, Paul Nolan,
Flannery O'Connor. 166

George Marion O'Donnell, Guy Owen, Edd
Winfield Parks, James Robert Peery,
Walker Percy 175

William Alexander Percy. 177

Julia Peterkin, Robert Deane Pharr,
Thomas Hal Phillips, Ovid Williams
Pierce, Katherine Anne Porter. 178

Reynolds Price, John Crowe Ransom. 181

Beatrice Witte Ravenel, Byron Herbert
Reece, Ishmael Reed, Willis Richardson,
Elizabeth Madox Roberts, Robert Rylee,
Sonia Sanchez. 184

Anderson M. Scruggs, James Seay, Mary Lee
Settle, Hubert A. Shands, Lillian Smith,
Elizabeth Spencer, Randall Stewart 185

Thomas Sigismund Stribling, Jesse Stuart,
William Styron 186

Allen Tate 191

Peter Taylor, Jean Toomer. 193

John Donald Wade 196

Alice Walker, Margaret Walker, Richard
Walser, Robert Penn Warren 197

Richard Weaver, Eudora Welty 202

James Whitehead, Sylvia Wilkinson,
Tennessee Williams 207

Calder Willingham, Anne Goodwin Winslow,
Thomas Wolfe 211

Tom Wolfe. 215

Richard Wright 216

Stark Young, Miscellaneous 222

V. GENERAL. 239

Preface

This checklist integrates in a single alphabet the first eight annual bibliographies prepared by the Committee on Bibliography of the Society for the Study of Southern Literature and regularly published in the Spring issues of the *Mississippi Quarterly*. It continues and supplements the information in *A Bibliographical Guide to the Study of Southern Literature*, edited by Louis D. Rubin, Jr. (Baton Rouge: Louisiana State University Press, 1969).

During the period covered by this volume, the late Paschal Reeves (University of Georgia) was chairman and bibliographer from 1968 through 1972, and was succeeded by James E. Kibler, Jr. (also University of Georgia). Other members who have served are Richard E. Amacher (Auburn University), 1968; the late John Q. Anderson (University of Houston), 1968–'73; Jackson R. Bryer (University of Maryland), 1968–'75; A. K. Butterworth, Jr. (University of South Carolina), 1974–'75; Raymond A. Cook (Valdosta State College), 1969–'71; J. Lasley Dameron (Memphis State University), 1970–'75; Maurice Duke (Virginia Commonwealth University), 1969–'75; O. B. Emerson (University of Alabama), 1968–'75; Ruel E. Foster (West Virginia University), 1968–'75; James A. Hart (University of British Columbia), 1968–'75; Bert Hitchcock (Auburn University), 1971–75; Patrick G. Hogan, Jr. (University of Houston), 1969–'71; M. Thomas Inge (Virginia Commonwealth University), 1968–'75; James E. Kibler, Jr. (University of Georgia), 1968–'75; Stephen E. Meats (University of Tampa), 1974–'75; Marion C. Michael (Auburn University [now at Texas Tech University]), 1968–'70; Warren O'Rourke (University of Alabama), 1969; Robert L. Phillips, Jr. (Mississippi State University), 1972–'75; Milton Rickels (University of Southwestern Louisiana), 1968–'75; Beverly Scafidel (University of South Carolina), 1975; Miriam J. Shillingsburg (Mississippi State University), 1973–'75, and Charles S. Watson (University of Alabama), 1968–'75.

From the beginning, brief informative annotations have been provided; in this volume, further cross-references have been inserted to assist the user. Entries from a number of publications not included in the *Mississippi Quarterly* checklists have been added here.

Although for the period it covers this checklist is inclusive to a much greater degree than was Rubin's necessarily more selective *A Bibliographical Guide*, it is not exhaustive; the completeness to which the Committee on Bibliography and the editor aspired has not been possible to achieve, but it is hoped that this conflation will be a useful addition to the instruments being developed, by the Society and others, for the study of Southern literature.

The Committee and the editor are grateful to Mrs. Martha Murphree and Mrs. Mary Ann Benoist for their help in assembling the manuscript.

Journal Abbreviations

Acta Litt Acad Hungaricae	Acta Litteraria Academiae Scientiarum Hungaricae (Budapest)
Af Forum	African Forum: A Quarterly Journal of Contemporary Affairs
Agenda	Agenda
AH	American Heritage
AI	American Imago
AL	American Literature
AlaHQ	Alabama Historical Quarterly
AlaR	Alabama Review
Am-Austriaca	Americana-Austriaca
Am Benedictine Rev	American Benedictine Review
Am Bk Collector	American Book Collector
Americana-Norvegica	Americana-Norvegica
Am Libraries	American Libraries
Am Lit Realism	American Literary Realism, 1870-1910
Am N&Q	American Notes and Queries
Am Schol	American Scholar
Am Speech	American Speech
Am Stud	American Studies
Am Stud in Scand	American Studies in Scandinavia
Am West	American West
Anglia	Anglia
Annali di Ca' Foscari	Annali di Ca' Foscari
Antigonish Rev	Antigonish Review
Antologia Vieussieux	Antologia Vieussieux
Apollo	Apollo
Appal Jour	Appalachian Journal
Appalachian Rev	Appalachian Review
AQ	American Quarterly
AR	Antioch Review
Arcadia	Arcadia
Archiv	Archiv für das Studium der Neueren Sprachen und Literaturen
ArielE	Ariel: A Review of International English Literature
Ark Lib	Arkansas Libraries
ArlQ	Arlington Quarterly
ArQ	Arizona Quarterly
Art Internat'l	Art International
Arts in Soc	Arts in Society
Arts in Virginia	Arts in Virginia
Atl	Atlantic Monthly
Atlanta Journal and Constitution Mag	Atlanta Journal and Constitution Magazine
ATQ	American Transcendental Quarterly
BA	Books Abroad
Bancroftiana	Bancroftiana (University of California)
Barat Rev	Barat Review
BB	Bulletin of Bibliography
BFLS	Bulletin de la Faculté des Lettres de Strasbourg
Bks and Bookmen	Books and Bookmen
Black Acad Rev	Black Academy Review: Quarterly of the Black World
Black Bks Bul	Black Books Bulletin
Black Schol	Black Scholar
Black World	Black World
BNYPL	Bulletin of the New York Public Library
Bookman	Bookman
Books at Iowa	Books at Iowa
Book World	Book World
Boston Univ Jour	Boston University Journal
Boundary 2	Boundary 2: A Journal of Postmodern Literature
Brit Jour of Aes	British Journal of Aesthetics
BSUF	Ball State University Forum
Bul Baud	Bulletin Baudelairien
BuR	Bucknell Review
BYUS	Brigham Young University Studies
Cabellian	The Cabellian: A Journal of the Second American Renaissance
Caliban	Caliban (Toulouse)
CamQ	Cambridge Quarterly
Can Lit	Canadian Literature
Can Rev Bks	Canadian Review of Books
Carleton Misc	Carleton Miscellany
Carrell	The Carrell: Journal of the Friends of the University of Miami (Fla.) Library
Carson-Newman Col Faculty Stud	Carson-Newman College Faculty Studies
Catholic Lib World	Catholic Library World
CE	College English
CEAAN	Center for Editions of American Authors Newsletter (MLA)
CEA Critic	CEA Critic
Centennial Rev	Centennial Review
ChiR	Chicago Review
Chri and Lit	Christianity and Literature
Chri Schol Rev	Christian Scholar's Review (formerly *Gordon Review*)
Cim Rev	Cimarron Review
Cithara	Cithara
Civil War Hist	Civil War History

CL	Comparative Literature	EJ	English Journal
CLA Jour	College Language Association Journal	ELH	Journal of English Literary History
CLS	Comparative Literature Studies	Ellen Glasgow Newsletter	Ellen Glasgow Newsletter
Coll Lit	College Literature	Emporia State Res Stud	Emporia State Research Studies
Colóquio/Letras	Colóquio/Letras	Encounter	Encounter (London)
ColQ	Colorado Quarterly	Eng Lang and Lit	English Language and Litera-
Columbia Forum	Columbia Forum (new series)		ture (Korea University)
Columbia Lib Columns	Columbia Library Columns	Eng Lang Notes	English Language Notes
Comment	Comment	Eng Lit in Transition	English Literature in Transi-
Commentary	Commentary		tion (1880–1920)
Commonwealth	Commonwealth (Richmond)	Eng Quart	English Quarterly
Comunitá	Comunitá (Milan)	Eng Rec	English Record
Concerning Poetry	Concerning Poetry	Eng Stud	English Studies
ConL	Contemporary Literature	Eng Stud in Africa	English Studies in Africa
	(formerly Wisconsin Studies		(Johannesburg)
	in Contemporary Literature)	Epoch	Epoch (Cornell University)
Conn Rev	Connecticut Review	L'Esprit Createur	L'Esprit Createur (Lawrence,
Conradiana	Conradiana: A Journal of		Kansas)
	Joseph Conrad	ESQ	Emerson Society Quarterly
Contemporary Poetry	Contemporary Poetry	Esquire	Esquire
Coranto	Coranto: Journal of the	Essays in Lit	Essays in Literature
	Friends of Libraries	ETC	ETC: A Review of General
	(U. S. C.)		Semantics
Cosmopolitan	Cosmopolitan	ETJ	Educational Theatre Journal
Costerus	Costerus: Essays in English	Explicator	Explicator
	and American Language and	Extrap	Extrapolation
	Literature	Fabula	Fabula
Cresset	Cresset (Valparaiso	Faulkner Concordance	The Faulkner Concordance
	University)	Newsl	Newsletter
CRev Am Stud	Canadian Review of American	FCHQ	Filson Club Historical
	Studies		Quarterly
Crisis	Crisis	FHQ	Florida Historical Quarterly
Critical Inquiry	Critical Inquiry: A Voice	Fiction Internat'le	Fiction Internationale
	for Reasoned Inquiry into	Filología Mod	Filología Moderna (Madrid)
	Significant Creations of	Flannery O'Connor	Flannery O'Connor Bulletin
	the Human Spirit	Bul	
Criticism	Criticism (Wayne State	Forum H	Forum (Houston)
	University)	Forum for Mod Lang	Forum for Modern Language
Critique	Critique: Studies in Modern	Stud	Studies (St. Andrews,
	Fiction		Scotland)
Critique	Critique (Paris)	Four Quarters	Four Quarters
Crit Quart	Critical Quarterly	French Rev	French Review
Crit Rev	Critical Review	Furman Mag	Furman Magazine
Cuad Hisp	Cuadernos Hispanoamericanos	Furman Stud	Furman Studies
	(Madrid)	GaR	Georgia Review
Cweal	Commonweal	Genre	Genre
Daedalus	Daedalus (Proceedings of the	Ger-Am Stud	German-American Studies
	American Academy of Arts	German Quart	German Quarterly
	and Sciences)	Germano-Slavica	Germano-Slavica
Dal Rev	Dalhousie Review	GHQ	Georgia Historical Quarterly
Delta Rev	Delta Review	Gordon Rev	Gordon Review (now Christian
Denver Quart	Denver Quarterly		Scholar's Review)
Descant	Descant	Great Lakes Rev	Great Lakes Review
Diacritics	Diacritics: A Review of	Harper's	Harper's Magazine
	Contemporary Criticism	Hartford Stud in Lit	Hartford Studies in Literature
Dickens Stud	Dickens Studies Newsletter	Harvard Lib Bul	Harvard Library Bulletin
Newsletter		Hasifrut	Hasifrut: Quarterly for the
Dickensian	Dickensian		Study of Literature
Diliman Rev	Diliman Review (Quezon City)	Hebrew Univ Stud in	Hebrew University Studies in
Dissent	Dissent	Lit	Literature
Drama & Theatre	Drama and Theatre (formerly	Hemingway Notes	Hemingway Notes
	First Stage [Purdue	Hisp Mod	Hispánica Moderna
	University])	Hist Mag of the Prot	Historical Magazine of the
DramaR	Drama Review	Epis Ch	Protestant Episcopal Church
DuR	Duquesne Review	HLQ	Huntington Library Quarterly
Durham Univ Jour	Durham University Journal	Hollins Critic	Hollins Critic
EA	Etudes Anglaises	HudR	Hudson Review
Early Am Lit	Early American Literature	Humanitas	Humanitas (Brescia)
Edda	Edda		
EIC	Essays in Criticism (Oxford)		

Hungarian Stud in Eng	Hungarian Studies in English (L. Kossuth University, Debrecen)
I Eng Yearbk	Iowa English Bulletin: Yearbook
Illinois Quart	Illinois Quarterly
Independent Shavian	Independent Shavian
Indian Jour of Am Stud	Indian Journal of American Studies
Indian Jour of Eng Stud	Indian Journal of English Studies
Internat'l Fiction Rev	International Fiction Review
In Touch	In Touch
Iowa Rev	Iowa Review
Iowa State Jour of Research	Iowa State Journal of Research
ItQ	Italian Quarterly
Jack London Newsl	Jack London Newsletter
JAF	Journal of American Folklore
Jahrbuch des Wiener Goethe-Vereins	Jahrbuch des Wiener Goethe-Vereins
Jahrbuch für Amerikastudien	Jahrbuch für Amerikastudien
JHI	Journal of the History of Ideas
JMiH	Journal of Mississippi History
JNH	Journal of Negro History
Jour Am Hist	Journal of American History
Jour Am Stud	Journal of American Studies
Jour of Aesthetics and Art Crit	Journal of Aesthetics and Art Criticism
Jour of Black Stud	Journal of Black Studies
Jour of Gen Ed	Journal of General Education
Jour of Hist Stud	Journal of Historical Studies
Jour of Mod Lit	Journal of Modern Literature
Jour of Narrative Tech	Journal of Narrative Technique
Jour of Pop Culture	Journal of Popular Culture
Jour of Psych	Journal of Psychology
Jour of Religious Thought	Journal of Religious Thought
Jour of Spanish Stud	Journal of Spanish Studies
Jour of the Karnitak Univ: Humanities	Journal of the Karnitak University: Humanities
Jour of the Ohio Folklore Soc	Journal of the Ohio Folklore Society
Jour of the Rutgers Univ Lib	Journal of the Rutgers University Library
JR	Journal of Religion
JSH	Journal of Southern History
K & L	Kunst und Literatur
Kalki	Kalki: Studies in James Branch Cabell
Kansas Quart	Kansas Quarterly
KHSR	Kentucky Historical Society Register
KR	Kenyon Review
Ky Folklore Record	Kentucky Folklore Record
Ky Romance Quart	Kentucky Romance Quarterly
La Hist	Louisiana History
Lang and Style	Language and Style
La Stud	Louisiana Studies
Laurel Rev	Laurel Review
Lettres Romanes	Les Lettres Romanes
Letture	Letture
Lib Chron	Library Chronicle (University of Pennsylvania)
Lib Chron of the Univ of Texas	Library Chronicle of the University of Texas
Lib Notes	Library Notes
Lincoln Herald	Lincoln Herald
Listener	Listener
Listening	Listening
Lit and Ideology	Literature and Ideology
Lit and Psych	Literature and Psychology
Lit/Film Quart	Literature/Film Quarterly
Lit Half-Yearly	Literary Half-Yearly
Literary Criterion	Literary Criterion (University of Mysore, India)
Lit Rev	Literary Review (Fairleigh Dickinson University)
Lock Haven Rev	Lock Haven Review (Lock Haven State College, Pa.)
London Mag	London Magazine
LWU	Literatur in Wissenschaft und Unterricht (Kiel)
Mankato State Coll Stud	Mankato State College Studies
MarkR	Markham Review
Mary Wollstonecraft Jour	Mary Wollstonecraft Journal
Mary Wollstonecraft Newsletter	Mary Wollstonecraft Newsletter
Mass Rev	Massachusetts Review
Mass Stud in Eng	Massachusetts Studies in English
McNeese Rev	McNeese Review
Medit Rev	Mediterranean Review
Menckeniana	Menckeniana
Merkur	Merkur
MFS	Modern Fiction Studies
MHM	Maryland Historical Magazine
Mich Academician	Michigan Academician (supersedes *Papers of the Michigan Academy of Arts, Sciences, and Letters*)
Mich Quart Rev	Michigan Quarterly Review
Midcontinent Am Stud Jour	Midcontinent American Studies Journal
Mid-South Folk	Mid-South Folklore
Midstream	Midstream
Midwest Quart	Midwest Quarterly
Minn Rev	Minnesota Review
MissFR	Mississippi Folklore Register
Mississippi Rev	Mississippi Review
Missouri Hist Rev	Missouri Historical Review
Missouri Hist Soc Bul	Missouri Historical Society Bulletin
Miss Quart	Mississippi Quarterly
MLQ	Modern Language Quarterly
Mod Age	Modern Age
Mod Drama	Modern Drama
Mod Lang Stud	Modern Language Studies
Mod Occasions	Modern Occasions
Mod Poetry Stud	Modern Poetry Studies
Mod Rev	Modern Review
Mod Språk	Moderna Språk
Moreana	Moreana (Angers)
Mosaic	Mosaic: A Journal for the Comparative Study of Literature and Ideas
MP	Modern Philology
MSS	Manuscripts
MTJ	Mark Twain Journal
Music and Letters	Music and Letters (London)
MVC Bul	Missouri Valley Collections Bulletin, John Willard Brister Library, Memphis State University
NALF	Negro American Literature Forum

Names	Names	PQ	Philological Quarterly
N & Q	Notes and Queries	PR	Partisan Review
Nassau Rev	Nassau Review	*Prés Af*	Presénce Africaine
Nath Hawthorne Jour	Nathaniel Hawthorne Journal	*Proc of Names Inst*	Proceedings of the Names Institute
Nation	Nation		
Nature Stud	Nature Studies	*Proc of the Am Anti-quarian Soc*	Proceedings of the American Antiquarian Society
NCarF	North Carolina Folklore		
NCF	Nineteenth-Century Fiction	*Proc of the Gulf Coast Hist and Humanities Conf*	Proceedings of the Gulf Coast History and Humanities Conference
NCHR	North Carolina Historical Review		
NConL	Notes on Contemporary Literature	*Proof*	Proof: Yearbook of American Bibliographical and Textual Studies
NDQ	North Dakota Quarterly		
Negro Digest	Negro Digest	*Prose*	Prose
Negro Hist Bul	Negro History Bulletin	*PrS*	Prairie Schooner
NEQ	New England Quarterly	*Psych Today*	Psychology Today
Neueren Sprachen	Die Neueren Sprachen	*PsyR*	Psychology Review
New Dominion Life Style	New Dominion Life Style	*Pub of Am Dialect Soc*	Publications of the American Dialect Society
New England Galaxy	New England Galaxy	PULC	Princeton University Library Chronicle
New Letters	New Letters (formerly *University Review*)		
New Lit Hist	New Literary History	PW	Publishers' Weekly
New Orleans Rev	New Orleans Review	QJLC	Quarterly Journal of the Library of Congress
New Rep	New Republic		
Newsweek	Newsweek	QJS	Quarterly Journal of Speech
New Yorker	New Yorker	*Quadrant*	Quadrant: An Australian Bi-monthly
North Am Rev	North American Review		
Northwest Rev	Northwest Review	*Quinzaine Littéraire*	Quinzaine Littéraire
Notes on Miss Writers	Notes on Mississippi Writers	RALS	Resources for American Literary Studies
Notre Dame Eng Jour	Notre Dame English Journal		
Novel	Novel: A Forum on Fiction (Brown University)	*Ramparts*	Ramparts
		RANAM	Recherches Anglaises et Américaines
NRF	Nouvelle Revue Française		
Nuova Antologia	Nuova Antologia	*Re:A&L*	Re: Arts and Letters
NYRB	New York Review of Books	*Ren 2*	Renaissance 2: A Journal of Afro-American Studies (Yale)
NYTBR	New York Times Book Review		
NY Times	New York Times		
Obsidian	Obsidian	*Renascence*	Renascence
Occasional Rev	Occasional Revue	*Rendezvous*	Rendezvous: Journal of Arts and Letters
Ohio Hist	Ohio History		
Ohio Rev	Ohio Review (formerly *Ohio University Review*)	*Research Stud*	Research Studies (Washington State University)
Ohio Univ Rev	Ohio University Review	*Rev Belge de Philologie et d'Histoire*	Revue Belge de Philologie et d'Histoire
Old Northwest	The Old Northwest: A Journal of Regional Life and Letters		
		Rev d'Esthétique	La Revue d'Esthétique
Pacific Coast Phil	Pacific Coast Philology	*Rev d'Histoire Littéraire*	Revue d'Histoire Littéraire de la France
Papeles de Son Armadans	Papeles de Son Armadans (Mallorca)	*Rev de Litt Comp*	Revue de Littérature Comparée
Papers on Lang and Lit	Papers on Language and Literature	*Rev Nacional de Cultura*	Revista Nacional de Cultura (Venezuela)
Paris Rev	Paris Review	*Richmond Mercury Book Review*	The Richmond Mercury Book Review
Parnassus	Parnassus: Poetry in Review		
PBSA	Papers of the Bibliographical Society of America	*Richmond Times-Dispatch*	Richmond Times-Dispatch
Pembroke Mag	Pembroke Magazine	RLM	La Revue des Lettres Modernes
Person	The Personalist		
Phylon	Phylon	RLMC	Rivista di Letteratura Moderne e Comparate (Firenze)
Players	Players: Magazine of American Theatre		
		RLV	Revue des Langues Vivantes
PMASAL	Publications of the Michigan Academy of Arts, Sciences, and Letters	*Rocky Mt MLA Bul*	Rocky Mountain Modern Language Association Bulletin
PMLA	Publications of the Modern Language Association	*Romance Notes*	Romance Notes (University of North Carolina)
Poe Newsletter	Poe Newsletter	*Romanian Rev*	Romanian Review
Poe Stud	Poe Studies (formerly *Poe Newsletter*)	*Romanic Rev*	Romanic Review
		Roots	Roots (Houston, Texas)
Poet and Critic	Poet and Critic	RTE	Research in the Teaching of English
Poetica	Poetica	*Russ Rev*	Russian Review

SA	Studi Americani (Roma)
SAB	South Atlantic Bulletin
Sahara	Sahara
Salmagundi	Salmagundi
Sandlapper	Sandlapper
SAQ	South Atlantic Quarterly
Satire Newsl (SNL)	Satire Newsletter
SatR	Saturday Review
SB	Studies in Bibliography: Papers of the Bibliographical Society of the University of Virginia
SBHC	Studies in Browning and His Circle
SBL	Studies in Black Literature
Scand S	Scandinavian Studies
SCHM	South Carolina Historical Magazine
Sci Fic Stud	Science Fiction Studies
Scriblerian	The Scriblerian: A Newsletter Devoted to Pope, Swift, and Their Circle
Semiotica	Semiotica: Revue Publiée par l'Association Internationale de Sémiotique
SFQ	Southern Folklore Quarterly
Shaw Rev	Shaw Review
Shen	Shenandoah
SHQ	Southwestern Historical Quarterly
SHR	Southern Humanities Review
Sigma	Sigma: Revista Trimestrale di Letteratura (Turin)
Sin Nombre	Sin Nombre (Puerto Rico)
SLI	Studies in the Literary Imagination
SoCarRev	South Carolina Review
So Lit Jour	Southern Literary Journal
So Quart	Southern Quarterly
So Speech Comm Jour	Southern Speech Communication Journal (formerly Southern Speech Journal)
So Speech Jour	Southern Speech Journal (now Southern Speech Communication Journal)
Sou Central Bul	South Central Bulletin
Sou Dakota Rev	South Dakota Review
Soundings	Soundings: A Journal of Interdisciplinary Studies (formerly Christian Scholar)
SouR	Southern Review
Southern Rev (SnRev)	Southern Review (Adelaide)
Sov Lit	Soviet Literature
SP	Studies in Philology
Spec	Spectator
Spectrum	Spectrum
Sp Monographs	Speech Monographs
SR	Sewanee Review
SSC Rev	Shippensburg State College Review
Steinbeck Quart	Steinbeck Quarterly
St. Louis Univ Research Jour	St. Louis University Research Journal
Studia Neophilologica	Studia Neophilologica
Studies by Members of SCMLA (So Central Bul)	Studies by Members of SCMLA (South Central Bulletin)
Stud in Am F	Studies in American Fiction
Stud in Am Humor	Studies in American Humor
Stud in Eng Lit	Studies in English Literature (Japan)
Stud in Romanticism	Studies in Romanticism
Stud in the Novel	Studies in the Novel
Stud in the Twentieth Cent	Studies in the Twentieth Century
Stud SF	Studies in Short Fiction
Style	Style (University of Arkansas)
SWR	Southwest Review
TCL	Twentieth Century Literature
Tel Quel	Tel Quel
Tenn Hist Quart	Tennessee Historical Quarterly
Tenn Poetry Jour	Tennessee Poetry Journal
Tenn Stud in Lit	Tennessee Studies in Literature
Tex Quart	Texas Quarterly
Tex Stud in Lit and Lang	Texas Studies in Literature and Language
TFSB	Tennessee Folklore Society Bulletin
Theatre Annual	Theatre Annual
Theoria	Theoria: A Journal of Studies in the Arts, Humanities and Social Sciences
Thought	Thought
Time	Time
TLS	[London] Times Literary Supplement
Topic	Topic (Washington and Jefferson College)
Tri-Quart	Tri-Quarterly (Evanston, Illinois)
Tulane Stud in Eng	Tulane Studies in English
Twentieth Century Stud	Twentieth Century Studies
UHQ	Utah Historical Quarterly
Unisa Eng Stud	Unisa English Studies
Univ Bookman	University Bookman
Univ Col Quart	University College Quarterly
Univ of Miss Stud in English	University of Mississippi Studies in English
Univ of Portland Rev	University of Portland Review
Univ of Windsor Rev	University of Windsor Review
Univ Rev	University Review
UTQ	University of Toronto Quarterly
Va Cavalcade	Virginia Cavalcade
Vanderbilt Alumnus	Vanderbilt Alumnus
Ventures	Ventures: Magazine of the Yale Graduate School
VMHB	Virginia Magazine of History and Biography
VQR	Virginia Quarterly Review
A Wake Newslitter	A Wake Newslitter
WAL	Western American Literature
Walt Whit Rev	Walt Whitman Review
Weimarer Beiträge	Weimarer Beiträge
West Va Univ Bul: Phil Papers	West Virginia University Bulletin: Philological Papers
WF	Western Folklore
WHR	Western Humanities Review
Wichita State Univ Bul	Wichita State University Bulletin
WMQ	William and Mary Quarterly
WVH	West Virginia History
XUS	Xavier University Studies

YCGL	Yearbook of Comparative and General Literature	*YULG*	Yale University Library Gazette
Yearbok of Eng Stud	Yearbook of English Studies	*ZAA*	Zeitschrift für Anglistik und Amerikanistik (East Berlin)
YR	Yale Review		

I. Colonial (1607–1800)

[ALSOP, GEORGE] Wardenaar, Leslie A. "Humor in the Colonial Promotional Tract: Topics and Techniques." *Early Am Lit*, 9 (Winter 1975), 286–300.
Treats exaggeration of Indian crudities which poke fun at English gullibility.

[BEVERLEY, ROBERT] Hawke, David F., ed. *The History and Present State of Virginia: A Selection*, by Robert Beverley. Indianapolis: Bobbs-Merrill, 1971.
A slightly abridged edition of the 1705 *History* with an introduction to the book as "one of the liveliest, wittiest, and best written accounts we have in colonial America."

[BLAIR, JAMES] Bain, Robert. "A Note on James Blair and the Southern Plain Style." *So Lit Jour*, 4 (Fall 1971), 68–73.
Blair's stylistic theory and practice in his sermons and in *The Present State of Virginia and the College* are a plain way of writing, a style that did not die with Jefferson and Madison but persisted in the works of a great many writers, especially those of the New South.

_____. "The Composition and Publication of *The Present State of Virginia and the College*." *Early Am Lit*, 6 (Spring 1971), 31–54.
Traces the events involved in the preparation and publication of *The Present State of Virginia and the College*.

_____. See MISCELLANEOUS (Colonial--2nd Bain entry).

Rouse, Parke, Jr. *James Blair, King-Maker of Virginia*. Chapel Hill: Univ of North Carolina Press, 1971.
A biography.

_____. "James Blair of Virginia." *Hist Mag of the Prot Epis Ch*, 43 (June 1974), 189–193.
A brief overview of Blair's life.

[BOTSFORD, JOHN] Kable, William. "Addenda to Wright: Botsford's *The Spiritual Voyage*." *PBSA*, 65 (1st Qtr. 1971), 72–74.
An account of the first work of prose fiction written and published in South Carolina.

[BYRD, WILLIAM I] Marambaud, Pierre. "Colonel William Byrd I: A Fortune Founded on Smoke." *VMHB*, 82 (October 1974), 430–457.

A study of, and quotations from, Byrd's business letters.

_____. William Byrd I: A Young Virginia Planter in the 1670's." *VMHB*, 81 (April 1973), 131–150.
Traces Byrd's movements and activities during the decade in question.

[BYRD, WILLIAM II] Arner, Robert D. "Westover and the Wilderness: William Byrd's Images of Virginia." *So Lit Jour*, 7 (Spring 1975), 105–123.
In his writings Byrd used the pastoral, the epic, and the romance in an attempt to establish Virginia's ties with the civilized and cultivated world of England.

Beatty, Richmond C. *William Byrd of Westover*, ed. M. Thomas Inge. Hamden, Conn.: Archon, 1970.
Reprints the 1932 biography, with a new preface summarizing the scholarship since 1932 and an annotated bibliography by the editor.

Berger, Arthur A. See GENERAL.

Core, George. "*The Prose Work of William Byrd of Westover: Narratives of a Colonial Virginian*, ed. Louis B. Wright." *ArlQ*, 2 (Summer 1969), 154–157.
An essay-review which maintains that as a result of Wright's labor of over thirty years "Byrd's reputation as a man of letters may now be coming into the full bloom of its beauty and the full vigor of its strength."

_____. "Two Views of Colonel William Byrd." *So Lit Jour*, 4 (Spring 1972), 117–121.
Pierre Marambaud's biography of Byrd (*William Byrd of Westover, 1674–1744*) is more historical than literary. Beatty's biography (*William Byrd of Westover*) is written with "an idiomatic flair that subtly echoes Byrd's own best style" and bears re-reading for its distinguished prose.

Cutting, Rose Marie. "America Discovers Its Literary Past: Early American Literature in Nineteenth-Century Anthologies." *Early Am Lit*, 9 (Winter 1975), 226–251.
This discussion of nineteenth-century anthologies includes some commentary on the Duyckincks' remarks on William Byrd in their *Cyclopedia*.

Davis, Richard B. "William Byrd: Taste and Tolerance," in *Major Writers of Early American Literature*, ed. Everett Emerson. Madison: Univ. of Wisconsin Press, 1972.
   An examination of Byrd's life and writings, against the intellectual milieu of his time, characterized by a union of "wit and utility."

Dolmetsch, Carl R. "William Byrd of Westover." *EA*, 27 (July-September 1974), 320-323.
   A review-essay of Pierre Marambaud's biograraphy of Byrd, arguing that Byrd's writings deserve further study as literature, not just as documents.

_____. "William Byrd II: The Augustan Writer as 'Exile' in His Own Country." *VQR*, 48 (Winter 1972), 145-149.
   An essay-review of Pierre Marambaud's book *William Byrd of Westover, 1674-1744*, the first new biography since Beatty's forty years ago. Updates our knowledge of Byrd; rescues him from antiquarians, and establishes his claims to our attention as a belletrist.

_____. "William Byrd II: Comic Dramatist." *Early Am Lit*, 6 (Spring 1971), 18-30.
   Examines the possibility that Byrd may have had a hand in the authorship of Colley Cibber's *The Careless Husband*.

Hatch, Alden. *The Byrds of Virginia: An American Dynasty, 1670 to the Present*. New York: Holt, Rinehart & Winston, 1969.
   Includes a brief biography (121 pages) of William Byrd II.

Helmcke, Hans. See GENERAL.

Marambaud, Pierre. *William Byrd of Westover, 1674-1744*. Charlottesville: Univ Press of Virginia, 1971.
   The first new biography of Byrd since Beatty's forty years ago. Contains extensive critical evaluations.

_____. "William Byrd of Westover: Cavalier, Diarist, and Chronicler." *VMHB*, 78 (April 1970), 144-183.
   A general article, carefully documented, about Byrd's contributions as a writer.

Parramore, T. C. See MISCELLANEOUS (Colonial).

Rubin, Louis D., Jr. See GENERAL--4th Rubin entry.

Simpson, Lewis P. "William Byrd and the South." *Early Am Lit*, 7 (Fall 1972), 187-195.
   An essay-review of Pierre Marambaud's *William Byrd of Westover, 1674-1744*.

[COOKE, EBENEZER] Arner, Robert D. *"Clio's* Rhimes: History and Satire in Ebenezer Cooke's *History of Bacon's Rebellion." So Lit Jour*, 6 (Spring 1974), 91-106.
   Cooke's *History* has a double focus with each image being related to the other by "the attitude of his persona."

_____. "Ebenezer Cooke: Satire in the Colonial South." *So Lit Jour*, 8 (Fall 1975), 153-164.

An essay-review of *Ebenezer Cooke: The Sot-Weed Canon*, by Edward H. Cohen; Cohen is "more concerned with consolidating what was already known about Cooke than with advancing our understanding of his poetry and its place in an American and distinctly Southern literary tradition."

_____. "Ebenezer Cooke's *The Sot-Weed Factor*: The Structure of Satire." *So Lit Jour*, 4 (Fall 1971), 33-47.
   The Sot-Weed Factor is richer and more complex than is commonly supposed.

_____. "Ebenezer Cooke's *Sotweed Redivivus*: Satire in the Horatian Mode." *Miss Quart*, 28 (Fall 1975), 489-496.
   Analysis of Cooke's poem in terms of the influence of Horace.

Cohen, Edward H. *Ebenezer Cooke: The Sot-Weed Canon*. Athens: Univ of Georgia Press, 1975.
   A biographical-critical commentary on the life and burlesque poetry of the colonial satirist, lawyer, and poet-laureate of Maryland.

_____. "The Elegies of Ebenezer Cooke." *Early Am Lit*, 4, no. 2 (1969), 49-72.
   Cooke's four elegies, traditional in form, are valuable for what they reveal about Cooke himself.

_____. "The 'Second Edition' of *The Sot-Weed Factor." AL*, 42 (November 1970), 289-303.
   Argues, from a reading of Cooke MSS, that a second edition of *The Sot-Weed Factor*, although never located, may very well have existed.

Diser, Philip E. "The Historical Ebenezer Cooke." *Critique*. 10, no. 3 (1968), 48-59.
   Relates Cooke, a Maryland poet, to John Barth's *The Sot-Weed Factor*.

[DAVIES, SAMUEL] Davis, Richard B., ed. *Collected Poems of Samuel Davies, 1723-1761*. Gainesville, Fla.: Scholars' Facsimiles and Reprints, 1968.
   Facsimiles of Davies' one published volume of poetry and texts of some other poems.

Dolmetsch, Carl R. "The Apostle as Southerner." *So Lit Jour*, 4 (Fall 1971), 74-82.
   An essay-review of *Samuel Davies: Apostle of Dissent in Colonial Virginia*, by George William Pilcher--a long-awaited biography that rescues this "Presbyterian Apostle to Virginia" from obscurity.

Larson, Barbara A. "Samuel Davies and the Rhetoric of the New Light." *Sp Monographs*, 38 (August 1971), 207-216.
   Discusses Davies' sermons as they reflected New Light philosophy.

Pilcher, George William. *Samuel Davies: Apostle of Dissent in Colonial Virginia*. Knoxville: Univ of Tennessee Press, 1971.
   A biography of the poet, pamphleteer, sermon author, and hymn writer active in Virginia during the Great Awakening.

[DIGGES, THOMAS ATWOOD] Elias, Robert H., and Michael N. Stanton. "Thomas Atwood Digges and

Adventures of Alonso: Evidence from Robert Southey." *AL*, 44 (March 1972), 118-122.
   Cites evidence to prove that Digges is the author of *Adventures of Alonso*.

[GAVIN, ANTHONY] Gundersen, Joan R. "Anthony Gavin's *A Master-Key to Popery*: A Virginia Parson's Best Seller." *VMHB*, 82 (January 1974), 39-46.
   Contains comments on the book and biographical information about the author.

[HAMMOND, JOHN] Arner, Robert D. "A Note on John Hammond's *Leah and Rachel*." *So Lit Jour*, 6 (Fall 1973), 77-80.
   Jacob's story furnishes parallels to the colonial experience.

[JEFFERSON, THOMAS] Adair, Douglass. See MISCELLANEOUS (Colonial).

Beloff, Max. "A 'Founding Father': The Sally Hemings Affair." *Encounter*, 43 (September 1974), 52-56.
   This essay-review of Fawn Brodie's *Thomas Jefferson: An Intimate Portrait* explores Jefferson's attitudes toward women, race, and slavery.

Benson, Randolph. *Thomas Jefferson as Social Scientist*. Cranbury, N. J.: Fairleigh Dickinson Univ Press, 1971.
   A study of Jefferson's social thought which argues that he was a proto-sociologist whose work has strong contemporary relevance to modern problems.

Berkhofer, Robert F., Jr. "Jefferson, the Ordinance of 1784, and the Origins of the American Territorial System." *WMQ*, 29 (April 1972), 231-262.
   Challenges the role usually attributed to Jefferson in the composition of the Ordinance of 1784.

Binger, Carl. *Thomas Jefferson: A Well-Tempered Mind*. New York: Norton, 1970.
   An analysis of Jefferson's mind by a psychiatrist who finds that Jefferson's inner harmony and reconciliation of the masculine and feminine opposites released his singular creativeness.

Boyd, Julian P. "Jefferson's Expression of the American Mind." *VQR*, 50 (Autumn 1974), 538-562.
   An account of Jefferson's preparation for statesmanship which enabled him to speak out in 1774 on the question of constitutional rights.

Brent, Robert. "Puncturing Some Jeffersonian Mythology." *So Quart*, 6 (January 1968), 175-190.
   Jefferson did not believe in every man's right to vote nor in an unqualified states-rights philosophy.

Briceland, A. V. See MISCELLANEOUS (Antebellum).

Brodie, Fawn M. "The Great Jefferson Taboo." *AH*, 23 (June 1972), 48-57; 97-100.
   Discusses the possibility that Jefferson fathered children by his slave woman Sally Hemings.

_____. *Thomas Jefferson: An Intimate Portrait*. New York: Norton, 1974.

   A biography of Jefferson emphasizing the Sally Hemings story.

Cohen, William. "Thomas Jefferson and the Problem of Slavery." *Jour Am Hist*, 56 (December 1969), 503-527.
   Discusses the paradox of Jefferson's defending freedom and holding slaves at the same time, and concludes that this paradox arose from a complex of factors: his belief in Negro inferiority, a societal environment which took slavery for granted, and his ownership of 10,000 acres and 200 slaves.

Cooke, J. W. "Jefferson on Liberty." *JHI*, 34 (October-December 1973), 563-576.
   Seeks to define Jefferson's concept of liberty.

Cox, R. Merritt. "Thomas Jefferson and Spanish: 'To Every Inhabitant Who Means to Look Beyond the Limits of His Farm.'" *Romance Notes*, 14 (Autumn 1972), 116-121.
   Deals with Jefferson's efforts to encourage the study of the Spanish language.

Davis, Richard B. "Our Thomas Jefferson." *So Lit Jour*, 3 (Spring 1971), 120-124.
   An essay-review of two biographies that are "significant contributions" toward painting "a complete portrait" of Jefferson. These are *Jefferson the President, First Term 1801-1805*, by Dumas Malone; and *Thomas Jefferson: A Well-Tempered Mind*, by Carl Binger. The reviewer discusses a third book on Jefferson published in 1970, "our best one-volume biography," *Thomas Jefferson and the New Nation*, by Merrill D. Peterson.

_____. See MISCELLANEOUS (Colonial--1st and 3rd Davis entries).

Farber, J. Z., photographs, and W. D. Garrett, text. *Thomas Jefferson Redivivus*. Barre, Mass.: Barre Publishers, 1971.
   A photo-biography of Jefferson combining Farber's photographs with extracts from Jefferson's writings and editorial comment by Garrett.

Farrison, W. Edward. See BROWN, WILLIAM WELLS (Antebellum--1st Farrison entry).

Gittleman, Edwin. "Jefferson's 'Slave Narrative': The Declaration of Independence as a Literary Text." *Early Am Lit*, 8 (Winter 1974), 239-256.
   Discusses the *Declaration* as a basic non-fiction prose writing worthy of literary analysis.

Goff, Frederick R. "Jefferson the Book Collector." *QJLC*, 29 (January 1972), 32-47.
   Deals with the sources and kinds of books Jefferson collected.

Hay, Robert P. "The Glorious Departure of the American Patriarchs: Contemporary Reactions to the Deaths of Jefferson and Adams." *JSH*, 35 (November 1969), 543-555.
   Deals with national reaction to the deaths of Jefferson and Adams.

Libman, Valentina. See GENERAL.

Lynd, Staughton. "Beard, Jefferson and the Tree of Liberty." *Mid-Cont Am Stud Jour*, 9 (Spring 1968), 8-22.
    Charles Beard's misunderstanding of the Constitution resulted from his acceptance of "an error in Jefferson's perception of his own time."

Malone, Dumas. "Mr. Jefferson's Private Life." *Proc of the Am Antiquarian Soc*, 84 (1974), 65-72.
    Though it is difficult to prove Jefferson's innocence, it is unlikely that he was the father of Sally Hemings' children.

_____. "Presidential Leadership and National Unity: The Jeffersonian Example." *JSH*, 35 (February 1969), 3-17.
    Considers "the exercise of the presidential office by Jefferson with special reference to certain aspects of this which seem to have relevance today."

Martin, John S. "Rhetoric, Society and Literature in the Age of Jefferson." *Mid-Cont Am Stud Jour*, 9 (Spring 1968), 77-90.
    Defines the change in the idea of rhetoric which occurred in late eighteenth-century America and illustrates the new rhetoric with some examples of imagery, scene, and the impersonal persona from Jefferson's First Inaugural and *Notes*.

McColley, Robert. See MISCELLANEOUS (Colonial).

McLoughlin, William G. "Thomas Jefferson and the Beginning of Cherokee Nationalism, 1806 to 1809." *WMQ*, 32 (October 1975), 547-580.
    Explores the relationship between President Jefferson and the powerful Cherokee nation.

Mintz, Max M. "A Conversation Between Thomas Jefferson and Gouveneur Morris: The Author of the Declaration of Independence and the Penman of the Constitution." *Conn Rev*, 9 (November 1975), 21-26.
    A hypothetical conversation on the philosophy of government on the occasion of Morris' visit to Paris in 1789.

Mirkin, Harris G. "Rebellion, Revolution, and the Constitution: Thomas Jefferson's Theory of Civil Disobedience." *Am Stud*, 13 (Fall 1972), 61-74.
    A presentation and assessment of the place of revolution and rebellion in Jefferson's political theory and rhetoric.

Montgomery, Henry C. "Epicurus at Monticello," in *Classical Studies Presented to Ben Edwin Perry by His Students and Colleagues at the University of Illinois, 1924-1960*. Urbana: Univ of Illinois Press, 1969.
    Deals with Jefferson's Epicurean leanings.

Morse, John T., Jr. *Thomas Jefferson*. Giants of America: Founding Fathers. New Rochelle, N. Y.: Arlington House, 1970.
    Reprints the 1898 edition of this biography.

Peterson, Merrill D. *Thomas Jefferson and the New Nation*. New York: Oxford Univ Press, 1970.
    A biographical examination of Jefferson's life and mind in his private and public lives with emphasis on three themes--democracy, nationality, and enlightenment; includes a chapter on *Notes on the State of Virginia* and a selected bibliography.

Sheehan, Bernard W. "Paradise and the Noble Savage in Jeffersonian Thought." *WMQ*, 26 (July 1969), 327-359.
    Deals with Utopian concepts of the Indian during the Jeffersonian era.

_____. "The Quest for Indian Origins in the Thought of the Jeffersonian Era." *Mid-Cont Am Stud Jour*, 9 (Spring 1968), 34-51.
    A discussion of various theories of the origin of the Indians, with emphasis on Jefferson's own scientific approach and his study of Indian languages.

Skallerup, Harry R. "'For His Excellency Thomas Jefferson, Esq.': The Tale of a Wandering Book." *QJLC*, 31 (1974), 116-121.
    Traces the location of a book owned by Jefferson but not in the Jefferson collection in the Library of Congress.

Stafford, John S. "The Power of Sympathy." *Mid-Cont Am Stud Jour*, 9 (Spring 1968), 52-57.
    Though Jefferson's age was very much a part of the Age of Reason, "sympathy and the heart" were an important part in Jefferson's thinking as well as that of many others.

van Pelt, C. B. "Thomas Jefferson and Maria Cosway." *AH*, 22 (August 1971), 24-29; 102-103.
    Chronicles Jefferson's infatuation, in France in 1786, with Maria Cosway, wife of the artist Richard Cosway.

Yellin, Jean F. See MISCELLANEOUS (Antebellum).

[LEWIS, RICHARD] Lemay, J. A. Leo. "Richard Lewis and Augustan American Poetry." *PMLA*, 83 (March 1968), 80-101.
    A study of the Maryland poet, "the best neoclassic poet of colonial America."

[MADISON, JAMES] Adair, Douglass. See MISCELLANEOUS (Colonial).

Brant, Irving. *The Fourth President: A Life of James Madison*. Indianapolis: Bobbs-Merrill, 1970.
    A one-volume abridgement of Brant's six-volume biography, 1941-1961.

Gay, Sydney H. *James Madison*. Giants of America: Founding Fathers. New Rochelle, N. Y.: Arlington House, 1970.
    Reprints the 1898 edition of this biography.

Ketcham, Ralph. *James Madison: A Biography*. New York: Macmillan, 1971.
    A chronological biography which draws upon source material until recently unavailable.

Mason, Julian. "Madison's August 1791 Letter Praising Freneau." *Early Am Lit*, 9 (Winter 1975), 325-327.
    Prints and comments on this letter.

McColley, Robert. See MISCELLANEOUS (Colonial).

Riemer, Neal. *James Madison*. Great American Thinkers Series. New York: Twayne, 1968.
A biography designed to illuminate Madison as a creative political theorist on the concept of a republican government.

Schultz, Harold S. *James Madison*. Twayne's Rulers and Statesmen of the World Series, no. 13. New York: Twayne, 1970.
A biography with emphasis on Madison's personality, philosophy, strategy, and political theory.

[MARTIN, ALEXANDER] Walser, Richard. "Alexander Martin, Poet." *Early Am Lit*, 6 (Spring 1971), 55-61.
A discussion of the poetry of Alexander Martin (1740-1807), North Carolina governor and senator.

[MURRAY, WILLIAM VANS] Mason, Julian. "William Vans Murray: The Fancy of a Poet." *Early Am Lit*, 6 (Spring 1971), 63-68.
Publication and discussion of two previously unpublished poems by this Maryland poet found in his papers at the Library of Congress.

[PARKS, WILLIAM] Arner, Robert D. "The Short, Happy Life of the Virginia 'Monitor.'" *Early Am Lit*, 7 (Fall 1972), 130-147.
Discusses the *Monitor* essays as a reflection of colonial life.

[PERCY, GEORGE] Barbour, Philip L. "The Honorable George Percy: Premier Chronicler of the First Virginia Voyage." *Early Am Lit*, 6 (Spring 1971), 7-17.
A biographical sketch precedes an examination of Percy's account of the Jamestown colony.

[PINCKNEY, ELIZA LUCAS] Baskett, Sam S. "Eliza Lucas Pinckney: Portrait of an Eighteenth Century American." *SCHM*, 72 (October 1971), 207-219.
Quotations from and a treatment of several excerpts from Mrs. Pinckney's *Letterbook*.

Pinckney, Elise, ed. *The Letterbook of Eliza Lucas Pinckney*. Chapel Hill: Univ of North Carolina Press, 1972.
Title is descriptive.

_____, ed. "Letters of Eliza Lucas Pinckney, 1768-1782." *SCHM*, 76 (1975), 143-170.
An edited transcription of letters owned by the South Carolina Historical Society, with a brief description of the collection.

[REID, JAMES] Davis, Richard B. "James Reid, Colonial Virginia Poet and Moral and Religious Essayist." *VMHB*, 79 (January 1971), 3-19.
Presents a heretofore unknown manuscript and printed materials by Reid.

[SMITH, JOHN] Arner, Robert D. "John Smith, the 'Starving Time,' and the Genesis of Southern Humor: Variation on a Theme." *La Stud*, 12 (Spring 1973), 383-390.
Smith may have invented the original Southwestern humor with its legacy of dark humor.

Bain, Robert. See MISCELLANEOUS (Colonial--2nd Bain entry).

Barbour, Philip L. "Captain John Smith and the London Theatre." *VMHB*, 83 (July 1975), 277-279.
Presents evidence that "some scene or scenes from Smith's life" were presented on the stage of London's Fortune Theatre.

_____. "The Earliest Reconnaissance of the Chesapeake Bay Area: Captain John Smith's Map and Indian Vocabulary," Part I. *VMHB*, 79 (July 1971), 280-302.
A listing of Indian place names recorded by Smith and an investigation of Smith's Indian vocabulary.

_____. "The Earliest Reconnaissance of the Chesapeake Bay Area: Captain John Smith's Map and Indian Vocabulary," Part II. *VMHB*, 80 (January 1972), 21-51.
The second part of a listing of Indian place names recorded by Smith and an investigation of Smith's Indian vocabulary.

_____. "A Note on the Discovery of the Original Will of Captain John Smith: With a Verbatim Transcription." *WMQ*, 25 (1968), 625-628.
Title is descriptive.

Craven, Wesley F. "A New Edition of the Works of Captain John Smith." *WMQ*, 29 (July 1972), 479-486.
An assessment of the publishing history of Smith's works and announcement of plans for a modern edition.

Emerson, Everett H. *Captain John Smith*. Twayne's U. S. Authors Series, no. 177. New York: Twayne, 1971.
The first extensive study of Smith as a writer considered in the context of his own life and the travel-narrative tradition of his time.

Hawke, David F., ed. *Captain John Smith's History of Virginia: A Selection*. Indianapolis: Bobbs-Merrill, 1970.
An abridgement of Smith's writings on Virginia in a modernized text with an introductory appreciation by the editor.

Herbst, Jurgen. "The New Life of Captain John Smith." *Hist Mag of the Prot Epis Ch*, 44 (March 1975), 47-68.
It was his spirit and will "that allowed John Smith to experience growth, rebirth, and regeneration."

Weixlmann, Joseph. See BARTH, JOHN (Contemporary--2nd Weixlmann entry).

[WASHINGTON, GEORGE] Flexner, James T. "I Walk on Untrodden Ground." *AH*, 20 (October 1969), 25ff.
Deals with Washington's early days in the White House.

_____. "Soldier's Return." *AH*, 20 (February 1969), 11ff.
Deals with Washington's return to Mount Vernon after the war.

I. Colonial (1607-1800)

_____. "The President's Progress." _AH_, 20 (June 1969), 73ff.
Deals with Washington's election and inauguration.

_____. "The Trumpet Sounds Again." _AH_, 20 (April 1969), 65-73.
Deals with Washington's reentry into public life following his retirement after the war.

Hay, Robert P. "George Washington: American Moses." _AQ_, 21 (Winter 1969), 780-791.
Discusses ways in which Washington was compared to Moses until late in the nineteenth century.

Lodge, Henry C. _George Washington._ Giants of America: Founding Fathers. New Rochelle, N. Y.: Arlington House, 1970.
Reprints the revised 1898 edition of this biography, two volumes in one.

McColley, Robert. See MISCELLANEOUS (Colonial).

Wagner, Paul R. "Books from the Library of George Washington now in the Princeton University Library." _PULC_, 32 (1971), 111-115.
A listing.

Walne, Peter. "George Washington and the Fairfax Family: Some New Documents." _VMHB_, 77 (October 1969), 441-463.
Reprints hitherto unpublished letters by Washington.

_____, ed. "A Mystery Resolved: George Washington's Letter to Governor Dinwiddie." _VMHB_, 79 (April 1971), 131-144.
This article identifies the sources and locations of scattered pages of a Washington letter first published by Jared Sparks in 1837.

[WHITEFIELD, GEORGE] Davis, William V., ed. _George Whitefield's Journals (1737-1741) to Which Is Prefaced His "Short Account" (1746) and "Further Account" (1747)._ Gainesville, Fla.: Scholars' Facsimiles and Reprints, 1969.
Covers Whitefield's first two visits to America.

Morgan, D. T., Jr. "George Whitefield and the Great Awakening in the Carolinas and Georgia, 1739-1740." _GHQ_, 54 (Winter 1970), 517-539.
Chronicles Whitefield's arrival and influence in the Carolinas and Georgia.

O'Connell, N. J. "George Whitefield and Bethesda Orphan-House." _GHQ_, 54 (Spring 1970), 40-62.
Chronicles Whitefield's efforts in establishing the Georgia orphanage, emphasizing his possible motives for this endeavor.

[MISCELLANEOUS] Adair, Douglass. _Fame and the Founding Fathers: Essays by Douglass Adair_, ed. Trevor Colburn. New York: Norton, 1974.
Two essays treat Madison, and "The Jefferson Scandals" argues that Jefferson was not the father of Sally Hemings' children.

Bain, Robert A. "Some Maryland Muses." _So Lit Jour_, 5 (Spring 1973), 124-130.

An essay-review of _Men of Letters in Colonial Maryland_, by J. A. Leo Lemay, which contends that this is an important book about early American writing and the culture that produced it.

_____. "Two Colonials in Virginia: Captain John Smith and James Blair." _So Lit Jour_, 4 (Spring 1972), 107-116.
In _Captain John Smith_, Everett H. Emerson offers readers essential information about Smith as well as an original contribution to scholarship. Parke Rouse, Jr., in _James Blair of Virginia_ "spins the yarn of Blair's life in graceful and vigorous prose."

Breslaw, Elaine G. "Wit, Whimsy and Politics: The Uses of Satire by the Tuesday Club of Annapolis, 1744 to 1756." _WMQ_, 32 (April 1975), 295-306.
A close study of the records of the Tuesday Club reveals "a varied and rich intellectual life behind the facade of jocularity."

Christadler, Martin. _Der amerikanische Essay 1720-1820._ Heidelberg: Carl Winter, 1968.
An extensive study of the essay form in Colonial American literature, with references to Jefferson and other Southern authors; in German.

Curtis, M. J. "Charles-Town's Church Street Theater." _SCHM_, 70 (July 1969), 149-154.
A description of "the most commodious" theater on the continent in 1773.

Davis, Richard B. _American Literature Through Bryant._ Goldentree Bibliographies in Language and Literature. New York: Appleton-Century-Crofts, 1969.
Selective checklists of works by and criticism and scholarship on several Southern figures, including Byrd, Smith, Jefferson, Washington, and Taylor.

_____. "The Intellectual Golden Age in the Colonial Chesapeake Bay Country." _VMHB_, 78 (1970), 131-143.
Answers charges that the people of eighteenth-century Virginia and Maryland lacked intellectuality.

_____. _Literature and Society in Early Virginia: 1608-1840._ Baton Rouge: Louisiana State Univ Press, 1973.
A collection of earlier published essays on such writers as William Fitzhugh, Byrd, Davies, Jefferson, and others.

_____. "Neglected 'Literary' Materials for Writing an Intellectual History of the Colonial South," in _From Irving to Steinbeck_, ed. Motley F. Deakin and Peter Lisca. Gainesville: Univ of Florida Press, 1972.
Wills, sermons, and letters are literary materials neglected by intellectual historians.

_____. "Three Poems from Colonial North Carolina." _NCHR_, 47 (Winter 1969), 33-41.
A reprinting of three early North Carolina verses, including the earliest known North Carolina poem, published in the Charleston _South Carolina Gazette_ in 1737.

Edgar, W. B. "Notable Libraries of Early South Carolina." _SCHM_, 72 (April 1971), 105-110.

A record of large private libraries in colonial South Carolina.

_____. "Some Popular Books in Colonial South Carolina." *SCHM*, 72 (July 1971), 174-178.
A listing showing the titles (religion, philosophy, literature, classics, legal, practical, scientific, and periodical) of some 2,314 inventories conducted in South Carolina from 1679-1776.

Howard, E. G. "An Unknown Maryland Imprint of the Eighteenth Century." *PBSA*, 63 (1969), 200-203.
Pertains to the Reverend Isaac Campbell's *A Rational Enquiry Into...Civil Government.*

Jones, Howard M. *The Literature of Virginia in the Seventeenth Century.* Charlottesville: Univ Press of Virginia, 1968.
A revised edition of the volume first published in 1946.

Lemay, J. A. Leo. *Men of Letters in Colonial Maryland.* Knoxville: Univ of Tennessee Press, 1972.
A general historical and critical study of Maryland's colonial writing, with full assessments of Andrew White, John Hammond, George Alsop, Ebenezer Cooke, William Parks, Richard Lewis, Jonas Green, Dr. Alexander Hamilton, James Sterling, and Thomas Bacon.

Lindgren, W. H., III. "Agricultural Propaganda in Lawson's *A New Voyage to Carolina.*" *NCHR*, 49 (Autumn 1972), 333-344.
A caution against taking Lawson's details in his 1708 publication as facts.

McColley, Robert. "Jefferson's Rivals: The Shifting Character of the Federalists." *Mid-Cont Am Stud Jour*, 9 (Spring 1968), 23-33.
A study of the characteristics of Federalism during three periods: 1785-1789, 1789-1800, and 1800-1815, with references to Washington, Jefferson, and Madison.

Merrens, H. R. "A View of Coastal South Carolina in 1778: The Journal of Ebenezer Hazard." *SCHM*, 73 (October 1972), 177-193.
A transcription of an unusually reliable travel account.

Moore, Jack B. "Images of the Negro in Early American Short Fiction." *Miss Quart*, 22 (Winter 1968-69), 47-57.
In the last decade of the eighteenth century, non-professional writers used stereotyped Negro characters as abolitionist propaganda, and the treatment of them was sentimental.

Parramore, T. C. "The 'Country Distemper' in Colonial North Carolina." *NCHR*, 48 (Winter 1971), 44-52.
Researches the facts concerning certain statements made by William Byrd, John Lawson, and others.

Pickering, Sam, Jr. "Literature and Society in Colonial Virginia." *Tenn Hist Quart*, 32 (Fall 1973), 290-295.

An essay-review of Richard Beale Davis' *Literature and Society in Early Virginia, 1608-1840.*

Porter, Dorothy, ed. *Early Negro Writing: 1760-1837.* Boston: Beacon Press, 1971.
An anthology of historical documents and writings including material about the South by Southern slaves.

Quinn, David B., ed. "A List of Books Purchased for the Virginia Company." *VMHB*, 77 (July 1969), 347-360.
Lists and discusses books sent to seventeenth-century Virginia.

Renwick, John. "Bélisaire in South Carolina, 1768." *Jour Am Stud*, 4 (July 1970), 19-38.
A speculative attempt "to gauge the reasons for the impact that Jean-François Marmontel's didactic novel had in South Carolina in moral and political terms."

Ritchey, David. "The Baltimore Theatre and the Yellow Fever Epidemic." *MHM*, 67 (Fall 1971), 298-301.
An account of William Godwin and his Maryland Company and the problems they encountered during the season of 1793.

_____. "Baltimore's Eighteenth-Century French Theatre." *So Speech Comm Jour*, 38 (Winter 1972), 164-167.
During the 1790's "the French performed the only native drama presented in Baltimore in the eighteenth century."

Roaten, Darnell. "Denis Braud: Some Imprints in the Bancroft Library." *PBSA*, 62 (2nd Qtr. 1968), 252-254.
Some additions to Douglas McMurtrie's *Early Printing in New Orleans, 1764-1810.*

Robbins, W. L., ed. and trans. "John Tobler's Description of South Carolina (1753-1754)." *SCHM*, 71 (1970), 141-161; 257-265.
German tracts recommending emigration to South Carolina.

Robinson, S. C. "Mark Catesby: A Forerunner of Audubon." *Sandlapper*, 5 (May-June 1972), 59-64.
An outline of the naturalist Catesby's career in the South, concentrating on South Carolina.

Rouse, Parke, Jr. "The Raucous, Ribald Rousers of Virginia's Pioneer Newsmen." *Commonwealth* (Richmond), 35 (1968), 28-31.
Discusses humor in Virginia newspapers of the colonial period.

Shillingsburg, Miriam J. "South Carolina Copyright Legislation, 1783-94." *Proof*, 3 (1973), 357-361.
There is a gap of five years between the pre-Federal copyright laws passed in South Carolina and the Federal copyright law of 1790. However, books were published in South Carolina during this period, and one may thus speculate that records for the five-year gap may yet be found.

Silverman, Kenneth, ed. *Colonial American Poetry.* New York: Hafner, 1968.
    Contains a section on "Southern Verse," with a critical introduction, and prints poetry by William Byrd and numerous others, much of it from previously unpublished manuscripts.

Skaggs, David C. "Thomas Cradock and the Chesapeake Golden Age." *WMQ,* 30 (January 1973), 93-116.
    Less-known figures such as Cradock well demonstrate the intellectual activity in the Chesapeake area.

Skeen, C. E., ed. *A Description of Louisiana by Thomas Jeffreys from his Natural and Civil History of the French Dominions in North and South America. MVC Bulletin* no. 6. Memphis, Tenn.: Memphis State Univ, 1973.
    Facsimile reprint, with notes and an introduction, of an excerpt from a 1750 work notable for Jeffreys' distinctive maps.

Slotkin, Richard. *Regeneration Through Violence: The Mythology of the American Frontier, 1660-1860.* Middletown, Conn.: Wesleyan Univ Press, 1973.
    Traces the development of a myth of regeneration through violent confrontation between the dark forces of nature and humanity in frontier literature; numerous Southerners, from Byrd through Simms, are treated.

Wages, Jack D. "Mock Wills: Parody in the Colonial South." *Satire Newsl,* 9 (Spring 1972), 192-194.
    Reprints mock wills from the *Virginia Gazette* and the *Maryland Gazette.*

Watson, H. R. "The Books They Left: Some 'Liberies' in Edgecombe County, 1733-1783." *NCHR,* 48 (Summer 1971), 245-257.
    Inventories of books in Edgecombe County, North Carolina.

Williams, H. G. "John Miller and His Descendents." *SCHM,* 72 (April 1971), 104.
    A brief note on a colonial South Carolina printer.

Winton, Calhoun. "The Colonial South Carolina Book Trade." *Proof,* 2 (1972), 71-87.
    Though few books were printed in colonial South Carolina, many were brought in by colonists or imported.

II. Antebellum (1800–1865)

[ALLSTON, WASHINGTON] Ringe, Donald A. "Early American Gothic: Brown, Dana, and Allston." *ATQ*, 19 (Summer 1973), 3–8.
 Discusses Gothic elements in Allston's *Monaldi: A Tale.*

Welsh, John R. "An Anglo-American Friendship: Allston and Coleridge." *Jour Am Stud*, 5 (April 1971), 81–91.
 Traces the Allston-Coleridge relationship, using Coleridge's letters and notebooks, Allston's reminiscences, and accounts of others.

[BALDWIN, JOSEPH GLOVER] Dillingham, William B. See MISCELLANEOUS (Antebellum).

Hansen, Arlen J. See GENERAL.

Rubin, Louis D., Jr. See GENERAL––4th Rubin entry.

[BLEDSOE, ALBERT TAYLOR] Cooke, J. W. "Albert Taylor Bledsoe: An American Philosopher and Theologian of Liberty." *SHR*, 8 (Spring, 1974), 215–228.
 Bledsoe's "ultimate significance as a thinker rests upon the considerable intellectual ingenuity and sympathy he displayed in trying to rescue men from the baleful consequences of Jonathan Edwards' theology" and upon his able defense of Southern society.

Davis, Michael. See MISCELLANEOUS (Antebellum).

[BROWN, WILLIAM WELLS] Abramson, Doris M. "William Wells Brown: America's First Negro Playwright." *ETJ*, 20 (October 1968), 370–375.
 Analyzes *The Escape* and concludes that it is "an interesting document both from a social and a theatrical point of view."

Brown, William Wells. *Clotel, or The President's Daughter.* New York: Collier Books, Macmillan, 1970.
 Reprints the first novel by a black, concerning an illegitimate daughter of Thomas Jefferson and a slave mistress, with an introductory appreciation by Arthur Davis.

Butterfield, Stephen T. "The Use of Language in the Slave Narrative." *NALF*, 6 (Fall 1972), 72–78.
 Brown's narrative is one of the ones discussed in this treatment of the devices of the narratives as influences on contemporary black autobiography.

Clark, James W., Jr. See MISCELLANEOUS (Antebellum).

Farrison, W. Edward. "Clotel, Thomas Jefferson, and Sally Hemings." *CLA Jour*, 17 (1973), 147–174.
 Since the chronology of *Clotel* indicates that Jefferson could not have been the father of Clotel and Althea, one must question whether he was the father of Sally Hemings' children.

_____. *"The Kidnapped Clergyman* and Brown's *Experience."* *CLA Jour*, 18 (June 1975), 507–515.
 The unpublished *Experience*, not *The Escape*, was Brown's first drama; points out parallels between *Experience* and the anonymous anti-slave drama *The Kidnapped Clergyman.*

_____. "One Ephemera After Another." *CLA Jour*, 13 (December 1969), 192–197.
 A review of *William Wells Brown and Clotelle*, edited by J. Noel Heermance.

_____. *William Wells Brown, Author and Reformer.* Chicago: Univ of Chicago Press, 1969.
 The first full-length study of Brown; focuses particularly on him as reformer.

Fleming, Robert E. See GENERAL––both Fleming entries.

Heermance, J. Noel. *William Wells Brown and Clotelle.* Hamden, Conn.: Archon, 1969.
 A biographical account of America's first black novelist, dramatist, and travel writer, and an assessment of his slave *Narrative* and his novel *Clotelle*, reprinted in facsimile in the book.

Isani, Mukhtar A. See GENERAL.

Nichols, Charles H. See MISCELLANEOUS (Antebellum).

Osofsky, Gilbert. See MISCELLANEOUS (Antebellum).

Pawley, Thomas. "The First Black Playwrights." *Black World*, 21 (April 1972), 16–24.
 Part of the article deals with Brown as an early black playwright not interested in the staging of his dramas but rather in "seeking novel ways of representing the horrors of slavery and promoting the anti-slavery cause."

Shockley, Ann A. See MISCELLANEOUS (Antebellum).

Smith, Sidonie. See GENERAL.

Yellin, Jean F. See MISCELLANEOUS (Antebellum).

[BRUCE, EDWARD CALEDON] Simms, L. Moody, Jr.
"Edward Caledon Bruce: Virginia Artist and
Writer." *Va Cavalcade*, 23 (Winter 1974), 30-37.
Bruce (1825-1901) wrote stories and articles
for *Harper's Magazine* and published one book.

[CARUTHERS, WILLIAM ALEXANDER] Davis, Curtis C.
"Introduction" to *The Knights of the Golden
Horse-Shoe*. Chapel Hill: Univ of North
Carolina Press, 1970.
Examines the composition, publication, and
historical background of this romantic novel
set in pre-Revolutionary Virginia, reprinted
from the 1845 text.

[CHIVERS, THOMAS HOLLEY] Camp, James, et al.
See MISCELLANEOUS (Antebellum).

Rosenfeld, Alvin H. See POE, EDGAR ALLAN
(Antebellum).

Tucker, Edward L., ed. "A New Letter by Thomas
Holley Chivers." *GHQ*, 55 (Winter 1971),
582-584.
A brief biographical note precedes the printing of a letter from Chivers to the *Augusta
Chronicle and Sentinel* dealing with a medical
problem.

[COBB, JOSEPH B.] Mohr, Clarence L. "Candid Comments from a Mississippi Author." *Miss Quart*,
25 (Winter 1972), 83-93.
Two letters (1844 and 1851) of Joseph B.
Cobb's show that he combined politics with
literary effort.

Rogers, Tommy W. "The Folk Humor of Joseph B.
Cobb." *Notes on Miss Writers*, 3 (Spring 1970),
13-35.
A description of Cobb's *Mississippi Scenes*
(1851) as falling in the genre of Southern and
Southwestern humor.

_____. "Joseph B. Cobb: Antebellum Humorist and
Critic." *Miss Quart*, 22 (Spring 1969), 131-136.
Mississippi planter and politician, Cobb
wrote short stories, novels, frontier humor, and
critical reviews; though he achieved no lasting
reputation, he was productive in the avocation
of belles-lettres.

_____. "Joseph B. Cobb: Continuation of a Dis-
tinguished Lineage." *GHQ*, 56 (Fall 1972),
404-414.
Rogers examines Cobb's contributions to
Southwestern humor, particularly Cobb's book,
Mississippi Scenes.

_____. "Joseph B. Cobb: The Successful Pursuit of
Belles Lettres." *McNeese Rev*, 20 (1971-72),
70-83.
A study of themes and characters in Cobb's
Mississippi Scenes.

[COOKE, JOHN ESTEN] Barnett, Louise K. See
GENERAL.

Grant, William A. See MISCELLANEOUS (Antebellum).

Welsh, John R., ed. *John Esten Cooke's Autobiographical Memo*. Dept. of English Bibliographical
Series, no. 4. Columbia: Univ of South
Carolina Press, 1969.
First publication of an autobiographical memo
sent by Cooke to W. G. Simms in 1867, with preface, transcription, and notes by the editor.

[COOKE, PHILIP PENDLETON] Allen, John D., ed.
Philip Pendleton Cooke: Poet, Critic, Novelist.
Johnson City, East Tennessee State Univ, 1969.
A collection of poetry, short fiction, and
essays and letters by the Virginia gentleman-
poet, with a biographical introduction, critical
forewords, and a bibliography.

Jackson, David K. "The Writings of Philip Pendleton
Cooke." *So Lit Jour*, 2 (Spring 1970), 156-158.
An essay-review of *Philip Pendleton Cooke:
Poet, Critic, Novelist*, edited by John D. Allen,
in which Jackson finds that "the selections made
by Mr. Allen reveal Cooke as a talented poet and
ballad maker, a discerning critic, an amateurish
novel writer, and a cultivated Virginia
gentleman."

Tucker, Edward L. "Philip Pendleton Cooke." *Va
Cavalcade*, 19 (Winter 1970), 42-46.
A biographical sketch and information on
Poe's aid in getting Cooke into print.

_____. "Philip Pendleton Cooke and *The Southern
Literary Messenger*: Selected Letters." *Miss
Quart*, 27 (Winter 1973-74), 79-99.
Eight previously unpublished letters of
Cooke primarily to John R. Thompson and Benjamin
Blake Minor on Cooke's writings for the
Messenger.

[CROCKETT, DAVY] Arpad, Joseph J., ed. *A Narrative
of the Life of David Crockett*. New Haven, Conn.:
College & Univ Press, 1972.
Reprints the text of the first 1834 edition,
with printing errors corrected, and provides a
biographical and critical introduction.

Mason, Melvin R. "*The Lion of the West*: Davy
Crockett and Frances Trollope." *Studies by
Members of SCMLA (So Central Bul)*, 19
(Winter 1969), 143-145.
Suggests that Nimrod Wildfire in Paulding's
play is a caricature of Crockett.

Shackford, James A., and Stanley J. Folmsbee, eds.
*A Narrative of the Life of David Crockett of the
State of Tennessee*. Knoxville: Univ of
Tennessee Press, 1973.
An annotated facsimile of the 1834 edition.

West, James L. W. III. See MISCELLANEOUS
(Antebellum).

[CUSTIS, GEORGE WASHINGTON PARKE] Crowson, E. T.
"George Washington Parke Custis: The Child of
Mount Vernon." *Va Cavalcade*, 22 (Winter 1973),
37-47.
Biographical information on George
Washington's foster son, who composed several
plays.

[DAVIS, JEFFERSON] Hattaway, Herman. "A Note on Jefferson Davis as an Inspiring Speaker." *Miss Quart*, 22 (Spring 1969), 147-149.
Though historians have labelled Davis an ineffective speaker, in this instance he was received with enthusiasm.

Hunchett, William. "Reconstruction and the Rehabilitation of Jefferson Davis: Charles G. Halpine's *Prison Life*." *Jour Am Hist*, 56 (September 1969), 280-290.
Points out that John J. Craven's *Prison Life of Jefferson Davis* was largely ghost-written by Charles G. Halpine and contained many falsifications distasteful to Davis himself.

Muldowny, John. "Jefferson Davis: The Postwar Years." *Miss Quart*, 23 (Winter 1969-70), 17-33.
After unsuccessful business ventures in the postwar years, Davis found retreat at Beauvoir, the gift of a friend, where he wrote his history of the war and lived a rather dull life.

Smiley, David L. "*The Papers of Jefferson Davis*, Volume 1, *1808-1840*, ed. Haskell M. Monroe, Jr., and James T. McIntosh." *WVH*, 33 (July 1972), 429-430.
An essay-review which comments on the difficulties of writing on such a controversial figure and commends the scholarship of the work.

[DOUGLASS, FREDERICK] Aptheker, Herbert. "Frederick Douglass Calls for Black Suffrage in 1866." *Black Schol*, 5 (December 1973-January 1974), 10-16.
Reprints for the first time Douglass' "An Appeal to Congress for Impartial Suffrage," which appeared first in the *Atlantic* in 1866.

_____. See GENERAL.

Baker, Houston A., Jr. See GENERAL--1st, 3rd, and 4th Baker entries.

Bontemps, Arna. *Free at Last: The Life of Frederick Douglass*. New York: Dodd, Mead, 1971.
A full biographical account of Douglass' life and career as a reformer.

Broderick, John C., et al. See GENERAL.

Clark, James W. See MISCELLANEOUS (Antebellum).

Clasby, Nancy T. "Frederick Douglass's *Narrative*: A Content Analysis." *CLA Jour*, 14 (March 1971), 242-250.
Reviews Douglass' growing awareness of the cruelty of slavery as it is recorded in the early *Narrative*. "Douglass's vision of slavery, suffused with anger and sadness, is that of an outraged idealist."

Fulkerson, Gerald. "Exile as Emergence: Frederick Douglass in Great Britain, 1845-1847." *QJS*, 60 (February 1974), 69-82.
Douglass went to Great Britain as a "subordinate" in the ranks of abolitionists but because of the British reaction to him he returned to the United States as an "emerging leader."

Gayle, Addison, Jr. See GENERAL--1st Gayle entry.

Grumbach, Doris. See GENERAL.

Jaskoski, Helen. See GENERAL.

Johnson, Paul D. "'Goodby to Sambo': The Contribution of Black Slave Narratives to the Abolition Movement." *NALF*, 6 (Fall 1972), 79-84.
The narratives were intended to expose the evils of slavery and "to build a sympathetic picture of the narrator." Douglass' narrative is discussed at some length.

Kinnamon, Keneth. See GENERAL.

Minter, David. "Conceptions of Self in Black Slave Narratives." *ATQ*, 24 (Fall 1974, Part 1), 62-68.
Douglass' narrative reveals his progress from passive adjustment of self to the world to self-fashioning which led "to new identity, a different self in a changing world."

Nichols, Charles H. See MISCELLANEOUS (Antebellum).

Nichols, William W. "Individualism and Autobiographical Art: Frederick Douglass and Henry Thoreau." *CLA Jour*, 16 (December 1972), 145-158.
My Bondage and My Freedom and *Walden* are similar in that both deal with the quest for human freedom, but the focuses of the two works are different because of their authors' differing views on individualism.

Perry, Patsy B. "Before *The North Star*: Frederick Douglass' Early Journalistic Career." *Phylon*, 35 (March 1974), 96-107.
During 1847 Douglass gained valuable journalistic experience from both the *National Anti-Slavery Standard* and *The Ram's Horn* before establishing *The North Star*, his own abolitionist journal.

_____. "The Literary Content of *Frederick Douglass' Paper* Through 1860." *CLA Jour*, 17 (1973), 214-229.
In his *Paper* Douglass sought to stimulate literary appreciation.

Quarles, Benjamin. "Frederick Douglass: Black Imperishable." *QJLC*, 29 (July 1972), 159-161.
A speech made on the occasion of the coming of Douglass' papers to the Library of Congress.

Shockley, Ann A. See MISCELLANEOUS (Antebellum).

Stone, Albert E. "Identity and Art in Frederick Douglass's *Narrative*." *CLA Jour*, 17 (1973), 192-213.
The *Narrative* concerns Douglass' search for identity and makes use of "metaphors of self" to represent the discovered self.

[DRAYTON, JOHN G.] Lashley, Dolores. "John Grimké Drayton." *Sandlapper*, 5 (February 1972), 39-43, 66-69.
A summary of the contributions of John G. Drayton of Charleston (1815-1891).

[ELLIOTT, WILLIAM] Anderson, Charles R. "Thoreau Takes a Pot Shot at *Carolina Sports*." *GaR*, 22 (Fall 1968), 289-299.

II. Antebellum (1800-1865)

An account of Elliott's sporting book (1846) and Thoreau's reaction to it.

Scafidel, Beverly. "William Elliott, Planter and Politician: New Evidence from the Charleston Newspapers, 1831-1856," in *South Carolina Journals and Journalists*. Columbia, S. C.: Southern Studies Program, 1975, pp. 109-119.
Points out the need for further study and location of Elliott's fugitive works in antebellum newspapers.

Rubin, Louis D., Jr. See GENERAL--8th Rubin entry.

[EVANS, CHARLES N. B.] Stokes, Durward T. "A Newly Discovered Letter from the Fool Killer." *NCarF*, 17 (May 1969), 3-8.
One of the letters from "Jesse Holmes, the Fool Killer," which appeared in Evans' *The Milton Chronicle*.

[FALKNER, WILLIAM CUTHBERT] Anderson, Hilton. "Colonel Falkner's Preface to *The Siege of Monterrey*." *Notes on Miss Writers*, 3 (Spring 1970), 36-40.
A reprinting of the preface.

_____. "*The White Rose of Memphis*: A Clarification." *Notes on Miss Writers*, 1 (Fall 1968), 64-67.
Makes a case for Colonel Falkner's novel, which "does not belong in the moonlight-and-magnolia school," and mentions two little-known studies of Colonel Falkner.

McHaney, Thomas L. See FAULKNER, WILLIAM (Contemporary--4th McHaney entry).

Robinson, Clayton. See GENERAL.

[HARRIS, GEORGE WASHINGTON] Austin, James C., and Donald A. Koch. See GENERAL.

Blair, Walter. See GENERAL

Current-Garcia, Eugene. "Sut Lovingood's Rare Ripe Southern Garden." *Stud SF*, 9 (Spring 1972), 117-129.
"However repellent they may be, Sut and his world symbolize--in one sense--the old South's vigor and fertility."

Davis, Michael. See MISCELLANEOUS (Postbellum).

Dillingham, William B. See MISCELLANEOUS (Antebellum).

Gray, R. J. See CALDWELL, ERSKINE (Contemporary).

Hansen, Arlen J. See GENERAL.

Howell, Elmo. "Timon in Tennessee: The Moral Fervor of George Washington Harris." *GaR*, 24 (Fall 1970), 311-319.
Sut is inspired by "principle of right reason in human conduct" more than by crass prejudice.

Inge, M. Thomas, ed. "Early Appreciations of George W. Harris by George Frederick Mellen." *Tenn Hist Quart*, 30 (Summer 1971), 190-204.

A reprinting of four essays (1909, 1909, 1911, 1914) originally published in the Knoxville *Sentinel*; Mellen's appreciations, Inge says, are perhaps more important for "their use of original research on Harris's life and times."

Leary, Lewis. See GENERAL--1st Leary entry.

Plater, Ormonde. "Before Sut: Folklore in the Early Works of George Washington Harris." *SFQ*, 34 (June 1970), 104-115.
In Harris' early works humor derives from (1) contrast of wisdom and foolishness and (2) sex.

_____. "The Lovingood Patriarchy." *Appal Jour*, 1 (Spring 1973), 82-93.
Deals with the self-degradation of Sut's father which brings about a matriarchal dominance in the Lovingood family.

[HENTZ, CAROLINE LEE] Hentz, Caroline Lee. *The Planter's Northern Bride*. Southern Literary Classics Series. Chapel Hill: Univ of North Carolina Press, 1970.
A reprint of the 1854 first edition with an introduction to the cultural significance of this reply to *Uncle Tom's Cabin* by Rhoda Coleman Ellison.

[HOLMES, GEORGE FREDERICK] Crowson, E. T. "George Frederick Holmes and Auguste Comte." *Miss Quart*, 22 (Winter 1968-69), 59-70.
Holmes, first chancellor of the University of Mississippi and reviewer and critic for literary and religious magazines, wrote at length on Comtean positivism and corresponded with the French philosopher.

Gillespie, N. C. "George Frederick Holmes and the Philosophy of History." *SAQ*, 67 (Summer 1968), 486-498.
Holmes anticipated later historians by searching through past civilizations to find clues to the outcome of "his own world's tribulations."

[HOOPER, JOHNSON JONES] Hoole, W. Stanley. See GENERAL.

Rachal, John. See CLEMENS, SAMUEL LANGHORNE (Postbellum--2nd Rachal entry).

Smith, Winston. "*Simon Suggs* and the Satiric Tradition," in *Essays in Honor of Richebourg Gaillard McWilliams*, ed. Howard Creed. Birmingham, Ala.: Birmingham-Southern College, 1970.
Classifies *Simon Suggs* as a picaresque novel and compares it with other works in the same category.

Wellman, Manly W. "Introduction" to *Adventures of Captain Simon Suggs*. Chapel Hill: Univ of North Carolina Press, 1969.
A general summary of biographical and critical material on Hooper and his picaresque creation, and a brief bibliography.

West, H. C. "Simon Suggs and His Similes." *N Car F*, 16 (May 1968), 43-57.
Hooper uses similes sparingly but effectively.

Williams, Benjamin B. See GENERAL.

[HORTON, GEORGE MOSES] Farrison, W. Edward. "George
Moses Horton: Poet for Freedom." *CLA Jour*, 14
(1971), 227-241.
An account of this slave-poet's life and work.

Reeves, William J. See GENERAL.

Shockley, Ann A. See MISCELLANEOUS (Antebellum).

Walser, Richard. "Newly Discovered Acrostic by
George Moses Horton." *CLA Jour*, 19
(December 1975), 258-260.
Prints an acrostic which the slave-poet
Horton, as with others of his acrostics, wrote
to order and sold to a student at the University
of North Carolina.

[HUNDLEY, DANIEL R.] Rogers, Tommy W. "D. R.
Hundley: A Multi-Class Thesis of Social
Stratification in the Antebellum South." *Miss
Quart*, 23 (Spring 1970), 135-154.
Hundley (1832-1862), Alabama planter, lawyer,
banker, and amateur sociologist, made one of the
earliest attempts at class analysis in his
Social Relations in Our Southern States (1860).

[INGRAHAM, JOSEPH HOLT] Anon. *HLQ*, 38
(August 1975), 373-374.
A note on Ingraham's works in the Harvard
Library.

Blanck, Jacob. "Two Revisions in the Bibliography
of Joseph Holt Ingraham." *YULG*, 42
(January 1968), 158-161.
Corrects items listed in the *Bibliography of
American Literature*.

Weathersby, Robert W., II. "J. H. Ingraham and
Tennessee: A Record of Social and Literary
Contributions." *Tenn Hist Quart*, 34 (Fall 1975),
264-272.
In Nashville, where he studied theology,
Ingraham "would lobby for a system of tax-
financed public schools,...aid the welfare of
the state's prisoners, and begin the publication
of one of the best selling Biblical novels of
the nineteenth century."

[JONES, JOHN BEAUCHAMP] Lapides, Frederick R.
"John Beauchamp Jones: A Southern View of the
Abolitionists." *Jour of the Rutgers Univ Lib*,
33 (June 1970), 63-73.
Deals mainly with Jones's *Secession Coercion,
and Civil War: the Story of 1861* (1861) in
which there is a vision in a dream of war between the North and the South, with the North
seceding from the Union and being defeated by
the South.

[KENNEDY, JOHN PENDLETON] Grant, William A. See
MISCELLANEOUS (Antebellum).

Rose, Alan H. "The Image of the Negro in the Pre-
Civil War Novels of John Pendleton Kennedy and
William Gilmore Simms." *Jour Am Stud*, 4
(February 1971), 217-231.
It is "this sense of imminent destruction
which accounts for the compulsive rigour with
which the hint of Negro demonism is suppressed
in the novels of Kennedy and Simms."

Sutton, Robert P. See MISCELLANEOUS (Antebellum).

Yellin, Jean F. See MISCELLANEOUS (Antebellum).

[LEGARÉ, HUGH SWINTON] Evans, Elizabeth. "The
Friendship of Alexander Hill Everett and Hugh
Swinton Legaré." *Miss Quart*, 28 (Fall 1975),
497-504.
Includes unpublished letters and commentary.

Welsh, John R. See MISCELLANEOUS (Antebellum).

[LEGARÉ, JAMES MATHEWES] Davis, Curtis C. *That
Ambitious Mr. Legaré*. Columbia: Univ of South
Carolina Press, 1971.
A biography of the life and times of poet
James M. Legaré (1823-59) of South Carolina, with
a collected edition of his poems, and biblio-
graphical notes and appendices.

Jacobs, Robert D. "James Mathewes Legaré: Nearly
Forgotten but Not Lost." *So Lit Jour*, 4
(Spring 1972), 122-127.
"Poor Legaré, as Mr. Davis [Curtis Carroll
Davis] presents him [*That Ambitious Mr. Legaré*],
wrote poetry with his right hand, wrote fiction
with his left, and somehow with ambidextrous
talent, did passable painting and inspired
tinkering with both."

Kibler, James E. "C. C. Davis' *That Ambitious
Mr. Legaré: The Life of James M. Legaré of
South Carolina, Including a Collected Edition of
His Verse*." *GaR*, 26 (Fall 1972), 385-389.
An essay-review that cites reference for two
new Legaré poems not in Davis.

_____. Legaré's First Poems and His Early Career."
So Lit Jour, 6 (Fall 1973), 70-76.
A significant relationship between the poet
and Simms existed, as a consequence of which the
older writer advanced the young poet's
reputation.

[LEWIS, HENRY CLAY] Israel, Charles. "Henry Clay
Lewis's *Odd Leaves*: Studies in the Surreal and
Grotesque." *Miss Quart*, 28 (Winter 1974-75),
61-69.
Examines and defines Lewis's "conscious
artistic use of violence, grotesque episodes and
images, and surreal humor to create a consistent
world view."

Rose, Alan H. "The Image of the Negro in the Writings of Henry Clay Lewis." *AL*, 41 (May 1969),
255-263.
Discusses the "demonic" Negro in Lewis' works.

[LONGSTREET, AUGUSTUS BALDWIN] Hansen, Arlen J.
See GENERAL.

Harwell, Richard. "Introduction," *Georgia Scenes*,
by A. B. Longstreet. Savannah, Ga.: Beehive
Press, 1975.
A brief biographical and historical
appreciation.

Inge, M. Thomas. See WADE, JOHN DONALD.

Longstreet, Augustus Baldwin. "A Night in the Cars."
Miss Quart, 23 (Spring 1970), 169-174.

A reprinting of the sketch from the *Southern Miscellany* (1842).

Rubin, Louis D., Jr. See GENERAL--4th Rubin entry.

Scafidel, James R. "A. B. Longstreet and Secession: His Contributions to Columbia and Charleston Newspapers, 1860-1861," in *South Carolina Journals and Journalists*. Columbia, S. C.: Southern Studies Program, 1975, pp. 77-87.
    A study and listing of previously unnoticed newspaper pieces which clarify Longstreet's attitudes toward secession and the Civil War.

Smith, Gerald. "Augustus Baldwin Longstreet and John Wade's 'Cousin Lucius.'" *GHQ*, 56 (Summer 1972), 276-281.
    There is an "affinity" between the hero of Wade's "The Life and Death of Cousin Lucius," included in *I'll Take My Stand*, and the life of A. B. Longstreet, whose biography Wade had written several years earlier.

[McNUTT, ALEXANDER] Howell, Elmo. "Governor Alexander G. McNutt of Mississippi: Humorist of the Old Southwest." *JMiH*, 35 (May 1973), 153-165.
    Identifies McNutt as the "Turkey Runner" and cites his use of a man who worked for him as Chunkey and Jim in his sketches.

[NOLAND, CHARLES] Williams, Leonard. "An Early Arkansas 'Frolic': A Contemporary Account." *Mid-South Folk*, 2 (1974), 39-42.
    Includes information about Noland and describes the "frolic."

[POE, EDGAR ALLAN] Anon. "The Detached Terrorism of Poe." *TLS*, no. 3,595 (February 22, 1971), 95-96.
    An essay-review of the following books: Edgar Allan Poe, *Poems*. Illus. W. Heath Robinson; Sidney P. Moss, *Poe's Major Crisis*; Michael Allen, *Poe and the British Magazine Tradition*; Robert D. Jacobs, *Poe: Journalist and Critic*; Burton R. Pollin, *Discoveries in Poe*; Thomas Ollive Mabbott, ed. *Collected Works of Edgar Allan Poe*, Vol. I: *Poems*; and Floyd Stovall, *Edgar Poe the Poet*.

Adams, John F. "Classical Raven Lore and Poe's Raven." *Poe Stud*, 5 (December 1972), 53.
    A discussion of symbolism and irony in Poe's "The Raven."

Aderman, Ralph M. "Poe in Rumania: A Bibliography." *Poe Newsletter*, 3 (June 1970), 19-20.
    Lists important Rumanian translations and critical studies of Poe.

Alexander, Jean. *Affidavits of Genius, Edgar Allan Poe and the French Critics, 1874-1924*. Port Washington, N. Y.: The Kennikat Press, 1971.
    Essays (in translation) by fifteen French poets and critics, from E. D. Forgues and Baudelaire to Mallarmé and Valéry.

Allen, Bruce A. "Delight and Terror." *HudR*, 26 (Winter 1973-74), 735-742.
    Essay-review of Daniel Hoffman's *Poe, Poe, Poe, Poe, Poe, Poe, Poe* which concludes that Hoffman "revitalizes" Poe.

Allen, Michael. *Poe and the British Magazine Tradition*. New York: Oxford Univ Press, 1969.
    Focusing upon Poe's career as a journalist between 1835 and 1849, Allen delineates the formulas and conventions Poe adopted from his reading in popular British journals in order to preserve his artistic integrity against the ruinous demands of a mass reading audience.

Alsen, Eberhard. "Poe's Theory of Hawthorne's Indebtedness to Tieck." *Anglia*, 91 (1973), 342-356.
    In his first review of *Twice-Told Tales*, Poe did not accuse Hawthorne of heavy indebtedness to Tieck because he himself was not yet thoroughly familiar with Tieck's work; by the time of his second review he was.

Amur, G. S. "'Heart of Darkness' and 'The Fall of the House of Usher.'" *Literary Criterion*, 9 (Summer 1971), 59-70.
    Points out similarities and differences in structure, symbols, theme, and the role of the narrator and hero in these two works.

Amyot, Gerald F. "Contrasting Visions of Death in the Poetry of Poe and Whitman." *Walt Whit Rev*, 19 (September 1973), 103-111.
    Whitman's view of death is optimistic, whereas Poe's is not.

Anderson, Carl L. *Poe in Northlight: The Scandinavian Response to His Life and Work*. Durham, N. C.: Duke Univ Press, 1973.
    Surveys Poe's reception in Denmark, Norway, and Sweden, with special attention to the interpretations of Strindberg and Ola Hansson.

Anderson, Imbert E. "El cuervo de Poe." *Rev Nacional de Cultura*, 33 (January-December 1973), 195-198.
    Deals with the symbolic significance of the raven.

Armistead, J. M. "Poe and Lyric Conventions: The Example of 'For Annie.'" *Poe Stud*, 8 (June 1975), 1-5.
    As a love lyric, Poe's "For Annie" is transitional, revealing Poe's capacity to create a new genre from old forms and "to transform egotistical expression into formal, publicly pleasing artifice."

Asociación Argentina de Estudios Americanos. *Sextas jornadas de historia y literatura norteamericana y rioplatense*. Buenos Aires, 1971.
    Contains two essays on Poe, one by L. Scott Catlett on *Eureka* and one by Angel Vilanova on Poe's critical theories.

Asselineau, Roger. *Edgar Allan Poe*. University of Minnesota Pamphlets on American Writers, no. 89. Minneapolis: Univ of Minnesota Press, 1970.
    A critical introduction.

_____. "Introduction," *Les aventures d'Arthur Gordon Pym*. Paris: Aubier-Montaigne, 1973.
    A bilingual edition using Baudelaire's translation. The introduction surveys criticism on this work.

Avni, Abraham. See GENERAL.

Babcock, C. Merton. "The Wizards of Baltimore: Poe and Mencken." *Tex Quart*, 13 (Autumn 1970), 110–115.
    Poe and Mencken were alike in their merciless attacks on authors and literary fads and fashions.

Baker, Christopher P. "Spenser and 'The City in the Sea.'" *Poe Stud*, 5 (December 1972), 55.
    The Faerie Queen offers a parallel for Poe's poem.

Bales, Kent. "Poetic Justice in 'The Cask of Amontillado.'" *Poe Stud*, 5 (December 1972), 51.
    Discusses the rich ironic effects of Montresor's confession.

Bandy, W. T. "The Date of Poe's Burial." *Poe Stud*, 4 (December 1971), 47–48.
    The correct date of Poe's funeral was October 8, 1849.

_____, ed. *Edgar Allan Poe: sa vie et ses ouvrages*, by Charles Baudelaire. Toronto: Univ of Toronto Press, 1973.
    An annotated edition of the 1852 essay, the earliest foreign study of Poe.

_____. "More on 'The Angel of the Odd.'" *Poe Newsletter*, 3 (June 1970), 22.
    Comments upon the accuracy of Baudelaire's translation of a phrase in Poe's "The Angel of the Odd" and clarifies Poe's reference in the story to Griswold's edition of *The Curiosities of American Literature*.

_____, ed. *Seven Tales by Edgar Allan Poe*. New York: Schocken Books, 1971.
    A bilingual (Baudelaire's French translation) edition.

_____. "Taine on Poe: Additions and Corrections." *Poe Stud*, 7 (December 1974), 48.
    Points to errors in an article on Taine and Poe appearing in *Poe Stud* in December 1973.

Banta, Martha. "American Apocalypses: Excrement and Ennui." *SLI*, 7 (Spring 1974), 1–30.
    Poe is included in this discussion of writers who seem to view America as the place where the Apocalypse will occur.

_____. "Benjamin, Edgar, Humbert, and Jay." *YR*, 60 (June 1971), 532–549.
    Discusses the American Dream and the influence of Poe and Franklin on *Lolita* and *The Great Gatsby*.

Barthes, Roland. "Analyse textuelle d'un conte d'Edgar Poe," in *Sémiotique narrative et textuelle* (Collection L). Paris: Larousse, 1973.
    The story analyzed is "M. Valdemar."

Barzun, Jacques. "A Note on the Inadequacy of Poe as a Proofreader and of His Editors as French Scholars." *Romanic Rev*, 61 (February 1970), 23–26.
    Poe and his editors misspelled French words and misused accent marks.

Battilana, Marilla. "Edgar Allan Poe, nostro contemporaneo." *Annali di Ca' Foscari*, 8, no. 2 (1969), 1–10.
    Deals with reasons for Poe's appeal to twentieth-century readers.

Baym, Max I. See GENERAL.

Beaver, Harold. "Introduction," *The Narrative of Arthur Gordon Pym of Nantucket*. Baltimore, Md.: Penguin Books, 1975.
    A text based on the first American edition, with critical introduction, notes, and commentary.

Bell, H. H., Jr. "'The Masque of the Red Death'—An Interpretation." *SAB*, 38 (November 1973), 101–105.
    Prospero's seven colored apartments represent the seven decades of a madman's life; each color is appropriate to the decade.

Benton, Richard P. "Edgar Allan Poe: Current Bibliography." *Poe Newsletter*, 2 (January 1969), 4–12.
    This annotated bibliography covers principally the years 1966–1968.

_____. "Edgar Allan Poe: Current Bibliography." *Poe Newsletter*, 3 (June 1970), 11–16.
    This annotated bibliography covers principally the years 1968–1969.

_____. "Edgar Allan Poe: Current Bibliography." *Poe Stud*, 4 (December 1971), 38–44.
    This annotated bibliography covers principally the years 1970–1971.

_____. "'Eureka: A Prose Poem,' New Edition with Line Numbers, Exploratory Essay, and Bibliographical Guide." *ATQ*, 22 (Spring 1974), 1–77.
    Contains the complete text.

_____. "G. R. Thompson's New Reading of Poe." *ATQ*, 24 (Fall 1974, Supp.), 1–3.
    An essay-review of Thompson's *Poe's Fiction: Romantic Irony in the Gothic Tales*, which surveys some previous Poe criticism and concludes that Thompson's is "the most important book since Davidson's and Quinn's, whose work he goes well beyond."

_____. "'The Masque of the Red Death'—The Primary Source." *ATQ*, 1 (1st Qtr. 1969), 12–13.
    Suggests that the source is Letter XVI of Willis' *Pencillings by the Way*.

_____. "'The Mystery of Marie Rogêt'—A Defense." *Stud SF*, 6 (Winter 1969), 144–151.
    Argues that the story has more values than generally recognized. Sees the story as a masterpiece of detective fiction.

_____. "Poe's 'Lionizing': A Quiz on Willis and Lady Blessington." *Stud SF*, 5 (Spring 1968), 239–244.
    Argues that Poe's satirical skit "Lionizing" (*Southern Literary Messenger*, 1835) aims not only at N. P. Willis but also at Lady Blessington and her circle and that the source of the skit is Willis' first two letters to the *New York Mirror*.

_____. "Reply to Professor Thompson." *Stud SF*, 6 (Fall 1968), 97.
     Argues that Poe intended N. P. Willis, not Bulwer-Lytton, as the major target of satire in "Lionizing."

_____. "The Study of Poe--Past and Present." *ESQ*, no. 60 (Fall 1970, Part 1, Supp.), 3.
     Traces critical attitudes toward Poe.

_____. "'The System of Dr. Tarr and Prof. Fether': Dickens or Willis?" *Poe Newsletter*, 1 (April 1968), 7-9.
     Argues that the source is not Dickens.

Berke, Richard. "Poe's *Eureka*--Equivocation or Epiphany?" *Nassau Rev*, 3, no. 1 (1975), 32-42.
     In this work Poe conceives of an ultimate Unity of Nothingness.

Bickman, Martin. "Animatopoeia: Morella as Siren of the Self." *Poe Stud*, 8 (December 1975), 29-32.
     Explores elements of Jungian psychology and metaphysics in "Morella."

Blish, James. "The Climate of Insult." *SR*, 80 (Spring 1972), 340-346.
     Describes Poe as a technical innovator in the field of narrative and as the portraitist of a species of sensibility more common in our own time than in Poe's.

Boos, Florence and William. "A Source for the Rimes of Poe's 'The Raven': Elizabeth Barrett Browning's 'A Drama of Exile.'" *Mary Wollstonecraft Jour*, 2, no. 2 (1974), 30-31.
     Title is descriptive.

Borowitz, Helen O. "Visions of Salome." *Criticism*, 14 (Winter 1972), 12-21.
     Includes discussion of Poe's influence on the French symbolists and on concepts of Salome.

Braddy, Haldeen. "Edgar Allan Poe's Princess of Long Ago." *Laurel Rev*, 9 (Fall 1969), 23-31.
     Argues that Poe was primarily a poet of lyric love which concretized about the image of the "Lost Princess."

_____. *Three Dimensional Poe*. El Paso: Texas Western Press, 1973.
     Four brief surveys of Poe's life, verse, stories, and essays that reflect "the frustrating confines of worldly reality," plus a checklist of scholarship, 1949-1970.

Bramsbäck, Birgit. "The Final Illness and Death of Edgar Allan Poe: An Attempt at Reassessment." *Studia Neophilologica*, 42 (1970), 40-59.
     Poe's symptoms before his death were those of delirium tremens, which Poe could well have suffered from because of an acute infection, not because of drinking.

Brie, Hartmut. "Die Theorie des poetischen Effekts bei Poe und Mallarmé." *Neueren Sprachen*, 21 (August 1972), 473-481.
     Mallarmé was heavily influenced by Poe's poetic theories, but his aims in applying them were different.

Bronzwaer, W. "Deixis as a Structuring Device in Narrative Discourse: An Analysis of Poe's 'The Murders in the Rue Morgue.'" *Eng Stud*, 56 (August 1975), 345-359.
     A study of tense reveals how Poe directs attention from the "horror story" of the murders to the "detective story" of solving them.

Brooks, Cleanth. "Edgar Poe as an Interior Decorator." *Ventures*, 8 (1968), 41-46.
     Discusses the ways Poe uses furnishings in houses in his stories to reflect states of mind.

_____. See GENERAL--2nd Brooks entry.

Brooks, Curtis M. "The Cosmic God: Science and the Creative Imagination in *Eureka*." *ATQ*, 26 (Spring 1975), 60-68.
     Eureka represents Poe's reconciliation of science and poetry.

Broussard, Louis. *The Measure of Poe*. Norman: Univ of Oklahoma Press, 1969.
     Examines Poe's work in the light of philosophical ideas expressed in *Eureka*, and traces his critical reputation to the present; includes an exhaustive bibliography of criticism listing books published since 1849 and essays since 1925.

Bruns, Gerald L. "Poetry as Reality: The Orpheus Myth and Its Modern Counterparts." *ELH*, 37 (1970), 263-286.
     Contains some discussion of Poe's "The Power of Words."

Buchloh, Paul G. See GENERAL.

Bulgheroni, Marisa. See GENERAL.

Bungert, Hans. See GENERAL.

Burns, Shannon. "'The Cask of Amontillado': Montresor's Revenge." *Poe Stud*, 7 (June 1974), 25.
     Suggests that Montresor's account of his revenge is "addressed to the bones of his ancestors."

Burt, Donald C. "Poe, Bradbury, and the Science Fiction Tale of Terror." *Mankato State Coll Stud*, 3 (December 1968), 76-84.
     Though Poe and Bradbury see the forces of destruction as coming from different sources, there are many similarities in their works.

Butterfield, R. W. "Total Poe." *EIC*, 22 (April 1972), 196-206.
     An essay-review of *The Poems*, edited by Thomas Ollive Mabbott, Volume I of the *Harvard Collected Works of Edgar Allan Poe*, which sees Poe's importance and great achievement in his being the first author of a new, twentieth-century literature.

Cady, Edwin H. See GENERAL.

Cameron, Kenneth W. "Another Poe Letter for Sale." *ESQ*, no. 63 (Spring 1971), 37.
     Reproduction of a letter from Poe to Ezra Holden.

_____. "Notes on Young Poe's Reading." *ATQ*, 24 (Fall 1974, Supp.), 33-34.
　　A listing of books Poe checked out of the University of Virginia Library.

_____, ed. *The Philosophy of Animal Magnetism.* *ATQ*, 24 (Fall 1974, Part 1), 69 ff.
　　Reproduces this work; Cameron's introduction offers evidence that it was written by Poe.

_____. "Young Poe and the Army--Victorian Editing." *ATQ*, 20 (Fall 1973, Supp., Part 4), 154-193.
　　Scholars once had to and still frequently rely on poorly edited transcripts of documents. The article contains xeroxes of the originals of letters concerning Poe at West Point.

Camp, James, et al. See MISCELLANEOUS (Antebellum).

Campbell, Felicia F. "A Princedom by the Sea." *Lock Haven Rev*, no. 10 (1968), 39-46.
　　Discusses Poe's influence on Nabokov's *Lolita*.

Campbell, J. P. "Deceit and Violence: Motifs in *The Narrative of Arthur Gordon Pym*." *EJ*, 59 (February 1970), 206-212.
　　The motifs of deceit and violence recur throughout the novel as Pym comes to terms with the world through treachery and brutality.

Campos, Haraldo. "Edgar Allan Poe: Una engenharia de avessos." *Colóquio/Letras*, 3 (1971), 5-16.
　　Concerns sound effects in "The Raven" and discusses Portuguese translations of the poem.

Canario, John W. "The Dream in 'The Tell-Tale Heart.'" *Eng Lang Notes*, 7 (March 1970), 194-197.
　　The tale is a hallucinatory nightmare in which the narrator and old man are doubles, representing the mind and the mortal body respectively.

Candelaria, Cordelia. "On the Whiteness at Tsalal: A Note on *Arthur Gordon Pym*." *Poe Stud*, 6 (June 1973), 26.
　　Argues that the image of "devastating snow" helps to explain *Pym*'s closing chapter.

Carlson, Eric W., ed. *Edgar Allan Poe: "The Fall of the House of Usher."* Columbus, Ohio: Charles E. Merrill, 1971.
　　Reprints the text of the story and fifteen critical essays, 1923-1968, in casebook format.

_____. *Poe on the Soul of Man.* Baltimore, Md.: Edgar Allan Poe Society and the Enoch Pratt Free Library, 1973.
　　Believes that the central theme of Poe's work is the soul of man.

Carringer, Robert L. "Circumscription of Space and Form in Poe's *Arthur Gordon Pym*." *PMLA*, 89 (May 1974), 506-516.
　　The curious form of this work results from a conflict between Poe's psychological inclination and the requirements of an unfamiliar genre.

Casale, Ottavio M. "The Battle of Boston: A Re-valuation of Poe's Lyceum Appearance." *AL*, 45 (November 1973), 423-428.
　　Points out Poe's attempts at defending himself when he appeared before Boston's literati on October 16, 1845.

_____. "Poe on Transcendentalism." *ESQ*, 50 (1st Qtr. 1968), 85-97.
　　An omnium-gatherum of Poe's references to transcendentalism, designed to show that Poe was not as completely anti-transcendental as he is usually considered to be.

Cauthen, I. B., Jr. "Another Mallarmé-Manet Book-plate for Poe's *Raven*." *Poe Stud*, 5 (December 1972), 56.
　　On autographed bookplates for Poe's *Raven* signed "S. Mallarmé" and "E. Manet."

Cecil, L. Moffitt. "Poe's Wine List." *Poe Stud*, 5 (December 1972), 41-42.
　　Poe's allusions to wines in his tales reflect his satiric mode.

Cevasco, G. A. "*A Rebours* and Poe's Reputation in France." *Romance Notes*, 13 (Winter 1971), 255-261.
　　It was the hero's praise of Poe in Huysmans' *A Rebours* that brought about Poe's popularity in France.

Chandler, Alice. "'The Visionary Race': Poe's Attitudes Toward His Dreamers." *ESQ*, no. 60 (Fall 1970, Part 2, Supp.), 73-81.
　　In his dreamworld visions Poe ultimately concluded that matter and spirit are one.

Cirlot, Juan-Eduardo. "El pensamiento d'Edgar Poe." *Papeles de Son Armadans*, 52 (January 1969), 239-244.
　　Deals chiefly with Poe's preoccupation with death.

Cixous, Hélène. "Poe re-lu: une poétique du revenir." *Critique*, 28 (1972), 299-327.
　　Deals with the themes of love and death in Poe's works.

Clark, C. E. Frazer, Jr. "Two Unrecorded Notices of Poe's Parents." *Poe Stud*, 4 (December 1971), 37.
　　"Two acting notices of Poe's mother and one notice of his father appear in *The Repertory* (Boston)."

Clark, George P. "A Further Word on Poe and *Lolita*." *Poe Newsletter*, 3 (December 1970), 39.
　　Nabokov's Humbert in *Lolita* is compared to Poe's Montresor of "The Cask of Amontillado."

_____. "Two Unnoticed Recollections of Poe's Funeral." *Poe Newsletter*, 3 (June 1970), 1-2.
　　Charles William Hubner and Colonel J. Alden Weston attended Poe's funeral and have recorded a description of Poe's "hasty interment."

Clark, Harry H. See GENERAL.

Claudel, Alice M. "Poe as Voyager in 'To Helen.'" *ESQ*, no. 60 (Fall 1970, Part 1, Supp.), 33-37.
　　Poe links Greek and Christian traditions in this poem.

_____. "What Has Poe's 'Silence' to Say?" *BSUF*, 10 (Winter 1969), 66-70.

    The silence is the death of poetry; the lynx at the end of the poem may represent escape from the silence.

Colquitt, Betsy F. See GENERAL.

Colwell, James L., and Gary Spitzer. "'Bartleby' and 'The Raven': Parallels of the Irrational." *GaR*, 23 (Spring 1969), 37-43.

    Compares "Bartleby" and "The Raven" according to mood, theme, method, and structure.

Cooney, James F. "'The Cask of Amontillado': Some Further Ironies." *Stud SF*, 11 (Spring 1974), 195-196.

    An awareness of the story's "Roman Catholic cultural and theological materials adds to the irony and transforms a clever trick into an episode of horror."

Covici, Pascal, Jr. "Toward a Reading of Poe's *Narrative of Arthur Gordon Pym*." *Miss Quart*, 21 (Spring 1968), 111-118.

    Contrary to Poe's usual obsession with death, Dick Peters in *Pym*, Poe's longest sustained narrative, is concerned with life.

Cox, James M. "Edgar Poe: Style as Pose." *VQR*, 44 (Winter 1968), 67-89.

    Deals with Poe's "theatrical" poses in his fiction.

Dameron, J. Lasley, et al. "Current Poe Bibliography." *Poe Stud*, 6 (December 1973), 36-42.

    Supplements Richard P. Benton's checklist of Poe criticism and scholarship appearing in *Poe Stud*, 4 (1971), 38-45.

_____, et al. "Current Poe Bibliography." *Poe Stud*, 8 (June 1975), 15-21.

    Supplements the checklist appearing in *Poe Stud*, 6 (1973), 36-42.

_____, et al. "Current Poe Bibliography." *Poe Stud*, 8 (December 1975), 43-46.

    Supplements the checklist appearing in *Poe Stud*, 8 (June 1975), 15-21.

_____, and Irby B. Cauthen, Jr. *Edgar Allan Poe: A Bibliography of Criticism*. Charlottesville: Univ Press of Virginia, 1974.

    Lists and annotates criticism from 1827-1967.

_____. *Edgar Allan Poe: A Checklist of Criticism, 1942-1960*. Charlottesville: Univ Press of Virginia, 1968.

    A comprehensive bibliography.

_____. "Poe and *Blackwood's* Alexander Smith on Truth and Poetry." *Miss Quart*, 22 (Fall 1969), 355-359.

    Poe read Smith's critical essay "The Philosophy of Poetry" and voices some of the same concepts in his own criticism.

_____. "Poe and *Blackwood's* Thomas Doubleday on the Art of Poetry." *Eng Stud*, 49 (December 1968), 540-542.

    Notes similarities between Poe's "Philosophy of Composition" and Doubleday's "How Far Is Poetry an Art," *Blackwood's*, 11 (February 1822).

_____. "Symbolism in the Poetry of Poe and Stephen Crane." *ESQ*, no. 60 (Fall 1970, Part 1, Supp.), 22-28.

    Similarities in the use of the grotesque and the bizarre indicate that Crane was influenced by Poe.

_____. "Thomas Ollive Mabbott on the Canon of Poe's Reviews." *Poe Stud*, 5 (December 1972), 56-57.

    Lists essays and reviews appearing in the Virginia edition which should not be attributed to Poe.

D'Avanzo, Mario L. "'Like Those Nicéan Barks': Helen's Beauty." *Poe Stud*, 6 (June 1973), 26-27.

    Suggests that "Nicéan Barks" in Poe's first "To Helen" could allude to "a tradition, or figure, in Grecian art that is called a 'Nike.'"

Davidson, Gustav. "Poe's 'Israfel.'" *Literary Rev*, 12 (1968), 86-91.

    Deals with the source of the name.

Davis, June and Jack L. "An Error in Some Recent Printings of 'Ligeia.'" *Poe Newsletter*, 3 (June 1970), 21.

    In some printings of "Ligeia" the word "my" is erroneously substituted for "her" at a crucial point, an error that weakens "the dramatic effect of this meticulously structural tale."

_____, and _____. "Poe's Ethereal Ligeia." *Rocky Mt MLA Bul*, 24 (December 1970), 170-176.

    The events of the story are both literal and psychological.

Davis, Richard B. "Poe Criticism: Some Advances Toward Maturity." *Miss Quart*, 23 (Winter 1969-70), 67-76.

    An essay-review evaluating new books: Hubbell (ed.), *Edgar Allan Poe: 'Tales' and 'The Raven and Other Poems'*; Mabbott (ed.), *Edgar Allan Poe*. Vol. I. *Poems*; Stovall, *Edgar Poe the Poet*; Broussard, *The Measure of Poe*; Allen, *Poe and the British Magazine Tradition*; and Jacobs, *Poe, Journalist and Critic*.

Davison, Ned J. "'The Raven' and 'Out of the Cradle Endlessly Rocking.'" *Poe Newsletter*, 1 (April 1968), 5-6.

    Suggests that Whitman's "Out of the Cradle" may have been influenced by "The Raven."

DeFalco, Joseph M. "The Source of Terror in Poe's 'Shadow--A Parable.'" *Stud SF*, 6 (Fall 1969), 643-648.

    The source of the terror is Poe's presentation of "the loss of individuality at death as a revelational climax."

_____. "Whitman's Changes in 'Out of the Cradle' and Poe's 'Raven.'" *Walt Whit Rev*, 16 (March 1970), 22-27.

    Contrasts Whitman's use of the mockingbird as a symbol of hope with Poe's use of the raven.

DeGrazia, Emilio. "Edgar Allan Poe, George Lippard and the 'Spermaceti and Walnut-Coffin Papers.'" *PBSA*, 66 (1st Qtr. 1972), 58-60.
George Lippard, not Poe, is the author of the "Papers."

_____. "Poe's Devoted Democrat, George Lippard." *Poe Stud*, 6 (June 1973), 6-8.
Poe's young friend Lippard, a writer of popular romances, greatly admired Poe, although he did not share Poe's aesthetic principles and critical standards.

Delaney, Joan. "Poe's 'The Gold-Bug' in Russia: A Note on First Impressions." *AL*, 42 (November 1970), 375-379.
Notes that Poe's first acceptance in Russia was in the realm of children's literature.

Delesalle, Jean-François. "Edgar Poe et les *Petits poèmes en prose*." *Bul Baud*, 8 (April 1973), 19-21.
Poe's *Marginalia XVI* is clearly echoed in at least two ways in Baudelaire's *Petits poèmes en prose*.

Dendinger, Lloyd N. "The Ghoul-Haunted Woodland of Robert Frost." *SAB*, 38 (November 1973), 87-94.
In his allegorical use of nature, Frost, like Poe, takes interest in a reality beyond the natural world.

Dowell, Richard W. "The Ironic History of Poe's 'Life in Death': A Literary Skeleton in the Closet." *AL*, 42 (January 1971), 478-486.
Discusses circumstances surrounding Poe's composition of "Life in Death," which later became "The Oval Portrait."

Doyle, Charles C. "The Imitating Monkey: A Folktale Motif in Poe." *NCarF*, 23 (August 1975), 89-91.
Discusses folktale antecedents of Poe's orangutang in "The Murders in the Rue Morgue."

Drabeck, Bernard A. "'Tarr and Fether'--Poe and Abolitionism." *ATQ*, 14 (Spring 1972), 177-184.
The insane insurrectionists represent slaves; the superintendent represents "the aberrant Southern abolitionist"; and the narrator represents "the ignorant, intrusive Northerner."

Drake, William. "The Logic of Survival: *Eureka* in Relation to Poe's Other Works." *ATQ*, 26 (Spring 1975), 15-22.
Eureka brings Poe's thinking to a resolution in the realization that "one's dreams were legitimate if they were not at odds with the truth of experience, which included pain as well as pleasure and death as well as life."

Driskell, Daniel. "Lucretius and 'The City in the Sea.'" *Poe Stud*, 5 (December 1972), 54-55.
Parallels between Lucretius' *De Rerum Natura* and Poe's lyric.

Durzak, Manfred. "Die kunst-theoretische Ausgangsposition Stefan Georges zur Wirkung Edgar Allan Poes." *Arcadia*, 4 (1969), 164-178.
Argues that George was influenced by Poe's aesthetic theory.

_____, et al., eds. *Texte und Kontexte: Studien zur deutschen und vergleichenden Literaturwissenschaft. Festschrift für Norbert Fuerst zum 65. Geburstag.* Bern: Francke, 1973.
Contains an essay comparing the literary theories of Sakutaro Hagiwara and Poe.

Eakin, Paul J. "Poe's Sense of an Ending." *AL*, 45 (March 1973), 1-22.
In his endings Poe was making "daring attempts to construct fiction commensurate with final knowledge."

Eddings, Dennis W. "Poe's 'Dream-Land': Nightmare or Sublime Vision?" *Poe Stud*, 8 (June 1975), 5-8.
Poe's "Dream-Land," although a "vision of the chaotic, disharmonic world of physical reality," affirms the power of the imagination to transcend this disharmony.

Edgar A. Poe. Verona: Editorial Prensa Española, 1971. Los Gigantes Series, no. 7.
Introductory essays on Poe in Spanish, with Spanish translations of some of Poe's works.

Edwards, C. Hines, Jr. See FAULKNER, WILLIAM (Contemporary--2nd Edwards entry).

Ehrlich, Heyward. "The *Broadway Journal* (1): Briggs's Dilemma and Poe's Strategy." *BNYPL*, 73 (February 1969), 74-93.
An account of the magazine based on papers of both Briggs and Poe.

_____. "The 'Mysteries' of Philadelphia: Lippard's *Quaker City* and 'Urban Gothic.'" *ESQ*, 18 (1972), 50-65.
Contains discussion of Poe's relation with Lippard while Poe was living in Philadelphia.

Elagin, Ivan. "Poe in Blok's Literary Heritage." *Russ Rev*, 32 (October 1973), 403-412.
Deals with Poe's "sporadic" influence on Blok.

Elkins, William R. "The Dream World and the Dream Vision: Meaning and Structure in Poe's Art." *Emporia State Res Stud*, 17 (September 1968), 5-17.
Using "MS Found in a Bottle" to support the thesis that Poe's works reflect his own struggle for identity, which is only to be found in the imagination.

Ellyson, Louise. "A Few Kind Words for Rosalie." *New Dominion Life Style*, 2 (February 1975), 6-10.
Biographical appreciation for Poe's sister, Rosalie.

Empiric, Julienne H. "A Note on 'Annabel Lee.'" *Poe Stud*, 6 (June 1973), 23.
The narrator of "Annabel Lee" expresses a child-like, grotesque vision of reality.

Englekirk, John E. "Crónica de 'El cuervo' de Cazenueve." *Hisp Mod*, 34 (1968), 612-629.
An account of a translation of "The Raven" by Felipe G. Cazenueve, published in 1890 in Eagle Pass, Texas.

Erickson, John D. "Valéry on Leonardo, Poe and Mallarmé." *L'Esprit Createur*, 13 (Fall 1973), 252-259.

An essay-review on *Paul Valéry: Leonardo, Poe and Mallarmé*, the eighth volume in the Bollingen *Collected Works of Paul Valéry*, a collection of essays on the three named artists. The article also contains discussion of why Valéry was attracted to Poe.

Evans, Walter. "Poe's Revisions in His Reviews of Hawthorne's *Twice-Told Tales*." *PBSA*, 66 (1972), 407-419.

Discusses the significance of Poe's revisions in focusing on the importance of skillful construction.

Fabre, Michel. See WRIGHT, RICHARD.

Falk, Doris V. "Poe and the Power of Animal Magnetism." *PMLA*, 84 (May 1969), 536-546.

Since Poe's tales of mesmerism derive from the concept of animal magnetism, a cohesive force which organizes both mind and matter, these tales bear a relation to his other works.

_____. "Thomas Low Nichols, Poe, and the 'Balloon Hoax.'" *Poe Stud*, 5 (December 1972), 48-49.

Poe "undermines his own success with the 'Balloon Hoax.'"

Finger, Hans, ed. *Interpretationen zu Irving, Melville, und Poe*. Frankfurt: Diesterweg, 1971.

Introductory essays in German.

Finholt, Richard D. "The Vision at the Brink of the Abyss: 'A Descent into the Maelstrom' in the Light of Poe's Cosmology." *GaR*, 27 (Fall 1973), 356-366.

The effectiveness of Poe's story derives "not so much from the drama of the sailor's duel with the Maelstrom as from the vision he wins at its brink"; it is "a vision of the nature of the cosmos and man's place in it."

Fisher, Benjamin F., IV. "Blackwood Articles á la Poe: How to Make a False Start Pay." *RLV*, 39 (1973), 418-432.

Deals with Poe's technique of beginning a story one way and altering it to another.

_____. "Dickens and Poe: *Pickwick* and 'Ligeia.'" *Poe Stud*, 6 (June 1973), 14-16.

Examines Poe's borrowing from and modification of Dickens' "A Madman's MS," a tale from the *Pickwick Papers*.

_____. "Poe, Blackwood's and 'The Murders in the Rue Morgue.'" *Am N&Q*, 12 (March 1974), 109-110.

An account of an ape in a *Blackwood's* article is a possible source.

_____. "Poe's 'Metzengerstein': Not a Hoax." *AL*, 42 (January 1971), 487-494.

Compares the first published text with the final published version to prove that the story is an early venture, by Poe, into Gothic fiction.

_____. "Poe's 'Usher' Tarred & Fethered." *Poe Stud*, 6 (December 1973), 49.

Discusses burlesque elements in Poe's "The System of Dr. Tarr and Professor Fether" and in "The Fall of the House of Usher."

_____. "To 'The Assignation' from 'The Visionary' and Poe's Decade of Revising." *Lib Chron*, 39 (1973), 89-105.

The original magazine versions of these two works should be reprinted in order to aid study of Poe's methods of composition and revision.

Fletcher, Richard M. *The Stylistic Development of Edgar Allan Poe*. The Hague: Mouton, 1973.

A close analysis of Poe's word device and vocabulary which asserts that he was more obsessed with sound that sense in his prose and poetry.

Flory, Wendy S. "Rehearsals for Dying in Poe and Emily Dickinson." *ATQ*, 18 (Spring 1973), 13-18.

Both Poe and Dickinson frequently sought to convey the experience of death; both believed that the search "for the meaning of human existence" would continue after death; and both "consistently recur to states of paralysis and vertigo."

_____. "Usher's Fear and the Flaw in Poe's Theories of the Metamorphosis of the Senses." *Poe Stud*, 7 (June 1974), 17-19.

In "Usher," Poe evades a flaw in his theory of metamorphosis--a theory that assumes that "the senses persist after the death of the physical body"--by depicting Roderick Usher as a weak character.

Forclaz, Roger. "Edgar Poe et la psychoanalyse." *RLV*, 36 (1970), 272-288, 375-389.

Rejects psychoanalytic interpretations of Poe and his work.

_____. "Edgar Poe et les animaux." *RLV*, 39 (1973), 483-496.

Deals with Poe's use of animals in his fiction.

_____. "Le monde d'Edgar Poe." Berne: Herbert Lang; Frankfort: Peter Lang, 1974. (Volume 17 in the Europäische Hochschulschriften, Series 14.)

A study of the world in which Poe actually lived and the world which he created.

Fraiberg, Louis. "Poe's Intimations of Mortality." *Hartford Stud in Lit*, 5 (1973), 106-125.

Poe was torn between an unconscious wish to die and a fear of dying. The wish prevailed.

Freehafer, John. "Poe's 'Cask of Amontillado': A Tale of Effect." *Jahrbuch für Amerikastudien*, 13 (1968), 134-142.

Discusses the devices Poe used to carry out his intention of creating a "tale of effect."

Freeman, Fred B., Jr. "A Note on Poe's 'Miss B.'" *AL*, 43 (March 1971), 115-117.

Short biographical notes on Eliza J. Butterfield, a lady favored by Poe's attention.

_____. "Poe's 'Miss B' and 'Annie.'" *Am N&Q*, 12 (January 1974), 79-80.
    Information on Eliza Butterfield and Annie Richmond, both "candidates" for Poe's "last love"; the two women were buried only thirty feet from each other.

_____. "Poe's Lowell Trips." *Poe Stud*, 4 (December 1971), 23-24.
    On the relationship between Poe and Mrs. Annie Richmond.

Freese, Peter. See CAPOTE, TRUMAN (Contemporary).

Friedl, Herwig. "Die Bedeutung der Perspektiv in den Landschaftsskizzen von Edgar Allan Poe." *Archiv*, 210 (1973), 86-93.
    Deals with nature and art in Poe's landscapes.

_____. "Poe und Lanier. Ein Vergleich ihrer Versdichtung." *Jahrbuch für Amerikastudien*, 15 (1970), 123-140.
    Concentrates on differences in techniques and objectives in the poetry of Poe and Lanier.

Frushell, Richard C. "An Incarnate Night-Mare: Moral Grotesquerie in 'The Black Cat.'" *Poe Stud*, 5 (December 1972), 43-44.
    Poe's cats are "progressively emblematic of the perversity of the narrator."

Furrow, Sharon. "Psyche and Setting: Poe's Picturesque Landscapes." *Criticism*, 15 (Winter 1973), 16-27.
    Concerns Poe's pictorial presentation of the natural world, his landscapes and seascapes.

Gaillard, Dawson. "Poe's *Eureka*: The Triumph of the Word." *ATQ*, 26 (Spring 1975), 42-46.
    Poe is concerned in *Eureka* to convey his belief that only through language, "only by saying can we initiate the experience of being in a universe of divine immanence."

Gale, Robert L. *Barron's Simplified Approach to Edgar Allen* [sic] *Poe.* Woodbury, N. Y.: Barron's Educational Series, 1969.
    A student guide to the stories, poems, and criticism.

_____. *Plots and Characters in the Fiction and Poetry of Edgar Allan Poe.* Hamden, Conn.: Archon Books, 1970.
    Plot and content summaries of the tales and poems, a character index, and chronologies of Poe's life and works.

Gargano, James W. "Art and Irony in 'William Wilson.'" *ESQ*, no. 60 (Fall 1970, Part 1, Supp.), 18-22.
    The story is ironic because a deranged William Wilson lives in an orderly society.

_____. "Poe's 'Morella': A Note on Her Name." *AL*, 47 (May 1975), 259-264.
    Suggests that "the first three letters of [Morella's] name contain a resonant Latin root for 'death' and that the last four constitute a diminutive."

_____. "The Theme of Time in 'The Tell-Tale Heart.'" *Stud SF*, 5 (Summer 1968), 378-382.
    The unreliability of the narrator's description of himself and of his actions and "a set of internally consistent symbols that are charged with meaning" make this more than a mere tale of terror.

Garmon, Gerald M. "Emerson's 'Moral Sentiment' and Poe's 'Poetic Sentiment': A Reconsideration." *Poe Stud*, 6 (June 1973), 19-21.
    An examination of Emerson's "Moral Sentiment" and Poe's "Poetic Sentiment" demonstrates that the terms posit largely similar attitudes toward art and morality.

_____. "Roderick Usher: 'Portrait of the Madman as an Artist.'" *Poe Stud*, 5 (June 1972), 11-14.
    Roderick Usher longs for freedom but is destroyed by his environment and heredity.

Garrett, Walter. "The 'Moral' of 'Ligeia' Reconsidered." *Poe Stud*, 4 (June 1971), 19-20.
    Ligeia's resurrection effects an allegorical unification of God and universe.

Garrison, Joseph M., Jr. "The Irony of 'Ligeia.'" *ESQ*, no. 60 (Fall 1970, Part 1, Supp.), 13-17.
    The irony lies in the fact that the narrator, wishing to regain Ligeia, is left alone.

Gendre, André. "Gaston Bachelard et *les Aventures d'Arthur Gordon Pym* d'Edgar Poe." *Lettres Romanes*, 26 (May 1972), 169-180.
    Contrary to some earlier views, Bachelard does show, in his *L'Eau et les rêves* and in the introduction to his edition of Poe's *Pym* in "Voyages imaginaires," that his criticism can encompass a whole work rather than fragmentary aspects.

Gerber, Gerald E. "The Coleridgean Context of Poe's *Blackwood* Satires." *ESQ*, no. 60 (Fall 1970, Part 2, Supp.), 87-91.
    Coleridge's influence is particularly evident in "The Psyche Zenobia" and "The Scythe of Time."

_____. "Milton and Poe's 'Modern Woman.'" *Poe Newsletter*, 3 (December 1970), 25-26.
    Milton was a convenient source for the satiric depiction of Signora Psyche Zenobia, the modernist heroine of Poe's "How to Write a Blackwood Article" and "A Predicament."

_____. "Poe and *The Manuscript*." *Poe Stud*, 6 (June 1973), 27.
    Points to similarities between three of Poe's tales and works appearing in *The Manuscript*, a periodical published in New York 1827-1828.

_____. "Poe's Odd Angel." *NCF*, 23 (June 1968), 88-93.
    Poe is burlesquing "the spirit of reform."

Goetz, Thomas H. "Taine on Poe: A Neglected French Critic." *Poe Stud*, 6 (December 1973), 35-36.
    In a brief letter to Charles Baudelaire, Taine expresses admiration for Poe, but considers *Eureka* "too akin to philosophy."

Gogol, John M. "Two Russian Symbolists on Poe." *Poe Newsletter*, 3 (December 1970), 36-37.
Translations of two poems on Poe by Konstantin Balmont (1867-1943), and a translation of Alexander Blok's review (1906) of Balmont's translation of Poe's works.

Goldhurst, William. "Edgar Allan Poe and the Conquest of Death." *New Orleans Rev*, 1 (Summer 1969), 316-319.
Argues that Poe was not morbidly preoccupied with death.

_____. "Poe's Multiple 'King Pest': A Source Study." *Tulane Stud in Eng*, 20 (1972), 107-121.
Suggests that a source can be found in what Poe had read about the London plague and what he had read in German myth and folklore.

_____. "Sport of 'Poe Creating' Continues." Richmond *Times-Dispatch*, October 15, 1972, p. F-3.
Poe is best understood by attention to his technical virtuosity as a writer rather than by his life.

_____, et al. "Three Observations on 'Amontillado' and *Lolita*." *Poe Stud*, 5 (December 1972), 51.
Points out similarities between Poe's story and Nabokov's *Lolita*.

Graham, D. B. "Yone Noguchi's 'Poe Mania.'" *MarkR*, 4 (May 1974), 58-60.
An account of accusations and responses to them that Noguchi plagiarized from Poe's poetry.

Granger, Byrd H. "Devil Lore in 'The Raven.'" *Poe Stud*, 5 (December 1972), 53-54.
Concludes that Poe's narrator damns himself.

Gravely, William H., Jr. "A Few Words of Clarification on 'Hans Pfaal.'" *Poe Stud*, 5 (December 1972), 56.
On the composition date of "Pfaal."

_____. "New Sources for Poe's 'Hans Pfaal.'" *Tenn Stud in Lit*, 17 (1972), 139-149.
"Poe's most significant sources are scientific rather than fictional."

_____. "A Note on the Composition of Poe's 'Hans Pfaal.'" *Poe Newsletter*, 3 (June 1970), 2-5.
Poe's most significant sources of "Hans Pfaal" are scientific, not fictional.

Greer, H. Allan. "Poe's 'Hans Pfaal' and the Political Scene." *ESQ*, no. 60 (Fall 1970, Part 2, Supp.), 67-73.
Deals with Poe's purposes in writing "Hans Pfaal."

Grieve, A. I. "Rossetti's Illustrations to Poe." *Apollo*, 97 (February 1973), 142-145.
Comments on Poe's influence on Rossetti's painting, reproduces paintings that reflect that influence and some of Rossetti's illustrations for Poe works.

Gross, Seymour. "*Native Son* and 'The Murders in the Rue Morgue': An Addendum." *Poe Stud*, 8 (June 1975), 23.
Points out evidence that Richard Wright had read Poe's story during the composition of *Native Son*.

Grossman, Joan D. *Edgar Allan Poe in Russia: A Study in Legend and Literary Influence*. Wurzburg: Jal-Verlag, 1973.
Surveys the ups and downs in Poe's reputation in Russia and the nature and extent of his influence on Russian writers.

Guidacci, Margherita. "Su un racconto di Poe: 'La maschera della morte rossa.'" *Humanitas*, 10 (1974), 721-730.
Analyzes "The Masque of the Red Death" and compares it with Hawthorne's "Howe's Masquerade."

Halliburton, David. *Edgar Allan Poe: A Phenomenological View*. Princeton, N. J.: Princeton Univ Press, 1973.
Deals with the "internal dynamics" and "signifying intention" of Poe's works.

Hammond, Alexander. "Further Notes on Poe's Folio Club Tales." *Poe Stud*, 8 (December 1975), 38-42.
Discusses the Folio Club stories as a group, with particular attention to "Raising the Wind; or Diddling Considered as One of the Exact Sciences," "Loss of Breath. A Tale à la Blackwood," "Siope--A Fable," and "King Pest the First."

_____. "Poe's 'Lionizing' and the Design of *Tales of the Folio Club*." *ESQ*, 18 (3rd Qtr. 1972), 154-165.
Studies sources for Poe's "Lionizing" and examines the story as it relates to the overall content of *Tales of the Folio Club*.

_____. "A Reconstruction of Poe's 1833 *Tales of the Folio Club*." *Poe Stud*, 5 (December 1972), 25-32.
Identifies Poe's *Tales of the Folio Club* on the basis of bibliographic and textual evidence.

Harap, Louis. "Edgar Allan Poe and Journalism." *ZAA*, 19, no. 2 (1971), 164-181.
Deals with the differences between Poe's theories as a literary critic and as a journalist.

Harkey, Joseph H. "A Note on Fortunato's Coughing." *Poe Newsletter*, 3 (June 1970), 22.
Close attention to Fortunato's coughing fit in Poe's "The Cask of Amontillado" reveals "a high degree of artistic subtlety."

Harp, Richard L. "A Note on the Harmony of Style and Theme in Poe's *Narrative of Arthur Gordon Pym*." *CEA Critic*, 36 (March 1974), 8-11.
Contends that the attention to detail in Pym's narrative is essential to the central theme of the book.

Harris, Kathryn M. "Ironic Revenge in Poe's 'The Cask of Amontillado.'" *Stud SF*, 6 (Spring 1969), 333-335.
Understanding the mason-Catholic conflict makes this a more coherent tale than has been recognized. The trowel as a symbol of brotherhood and an instrument of death provides an irony that gives coherence to the tale

and to Montresor's sarcasms, and suggests a motive for the murder.

Haskell, John D. "Poe, Literary *Soirées*, and Coffee." *Poe Stud*, 8 (December 1975), 47.
  Concerns Poe's visits to the Amity Place home of John Russell Bartlett in New York City.

Haswell, Henry. "Baudelaire's Self-Portrait of Poe: 'Edgar Allan Poe: sa vie et ses ouvrages.'" *Romance Notes*, 10 (Spring 1969), 253-260.
  In spite of the fact that Baudelaire plagiarized most of this essay from the *Southern Literary Messenger*, he still succeeded in manipulating the facts "in order to re-create Poe in his own image."

Hatvary, George E. "The Whereabouts of Poe's 'Fifty Suggestions.'" *Poe Stud*, 4 (December 1971), 47.
  On documenting the first appearance of Poe's "Fifty Suggestions."

Hayter, Alethea. *Opium and the Romantic Imagination*. Berkeley: Univ of California Press, 1968.
  There is no evidence that Poe took opium or that, if he did, he was addicted to it.

Heaney, Howell J. "'The Raven' Revisited." *MSS*, 25 (1973), 87-95.
  Deals chiefly with the Gimbel collection of Poe in the Free Library of Pennsylvania.

Helms, Randel. "Another Source for Poe's *Arthur Gordon Pym*." *AL*, 41 (January 1970), 572-575.
  Finds in Jane Porter's novel *Sir Edward Seaward's Narrative of His Shipwreck* a possible source for *Pym*.

Henninger, Francis J. "The Bouquet of Poe's Amontillado." *SAB*, 35 (March 1970), 35-40.
  The ending of "The Cask of Amontillado" is startling since Montresor realizes that he has taken his revenge on a man gone mad.

Hess, Jeffrey A. "Sources and Aesthetics of Poe's Landscape Fiction." *AQ*, 22 (Summer 1970), 177-189.
  Attempts to link Poe's fictional landscapes to particular books and paintings of the early nineteenth century.

Hinden, Michael. "Poe's Debt to Wordsworth: A Reading of 'Stanzas.'" *Stud in Romanticism*, 8 (Winter 1969), 109-120.
  Supports the thesis that "Stanzas" was influenced by Wordsworth's "Intimations" ode.

Hinz, Evelyn J. "The Source of *The Narrative of Arthur Gordon Pym of Nantucket* of Edgar Allan Poe." *Satire Newsl*, 9 (Spring 1972), 138-143.
  A satire on source-hunting.

_____. "'Tekeli-li': *The Narrative of Arthur Gordon Pym* as Satire." *Genre*, 3 (December 1970), 379-399.
  Treats *Pym* as a Menippean satire.

Hirsch, David H. "Another Source for 'The Pit and the Pendulum.'" *Miss Quart*, 23 (Winter 1969-70), 35-43.

Proposes another *Blackwood's* article as an additional source for the story and cites parallel passages.

_____. "The Pit and the Apocalypse." *SR*, 76 (October-December 1968), 632-652.
  Suggests that Poe's use of Biblical allusions creates a style that raises "The Pit and the Pendulum" above the realm of pure horror.

Hoberg, Perry F. "'Poe' Trickster-Cosmologist." *ATQ*, 26 (Spring 1975), 30-37.
  Deals with *Eureka*.

Hoffman, Daniel. "I Have Been Faithful to You in My Fashion: The Remarriage of Ligeia's Husband." *SouR*, 8 (Winter 1972), 89-105.
  Analyzes Poe's Ligeia for her meanings as female myth figure and as psychological archetype.

_____. *Poe Poe Poe Poe Poe Poe Poe*. Garden City, N. Y.: Doubleday, 1972.
  A highly personal reading of Poe's work, based on a lifetime's acquaintance, which attempts to elucidate the full range of emotion Poe's writing stirs in the reader.

_____. "Send-Ups." *London Mag*, 9 (January 1970), 30-36.
  Deals with Poe's "exploring" mind.

Hoffman, Gerhard. "Raum und Symbol in den Kurzgeschichten Edgar Allan Poes." *Jahrbuch für Amerikastudien*, 16 (1971), 102-107.
  Deals with the symbolic significance of the settings of "The Fall of the House of Usher" and "The Masque of the Red Death."

Hoffmeister, Charles C. "'William Wilson' and *The Double*: A Freudian Insight." *Coranto*, 9, no. 2 (1974), 24-27.
  William Wilson and Dostoyevsky's Golyadkin see themselves differently from the Freudian point of view, but neither can accept his conception of himself.

Hogue, L. Lynn. "Eroticism in Poe's 'For Annie.'" *ESQ*, no. 60 (Fall 1970, Part 2, Supp.), 85-87.
  "For Annie" is the only one of Poe's poems that is explicitly erotic.

Hollander, John. "The Music of Silence." *Prose*, 7 (1973), 79-91.
  In Poe's works silence "suggests an emblem of the poetic mind's awareness of its own listening, and a reciprocal picture of the uncommunicativeness of nature, her blank pages."

Holman, Harriet R. "Hog, Bacon, Ram and Other 'Savans' in *Eureka*: Notes Toward Decoding Poe's Encyclopedic Satire." *Poe Newsletter*, 2 (1969), 49-55.
  On the importance of *Eureka* in interpreting Poe as satirist.

_____. "Longfellow in 'The Rue Morgue.'" *ESQ*, no. 60 (Fall 1970, Part 2, Supp.), 58-60.
  In Poe's "The Murders in the Rue Morgue" the references to a "little fellow" are to Longfellow.

_____. "Splitting Poe's 'Epicurean Atoms': Further Speculation on the Literary Satire of *Eureka*." *Poe Stud*, 5 (December 1972), 33-37.
Poe's concept of "Epicurean Atoms" is applied with irony and satire.

Holoquist, Michael. "Whodunit and Other Questions: Metaphysical Detective Stories in Post-War Fiction." *New Lit Hist*, 3 (Autumn 1971), 135-156.
Poe's contributions to detective fiction are mentioned.

Howarth, William L., ed. *Twentieth Century Interpretations of Poe's Tales*. Englewood Cliffs, N. J.: Prentice-Hall, 1971.
Reprints ten excerpts and abridgements, five full essays, and includes a chronology, a selected bibliography, and an original introduction by the editor.

Hubbell, Jay B. "The Literary Apprenticeship of Edgar Allan Poe." *So Lit Jour*, 2 (Fall 1969), 99-105.
Poe mastered the craft of poetry, criticism, and fiction by playing "the sedulous ape" to the various writers whom he admired or disliked.

_____, ed. *'Tales' and 'The Raven and Other Poems.'* Columbus, Ohio: Charles E. Merrill, 1970.
Facsimile reproduction of the first editions of *Tales* (1845) and *The Raven and Other Poems* (1845), with an introduction to Poe's life and reputation.

_____. See GENERAL.

Hubert, Thomas. "The Southern Element in Poe's Fiction." *GaR*, 28 (Summer 1974), 200-211.
Southern qualities in Poe's fiction include "the high formalism of his prose style; his idealization of woman; his espousal of agrarian ideals along with an antipathy for industrialism...."

Humma, John B. "Poe's 'Ligeia': Glanvill's Will or Blake's Will?" *Miss Quart*, 26 (Winter 1972-73), 55-62.
Will as evil is the motivating force of the story.

Hussey, John P. "'Mr. Pym' and 'Mr. Poe': The Two Narrators of 'Arthur Gordon Pym.'" *SAB*, 39 (May 1974), 22-32.
Pym is unconcerned with questions of larger meaning, which originate with the "Mr. Poe" of the Preface.

_____. "Narrative Voice and Classical Rhetoric in *Eureka*." *ATQ*, 26 (Spring 1975), 37-42.
The narrator of *Eureka* is the "apotheosis" of the successful "rhetorician"; he "utters Poe's version of an epideictic oration on the sublime."

Hyneman, Esther F. *Edgar Allan Poe: An Annotated Bibliography of Books and Articles in English, 1827-1973*. Boston: G. K. Hall and Co., 1974.
A volume in the Research Bibliographies in American Literature Series.

Idol, John L., Jr. "William Cowper Brann on Edgar Allan Poe." *Poe Stud*, 7 (June 1974), 24-25.
Cites adverse comments on Poe by a notable American magazinist and journalist of the late nineteenth century.

Inge, M. Thomas, and Gloria Downing. "Unamuno and Poe." *Poe Newsletter*, 3 (December 1970), 35-36.
A translation of Miguel de Unamuno y Jugo's response to Ernesto Montenegro's review of John W. Robertson's *Edgar A. Poe: A Psychopathic Study* appearing in *La Nación*, August 19, 1923.

_____. See GENERAL--2nd Inge entry.

Isani, Mukhtar A. "A Further Word on Poe and Alexander Crane." *Poe Stud*, 7 (December 1974), 48.
Compares two interviews of Crane, an office boy in the office of the *Broadway Journal*, who relates his impressions of Poe.

_____. "Reminiscences of Poe by an Employee of the *Broadway Journal*." *Poe Stud*, 6 (December 1973), 33-34.
A summary of an interview, first appearing in the *London Academy*, 63 (September 1902), 280, with the aged Alexander Crane, who had been an office boy for Poe's *Broadway Journal*.

_____. "Some Sources for Poe's 'Tale of the Ragged Mountains.'" *Poe Stud*, 5 (December 1972), 38-40.
Poe's Indian episode in "Tale of the Ragged Mountains" is intended as burlesque.

Jackson, David K. "Addendum to a Footnote: 'The Bells.'" *Poe Stud*, 8 (December 1975), 47.
On George Newell Lovejoy's fictitious account of Poe's writing of "The Bells."

_____. "A Poe Hoax Comes Before the U. S. Senate." *Poe Stud*, 7 (December 1974), 47-48.
Explains how Poe's "The Journal of Julius Rodman" can be "found in U. S. Senate Document of the 26th Congress, 1st Session, Volume IV (1839-40)...."

_____. "A Typographical Error in the B Version of Poe's 'Sonnet--To Science.'" *Poe Newsletter*, 3 (June 1970), 21.
Discusses a misspelling appearing in *The Philadelphia Saturday Evening Post* version of Poe's sonnet in the light of possible textual discrepancies found in other versions.

Jacobs, Robert D. *Poe: Journalist and Critic*. Baton Rouge: Louisiana State Univ Press, 1969.
Instead of explicating Poe's esthetic principles as a journalist and critic, Jacobs attempts to evaluate his success in applying the theories to the work of others by a chronological review of his criticism, also taking into account such external matters as popular trends of thought and the practical pressures of the journalistic world.

_____. "The Seven Faces of Poe." *So Lit Jour*, 6 (Spring 1974), 107-123.
An essay-review of Daniel Hoffman's *Poe Poe Poe Poe Poe Poe Poe*, which finds the work an

"extraordinary book" and a challenging study of Poe by one who identified with Poe to the extent that he had "to devise some strategy to maintain the psychic balance of a literary critic."

Jacobs, William Jay. *Edgar Allan Poe: Genius in Torment*. New York: McGraw-Hill, 1975.
A biography and critical estimate of Poe for the juvenile reader.

Jannaccone, Pasquale. "The Aesthetics of Edgar Poe." Trans. Peter Mitilineos. *Poe Stud*, 7 (June 1974), 1-13.
This nineteenth-century essay states that Poe's aesthetic owes much to Coleridge's *Biographia Literaria* and, among other things, to certain stylistic features Poe found in Shelley's short poems.

Jeffrey, David K. "The Johnsonian Influence: *Rasselas* and Poe's 'The Domain of Arnheim.'" *Poe Newsletter*, 3 (December 1970), 26-29.
Poe's Arnheim and Johnson's "Amhara" are physically comparable and can be associated with the meaning of death.

Joseph, Gerhard J. "Poe and Tennyson." *PMLA*, 88 (May 1973), 418-428.
The delight of both poets in sound for its own sake led them to a comparable strategy in showing the soul's attempt to escape gross materiality.

Kaplan, Harold. See GENERAL.

Karatson, André. *Edgar Allan Poe et le groupe des ecrivains du 'Nyugat' in Hongrie*. Paris: Presses Universitaires de France, 1971.
Discusses Poe as a major influence on Hungarian poets.

Kehler, Joel R. "New Light on the Genesis and Progress of Poe's Landscape Fiction." *AL*, 47 (May 1975), 173-183.
Traces the various influences on Poe's story "The Landscape Garden."

Kelley, David J. "Delacroix, Ingres et Poe: Valeurs picturales et valeurs littéraires dans l'oeuvre critique de Baudelaire." *Rev d'Histoire Littéraire*, 71 (July-August 1971), 606-614.
Though Baudelaire thought of Delacroix and Ingres as being different, he used some of the same language in speaking of Ingres that he did in pointing out similarities between Poe and Delacroix.

Kennedy, J. Gerald. "Jeffrey Aspern and Edgar Allan Poe: A Speculation." *Poe Stud*, 6 (June 1973), 17-18.
Suggests that James's Jeffrey Aspern in *The Aspern Papers* could be Poe.

_____. "The Preface as a Key to the Satire in *Pym*." *Stud in the Novel*, 5 (Summer 1973), 191-196.
Poe's actual intention in *Pym*—to satisfy Harper Brothers' requirements for a long work, to dupe the reading public, and to salvage his own self-respect—may be seen by understanding the deftly ironic Preface.

Kesterson, D. B., ed. *Critics on Poe*. Coral Gables, Fla.: Univ of Miami Press, 1973.
Reprints thirty-nine critical excerpts and full essays on Poe's poetry and fiction, 1845-1969, with a chronology and selected bibliography.

Ketterer, David. "Poe's Usage of the Hoax and the Unity of 'Hans Pfaal.'" *Criticism*, 13 (Fall 1971), 377-385.
A defense of the unity of "Hans Pfaal" through a presentation of what the hoax really is in the story and of its relation to Poe's theory of reality.

_____. "Protective Irony and 'The Full Design' of *Eureka*." *ATQ*, 26 (Spring 1975), 46-55.
Eureka is a "cosmological structure based on aesthetic principles."

_____. "The S[cience] F[iction] Element in the Work of Poe: A Chronological Survey." *Sci Fic Stud*, 1 (1974), 197-213.
Title is descriptive.

_____. See GENERAL.

Kilburn, Patrick E. "Poe's 'Evening Star.'" *Expl*, 28 (May 1970), Item 76.
Poe indicates a preference for love over chastity in this poem.

Kimball, William J. "Poe's *Politian* and the Beauchamp-Sharp Tragedy." *Poe Stud*, 4 (December 1971), 24-27.
"Poe's *Politian* parallels the Beauchamp-Sharp Story, known as the 'Kentucky Tragedy.'"

Kime, Wayne R. "Poe's Use of Irving's *Astoria* in 'The Journal of Julius Rodman.'" *AL*, 40 (May 1968), 215-222.
Presents parallel texts to show similarities and differences between Poe's hoax and Irving's *Astoria* in character, incident, and minor details.

_____. "Poe's Use of Mackenzie's *Voyages* in 'The Journal of Julius Rodman.'" *WAL*, 3 (Spring 1968), 61-67.
Poe used *Voyages* to develop his "pseudo-realistic" background for "Rodman."

Knowlton, Edgar C., Jr. "Poe's Debt to Father Bouhours." *Poe Stud*, 4 (December 1971), 27-29.
Discusses Poe's acquaintance with Father Dominique Bouhours' *La Manière de bien Penser*.

Koster, Donald N. "Poe, Romance and Reality." *ATQ*, 19 (Summer 1973), 8-12.
"Ligeia" is not a work of the supernatural but instead is a realistic probing of the human psyche; the narrator is revealing that he has murdered Ligeia as well as Rowena.

La Guardia, David M. "Poe, *Pym*, and Initiation." *ESQ*, no. 60 (Fall 1970, Part 2, Supp.), 82-84.
Pym is the initiate artist.

Lange, Victor, and Hans-Gert Roloff, eds. *Dichtung Sprache, Gesellschaft: Akten des IV. Internationalen Germanisten Kongresses 1970 in Princeton*. Frankfurt: Athenäum, 1971.

Contains an essay by Liselotte Dieckmann on Poe and E. T. A. Hoffmann.

Lawson, Lewis. "Poe and the Grotesque: A Bibliography, 1695-1965." *Poe Newsletter*, 1 (April 1968), 9-10.
    Bibliographical references to sources which Poe might have used in arriving at his concept of the grotesque, and articles on his use of the grotesque.

Leary, Lewis. "Edgar Allan Poe: The Adolescent as Confidence Man." *So Lit Jour*, 4 (Spring 1972), 3-21.
    A brief analysis of several of Poe's major works reveals Poe as a beguiler, a trickster, a literary confidence man, whose spirit is with us still.

_____. "Miss Octavia's Autograph Album and Edgar Allan Poe." *Columbia Lib Columns*, 17 (February 1968), 9-15.
    Deals with the significance for Poe biography of a poem, supposedly written by Poe, in Octavia Walton's album.

Lease, Benjamin. "John Neal and Edgar Allan Poe." *Poe Stud*, 7 (December 1974), 38-41.
    "Poe's expressions of nationalistic sentiment, his involvement with *Blackwood's*, his ironic mode...are better understood against the background of his...relationship with John Neal."

LeClair, Thomas. "Poe's *Pym* and Nabokov's *Pale Fire*." *NConL*, 3 (March 1973), 2-3.
    Discusses the similarities of visions experienced by characters in both works.

Lee, Grace F. "The Quest of Arthur Gordon Pym." *So Lit Jour*, 4 (Spring 1972), 22-23.
    In Pym's voyage "all matter is subsumed into unity" and his quest within himself takes him back to "the universal essence of being."

Lees, Daniel E. "An Early Model for Poe's 'The Raven.'" *Papers on Lang and Lit*, 6 (Winter 1970), 92-95.
    Poe may have been influenced by an article about ravens and by a poem called "The Owl"-- both in *Blackwood's*.

Leibman, Mary C. "Dr. Maudsley, Forgotten Poe Diagnostician." *Poe Stud*, 5 (December 1972), 55.
    A British physician authors an 1860 article on Poe's "psychological condition."

Lentricchia, Frank. "Four Types of Nineteenth Century Aesthetic." *Jour of Aesthetics and Art Crit*, 26 (Spring 1968), 351-366.
    Poe's theory allows for both the transparent and the opaque in poetry.

Lerner, Arthur. *Psychoanalytically Oriented Criticism of Three American Poets: Poe, Whitman, and Aiken.* Rutherford, N. J.: Fairleigh Dickinson Univ Press, 1970.
    Subjects eight poems by Poe to psychoanalytical criticism in a brief study.

Levine, Richard A. "The Downward Journey of Purgation: Notes on an Imagistic Leitmotif in *The Narrative of Arthur Gordon Pym*." *Poe Newsletter*, 2 (April 1969), 29-31.
    The imagery of above and below supports the conclusion that the story concerns the conflict between the rational and irrational, the conscious and the unconscious.

Levine, Stuart. *Edgar Poe: Seer and Craftsman.* Deland, Fla.: Everett/Edwards, 1972.
    A comprehensive reading of the fiction which focuses on Poe's craftsmanship rather than on his life.

_____, and Susan. "History, Myth, Fable, Satire: Poe's Use of Jacob Bryant." *ESQ*, 21 (4th Qtr. 1975), 197-214.
    Discusses the influence of Bryant's *Mythology* on Poe and Poe's reaction to the errors in Bryant.

_____. *The Short Fiction of Edgar Allan Poe.* Indianapolis, Indiana: Bobbs-Merrill, 1975.
    A thoroughly annotated critical edition of sixty-nine stories arranged by type and subject matter.

Lévy, Maurice. "Edgar Poe et la tradition 'gothique.'" *Caliban*, 5, no. 1 (1968), 35-51.
    Sets Poe in the Gothic tradition by pointing out similarities in various Poe works and Gothic novels such as *The Castle of Otranto*; Poe's works, however, are more artistic and have an added psychological element.

_____. (Richard Henry Haswell, trans.) "Poe and the Gothic Tradition." *ESQ*, 18 (1st Qtr. 1972), 19-29.
    Poe was undoubtedly interested in an array of manias, but his stories nevertheless are deeply indebted to the traditional motifs of Gothic fiction.

_____. "*Pym*, Conte Fantastique?" *EA*, 27 (January-March 1974), 38-44.
    Discusses the aspects of fantasy and reality in *The Narrative of Arthur Gordon Pym*.

Libman, Valentina. See GENERAL.

Lieber, Todd M. *Endless Experiments: Essays on the Heroic Experience in American Romanticism.* Columbus: Ohio State Univ Press, 1973.
    The book deals with the dualism of romanticism in American literature; the chapter on Poe is entitled "The Apocalyptic Imagination of A. Gordon Pym."

Liebman, Sheldon. "Poe's Tales and His Theory of the Poetic Experience." *Stud SF*, 7 (Fall 1970), 582-596.
    Poe's tales "objectify the two central events of the poetic experience: (1) pursuit of Beauty and Knowledge and (2) the making of a poem."

Lima, Robert. "A Borges Poem on Poe." *Poe Stud*, 6 (June 1973), 29-30.
    Lima's translation of a brief poem on Poe by Jorge Luis Borges, the noted Argentine author.

Link, Franz H. *Edgar Allan Poe: Ein Dichter Zwischen Romantick Und Moderne*. Frankfurt am Main: Athenaum Verlag, 1968.
A comprehensive study of Poe's art and philosophy with emphasis on his place between Romanticism and Modernism.

Ljungquist, Kent. "Poe and the Sublime: His Two Short Sea Tales in the Context of an Aesthetic Tradition." *Criticism*, 17 (Spring 1975), 131-151.
Sees, in the development of Poe's art, a use of and later abandonment of the aesthetic of the sublime.

Loberger, Gordon J. "Poe's Use of *Page* and *Lore* in 'Tamerlane.'" *Poe Newsletter*, 3 (December 1970), 37-38.
Poe's "page of early lore" (1. 82) in "Tamerlane" relates to the love theme found throughout the poem.

Lombard, Charles. "Poe and French Romanticism." *Poe Newsletter*, 3 (December 1970), 30-35.
Poe was to a degree indebted to chief French Romantics like Mme. de Staël, George Sand, Lamartine, and Victor Hugo.

Lord, John B. "Two Phonological Analyses of Poe's 'To Helen.'" *Lang and Style*, 3 (Spring 1970), 147-158.
An analysis of sound patterns reveals overlapping themes in this poem.

Lundquist, James. "The Moral of Averted Descent: The Failure of Sanity in 'The Pit and the Pendulum.'" *Poe Newsletter*, 2 (April 1969), 25-26.
Points out Kafkian qualities in this story.

Lynen, John F. *The Design of the Present: Essays on Time and Form in American Literature*. New Haven: Yale Univ Press, 1969.
Analyzes the work of seven major American authors, including Poe, to test the theory that the formal structure of a work of literature is partly determined by its assumptions concerning time, and that the American tradition derives from a fusion of Puritan theology and national individualism.

Mabbott, Thomas O. "The Books in the House of Usher." *Books at Iowa*, 19 (1973), 3-7.
Poe put only real books in Usher's library.

_____, ed. *Collected Works of Edgar Allan Poe. Volume I. Poems*. Cambridge: Belknap Press of Harvard Univ Press, 1969.
Contains 101 poems by or attributed to Poe.

Maekawa Shunichi. See GENERAL.

Mann, K. H. See GENERAL.

Marcadé, Bernard. "Pour une psychogéographie de l'espace fantastique: Les architectures arabesques et grotesques chez E. A. Poe." *La Rev d'Esthétique*, 27 (1974), 41-56.
A treatment of the psychological landscape in Poe's works.

Marder, Daniel. "Exiles at Home in American Literature." *Mosaic*, 8 (Spring 1975), 49-75.
Includes discussion of James, Cooper, Irving, Melville, Hawthorne, and Poe as variations on the exile theme. With Poe, it is not so much a question of a homeland he is seeking or lamenting as it is a matter of an estranged personality.

Marler, Robert F. "From Tale to Short Story: The Emergence of a New Genre in the 1850's." *AL*, 46 (May 1974), 153-169.
Discusses Poe's legacies to the writers of the 1850's, a period that saw the decay of the tale and the rise of the short story as an independent genre.

Marovitz, Sanford E. "Poe's Reception of C. W. Webber's Gothic Western, 'Jack Long; or, The Shot in the Eye.'" *Poe Stud*, 4 (June 1971), 11-13.
Webber's story drew Poe's approval and high praise.

Marrs, Robert L. "'The Fall of the House of Usher': A Checklist of Criticism Since 1960." *Poe Stud*, 5 (June 1972), 23-24.
Supplements listings found in three recent studies devoted to "Usher."

_____. "Fugitive Poe References: A Bibliography." *Poe Newsletter*, 2 (January 1969), 12-18.
Lists and annotates recent books, essays, and miscellaneous publications that do not expressly focus on Poe and are not generally listed in standard bibliographies of Poe criticism. See also Judy Osowski, "Fugitive Poe References: A Bibliography," *Poe Newsletter*, 3 (June 1970), 16-19.

Marsh, John L. "The Psycho-Sexual Reading of 'The Fall of the House of Usher.'" *Poe Stud*, 5 (June 1972), 8-9.
Emphasizes the significance of perverse sensuality in understanding Poe's story.

Martin, Bruce K. "Poe's 'Hop-Frog' and the Retreat from Comedy." *Stud SF*, 10 (Summer 1973), 288-290.
The ultimate effect of this story is horror.

Martindale, Colin. "Archetype and Reality in 'The Fall of the House of Usher.'" *Poe Stud*, 5 (June 1972), 9-11.
"Both the narrator and 'The Mad Trist' contribute significantly to symbolic meaning."

_____. "Transformation and Transfusion of Vitality in the Narratives of Poe." *Semiotica*, 8 (1973), 46-59.
In Poe's stories opposites are ultimately reconciled.

Mazow, Julia. "The Survival Theme in Selected Tales of Edgar Allan Poe." *Stud in Am F*, 3 (Autumn 1975), 216-223.
Title is descriptive.

_____. "The Undivided Consciousness of the Narrator in *Eureka*." *ATQ*, 26 (Spring 1975), 55-60.

II. ANTEBELLUM (1800-1865)

The narrator of *Eureka* guides us to the understanding that "the periodic return to an undivided consciousness makes it possible for man to deal with despair and meaninglessness."

McCarthy, Kevin M. "'Sameness' Versus 'Saneness' in Poe's 'Morella.'" *Am N&Q*, 11 (June 1973), 149-150.
"Sameness" should be the word used in a correct text because Poe is dealing with two persons having the same consciousness.

_____. "Unity and Personal Identity in *Eureka*." *ATQ*, 26 (Spring 1975), 22-26.
"*Eureka*...is a compendium of ideas Poe borrowed from Locke concerning unity and personal identity"; Poe had used these ideas differently in earlier stories.

McElderry, B. R., Jr. "T. S. Eliot on Poe." *Poe Newsletter*, 2 (1969), 32-33.
The French Symbolists' admiration for Poe aroused Eliot's interest in him.

McElrath, Joseph R. "Poe's Conscious Technique." *Northeast MLA Newsletter*, 2 (1970), 38-43.
Concerns Poe's own use of devices satirized in "How to Write a Blackwood Article" and "A Predicament."

McElroy, M. D. "Poe's Last Partner: E. H. N. Patterson of Oquawka, Illinois." *Papers on Lang and Lit*, 7 (Summer 1971), 252-271.
Deals with a projected journal which Patterson wanted Poe to edit; Poe died before any definite plans could be made.

McKeithan, D. M. "Poe and the Second Edition of Hawthorne's *Twice-Told Tales*." *Nath Hawthorne Jour*, 4 (1974), 257-269.
Discusses the influence of the second edition on Poe's "The Oval Portrait" and "The Masque of the Red Death" and on his theory of the short story.

McLean, Robert C. "Poe in the Marketplace." *Poe Stud*, 5 (June 1972), 21-23.
Discusses current publications on Poe competing for the freshman-sophomore "market" in English study.

Merivale, Patricia. "The Raven and the Bust of Pallas: Classical Artifacts and the Gothic Tale." *PMLA*, 89 (October 1974), 960-966.
Discusses the use of classical statues by Poe and later writers.

Miller, John C. "The Birthdate of John Henry Ingram." *Poe Stud*, 7 (June 1974), 24.
Ingram's identification with Poe may have "led him to change his real birthyear to the year of Poe's death."

_____. "The Exhumations and Reburials of Edgar and Virginia Poe and Mrs. Clemm." *Poe Stud*, 7 (December 1974), 46-47.
Drawing facts from several newspapers, the article accounts for the burials of Poe, his wife, and his mother-in-law "in a corner lot at the juncture of Fayette and Greene Streets in Baltimore."

_____. "John Bannister Tabb's Defense of Edgar Allan Poe." *Va Cavalcade*, 24 (Spring 1975), 156-163.
Tabb tried mightily to salvage Poe's reputation through poems he wrote after the Civil War.

Miranda, J. E. "Edgar Allan Poe o la existencia amenazada." *Cuad Hisp*, 228 (December 1968), 775-780.
Believes that Poe affirmed the power of human will and reason.

Mize, George E. "The Matter of Taste in Poe's 'Domain of Arnheim' and 'Landor's Cottage.'" *Conn Rev*, 6 (October 1972), 93-99.
Both works reveal Poe's awareness of the interest in landscape gardening during his time and also represent an attempt to escape "from the sordid poverty around him."

Mokashi-Punekar, S. "Indra--the Mind of Edgar Allan Poe." *Jour of the Karnatak Univ: Humanities*, 65 (1972), 119-133.
Poe's philosophy is alien to Western thinking.

Moldenhauer, Joseph J. "Beyond the Tamarind Tree: A New Poe Letter." *AL*, 42 (January 1971), 468-477.
Reproduces and comments on a letter from Poe to Thomas Wyatt, affording a view of Poe's connections with Philadelphia printers *circa* 1840.

_____. *Descriptive Catalogue of Edgar Allan Poe Manuscripts in The Humanities Research Center Library*. Austin: Univ of Texas, 1973.
Describes the Koester Collection.

_____. "Imagination and Perversity in *The Narrative of Arthur Gordon Pym*." *Tex Stud in Lit and Lang*, 13 (Summer 1971), 267-280.
"Less equivocally than any other work of Poe's, *The Narrative of Arthur Gordon Pym* associates the artistic imagination with the imp of the perverse. Pym's adventures are dictated by his creative and masochistic inner self."

_____. "Murder as a Fine Art: Basic Connections Between Poe's Aesthetics, Psychology, and Moral Vision." *PMLA*, 83 (May 1968), 284-297.
Poe's aesthetic idea of unity is expressed on all levels of theme and form and is a self-contained metaphysics.

_____. "Poe Manuscripts in Austin." *Lib Chron of the Univ of Texas*, no. 3 (May 1971), 82-87.
Description of the Koester Collection at the University of Texas.

Monteiro, George. "Edgar Poe and the New Knowledge." *So Lit Jour*, 4 (Spring 1972), 34-40.
Poe early declared war upon the new knowledge, voicing the objection of the romanticists that the scientific attitude reduces everything to prosaic reality.

Moore, Rayburn S. "'Prophetic Sounds and Loud': Allen, Stovall, Mabbott, and other Recent Works on Poe." *GaR*, 25 (Winter 1971), 481-488.
A survey and appraisal of recent criticism on Poe and his works.

Moskowitz, Sam, ed. *The Man Who Called Himself Poe*. Garden City, N. Y.: Doubleday, 1969.
A collection of literary materials in which Poe appears as an integral character; includes nine mystery and science-fiction tales and six poems.

Moss, Sidney P. "Duyckinck Defends Mr. Poe Against New York's Penny-A-Liners." *Papers on Lang and Lit*, 5 (Summer 1969--Supplement), 74-81.
Deals with the general rejection of Poe by literary circles after the publication of the first installment of his "The Literati of New York City," and prints an article which defends Poe by pointing out the status of his reputation in America, England, and France.

_____. "Poe as Probabilist in Forgues' Critique of the *Tales*." *ESQ*, no. 60 (Fall 1970, Part 1, Supp.), 4-13.
A condensed version of Forgues' *Studies of English and American Fiction: The Tales of Edgar A. Poe*.

_____. *Poe's Major Crisis: His Libel Suit and New York's Literary World*. Durham, N. C.: Duke Univ Press, 1970.
A collection of documents arranged in chronological order with commentary relating to Poe's libel suit against the owner of the New York *Mirror* (1846-1847) and its effect on his life and career.

Mulqueen, James E. "The Meaning of Poe's 'Ulalume.'" *ATQ*, 1 (1st Qtr. 1969), 27-30.
Astarte serves as a symbol of a "Life Principle," not as a sexual symbol.

_____. "The Poetics of Emerson and Poe." *ESQ*, no. 55 (2nd Qtr., Part 1, 1969), 5-11.
Though the two share similarities, they differ in their aesthetic theories.

Murphy, Christina J. "The Philosophical Pattern of 'A Descent into the Maelström.'" *Poe Stud*, 6 (June 1973), 25-26.
Eureka and "The Descent into the Maelström" depict intuitive experiences that bring profound realizations of the nature of the universe.

Murtuza, Athar. "An Arabian Source for Poe's 'The Pit and the Pendulum.'" *Poe Stud*, 5 (December 1972), 52.
Discusses George Sales's commentary on and translation of the Koran as a possible source.

Nethery, Wallace. "Poe and Charles Lamb." *Poe Newsletter*, 3 (December 1970), 38.
Deals with Poe's opinion of Lamb's style.

Nettesheim, Josefine. "Kriminelles, Kriminalistiches und Okkultes in der Dichtung der Droste und Edgar Allan Poes." *Jahrbuch des Wiener Goethe-Vereins*, 74 (1970), 136-146.
Discusses similarities in the treatment of the criminal and the occult in the works of Poe and Annette von Droste-Hülshoff.

Newlin, Paul A. "Scott's Influence on Poe's Grotesque and Arabesque Tales." *ATQ*, 2 (1969), 9-12.

Poe took the terms *grotesque* and *arabesque* from Scott's "On the Supernatural in Fictitious Composition"; furthermore, he may have based his definitions of the terms on this essay.

Obuchowski, Peter. "Unity of Effect in Poe's 'The Fall of the House of Usher.'" *Stud SF*, 12 (Fall 1975), 407-412.
"The unity of effect in this story is achieved through the careful selection of details and actions to present in the narrator (and by extension in the reader) the terror in one's losing his mind."

Ocano, Armando. *Edgar Allan Poe*. Madrid: Ediciones y Publicaciones Españolas, S. A., 1971.
A biography in Spanish.

O'Connor, Roger. "Letters, Signatures, and 'Juws' in Poe's 'Autography.'" *Poe Newsletter*, 3 (June 1970), 21-22.
Suggests that Poe's comic frame in treating Joseph Miller in the "Autography" extends to matters of printing and style.

Oelke, Karl E. "Poe at West Point--A Revaluation." *Poe Stud*, 6 (June 1973), 1-6.
Poe had time and opportunity for intellectual pursuits while at West Point from June 1830 to February 1831.

Orvell, Miles D. "'The Raven' and the Chair." *Poe Stud*, 5 (December 1972), 54.
Suggests a subconscious source for Poe's raven.

_____. See O'CONNOR, FLANNERY (Contemporary--2nd Orvell entry).

Osowski, Judy. "Fugitive Poe References: A Bibliography." *Poe Newsletter*, 3 (June 1970), 16-19.
Primarily lists and annotates recent books, essays, and miscellaneous publications (since about 1960) that do not expressly focus on Poe and are not generally listed in standard bibliographies of Poe criticism; see also "Fugitive Poe References: A Bibliography," Robert L. Marrs, *Poe Newsletter*, 2 (January 1969), 12-18.

_____. "Fugitive Poe References: A Bibliography." *Poe Stud*, 4 (December 1971), 44-46.
Lists and annotates recent books, essays, and miscellaneous publications (principally 1964-1970) that do not expressly focus on Poe.

_____. "Fugitive Poe References: A Bibliography." *Poe Stud*, 8 (June 1975), 21-22.
Lists current publications that do not focus on Poe, but which discuss him within a larger perspective or special angle of vision.

_____. "T. S. Eliot on 'Poe the Detective.'" *Poe Newsletter*, 3 (December 1970), 39.
Eliot develops admiration for Poe as a writer of detective stories.

Ostrom, John. "Fourth Supplement to *The Letters of Poe*." *AL*, 45 (January 1974), 513-536.
Prints and comments on Poe letters found since the 1966 edition was published.

Ousby, Ian V. K. "'The Murders in the Rue Morgue' and 'Doctor D'Arsac': A Poe Source." *Poe Stud*, 5 (December 1972), 52.
Points to verbal parallels.

Paul, Raymond. *Who Murdered Mary Rogers?* Englewood Cliffs, N. J.: Prentice-Hall, 1971.
After evidence is carefully considered, Mary's fiancé, Daniel Payne, is determined to have killed her.

Pauly, Thomas H. "'Hop-Frog'--Is the Last Laugh Best?" *Stud SF*, 11 (Summer 1974), 307-309.
In this tale, whose dramatic impact "hinges upon a central definition of comedy," Hop-Frog himself is the most notable victim of the joke.

Pavnaskar, Sadanand R. "Indian Translations of Edgar Allan Poe: A Bibliography with a Note." *Indian Jour of Am Stud*, 1, no. 4 (1971), 103-110.
Title is descriptive.

_____. "Poe in India: A Bibliography, 1955-1969." *Poe Stud*, 5 (December 1972), 49-50.
Discusses Poe's reception in India, and includes a checklist of translations and criticism.

Pemberton, J. M. "Poe's 'To Helen': Functional Wordplay and a Possible Source." *Poe Newsletter*, 3 (June 1970), 6-7.
Poe was aware that in the original Greek "Helen" connotes "brightness" and "light."

Phillips, H. Wells. "Poe's Usher: Precursor of Abstract Art." *Poe Stud*, 5 (June 1972), 14-16.
On the "abstractness" of Usher's paintings.

Pitcher, Edward W. "Anagrams in Poe's Stories." *Am N&Q*, 12 (May/June 1974), 167-169.
Offers several anagrammatic interpretations of names in Poe's works and suggests that our understanding of the work is greater if we recognize such anagrams.

Pochmann, Henry A., and Gay Wilson Allen. See GENERAL.

Poe, Edgar Allan. "New Letter of Edgar Allan Poe." *ESQ*, 51 (2nd Qtr. 1968), 51-52.
To Dr. Francis Lieber (June 18, 1836) soliciting a contribution for the *Southern Literary Messenger*.

Pollin, Burton R. "Another Source of 'The Bells' by Poe: A *Broadway Journal* Essay." *Miss Quart*, 27 (Fall 1974), 467-473.
Presents a case for an 1845 essay in the *Broadway Journal* having influenced Poe's 1849 revision of "The Bells."

_____. "Contemporary Reviews of *Eureka*: A Checklist." *ATQ*, 26 (Spring 1975), 26-30.
Title is descriptive.

_____. "Dean Swift in the Works of Poe." *N&Q*, 20 (July 1973), 244-246.
Examples cited in Poe's work show a special fondness of *Gulliver's Travels*.

_____. "'Delightful Sights,' a Possible Whitman Article in Poe's *Broadway Journal*." *Walt Whit Rev*, 15 (1969), 180-187.
An anonymous article printed in the *Broadway Journal* while Poe was editor may have been written by Whitman.

_____, comp. *Dictionary of Names and Titles in Poe's Collected Works*. New York: Da Capo, 1968.
The index is cross-referenced to Harrison's edition of Poe's works.

_____. *Discoveries in Poe*. Notre Dame: Univ of Notre Dame Press, 1970.
Traces the European backgrounds and authors which influenced Poe's work and upon which he drew for material and inspiration, especially the work of Hugo Béranger, Byron, Mary Shelley, and William Godwin.

_____. "Dubartas and Victor Hugo in Poe's Criticism." *Miss Quart*, 23 (Winter 1969-70), 45-55.
References to these two writers in Poe's criticism exemplify "Poe's habit of using names to validate his own literary authority."

_____. "An 1839 Review of Poe's *Tales* in Willis' *The Corsair*." *Poe Stud*, 5 (December 1972), 56.
A significant contemporary review possibly by Dr. Timothy O. Porter.

_____. "Figs, Bells, Poe, and Horace Smith." *Poe Newsletter*, 3 (June 1970), 8-10.
Analyzes Poe's knowledge and use of the writings of Horace Smith, a popular British writer of poetry, essays, novels, and tales.

_____. "Light on 'Shadow' and Other Pieces by Poe; or, More of Thomas Moore." *ESQ*, 18 (3rd Qtr. 1972), 166-173.
Examines the influence of Thomas Moore on some of Poe's stories and adds to the evidence for the influence of Moore on Poe.

_____. "More Music to Poe." *Music and Letters*, 54 (October 1973), 391-404.
Two hundred additions to the list of music based on Poe's poetry.

_____. "More on Lippard and Poe." *Poe Stud*, 7 (June 1974), 22-23.
Cites passages from George Lippard's reviews of Poe's writings as well as from Lippard's obituary notice on Poe.

_____. "Names Used for Humor in Poe's Tales." *Proc of Names Inst*, East Texas State University, Fall 1972, pp. 51-57.
Treats proper names used for satire and those which are a play on words. Shows Poe to be "possessed of high spirits."

_____. "*Nicholas Nickleby* in 'The Devil in the Belfry.'" *Poe Stud*, 8 (June 1975), 23.
Some of the comments and atmospheric touches in "The Devil in the Belfry" came from Dickens' *Nicholas Nickleby*.

_____. "*Notre-Dame de Paris* in Two of Poe's Tales." *RLV*, 34 (August 1968), 354-365.

A passage from Hugo's novel is cited as an influence on "A Tale of the Ragged Mountains" and "The Cask of Amontillado."

_____. "Place Names in Poe's Creative Writings." *Poe Stud*, 6 (December 1973), 43-48.
Listing supplements Professor Pollin's *Names and Titles in Poe's Collected Works* (1968).

_____. "Poe and Henry James: A Changing Relationship." *Yearbk of Eng Stud*, 3 (1973), 232-242.
James's interest in Poe went through an early fascination, later disenchantment, and finally a rediscovery that is reflected especially in *The Sacred Fount* and *The Golden Bowl*.

_____. "Poe and the *Boston Notion*." *Eng Lang Notes*, 8 (September 1970), 23-28.
The *Boston Notion*, a literary paper, was at times friendly, at times hostile to Poe and his writings.

_____. "Poe and the Incubator." *Am N&Q*, 12 (May/June 1974), 146-149.
Concerns "The Thousand-and-Second Tale of Scheherazade" term for a poultry incubator.

_____. "Poe as Edward S. T. Grey." *BSUF*, no. 3 (1973), 44-46.
Deals with the significance of Poe's use of this pseudonym.

_____. "Poe as Probable Author of 'Harper's Ferry.'" *AL*, 40 (May 1968), 164-178.
Considers evidence that Poe may have written this article published in *Graham's Magazine* (February 1848).

_____. "Poe as Scriblerian." *Scriblerian*, 1 (Spring 1969), 30-31.
Offers supplementary evidence that Poe was the author of the anonymously published "The Atlantis, a Southern World..."

_____. *Poe, Creator of Words*. Baltimore, Md.: Enoch Pratt Free Library, 1974.
A glossary of words and proper names invented by Poe.

_____. "Poe, Freeman Hunt, and Four Unrecorded Reviews of Poe's Works." *Tex Stud in Lit and Lang*, 16 (Summer 1974), 305-313.
Describes the relationship between Poe and Hunt and discusses Hunt's review of Poe in his *Merchant's Magazine*.

_____. "Poe in the *Boston Notion*." *NEQ*, 62 (December 1969), 585-589.
Biography of Poe in the *Notion*, April 29, 1843.

_____. "Poe's 'Diddling': The Source of Title and Tale." *So Lit Jour*, 2 (Fall 1969), 106-111.
For one of his tales Poe took from James Kenney's farce "Raising the Wind" the title and the name of his character Jeremy Diddler and also a "good-humored raillery" at respectable middle-class success.

_____. "Poe's Dr. Ollapod." *AL*, 42 (March 1970), 80-82.
Traces the source of Dr. Ollapod, from Poe's "The Scythe of Time," to the character by that name found in *The Poor Gentleman*, a popular play by George Colman, Jr.

_____. "Poe's 'Eldorado' Viewed as a Song of the West." *PrS*, 46 (Fall 1972), 228-235.
Poe's poem, borrowing from "Tom-a-Bedlam Song" and echoing "The Man for *Galway*" doggerel and/or the drinking song "Wreath the Bowl," should be regarded as a popular ballad based on a major topic of the day.

_____. "Poe's Illustration for 'The Island of the Fay': A Hoax Detected." *Mystery and Detection Annual* (1972), 33-45.
Poe redesigned, with the help of a friend, a print to illustrate his story.

_____. "Poe's Literary Use of 'Oppodeldoc' and Other Patent Medicines." *Poe Stud*, 4 (December 1971), 30-32.
On Poe's playful allusions to patent medicines.

_____. "Poe's 'Mystification': Its Source in Fay's *Norman Leslie*." *Miss Quart*, 25 (Spring 1972), 111-130.
Poe's burlesque on duelling in "Mystification" (1837) derives from T. S. Fay's novel.

_____. "Poe's *Narrative of Arthur Gordon Pym* and the Contemporary Reviewers." *Stud in Am F*, 2 (1974), 37-56.
Explores the work's contemporary reception.

_____. "Poe's Pen of Iron." *ATQ*, 2 (2nd Qtr. 1969), 16-18.
Suggests a source of Poe's pseudonym Launcelot Canning and for a motto he used in a prospectus for a magazine he hoped to found.

_____. "Poe's 'Shadow' as a Source of His 'The Masque of the Red Death.'" *Stud SF*, 6 (Fall 1968), 104-106.
Suggests numerous parallels of detail, imagery, and situation between Poe's 1835 story "Shadow: A Parable" and his 1842 story "The Masque of the Red Death."

_____. "Poe's 'Some Words with a Mummy.'" *ESQ*, no. 60 (Fall 1970, Part 2, Supp.), 60-67.
Deals with the sources of this work.

_____. "Poe's 'Sonnet--To Zante': Sources and Associations." *CLS*, 5 (September 1968), 303-315.
Sources and inspiration for this sonnet are cited as Chateaubriand, Keats, and Byron.

_____. "Poe's Use of D'Israeli's *Curiosities* to Belittle Emerson." *Poe Newsletter*, 3 (December 1970), 38.
Discusses the source of Poe's inappropriate parallel of Emerson with Sallust-Arruntius.

_____. "Poe's Use of Material from Bernardin de Saint-Pierre's *Etudes*." *Romance Notes*, 12 (Spring 1971), 331-338.

The *Etudes* may have influenced Poe in his writing of "Manuscript Found in a Bottle," "Scheherezade," and "A Descent into the Maelström."

_____. "Poe's Use of the Name Ermengarde in 'Eleonora.'" *N&Q*, 17 (September 1970), 323-333.
Poe knew Scott's *The Betrothed* and used the name of "the ancient Lady of Baldringham" in "Eleonora."

_____. "Politics and History in Poe's 'Mellonta Tauta': Two Allusions Explained." *Stud SF*, 8 (Fall 1971), 627-631.
Clarifies the allusions in this tale, an expression of Poe's disenchantment with the rule of the common man, to the Washington Monument Association of New York and to Senator Thomas Hart Benton.

_____. "A Spurious Poe Letter to A. N. Howard." *Poe Stud*, 6 (June 1973), 27-28.
Lists evidence that a Poe letter to A. N. Howard, editor of the *New York Mirror*, is a blatant forgery.

_____. "The Temperance Movement and Its Friends Look at Poe." *Costerus* [Amsterdam], 2 (1972), 120-144.
Poe's career as a writer coincided with the rise of the temperance movement, and this may account for the widespread acceptance of Griswold's charges.

_____. "Three More Early Notices of *Pym* and the Snowden Connection." *Poe Stud*, 8 (December 1975), 32-35.
Discusses early notices of *Pym* from *Alexander's Weekly Messenger, Sunday Morning News* (New York) and *Snowden's Lady's Companion.*

_____. "*Undine* in the Works of Poe." *Stud in Romanticism*, 14 (Winter 1975), 59-74.
Examines the relationship between *Undine* and Poe's critical theory, and the influence of *Undine* on the construction and language of certain of Poe's works.

_____. "Victor Hugo and Poe." *Rev de Litt Comp*, 42 (1968), 494-519.
On echoes of Hugo in Poe's works.

Porte, Joel. *The Romance in America: Studies in Cooper, Poe, Hawthorne, Melville, and James.* Middletown, Conn.: Wesleyan Univ Press, 1969.
The fiction of five American authors is examined in the context of the tradition of non-realistic romance as a nineteenth-century American genre, characterized by a "self-conscious need to define its own aims."

Prior, Linda T. "A Further Word on Richard Wright's Use of Poe in *Native Son.*" *Poe Stud*, 5 (December 1972), 52-53.
Discusses Wright's use of Poe's "The Murders in the Rue Morgue."

Pry, Elmer R. "A Folklore Source for 'The Man that Was Used Up.'" *Poe Stud*, 8 (December 1975), 46.
The basic idea of the story may come from folk narrative about the Indian.

Quinn, Patrick F. "Poe: A Most Immemorial Year." *So Lit Jour*, 2 (Fall 1969), 112-122.
An essay-review of *Poe and the British Magazine Tradition*, by Michael Allen; *Poe: Journalist and Critic*, by Robert D. Jacobs; and *Collected Works of Edgar Allan Poe*, Vol. I, *Poems* edited by Thomas Ollive Mabbott.

_____. "Poe: Between Being and Nothingness." *So Lit Jour*, 6 (Fall 1973), 81-100.
Essay-review of three books on Poe by (1) Carl L. Anderson, who shows what Poe has meant to the culture of Scandinavia, (2) G. R. Thompson, who puts Poe on the side of Nothingness, and (3) David Halliburton, who puts Poe on the side of Being.

Rayan, Krishna. "Edgar Allan Poe and Suggestiveness." *Brit Jour of Aes*, 9 (1969), 73-79.
Poe made a valuable contribution to critical terminology by introducing the term *suggestiveness* in the sense of the French Symbolists' *la suggestion.*

Reece, James B. "An Error in Some Reprintings of Poe's 1847 Critique of Hawthorne." *Poe Stud*, 4 (December 1971), 47.
Corrects an error in textual transmission.

_____. "Poe's 'Dream-Land' and the Imagery of Opium Dreams." *Poe Stud*, 8 (June 1975), 24.
Notes the similarities between the imagery of Poe's "Dream-Land" and current literature describing opium dreams.

_____. "A Reexamination of a Poe Date: Mrs. Ellet's Letters." *AL*, 42 (May 1970), 157-164.
Places the date of Poe's letters to Mrs. Elizabeth F. Ellet as January 1846, not June of that year as is normally believed. Also clarifies points about Poe's "Literati" sketches.

Reed, Kenneth T. "'Ligeia': The Story as a Sermon." *Poe Stud*, 4 (June 1971), 20.
Poe could have structured "Ligeia" in line with the five-part sermon plan recommended by contemporary books on homiletics.

Reeder, Roberta. "'The Black Cat' as a Study in Repression." *Poe Stud*, 7 (June 1974), 20-22.
Examines the story in terms of Jungian psychology.

Rees, Thomas R. "Why Poe? Some Notes on the Artistic Qualities of the Prose of Edgar Allan Poe." *Forum H*, 12, no. 1 (1974), 10-15.
Discusses reasons for Poe's popularity as a writer.

Regan, Robert. "Hawthorne's 'Plagiary'; Poe's Duplicity." *NCF*, 25 (December 1970), 281-298.
Believes that Poe was testing his readers when he accused Hawthorne of having plagiarized from "William Wilson" in "Howe's Masquerade."

Reilly, John E. "Current Poe Activities." *Poe Stud*, 8 (December 1975), 47-48.
Cites a variety of current scholarly activities and publications.

_____. "The Lesser Death-Watch and 'The Tell-Tale Heart.'" *ATQ*, 2 (2nd Qtr. 1969), 3-9.
    The sound that the narrator hears is that of the insect called a lesser death-watch. The sound is sometimes there, sometimes not, because the narrator suffers from paranoid schizophrenia.

_____. "Poe in Pillory: An Early Version of a Satire by A. J. H. Duganne." *Poe Stud*, 6 (June 1973), 9-12.
    Duganne, a minor American writer, ridicules Poe as poet and critic in the fashion of Lowell's *A Fable for Critics*.

_____. Untitled. *Miss Quart*, 28 (Fall 1975), 531-535.
    Review of *Edgar Allan Poe: A Bibliography of Criticism, 1827-1967*, by J. Lasley Dameron and Irby B. Cauthen, Jr., and of *Edgar Allan Poe: An Annotated Bibliography of Books and Articles in English, 1827-1973*, by Esther Hyneman.

Rein, David M. "The Appeal of Poe Today." *ESQ*, no. 60 (Fall 1970, Part 1, Supp.), 29-33.
    There are several reasons for Poe's popularity, but the most important is the appeal of his horror stories.

Reiss, T. J. "The Universe and the Dialectic of Imagination in Edgar Allan Poe." *EA*, 27 (January-March 1974), 16-25.
    Discusses Poe's view of the universe presented in *Eureka*; through "repeated destruction and re-formation: the universe will pulsate for all eternity."

Ricardou, Jean. "L'or du sacrabée." *Tel Quel*, 34 (1968), 42-57.
    Deals with the significance of east and west in "The Gold Bug."

Richard, Claude. "Poe and the Yankee Hero: An Interpretation of 'Diddling Considered as One of the Exact Sciences.'" *Miss Quart*, 21 (Spring 1968), 93-109.
    Considered an early piece, the sketch may be a parody of the Yankee of popular drama and humor.

_____. "Poe and Young America." *SB*, 21 (1968), 25-58.
    Poe "kowtowed" to the Young America group during 1844-1846 because he hoped that doing so would further his ambitions for publication.

_____. "Poe et Hawthorne." *EA*, 22 (October-December 1969), 351-361.
    Deals with Poe's contradiction of himself in his two reviews of Hawthorne's *Twice-Told Tales*.

_____. "Poe Studies in Europe: France." *Poe Newsletter*, 2 (1969), 20-23.
    Evaluates recent French criticism on Poe.

_____, ed. *RLM*, nos. 193-198 (1969).
    An issue devoted to Poe, consisting mainly of essays previously published in English (by Wilbur and Tate, for example), here translated into French; includes a bibliography compiled by Richard and a 1968 essay, also by Richard.

Richmond, Lee J. "Edgar Allan Poe's 'Morella': Vampire of Volition." *Stud SF*, 9 (Winter 1972), 93-94.
    Through "veiled ironies that clarify the narrator's characterization," we discover Poe's secondary use of "the machinery of gothic sensationalism" to "dramatize a primary interest in the possibilities of the human psyche to affirm itself over and beyond matter."

Ridgely, J. V. "The Continuing Puzzle of *Arthur Gordon Pym*: Some Notes and Queries." *Poe Newsletter*, 3 (June 1970), 5-6.
    Raises questions in regard to *Pym*'s sources, published texts and language.

_____. "Tragical-Mythical-Satirical-Hoaxical Problems of Genre in *Pym*." *ATQ*, 24 (Fall 1974, Part 1), 4-9.
    A survey of previous critical categorizations of *Pym*, with suggestions about what should be taken into account in future studies of the same kind.

Robbins, J. Albert. *Checklist of Edgar Allan Poe*. Columbus, Ohio: Charles E. Merrill, 1969.
    Selective checklist of primary and secondary materials.

_____. "Edgar Poe and the Philadelphians: A Reminiscence by a Contemporary." *Poe Stud*, 5 (December 1972), 45-48.
    Deals with Poe among Philadelphia journalists from 1839 to 1844.

_____. "A Review of *Edgar Poe the Poet: Essays New and Old on the Man and His Work* [Stovall]." *SAQ*, 69 (Spring 1970), 296-297.
    The essays reflect the common sense, insight, and knowledge of the author.

_____. "The State of Poe Studies." *Poe Newsletter*, 1 (April 1968), 1-2.
    Deals with what needs to be done in Poe scholarship.

_____. See GENERAL--all Robbins entries.

Roberts, Leonard. See MISCELLANEOUS (Antebellum).

Robinson, David. "The Romantic Quest in Poe and Emerson: 'Ulalume' and 'The Sphinx.'" *ATQ*, 26 (Spring 1975, Supp.), 26-30.
    Both poems should be read as "comments on human psychology.... Poe finds himself in the paradox of wanting a peaceful state, but abhorring death. In the end his narrator realizes that they are the same."

_____. "'Ulalume'--The Ghouls and the Critics." *Poe Stud*, 8 (June 1975), 8-10.
    The ghouls in Poe's "Ulalume" lead the speaker to remorse and frustration.

Robinson, E. Arthur. "'New Approaches' in Poe Criticism." *Poe Stud*, 4 (December 1971), 48-50.
    An essay-review of *New Approaches to Poe: A Symposium*, ed. Richard P. Benton. Hartford, Conn.: Transcendental Books, 1970.

_____. "Thoreau and the Deathwatch in Poe's 'The Tell-Tale Heart.'" *Poe Stud*, 4 (June 1971), 14-16.
 Poe and Thoreau "use an obscure insect to symbolize inexorable changes of nature," the former emphasizing the terror of death in a Gothic mode.

Roche, A. John. "Another Look at Poe's Dr. Ollapod." *Poe Stud*, 6 (June 1973), 28.
 Suggests that Poe's Dr. Ollapod in his "A Predicament" could allude in part to Willis Gaylord Clark of the *Knickerbocker Magazine*.

Rocks, James E. "Conflict and Motive in 'The Cask of Amontillado.'" *Poe Stud*, 5 (December 1972), 50-51.
 Poe's story in the light of the "forthright Catholic reaction against Freemasonry."

Rose, Marilyn G. "Poe's 'The City in the Sea': A Conjecture." *ESQ*, 50 (1st Qtr. 1968), 58-59.
 If "viol" is taken as a French pun, the poem becomes a condemnation of the life cycle.

Rosenfeld, Alvin H. "The Poe-Chivers Controversy: A New Letter." *BB*, 23 (1969), 89-93.
 Concerns the acquisition by the Brown Library of a letter by Chivers disclaiming any indebtedness to Poe's "The Raven."

Rosenthal, Bernard. "Poe, Slavery, and the *Southern Literary Messenger*: A Reexamination." *Poe Stud*, 7 (December 1974), 29-38.
 Presents evidence that the "Paulding-Drayton Review," a review of two books on slavery appearing in the April 1836 issue of the *SLM*, should be included in the Poe canon.

Rountree, Thomas J. "Poe's Universe: 'The House of Usher' and the Narrator." *Tulane Stud in Eng*, 20 (1972), 123-134.
 Discusses "Usher" and "Eureka" as stories in which Poe emphasized the theory of cyclic unity.

Rubin, Larry. See WOLFE, THOMAS (Contemporary).

Rubin, Louis D., Jr. See GENERAL--3rd Rubin entry.

Russ, Joanna. "Dream Literature and Science Fiction." *Extrap*, 11 (December 1969), 6-14.
 Gives the characteristics of dream literature (as a category of science fiction and fantasy) and, among others, places Poe's "The Assignation" in this category.

Russell, J. Thomas. *Edgar Allan Poe: The Army Years*. U. S. M. A. Bul, no. 10. West Point, N. Y.: U. S. Military Acad, 1972.
 Briefly surveys Poe's attendance at the Academy and deals with the amount of the contributions subscribed by cadets to Poe's *Poems* in 1831.

Salzberg, Joel. "The Gothic Hero in the Transcendental Quest: Poe's 'Ligeia' and James's 'The Beast in the Jungle.'" *ESQ*, 18 (2nd Qtr. 1972), 108-114.
 Finds a "similar thematic design" in the two stories.

_____. "Preposition and Meaning in Poe's 'The Spectacles.'" *Poe Newsletter*, 3 (June 1970), 21.
 A curious printing error occurs in the text of "The Spectacles" appearing in the Modern Library edition of *The Complete Tales and Poems of Edgar Allan Poe* (New York, 1937) and in the Doubleday edition, *Complete Stories and Poems of Edgar Allan Poe* (Garden City, N. Y., 1966).

Sands, Kathleen. "The Mythic Initiation of Arthur Gordon Pym." *Poe Stud*, 7 (June 1974), 14-16.
 The initiation motif gives *Pym* unity, bridging "the seeming break between the *Grampus* and *Jane Guy* adventures."

Sanford, Charles L. "Edgar Allan Poe: A Blight upon the Landscape." *AQ*, 20 (Spring 1968), 54-66.
 Sees Poe's major theme as "dispossession from Paradise" and as related to a cultural drive for "a paradisiacal fulfillment in the New World."

Santraud, J. M. "Dans le sillage de la baleinière d'Arthur Gordon Pym: *Le Sphinx des Glaces, Dan Yack*." *EA*, 54 (July-September 1972) 353-366.
 Points out parallels in *Pym*, Jules Verne's *Le Sphinx des Glaces*, and Blaise Cendrar's *Dan Yack*.

Schaefer, Charles W. "Poe's *Eureka*: The Macrocosmic Analogue." *Jour of Aesthetics and Art Crit*, 29 (Spring 1971), 353-365.
 Eureka is Poe's last statement of his aesthetics; in it poetry and philosophy are joined.

Scherting, Jack. See CLEMENS, SAMUEL LANGHORNE (Postbellum).

Schuster, Richard. "More on the 'Fig-Pedlar.'" *Poe Newsletter*, 3 (June 1970), 22.
 Discusses the origin of a specific parody found in Poe's "How to Write a Blackwood Article."

Schwaber, Paul. "On Reading Poe." *Lit and Psych*, 21, no. 2 (1971), 81-99.
 In his writing, as in his personal life, Poe disciplined madness by reason--for example, with the reasonable narrator.

Schwartz, Arthur. "The Transport: A Matter of Time and Space." *CEA Critic*, 31 (December 1968), 14-15.
 Deals with diction, rhythm, and syntax in "To Helen."

Seelye, John. "Edgar Allan Poe: *Tales of the Grotesque and Arabesque*," in *Landmarks of American Writing*, ed. Hennig Cohen, pp. 101-110.
 Poe's idiosyncratic collection of stories reflects the consciousness of a "claustrophobic, sitting in his room and looking out into a mirror at himself sitting in his room."

Senelick, Laurence. "Charles Dickens and 'The Tell-Tale Heart.'" *Poe Stud*, 6 (June 1973), 12-14.
 On Poe's possible use of a Dickens tale in composing this story.

Serio, John N. "From Edwards to Poe." *Conn Rev*, 6 (October 1972), 88-92.

Poe's works reflect both Puritan mysticism and the Puritan concept of human depravity.

Sheehan, Peter J. "Dirk Peters: A New Look at Poe's *Pym*." *Laurel Rev*, 9, no. 2 (1969), 60-70.
Pym represents the imaginative, Peters the rational side.

Shulman, Robert. "Poe and the Powers of the Mind." *ELH*, 37 (June 1970), 245-262.
In Poe's stories disintegration of the psyche seldom leads to union with "Divine Unity and Beauty," as one might expect it would.

Sims, James H. "Death in Poe's Poetry: Variations on a Theme." *Costerus*, 9 (1973), 159-180.
Identifies six approaches Poe used in dealing with the subject of death, only death "as an unpleasant end" being unpleasant to contemplate.

Sippel, Erich W. "Bolting the Whole Shebang Together: Poe's Predicament." *Criticism*, 15 (Fall 1973), 289-308.
An examination of the philosophical questions and their answers that Poe struggles with in his writing.

Sloane, David E. E. "Gothic Romanticism and Rational Empiricism in Poe's 'Berenice.'" *ATQ*, 19 (Summer 1973), 19-26.
Among other things, the article concerns the significance of Berenice's teeth and points out a possible medical source for the emphasis that Poe places on them; the whole story is a "statement on the dangers of empiricism."

_____, and Benjamin F. Fisher, IV. "Poe's Revisions in 'Berenice': Beyond the Gothic." *ATQ*, 24 (Fall 1974, Supp. 2), 19-23.
Deals with the changes that Poe made to de-emphasize "excessive terror" and to give the story "psychological tone."

Smith, Allan. "The Psychological Context of Three Tales by Poe." *Jour Am Stud*, 7 (December 1973), 279-292.
Concludes that Poe's aesthetic cannot "aspire to the full imaginative reordering of reality into an ideal realm" because it "prevents the reader from employing images that will not be universally understood, and encourages the use of hackneyed and sterile metaphors."

Smith, Herbert F. "Is Roderick Usher a Caricature?" *Poe Stud*, 6 (December 1973), 49-50.
Compares Poe's Usher to James Gates Percival (1795-1856)--"American poetaster, lexicographer, geologist, and neurotic."

Smith, Patricia. "Poe's Arabesque." *Poe Stud*, 7 (December 1974), 42-45.
The word "Arabesque" in Poe evokes "the sense of impending death" and suggests "that the nature of that death is some sort of dissolution into Unity."

Smuda, Manfred. "Variation und Innovation: Modelle literarischer Möglichkeiten der Prosa in der Nachfolge Edgar Allan Poes." *Poetica*, 3 (1970), 165-187.

Poe created both "true art" (the short story) and "trivial art" (the detective story).

Soule, George H., Jr. "Another Source for Poe: Trelawny's *The Adventures of a Younger Son*." *Poe Stud*, 8 (December 1975), 35-37.
Finds parallels between Trelawny's sea narrative and some of Poe's tales, notably "MS. Found in a Bottle," *Pym*, and "William Wilson."

St. Armand, Barton L. "Poe's 'Sober Mystification': The Uses of Alchemy in 'The Gold-Bug.'" *Poe Stud*, 4 (June 1971), 1-7.
"The Gold-Bug" demonstrates Poe's use of the philosophy of alchemy to achieve a plausible and coherent tale.

_____. "'Seemingly Intuitive Leaps': Belief and Unbelief in *Eureka*." *ATQ*, 26 (Spring 1975), 4-15.
Argues that in this work Poe "abandoned the Romantic doctrine of [divine] inspiration, and substituted for it a more practical philosophy of insight and intuition."

_____. "Usher Unveiled: Poe and the Metaphysic of Gnosticism." *Poe Stud*, 5 (June 1972), 1-8.
Considers Poe's "The Fall of the House of Usher" in the light of a metaphysic based on Gnosticism.

Stauffer, Donald B. "Poe's View on the Nature and Function of Style." *ESQ*, no. 60 (Summer 1970, Part 1), 23-30.
Summarizes Poe's views and concludes that they are unclear to us because Poe himself was unclear about them.

Stein, Allen F. "Another Source for 'The Raven.'" *Am N&Q*, 9 (February 1971), 85-86.
A blackbird representing mournful remembrance in *Puffer Hopkins*, a novel by Poe's contemporary Cornelius Mathews, is suggested as the source.

Stein, A. M. "The Detective Story--How and Why." *PULC*, 36 (Autumn 1974), 19-46.
Includes brief discussion of Poe's detective stories.

Stern, Madeleine B. "Poe: 'The Mental Temperament' for Phrenologists." *AL*, 40 (May 1968), 155-163.
Deals with sketches by the Fowlers of Poe, as a phrenological phenomenon, published after Poe's death.

_____. See GENERAL.

Stone, Edward. See GENERAL.

Stovall, Floyd. *Edgar Poe the Poet*. Charlottesville: Univ Press of Virginia, 1969.
A critical interpretation of Poe's poetry and poetic theory which characterizes him as an intuitive and skillful craftsman.

Strandberg, Victor. "Poe's Hollow Men." *Univ Rev*, 35 (March 1969), 203-212.
Poe was this country's "first fullfledged hollow man."

Strickland, Edward. "Poe's 'Ulalume,' Stanza 10." *Expl*, 34 (November 1975), Item 19.
Argues that in this stanza Ulalume has arisen.

Stromberg, Jean S. "The Relationship of Christian Concepts to Poe's *Grotesque Tales*." *Gordon Rev*, 11 (Fall 1968), 144-158.
    Poe assigned roles usually associated with Christ to man.

Stronks, James. "A Poe Source for Faulkner? 'To Helen' and 'A Rose for Emily.'" *Poe Newsletter*, 1 (April 1968), 11.
    Faulkner's image of Emily as an idol in the window could have been suggested by Poe's image of Helen in the window-niche.

Sweeney, Gerard M. "Beauty and Truth: Poe's 'A Descent into the Maelström.'" *Poe Stud*, 6 (June 1973), 22-25.
    Poe's emphasis upon the value of aesthetic intuition and his use of the frame narrative contribute to the artistry of this work.

Sweet, Charles A., Jr. "Retapping Poe's 'Cask of Amontillado.'" *Poe Stud*, 8 (June 1975), 10-12.
    Suggests that Fortunato is Montresor's "mirror image"; hence Montresor's revenge "is not a ritual of sacrifice, but of scapegoating."

Tanselle, G. Thomas. "The State of Poe Bibliography." *Poe Newsletter*, 2 (January 1969), 1-3.
    Approves of the state of Poe criticism but concludes that a definitive bibliography is still needed.

Tate, Allen. "The Poetry of Edgar Allan Poe." *SR*, 76 (Spring 1968), 214-230.
    A brief comment on Poe's poetry culminating with analyses of "The City in the Sea," "To Helen," "The Sleeper," and "The Raven."

_____. See GENERAL.

Teunissen, John J., and Evelyn J. Hinz. "Poe's *Journal of Julius Rodman* as Parody." *NCF*, 27 (December 1972), 317-338.
    "...the donneé of the *Journal* is that it is the work not of Poe but of Rodman and that the seeming plagiarisms are the means to a satiric end."

_____, and _____. "'Quaint and Curious' Backgrounds for Poe's 'Raven.'" *SHR*, 7 (Fall 1973), 411-419.
    "By way of the Ovidean and biblical allusions," the poem becomes a dramatic monologue, similar to Browning's "Porphyria's Lover."

Thomas, Dwight. "James F. Otis and 'Autography': A New Poe Correspondent." *Poe Stud*, 8 (June 1975), 12-15.
    Identifies a Griswold MS. (796) in the Boston Public Library as a letter to Poe from James F. Otis, who was to be included in Poe's "Autography."

Thompson, G. R. "Dramatic Irony in 'The Oval Portrait': A Reconsideration of Poe's Revisions." *Eng Lang Notes*, 6 (December 1968), 107-114.
    In revising "Life in Death" into "The Oval Portrait" Poe, through the use of dramatic irony, intensified the theme of the romantic imagination.

_____. "The Face in the Pool: Reflections on the Doppelgänger Motif in 'The Fall of the House of Usher.'" *Poe Stud*, 5 (June 1972), 16-21.
    Poe uses the narrator to enhance effect and meaning.

_____, ed. *Great Short Works of Edgar Allan Poe*. New York: Harper & Row, 1970.
    A paperback anthology of thirty-one poems, thirty-one tales, and three critical essays with an introduction, bibliographical essay, and chronology by the editor.

_____. "Is Poe's 'A Tale of the Ragged Mountains' a Hoax?" *Stud SF*, 6 (Summer 1969), 454-460.
    Argues that the story is a cleverly constructed ratiocinative hoax consisting of "at least three levels of irony operating simultaneously...."

_____. "On the Nose: Further Speculations on the Sources and Meanings of Poe's 'Lionizing.'" *Stud SF*, 6 (Fall 1968), 94-96.
    Suggests as source or motivation an article of June 1827 in the *Edinburgh Review*, the desire to satirize Bulwer-Lytton and to equate nose with style.

_____. *Poe's Fiction: Romantic Irony in the Gothic Tales*. Madison: Univ of Wisconsin Press, 1973.
    Reconciles the Gothic and comic faces of Poe by reading the fiction as "an intricately structured body of work reflecting Poe's comic, satiric, hoaxical, ironic temperament."

_____. "Poe's 'Flawed Gothic': Absurdist Techniques in 'Metzengerstein' and the *Courier* Satires." *ESQ*, no. 60 (Fall 1970, Parts 1 & 2, Supp.), 38-58.
    Poe may deliberately have sought to be comic and satiric in his Gothic tales.

_____. "Poe's Reading of *Pelham*: Another Source for 'Tintinnabulation' and Other Piquant Expressions." *AL*, 41 (May 1969), 251-254.
    Title is descriptive.

_____. "'Proper Evidences of Madness': American Gothic and the Interpretation of 'Ligeia.'" *ESQ*, 18 (1st Qtr. 1972), 30-49.
    The pattern of the detective story can be found in Poe's Gothic tales. "Ligeia" is specifically examined.

_____. "Unity, Death, and Nothingness--Poe's 'Romantic Skepticism.'" *PMLA*, 85 (March 1970), 297-300.
    It is inaccurate to maintain that Poe's vision of death is ecstatic; his themes present a tension between hope and despair, reason and madness, which is "skeptical."

"Three New Poe Letters." *ATQ*, 14 (Spring 1972, Part 2), 89-92.
    Facsimiles of these letters.

Timmerman, John. "Edgar Allan Poe: Artist, Aesthetician, Legend." *Sou Dak Rev*, 10 (Spring 1972), 60-70.
    Poe's legendary status has obscured the consistency of his aesthetic theory.

Travis, Mildred K. "The Idea of Poe in *Pierre*."
ESQ, 50 (1st Qtr. 1968), 59–62.
Suggests that Melville's use of Poe's themes
and critical theories constitutes a unifying
quality in *Pierre*.

_____. "A Note on 'The Bell-Tower': Melville's
'Blackwood Article.'" *Poe Stud*, 6 (June 1973),
28–29.
Poe's duo "How to Write a Blackwood Article"
and "A Predicament" may have aided Melville in
composing "The Bell-Tower."

Trieber, J. Marshall. "The Scornful Grin: A Study
of Poesque Humor." *Poe Stud*, 4 (December 1971),
32–34.
"On Poe's 'humor of scorn, wherein our own
superiority is tacitly affirmed.'"

Troubetzkoy, Ulrich. "The Artist James Carling."
New Dominion Life Style, 2 (June–July 1975),
27–33.
Profile of a nineteenth-century illustrator
of Poe's works who lost the *Harper's* magazine
competition to Gustave Doré.

Tucker, Edward L. See COOKE, PHILIP PENDLETON
(Antebellum).

_____. See MISCELLANEOUS (Antebellum).

Tuerk, Richard. "John Sartain and E. A. Poe."
Poe Stud, 4 (December 1971), 21–23.
Presents Sartain's essay on Poe appearing in
the *Boston Evening Transcript*, February 25,
1893.

_____. "Sadakichi Hartmann's 'How Poe Wrote the
Raven': A Biochemical Explanation." *MarkR*, 3
(February 1973), 81–85.
Hartmann's theory was that creativity is the
result of a chemical change in the mind, and
that such a change accounts for Poe's writing
of "The Raven."

Tynan, Daniel J. "J. N. Reynolds' *Voyage of the
Potomac*: Another Source for *The Narrative of
Arthur Gordon Pym*." *Poe Stud*, 4
(December 1971), 35–37.
Poe borrowed directly from Reynolds' *Voyage
of the Potomac*, especially wording.

Vanderbilt, Kermit. "Art and Nature in 'The Masque
of the Red Death.'" *NCF*, 22 (March 1968),
379–389.
Prospero is the "artist-hero" unable to
transcend or master nature.

Varnado, S. L. "Poe's Raven Lore: A Source
Note." *Am N&Q*, 7 (November 1968), 35–38.
A passage on the raven in Graham Dalyell's
The Darker Superstitions of Scotland (1834) was
probably a source of "The Raven."

Veler, Richard P., ed. *Papers on Poe: Essays in
Honor of John Ward Ostrom*. Springfield, Ohio:
Chantry Music Press of Wittenberg Univ, 1972.
A festschrift containing seventeen original
essays on aspects of Poe's writings and life,
with a tribute to Ostrom by Richard B. Davis.

Virtanen, Reino. "Allusions to Poe's Poetic Theory
in Valéry's *Cahiers*," in *Poetic Theory/Poetic
Practice: Papers of the Midwest MLA*, ed. Robert
Scholes. Iowa City: Midwest MLA, 1969.
Concerns Valéry's interest in Poe's "abstract
intelligence."

Vitanza, Victor J. "Edgar Allan Poe's *The Narrative
of Arthur Gordon Pym*: An Anatomy of Perverse-
ness." *EA*, 27 (January–March 1974), 26–37.
Argues that Pym is driven by the "impulse of
the Perverse" through the conscious and precon-
scious to the subconscious mind. Describes the
voyage as "a regression from civilization to
barbarianism to the brink of the original unity
of all things."

Vitt-Maucher, Gisela. "E. T. A. Hoffmanns 'Ritter
Gluck' und E. A. Poes 'The Man of the Crowd':
Eine Gegenüberstellung." *German Quart*, 43
(1970), 35–46.
Poe's story is more psychological than
Hoffman's, the latter being a fantasy emphasiz-
ing the alienated artist.

Voss, Arthur. See GENERAL.

Wages, Jack D. "Isaac Asimov's Debt to Edgar Allan
Poe." *Poe Stud*, 6 (June 1973), 29.
Asimov, "with numerous backward glances to
Poe's work, has successfully amalgamated the
detective story with science fiction."

Walcutt, Charles C., and J. E. Whitesell. See
GENERAL.

Wallace, Alfred R. *Edgar Allan Poe: A Series of
Seventeen Letters Concerning Poe's Scientific
Erudition in Eureka and His Authorship of
Leonainie*. *ATQ*, 24 (Fall 1974, Supp.), 45–49.
A reprinting of letters written by Wallace
to Ernest Marriott about Poe; Wallace had the
letters privately printed in 1930.

Walsh, John. *Poe the Detective: The Curious Circumstances Behind "The Mystery of Marie Roget."*
New Brunswick, N. J.: Rutgers Univ Press, 1968.
An attempt to test Poe's claim that he
solved a murder mystery without leaving his
study in "The Mystery of Marie Roget."

Walsh, Thomas F. "The Other William Wilson." *ATQ*,
10 (Spring 1971), 17–26.
Examines the divided personality, the double
self, in Poe's story.

Watson, Charles N., Jr. "Premature Burial in
'Arthur Gordon Pym' and 'Israel Potter.'" *AL*,
47 (March 1975), 105–107.
A close study of Melville's story offers
further evidence that he read and was influenced
by Poe.

Weidman, Bette S. "*The Broadway Journal* (2): A
Casualty of Abolition Politics." *BNYPL*, 73
(February 1969), 94–113.
Investigation of the magazine in the context
of the abolition movement. Relatively little
mention of Poe.

Weiner, Bruce I. "Poe's Subversion of Verisimilitude." *ATQ*, 24 (Fall 1974, Supp. 2), 2-8.
    Deals with Poe's manipulation of the "rhet-
oric of verisimilitude" in "The Premature
Burial" and "Von Kempelen and His Discovery"
for the purpose of "undermin[ing] the illusion
of truth and expos[ing] the artifice."

Wells, Daniel A. "'Bartleby the Scrivener,' Poe,
and the Duyckinck Circle." *ESQ*, 21 (1st Qtr.
1975), 35-39.
    Poe may have been a model for Nippers in
Melville's story.

Wertz, S. K., and Linda L. "On Poe's Use of 'Mystery.'" *Poe Stud*, 4 (June 1971), 7-10.
    "Mystery" in Poe's fiction is "that which
involves the subject and the reader in preter-
natural or abnormal speculations."

Westburg, Barry. "How Poe Solved the Mystery of
Barnaby Rudge." *Dickens Stud Newsletter*, 5
(June 1974), 38-40.
    Explains possible reasons why Poe's con-
clusions about the murderer in Dickens' novel,
made before it was finished, turned out to be
wrong.

Whitla, William. "Sources for Browning in Byron,
Blake, and Poe." *SBHC*, 2 (Spring 1974), 7-16.
    "The Raven" could be a source for Browning's
"The Householder."

Whitman, Sarah Helen. *Edgar Poe and His Critics*.
ATQ, 24 (Fall 1974, Supp. 2), 29 ff.
    A reprinting of a work published in 1860.

Wilbur, Richard. "Introduction," *The Narrative of
Arthur Gordon Pym* by Edgar Allan Poe. Boston:
David R. Godine, 1973.
    An autobiographical interpretation of Poe's
Pym as the product of sexual and existential
fears.

Wilson, James D. "Incest and American Romantic
Fiction." *SLI*, 7 (Spring 1974), 31-50.
    Includes a discussion of Poe's treatment of
the effects of narcissism.

Woodberry, George E., ed. "Poe in Philadelphia:
Selections from The Correspondence of Edgar
Allan Poe." (Reprinted from the September 1894
issue of *The Century Magazine*.) *Am Bk Collector*, 25 (January-February 1975), 6-14.
    A short introduction concerning Poe's life
in Philadelphia and a selection of letters to
and from Poe during the years 1839-1843.

Woodbridge, Hensley C. "Poe in Spanish America:
Addenda and Corrigenda." *Poe Stud*, 4
(December 1971), 46.
    Comments on four recent items touching on
Poe's reputation in Spanish America.

_____. "Poe in Spanish America: A Bibliographical
Supplement." *Poe Newsletter*, 2 (January 1969),
18-19.
    Items concerning Poe's reputation in South
America.

Woodress, James. See GENERAL--3rd and 4th Woodress
entries.

_____. See GENERAL (both Woodress entries)

Woodson, Thomas, ed. *Twentieth Century Interpretations of The Fall of the House of Usher*.
Englewood Cliffs, N. J.: Prentice-Hall, 1969.
    Reprints fifteen critical essays and excerpts,
with a chronology of Poe's career, a brief selected bibliography, and an original introductory essay by the editor.

Yonce, Margaret. "The Spirited Descent into the
Maelström: A Debt to 'The Rime of the Ancient
Mariner.'" *Poe Newsletter*, 2 (April 1969),
26-29.
    The journeys in both works are archetypal
quests for spiritual transcendence.

Zimmerman, Melvin. "Baudelaire's Early Conceptions
of Poe's Fate." *Rev de Litt Comp*, 44 (1970),
117-120.
    Baudelaire's 'L'Irrémédiable' reveals his
feeling that Poe was the victim of a "diabolical
Providence."

[POTTER, REUBEN] Karras, Bill, ed. "First Impressions of Mexico, 1828, by Reuben Potter." *SHQ*,
79 (July 1975), 55-68.
    Contains a letter from Potter to his brother;
a bibliographical headnote by the editor describes Potter as a diplomat, historian, and
poet.

[RUSSELL, IRWIN] Metcalf, Patricia. "A lean, pale,
sallow, shabby, striking young man." *Listener*,
86 (December 30, 1971), 904-905.
    Comments by Russell's niece on his interest
in Negro dialect and on the possibility that
Russell was the model for James's Basil Ransom.

Simms, L. Moody, Jr. "Irwin Russell and Negro Dialect Poetry: A Note on Chronological Priority
and True Significance." *Notes on Miss Writers*,
2 (Fall 1969), 67-73.
    Discounts statements that Russell was the
pioneer in using Negro character and dialect.

[SIMMS, WILLIAM GILMORE] Aaron, Daniel. See
GENERAL.

Barnett, Louise K. See GENERAL.

Bruccoli, Matthew. See GENERAL.

Bush, Lewis M. "Werther on the Alabama Frontier:
A Reinterpretation of Simms's *Confession*." *Miss
Quart*, 21 (Spring 1968), 119-130.
    Simms's *Confession; or, The Blind Heart* (1841),
an early forerunner of the psychological novel,
was influenced by Goethe's *Werther* in concept
and autobiographical detail.

Bush, Robert. "Introductions" to *The Writings of
W. G. Simms*, Vol. III, *As Good As Comedy*, and
Paddy McGann, ed. J. B. Meriwether. Columbia:
Univ of South Carolina Press, 1972.
    Historical and critical introductions to the
two novels, the first published once in 1852 and
the second published only in the *Southern*

Illustrated News in 1863, issued in CEAA-approved texts.

Christopherson, Merrill. "Simms' Northern Speaking Tour in 1856: A Tragedy." *So Speech Jour*, 36 (Winter 1970), 139-151.
    Examines the question as to why Simms could not adapt to the hostile audiences he met on his Northern tour.

Clark, Harry H. See GENERAL.

Colquitt, Betsy F. See GENERAL.

Davidson, Donald, and Mary C. Simms Oliphant. "Introduction" to *The Writings of W. G. Simms*, Vol. I, *Voltmeier or The Mountain Men*, ed. J. B. Meriwether. Columbia: Univ of South Carolina Press, 1969.
    Recounts the historical background and critical significance of this novel issued as a book for the first time in a CEAA-approved text.

Doxey, William S. "Dogs and Dates in Simms' *The Yemassee*." *ATQ*, 1 (1st Qtr. 1969), 41-43.
    Simms's comparison of the dog named Dugdale to dogs used by the French against insurrectionists in Haiti bears close resemblance to a description written by someone else thirty years earlier; this may be what Simms had in mind when he referred in his Preface to a "slight anachronism" in the novel.

Gilkes, Lillian. "Park Benjamin, Henry William Herbert, and William Gilmore Simms: A Case of Mistaken Identity." *So Carolina Rev*, 3 (June 1971), 66-77.
    Title is suggestive.

Gross, Theodore L. See GENERAL--1st Gross entry.

Guilds, John C. "The Achievement of William Gilmore Simms: His Short Stories." *Spectrum*, 2 (1972), 25-35.
    Discusses Simms's skill as a short-story writer.

_____. "The Literary Criticism of William Gilmore Simms." *So Carolina Rev*, 2 (November 1969), 49-56.
    Simms's literary criticism is judicious, farsighted, and commonsensical.

_____. "The 'Lost' Number of the *Southern Literary Gazette*." *SB*, 22 (1969), 266-273.
    Discusses the twelfth number of the *Southern Literary Gazette* (November 1, 1829), especially William Gilmore Simms's contributions to it.

_____. "Simms and the *Southern and Western*," in *South Carolina Journals and Journalists*. Columbia, S. C.: Southern Studies Program, 1975, pp. 45-59.
    A study of Simms's editorship of this periodical in 1845.

_____. "Southern Literary Magazines, V: Simms as Editor and Prophet: The Flowering and Early Death of the Southern *Magnolia*." *So Lit Jour*, 4 (Spring 1972), 69-92.

Pessimistic about the outcome of such arrangements, Simms became editor of the *Magnolia*, which under him became less concerned with literature that entertained and more concerned about literature that provoked thought.

_____, ed. *Stories and Tales*. *The Writings of William Gilmore Simms*. Vol. V. Columbia: Univ of South Carolina Press, 1974.
    Includes fifteen uncollected or unpublished stories with texts edited according to CEAA standards and an introduction by the editor.

_____. "William Gilmore Simms and the *Southern Literary Gazette*." *SB*, 31 (1968), 59-92.
    Deals with the years that Simms edited this journal; lists his contributions of poems and essays.

Hoge, James O. "Byron's Influence on the Poetry of William Gilmore Simms." *Essays in Lit*, 2 (Spring 1975), 87-96.
    Discusses Simms's interest in the English Romantics and traces Byron's influences on Simms's verse.

Holman, C. Hugh. See GENERAL.

Hoole, W. S. See GENERAL.

Howell, Elmo. "The Concept of Character in Simms's Border Romances." *Miss Quart*, 22 (Fall 1969), 303-312.
    Simms's five novels set in the Old Southwest (Georgia, Alabama, Tennessee, and Kentucky) present less aristocratic Southerners than his other novels but reveal a concept of character and honor "widely at variance from that of his Northern neighbors."

_____. "William Gilmore Simms and the American Indian." *So Car Rev*, 5 (June 1973), 57-64.
    Simms viewed the Indian as being essentially inferior.

Hubert, Thomas. "Simms's Use of Milton and Wordsworth in *The Yemassee*: An Aspect of Symbolism in the Novel." *So Car Rev*, 6 (November 1973), 58-65.
    The rattlesnake in chapter twenty of the novel "is a descendant of the Miltonic serpent which seduced Eve," and Simms "appropriated" some of the language of Wordsworth used in his "description of the 'sublime' in nature."

Kibler, James E., Jr. "A New Letter of Simms to Richard Henry Wilde: On the Advancement of Sectional Literature." *AL*, 44 (January 1973), 667-670.
    Includes the edited letter, with an introduction on its importance regarding Southern literature and the Simms/Wilde relationship.

_____. "Simms' Indebtedness to Folk Tradition in 'Sharp Snaffles.'" *So Lit Jour*, 4 (Spring 1972), 55-68.
    In "Sharp Snaffles" Simms draws on his 1847 journey to the mountains of western North Carolina, where he heard hunters tell tall yarns.

_____. "Simms's Editorship of the Columbia *Phoenix* of 1865," in *South Carolina Journals and Journalists*. Columbia, S. C.: Southern Studies Program, 1975, pp. 61-75.
  A study of Simms's editorial policy, his contributions to this newspaper, and what the paper reveals about the history of the last days of the war and federal occupation in central South Carolina.

_____. See LEGARÉ, JAMES MATHEWES (Antebellum-- 2nd Kibler entry).

Kolodny, Annette. *The Lay of the Land. Metaphor as Experience and History in American Life and Letters*. Chapel Hill: Univ of North Carolina Press, 1975.
  Treats., among works of other writers, Simms's romances and the view of the landscape which they present.

_____. "The Unchanging Landscape: The Pastoral Impulse in Simms's Revolutionary War Romances." *So Lit Jour*, 5 (Fall 1972), 46-67.
  In his fiction with an impulse to experience the land as woman, Simms became the leading spokesman for Southern culture.

Lease, Benjamin. "William Gilmore Simms, A New Letter." *GHQ*, 54 (Fall 1970), 427-430.
  Prints a letter from Simms to John Neal, inviting the latter to submit to the *Magnolia*, a journal under Simms's editorship.

McHaney, Thomas L. "An Early 19th Century Literary Agent: James Lawson of New York." *PBSA*, 64 (2nd Qtr. 1970), 177-192.
  A discussion of the correspondence between Simms and his literary agent.

Meats, Stephen E. "Introduction," *Joscelyn*. Columbia: Univ of South Carolina Press. Centennial edition, 1975.
  A critical introduction to this first book publication of *Joscelyn*.

Meriwether, James B., ed. *Simms Newsletter*. Columbia, S. C.: Southern Studies Program.
  An occasional mimeographed newsletter reporting Simms projects begun and completed.

Perkins, George. See GENERAL.

Powell, William E. "Motif and Tale-Type of Simms's 'Grayling.'" *SFQ*, 35 (June 1971), 157-159.
  Simms's work is a literary treatment of a folk story and deserves inclusion in E. W. Baughman, *Type and Motif-Index of the Folktale of England and North America*.

Rees, Robert A., and Marjorie Griffin. "William Gilmore Simms and *The Family Companion*." *SB*, 24 (1971), 109-129.
  The printing, with an introduction, of eight letters (1841-1842) from Simms to Mr. or Mrs. Benjamin F. Griffin regarding their ill-fated periodical *The Family Companion*; Rees and Griffin say the letters "add a chapter to our understanding of Simms and his relationship to Southern periodicals."

Ridgely, J. V. "Simms's Concept of Style in the Historical Romance." *ESQ*, no. 60 (Summer 1970, Part 1), 16-23.
  Simms believed that the historical romance should be modeled upon the epic and drama.

_____. "Two Unreprinted Short Novels: Volume II of the Centennial Simms." *So Lit Jour*, 5 (Spring 1973), 80-87.
  A review of the Centennial edition of *As Good As a Comedy* and *Paddy McGann*.

Roberts, Leonard. See MISCELLANEOUS (Antebellum).

Rose, Alan H. See KENNEDY, JOHN PENDLETON (Antebellum).

Rubin, Louis D., Jr. See MISCELLANEOUS (Postbellum).

_____. See GENERAL--1st and 6th Rubin entries.

Shillingsburg, Miriam J. "From Notes to Novel: Simms's Creative Method." *So Lit Jour*, 5 (Fall 1972), 89-107.
  On a trip to upper South Carolina watering places with his family in 1847 Simms had in mind writing a book using the notes he kept on the trip, but instead of writing a single book he drew on the notes several times later in his career.

_____. "'The Idylls of the Apalachian': An Unpublished Lecture by William Gilmore Simms." *Appal Jour*, 1 (Autumn 1972), 2-11 (Part 1); 1 (Spring 1973), 146-160 (Part 2).
  First printing of a lecture on the subject of "The Apalachian: A Southern Idyll," slated for delivery in the North but cancelled because of sectional animus.

_____. "Politics and Art: Toward Seeing Simms as a Whole." *So Lit Jour*, 7 (Spring 1975), 132-145, 148.
  A review-essay of *The Politics of a Literary Man: William Gilmore Simms*, by Jon L. Wakelyn, and of *Stories and Tales*, ed. John C. Guilds, which concludes that both present a record of the life and career of Simms that contributes toward seeing him "as a whole."

_____. "Simms's Reviews of Shakespeare on the Stage." *Tenn Stud in Lit*, 16 (1971), 121-135.
  A look at Simms's reviews (some newly ascribed to him) of Shakespearean productions in New York, Charleston, and New Orleans.

Simpson, Lewis P. See GENERAL--3rd Simpson entry.

Thomas, C. E. "Mary C. Simms Oliphant." *Sandlapper*, 4 (January 1971), 13-16.
  A description of the scholarship of Mrs. Oliphant, particularly of her work on her grandfather, W. G. Simms.

Tomlinson, David. "Southern Literary Magazines, VI: *Simms's Monthly Magazine: The Southern and Western Monthly Magazine and Review*." *So Lit Jour*, 8 (Fall 1975), 95-125.
  With Simms as the editor in its entire twelve issues, this journal was a solid publication

with a strong editorial position that seldom allowed prejudices to take precedence over fair literary judgment.

Vauthier, Simone. "Légende du Sud: presentation de William Gilmore Simms." *BFLS*, 47 (1969), 259-290.
    A detailed examination and evaluation of Simms's concept of the South.

_____. "Of Time and the South: The Fiction of William Gilmore Simms." *So Lit Jour*, 5 (Fall 1972), 3-45.
    In his novels Simms attempted to project "through the creative interweaving of legends, traditions, and facts a compelling image of the South," linking past, present, and future.

_____. "Une aventure du récit fantastique: *Paddy McGann, or, The Demon of the Stump* de William Gilmore Simms." *RANAM*, 6 (1973), 78-104.
    A critical study.

Wakelyn, Jon L. *The Politics of a Literary Man: William Gilmore Simms*. Contributions in American Studies, no. 5. Westport, Conn.: Greenwood Press, Inc., 1973.
    Considers Simms's political views and objectives to be the motivating forces in his writing.

Watson, Charles S. "A New Approach to Simms: Imagery and Meaning in *The Yemassee*." *Miss Quart*, 26 (Spring 1973), 155-163.
    The most prominent imagery in the novel is that of wild animals, used by the Indians as symbols of freedom; dogs as symbols of slavery; and the "true" man and "false" man used by the settlers.

_____. "William Gilmore Simms: An Essay in Bibliography." *RALS*, 3 (Spring 1973), 3-26.
    Assesses the history of scholarship on Simms.

Weidman, Bette S. "White Men's Red Man: A Penitential Reading of Four American Novels." *Mod Lang Stud*, 4, no. 2 (1974), 14-26.
    Includes discussion of Simms's *The Yemassee*.

Wimsatt, Mary Ann. "Leonard Voltmeier's 'Invictus': Volume One of the *Centennial Simms*." *So Lit Jour*, 2 (Spring 1970), 135-147.
    An essay-review that maintains that *Voltmeier*, the first volume in a major publishing effort, affords a new look at Simms and "suggests the need for reevaluating his role in Southern letters."

_____. "Simms as Novelist of Manners: *Katharine Walton*." *So Lit Jour*, 5 (Fall 1972), 68-88.
    Beginning with *Katharine Walton* (1851), Simms's social criticism, expressed through "manner," punctures "the pretensions of shallow socialites with lightly-pointed satire."

_____. "*The Writings of William Gilmore Simms: Centennial Edition*, ed. John Caldwell Guilds. Vol. I, *Voltmeier: or The Mountain Men*." *SAQ*, 71 (Summer 1972), 443-445.

An essay-review that discusses some of Simms's problems, summarizes the plot of *Voltmeier*, and expresses appreciation for the Simms edition.

Yellin, Jean F. See MISCELLANEOUS (Antebellum).

[TAYLOR, JOHN] Duke, Maurice. "John Taylor of Caroline, 1753-1824: Notes Toward a Bibliography." *Early Am Lit*, 6 (Spring 1971), 69-72.
    Notes on locations of materials relating to Taylor.

[THOMPSON, WILLIAM TAPPAN] Ellison, George R. "William Tappan Thompson and the *Southern Miscellany*, 1842-1844." *Miss Quart*, 23 (Spring 1970), 155-168.
    To illustrate the need for study of the original sources of publication of Southwestern humor, an analysis is made of the content of this magazine with emphasis on Thompson's contributions.

Thompson, W. T. *Major Jones's Courtship*. Atlanta: Cherokee Publishing Co., 1973.
    Facsimile reprint of the 1872 revision of the 1840 edition of a classic in Southern humor, with a biographical note by W. B. Willingham.

[THORPE, THOMAS BANGS] Hayne, Barrie. "Yankee in the Patriarchy: T. B. Thorpe's Reply to *Uncle Tom's Cabin*." *AQ*, 20 (Summer 1968), 180-195.
    Thorpe's "mixed" reaction to Mrs. Stowe is revealed in his novel *The Master's House*.

Lemay, J. A. Leo. "The Text, Tradition, and Themes of 'The Big Bear of Arkansas.'" *AL*, 47 (November 1975), 321-342.
    A thorough study of all aspects of the story which "celebrates the *joie de vivre* of the jest, a *joie de vivre* diminishing as the next stage of culture supersedes the heroic, primitive stage when man existed in near unity with nature."

Tyner, Troi. See FAULKNER, WILLIAM (Contemporary).

[TUCKER, GEORGE] Noble, Donald R., Jr. "Introduction" to *The Valley of the Shenandoah*. Chapel Hill: Univ of North Carolina Press, 1970.
    Outlines Tucker's career and assesses the place of this Virginia novel, reprinted from the 1824 text, in the development of Southern fiction and the plantation-novel tradition.

Sutton, Robert P. See MISCELLANEOUS (Antebellum).

Yellin, Jean F. See MISCELLANEOUS (Antebellum).

[TUCKER, NATHANIEL BEVERLEY] Sutton, Robert P. See MISCELLANEOUS (Antebellum).

Tucker, Nathaniel Beverley. *The Partisan Leader: A Tale of the Future*. Chapel Hill: Univ of North Carolina Press, 1971.
    A reprint of the 1836 novel written to warn the South against repressive measures of the Federal government and Jacksonian democracy, with a historical appreciation by C. Hugh Holman.

Wrobel, Arthur. "'Romantic Realism': Nathaniel Beverley Tucker." *AL*, 42 (November 1970), 325-335.
 A study of Tucker's novels, arriving at the conclusion that although he and his contemporaries tried "to observe the truths of human nature," they failed because they truckled to a public reared on Sir Walter Scott and the moralistic Scottish reviewers.

[TURNER, NAT] Foner, Eric, ed. *Nat Turner*. Great Lives Observed Series. Englewood Cliffs, N. J.: Prentice-Hall, 1971.
 A collection of historical and cultural materials concerned with Nat Turner and the Southampton Insurrection of 1831, with an introduction, chronology, and bibliographical note by the editor.

Gross, Seymour L., and Eileen Bender. "History, Politics and Literature: The Myth of Nat Turner." *AQ*, 23 (October 1971), 487-518.
 Discusses Turner's biography, Styron's treatment of it in *The Confessions of Nat Turner*, and "the black campaign against Styron's novel."

Nichols, Charles H. See MISCELLANEOUS (Antebellum).

Oates, Stephen B. *The Fires of Jubilee: Nat Turner's Fierce Rebellion*. New York: Harper & Row, 1975.
 An historical reconstruction and a biographical narrative of the life and times of Nat Turner.

Tragle, Henry I., compiler. *Nat Turner's Slave Revolt--1831*. *Jackdaw No. A-1*. New York: Grossman, 1972.
 A collection of twelve facsimiles of contemporary documents and five broadsheets prepared by the compiler on Turner's revolt, contained in an envelope.

_____, ed. *The Southampton Slave Revolt of 1831*. Amherst: Univ of Massachusetts Press, 1971.
 A compilation of contemporary newspaper accounts, the trial transcript, unpublished letters and documents, and other source materials for a study of Nat Turner's insurrection.

[WALKER, DAVID] Pease, William H. and Jane H. "Walker's *Appeal* Comes to Charleston: A Note and Documents." *JNH*, 59 (July 1974), 287-292.
 Information on the effect Walker's *Appeal* had when distributed in Charleston, South Carolina.

[WIRT, WILLIAM] Robert, Joseph C. "William Wirt, Virginian." *VMHB*, 80 (October 1972), 387-441.
 A well-documented biographical article on Wirt.

Wirt, William. *The Letters of the British Spy*. Southern Literary Classics Series. Chapel Hill: Univ of North Carolina Press, 1970.
 A reprint of the 1832 revised edition (originally published in 1803) of the letters of a lawyer about life in Virginia, with an introductory appreciation by Richard Beale Davis.

[MISCELLANEOUS] Alford, Terry L. "Letter from Liberia, 1848." *Miss Quart*, 22 (Spring 1969), 150-151.
 A letter from one of twenty-one slaves emancipated in 1836, reporting from the new home in Africa.

Andrews, J. C. *The South Reports the Civil War*. Princeton: Princeton Univ Press, 1970.
 A historical study of Southern journalism and its influence on the war effort, 1861-1865.

Bergeron, Jeanette. "Occupation Newspapers of South Carolina, 1862-1865," in *South Carolina Journals and Journalists*. Columbia, S. C.: Southern Studies Program, 1975, pp. 135-145.
 On the Northern propaganda presses in South Carolina during the Civil War.

Berthoff, Warner. *Fictions and Events: Essays in Criticism and Literary History*. New York: Dutton, 1971.
 Includes "Edmund Wilson and His Civil War," a critique of *Patriotic Gore*.

Blasingame, John W. "The Planter on the Couch: Earl Thorpe and the Psychodynamics of Slavery." *JNH*, 60 (April 1975), 320-331.
 A review-essay on Thorpe's *The Old South: A Psychohistory*.

Braden, W. W., ed. *Oratory in the Old South: 1828-1860*. Baton Rouge: Louisiana State Univ Press, 1970.
 Contains ten essays by rhetorical critics which examine the major oratorical movements in antebellum Southern politics, including a full essay on John C. Calhoun as a master dialectician, and an annotated bibliography.

Briceland, A. V. "Ephraim Kirby: Mr. Jefferson's Emissary on the Tombigbee--Mobile Frontier in 1804." *AlaR*, 24 (April 1971), 83-113.
 Discusses some of the activities of Jefferson's territorial land commissioner.

Bridges, Katherine. "'All Well at Natchitoches': A Louisiana City on the Stage." *La Stud*, 10 (Summer 1971), 85-91.
 History of a dramatic sketch presented in London and New York in the 1820's and 1830's by English actor Charles Mathews.

Calhoun, Richard J. *"Southern Literary Magazines, III*: The Ante-Bellum Literary Twilight: *Russell's Magazine*." *So Lit Jour*, 3 (Fall 1970), 89-110.
 Calhoun thinks that "not much of a case for the importance of *Russell's* can be based on the overall quality of its short stories, poems, and essays." It does deserve credit as the discoverer of Henry Timrod.

Camp, James, X. J. Kennedy, and Keith Waldrop, eds. *Pegasus Descending: A Book of the Best Bad Verse*. New York: Macmillan, 1971.
 Includes excerpts from and notes on Chivers and Poe.

Cardwell, Guy A. "The Plantation House: An Analogical Image." *So Lit Jour*, 2 (Fall 1969), 3-21.

In Southern life as in Southern fiction the plantation house was a dramatic center, bringing everything to a focus.

Clark, James W., Jr. "The Fugitive Slave as Humorist." *Stud in Am Humor*, 1 (October 1974), 73-78.
  A study of humor in the writings of William Wells Brown, Frederick Douglass, and others.

Clifton, James M. "The Ante-Bellum Rice Planter as Revealed in the Letterbook of Charles Manigault, 1846-1848." *SCHM*, 74 (July 1973), 119-127, 300-310.
  Concerning rice planting on the Cooper and Savannah Rivers.

Cohen, Hennig, and W. B. Dillingham, eds. *Humor of the Old Southwest*. Athens: Univ of Georgia Press, 1975.
  A second printing of the standard anthology first published in 1964.

Connelly, Thomas L. "Editorial Opinion in South Carolina's Wartime Press," in *South Carolina Journals and Journalists*. Columbia, S. C.: Southern Studies Program, 1975, pp. 211-224.
  Demonstrates the need for historians to examine the newspapers of the lower South to ascertain their opinions. Too much focus has been placed on the Virginia area.

Coulter, E. Merton. "The Great Georgia Railway Disaster Hoax on the London *Times*." *GHQ*, 56 (Spring 1972), 25-50.
  The editor of the London *Times* apparently believed a wild humor tale involving duels and murders on the Central of Georgia railroad.

Cox, Leland. "Realistic and Humorous Writings in Ante-Bellum Charleston Magazines," in *South Carolina Journals and Journalists*. Columbia, S. C.: Southern Studies Program, 1975, pp. 177-205.
  Contrary to popular notion, the period from 1828-1860 in South Carolina offers a wealth of significant *realistic* writing. An appendix lists these works, singling out those of O. B. Mayer of the Dutch Fork as of particular merit.

Daniel, W. Harrison. "Protestantism and Patriotism in the Confederacy." *Miss Quart*, 24 (Spring 1971), 117-134.
  In sermons of the clergy and in writings in church newspapers, patriotism, religious faith, and duty were closely associated.

Davis, Charles E., and Martha B. Hudson. "Humor of the Old Southwest: A Checklist of Criticism." *Miss Quart*, 27 (Spring 1974), 179-199.
  General and individual author listings.

Davis, Richard B. "Charleston in Its Golden Age: Unique or Archetypal?" *So Lit Jour*, 2 (Fall 1969), 148-151.
  An essay-review of *Charleston in the Age of the Pinckneys*, by George C. Rogers, Jr., which concludes that the book falls short in not developing an intellectual history for Charleston.

Degler, Carl N. *The Other South: Southern Dissenters in the Nineteenth Century*. New York: Harper & Row, 1973.
  A study of white Southerners who rejected the social and intellectual patterns of the region by opposing slavery, supporting the Union, and becoming Republicans during Reconstruction.

Dickson, Bruce D., Jr. "The 'John and Old Master' Stories of the World of Slavery: A Study of Folktales and History." *Phylon*, 35 (December 1974), 418-429.
  The central feature of every story in this cycle is interaction between John and Old Master in which the normal rules governing relations between slave and master are broken; thus, the stories embody an ongoing conflict and are symbolic descriptions of the way antebellum Southerners viewed the slave system.

Dillingham, William B. "Days of the Tall Tale." *SouR*, 4 (Spring 1968), 569-577.
  An essay-review of new editions of Weems's *Life of Washington*, J. G. Baldwin's *The Flush Times of California*, and of two new critical studies, one of Paul Bunyan and one of George Washington Harris.

Fucilla, Joseph G. "The Study of Italian in Mississippi Schools (1829-1860)." *Miss Quart*, 26 (Winter 1972-73), 63-70.
  Because Italy was the high point of European travel for cultivated Americans of the nineteenth century, the study of Italian in Mississippi, as elsewhere in the South, was widespread until it was superseded by "utilitarianism" in American education.

Grant, William A. *"The Virginians*: A Thackeray Novel about the Old Dominion." *Va Cavalcade*, 22 (Autumn 1972), 10-15.
  John Pendleton Kennedy, John Esten Cooke, and John Reuben Thompson, editor of the *Southern Literary Messenger*, helped with Thackeray's research, but the novel drew angry reactions because of the unflattering portrayal of Washington.

Green, Alan W. C. "'Jim Crow,' 'Zip Coon': The Northern Origins of Negro Minstrelsy." *Mass Rev*, 9 (Spring 1970), 385-397.
  Character traits thought of as "typically Negro" appeared early in the theater.

Griffith, Lucille. "Anne Royal in Alabama." *AlaR*, 21 (January 1968), 53-63.
  Information on Anne Royal's travel book (1830) describing the Alabama frontier.

Gutman, Herbert G. "The World Two Cliometricians Made." *JNH*, 60 (January 1975), 53-227.
  This monograph-length review contends that, although *Time on the Cross* may have "importance as economic history," it "cannot be taken seriously as social history."

Haberland, Paul M. "The Reception of German Literature in Baltimore's Literary Magazines." *Ger-Am Stud*, 7 (1974), 69-92.
  Deals with the varying reactions of the people of Baltimore to German literature.

II. Antebellum (1800-1865)

Harrell, Laura D. S. "The Development of the Lyceum Movement in Mississippi." *JMiH*, 31 (August 1969), 187-201.
Title is descriptive.

Harwell, Richard B. "Brief Candle: The Confederate Theatre." *Proc of the Am Antiquarian Soc*, 8 (April 21, 1971), 41-160.
Deals with the Richmond Theatre and its successor, the New Richmond Theatre.

Hauck, Richard B. "Predicting a Native Literature: William T. Porter's First Issue of the *Spirit of the Times*." *Miss Quart*, 22 (Winter 1968-69), 77-84.
Reprints two editorials from a rare first issue of the *Spirit* and shows that Porter anticipated the kind of material his paper would publish--humor, fiction, travel, natural history.

Hill, West T., Jr. *The Theatre in Early Kentucky: 1790-1820*. Lexington: Univ Press of Kentucky, 1971.
A detailed historical account of the first established theatrical productions in the early West during the period when Lexington, Frankfort, and Louisville were the major centers of dramatic activity.

Hummel, Ray O., Jr., ed. *Southeastern Broadsides Before 1877: A Bibliography*. Richmond: Virginia State Library, 1971.
Describes broadsides published in ten Southern states before 1877 and located in fifty-five libraries and archives in the region, with seventeen reproductions, indexed by states.

Inge, M. Thomas. "Literary Humor of the Old Southwest: A Brief Overview." *La Stud*, 7 (Summer 1968), 132-143.
A survey of pre-Civil War humor in the South; discusses the influence of this writing on Mark Twain and contemporary Southern writers and the reprinting of it in England.

_____, ed. *The Frontier Humorists: Critical Views*. Hamden, Conn.: Archon Books, 1975.
Reprints twenty essays on the humorists of the South with an introduction on the development of this school of writing and a checklist of other scholarship.

Jacobs, Robert D. "*Southern Literary Magazines*, I: Campaign for a Southern Literature: *The Southern Literary Messenger*." *So Lit Jour*, 2 (Fall 1969), 66-98.
The *Messenger*'s efforts to inform the nation of the "history, topography, and manners' of the South and have Southern people judged fairly "pointed the way toward the greatest accomplishment of Southern literature."

Kennedy, J. Gerald. "The Magazine Tales of the 1830's." *ATQ*, 24 (Fall 1974, Supp. 2), 23-28.
A survey of the types of tales that appeared in magazines, including Southern ones, of this period. Poe is referred to frequently, Simms briefly.

Killion, R. G. "Reminiscences of the 'Peculiar Institution.'" *Sandlapper*, 5 (October 1972), 49-54, 68.
Transcriptions of interviews with slaves made in the 1850's in South Carolina and Georgia.

Kimball, W. J. "The 'Kentucky Tragedy': Romance or Politics." *FCHQ*, 48 (January 1974), 16-26.
Selected references which "are representative of the basic feelings and thoughts of the main actors in this drama."

Korn, B. W. "Additional Benjamin and Alexander Levy Imprints." *PBSA*, 62 (2nd Qtr. 1968), 245-252.
This note brings up to date Mr. Korn's article, "Benjamin Levy: New Orleans Printer and Publisher," *PBSA*, 54 (1960).

Krumpelmann, John T. "*Tokeah*, the First English-Language Novel in Our Southwest." *So Central Bul*, 28 (Winter 1968), 142-143.
Charles Sealsfield endeavored in 1829 to do for the Indians of the South-Southwest what Cooper did for them elsewhere.

Lieber, Todd M. "The Significance of the Frontier in the Writing of Antebellum Southern History." *Miss Quart*, 22 (Fall 1969), 337-354.
Early in the twentieth century such historians as Phillips, Crane, Dodd, and Craven reflect an awareness of Frederick Jackson Turner's frontier thesis.

Margolies, Edward. "Ante-Bellum Slave Narratives: Their Place in American Literary History." *SBL*, 4 (Autumn 1973), 1-8.
Discusses the propaganda element and the image of the Negro presented in the narratives.

McFaul, John M. "Expediency vs. Morality: Jacksonian Politics and Slavery." *Jour Am Hist*, 62 (June 1975), 24-40.
A running description of the uneasy controversies of Jacksonian politicians attempting to placate Abolitionists, slave-owners, and Unionists; Unionists won out for the moment.

McNair, Donald. "Backwoods Humor in the Pendleton, S. C. *Messenger*, 1810-1851," in *South Carolina Journals and Journalists*. Columbia, S. C.: Southern Studies Program, 1975, pp. 225-232.
Traces the roots of Southern humor in this the first Upcountry Carolina newspaper.

Miles, Edwin A. "The Old South and the Classical World." *NCHR*, 48 (Summer 1971), 258-275.
A tracing of the reasons for the antebellum South's admiration for the classical world.

Miles, Elton. *Southwest Humorists*. Southwest Writers Series, no. 26, Austin: Steck-Vaughn, 1969.
Traces the roots of humor of the Southwest (Texas, Oklahoma, New Mexico, and Arizona) back to the humor of the Old Southwest (bounded by Tennessee, Georgia, and Louisiana).

Mohr, Clarence L. "Southern Blacks in the Civil War: A Century of Historiography." *JNH*, 59 (April 1974), 177-195.

Not until 1935 and after did historians begin to present a realistic account of blacks during the Civil War.

Moore, Rayburn S. "The Magazine and the Short Story in the Ante-Bellum Period." *SAB*, 38 (May 1973), 44-51.
    An evaluation of the influence of editors, publishing houses, and the public on short-story writers for magazines.

Mower, George R. "The Kentucky Tragedy, a Source of *Pierre*." *Ky Folklore Record*, 15 (January-March 1969), 1-2.
    Discusses Melville's possible use of *The Confession of Jeroboam O. Beauchamp*.

Musgrave, Marian E. "Patterns of Violence in Pro-Slavery and Anti-Slavery Fiction." *CLA Jour*, 16 (June 1973), 426-437.
    The works of several Southerners are used as examples to support the thesis that blacks were stereotyped in both pro- and anti-slavery fiction.

Myers, Robert M., ed. *The Children of Pride: A True Story of Georgia and the Civil War*. New Haven: Yale Univ Press, 1972.
    A collection of 1200 letters by family and friends of Charles Colcock Jones of Liberty County, Georgia, arranged as a chronological narrative, 1854-1868, and providing a panoramic view of plantation life before and during the war.

Nichols, Charles H., ed. *Black Men in Chains: Narratives by Escaped Slaves*. New York: Lawrence Hill & Co., 1972.
    Collects sixteen slave narratives including those by Nat Turner, Frederick Douglass, W. W. Brown, and other Southern blacks.

Norse, Clifford C., ed. "'My Love to Them All': The Letters of Private Benjamin Stone, C. S. A., to His Sister." *Miss Quart*, 23 (Spring 1970), 175-179.
    Excerpts showing the lighter side of the war.

Norton, Wesley. "Religious Newspapers in Ante-bellum Texas." *SHQ*, 79 (October 1975), 145-165.
    Explores the wide variety of functions performed by religious newspapers and analyzes the reasons for their decline.

Oates, Stephen B. "'In Thine Own Image': Modern Radicals and John Brown." *SAQ*, 73 (Autumn 1974), 417-427.
    Unable to resolve a contradiction of slavery in a Republic, both Christian and free, the U. S. "invited a messianic rebel like Brown to appear."

Osofsky, Gilbert, ed. *Puttin' on Old Massa*. New York: Harper & Row, 1969.
    Reprints the slave narratives of Henry Bibb (1849), William Wells Brown (1847), and Solomon Northup (1853), with a historical appreciation by the editor.

Rawick, George P. *From Sundown to Sunup: The Making of the Black Community*. Westport, Conn.: Greenwood Publishing Co., 1972.

A historical and sociological analysis, through an examination of slave narratives, of the techniques whereby blacks retained a distinctive culture; serves as an introduction to a nineteen-volume set of reprints entitled "The American Slave: A Composite Autobiography."

Rees, Robert A., and Marjorie Griffin. "Index and Author Guide to the *Family Companion* (1841-43)." *SB*, 25 (1972), 205-212.
    One of the best Georgia antebellum monthlies, the *Family Companion and Ladies' Mirror* was published in Macon between October 1841 and February 1843.

Ritchey, David. "Columbia Garden: Baltimore's First Pleasure Garden." *So Speech Com Jour*, 39 (Spring 1974), 241-247.
    In the summer seasons between 1805 and 1807, audiences visited Columbia Garden to dine, to stroll in the lamp-lighted grounds, and to enjoy the theatrical performance.

Roberts, Leonard. "Beauchamp and Sharp: A Kentucky Tragedy." *Ky Folklore Record*, 14 (January-March 1968), 14-19.
    Poe's *Politian* and Simms's *Beauchamp* make fictional uses of an actual incident.

Rogers, George C., Jr. *Charleston in the Age of the Pinckneys*. Norman: Univ of Oklahoma Press, 1969.
    An account of the city of Charleston, South Carolina, from the 1730's through the 1860's when its cultural and economic success and influence were dominated by the Pinckney family and such men as John C. Calhoun and Hugh Swinton Legaré.

Rogers, Tommy W. "Origin and Cultural Assimilation of the Population of Louisiana." *Miss Quart*, 25 (Winter 1971), 45-67.
    New Orleans, as the largest city in the antebellum South and the second seaport in the nation, induced a higher proportion of foreign immigrants into Louisiana's population than elsewhere in the region.

Ruoff, John C. "Frivolity to Consumption: Or, Southern Womanhood in Antebellum Literature." *Civil War Hist*, 18 (1972), 213-229.
    From a study of works by several antebellum Southern writers, one can conclude that plantation society was not a matriarchy.

Rust, R. D., ed. *Glory and Pathos: Responses of Nineteenth-Century American Authors to the Civil War*. Boston: Holbrook Press, 1970.
    An anthology of literary and historical documents written during the war years, with eight Southerners represented; critical introductions.

Schwaab, Eugene L., ed. (with the collaboration of Jacqueline Bull). *Travels in the Old South*. Lexington: Univ Press of Kentucky, 1973.
    An anthology of original accounts of travel in the South from 1783 to 1860 published in magazines in the U. S., in two volumes with period illustrations.

Schweninger, Loren. "A Slave Family in the Ante
Bellum South." *JNH*, 60 (January 1975), 29-44.
A history and analysis of the Thomas-Rapier
slave family, 1790-1850.

Scott, John A., ed. *Journal of a Residence on a
Georgian Plantation in 1838-1839 by Frances
Anne Kemble*. New York: New Am Library, 1975.
A modern edition of the 1863 account by the
British actress, written while she was living
on her husband's plantation.

Sederberg, Nancy B. "Antebellum Southern Humor in
the *Camden Journal*: 1826-1840." *Miss Quart*,
27 (Winter 1973-74), 41-74.
Commentary on the Southern humor contributions and on the different editors of the
Journal; includes an annotated checklist.

Shingleton, Royce G. "The Utility of Leisure:
Game as a Source of Food in the Old South."
Miss Quart, 25 (Fall 1972), 429-445.
Despite the notion that pork was the main
meat eaten by all classes in the Old South,
sporting literature shows that venison and wild
fowl were more widely consumed than hogmeat.

Shockley, Ann A. "American Anti-Slavery Literature:
An Overview--1693-1859." *Negro Hist Bull*, 37
(April 1974), 232-235.
Brief references to a number of writers,
including Douglass, W. W. Brown, and George
Moses Horton.

Shrell, Darwin. "Hunting in the Old South." *SouR*,
4 (Spring 1968), 467-470.
An essay-review of Clarence Gohdes' edition
of Southern hunting narratives.

Simpson, Lewis P. "The Civil War: Written and
Unwritten." *So Lit Jour*, 7 (Fall 1974),
132-145.
A review-essay of Daniel Aaron's *The Unwritten War: American Writers and the Civil War*,
which finds this work a "fine study" that challenges its readers "to search out the problem
of the difference between occasion and principle
in the literature of the Civil War."

Starobin, R. S., ed. *Denmark Vesey: The Slave
Conspiracy of 1822*. Great Lives Observed
Series. Englewood Cliffs, N. J.: Prentice-
Hall, 1970.
A collection of historical and cultural
documents about the Vesey revolt in Charleston,
South Carolina.

Steen, Ivan D. "Charleston in the 1850's: As
Described by British Travelers." *SCHM*, 71
(1970), 36-45.
Title is descriptive.

Sutton, Robert P. "Nostalgia, Pessimism, and
Malaise: The Doomed Aristocrat in Late-
Jeffersonian Virginia." *VMHB*, 76
(January 1968), 41-55.
Includes discussion of Kennedy's *Swallow
Barn*, N. B. Tucker's *Partisan Leader* and *George
Balcombe*, and George Tucker's *Valley of the
Shenandoah*.

Thomas, Charles E., ed. "The Diary of Anna Hasell
Thomas (July 1864-May 1865)." *SCHM*, 74
(July 1973), 128-143.
A reproduction of the diary.

Towery, Patricia. "Censorship of South Carolina
Newspapers, 1861-1865," in *South Carolina Journals and Journalists*. Columbia, S. C.: Southern Studies Program, 1975, pp. 147-160.
On the mild censorship of the press by the
officials of the Confederacy.

Tucker, Edward L. "'A Rash and Perilous Enterprize':
The Southern Literary Messenger and the Men Who
Made It." *Va Cavalcade*, 21 (Summer 1971),
14-20.
An account of the editors, including Poe.

Wander, P. C. "The Savage Child: The Image of the
Negro in the Pro-Slavery Movement." *So Speech
Comm Jour*, 37 (Summer 1972), 335-360.
Wander studies *De Bow's Review*, the *Southern
Literary Messenger*, and the *Southern Quarterly
Review* for the period 1850 to 1860.

Waring, Joseph I., ed. "The Diary of William G.
Hinson During the War of Secession." *SCHM*, 75
(April 1974), 111-120.
A reproduction of the diary.

Watson, Charles S. "Jeffersonian Republicanism in
William Ioor's *Independence*, the First Play of
South Carolina." *SCHM*, 69 (July 1968), 194-203.
This play, which emphasized the values of
simple rural life, was influenced by Jefferson's
Notes on Virginia.

_____. "Stephen Cullen Carpenter, First Drama
Critic of the Charleston *Courier*." *SCHM*, 69
(October 1968), 243-252.
Presents Carpenter's concepts of what the
theater should do and be like.

Welsh, John R. "Southern Literary Magazines, IV:
An Early Pioneer: Legaré's *Southern Review*."
So Lit Jour, 3 (Spring 1971), 79-97.
The *Southern Review*, accurately described as
"Legaré's Review," had its genesis in regional
or local pride and with its political and schol-
arly interests was never a genuine literary
journal.

West, James L. W. III. "Early Backwoods Humor in
the Greenville *Mountaineer*, 1826-1840." *Miss
Quart*, 25 (Winter 1971), 69-82.
A survey of this small-town weekly shows a
steady stream of types of humor that prepared
the way for later, more skillful writers in the
genre. Includes a bibliography of Crockett
material.

Wilson, Major L. "The Controversy over Slavery Expansion and the Concept of the Safety Valve:
Ideological Confusion in the 1850's." *Miss
Quart*, 24 (Spring 1971), 135-153.
The conflict finally came to be a question
of who should shape the future of the nation
and not what shape the future ought to have.

Wilt, Napier. *Some American Humorists*. New York: Johnson Reprint, 1970.

Reprints the 1929 edition of this critical anthology which included W. T. Thompson, J. J. Hooper, G. W. Harris, and C. H. Smith, with a new introduction by Martin Roth, who provides new critical commentary on these figures.

Yellin, Jean F. *The Intricate Knot: Black Figures in American Literature, 1776-1863*. New York: New York Univ Press, 1972.

A thematic study of the characterization of the black in pre-Civil War writing, with full discussions of writings by Jefferson, George Tucker, J. K. Paulding, J. P. Kennedy, W. G. Simms, W. W. Brown, and others.

III. Postbellum (1865–1920)

[ALLEN, JAMES LANE] Bottorff, William K. "James Lane Allen (1849-1925)." *Am Lit Realism*, 2 (Summer 1969), 121-124.
A bibliographical essay.

Eaton, Clement. See GENERAL.

Rhode, Robert D. See MISCELLANEOUS (Postbellum).

[BONNER, SHERWOOD] Biglane, Jean N. "Sherwood Bonner: A Bibliography of Primary and Secondary Materials." *Am Lit Realism*, 5 (Winter 1972), 39-60.
Listing is divided as follows: I. A. Separate Publications (chronologically arranged); I. B. Periodical Contributions (chronologically arranged); I. C. Newspaper Contributions; I. D. Anthology Selections from Separate Publications; I. E. Manuscripts and Letters; II. A. Major Dissertations and Theses; II. B. Major Biographical and Critical Articles; II. C. Book Reviews. All entries in Part II are annotated.

Frank, William L. "Sherwood Bonner's Diary for the Year 1869." *Notes on Miss Writers*, 3 (Winter 1971), 111-130.
The first of three transcriptions of the complete diary.

_____. "Sherwood Bonner's Diary for the Year 1869." *Notes on Miss Writers*, 4 (Spring 1971), 22-40.
Section II of the diary.

_____. "Sherwood Bonner's Diary for the Year 1869." *Notes on Miss Writers*, 4 (Fall 1971), 64-83.
Section III of the diary.

Moore, Rayburn S. "'Merlin and Vivien'? Some Notes on Sherwood Bonner and Longfellow." *Miss Quart*, 28 (Spring 1975), 181-184.
A brief account of the relationship between Bonner and Longfellow which includes a letter from Harriet Waters Preston to Paul Hamilton Hayne on the subject and also a suggestion that Ellen Olney Kirk's novel *The Story of Margaret Kent* (1886) was based on that relationship.

Pierle, Robert C. "Sherwood Who? A Study in the Vagaries of Literary Evaluation." *Notes on Miss Writers*, 1 (Spring 1968), 18-22.
Concerns Miss Bonner and her literary reputation in the nineteenth century.

Polk, Noel E. See MISCELLANEOUS (Postbellum--1st Polk entry).

Simms, L. Moody, Jr. "Sherwood Bonner: A Contemporary Appreciation." *Notes on Miss Writers*, 2 (Spring 1969), 25-33.
Largely a reprinting of an essay in *Harper's* for August 11, 1883.

[CABELL, JAMES BRANCH] Anderson, Poul. "Something about the Gods." *Kalki*, 3, no. 1 (1969), 20-21.
Deals with Cabell's use of Scandinavian mythology in *The Silver Stallion*.

Austin, Bliss. "Dartmoor Revisited." *Kalki*, 3, no. 4 (1969), 131-134.
Concerns a legend about Sir Richard Cabell as a source of Conan Doyle's *The Hound of the Baskervilles*; the article was motivated by J. B. Cabell's *Ladies and Gentlemen*.

Blish, James. "Cabell as Kabbalist." *Kalki*, 3, no. 1 (1969), 11-12.
Deals with Cabell's concept of the demiurge.

_____. "Cabell as Voluntarist." *Kalki*, 3, no. 4 (1969), 120-122.
Philosophically Cabell was a voluntarist, but still the world outside his own mind was real.

_____. "The Long Night of a Virginia Author." *Jour of Mod Lit*, 2 (1972), 393-405.
Deals with Cabell's trilogy *The Nightmare Has Triplets*.

Boardman, John. "The Two Cabells." *Kalki*, 3, no. 3 (Summer 1969), 83-85.
Deals with the implications of Cabell's appearances as Horvendile and Felix Kennaston in his works.

Brussell, I. R. "The First Fifty Years of *Jurgen*." *Cabellian*, 1 (1969), 74.
A brief summary of the various editions.

Buford, R. "The Life of James Branch Cabell." *The Richmond Mercury Book Review*, 1 (December 6, 1972), 1, 14-15.
A biographical summary of Cabell's career with emphasis on his Virginia background and experience.

Bungert, Hans. See GENERAL.

Canary, Robert H. "Cabell's Dark Comedies." *Miss Quart*, 21 (Spring 1968), 83-92.
 Cabell's novels, first thought to be light comedies about sex, are shown to have darker themes.

Carson, Betty F. See MISCELLANEOUS (Contemporary).

Carter, Lin. "Horvendile--Link Between Cabell and Tolkien." *Kalki*, 3, no. 3 (Summer 1969), 85-87.
 Traces possible sources of Horvendile as well as Tolkien's Eärendil.

Chancellor, Ann. "Messire Jurgen." *Kalki*, 3, no. 1 (1969), 3-8.
 Deals with the reversals of elements of the medieval epic and with reversals in Jurgen himself; Jurgen discovers not only that he cannot find justice but that he never really wanted justice.

Cheslock, Louis. "*The Jewel Merchants*, an Opera: A Case History." *Cabellian*, 4 (Spring 1972), 68-84.
 An account by the composer of the transformation of Cabell's play into an opera, with excerpts of letters from Cabell, Mencken, and others.

Churchill, Allen. See MISCELLANEOUS (Contemporary).

Cover, James P. "Notes on *Jurgen*." *Kalki*, 3, no. 1 (1969), 13-15; 3, no. 2 (1969), 70-72; 3 (Summer 1969), 92-97, 104-107; 3 (Fall 1969), 136-142.
 Explanatory notes on the terms Cabell uses in *Jurgen*.

Cranwell, John P., and James P. Cover. "Notes on *Figures of Earth*." *Kalki*, 2, no. 4 (1968), 91-95; 3, no. 1 (1969), 22-23.
 Explanatory notes on terms Cabell uses in this novel.

Dameron, Penn. "Inside Book Two of James Branch Cabell's *The Silver Stallion*." *Cabellian*, 3 (Autumn 1970), 22-23.
 Deals with the significance of the realism of the character Gonfal.

Davis, Joe Lee. "Cabell and Santayana in the Neo-Humanist Debate." *Cabellian*, 4 (Spring 1972), 55-67.
 Both Cabell and Santayana joined in the attack on the New Humanists, Cabell in his book of essays on his contemporaries, *Some of Us: An Essay in Epitaphs* (1930).

_____. "Recent Cabell Criticism." *Cabellian*, 1, no. 1 (1968), 1-12.
 An evaluation of some older criticism and of a number of recent critical works on Cabell.

Duke, Maurice. "Acquisitions of the Cabell Library Since August 1970." *Cabellian*, 3 (Spring 1971), 81.
 In addition to books and articles are twenty-seven letters from Cabell to Maurice J. Speiser, a Philadelphia attorney, between April 1921 and October 1934.

_____. "James Branch Cabell's Personal Library." *SB*, 23 (1970), 207-216.
 A description of Cabell's collection of books, manuscripts, letters, and memorabilia.

_____. "James Branch Cabell's Personal Library: A Summary." *Cabellian*, 1, no. 1 (1968), 27-30.
 A description with a listing of some of the works in the library that should be of particular interest to Cabell scholars.

_____. "Letters of George Sterling to James Branch Cabell." *AL*, 44 (March 1972), 146-153.
 Edited correspondence that Sterling wrote Cabell between 1919 and 1926.

_____. "Recent Acquisitions of the Cabell Library." *Cabellian*, 2 (Autumn 1969), 21-22.
 Cabell's personal library and papers are now in the library of Virginia Commonwealth University.

_____. See GENERAL.

Flora, Joseph M. "*Jurgen* in the Classroom." *Cabellian*, 1, no. 1 (1968), 31-33.
 Deals with the ways by which *Jurgen* can appeal to undergraduates; it should be read slowly as a romance, not as a novel. The article also contains some discussion of Faulkner's use of myth in *The Sound and the Fury*.

_____. "Vardis Fisher and James Branch Cabell: a Postscript." *Cabellian*, 3 (Autumn 1970), 7-9.
 Discusses Cabell's influence on Fisher's *Forgive Us Our Virtues*.

_____. "Vardis Fisher and James Branch Cabell: An Essay on Influence and Reputation." *Cabellian*, 2 (Autumn 1969), 12-16.
 Traces Cabell's considerable influence on Fisher, especially in the Vridar Hunter tetralogy.

French, Warren. See MISCELLANEOUS (Contemporary--4th French entry).

Gabbard, G. H. "Deems Taylor's Musical Version of *Jurgen*." *Cabellian*, 3 (Autumn 1970), 12-15.
 Deals with the history of the performance of the tone-poem.

_____. "Source Notes: Now about *The Silver Stallion*." *Kalki*, 3, no. 1 (1969), 33.
 Explanatory notes.

Godshalk, William L. "Cabell's *Cream of the Jest* and Recent American Fiction." *So Lit Jour*, 5 (Spring 1973), 18-31.
 Deals with ways in which Cabellian "skepticism, fantasy, and comedy" foreshadow similar elements in recent American fiction, including that of Barth.

Haight, A. L. See GENERAL.

Halper, Nathan. "Joyce and James Branch Cabell." *A Wake Newslitter*, 6 (August 1969), 51-60.
 Deals with similarities in interests and techniques of these two writers.

Hartman, Harry. "'The Comstock Lewd': *Jurgen* and the Law--Updated." *Kalki*, 3, no. 1 (1969), 16-19.
 Deals with how *Jurgen* might fare under more recent court rulings concerning obscenity.

Herrick, Thomas C. "Sides of *Jurgen*: II. Ch. 51: Of Compromises with Time." *Kalki*, 3 (Fall 1969), 128-129.
Jurgen's adventures bring him to a realization that there is a kind of justice in the fact that his first and his second youth have brought him to the same place.

Hoyt, Charles A. See GENERAL.

Hubbell, Jay B. See GENERAL.

Inge, M. Thomas. "The Unheeding South: Donald Davidson on James Branch Cabell." *Cabellian*, 2 (Autumn 1969), 17-20.
While Davidson, as reviewer in the twenties, was unusually perceptive in most instances, he found in Cabell "a stumbling block."

Ingrasci, Hugh J. "The Cabellian Picara as Women's Liberationist." *Cabellian*, 4 (Spring 1972), 89-95.
Actually a discussion of *The Unpredictable Adventure* (1935) by Claire Myers Spotswood (Wanders), a Cabell disciple who had not yet grasped the master's work.

Jenkins, William D. "Elementary, My Dear Cabell." *Kalki*, 3 (Fall 1969), 134-135.
Suggests that the reference to the "Ferrers business" in "In the Second April" may be a "theft" designed to get back at Conan Doyle for making use of the Sir Richard Cabell legend in *The Hound of the Baskervilles*.

_____. "The Shirt of Nessus." *Kalki*, 3, no. 1 (1969), 9-10.
Jurgen's easy wearing of the shirt symbolizes his contentment with monogamy; the wives Florimel, Chloris, and Anaïtis represent aspects of Lisa.

Johannsen, Kris. "Sides of *Jurgen*: III. Color in *Jurgen*." *Kalki*, 3 (Fall 1969), 129-130.
Multi-colored things in the novel indicate a world of illusion; black or white, in one way or another, indicates reality.

MacDonald, Edgar E. "Cabell Criticism: Past, Present, and Future." *Cabellian*, 1, no. 1 (1968), 21-25.
Some recent criticism has shown the error in the earlier general view of Cabell's works as escapist, unaffected by their author's regional background.

_____. "Cabell's Game of Hide and Seek." *Cabellian*, 4 (Autumn 1971), 9-16.
Cabell's effort from 1926 to 1929 to "whip his diverse essays, poems, tales, and novels into a 'Biography of Universal Man' did not wholly succeed."

_____. "Cabell's Hero: Cosmic Rebel." *So Lit Jour*, 2 (Fall 1969), 22-42.
The Cabellian hero takes on "the coloration" of Don Juan and Faust and "even enacts scenes from their legends."

_____. "Cabell's Richmond Trial." *So Lit Jour*, 3 (Fall 1970), 47-71.
Cabell suffered from the fact that his mother's name was involved in the gossip surrounding a Richmond murder.

_____. "The Glasgow-Cabell Entente." *AL*, 41 (March 1969), 76-91.
Discusses the personal relationship between the two writers.

_____. "The Influence of Provençal Poetry on James Branch Cabell." *Cabellian*, 3 (Autumn 1970), 1-6.
Cabell's early acquaintance with Provençal poetry through C. C. Fauriel's *History of Provençal Poetry* became a permanent infatuation that influenced many of his important works.

_____. "The Storisende Edition: Some Liabilities." *Cabellian*, 1 (1969), 64-67.
Maintains that Cabell's survival "is surely in spite of it rather than because of it."

_____. See GLASGOW, ELLEN (Postbellum--4th MacDonald entry).

Martin, Jay. See MISCELLANEOUS (Contemporary).

McNeill, Warren A. "Cabellian Harmonics--Why and How?" *Cabellian*, 2 (Spring 1970), 55-58.
The background of McNeill's writing of his early study, *Cabellian Harmonics* (1928), with numerous excerpts from Cabell's letters.

_____. "James Branch Cabell 'In Time's Hourglass.'" *Cabellian*, 3 (Spring 1971), 64-70.
Notes and recollections of visits with Cabell between 1926 and 1932.

Meyer, Gerard P. "Young Jurgen: A Comedy of Derision." *Cabellian*, 3 (Autumn 1970), 16-21.
A pastiche in the style of Cabell, written by Meyer and first published in 1929 in *The Morningside*, a literary magazine published at Columbia College.

Morley-Mower, Geoffrey F. "James Branch Cabell's Flirtation with Clio: The Story of a Collaboration." *YULG*, 47 (July 1972), 15-27.
Details of Cabell's collaboration with historian A. J. Hanna in producing *The St. John's* in the "Rivers of America" series.

Nevius, Blake. See MISCELLANEOUS (Contemporary).

Paluka, Frank. See GENERAL.

Peter, Emmett, Jr. "Another Mirror for Pigeons." *Kalki*, 3 (Summer 1969), 88-91.
Episodes in *The Arabian Nights* help to explain the meaning of Cabell's symbol of the pigeon and the mirror.

Rothman, Julius. "The Danish *Jurgen*." *Cabellian*, 3 (Spring 1971), 79-80.
An account of a translation published in Copenhagen in 1942.

_____. "Dissertations on Cabell." *Cabellian*, 1 (1969), 77-78.
A list of the eleven dissertations on Cabell from 1954 through 1968.

_____. "Jurgen, the Rabelaisian Babbitt."
Cabellian, 1, no. 1 (1968), 35-40.
  Jurgen should be read as a mock-heroic satire
of man's inability to overcome his animal
nature.

_____. "A Short History of *The Cabellian*." *Nassau
Rev*, 2, no. 4 (1973), 59-64.
  The history of the journal published from
1968-1972.

Rubin, Louis D., Jr. See GENERAL--3rd Rubin
  entry.

Ruland, Richard. "Mencken and Cabell." *Cabellian*,
  1, no. 1 (1968), 13-20.
  Deals with various aspects of the relationship between the two writers, including
Mencken's defense of *Jurgen* and his evaluation
of Cabell as being a "type of true artist."

Schilmeister, Deborah. "Sides of *Jurgen*: I.
  Revelations of a Sunrise." *Kalki*, 3
  (Fall 1969), 123-127.
  As an "embodiment of human kind," Jurgen
reveals that man's problem is to adjust "to his
fate"; in maturity he resigns himself to and
"makes the best" of what he cannot change.

Schlegel, Dorothy B. "Cabell and His Critics."
  Cabellian, 3 (Spring 1971), 50-63.
  Revised version of a lecture which appeared
in *The Dilemma of the Southern Writer*, ed.
R. K. Meeker (Farmville, Va., 1961), pp. 119-
142.

_____. "Cabell's Comic Mask." *Cabellian*, 4
(Autumn 1971), 1-8.
  Cabell's "comic mask served through most of
his career to hide the deep sense of tragedy
which lay at the heart of much of his work."

_____. "Cabell's Translation of Virginia." *Cabel-
lian*, 2 (Autumn 1969), 1-11.
  Discusses the genesis and development of
Poictesme as "a vehicle to satirize the shortcomings of his own society."

_____. "A Case of Literary Piracy?" *Cabellian*, 1
(1969), 58-63.
  Cabell's borrowings from Lambright's
Gasparilla in *There Were Two Pirates* are
treated as a joke on the critics.

_____. "James Branch Cabell: A Latter-Day En-
lightener." *CLA Jour*, 12 (March 1969),
223-236.
  Cabell wrote for the most part in the tradition of the eighteenth-century Enlighteners.

Schley, Margaret A. "The Demiurge in Jurgen."
  Cabellian, 4 (Spring 1972), 85-87.
  Offers a suggestion that Cabell names his
famous protagonist because "this character was
moved, principally, by the demiurge."

Siegle, Lin C. "Dating in *Figures of Earth*."
  Cabellian, 4 (Autumn 1971), 17-21.
  Inclusion of medieval holidays enriches the
interpretation of Manuel's life and "emphasizes
the mythic dimensions of the book."

Spencer, Paul. "'After the Style of Maurice
  Hewlett.'" *Kalki*, 3 (Fall 1969), 143-146.
  Deals with the relationship between Cabell
and Hewlett and possible minor influences of
Hewlett on Cabell.

Tarrant, Desmond. "Cabell's *Hamlet Had an Uncle* and
  Shakespeare's *Hamlet*." *Cabellian*, 3
  (Autumn 1970), 10-11.
  Suggests that *Hamlet Had an Uncle* may be "the
subtlest of Cabell's later works of art."

_____. "James Branch Cabell." *Menckeniana*, 33
(Spring 1970), 4-9.
  A consideration of Cabell's achievements as a
novelist.

_____. "James Branch Cabell (1879-1958)." *Cabel-
lian*, 1 (1969), 53-57.
  An appreciative summary of Cabell's total
work.

Untermeyer, Louis. *James Branch Cabell: The Man
  and His Masks*. Richmond: Mrs. James Branch
  Cabell, 1970.
  Cabell satirized the issues of his day with
skillful artifice. An address for the Associates of the Cabell Library, Virginia Commonwealth University, delivered February 18, 1970.

Wagenknecht, Edward, ed. *The Letters of James
  Branch Cabell*. Norman: Univ of Oklahoma Press,
  1975.
  A selection of letters to more than twenty
correspondents written between 1915 and 1958.

Warner, Richard. "The Illusion of Diabolism in the
  Cabellian Hero." *Novel*, 8 (Spring 1975),
  241-245.
  Refutes the evidence that Cabell's characters
act out of an innate sense of diabolism.

Welch, Emmons. "*Beyond Life* and *Jurgen*: The Demi-
  urge." *Cabellian*, 2 (Spring 1970), 48-53.
  Beyond Life is the "lens" through which
Jurgen is analyzed.

Woodress, James. See GENERAL--1st Woodress entry.

[CABLE, GEORGE WASHINGTON] Aaron, Daniel. See
  GENERAL.

Bridges, Katherine. See GENERAL.

Buchloh, Paul G. See GENERAL.

Bungert, Hans. See GENERAL.

Butcher, Philip. "Cable to Boyesen on *The
  Grandissimes*." *AL*, 40 (November 1968),
  392-394.
  An unpublished letter of Cable (December 28,
1878), during a yellow-fever epidemic, to Pro-
fessor H. H. Boyesen of Cornell, who helped
Cable publish *Old Creole Days* and *The
Grandissimes*.

_____. "George W. Cable and George W. Williams:
An Abortive Collaboration." *JNH*, 53
(October 1968), 334-344.

Deals with Cable's work in behalf of black civil rights, including his collaboration with Williams, cut short by Williams' death but resulting eventually in the founding of the *Journal of Negro History*.

_____. "Two Early Southern Realists in Revival." *CLA Jour*, 14 (September 1970), 91–95.
Cable and Chopin are now being recognized and appreciated as pioneers of sociological and psychological realism.

Campbell, Michael L. "The Negro in Cable's *The Grandissimes*." *Miss Quart*, 27 (Spring 1974), 165–178.
Cable's success in using four central black characters "to give an authentic and balanced treatment of the race problem" in the New Orleans society of his time argues for an organic connection between the novel's elements of romantic melodrama and social realism.

Chametzky, Jules. See MISCELLANEOUS (Postbellum).

Clark, Harry H. See GENERAL.

Clark, William B. See GENERAL.

Cleman, John. "The Art of Local Color in George W. Cable's *The Grandissimes*." *AL*, 47 (November 1975), 396–410.
Concludes that the novel should be read as a special kind of romantic one rather than as an early example of fictional realism.

Doughty, Nanelia S. See MISCELLANEOUS (Postbellum).

Eaton, Richard B. "George W. Cable and the Historical Romance." *So Lit Jour*, 8 (Fall 1975), 82–94.
In *The Grandissimes* Cable reflects the literary realism of his own time while responding to the artistic requirements of the historical romance.

Egan, Joseph J. "'Jean-ah-Poquelin': George Washington Cable as Social Critic and Mythic Artist." *MarkR*, 2 (May 1970), 6–7.
This short story reveals Cable's concern to give "mythic form to man's moral-sociological predicament."

Evans, William. "French-English Literary Dialect in *The Grandissimes*." *Am Speech*, 46 (Fall-Winter 1971), 210–222.
Deals with Cable's accurate use of Creole dialects.

Godbold, E. Stanly, Jr. See MISCELLANEOUS (Postbellum).

Howell, Elmo. "Cable and the Creoles: A Note on 'Jean-ah-Poquelin.'" *XUS*, 9 (Winter 1970), 9–15.
The story reveals Cable's "admiration of the stubbornness of spirit of a people tragically brought to bay by circumstance."

_____. "George Washington Cable's Creoles: Art and Reform in *The Grandissimes*." *Miss Quart*, 26 (Winter 1972–73), 43–53.

Cable's views on social reform, largely ignored in his own time, are part of the revival of interest in his work. He fails in attempting to create a true Southern atmosphere, largely because of a lack of affections.

Inge, M. Thomas. See FAULKNER, WILLIAM--4th Inge entry.

Libman, Valentina. See GENERAL.

Paluka, Frank. See GENERAL.

Perret, Joseph J. "The Ethnic and Religious Prejudices of G. W. Cable." *La Stud*, Winter 1972, pp. 263–273.
As the first to call attention to these ethnic and religious prejudices, Cable was in many ways unique.

Randel, William. "*Koango* and Its Libretto." *Music and Letters*, 52 (April 1971), 141–156.
In writing the libretto for Delius' opera, Charles Francis Keary probably did not read *The Grandissimes*.

Rhode, Robert D. See MISCELLANEOUS (Postbellum).

Ringe, Donald A. "The 'Double Center': Character and Meaning in Cable's Early Novels." *Stud in the Novel*, 5 (Spring 1973), 52–62.
The double heroes, Frowenfeld and Honore Grandissime and Dr. Sevier and John Richling, learn from each other to temper their viewpoints if meaningful social change is to occur.

Rubin, Louis D., Jr. "The Division of the Heart: Cable's *The Grandissimes*." *So Lit Jour*, 1 (Spring 1969), 27–47.
The Grandissimes is the first "modern" Southern novel in that it is the first novel by a Southerner to deal seriously with the relationships of whites and blacks.

_____. *George W. Cable: The Life and Times of a Southern Heretic*. Pegasus American Authors Series. New York: Pegasus, 1969.
A critical biography of Cable concentrating on the relationship of his work to the Genteel Tradition; unlike the others in that tradition, he was "a Southern writer who alone in his time broke through the trappings of local color and costume romance and sought to depict his native region in the rich daylight of reality."

_____. See MISCELLANEOUS (Postbellum).

_____. See GENERAL--6th Rubin entry.

Stone, Edward. See GENERAL.

Turner, Arlin. *George W. Cable*. Southern Writers Series. Austin: Steck-Vaughn, 1969.
As a novelist and reformer, Cable is viewed as "the recorder, interpreter, and prophet of change."

_____. "George W. Cable on Prison Reform." *HLQ*, 36 (November 1972), 69–75.
Reprints a Cable letter of November 1882.

_____. See CLEMENS, SAMUEL LANGHORNE (Postbellum).

Voss, Arthur. See GENERAL.

Weaver, William. See CLEMENS, SAMUEL LANGHORNE
(Postbellum--3rd Weaver entry).

[CHESNUTT, CHARLES WADDELL] Andrews, William L.
"Chesnutt's Patesville: The Presence and In-
fluence of the Past in *The House Behind the
Cedars*." *CLA Jour*, 15 (March 1972), 284-294.
Chesnutt uses the actual description of
Fayetteville, North Carolina, which he calls
Patesville, to show that the race pride and
traditions of the town have remained unchanged
with the passing of time.

_____. "Reconsideration of *Charles Waddell
Chesnutt: Pioneer of the Color Line*." *CLA
Jour*, 19 (December 1975), 136-151.
Deals with oversimplifications in Helen
Chesnutt's biography of her father.

_____. "The Significance of Charles W. Chesnutt's
'Conjure Stories.'" *So Lit Jour*, 7
(Fall 1974), 78-99.
Chesnutt maintained a balance between the
demands of popular local-color realism and "the
obligation of the artist to reveal 'truth to
nature.'"

_____. "Two New Books on Charles W. Chesnutt."
Miss Quart, 28 (Fall 1975), 511-520.
An essay-review of *The Short Fiction of
Charles W. Chesnutt*, edited by Sylvia Render,
and of *Charles W. Chesnutt: America's First
Great Black Novelist*, by J. Noel Heermance.

Baldwin, Richard E. "The Art of *The Conjure Woman*."
AL, 43 (November 1971), 385-398.
Discusses the devices Chesnutt uses in this
work to achieve his purpose of gradually
accustoming the white mind to the idea of black
equality.

Bigsby, C. W. E. See MISCELLANEOUS (Contemporary).

Bone, Robert. See GENERAL.

Britt, David D. "Chesnutt's Conjure Tales: What
You See Is What You Get." *CLA Jour*, 15
(March 1972), 269-283.
In *The Conjure Woman*, the stories are deliberately structured to allow the reader to be
deceived about the more significant levels of
meaning.

Chametzky, Jules. See MISCELLANEOUS (Postbellum).

_____. See GENERAL.

Corrigan, Robert A. See GENERAL--1st Corrigan
entry.

Cunningham, Joan. "The Uncollected Short Stories
of Charles Waddell Chesnutt." *NALF*, 9
(Summer 1975), 57-58.
The critics' neglect of Chesnutt's uncollected short stories results in an "incomplete
assessment of his range of characters, settings,
themes, and style."

Dixon, Melvin. "The Teller as Folk Trickster in
Chesnutt's *The Conjure Woman*." *CLA Jour*, 18
(December 1974), 186-197.
Deals with Julius' (and Chesnutt's) purpose
in telling the tales.

Everett, Chestyn. See GENERAL.

Farnsworth, Robert M. "Introduction" to *The Conjure
Woman*. Ann Arbor: Univ of Michigan Press,
1969.
Chesnutt's first book of stories "illustrates
the terms under which the white American reading
public at the end of the nineteenth century was
willing to let an Afro-American put his foot on
the ladder of literary success."

Fleming, Robert E. See GENERAL--both Fleming
entries.

Gartner, Carol B. "Charles W. Chesnutt: Novelist
of a Cause." *MarkR*, 3 (October 1968), 5-12.
Deals with Chesnutt's use of his works to
advance the black cause.

Gayle, Addison, Jr. See GENERAL.

Giles, James R. "Chesnutt's Primus and Annie: A
Contemporary View of *The Conjure Woman*." *MarkR*,
3 (May 1972), 46-49.
The episode of Primus and Annie is an example
of racism.

Heermance, J. Noel. *Charles W. Chesnutt: America's
First Great Black Novelist*. Hamden, Conn.:
Archon Books, 1974.
A critical study of Chesnutt's works.

Hemenway, Robert. "'Baxter's Procrustes': Irony
and Protest." *CLA Jour*, 18 (December 1974),
172-185.
Satirizes the narrow outlook of such clubs
as the Rowfant Club, in which Chesnutt was once
denied membership; the true artist is not just
a person who can write only about whites.

_____. "Gothic Sociology: Charles Chesnutt and
the Gothic Mode." *SLI*, 7 (Spring 1974), 101-119.
The Conjure Woman is Gothic, being filled
with tales of magic, ghosts, "hants," and the
occult. Yet the book is not a part of the
Gothic tradition, primarily because Chesnutt
found the Gothic sociology inadequate to his
purpose.

_____. See GENERAL.

Hill, Mildred. See GENERAL.

Hovet, Theodore R. "Chesnutt's 'The Goophered
Grapevine' as Social Criticism." *NALF*, 7
(Fall 1973), 86-88.
This story is "a parable which explains the
consequences of an unbounded faith in economic
progress and the way such a belief serves to
conceal the cost in human dignity."

Hoyt, Charles A. See GENERAL.

Jaskoski, Helen. See GENERAL.

Keller, Dean H. "Charles Waddell Chesnutt (1858-1932)." *Am Lit Realism*, no. 3 (Summer 1968), 1-4.
   A bibliographical essay.

Kinnamon, Keneth. See GENERAL.

Margolies, Edward. See MISCELLANEOUS (Contemporary--2nd Margolies entry).

Mason, Julian. "The Stories of Charles W. Chesnutt." *So Lit Jour*, 1 (Autumn 1968), 89-94.
   An essay-review of *The Wife of His Youth and Other Stories of the Color Line*.

McDowell, Robert E., and George Fortenberry. See MISCELLANEOUS (Contemporary).

Polk, Noel E. See MISCELLANEOUS (Postbellum--1st Polk entry).

Reilly, John M. "The Dilemma in Chesnutt's *The Marrow of Tradition*." *Phylon*, 32 (Spring 1971), 31-38.
   Chesnutt portrays ironically the paradox of racism in a nominally democratic America, documenting so powerfully the corruption of white society that it is difficult to believe his hero's aspirations to integrate into it.

Render, Sylvia L., ed. *The Short Fiction of Charles W. Chesnutt*. Washington, D. C.: Howard Univ Press, 1974.
   A collection of Chesnutt's short fiction.

Sedlack, Robert P. "The Evolution of Charles Chesnutt's *The House Behind the Cedars*." *CLA Jour*, 19 (December 1975), 125-135.
   The novel evolved from a short story called "Rena," which attacked racial prejudice "obliquely," through a "broken-back novelette" with prejudiced characters of both races, to the novel that blames white racism alone for prejudice.

Smith, Robert A. "A Pioneer Black Writer and the Problems of Discrimination and Miscegenation." *Costerus*, 9 (1973), 181-183.
   A brief survey of the stories in *The Wife of His Youth and Other Stories*, the first short stories about racial problems written by a black writer.

Taxel, Joel. "Charles Waddell Chesnutt's Sambo: Myth and Reality." *NALF*, 9 (Winter 1975), 105-108.
   Deals with Chesnutt's concepts of the uses of "Sambo" as revealed in *The Conjure Woman* and "The Passing of Grandison."

Teller, Walter. "Charles W. Chesnutt's Conjuring and Color-Line Stories." *Am Schol*, 42 (Winter 1972-73), 125-127.
   Chiefly an account of Chesnutt's career and his purposes in writing his various works.

Wade, Melvin and Margaret. See GENERAL.

Walcott, Ronald. "Chesnutt's 'The Sheriff's Children' as Parable." *NALF*, 7 (Fall 1973), 83-85.
   The story is a "parable of the Reconstruction South, with a biblical parallel." In it Chesnutt is concerned with the effects of the past on the present.

Wideman, John. "Charles W. Chesnutt: *The Marrow of Tradition*." *Am Schol*, 42 (Winter 1972-73), 128-134.
   Focuses on the artistic merits of the novel.

Wintz, Cary D. "Race and Realism in the Fiction of Charles W. Chesnutt." *Ohio Hist*, 81 (1972), 122-130.
   Chiefly a survey of Chesnutt's life and career.

[CHOPIN, KATE] Anon. "Love in Louisiana--Kate Chopin: A Forgotten Southern Novelist." *TLS*, October 9, 1970, p. 1163.
   An essay-review of *Kate Chopin: A Critical Biography*, by Per Seyersted, and *The Complete Works of Kate Chopin*, edited by Seyersted. Sees a deserved revival of interest in Chopin.

Andrews, William L. "An Addition to Kate Chopin's Poetry." *Am N&Q*, 13 (April 1975), 117-118.
   Reprints the text of "I Opened All the Portals Wide" and explains why the poem is of some importance.

Arner, Robert D. "Characterization and the Colloquial Style in Kate Chopin's 'Vagabonds.'" *MarkR*, 2 (1971), 110-112.
   The two types of language Chopin uses in this story indicate that Valcour is the narrator's other self.

_____. "Kate Chopin's Realism: 'At the 'Cadian Ball' and 'The Storm.'" *MarkR*, 2 (February 1970), 1-4.
   "The Storm" shows Chopin's movement away from the sentimental (typified in "At the 'Cadian Ball") to the realistic.

_____. "Landscape Symbolism in Kate Chopin's *At Fault*." *La Stud*, 9 (Fall 1970), 142-153.
   For various reasons, this novel is the most Southern of Chopin's works.

_____. "Pride and Prejudice: Kate Chopin's 'Désirée's Baby.'" *Miss Quart*, 25 (Spring 1972), 131-140.
   Despite recent critical claims that this short story is a failure, a detailed study of its theme, structure, and imagery reveals that it is surprisingly rich and complex.

Bender, Bert. "Kate Chopin's Lyric Short Stories." *Stud SF*, 11 (Summer 1974), 257-266.
   Chopin's stories are "lyric celebrations of life," and it is "bitterly ironic" that she should be classified as a local colorist.

Bonner, Thomas, Jr. "Kate Chopin's European Consciousness." *Am Lit Realism*, 8 (Summer 1975), 281-284.
   Deals chiefly with three Chopin stories with European settings, stories which reveal that Chopin had a "European consciousness" and was able to use it "as an integral aspect of her fiction."

Butcher, Philip. See CABLE, GEORGE WASHINGTON (Postbellum--3rd Butcher entry).

Chametzky, Jules. See MISCELLANEOUS (Postbellum).

Eaton, Clement. See GENERAL.

Espy, John. Untitled. *N Car F*, 25 (September 1970), 242-247.
    An essay-review of Per Seyersted's edition of *The Complete Works of Kate Chopin* and of his biography, *Kate Chopin: A Critical Biography*.

Koloski, Bernard J. "The Structure of Kate Chopin's *At Fault*." *Stud in Am F*, 3 (Spring 1975), 89-94.
    Title is descriptive.

_____. "The Swinburne Lines in *The Awakening*." *AL*, 45 (January 1974), 8-10.
    The lines quoted from the beginning of Swinburne's "The Cameo" create an atmosphere of death so that Edna's suicide should come as no surprise.

Leary, Lewis, ed. *The Awakening and Other Stories by Kate Chopin*. New York: Holt, Rinehart & Winston, 1970.
    Contains twenty stories and the novel in annotated texts with a critical introduction by the editor.

_____. "Kate Chopin and Walt Whitman." *Walt Whit Rev*, 16 (December 1970), 120-121.
    Discusses the ways Chopin's works reveal her reading of Whitman.

_____. "Kate Chopin, Liberationist?" *So Lit Jour*, 3 (Fall 1970), 138-144.
    An essay-review of Seyersted's biography and his edition of her works in which Leary finds Chopin more clearly revealed in her *Complete Works*, but the biographer tells us "almost everything that we need to know about Mrs. Chopin, the person."

_____. "Kate Chopin's Other Novel." *So Lit Jour*, 1 (Autumn 1968), 60-74.
    Whereas *The Awakening* shows a master skillfully at work, the earlier novel *At Fault* reveals an apprentice experimenting with rough designs later to be fashioned into art.

_____. See GENERAL--1st Leary entry.

May, John R. "Local Color in *The Awakening*." *SouR*, 6 (Autumn 1970), 1031-1040.
    Argues that the theme of the novel is developed directly and symbolically out of an integral local color.

Milliner, Gladys W. "The Tragic Imperative: *The Awakening* and *The Bell Jar*." *Mary Wollstonecraft Newsletter*, 2 (December 1973), 21-27.
    Deals with the frustrating consequences of the awakening of a woman such as Edna Pontellier to realization of herself.

Polk, Noel. See MISCELLANEOUS (Postbellum--1st Polk entry).

Potter, Richard H. "Kate Chopin and Her Critics: An Annotated Checklist." *Missouri Hist Soc Bul*, 26 (July 1970), 306-317.
    Title is descriptive.

_____. "Negroes in the Fiction of Kate Chopin." *Louisiana History*, 12 (Winter 1971), 41-58.
    Kate Chopin created a large number of Negro characters in her fiction. These are varied, realistic, and human, sometimes reflecting but usually going beyond the stereotypes.

Ringe, Donald A. "Cane River World: Kate Chopin's *At Fault* and Related Stories." *Studies in Am F*, 3 (Autumn 1975), 157-166.
    Thematic treatment.

_____. "Romantic Imagery in Kate Chopin's *The Awakening*." *AL*, 43 (January 1972), 580-588.
    Sees the novel as being one of a "powerful romantic" composition when its imagery is fully considered.

Rosen, Kenneth M. "Kate Chopin's *The Awakening*: Ambiguity as Art." *Jour Am Stud*, 5 (August 1971), 197-200.
    The sea imagery in *The Awakening* prefigures that of *The Old Man and the Sea* fifty-three years later.

Seyersted, Per, ed. *The Complete Works of Kate Chopin*. 2 vols. Baton Rouge: Louisiana State Univ Press, 1969. (Foreword by Edmund Wilson).
    Chopin's complete works except for three unfinished children's stories and some twenty poems.

_____. *Kate Chopin: A Critical Biography*. Baton Rouge: Louisiana State Univ Press, 1969.
    The first biography of the local-color writer Kate Chopin which examines the influence on her fiction of her life as author, critic, and defender of women's rights.

_____. "Kate Chopin (1851-1904)." *Am Lit Realism*, 3 (Spring 1970), 153-159.
    A bibliographical essay surveying work in print by and about Chopin and indicating areas in which further research is needed.

_____, ed. *"The Storm" and Other Stories by Kate Chopin: With "The Awakening."* (Feminist Press Reprint 5). Old Westbury, N. Y.: Feminist Press, 1974.
    Seyersted's introduction emphasizes the stir Chopin's works caused.

Skaggs, Peggy. "Three Tragic Figures in Kate Chopin's *The Awakening*." *La Stud*, 13 (Winter 1974), 345-364.
    Edna, Adèle, and Mademoiselle Reisz are all "tragic in [their] inability to achieve [their] full identity."

Spangler, George M. "Kate Chopin's *The Awakening*: A Partial Dissent." *Novel*, 3 (Spring 1970), 249-255.
    The Awakening deserves the present-day praise it is given except for the conclusion which is "unsatisfactory because it is fundamentally evasive."

Sullivan, Ruth, and Stewart Smith. "Narrative Stance in Kate Chopin's *The Awakening*." *Stud in Am F*, 1 (Spring 1973), 62-75.
    Discusses Edna Pontellier's human limitations.

Warnken, William P. "Kate Chopin and Henrik Ibsen: A Study of *The Awakening* and *A Doll's House*." *Mass Stud in Eng*, 4, no. 4; 5, no. 1 (Autumn 1974, Winter 1975--double issue), 43-49.
    Both writers were concerned with "the freedom of the individual spirit"; both Nora and Edna "experienced an awakening in a doll's house."

Wheeler, Otis B. "The Five Awakenings of Edna Pontellier." *SouR*, 11 (Winter 1975), 118-128.
    The Awakening rejects the Victorian myth of love, the two major functions of woman that the myth provided, and the romantic dream of "unlimited outward expansion of the self."

Wolff, Cynthia G. "Thanatos and Eros: Kate Chopin's *The Awakening*." *AQ*, 25 (October 1973), 449-471.
    Analyzes the personality and predicament of the main character of the novel.

Zlotnick, Joan. "A Woman's Will: Kate Chopin on Selfhood, Wifehood, and Motherhood." *MarkR*, 3 (October 1968), 1-5.
    Discusses Chopin's rejection of the contemporary view of wifehood and motherhood in her works.

[CLEMENS, SAMUEL LANGHORNE] Aaron, Daniel. See GENERAL.

Adams, Richard P. See GENERAL.

Agrawal, I. N. "Mark Twain's Visit to Allahabad." *Indian Jour of Am Stud*, 3, no. 1 (1973), 104-108.
    Quotations from the Allahabad newspapers on Twain's lecture in 1896.

Alsen, Eberhard. "The Futile Pursuit of Truth in Twain's 'What Is Man?' and Anderson's 'The Book of the Grotesque.'" *MTJ*, 17 (Winter 1974-75), 12-13.
    The old man and the ironic awareness that pursuit of truth might make one grotesque are central similarities in the two works.

_____. "Pudd'nhead Wilson's Fight for Popularity and Power." *WAL*, 7 (Summer 1972), 135-143.
    David Wilson, because he finds it impossible to change an "unenlightened community" is a pudd'nhead after all.

Anderson, Carl L. "Strindberg's Translations of American Humor." *Americana Norvegica*, 3 (1972), 153-194.
    Suggests that Strindberg made "arbitrary and sometimes drastic revision" in his translations and that Twain's humor influenced Scandinavian thought.

Anderson, D. M. "Basque Wine, Arkansas Chawin' Tobacco: Landscape, and Ritual in Ernest Hemingway and Mark Twain." *MTJ*, 16 (Winter 1971-72), 3-7.
    Discusses similarities between social criticism in *Huckleberry Finn* and *The Sun Also Rises*.

Anderson, Frederick. "Hazards of Photographic Sources." *CEAAN*, 1 (1968), 5.
    Deals with the preparation of the Twain-Henry Huttleston Rogers letters.

_____. Introduction, Note on Text, and Bibliography. *Pudd'nhead Wilson and Those Extraordinary Twins*. San Francisco: Chandler, 1968.
    A facsimile edition.

_____, ed. *Mark Twain: The Critical Heritage*. London: Routledge & Kegan Paul; New York: Barnes & Noble, 1971.
    A compilation of reviews and articles from British and American journals, 1869-1913, with the aim of reflecting Twain's developing reputation.

_____, et al., eds. *Mark Twain's Notebooks and Journals*. Vol. I: 1855-1873; Vol. II: 1877-1883. Berkeley: Univ of California Press, 1975.
    Thoroughly annotated texts of the notebooks recording travels and events which inspired creative writing.

_____. "Overlapping Texts." *CEAAN*, 1 (1968), 6-7.
    Deals with the difficulties of sorting out two sets of revisions in *The Mysterious Stranger* manuscripts.

_____. "Team Proofreading: Some Problems." *CEAAN*, 2 (1969), 15.
    Points out some difficulties encountered in oral proofreading of Twain materials.

_____, and Hamlin Hill. "How Samuel Clemens Became Mark Twain's Publisher: A Study of the James R. Osgood Contracts." *Proof*, 2 (1972), 117-143.
    Deals with Twain's relationship with James R. Osgood & Company which led ultimately to the establishment of Twain's publishing company, Charles L. Webster & Company.

Anderson, Thomas. See GENERAL.

Andrews, William L. "The Source of Mark Twain's 'The War Prayer.'" *MTJ*, 17 (Summer 1975), 8-9.
    When compared to its source in Chapter 57 of *Life on the Mississippi*, the changes in tone and emphasis reveal that Twain's moral and formal purpose in writing changed from 1882 to 1905.

"The Appert Collection of Mark Twain." *Bancroftiana*, 57 (January 1974), 5-6.
    Description of letters and Twain memorabilia at the University of California.

Arikawa, Shoji. "Huckleberry Finn in Japan." *Eng Rec*, 21 (February 1971), 20-26.
    Deals with the reasons that Huck appeals to Japanese students.

Arner, Robert D. "Acts Seventeen and *Huckleberry Finn*: A Note on Silas Phelps' Sermon." *MTJ*, 16 (Summer 1972), 12.
    Acts 17:29 points to the immoral and un-Christian center of Huck's world.

III. Postbellum (1865-1920)

Aspiz, Harold. "Mark Twain and 'Doctor' Newton." *AL*, 44 (March 1972), 130-136.
Examines Clemens' published comments about Newton.

_____. "The Other Half of Pudd'nhead's Dog." *MTJ*, 17 (Summer 1975), 10-11.
Suggests a source in P. T. Barnum's autobiography.

Austin, James C. "American Humor in France." *Papers on Lang and Lit*, 5 (Summer 1969--Supplement), 100-109.
Includes some discussion of Twain and quotes statements about his work by Mme. Bentzon, who translated "The Celebrated Jumping Frog."

Babcock, C. Merton. "Mark Twain as 'A Majority of One.'" *Univ Col Quart*, 15 (May 1970), 3-7.
Traces Twain's concern over the lack of "moral courage" in man and himself.

Baender, Paul. "Reflections Upon the CEAA by a Departing Editor." *RALS*, 4 (Autumn 1974), 131-144.
On editing, with many illustrations cited from the Iowa-California Twain edition.

_____. "Review Article: Two Books on Mark Twain." *PQ*, 47 (January 1968), 117-135.
An essay-review of Justin Kaplan's *Mr. Clemens and Mr. Twain* and of James M. Cox's *Mark Twain: The Fate of Humor*, which concludes that "partly because of their strategic faults these two books show how central and effective Clemens remains in our literary culture."

_____, ed. *What Is Man? And Other Philosophical Writers*. Vol. 19, *The Works of Mark Twain*. Berkeley: Univ of California Press, 1973.
A CEAA-approved edition of twenty philosophical works by Twain, including "Letters from the Earth," *Christian Science*, and *What Is Man?*, with annotations, textual notes, and an introduction by the editor.

Baetzhold, Howard G. "An Emendation in *A Connecticut Yankee*." *CEAAN*, 1 (1968), 10.
Deals with an emendation that should be made in Chapter 26.

_____. "Found: Mark Twain's 'Lost Sweetheart.'" *AL*, 44 (November 1972), 414-429.
Brings to light the brief acquaintance of Clemens with Laura M. Wright.

_____. *Mark Twain and John Bull: The British Connection*. Bloomington: Indiana Univ Press, 1970.
Traces and analyzes Twain's relationship with England from 1872 to his death and its influence on his life and thought.

Banasthali Patrika, 11 (July 1968). A special number on American literature, ed. Rameshwar Gupta.
Contains an essay comparing Huck Finn and Isabel Archer and one on unity in *Huckleberry Finn*.

Banta, Martha. "Escape and Entry in *Huckleberry Finn*." *MFS*, 14 (Spring 1968), 79-91.
Metaphorically, the River represents Huck's complex nature while the shore represents his "environmental nurture"; the "central movement of the novel...alternates between the raft and the shore, between escape and entry, between sleep and stimulation."

_____. "Rebirth or Revenge: The Endings of *Huckleberry Finn* and *The American*." *MFS*, 15 (Summer 1969), 191-207.
Both novels "continually test the possibilities of their heroes' codes of pleasure while dramatically proving the truth that the American must recognize the limitations of *human* nature even as he refuses to be diminished by self-destroying forces of *social* codes of revenge."

Barsness, John A. "Platform Manner in the Novel: A View from the Pit." *Midcontinent Am Stud Jour*, 10 (Fall 1969), 49-59.
The author argues that the techniques and themes of the oral storyteller influenced Mark Twain's writing.

Barton, Marion. "Shavian Mirth Recalled." *Independent Shavian*, 10 (Spring 1972), 48.
A reminiscence about a visit of Shaw and Clemens to the British House of Commons; the article is reprinted from the *New York Times*, April 19, 1933.

Baum, Joan. "Mark Twain on the Congo." *MTJ*, 17 (Summer 1974), 7-9.
Points out parallels between Mark Twain's propaganda pamphlet and Conrad's view of the Congo abuses.

Beaver, Harold. "Run, Nigger, Run: *Adventures of Huckleberry Finn* as a Fugitive Slave Narrative." *Jour Am Stud*, 8 (December 1974), 339-361.
Argues that Jim manipulates Huck into helping him escape and that he does not really gain freedom at the end of the book; instead the novel "comes to rest at the ambiguous heart of Huck's confusion: Silas Phelps's plantation..., whose very lay-out removes people to the status of non people...."

Beebe, Maurice, and John Feaster. "Criticism of Mark Twain: A Selected Checklist." *MFS*, 14 (Spring 1968), 93-139.
Divided into general studies of Twain's life and work, and discussions of individual works.

Beidler, Peter G. "The Raft Episode in *Huckleberry Finn*." *MFS*, 14 (Spring 1968), 11-20.
Questions Twain's deletion of the raft episode and considers the editorial problem that has resulted.

Bellamy, Joe David. "Two Eras, Two Epitaphs: Steamboating Life in the Works of Mark Twain and Richard Bissell." *BSUF*, 13, no. 4 (1972), 48-52.
Deals with *Life on the Mississippi* and *A Stretch on the River*.

Belson, Joel J. "The Nature and the Consequences of the Loneliness of Huckleberry Finn." *ArQ*, 26 (Autumn 1970), 243-248.

Pictures Huck as a character "completely apart from the adult world" and "completely apart from society." Huck's weapon for dealing with a hostile world is "concealment" and its companion--"overwhelming loneliness."

Benardete, Jane J. "*Huckleberry Finn* and the Nature of Fiction." *Mass Rev*, 9 (Spring 1968), 209-226.
On the thesis that Twain's novel is deliberately devised to show "fiction's power to distort life," Huck's "development" is thus his increasing preference for fiction over fact.

Bercovitch, Sacvan. "Huckleberry Bumppo: A Comparison of *Tom Sawyer* and *The Pioneers*." *MTJ*, 14 (Summer 1968), 1-5.
A comparison of structure and characterization in the two novels, leading to a tentative statement of Cooper's influence on Twain.

Berger, Sidney. "New Mark Twain Items." *PBSA*, 68 (3rd Qtr. 1974), 331-335.
About materials relating to printer's copy for *Pudd'nhead Wilson*.

Bergholz, Harry. "Strindberg's Anthologies of American Humorists, Bibliographically Identified." *Scand S*, 43 (1971), 335-343.
Includes very brief discussion of Strindberg's translations of "The Loves of Alonzo FitzClarence and Rosannah Ethelton" and "About Magnanimous-Incident Literature" and of other Swedish translations of Twain's work.

Bergmann, Frank. "Mark Twain and the Literary Misfortunes of John William DeForest." *Jahrbuch für Amerikastudien*, 13 (1968), 249-252.
Deals with Twain's rejection of DeForest's *Thousand and One Nights*.

Berkove, Lawrence I. "Language and Literature: The 'Poor Players' of *Huckleberry Finn*." *PMASAL*, 53 (1968), 291-310.
The way Mark Twain uses impersonation in *Huckleberry Finn* reveals determinism winning out over free will.

Bertolotti, D. S. "Structural Unity in 'The Man That Corrupted Hadleyburg.'" *MTJ*, 14 (Winter 1967-68), 19-20.
The letters written by Stephenson, appearing at the beginning of each section and forecasting the action to come, provide structural unity.

Bickley, R. Bruce, Jr. "Humorous Portraiture in Twain's News Writing." *Am Lit Realism*, 3 (Fall 1970), 395-398.
"These portraits from Twain's news writing reveal man as he is in reality--sometimes nobler but more often meaner than he appears or would have others believe."

Bie, Wendy A. "Mark Twain's Bitter Duality." *MTJ*, 16 (Summer 1972), 14-16.
The pervasive theme of duality between man's "low" impulses and his "high" morals culminates in Twain's late, suppressed works.

Birchfield, James. "Jim's Coat of Arms." *MTJ*, 14 (Summer 1969), 15-16.
The significance of Tom's insistence that Jim must have a coat of arms lies in the contrast it makes between his character and Huck's.

Blair, Walter, ed. *Mark Twain's Hannibal, Huck & Tom*. Berkeley: Univ of California Press, 1969.
A fully documented and annotated collection of unpublished writings about life in Hannibal, which influenced and inspired some of Twain's most memorable characters and greatest works of fiction.

_____. "Mark Twain's Other Masterpiece: 'Jim Baker's Blue-Jay Yarn.'" *Stud in Am Humor*, 1 (January 1975), 132-147.
A detailed study of the story Blair considers Twain's greatest work of short fiction.

_____. See GENERAL.

Blanck, Jacob. "BAL Addendum 3479: Twain's 'A Dog's Tale.'" *PBSA*, 62 (4th Qtr. 1968), 617.
Short addendum to the *Bibliography of American Literature*.

Bluefarb, Sam. See GENERAL.

Blues, Thomas. *Mark Twain and the Community*. Lexington: Univ Press of Kentucky, 1970.
Finds that a vision of the individual and the community in which the individual can assert his independence by flouting community standards is at the heart of Twain's early work and that the failure of the vision accounts for his later cynicism.

_____. "The Strategy of Compromise in Mark Twain's 'Boy Books.'" *MFS*, 14 (Spring 1968), 21-31.
A study of *Tom Sawyer*, *The Prince and the Pauper*, and *Huckleberry Finn*, which shows that in each book Twain "provided his hero with a victory over the community that in no way endangered his equable relation to it, a compromise resolution that had the important value of permitting triumph without isolation."

Bowen, James K., and Richard Van Der Beets, eds. *Adventures of Huckleberry Finn, With Abstracts of Twenty Years of Criticism*. Glenview, Ill.: Scott, Foresman, 1970.
Reprints the first American edition (1885) with forty brief abstracts of criticism (prepared by the critics) published between 1948 and 1968 and an original survey by Edgar M. Branch, "Mark Twain Scholarship: Two Decades."

Brack, O. M., Jr. "Mark Twain in Knee Pants: The Expurgation of *Tom Sawyer Abroad*." *Proof*, 2 (1972), 145-151.
A good portion of the American edition was set from copy in *St. Nicholas* which had been "censored" by Mary Mapes Dodge; the English edition is better because it was set from Twain's typescript.

Bradbury, Malcolm. "Introduction" to *Pudd'nhead Wilson* and *Those Extraordinary Twins*. Baltimore: Penguin, 1969.

The technical weaknesses and carefully controlled ironies of Twain's novel, and its reflections of the moral and social turbulence of the 1890's, contribute towards a paradoxical "problem comedy" which is one of the best late nineteenth-century American novels and perhaps Twain's most interesting.

_____. "Mark Twain in the Gilded Age." *Crit Quart*, 11 (Spring 1969), 65-73.
   Discusses Twain's relationship to the Gilded Age and its effect upon his work.

Branch, Edgar M. *Clemens of the "Call": Mark Twain in San Francisco*. Berkeley: Univ of California Press, 1969.
   Reprints two hundred items, arranged chronologically within topical groupings, written by Samuel Clemens as a local reporter for the San Francisco *Daily Morning Call* from June to October 1864; a full introduction, running commentary, and bibliographic appendices are provided by the editor.

_____. "Mark Twain Reports the Races in Sacramento." *HLQ*, 32 (February 1969), 179-186.
   Discusses Clemens as a newspaper reporter in California in 1866.

_____. "Samuel Clemens: Learning to Venture a Miracle." *Am Lit Realism*, 8 (Spring 1975), 91-99.
   Tales and sketches that Clemens wrote before October 1871 reveal his "extensive knowledge of romantic literature, and they clarify his love-hate involvement with that literature" and "suggest an affinity between his humor and an essentially romantic apprehension of experience."

Brand, John M. "The Incipient Wilderness: A Study of *Pudd'nhead Wilson*." *WAL*, 7 (Summer 1972), 125-134.
   On the symbolism of wilderness, east, and west in the novel.

Bray, Robert. "Mark Twain Biography: Entering a New Phase." *Midwest Quart*, 15 (April 1974), 286-301.
   A review-essay of Hamlin Hill's *Mark Twain: God's Fool*, which, after a survey of earlier biographies, concludes that Hill's offers a truer picture of Clemens' life and is thus a "far better biography than we have had."

Briden, E. F. "Samuel L. Clemens and Elizabeth Jordan: An Unpublished Letter." *MTJ*, 17 (Summer 1974), 11-13.
   Title is descriptive.

Broderick, John C. See GENERAL.

Brodwin, Stanley. "Blackness and the Adamic Myth in Twain's *Pudd'nhead*." *Tex Stud in Lit and Lang*, 15 (Spring 1973), 167-176.
   The novel is discussed as a thological study of man's nature modelled on the myth of the Fall of Man.

_____. "The Humor of the Absurd: Mark Twain's Adamic Diaries." *Criticism*, 14 (Winter 1972), 49-64.

This study of Mark Twain's version of the Genesis story argues that Twain's comic sense has theological roots.

_____. "Mark Twain's Masks of Satan: The Final Phase." *AL*, 45 (May 1973), 206-227.
   Studies Twain's use of the persona of the devil during the 1890's and 1900's.

Brogan, Howard O. "Early Experience and Scientific Determinism in Twain and Hardy." *Mosaic*, 7 (Spring 1974), 99-105.
   Their similar backgrounds led both Twain and Hardy to a belief in scientific determinism.

Brogunier, Joseph. "An Incident in *The Great Gatsby* and *Huckleberry Finn*." *MTJ*, 16 (Summer 1972), 1-3.
   Nick's account of the scene of Myrtle's death is like Huck's record of Sherburn killing Boggs.

Browne, R. B. *Mark Twain's Quarrel with Heaven*. New Haven, Conn.: College and Univ Press, 1970.
   An edition of "Captain Stormfield's Visit to Heaven" and two related sketches, with an introduction by the editor.

_____. See GENERAL.

Bruccoli, Matthew. See GENERAL.

Buchloh, Paul G. See GENERAL.

Budd, Louis J. "'Baxter's Hog': The Right Mascot for an Editor (With CEAA Standards) of Mark Twain's Political and Social Writings." *CEAAN*, 3 (1970), 3-10.
   Deals with the dilemmas faced in preparing these materials; defends the CEAA.

_____. "Did Mark Twain Write 'Impersonally' for the *New York Herald*?" *Lib Notes*, 43 (1972), 5-9.
   Though Mark Twain said that he had agreed to write two "impersonal" letters a week for the *Herald*, he wrote only three.

_____. "Mark Twain and the 'Quaker City.'" *So Lit Jour*, 1 (Autumn 1968), 112-116.
   An essay-review of *Mark Twain Abroad: The Cruise of the "Quaker City,"* by Dewey Ganzel.

_____. "Mark Twain Talks Mostly About Humor and Humorists." *Stud in Am Humor*, 1 (April 1974), 4-22.
   Examines Twain's statements about humor in his writings and in his interviews during his travels in 1895.

Bugliari, Jeanne. "The Picaresque as a Flaw in Mark Twain's Novels." *MTJ*, 15 (Summer 1971), 10-12.
   Twain was "Ensnared by the picaresque," and his novels are often the victims of excess didacticism, flat characterization, and lack of structure.

Bungert, Hans. See GENERAL.

Burg, David F. "Another View of *Huckleberry Finn*." *NCF*, 29 (December 1974), 299-319.

This novel "is a revolutionary work, an appropriate fusion of a modern antimoral metaphysics with a concomitantly modern form."

Burns, Graham. "Time and Pastoral: *The Adventures of Huckleberry Finn*." *Crit Rev*, 15 (1972), 52-63.
    Sees *Huck Finn*, like *Walden* and *Moby Dick*, as organized around a central highly pastoral image--an image placing civilized consciousness in an illuminating but ambiguous relation to the natural world, and both of these in a critical, antithetical relation to society.

Burns, Stuart. "St. Petersburg Re-visited: Helen Eustis and Mark Twain." *WAL*, 55 (Winter 1970), 99-112.
    Points out similarities between Eustis' *The Fool Killer* and *Huckleberry Finn*.

Burrison, John A. *"The Golden Arm," The Folk Tale and Its Literary Use by Mark Twain and Joel C. Harris*. Atlanta: George State Univ Research Paper, no. 19, 1968.
    Concludes that this tale is of white origin and compares it with Harris' version in *Uncle Remus*.

Bush, Robert. "Grace King and Mark Twain." *AL*, 44 (March 1972), 31-51.
    Based on letters and Miss King's notebooks, the article chronicles the relationship between the two writers.

Butcher, Philip. "'The Godfathership' of *A Connecticut Yankee*." *CLA Jour*, 12 (March 1969), 189-198.
    Shows the influence that George W. Cable had on Twain in the composition of this novel.

_____. "Mark Twain's Installment of the National Debt." *So Lit Jour*, 1 (Spring 1969), 48-55.
    Deals with Twain's paying the expenses of a black student to Yale.

Butler, M. D. "*Tom Sawyer, Detective*: The Last Emancipation." *Am N&Q*, 13 (April 1975), 116-117.
    Deals with the differences between a typescript of this work and the published version.

Byers, John R., Jr. "Mark Twain's Miss Mary Jane Wilks: Shamed or Shammed?" *MTJ*, 17 (Winter 1973-74), 13-14.
    Twain may have meant "shamming" instead of "shaming" in referring to Mary Jane Wilks in Chapter 28 of *Huckleberry Finn*.

_____. "Miss Emmeline Grangerford's Hymn Book." *AL*, 43 (May 1971), 259-263.
    Finds in Isaac Watts's "Alas! and did my Saviour bleed!" a possible source for Clemens' "Ode to Stephen Dowling Bots, Dec'd."

Cady, Edwin H. *The Light of Common Day: Realism in American Fiction*. Bloomington: Indiana Univ Press, 1971.
    An essay on the definition of realism includes discussion of *Huckleberry Finn* as picaresque novel and "boy book."

_____. See GENERAL.

Campbell, Frank, and Ina. "Mark Twain's Florentine Villas in 1964-65." *MTJ*, 15 (Summer 1971), 12-14.
    Deals with an attempt to locate the two villas.

Cardwell, Guy A. "The Bowdlerizing of Mark Twain." *ESQ*, 21 (3rd Qtr. 1975), 179-193.
    Scholarly opinion on Twain's acceptance of "editorial suggestions" from his wife and others remains biased.

_____. "*Life on the Mississippi*: Vulgar Facts and Learned Errors." *ESQ*, 19 (Summer 1973), 283-293.
    Discusses factual errors in scholarship on this work.

_____. "Mark Twain, James R. Osgood, and Those 'Suppressed' Passages." *NEQ*, 46 (June 1973), 163-188.
    Discusses changes Clemens made, or allowed to be made, in *Life on the Mississippi*.

_____. "Samuel Clemens' Magical Pseudonym." *NEQ*, 48 (June 1975), 175-193.
    A study of the various attitudes and meanings of Clemens' pseudonym.

_____. "A Surprising World: Amasa Delano in Kentucky." *MTJ*, 16 (Summer 1973), 12-13.
    Discusses real-life counterparts of a character in *The Gilded Age*.

Carrington, George C., Jr. *The Dramatic Unity of "Huckleberry Finn."* Columbus: Ohio State Univ Press, 1975.
    An attempt to resolve the critical dilemma posed by the ending of the novel, using a structuralist approach.

Carson, Herbert L. "Mark Twain's Misanthropy." *Cresset*, 33, no. 2 (1969), 13-15.
    Deals principally with *Huckleberry Finn*.

Cary, Richard. "In Further Defence of Harriet Shelley: Two Unpublished Letters by Mark Twain." *MTJ*, 16 (Summer 1973), 13-15.
    In these letters, Mark Twain holds Shelley wholly responsible for Harriet's death.

Casey, Daniel J. "Huckleberry Finn In Finland: A Comparison of Twain and Kivi." *Mod Språk*, 62, no. 4 (1968), 385-394.
    A comparison of *Huckleberry Finn* with Kivi's *Seven Brothers* to emphasize Huck's universality.

_____. "Universality in *Huckleberry Finn*: A Comparison of Twain and Kivi." *MTJ*, 14 (Winter 1967-68), 13-18.
    See annotation in the preceding item.

Cate, Hollis L. "Two American Bumpkins." *Research Stud*, 41 (March 1973), 61-63.
    Points out parallels between a rustic character in Sarah Kemble Knight's *Journal* and Nicodemus Dodge in *A Tramp Abroad*.

Cecil, L. Moffitt. "Tom Sawyer: Missouri Robin Hood." *WAL*, 4 (Summer 1969), 125-131.
Deals with the tick-running episode in Chapter VII.

Chambliss, Amy. "The Friendship of Helen Keller and Mark Twain." *GaR*, 24 (Fall 1970), 305-310.
A brief chronicle of Twain's friendship with Miss Keller.

Chellis, Barbara A. "Those Extraordinary Twins: Negroes and Whites." *AQ*, 21 (Spring 1969), 100-112.
In *Pudd'nhead Wilson*, Mark Twain attacks the fictions of race and shows that he is against slavery.

Christopher, J. R. "On the *Adventures of Huckleberry Finn* as Comic Myth." *Cim Rev*, 18 (1972), 18-27.
Classifies the characters according to three basic comic types.

Clark, Harry H. See GENERAL.

Clemens, S. L., W. D. Howells, and C. H. Clark, eds. *Mark Twain's Library of Humor*. New York: MSS Information Corp., 1969.
A reprint of the 1888 edition with a new Foreword by Clarence Gohdes outlining its importance.

Clerc, Charles. "Sunrise on the River: 'The Whole World' of *Huckleberry Finn*." *MFS*, 14 (Spring 1968), 67-78.
An analysis of the passage at the beginning of Chapter XIX.

Cloutier, Arthur C. "Dear Mister Seelye...Yours Truly, Tom Sawyer." *CE*, 34 (March 1973), 849-853.
Parodies Seelye's rewriting of *Huckleberry Finn*.

Clymer, Kenneth J. "John Hay and Mark Twain." *Missouri Hist Rev*, 67 (1973), 397-406.
An account of the friendship between these two men.

Coard, Robert L. "Huck Finn and Mr. Twain Rhyme." *Midwest Quart*, 10 (1969), 317-329.
Analyzes poetic elements in *Huckleberry Finn*.

_____. "Mark Twain's *The Gilded Age* and Sinclair Lewis's *Babbitt*." *Midwest Quart*, 13 (Spring 1972), 319-333.
Both works present a real world set against an implied ideal world.

Coburn, Mark D. "'Training is everything': Communal Opinion and the Individual in *Pudd'nhead Wilson*." *MLQ*, 31 (June 1970), 209-219.
Pudd'nhead Wilson is the "most starkly pessimistic of Twain's novels," revealing "a world in which no escape from the debilitating influence of training is possible."

Cohen, Edward H. "The Return to St. Petersburg." *I Eng Yearbk*, 23 (1973), 50-55.

Develops the thesis that Huck is unable to escape civilization.

Colwell, James L. "Huckleberries and Humans: On the Naming of Huckleberry Finn." *PMLA*, 86 (January 1971), 70-76.
Huck is appropriately named since the berry, which Twain learned of in 1868 in Hartford, does not submit to cultivation.

Coplin, Keith. "John and Sam Clemens: A Father's Influence." *MTJ*, 15 (Winter 1970), 1-6.
Most of the father figures in Twain's fiction are tyrannical or aloof. John Clemens was such a man.

Cox, James M. "The Approved Mark Twain: The Beginning of the End." *SouR*, 4 (Spring 1968), 542-550.
An essay-review of the first three volumes of Mark Twain's unpublished writings, opening with a history of the first posthumous publication, and assessing the light these new volumes throw on Mark Twain's techniques and themes.

_____. "Humor and America: The Southwestern Bear Hunt, Mrs. Stowe, and Mark Twain." *SR*, 83 (Fall 1975), 573-601.
Discusses the influence of old Southwestern humor on Mark Twain, especially in *Huckleberry Finn*.

_____. "Mark Twain and the South." *So Lit Jour*, 8 (Fall 1975), 144-152.
A review-essay of *Mark Twain and the South*, by Arthur C. Pettit, which the reviewer believes fills a real gap in Twain criticism.

_____. "Toward Vernacular Humor." *VQR*, 46 (Spring 1970), 311-330.
In this discussion of several writers, Twain's Huck Finn's use of double negatives is said to represent his negative view of society.

Cracroft, Richard H. "Distorting Polygamy for Fun and Profit: Artemus Ward and Mark Twain Among the Mormons." *BYUS*, 14 (Winter 1974), 272-288.
Deals with the two writers' misconceptions about the Mormons, Twain probably having borrowed from Ward.

_____. "The Gentle Blasphemer: Mark Twain, Holy Scripture and the Book of Mormon." *BYUS*, 11 (Winter 1971), 119-140.
Concentrates on Twain's burlesque of the "Mormon Bible" and of Mormon customs. Stresses Twain's constant efforts to be a humorist.

Crawford, John W. See GENERAL.

Cronin, Frank C. "The Ultimate Perspective in *Pudd'nhead Wilson*." *MTJ*, 16 (Winter 1971-72), 14-16.
The moral center of the book is the narrator.

Crowley, John W. "A Note on *The Gilded Age*." *Eng Lang Notes*, 10 (December 1972), 116-118.
An undiscovered letter of Charles Dudley Warner in response to a review in *Appleton's Journal* indicates the book was completed more quickly than supposed, supports the contention

that the authors were reacting to specific Washington scandals, and praises the reviewer's recognition of Twain's serious side.

_____. "The Sacerdotal Cult and the Sealskin Coat: W. D. Howells in *My Mark Twain*." *Eng Lang Notes*, 11 (June 1974), 287-292.
   Howells' ambivalence toward Twain and Boston appears in *My Mark Twain*.

Dahl, Curtis. "Mark Twain and Ben Ely: Two Missouri Boyhoods." *Missouri Hist Rev*, 66 (1972), 549-566.
   Ely, who lived in Marion County, Missouri, about the same time Clemens did, also described Hannibal.

D'Avanzo, M. L. "In the Name of Pudd'nhead." *MTJ*, 16 (Summer 1972), 13-14.
   Franklin's Poor Richard produced "solid pudding," inverted in Wilson to intellectual, not material, "pudd'n."

David, Beverly R. "The Pictorial *Huck Finn*: Mark Twain and His Illustrator, E. W. Kemble." *AQ*, 26 (October 1974), 331-351.
   A study, copiously illustrated with Kemble's art, of Twain's relationship to the New York illustrator.

Davidson, Loren K. "The Darnell-Watson Feud." *DuR*, 13 (1968), 76-95.
   A detailed account of the real-life feud on which the Grangerford-Shepherdson feud in *Huckleberry Finn* was based.

Debouzy, Marianne. *La Genèse de l'Esprit Revolté dans le Roman Américain, 1875-1915*. Paris: Lettres Modernes, Minard, 1968.
   Of the writers and their works considered, Twain's work is said to be "the apogee of the individual revolt."

Delaney, Paul. "The Avatars of the Mysterious Stranger: Mark Twain's Images of Christ." *Chri & Lit*, 24 (Fall 1974), 25-38.
   Points out similarities in Twain's use of Christian mythology in the three unfinished manuscripts of *The Mysterious Stranger*.

DeMott, Benjamin. "Speaking of Books: If the book which Mr. Mark Twain wrote warn't up to what these crickits wanted...." *NYTBR*, March 22, 1970, pp. 2, 32.
   Tongue-in-cheek commentary on critics' dissatisfaction with *Huckleberry Finn*.

Denton, Lynn W. "Mark Twain and the American Indian." *MTJ*, 16 (Winter 1971-72), 1-3.
   Discusses Twain's change from dislike to admiration of the Indian.

_____. "Mark Twain on Patriotism, Treason, and War." *MTJ*, 17 (Summer 1974), 4-7.
   By 1900 Mark Twain was a staunch patriot trying to persuade the nation it was wrong about Philippine involvement.

Dinan, John S. "Hank Morgan: Artist Run Amuck." *Mass Stud in Eng*, 3 (Spring 1972), 72-77.

Hank Morgan is the artist whose aesthetic distance makes him incapable of human sensibility.

Ditsky, John M. "Mark Twain and the Great Dark: Religion in *Letters From the Earth*." *MTJ*, 17 (Summer 1975), 12-19.
   These letters are a critically viable entity in which "The Great Dark" plays a crucial role in organizing Twain's "religious" views.

Donaldson, Scott. "Pap Finn's Boy." *SAB*, 36 (May 1971), 32-37.
   Only in *Huckleberry Finn* does Twain resolve the antithesis of environment and heredity, when Huck turns from society and pursues the life of a loner, which was his father's way.

Doughty, Nanelia S. See MISCELLANEOUS (Postbellum).

Doyle, Paul A. "Henry Harper's Telling of a Mark Twain Anecdote." *MTJ*, 15 (Summer 1970), 13.
   A Harper letter includes a retelling of Twain's account of the funeral of an impersonator of his.

Doyno, Victor A. "Over Twain's Shoulder: The Composition and Structure of *Huckleberry Finn*." *MFS*, 14 (Spring 1968), 3-9.
   A study of parallel patterns in the novel which dramatize the idea that "for Huck freedom exists, if at all, in the process of seeking freedom."

Duram, James C. "Mark Twain and the Middle Ages." *Wichita State Univ Bul: Univ Stud*, 47 (August 1971), 3-16.
   Mark Twain found the Middle Ages a dehumanizing period, to be reflected later in the Gilded Age.

Ellis, Helen E. "Mark Twain: The Influence of Europe." *MTJ*, 14 (Winter 1968-69), 14-18.
   Twain's dislike for Europeans and their culture had turned to admiration by the time of *A Tramp Abroad*, with an accompanying dislike for Americans and their culture. By the time of *A Connecticut Yankee* he had concluded that all human beings are weak.

Elsbree, Langdon. "Huck Finn on the Nile." *SAQ*, 69 (Autumn 1970), 504-510.
   The experiences of a Fulbright scholar in Cairo teaching American literature, especially *Huckleberry Finn*, in which there is a deep sense of loneliness and, as in Egypt now, the passing away of the frontier.

Emblen, D. L. "Mark Twain Alive and Well--Very Well Indeed--in Sweden." *MTJ*, 16 (Summer 1973), 16-18.
   Discusses Mark Twain's popularity in Sweden and his influence on Swedish writers.

Ensor, Allison. "The Birthplace of Samuel Clemens: A New Mark Twain Letter." *Tenn Stud in Lit*, 14 (1969), 31-34.
   Prints for the first time the original letter from Twain to George H. Morgan of Gainesboro, Tennessee, written on December 16, 1882. Accompanying the letter was a biographical sketch

showing Twain's birthplace to be Florida, Missouri.

_____. "A Clergyman Recalls Hearing Mark Twain." *MTJ*, 15 (Winter 1970-71), 6.
Joseph Fort Newton heard Mark Twain at a meeting of the St. Louis Press Club in 1902.

_____. "The Contributions of Charles Webster and Albert Bigelow Paine to *Huckleberry Finn*." *AL*, 40 (May 1968), 222-227.
Concerns changes by Webster and Paine in chapter headings supplied in tables of contents and in captions to drawings by Kemble in various editions.

_____. "The Downfall of Poor Richard: Benjamin Franklin as Seen by Hawthorne, Melville, and Mark Twain." *MTJ*, 17 (Winter 1974-75), 14-17.
Hawthorne's and Melville's attitudes were negative or caustic toward "perfectability," but Twain treated it humorously.

_____. "The House United: Mark Twain and Henry Watterson Celebrate Lincoln's Birthday, 1901." *SAQ*, 74 (Spring 1975), 259-268.
An account of Mark Twain's introduction of Henry Watterson as featured speaker at the Carnegie Hall celebration, in which he scathingly condemns the United States's occupation of the Philippines.

_____. "The Location of the Phelps Farm in *Huckleberry Finn*." *SAB*, 34 (May 1969), 7.
The location is in southeastern Arkansas, evidenced in the working notes for *Huckleberry Finn* and statements in *Tom Sawyer, Detective*.

_____. *Mark Twain and the Bible*. Lexington: Univ Press of Kentucky, 1969.
Explores Twain's attitudes towards the Bible and his uses of it in his writings.

_____. "Mark Twain's 'The War Prayer': Its Ties to Howells and Hymnology." *MFS*, 16 (Winter 1970-71), 535-539.
Deals with similarity of views in "The War Prayer" and Howells' "Editha."

_____. "The 'Opposition Line' to The King and The Duke in *Huckleberry Finn*." *MTJ*, (Winter 1968-69), 6-7.
Disputes the suggestion of W. Keith Kraus (*MTJ*, 14 [Winter 1967-68]) that the second set of Wilks brothers are imposters.

_____. "The 'Tennessee Land' of *The Gilded Age*: Fiction and Reality." *Tenn Stud in Lit*, 15 (1970), 15-23.
Points up autobiographical elements in *The Gilded Age*.

Eschholz, Paul A. "Mark Twain and the Language of Gesture." *MTJ*, 17 (Winter 1973-74), 5-8.
Points out examples of nonverbal communication in *Huckleberry Finn*, *A Connecticut Yankee*, and *Pudd'nhead Wilson*.

_____. "Twain's *The Tragedy of Pudd'nhead Wilson*." *Expl*, 31 (April 1973), Item 67.
Pudd'nhead's "victory" in court is ironic.

Etulain, R. W. See GENERAL.

Fetterley, Judith. "Disenchantment: Tom Sawyer in *Huckleberry Finn*." *PMLA*, 87 (January 1972), 69-74.
Tom's cruelty intensifies from *Tom Sawyer*, where it results from failure to consider the consequences of actions, to *Huckleberry Finn*, where it is a primary motive.

_____. "The Sanctioned Rebel." *Studies in the Novel*, 3 (Fall 1971), 293-304.
An analysis of Tom's various roles in *The Adventures of Tom Sawyer*.

_____. "Yankee Showman and Reformer: The Character of Mark Twain's Hank Morgan." *Tex Stud in Lit and Lang*, 14 (Winter 1973), 667-679.
Hank Morgan is discussed as an egotistical reformer and performer who manipulates and humiliates those around him.

Fisher, Marvin, and Michael Elliott. "*Pudd'nhead Wilson*: Half a Dog Is Worse than None." *SouR*, 8 (Summer 1972), 533-547.
A study of the novel through examination of the meanings of the terms *dog* and *half*.

Fite, Montgomery. "Mark Twain's Naming of Huckleberry Finn." *Am N&Q*, 13 (May 1975), 140-141.
On the aptness of the name.

Fleck, Richard F. "Mark Twain in the American Wilderness." *Nature Stud*, 25, no. 2 (1972), 12-14; 25, no. 3 (1972), 10-11.
Compares Twain's descriptions of nature in *Roughing It* with those of Robert Louis Stevenson, Whitman, Muir, and W. H. Hudson.

_____. "Mark Twain's Social Criticism in *The Innocents Abroad*." *Rocky Mt. MLA Bul*, 25 (June 1971), 39-48.
The novel reveals that Twain judged nations by the way they treated the common people.

Fortenberry, George. "The Unnamed Critic in William Dean Howells' *Heroines of Fiction*." *MTJ*, 16 (Winter 1971-72), 7-8.
Twain is that critic.

Foster, Edward F. "*A Connecticut Yankee* Anticipated: Max Adeler's *Fortunate Island*." *BSUF*, 9 (Autumn 1968), 73-76.
Points out parallels between these two works; there is no evidence that Twain had read Adeler's book.

Frederick, John T. *The Darkened Sky: Nineteenth Century American Novelists and Religion*. Notre Dame, Ind.: Univ of Notre Dame Press, 1969.
Contains a section on Twain which concludes that Twain's determinism was the result of evolutionary science.

Freimarck, John. "*Pudd'nhead Wilson*: A Tale of Blood and Brotherhood." *Univ Rev*, 34 (June 1968), 303-306.
A study of a "novel that is uniquely American, at once evoking the dream of democratic possibilities and examining the institution which destroyed it."

French, Bryant M., ed. *The Gilded Age*. Indianapolis: Bobbs-Merrill, 1972.
   An edition based on the second printing of the first edition with notes, annotations, and an introduction by the editor.

_____. "James Hammond Trumbull's Alternative Chapter Mottoes for *The Gilded Age*." PQ, 50 (1971), 271-280.
   Deals with the mottoes Hammond wrote in several foreign languages to point up the satire of each chapter.

Fuller, Daniel J. "Mark Twain and Hamlin Garland: Contrarieties in Regionalism." *MTJ*, 17 (Winter 1973-74), 14-18.
   Emphasizes the similarities and differences in the two writers' treatment of setting.

Gale, Robert L. *Plots and Characters in the Works of Mark Twain*. 2 vols. Hamden, Conn.: Archon Books, 1973.
   Covers all of Twain's published work.

Ganzel, Dewey. *Mark Twain Abroad: The Cruise of the "Quaker City."* Chicago: Univ of Chicago Press, 1968.
   An account of Twain as a passenger on a luxury cruise, about which he later wrote in *Innocents Abroad*.

Gardner, Joseph H. "Gaffer Hexam and Pap Finn." *MP*, 66 (November 1968), 155-156.
   Suggests that Gaffer Hexam's outburst against learning to read in *Our Mutual Friend* is a source for Pap Finn's tirade against Huck for the same reason in *Huckleberry Finn*.

_____. "Mark Twain and Dickens." *PMLA*, 84 (January 1969), 90-101.
   In spite of hostile remarks which can be explained, Mark Twain was a careful reader of Dickens for over fifty years; hence Dickens was an influence that must not be excluded.

Gargano, James W. "*Pudd'nhead Wilson*: Mark Twain as Genial Satan." *SAQ*, 74 (Summer 1975), 365-375.
   Train's portrayal of human absurdity in daily life as seen in *Pudd'nhead Wilson* demonstrates his view of "human nature as a marvelous machinery for projecting social and moral arrangements at odds with its capabilities for good and sane behaviour."

Gaston, Georg M. "The Function of Tom Sawyer in *Huckleberry Finn*." *Miss Quart*, 27 (Winter 1973-74), 33-39.
   Tom's sinister spirit pervades the novel; he is an enemy of the freedom and moral maturity toward which Huck is journeying; the controversial Phelps episode is appropriate because it demonstrates the failures of Tom's imagination.

Geismar, Maxwell. *Mark Twain: An American Prophet*. Boston: Houghton Mifflin, 1970.
   A study of Twain's literary career using autobiographical material to clarify meaning in the work.

_____. "Mark Twain on U. S. Imperialism, Racism and Other Enduring Characteristics of the Republic." *Ramparts*, 6 (May 1968), 65-71.
   Deals with Twain's essays on these subjects as "the fateful meeting of the man and his time."

_____, ed. *Mark Twain and the Three R's*. Indianapolis: Bobbs-Merrill, 1971.
   An anthology of Twain's radical social commentary dealing with race, religion, revolution, and related matters.

Gerber, John C. "Practical Editions: Mark Twain's *The Adventures of Tom Sawyer* and *Adventures of Huckleberry Finn*." *Proof*, 2 (1972), 285-292.
   Deals with the extent to which modern paperback editions of these works deviate from what Twain intended because they are based on editions which also deviate.

_____. "*Pudd'nhead Wilson* as Fabulation." *Stud in Am Humor*, 2 (April 1975), 21-31.
   Believes that the reason critics are baffled by the novel is that they treat it as a work of realism, whereas it is really in the tradition of fabulations.

_____, ed. *Studies in Huckleberry Finn*. Columbus, Ohio: Charles E. Merrill, 1971.
   Reprints five early reviews and eleven critical statements on the novel, 1913-1968.

Gervais, Ronald J. "*The Mysterious Stranger*: The Fall as Salvation." *Pacific Coast Phil*, 5 (1970), 24-33.
   Philip Traum is "an innocent devil" coming "to an already fallen world" to offer "the salvation of complete knowledge...."

Gibson, Donald B. "Mark Twain's Jim in the Classroom." *EJ*, 57 (February 1968), 196-199, 202.
   Twain was not able to overcome his limitations of background and could not resist the temptation to evoke laughter though compromising his morality and his art.

Gibson, William M., ed. *Mark Twain's Mysterious Stranger Manuscripts*. Berkeley: Univ of California Press, 1969.
   Presents for the first time the three unfinished manuscripts of *The Mysterious Stranger*, upon which Paine based his bowdlerized edition (1916), with a historical introduction, textual appendix, and editorial commentary.

_____. "Mark Twain's *Mysterious Stranger Manuscripts*: Some Questions for Textual Critics." *Rocky Mt. MLA Bul*, 22 (1968), 183-191.
   Discusses the various kinds of questions raised by the manuscripts.

Glick, Wendell. "The Epistemological Theme of *The Mysterious Stranger*," in R. B. Browne and Donald Pizer, eds., *Themes and Directions in American Literature*. Lafayette, Indiana: Purdue Univ Studies, 1969, pp. 130-147.
   Argues that Twain's theme is "the ubiquitous twentieth century idea of the breakdown of epistemological certainty."

III. Postbellum (1865-1920)

Goad, Mary Ellen. "The Image and the Woman in the Life and Writings of Mark Twain." *Emporia State Research Stud*, 19 (March 1971), 5-70.
Deals with Twain's relationships with his mother, his friend Mrs. Fairbanks, and his wife.

Gogol, J. M. "Nikolai Aseev and Mark Twain." *MTJ*, 16 (Summer 1973), 15-16.
Contains a translation of a poem by Aseev dealing with Twain's influence on Russian literature.

Goldstien, Neal L. "Mark Twain's Money Problem." *BuR*, 19 (Spring 1971), 37-54.
Twain's life and his writings reveal a preoccupation with and an ambivalent attitude toward money. His inability to resolve the split between money and idealism is explored, with particular attention to *Roughing It* and *A Connecticut Yankee*.

Goodyear, Russell H. "Huck Finn's Anachronistic Double Eagles." *Am N&Q*, 10 (November 1971), 39.
These golden coins were not issued until 1850, five to fifteen years after the date Twain sets for *Huckleberry Finn*.

Gordon, Caroline. "The Shape of the River." *Mich Quart Rev*, 12 (Winter 1973), 1-10.
A lecture given at the University of Michigan; deals with the river as metaphor for human conduct in Dante and Twain.

Gottfried, Leon. "The Odyssey as Form: An Exploratory Essay," in *Essays on European Literature in Honor of Liselotte Dieckmann*, ed. Peter U. Hohendahl, et al. St. Louis, Mo.: Washington Univ Press, 1972.
Includes discussion of *Huckleberry Finn*.

Goudie, Andrea. "'What Fools These Mortals Be!' A Puckish Interpretation of Mark Twain's Narrative Stance." *Kansas Quart*, 5, no. 4 (1973), 19-31.
As humorist Twain frequently took the distanced stance of a Puck observing human beings.

Graves, Wallace. "Mark Twain's 'Burning Shame.'" *NCF*, 23 (June 1968), 93-98.
Twain originally intended "The Royal Nonesuch" episode in *Huckleberry Finn* to be patterned after "The Burning Shame," an obscene story that he had heard.

Gregory, Ralph. "John A. Quarles: Mark Twain's Ideal Man." *Missouri Hist Soc Bul*, 25 (April 1969), 229-235.
Deals with the influence of his uncle on Mark Twain.

Grenander, M. E. "Mark Twain's English Lectures and George Routledge & Sons." *MTJ*, 17 (Summer 1975), 1-4.
Transcriptions and commentary on Twain's relationship with publishers in the 1870's.

Gribben, Alan. "The Dispersal of Samuel L. Clemens' Library Books." *RALS*, 5 (Autumn 1975), 147-165.
Deals with what happened to the books in Twain's library.

_____. "Mark Twain, Phrenology and the 'Temperments': A Study of Pseudoscientific Influence." *AQ*, 24 (March 1972), 45-68.
Explores Clemens' attitudes toward phrenology.

Griffith, Clark. "Merlin's Grin: From 'Tom' to 'Huck' in *A Connecticut Yankee*." *NEQ*, 48 (March 1975), 28-46.
The author studies the ways in which Twain employs Merlin as a character in the novel.

Haight, A. L. See GENERAL.

Hakac, John. "*Huckleberry Finn*: A Copy Inscribed in 1903." *Am Bk Collector*, 20 (January 1970), 7-9.
An inscription points to Twain's "likening one of his books to a bottle of whiskey."

Hansen, Arlen J. See GENERAL.

Hansen, Chadwick. "The Once and Future Boss: Mark Twain's Yankee." *NCF*, 28 (June 1973), 62-73.
The character of the Yankee, Hank Morgan, "lies at the heart of *A Connecticut Yankee in King Arthur's Court* and gives to that novel a terrible and inexorable power."

Hanson, R. Galen. "Bluejays and Man: Twain's Exercise in Understanding." *MTJ*, 17 (Winter 1973-74), 18-19.
In "What Stumped the Bluejays" Twain is using the bluejays to satirize "human collective behavior."

Harkey, Joseph H. "When Huck Finn Smouched That Spoon." *MTJ*, 15 (Summer 1970), 14.
Deals with meanings of "smouch."

Harrell, Don W. "A Chaser of Phantoms: Mark Twain and Romanticism." *Midwest Quart*, 13 (Winter 1972), 201-212.
Deals with images in Twain's works which suggest a desire to escape reality.

_____. "Mark Twain's *Joan of Arc*: Fact or Fiction?" *MarkR*, 4 (October 1975), 95-97.
"...when fiction becomes a matter of entering an even worse fire than reality, the result is a frustrated effort, born of grief, neither history nor entirely fiction--that is, *Joan of Arc*."

Harris, Helen L. "Mark Twain's Response to the Native American." *AL*, 46 (January 1975), 495-505.
Twain's works reveal a hostile attitude toward Indians. Though the notebook entries of his later years indicate that he was more aware that injustice had been done to the Indians, his public "silence...gave consent to that injustice."

Harrison, Stanley R. "Mark Twain's Requiem for the Past." *MTJ*, 16 (Summer 1972), 3-10.
Twain's development as man and author paralleled the maturing of the nation.

Hart, John E. "Heroes and Houses: The Progress of Huck Finn." *MFS*, 14 (Spring 1968), 39-46.
In *Huckleberry Finn* houses, "including sheds and rafts, huts and mansions, and sometimes rows

of houses," symbolize "civilization, a container of ambiguities," and "serve to identify the steps and progress of the hero in his quest and adventures."

Hasley, Louis. "The Durable Humor of Bill Nye." *MTJ*, 15 (Winter 1970–71), 7–10.
Includes discussion of parallels between the lives of Nye and Clemens and mention of their several meetings with each other.

Hauck, Richard B. See GENERAL.

Henderson, Harry B., III. See GENERAL.

Hilfer, Anthony C. See MISCELLANEOUS (Contemporary).

Hill, Hamlin. "Mark Twain and His Enemies." *SouR*, 4 (Spring 1968), 520–529.
An essay-review of several books, mostly devoted to Clemens' poses and to his relations with Bret Harte and Matthew Arnold.

_____. *Mark Twain: God's Fool*. New York: Harper & Row, 1973.
A biographical narrative of Clemens' last ten years with extensive quotation from letters and family papers.

_____. "Who Killed Mark Twain?" *Am Lit Realism*, 7 (Spring 1974), 119–124.
A survey of Twain scholarship and criticism, with indications of areas in which more work is still needed.

_____, and Walter Blair, eds. *The Art of Huckleberry Finn*. San Francisco: Chandler, 1969.
A revision of the 1962 casebook, with five essays added.

Hoffman, Michael J. "Huck's Ironic Circle." *GaR*, 23 (Fall 1969), 307–322.
Never rejecting society's standards, Huck must return to Tom's world.

Hook, Andrew. "Huckleberry Finn and Scotland." *Eng Record*, 21 (December 1970), 8–14.
Readers in Scotland respond to Huck's language and his religion.

Hough, Robert L. "Twain's Double-dating in *A Connecticut Yankee*." *N&Q*, 15 (November 1968), 424–425.
Analyzes Twain's deceptive use of dates to achieve suspense before the "eclipse" scene.

Howe, Irving. See GENERAL.

Howell, Elmo. "Huckleberry Finn in Mississippi." *La Stud*, 7 (Summer 1968), 167–172.
The setting for the end of *Huckleberry Finn* may be in Mississippi.

_____. "In Defense of Tom Sawyer." *MTJ*, 15 (Winter 1970), 17–19.
"Tom was for Mark Twain the general incarnation of a vanished world."

_____. "Mark Twain and the Civil War." *BSUF*, 13 (1972), 53–61.
Concludes that Twain's desertion from Marion's Raiders "laid the foundation for misanthropy and dissociation in his last years."

_____. "Mark Twain's Indiantown." *MTJ*, 15 (Summer 1971), 16–19.
Conjectures that Mark Twain may possibly have used Napoleon, Arkansas, as a model for Indiantown, a town in unfinished works.

_____. "Tom Sawyer's Mock Funeral: A Note on Mark Twain's Religion." *MTJ*, 16 (Winter 1972), 15–16.
At heart Mark Twain accepted the "old verities" of his culture, showing in Tom's "funeral" solidarity of community life.

_____. "Uncle John Quarles' Watermelon Patch." *Midwest Quart*, 9 (Spring 1968), 271–282.
Mark Twain drew heavily on memories of his visits to his uncle's farm.

_____. "Uncle Silas Phelps: A Note on Mark Twain's Characterization." *MTJ*, 14 (Summer 1968), 8–12.
Maintains that Mark Twain's portrait of Uncle Silas is his finest of a good man.

Hubbell, Jay B. See GENERAL.

Illiano, Antonio. "'Italian Without a Master': A Note for the Appreciation of Mark Twain's Undictionarial Translation as Exercise in Humor." *MTJ*, 17 (Summer 1974), 17–20.
Compares literal translations from Italian newspapers with Twain's humorous ones.

Jager, Ronald B. "Mark Twain and the Robber Barons: A View of the Gilded Age Businessman." *MTJ*, 17 (Winter 1974–75), 8–11.
Twain both excoriated and admired the uncertainty and excitement of business tycoons.

James, Stuart B. "The Politics of Personal Salvation: The American Literary Record." *Denver Quart*, 4 (Summer 1969), 19–45.
Huck Finn is among heroes of American novels who represent Tocquevillian and Turnerian individualism, a matter of feeling, not thinking.

Johnson, Ellwood. "Mark Twain's Dream Self in the Nightmare of History." *MTJ*, 15 (Winter 1970), 6–12.
The Mysterious Stranger is an example of Emersonian ideational determinism.

Jones, Joseph. "Mark Twain's *Connecticut Yankee* and Australian Nationalism." *AL*, 40 (May 1968), 227–231.
The favorable reception of *A Connecticut Yankee* is described from a contemporary review in the Sidney *Bulletin*.

Justus, James H. See GENERAL.

Kahn, Sholom, Jr. "Mark Twain as American Rabelais." *Hebrew Univ Stud in Lit*, 1 (1973), 47–75.
Points out Rabelaisian techniques in Twain's works.

Kaplan, Harold. See GENERAL.

III. POSTBELLUM (1865-1920)

Kaplan, Justin. "Introduction," *A Connecticut Yankee in King Arthur's Court*. Baltimore: Penguin, 1971.
    Summarizes biographical and philosophical backgrounds. Text of the novel follows the first English edition of December 6, 1889.

_____. *Mark Twain and His World*. New York: Simon & Schuster, 1974.
    A biography with copious illustrations, paintings, photographs, and sketches of the world that Mark Twain knew and the people who figured in his life.

_____. "On Mark Twain: 'Never Quite Sane in the Night.'" *PsyR*, 56, no. 1 (1969), 113-127.
    A reprinting of Chapter 16 of Kaplan's *Mr. Clemens and Mr. Twain*.

Kapoor, S. D. "Tradition and Innovation in *Huckleberry Finn*." *Mod Rev*, no. 762 (June 1970), 409-413.
    Deals with Twain's representation of contemporary reality.

Karpowitz, Steven. "Tom Sawyer and Mark Twain: Fictional Women and Real in the *Play* of Conscience with the Imagination." *Lit and Psych*, 23, no. 1 (1973), 5-12.
    Twain's unconscious feelings toward women find expression in *Tom Sawyer*.

Katz, Joseph. See GENERAL.

Kegel, Paul L. "Henry Adams and Mark Twain: Two Views of Medievalism." *MTJ*, 15 (Winter 1970-71), 11-21.
    Deals with similarities in Adams' *Mont-Saint-Michel and Chartres* and Twain's *The Prince and the Pauper* and *A Connecticut Yankee* and with differences in purposes and methods in these works.

Kerr, Howard. *Mediums, and Spirit-Rappers, and Roaring Radicals: Spiritualism in American Literature, 1850-1900*. Urbana: Univ of Illinois Press, 1972.
    The influence of the cult of spiritualism on a number of writers, including Twain, is discussed.

Kesterson, D. B., ed. *Critics on Mark Twain*. Coral Gables, Fla.: Univ of Miami Press, 1973.
    Reprints forty-four critical excerpts, essays, and appreciations on Twain's fiction, 1882-1971, with a chronology and selected bibliography.

Ketterer, David. "Epoch-Eclipse and Apocalypse: Special 'Effects' in *A Connecticut Yankee*." *PMLA*, 88 (October 1973), 1104-1114.
    The eclipse and related imagery signify that the sixth-century and nineteenth-century worlds are identical.

_____. See GENERAL.

Kimball, William J. "Samuel Clemens as a Confederate Soldier: Some Observations About 'The Private History of a Campaign That Failed.'" *Stud SF*, 5 (Summer 1968), 382-384.

    A note relating biographical data to Mark Twain's handling of events and attitudes in "The Private History."

Kinghorn, Norton D. "E. W. Kemble's Misplaced Modifier: A Note on the Illustrations for *Huckleberry Finn*." *MTJ*, 16 (Summer 1973), 9-11.
    On Kemble's illustration reflecting the modifier Huck misplaced when he referred to an "ancestor with a wooden handle."

Kiralis, Karl. "Two More Recently Discovered Letters by S. L. Clemens." *MTJ*, 16 (Summer 1973), 18-20.
    Prints the two letters.

_____. "Two Recently Discovered Letters by Mark Twain." *MTJ*, 15 (Winter 1970-71), 1-5.
    Letters in which Twain denies writing a review of Kate Field's performance in *The Gilded Age*.

Kirkham, Bruce. "Huck and Hamlet...." *MTJ*, 14 (Summer 1969), 17-19.
    Deals with the Shakespearean sources of the quotations Huck uses.

Klass, Philip. "An Innocent in Time: Mark Twain in King Arthur's Court." *Extrap*, 16 (1974), 17-32.
    Discusses *A Connecticut Yankee* as a significant first in areas which concern today's science fiction.

Kolb, Harold H., Jr. *The Illusion of Life: American Realism as a Literary Form*. Charlottesville: Univ Press of Virginia, 1969.
    Examines the contributions of James, Howells, and Twain to the developing realism of the mid-1880's.

Kolin, Philip C. "Mark Twain, Aristotle, and *Pudd'nhead Wilson*." *MTJ*, 15 (Summer 1970), 1-4.
    Deals with the ways *Pudd'nhead* resembles Aristotelian tragedy.

_____. "Mark Twain's *Pudd'nhead Wilson*--A Selected Checklist." *BB*, 28 (April-June 1971), 58-59.
    An unannotated listing of criticism of the novel.

Kraus, W. Keith. "Mark Twain's 'A Double-Barreled Detective Story': A Source for the Solitary Oesophagus." *MTJ*, 16 (Summer 1972), 10-12.
    Suggests that the source is Doyle's "A Study in Scarlet."

_____. "Huckleberry Finn: A Final Irony." *MTJ*, 14 (Winter 1967-68), 18-19.
    Suggests that the second set of Wilks brothers are imposters.

Krause, Sydney J. "The Pearl and 'Hadleyburg': From Desire to Renunciation." *Steinbeck Quart*, 7 (1974), 3-18.
    Deals with similarities in the treatment of greed in the two stories.

_____. "Steinbeck and Mark Twain." *Steinbeck Quart*, 6 (Fall 1973), 104-111.
    Points out similarities in background, tastes, and philosophy of the two writers.

Krauth, Leland. "Mark Twain: At Home in the Gilded Age." *GaR*, 28 (Spring 1974), 105-113.
  Twain's move from west to east was a continuation of his search for better "prospecting"; however, "he was still hunting for the same things," among them his "dream of family."

Kronenberger, Louis, and E. M. Beck. See GENERAL.

Kuhlmann, Susan. See GENERAL.

Lang, Hans J. See GENERAL.

Leary, Lewis. "The Bankruptcy of Mark Twain." *Carrell*, 9 (1968), 13-20.
  In dealing with Henry Huttleston Rogers and other tycoons, Twain "exchanged moral for financial bankruptcy."

_____. "Mark Twain Did Not Sleep Here: Tarrytown, 1902-1904." *MTJ*, 17 (Summer 1974), 13-16.
  Protest over tax-assessment and poor health in his family prevented occupancy of the Casey estate bought by Twain.

_____. "Mark Twain Himself." *SR*, 83 (Fall 1975), 708-713.
  An informal review of Mark Twain's *Notebooks and Journals*, Vol. I, 1855-1873, Vol. II, 1877-1883, and of Arthur G. Pettit's *Mark Twain and the South*.

_____, ed. *Mark Twain's Correspondence with Henry Huttleston Rogers*. Berkeley: Univ of California Press, 1969.
  An annotated collection of 464 letters exchanged from 1893 to 1909 between Twain and the millionaire Standard Oil executive and financier who served as the author's friend and business consultant, with historical introductions and editorial appendices.

_____. "More Letters from the *Quaker City*." *AL*, 42 (May 1970), 197-202.
  Publishes three letters from one of the owners of the *Quaker City* concerning the voyage when Twain was on board.

_____. "On Writing About Writers: Mark Twain and Howells." *SouR*, 4 (Spring 1968), 551-557.
  An essay-review principally of James M. Cox's *Mark Twain: The Fate of Humor*, including discussion of Mark Twain as an "invented voice" and "costumed presence."

_____. "Troubles with Mark Twain: Some Considerations on Consistency." *Stud in Am F*, 2 (Spring 1974), 89-103.
  Concerns textual problems in *Innocents Abroad* and *Huckleberry Finn*.

_____. See GENERAL--1st Leary entry.

Lee, L. L. "Mark Twain's Assayer: Some Other Versions." *MarkR*, 4 (May 1974), 47-48.
  Discusses a version of the assaying episode in Chapter 36 of *Roughing It* in Mormon folklore, and an "inept plagiarism" of Twain's telling of the story.

Lehan, Richard. "Recent Books: American Fiction." *NCF*, 25 (March 1971), 502-508.
  A review of *Mark Twain's Mysterious Stranger Manuscripts*, ed. William M. Gibson.

Lewis, Stuart A. "Pudd'nhead Wilson's Election." *MTJ*, 15 (Winter 1970), 21.
  Pudd'nhead Wilson's election is amply justified in the Ur-story, "Those Extraordinary Twins." Twain's carelessness allowed it to remain in the revised work.

_____. "Twain's *Huckleberry Finn*, Chapter XIV." *Expl*, 30 (March 1972), Item 61.
  Believes that Jim's wisdom is superior to Huck's.

Libman, Valentina. See GENERAL.

Light, Martin. "Sweeping Out Chivalric Silliness: The Example of *Huck Finn* and *The Sun Also Rises*." *MTJ*, 17 (Winter 1974-75), 18-21.
  Three quixotic elements of these works being satirized are reading idealistic literature, adventuring, and attraction to enchantments.

Lindborg, Henry J. "A Cosmic Tramp: Samuel Clemens's *Three Thousand Years Among the Microbes*." *AL*, 44 (January 1973), 652-657.
  Notes some of the philosophical influences on this work.

Livingston, James L. "Names in Mark Twain's *The Mysterious Stranger*." *Am N&Q*, 12 (March 1974), 108-109.
  On the meaning and symbolic significance of names in this work.

Lloyd, James B. "The Nature of Mark Twain's Attack on Sentimentality in *The Adventures of Huckleberry Finn*." *Univ of Miss Stud in English*, 13 (1972), 59-63.
  The criers in this story weep correctly, hypocritically, or sentimentally.

Lohner, Edgar. See GENERAL.

Long, Timothy. "Mark Twain's Speeches on Billiards." *MTJ*, 17 (Summer 1974), 1-3.
  On the relationship between the two accounts of Twain's 1906 billiard tournament speeches.

Lorch, Fred W. *The Trouble Begins at Eight: Mark Twain's Lecture Tours*. Ames: Iowa State Univ Press, 1968.
  Deals with Mark Twain's career on the lecture circuit, with five of his lectures.

Lowery, Robert E. "The Grangerford-Shepherdson Episode: Another of Mark Twain's Indictments of the Damned Human Race." *MTJ*, 15 (Winter 1970), 19-21.
  Grangerford and Shepherdson are symbolic names giving the significance to the universal struggle between settled farmer and nomad.

Lycette, Ronald. "Mark Twain Mapping His Territory." *ETC*, 29 (1972), 155-164.
  On the significance of "Twain's self-evaluation of his own educational development" in "Old Times on the Mississippi."

III. Postbellum (1865-1920)

Manierre, William R. "Huck Finn, Empiricist Member of Society." *MFS*, 14 (Spring 1968), 57-66.
A study of the first four chapters of the novel.

_____. "On Keeping the Raftsmen's Passage in *Huckleberry Finn*." *Eng Lang Notes*, 6 (December 1968), 118-122.
Twain would have improved the artistic structure of the book if he had left the passage in.

Mann, Carolyn. "Innocence in *Pudd'nhead Wilson*." *MTJ*, 14 (Winter 1968-69), 18-21, 11.
Though Twain "finds the human race despicable...he is searching for a way to interpret the evidence so that man will be 'not guilty.'"

"Mark Twain to Chatto & Windus." *CEAAN*, 3 (1970), 1-2.
Two letters complaining about copy editing and proofreading of the English edition of *Following the Equator*.

"Mark Twain's Last Manuscript." *Bancroftiana*, 55 (June 1973), 9.
Description of the manuscript of a portion of Twain's autobiography in the form of a letter to Howells.

Martin, Jay. "Mark Twain: The Fate of Primitivity." *So Lit Jour*, 2 (Fall 1969), 123-137.
An essay-review of *Mark Twain's Hannibal, Huck & Tom; Mark Twain's Mysterious Stranger Manuscripts; Mark Twain's Correspondence with Henry Huttleston Rogers 1893-1909; Mark Twain at Large;* and *Mark Twain and the Bible*. The reviewer concludes that these volumes offer the "exciting possibility that we may yet have a biography of the whole man."

Marx, Leo. "'Noble Shit': The Uncivil Response of American Writers to Civil Religion in America." *Mass Rev*, 14 (Autumn 1973), 709-739.
Part of the article deals with Twain and his use of the vernacular "to deflate overblown values."

Mattson, J. Stanley. "Mark Twain on War and Peace: The Missouri Rebel and 'The Campaign That Failed.'" *AQ*, 20 (Winter 1968), 783-794.
Though one cannot demonstrate that Twain was a pacifist, his views expressed in this work, that man and war are incompatible, are sincere.

Mauranges, J.-P. "Aliénation et Châtiment chez Mark Twain et Heinrich Böll." *RLV*, 39 (1973), 131-136.
Discusses similarities and differences in the treatment of the theme of an alienated society in Twain's "The Man That Corrupted Hadleyburg" and Böll's "Der Bahnhof von Zimpren."

May, John R. "The Gospel According to Philip Traum: Structural Unity in 'The Mysterious Stranger.'" *Stud SF*, 8 (Summer 1971), 411-422.
"The structural unity of 'The Mysterious Stranger' develops out of Philip Traum's mission of salvation to Theodor Fischer."

_____. See GENERAL.

Mayberry, George. "Huckleberry Finn Enriched." *Nation*, 207 (August 26, 1968), 154-157.
An evaluation of paperback editions of *Huckleberry Finn*.

Maynard, Reid. "Mark Twain's Ambivalent Yankee." *MTJ*, 14 (Winter 1968-69), 1-5.
Discusses three critical approaches to *A Connecticut Yankee* and approves the one that finds Twain's attitudes ambivalent.

McCarthy, Harold T. "Mark Twain's Pilgrim's Progress: *The Innocents Abroad*." *ArQ*, 26 (Autumn 1970), 249-258.
Traces Twain's increasing disillusionment with the Holy Land and the effect it had in moving Twain "closer to the memory of Hannibal and the river...the richest source of his creative process."

_____. See GENERAL.

McCullough, Joseph B. "A Listing of Mark Twain's Contributions to the Buffalo *Express*, 1869-1871." *Am Lit Realism*, 5 (Winter 1972), 61-70.
Clemens' contributions are divided into five categories--sketches, sketches and poems signed Carl Byng, editorials, people and things, and miscellaneous.

_____. "Mark Twain and Journalistic Humor Today." *EJ*, 60 (May 1971), 591-595.
Like Twain, contemporary American writers "mingle what humor they can find in the human situation with the terror and violence of the world."

_____. "Mark Twain and the Hy Slocum-Carl Byng Controversy." *AL*, 43 (March 1971), 42-59.
Discusses the probability that Slocum and Byng were pseudonyms used by Clemens during his tenure on the Buffalo *Express*.

McDermott, John F. "Mark Twain and the Bible." *Papers on Lit and Lang*, 4 (Spring 1968), 195-198.
Prints a letter in which Twain acknowledged that he had made up phony quotations from the Bible.

McElrath, Joseph R., Jr. "Mark Twain's America and the Protestant Work Ethic." *CEA Critic*, 36 (March 1974), 42-43.
An analysis of a passage from *A Connecticut Yankee*.

McIntyre, James P. "Three Practical Jokes: A Key to Huck's Changing Attitude Toward Jim." *MFS*, 14 (Spring 1968), 33-37.
"One of the most important thematic movements in the novel is Jim's emergence--in Huck's eyes-- out of the abstract to the concrete."

McKee, John D. "*Roughing It* as Retrospective Reporting." *WAL*, 5 (Summer 1970), 113-119.
Unlike contemporary journalism, Twain's reporting transcends facts and includes elements of his personality and his opinions in his humorous portrait of the West.

McMahan, Elizabeth E. "The Money Motif: Economic Implications in *Huckleberry Finn*." *MTJ*, 15 (Summer 1971), 5-10.
   The role of money in the novel helps to reveal Twain's attitudes towards Western civilization.

Mendelsohn, Edward. "Mark Twain Confronts the Shakespeareans." *MTJ*, 17 (Winter 1973-74), 20-21.
   Is Shakespeare Dead? was not so much an advocacy of Bacon as Shakespeare as it was a means of "exposing the superficiality of the Shakespeareans."

Mews, Siegfried. "Foreign Literature in German Magazines, 1870-1890." *YCGL*, 18 (1969), 36-47.
   Clemens was among the writers whose works were printed in German periodicals during this period.

_____. "German Reception of American Writers in the Late Nineteenth Century." *SAB*, 34 (March 1969), 7-9.
   Twain was among several writers who were very popular in Germany during this period.

Meyer, Horst E. "An Unnoticed Twain Letter." *MTJ*, 16 (Winter 1972), back cover.
   Reproduces Twain's first letter to his German publisher.

Miller, Bruce E. "*Huckleberry Finn*: The Kierkegaardian Dimension." *Illinois Quart*, 34 (September 1971), 55-64.
   Huck is Kierkegaardian in his retreat from society to seek another "communion."

Miller, J. Hillis. "Three Problems of Fictional Form: First Person Narration in *David Copperfield* and *Huckleberry Finn*," in *Experience in the Novel: Selected Papers from the English Institute*, ed. Roy Harvey Pearce. New York: Columbia Univ Press, 1968.
   When Huck can no longer use the language of the raft, he has left only two choices--the language of the "shore" or no language at all.

Miller, Leo. "Huckleberries and Humans." *PMLA*, 87 (March 1972), 314.
   Suggests that Twain may have decided to change Colonel Sellers' first name from Eschol to Mulberry because Eschol means "a bunch of grapes."

Miller, Ruth. "But Laugh or Die: A Comparison of *The Mysterious Stranger* and *Billy Budd*." *Lit Half-Yearly*, 11, no. 1 (1970), 25-29.
   Ultimately, *The Mysterious Stranger* says that the only way to deal with human ills is to laugh, not despair.

Miller, Theodore C. See WASHINGTON, BOOKER T. (Postbellum).

Miller, William C. "Samuel L. and Orion Clemens vs. Mark Twain and His Biographers (1861-1862)." *MTJ*, 16 (Summer 1973), 1-9.
   Seeks to correct biographical facts in *Roughing It*.

Millichap, Joseph R. "Calvinistic Attitudes and Pauline Imagery in *The Adventures of Huckleberry Finn*." *MTJ*, 16 (Winter 1971-72), 8-10.
   An attempt to clarify through the imagery "the puzzling ambiguity" of the novel's conclusion.

Mills, Nicolaus. *American and English Fiction in the Nineteenth Century: An Antigenre Critique and Comparison*. Bloomington: Indiana Univ Press, 1973.
   An attack on the theory that American fiction of the nineteenth century was romantic includes discussion of *Huckleberry Finn* and comparison of Huck and Pip in Dickens' *Great Expectations*.

_____. "Prison and Society in Nineteenth-Century American Fiction." *WHR*, 24 (Autumn 1970), 325-331.
   Deals with nineteenth-century novelists who viewed America and its society as a prison. Treats *Huckleberry Finn* briefly.

_____. "Social and Moral Vision in *Great Expectations* and *Huckleberry Finn*." *Jour Am Stud*, 4 (July 1970), 61-72.
   Comparison "clarifies the way Dickens's and Twain's moral vision shapes their writing and understanding of Victorian England and the ante-bellum South."

Mixon, Wayne. "Mark Twain, *The Gilded Age*, and the New South Movement." *SHR*, 7 (Fall 1973), 403-409.
   In *The Gilded Age*, Twain "administered a badly needed corrective to the unwarranted optimism of the burgeoning New South movement."

Monteiro, George. "New Mark Twain Letters." *MTJ*, 17 (Summer 1974), 9-10.
   Letters to the publishers of the *Atlantic Monthly*.

_____. "'Such as Mother Used to Make': An Addition to the Mark Twain Canon." *PBSA*, 67 (4th Qtr. 1973), 450-452.
   On a contribution Mark Twain made to the "Contributor's Club" in the *Atlantic Monthly*.

Morsberger, Robert E. "Pap Finn and the Bishop's Candlesticks: Victor Hugo in Hannibal." *CEA Critic*, 21 (April 1969), 17.
   Les Misérables is suggested as a source for Twain's burlesquing of Romanticism.

Mott, Bertram, Jr. "Twain's *Joan*: A Divine Anomaly." *EA*, 23 (July-September 1970), 245-255.
   Concludes that Twain was unable to respond to the divine.

Moyne, Ernest J. "Mark Twain and Baroness Alexandra Gripenberg." *AL*, 45 (November 1973), 370-378.
   Charts the details, and later literary consequences, of a meeting between Twain and Baroness Gripenberg, a Finnish author and a leader in Finland's woman suffrage and temperance movements.

Mulqueen, James E. "Huck Finn, Imagist Poet." *CEA Critic*, 37 (March 1975), 14-15.

Believes that Twain anticipated the Imagist movement in poetry.

Myers, Margaret. "Mark Twain and Melville." *MTJ*, 14 (Summer 1968), 5-8.
    Characterizes Twain's progression from nostalgia to disillusionment and Melville's progression from rebellion to submission as the loss of each writer's early dream.

Nagel, James. "*Huck Finn* and 'The Bear': The Wilderness and Moral Freedom." *Eng Stud in Africa*, 12 (March 1969), 59-63.
    Both Twain and Faulkner possess "the central poetic insight that American freedom should be moral as well as political, psychological as well as physical."

Nebeker, Helen E. "The Great Corrupter or Satan Rehabilitated." *Stud SF*, 8 (Fall 1971), 635-637.
    Satan is not the Corrupter in "The Man That Corrupted Hadleyburg"; rather, in the Calvinist ethos which Twain knew and detested, God is the Great Corrupter because He condemned man to his fallen nature.

Nibbelink, Herman. "Mark Twain and the Mormons." *MTJ*, 17 (Winter 1973-74), 1-5.
    Deals with the techniques Twain uses in poking fun at the Mormons.

Odessky, Marjory H. "The Impartial Friend: The Death of Mark Twain." *Jour of Hist Stud*, 2 (1969), 156-160.
    A factual account.

Orth, Michael. "*Pudd'nhead Wilson* Reconsidered or The Octoroon in the Villa Viviani." *MTJ*, 14 (Summer 1969), 11-15.
    Suggests that a source for *Pudd'nhead Wilson* is Mayne Reid's *The Quadroon; or, a Lover's Adventures in Louisiana*.

Ostrom, Alan. "Huck Finn and the Modern Ethos." *Centennial Rev*, 16, no. 2 (1972), 162-179.
    Deals with Huck's struggle between the individual and the social worlds.

Park, Martha M. "Mark Twain's Hadleyburg: A House Built on Sand." *CLA Jour*, 16 (June 1973), 508-513.
    Hadleyburg, like the house in the parable, was ruined because the foundation was not deep enough.

Parker, Hershel. "Three Mark Twain Editions." *NCF*, 28 (September 1973), 225-229.
    Review of *Mark Twain's Fables of Man*, ed. John S. Tuckey (textual editors, Kenneth M. Sanderson and Bernard L. Stein); the Iowa Center for Textual Studies edition of *Roughing It*; and (briefly) of the Bancroft Library edition of *The Great Landslide Case*.

Parsons, Coleman O. "Down the Mighty River with Mark Twain." *Miss Quart*, 22 (Winter 1968-69), 1-18.
    Discusses Twain's trip to gather material for *Life on the Mississippi*.

Patrick, Walton R. Untitled. *SHR*, 3 (Summer 1969), 293-295.
    An essay-review of Edward Wagenknecht's *Mark Twain: The Man and His Work* (1967) and James M. Cox's *Mark Twain: The Fate of Humor* (1966).

Pauly, Thomas H. "Directed Readings: The Contents Tables in *Adventures of Huckleberry Finn*." *Proof*, 3 (1973), 63-68.
    Twain did not write the Table of Contents to the novel; thus, the chapter summaries in the Table of Contents may not accurately reflect Twain's intentions.

_____. "The 'Science of Piloting' in Twain's 'Old Time': The Cub's Lesson on Industrialization." *ArQ*, 30 (Autumn 1974), 229-238.
    "Old Times on the Mississippi" reaches beyond the Cub's initiation to a larger consideration of the science of piloting and ultimately to Twain's artistic intentions; thus, it stands as an impressive literary accomplishment in its own right.

Pearce, Roy H. "Huck Finn in His History." *EA*, 24 (1971), 283-291.
    Huck "gains no sense of his own history and has no future"; he is just a passive observer.

Perkins, George. See GENERAL.

Pettit, Arthur G. "Mark Twain and the Negro, 1867-1869." *JNH*, 56 (April 1971), 88-96.
    Twain's use of the Negro for humorous purposes before 1867 changes to a more liberal attitude.

_____. *Mark Twain and the South*. Lexington: Univ Press of Kentucky, 1974.
    An analysis of Mark Twain's changing attitude towards the South and the black man.

_____. "Mark Twain, the Blood-Feud and the South." *So Lit Jour*, 4 (Fall 1971), 20-32.
    There are two Souths in Twain's literary imagination, one of nostalgia, the other of nausea and nightmare.

Pochmann, Henry A., and Gay Wilson Allen. See GENERAL.

Powers, Lyall. "The Sweet Success of Twain's Tom." *Dal Rev*, 53 (Summer 1973), 310-324.
    Argues that *The Adventures of Tom Sawyer* is "rigorously informed," formally organized through three principal narrative themes and three major motifs.

Prince, Gilbert. "Mark Twain's 'A Fable': The Teacher as Jackass." *MTJ*, 17 (Winter 1974-75), 7.
    The story satirizes the concept that the teacher should act as interpreter of experience.

Rachal, John. "David Wilson and Sam Clemens: The Public Image Vs. the Private Man." *Am N&Q*, 13 (September 1974), 6-8.
    Pudd'nhead's public image conflicted with the private cynicism of his Calendar; there was a similar dichotomy in Twain.

_____. "Scotty Briggs and the Minister: An Idea from Hooper's *Simon Suggs*?" *MTJ*, 17 (Summer 1974), 10–11.
  The gambling jargon is similar in *Roughing It* and "Simon Plays the Snatch Game."

Rackham, Jeff. "The Mysterious Stranger in 'The Campaign That Failed.'" *SHR*, 5 (Winter 1971), 63–67.
  By artistically re-creating the "facts" of his life and inserting the incident of the murdered stranger in this essay, "not only was Twain creating a modern anti-hero ten years before Stephen Crane's *Red Badge of Courage*, he was subtly injecting a critical condemnation of war" into an age which still looked back romantically upon the Civil War.

Reed, Kenneth T. "Mirth and Misquotation: Mark Twain in Petoskey, Michigan." *MTJ*, 15 (Summer 1970), 19–20.
  Deals with Twain's denial of a false story that he had attacked a man planning to start a volunteer newspaper.

Rees, Robert A. "*Captain Stormfield's Visit to Heaven* and *The Gates Ajar*." *Eng Lang Notes*, 7 (March 1970), 197–202.
  Contrary to the view expressed in Franklin E. Rogers' *Mark Twain's Satires and Burlesques* (1967), Twain not only satirized aspects of *The Gates Ajar* but also borrowed ideas which he used positively.

_____, and Richard D. Rust. "Mark Twain's 'The Turning Point of My Career.'" *AL*, 40 (January 1969), 524–535.
  Deals with textual problems of two MSS of Twain's "last work written for publication," in *Harper's Bazaar*, including his concern for style and expressing his philosophy in his last years.

Requa, Kenneth A. "Counterfeit Currency and Character in Mark Twain's 'Which Was It'?" *MTJ*, 17 (Winter 1974–75), 1–6.
  This unfinished novel presents variations on several later themes: money as temptation, existence as dream, and hypocrisy.

Reynolds, Albert E., II. "The California Gold Rush as a Basis for Literature." *Americana-Austriaca*, 2 (1970), 61–80.
  Includes mention of Twain's "Celebrated Jumping Frog."

Rhode, Robert D. See MISCELLANEOUS (Postbellum).

Rickels, Milton. "Samuel Clemens and the Conscience of Comedy." *SouR*, 4 (Spring 1968), 558–568.
  An essay-review of Norris Yates's *The American Humorist: Conscience of the Twentieth Century*, and of four recent scholarly studies of Samuel Clemens.

Righter, William. See GENERAL.

Ritunnano, Jeanne. "Mark Twain vs. Arthur Conan Doyle on Detective Fiction." *MTJ*, 16 (Winter 1971–72), 10–14.
  A treatment of "A Double-Barreled Detective Story."

Robbins, J. Albert. See GENERAL.

Robinson, Fred C. "Appropriate Naming in English Literature." *Names*, 20 (June 1972), 131–137.
  Includes comments on the appropriateness of the names Huck Finn and Tom Sawyer.

Robinson, William H., Jr. "Mark Twain: Senatorial Secretary." *Am West*, 10, no. 1 (1973), 16–17, 60–62.
  Deals with Twain as secretary to Senator William M. Stewart, for a brief time in 1867.

Rodgers, Paul C., Jr. "Artemus Ward and Mark Twain's 'Jumping Frog.'" *NCF*, 28 (December 1973), 273–286.
  Believes that Artemus Ward strongly influenced this story and that the story parabolically hints of Twain's identification with Ward's accomplishments and professional goals.

Rodnon, Stewart. "*The Adventures of Huckleberry Finn* and *Invisible Man*: Thematic and Structural Parallels." *NALF*, 4 (1970), 45–51.
  Title is descriptive.

Roemer, Kenneth M. "The Yankee(s) in Noahville." *AL*, 45 (May 1973), 434–437.
  Franklin H. North's *The Awakening of Noahville* (1898) was an "obvious attempt to rewrite" *A Connecticut Yankee* and thus offers "an interesting contemporary reaction" to Twain's book.

Rogers, Franklin R., and Paul Baender, eds. *Roughing It*. Berkeley: Univ of California Press, 1972.
  An edition of the novel according to CEAA standards, Volume 2 in *The Works of Mark Twain*, with a historical introduction on its composition by Rogers.

Rogers, Rodney O. "Twain, Taine, and Lecky: The Genesis of a Passage in *A Connecticut Yankee*." *MLQ*, 34 (December 1973), 436–447.
  Discusses the influence of Taine and Lecky on Twain's historical outlook in *A Connecticut Yankee* and the implications of "Twain's secretive use of source material" on "prevailing critical readings of the novel."

Ross, Michael L. "Mark Twain's *Pudd'nhead Wilson*: Dawson's Landing and the Ladder of Nobility." *Novel*, 6 (Spring 1973), 244–256.
  The novel attacks class-stratification; its "real subject" is "the presence in the New World of a variant of feudalism...."

Rowlette, Robert. "Mark Twain, Sarah Grand, and *The Heavenly Twins*." *MTJ*, 16 (Summer 1972), 17–18.
  Grand's popular *The Heavenly Twins* may have influenced Twain's deletion of the Siamese twins from *Pudd'nhead Wilson*.

_____. "Mark Twain's Barren Tree in *The Mysterious Stranger*: Two Biblical Parallels." *MTJ*, 16 (Winter 1971–72), 19–20.
  Discusses Twain's blending of two of Christ's miracles into the one performed by little Satan in chapter ten of the *Stranger*.

_____. *Mark Twain's Pudd'nhead Wilson: The Development and Design*. Bowling Green, Ohio: Bowling Green Univ Popular Press, 1971.
A study of the form and substance of Twain's controversial novel, with attention to its structure and integration of the themes of slavery, detection, and twinhood.

_____. "'Mark Ward on Artemus Twain': Twain's Literary Debt to Ward." *Am Lit Realism*, 6 (Winter 1973), 13-25.
Careful and specific examination of Twain's literary debt to Ward based on specific passages from both writers.

Rubin, Louis D., Jr. "The Begum of Bengal: Mark Twain and the South," in *Individual and Community: Variations on a Theme in American Fiction*, ed. K. H. Baldwin and D. K. Kirby. Durham, N. C.: Duke Univ Press, 1975, pp. 64-93.
Analyzes Twain as a Southern writer in the context of the private experience of the writer matching the public meaning of the time and place.

_____. "How Mark Twain Threw Off His Inhibitions and Discovered the Vitality of Formless Form." *SR*, 79 (Summer 1971), 426-433.
A review of Geismar's *Mark Twain: An American Prophet*.

_____. "Mark Twain: *The Adventures of Tom Sawyer*," in *Landmarks of American Writing*, ed. Hennig Cohen, pp. 157-171. New York: Basic Books, 1969.
Speculates about what the place of *Tom Sawyer* in Twain's canon would be had *Huckleberry Finn* not been completed; *Tom Sawyer* is "filled with honesty and truth,...a classic if ever there was one."

_____. "Three Installments of Mark Twain." *SR*, 78 (Autumn 1970), 678-684.
A review-essay of *Mark Twain's Hannibal, Huck and Tom*, ed. Walter Blair; *Mark Twain's Mysterious Stranger Manuscripts*, ed. William M. Gibson; and *Mark Twain's Correspondence with Henry Huttleston Rogers*, ed. Lewis Leary.

_____. See MISCELLANEOUS (Postbellum).

_____. See GENERAL--1st, 3rd, 6th, and 9th Rubin entries.

Rule, Henry B. "The Role of Satan in 'The Man That Corrupted Hadleyburg.'" *Stud SF*, 6 (Fall 1969), 619-629.
This story is one of Twain's several attempts "to rescue Satan from centuries of slander." The "mysterious stranger" in the story is Satan, and Hadleyburg is an ironic Eden, corrupt and hypocritical.

Rulon, Curt M. "Geographical Delimitation of the Dialect Areas in *The Adventures of Huckleberry Finn*." *MTJ*, 14 (Winter 1967-68), 9-12.
Finds only two areas represented in the novel.

Rust, Richard D. "Americanisms in *A Connecticut Yankee*." *SAB*, 33 (May 1968), 11-13.
Deals with the significance of the Americanisms and the fact that Twain uses them less frequently as the novel progresses.

Salzman, Jack. See GENERAL.

Sapper, Neil. "'I Been There Before': Huck Finn as Tocquevillian Individual." *Miss Quart*, 24 (Winter 1970-71), 35-45.
Huck qualifies as Tocqueville's individual who withdraws from the mass of his fellows into his own circle and willingly leaves society to itself.

Schäfer, Jürgen. "'Huckleberry, U. S.'" *Eng Stud*, 54 (1973), 334-335.
On the question of the origin of the word *huckleberry*.

Scheick, William J. "The Spunk of a Rabbit: An Allusion in *The Adventures of Huckleberry Finn*." *MTJ*, 15 (Summer 1971), 14-16.
The trick Huck uses to keep the men from inspecting the raft that Jim is on is like that used by Harris in the Uncle Remus story of the rabbit and the briar patch.

Scherting, Jack. "Poe's 'The Cask of Amontillado': A Source for Twain's 'The Man That Corrupted Hadleyburg.'" *MTJ*, 16 (Summer 1972), 18-19.
Offers thematic and structural parallels.

Schinto, Jeanne. "The Autobiographies of Mark Twain and Henry Adams: Life Studies in Despair." *MTJ*, 17 (Summer 1975), 5-7.
Both Twain and Adams question power derived from "moral sense" and find short-lived hope in the powerless child.

Schmitter, Dean M. *Mark Twain, A Collection of Criticism*. New York: McGraw-Hill, 1974.
Reprints thirteen critical essays and includes a bibliography of criticism.

Schmitz, Neil. "The Paradox of Liberation in *Huckleberry Finn*." *Tex Stud in Lit and Lang*, 13 (Spring 1971), 125-136.
"Having been shackled like an animal on the river, duped and betrayed at the Phelps farm, Jim suffers a final indignity--the affirmation of his 'fine qualities.'"

_____. "Twain, *Huckleberry Finn*, and the Reconstruction." *Am Stud*, 12 (Spring 1971), 59-67.
Tom's treatment of Jim is examined for what it reveals about the dilemma Mark Twain faced in including Jim's fate in the novel. The episode is compared to the hospital passage in Ellison's *Invisible Man*.

Schonhorn, Manuel. "Mark Twain's Jim: Solomon on the Mississippi." *MTJ*, 14 (Winter 1968-69), 9-11.
Deals with Chapter 14 of *Huckleberry Finn*.

Scott, Arthur L. *Mark Twain at Large*. Chicago: Henry Regnery, 1969.
Focusing upon Twain's years as a world traveler and the books he produced about the adventures and under the influence of foreign exposure, Scott traces the sources of and

explicates Twain's firm opinions about international affairs, other nationalities, and the quality of American life.

Scrivner, Buford, Jr. *"The Mysterious Stranger*: Mark Twain's New Myth of the Fall." *MTJ*, 17 (Summer 1975), 20-21.
The book inverts, yet parallels, the Christian interpretation of the fortunate fall.

Sears, Robert R., and Deborah Lapidus. "Episodic Analysis of Novels." *Jour of Psych*, 85 (1973), 267-276.
A tabulation of episodic themes in various Twain works, in preparation for evaluation of Twain's personality.

Seelye, John. "De ole true Huck: An Introduction." *Tri-Quart*, 16 (Autumn 1969), 5-10.
The introduction to Seelye's *The True Adventures of Huckleberry Finn*.

_____. *The True Adventures of Huckleberry Finn*. Evanston, Ill.: Northwestern Univ Press, 1970.
A rewriting of Twain's novel, which answers to the criticisms made by major Twain scholars, in the form of a satiric *tour de force*.

Serrano-Plaja, Arturo. *"Magic" Realism in Cervantes: Don Quixote as Seen Through Tom Sawyer and The Idiot*. Trans. Robert S. Rudder. Berkeley: Univ of California Press, 1970.
Tom Sawyer and *Huckleberry Finn* are viewed as artistic and literary extensions, from within, of Cervantes' world, Tom (Don Quixote) inventing the "magic" children's game which Huck (Sancho) follows.

Sharma, Mohan Lal. "Mark Twain's Passage to India." *MTJ*, 14 (Summer 1968), 12-14.
Summarizes Mark Twain's positive attitude towards India.

Shrell, Darwin H. "Twain's Owl and His Bluejays," in *Essays in Honor of Esmond Linworth Morilla*, ed. Thomas A. Kirby and William J. Olive. Baton Rouge: Louisiana State Univ Press, 1970.
A reading of "Baker's Bluejay Yarn" in the light of the Whittier Dinner address.

Simonson, Harold P. *The Closed Frontier: Studies in American Literary Tragedy*. New York: Holt, Rinehart, and Winston, 1970.
Defines *Huckleberry Finn* as a tragedy within the context of Turner's frontier thesis.

_____. "*Huckleberry Finn* as Tragedy." *YR*, 59 (June 1970), 532-548.
Huckleberry Finn is important in the development of American tragedy because it reveals for the first time in our literature the meaning of America's closed frontier.

Simpson, Claude M., ed. *Twentieth Century Interpretations of Adventures of Huckleberry Finn*. Englewood Cliffs, N. J.: Prentice-Hall, 1968.
Reprints nine selected essays and eight critical excerpts on the novel.

Simpson, Lewis P. "Mark Twain and the Pathos of Regeneration: A Second Look at Geismar's *Mark Twain*." *So Lit Jour*, 4 (Spring 1972), 93-106.
Geismar insists on Twain's relevance to the present as "an aged prophet speaking to us out of the depths of the Old Republic about an American pastoral destiny that could never be."

Skerry, Philip J. "*The Adventures of Huckleberry Finn* and *Intruder in the Dust*: Two Conflicting Myths of American Experience." *BSUF*, 13 (Winter 1972), 4-13.
Huck rejects society, but Chick accepts it.

Skow, John. "Quarter Twain." *Time*, 96 (November 30, 1970), 81-82.
Skow finds much to criticize and something to praise in Maxwell Geismar's *Mark Twain, an American Prophet*, saying that Twain never arrived at a consistent view of his world.

Smith, Dorothy J. "The American Railroad Novel." *MarkR*, 3 (October 1972), 61-71.
Includes discussion of *The Gilded Age* as an important early example of the railroad novel.

Smith, Lucian R. "Sam Clemens: Pilot." *MTJ*, 15 (Summer 1971), 1-5.
Debates the meaning of Clemens' career as a riverboat pilot to Clemens the man. Argues that wealth and prestige were Clemens' main reason for piloting and that the decline of these two factors was the reason for his not returning to the job after the war.

Solomon, Andrew. "Jim and Huck: Magnificent Misfits." *MTJ*, 16 (Winter 1972), 17-24.
Though Huck's thoughts and words are often bigoted, his feelings of empathy and humanity are true, and Jim is his equal.

Solomon, Jack. "*Huckleberry Finn* and the Tradition of *The Odyssey*." *SAB*, 33 (March 1968), 11-13.
Points out similarities in episodes, characters, and form.

Spangler, George M. "*Pudd'nhead Wilson*: A Parable of Property." *AL*, 42 (March 1970), 28-37.
Puts forth the thesis that "property, more particularly the obsession with property as a vitiating and reductive influence on human beings" is the theme on which is centered the coherence of the novel.

Spofford, William. "Mark Twain's Connecticut Yankee: An Ignoramus Nevertheless." *MTJ*, 15 (Summer 1970), 15-18.
The failure of Hank Morgan's revolution lies in the limitations of his character.

Standart, Phoebe, ed. *Your Personal Mark Twain*. New York: International Publishers, 1969.
A biographically arranged selection of excerpts from Twain's writings reflecting his opinions, as the subtitle reads, "on Ladies, Language, Liberty, Literature, Liquor, Love and other Controversial Subjects."

Stein, Allen F. "Return to Phelps Farm: *Huckleberry Finn* and the Old Southwestern Framing Device." *Miss Quart*, 24 (Spring 1971), 111-116.

The much debated ending of the novel may be better understood by comparing it to the narrative device used by humorists of the Old Southwest.

Stern, Madeleine B. "Mark Twain Had His Head Examined." *AL*, 41 (May 1969), 207-218.
    Deals with the results of Twain's examination by a phrenologist.

_____. See GENERAL.

Stessin, Lawrence. "The Businessman in Fiction." *Literary Rev*, 12 (Spring 1969), 281-289.
    Includes discussion of *A Connecticut Yankee*; Twain avoided stereotyping the businessman as a villain.

Stowell, Robert. "River Guide Books and Mark Twain's *Life on the Mississippi*." *MTJ*, 16 (Summer 1973), 21.
    The cub pilot did not have to do as much memorizing of details of the river as Twain said he did because navigational guidebooks were available.

Sturdevant, James R. "Mark Twain's Unpublished Letter to Tom Taylor--an Enigma." *MTJ*, 14 (Winter 1967-68), 8-9.
    Reprints a letter which may indicate that Taylor wanted to discuss the possibility of dramatizing *The Gilded Age*.

Sykes, Robert H. "A Source for Mark Twain's Feud." *West Va Hist*, 28 (1968), 191-198.
    Suggests that the source may be newspaper accounts of the Hatfield-McCoy feud.

Talbott, Linda Hood. "*Huck Finn*: Mark Twain at Midstream." *Nassau Rev*, 1 (Spring 1969), 44-60.
    Huckleberry Finn was written when Twain was in "midstream" in his outlook on life.

Tatham, Campbell. "'Dismal and Lonesome': A New Look at *Huckleberry Finn*." *MFS*, 14 (Spring 1968), 47-55.
    Huck does not, in the course of the novel, grow in moral stature; thus, "the Huck Finn who takes part in the events at the Phelps farm is a logical projection of the Huck Finn who at three crucial moments based his actions on his pathological fear of loneliness and his personal need for acceptance and comfort."

Taylor, Robert, Jr. "Sounding the Trumpets of Defiance: Mark Twain and Norman Mailer." *MTJ*, 16 (Winter 1972), 1-14.
    Both Twain and Mailer (and others) write in response to the "American myth" of material wealth.

Todd, W. B. "Problems in Editing Mark Twain," in *Bibliography and Textual Criticism*, ed. O. M. Brack, Jr., and Warner Barnes. Chicago: Univ of Chicago Press, 1969, pp. 202-208.
    Enumerates problems encountered in preparing the edition of Mark Twain's works at Iowa.

Towers, Tom H. "'Hateful Reality': The Failure of the Territory in *Roughing It*." *WAL*, 9 (Spring 1974), 3-15.

If disillusionment rather than initiation is seen as the central theme of *Roughing It*, the work achieves a greater unity than admitted by earlier critics.

Trachtenberg, Alan. "The Form of Freedom in *Adventures of Huckleberry Finn*." *SouR*, 6 (Autumn 1970), 954-971.
    An analysis of the formal problem in expressing the theme of freedom through the point of view which requires Huck to be both a character in and the narrator of the action.

Tracy, Robert. "Myth and Reality in *The Adventures of Tom Sawyer*." *SouR*, 4 (Spring 1968), 530-541.
    A study of realism, romantic melodrama, and archetypal myth.

Trensky, Anne. "The Bad Boy in Nineteenth-Century American Fiction." *GaR*, 27 (Winter 1973), 503-517.
    In this general discussion, there is comment on Twain's stories "The Story of the Bad Little Boy" and "The Story of the Good Little Boy" as being typical in that the bad boys remained within the framework of middle-class morality, unlike Huck, who rebels against it.

Tuckey, John S. "Hannibal, Weggis, and Mark Twain's Eseldorf." *AL*, 42 (May 1970), 235-240.
    Argues that the village boys in *The Mysterious Stranger* are modeled on European children rather than on those from Hannibal.

_____. *Mark Twain's Fables of Man*. Berkeley: Univ of California Press, 1972.
    A collection of thirty-six philosophical, historical, and religious fantasies written during periods of despair, in CEAA-approved texts, with an interpretive introduction by the editor and textual apparatus by Kenneth M. Sanderson and Bernard L. Stein.

_____. "Mark Twain's Later Dialogue: The 'Me' and the Machine." *AL*, 41 (January 1970), 532-542.
    Argues against the popular belief that Twain was a pessimist in his later years.

_____, ed. *Mark Twain's "The Mysterious Stranger" and the Critics*. Belmont, Calif: Wadsworth, 1968.
    Includes the text and reprinted criticism.

Turner, Arlin. "Mark Twain and the South: An Affair of Love and Anger." *SouR*, 4 (Spring 1968), 493-519.
    A study of Mark Twain's changing assessment of Southern life and institutions. The analysis rests on extensive knowledge of the Mark Twain-George W. Cable relationship and on study of Mark Twain's manuscript revisions.

Turner, D. R. *Arco Notes: Mark Twain's Huckleberry Finn*. New York: Arco Publishing, 1969.
    A study guide to the novel.

Twain, Mark. *King Leopold's Soliloquy*. New York: International Publishers, 1970.
    A new edition of Twain's 1906 pamphlet with an introduction by Stefan Heym, which draws parallels between conditions in the Congo then and now.

Underhill, Irving S. "A Dog's Tale." *Am Bk Collector*, 25 (March-April 1975), 17-19.
A bibliographical article about the pamphlet publication of Twain's short story "A Dog's Tale."

Untermeyer, Louis. *Treasury of Great Humor*. New York: McGraw-Hill, 1972.
Includes five excerpts from Twain with an introductory critical comment.

Vanderbilt, Kermit. "Correction and Further Note on Mark Twain and Longfellow." *MTJ*, 16 (Winter 1972), 24.
Twain wished to repudiate Longfellow's literary tradition.

Vandersee, Charles. "The Mutual Awareness of Mark Twain and Henry Adams." *Eng Lang Notes*, 5 (June 1968), 285-292.
Contrary to the belief that Twain and Adams never saw each other, the two did meet in 1886. Each showed an awareness of the other in his writings.

Vorpahl, Ben M. "'Very Much Like a Fire-Cracker': Owen Wister on Mark Twain." *WAL*, 6 (Summer 1971), 83-98.
Wister's ambivalent attitude toward Twain is revealed in a 1935 essay in *Harper's*.

Voss, Arthur. See GENERAL.

Wagenknecht, Edward. "*The Mark Twain Papers* and *Henry James: The Treacherous Years*." *Stud in the Novel*, 2 (Spring 1970), 88-98.
A review-essay pointing out the value to scholars of *The Mark Twain Papers*.

Walker, Franklin. *Irreverent Pilgrims: Melville, Browne, and Mark Twain in the Holy Land*. Seattle: Univ of Washington Press, 1974.
A comparative analysis of the journals and published writings of Melville, John Ross Browne, and Mark Twain about their travels to Jerusalem, Nazareth, and Bethlehem.

Walker, I. M. *Mark Twain*. Profiles in Literature Series. New York: Humanities Press, 1970.
Extracts from Twain's works arranged so as to demonstrate his major techniques as a humorist and stylist.

Walters, Thomas N. "Twain's Finn and Alger's Gilman: Picaresque Counter-Directions." *MarkR*, 3 (May 1972), 53-58.
Huck and Jed Gilman are picaresque heroes appearing in picaresque novels.

Warren, Robert Penn. "Mark Twain." *SouR*, 8 (Summer 1972), 459-492.
A presentation of Mark Twain's total artistic achievement, with particular attention to *Adventures of Huckleberry Finn* and *A Connecticut Yankee in King Arthur's Court*.

Watkins, T. H. "Mark Twain and His Mississippi." *Am West*, 10, no. 6 (1973), 12-19.
Historical background.

_____. *Mark Twain's Mississippi*. Palo Alto, Calif.: American West, 1974.
Mainly a picture book containing parts of the text of *Life on the Mississippi*.

Weaver, William. "Mark Twain and Kate Field Differ on Constitutional Rights." *MTJ*, 17 (Summer 1974), 16-17.
Letters on Mormon polygamy.

_____. "Samuel Clemens Lectures in Kentucky." *MTJ*, 17 (Summer 1974), 20-21.
Twain and the Kentuckians paid mutual compliments.

_____. "The Twain-Cable Lectures in Kentucky, 1884-1885." *KHSR*, 72 (April 1974), 134-142.
Twain as well as Cable received popular acclaim all along the tour.

Weeks, Lewis E., Jr. "Mark Twain and Hemingway: 'A Catastrophe' and 'A Natural History of the Dead.'" *MTJ*, 16 (Summer 1968), 15-17.
Points out similarities in Twain's description of the death of his brother Henry in *Life on the Mississippi* and Hemingway's description of the death of a soldier in "A Natural History of the Dead."

Weintraub, Rodelle, ed. "'Mental Telegraphy?': Mark Twain on G. B. S." *Shaw Rev*, 17 (May 1974), 68-70.
Publishes a sketch in which Clemens comments on echoes in a Shaw story ("Ariel Football: the New Game") of elements in his unpublished "The Late Rev. Sam Jones's Reception in Heaven"; also prints the Shaw story.

Welland, Dennis. "Samuel Clemens and His English Publishers," in *Art and Error: Modern Textual Editing*, ed. Ronald Gottesman and Scott Bennett. Bloomington: Indiana Univ Press, 1970, pp. 167-185.
Examines reasons for variations between British and American editions of the same book, drawing upon Twain's experience with his works as examples.

Wells, David M. "More on the Geography of 'Huckleberry Finn.'" *SAB*, 38 (November 1973), 82-86.
An attempt to locate Huck's landings on the Mississippi River and to note Twain's geographical errors.

Werge, Thomas. "Mark Twain and the Fall of Adam." *MTJ*, 15 (Summer 1970), 5-13.
Deals with the way Twain uses Adam, especially in *Huckleberry Finn* and "The Man That Corrupted Hadleyburg."

Wexman, Virginia. "The Role of Structure in *Tom Sawyer* and *Huckleberry Finn*." *Am Lit Realism*, 6 (Winter 1973), 1-11.
A study of structural pattern in relation to Twain's "developing attitude toward social reality."

Wheelock, C. Webster. "The Point of Pudd'nhead's Half-a-Dog Joke." *Am N&Q*, 8 (June 1970), 150-151.

Men who are aghast at killing an animal that is only partially the owner's property treat human beings as fractions daily since many slaves are only part Negro.

Wilson, Edmund. "The Fruits of the MLA: I. *Their Wedding Journey*." *NYRB*, September 26, 1968.
    Principally an attack on the MLA and on CEAA methods of dealing with Melville, Hawthorne, and Poe, but also on the methods used by scholars working with Twain materials.

_____. "The Fruits of the MLA: II. Mark Twain." *NYRB*, October 10, 1968.
    An attack on the methods used in the editing of the Mark Twain papers.

Wilson, James D. "*Adventures of Huckleberry Finn*: From Abstraction to Humanity." *SouR*, 10 (Winter 1974), 80-94.
    Presents Twain's treatment of abstract codes of behavior—Christianity, chivalry, hedonism, codes of vengeance and of pride—as opposed to concrete human values.

_____. "Hank Morgan, Philip Traum, and Milton's Satan." *MTJ*, 16 (Summer 1973), 20-21.
    Points out parallels in Book VI of *Paradise Lost* and a description of Hank Morgan in *A Connecticut Yankee*; in *The Mysterious Stranger* Philip Traum's analysis of man as an increasingly destructive creature provides evidence that Hank Morgan is typical of Western man.

_____. "'The Monumental Sarcasm of the Sciences': Science and Pseudoscience in the Thought of Mark Twain." *SAB*, 40 (May 1975), 72-82.
    Twain came to believe that science "had created a world bereft of meaning, permeated with moral chaos," which in turn "created a time ripe" for the pseudosciences, which take advantage of the weak and unfortunate.

Wilson, Mark K. "Mr. Clemens and Madame Blanc: Mark Twain's First French Critic." *AL*, 45 (January 1974), 537-556.
    Documented discussion of Madame Marie-Thérèse Blanc's writings on Clemens.

Woodress, James. See GENERAL—2nd, 3rd, and 4th Woodress entries.

Wysong, Jack P. "Samuel Clemens' Attitude Toward the Negro as Demonstrated in *Pudd'nhead Wilson* and *A Connecticut Yankee at King Arthur's Court*." *XUS*, 7 (July 1968), 41-57.
    An analysis of the two novels maintaining that, although Twain was opposed to slavery, he did not believe Negroes to be the equals of whites.

Yu, Beongcheon. "The Immortal Twins: An Aspect of Mark Twain." *Eng Lang and Lit* (Korea Univ), 22 (1968), 48-77.
    The progression in Twain's treatment of doubles reveals his growing concern with the problem of identity.

Zaraspe, Raquel S. "The Picaresque Tradition in Mark Twain." *Diliman Rev*, 17 (July 1969), 218-243.

Points out parallels in *Tom Sawyer*, *Huckleberry Finn*, and *A Connecticut Yankee*, and *Lazarillo de Tormes*.

Zwahlen, Christine. "Of Hell or of Hannibal." *AL*, 42 (January 1971), 562-563.
    Discusses Clemens' possible pun on Hell and Hannibal in the *Hannibal* (Missouri) *Journal* of May 6, 1853.

[COOGLER, JOHN BROWN GORDON] Coogler, J. G. *Purely Original Verse*. Columbia, S. C.: Neuffer-LaBorde Reprint (Eng. Dept., USC), 1974.
    Facsimile reprint of the 1897 edition of the poet immortalized by quotation in Mencken's "Sahara of the Bozart," with a new introduction by C. H. Neuffer and R. LaBorde.

[DICKSON, HARRIS] Brown, Calvin S. See FAULKNER, WILLIAM (Contemporary—2nd Brown entry).

Simms, L. Moody, Jr. "Harris Dickson and the Post-Civil War South." *Notes on Miss Writers*, 5 (Winter 1973), 80-83.
    A brief biographical sketch pointing out Dickson's four works dealing with the post-Civil War South.

[DIXON, THOMAS, JR.] Aptheker, Herbert. See GENERAL.

Baker, Donald G. See GENERAL.

Cook, Raymond A. *Fire From the Flint: The Amazing Careers of Thomas Dixon*. Winston-Salem, N. C.: John F. Blair, 1968.
    A thorough biography of the Baptist minister, lawyer, legislator, dramatist, and novelist responsible for *The Clansman* and *Birth of a Nation*, emphasizing neglected aspects of his career and recounting his ardent involvement in all the crucial social issues of his day.

_____. *Thomas Dixon*. New York: Twayne, 1974.
    A biographical and critical survey.

Davenport, F. Garvin, Jr. See MISCELLANEOUS (Contemporary).

Davis, Michael. See MISCELLANEOUS (Postbellum).

Dixon, Thomas, Jr. *The Clansman: An Historical Romance of the Ku Klux Klan*. The Novel as American Social History Series. Lexington: Univ Press of Kentucky, 1970.
    A reprint of the 1905 edition with an introduction to the novel's cultural and historical importance by Thomas D. Clark.

Godbold, E. Stanly, Jr. See MISCELLANEOUS (Postbellum).

Mellard, James M. See GENERAL.

Silva, Fred, ed. *Focus on the Birth of a Nation*. Englewood Cliffs, N. J.: Prentice-Hall, 1971.
    A collection of primary and secondary materials concerning the production and cultural impact of *The Birth of a Nation* (1915) based on Dixon's *The Clansman* and *The Leopard's Spots*.

[DORSEY, SARAH ANNE] Anderson, John Q. "Louisiana and Mississippi Lore in the Fiction of Sarah

Anne Dorsey (1829-1879)." *La Stud*, 11 (Fall 1972), 230-239.

Despite her attempt to use in her fiction local history, legend, and folkways, Mrs. Dorsey's four novels suffer generally from the weakness of popular fiction of the time.

[EDWARDS, HARRY STILLWELL] Lamplugh, George R. See MISCELLANEOUS (Postbellum).

Lanier, Doris. "James Whitcomb Riley, 'Bill' Nye, and Harry Stillwell Edwards: A Lecture Tour." *GHQ*, 57 (Summer 1973), 256-264.

In late November 1888 Edwards began a tour of South Carolina and Georgia with Riley and Nye.

[FOX, JOHN, JR.] Holman, Harriet R., ed. *John Fox and Tom Page as They Were*. Miami, Fla: Field Research Projects, 1970.

Collects in edited texts seventy-four letters exchanged between Fox and Thomas Nelson Page and two uncollected essays by Page, "The Mountains of the South" and "John Fox," with an introduction, notes, and index by the editor.

_____. "John Fox, Jr.: An Appraisal and Self-Appraisal: *Personal Sketch by John Fox, Jr. (1908)*." *So Lit Jour*, 3 (Spring 1971), 18-38.

Today Fox suffers neglect compounded by changing literary fashions and the refusal of his family to release information for biographical or critical work about him. "Personal Sketch," printed here, is "basic to any work done on Fox."

_____. "Interlude: Scenes from John Fox's Courtship of Fritzi Scheff as Reported by Richard Harding Davis." *So Lit Jour*, 7 (Spring 1975), 77-87.

In several letters to his mother Richard Harding Davis comments on Fox's courtship of Fritzi Scheff in the summer of 1908 in Marion, Massachusetts.

Polk, Noel E. See MISCELLANEOUS (Postbellum--1st Polk entry).

Titus, Warren I. *John Fox, Jr.* Twayne's U. S. Authors Series, no. 174. New York: Twayne, 1971.

A biographical-analytical study of Fox's fiction which is found to be of interest for its preservation of the life and culture of the Southern Appalachian Mountain region.

_____. "John Fox, Jr. (1862-1919)." *Am Lit Realism*, no. 3 (Summer 1968), 5-8.

A bibliographical essay.

Tucker, Edward L. "John Fox, Jr.: *Bon Vivant* and Mountain Chronicler." *Va Cavalcade*, 21 (Spring 1972), 18-29.

A sketch of the author of *The Trail of the Lonesome Pine* (1908), a novel which describes the conflict between Southern mountaineers and industry.

[GAYARRÉ, CHARLES] Bush, Robert. "Charles Gayarré and Grace King: Letters of a Louisiana Friendship." *So Lit Jour*, 7 (Fall 1974), 100-131.

The fact that much of Grace King's writing career was concerned with Creole life was due to the influence of Gayarré.

Polk, Noel E. See MISCELLANEOUS (Postbellum--1st Polk entry).

[GLASGOW, ELLEN] Buchloh, Paul G. See GENERAL.

Bush, Robert. See MISCELLANEOUS (Postbellum).

Carlton, Holt. "Ellen Glasgow: A Turn-of-the-Century Feminist?" *New Dominion Life Style*, 2 (August-September 1975), 30-33.

A biographical sketch relating Glasgow and her work to the trends of the times.

Duke, Maurice. "The First Novel by a Glasgow: Cary's *A Successful Failure*." *Ellen Glasgow Newsletter*, 1, no. 1 (1974), 7-9.

Deals with a novel by Ellen Glasgow's older sister and its possible influence on Ellen Glasgow.

_____. See GENERAL.

Eaton, Clement. See GENERAL.

Edmunds, P. W. See GENERAL.

Godbold, E. Stanly, Jr. *Ellen Glasgow and the Woman Within*. Baton Rouge: Louisiana State Univ Press, 1972.

The first full biographical account of Miss Glasgow's career with special attention to her private life and its contrast to her public reputation.

_____. See MISCELLANEOUS (Postbellum).

Godshalk, William L. "Addendum to Kelly: Ellen Glasgow's *The Voice of the People*." *PBSA*, 67 (1st Qtr. 1973), 68-69.

Adds some items to Kelly's *Ellen Glasgow: A Bibliography*.

_____, ed. *The Voice of the People*, by Ellen Glasgow. New Haven: College and Univ Press, 1972.

An edition of the 1900 novel with textual notes and a critical introduction by the editor.

Holman, C. Hugh. "April in Queenborough: Ellen Glasgow's Comedies of Manners." *SR*, 82 (Spring 1974), 263-283.

The Queenborough novels, portraying an inner division of the writer's own life, succeed admirably in that rare and difficult genre, the American comedy of manners.

_____. See GENERAL.

Inge, M. Thomas, ed. *Ellen Glasgow: Centennial Essays*. Charlottesville: Univ Press of Virginia, 1975.

Contains nine critical and biographical essays originally delivered at Mary Baldwin College and in Richmond.

MacDonald, Edgar E. "Biographical Notes on Ellen Glasgow." *RALS*, 3 (Autumn 1973), 249-253.

Certifies Ellen Glasgow's birthdate as 1873 and identifies the mysterious "Gerald B" alluded to in *The Woman Within*.

_____. "Ellen Glasgow: An Essay in Bibliography." *RALS*, 2 (Autumn 1972), 131-156.
    Assesses the history and quality of Glasgow scholarship.

_____, ed. *Ellen Glasgow Newsletter* (Box 565, Ashland, Va. 23005).

_____. "Glasgow, Cabell, and Richmond." *Miss Quart*, 27 (Fall 1974), 393-413.
    Describes the writing careers of Ellen Glasgow and James Branch Cabell, emphasizing the atmosphere of Richmond as it influenced these writers.

_____. "Lest Ellen Glasgow's 100th Anniversary Go Unnoticed...." Richmond *Times-Dispatch*, April 29, 1973, p. F-1.
    An appreciative reassessment of Glasgow's position in American letters on the occasion of her one hundredth birthday.

_____. "The Sheltered Image." *So Lit Jour*, 4 (Fall 1971), 83-86.
    An essay-review of *Without Shelter: The Early Career of Ellen Glasgow*, by J. R. Raper (1971), which analyzes Miss Glasgow's early works and enlightens the reader.

_____. See CABELL, JAMES BRANCH (Postbellum--4th MacDonald entry).

Murr, Judy S. "History in *Barren Ground* and *Vein of Iron*: Theory, Structure, and Symbolism." *So Lit Jour*, 8 (Fall 1975), 39-54.
    The lives of the heroines of these two novels "adhere to and are structured by a theory of history which insists that individual history is an endless, repetitive pattern of human endeavor, always ending in less than fulfillment."

Paluka, Frank. See GENERAL.

Payne, Ladell. "Ellen Glasgow's *Vein of Iron*: Vanity, Irony, Idiocy," in *Interculture: A Collection of Essays and Creative Writings Commemorating the Twentieth Anniversary of the Fulbright Program*. Vienna: Wilhelm Braumüller, 1975, pp. 260-267.
    The theme of *Vein of Iron* is that "man's endurance marks a triumph, however limited and irrational, of the human spirit" and that "there is nothing to affirm *but* life, existence in all its idiocy."

Perkins, George. See GENERAL.

Pratt, Annis. "Women and Nature in Modern Fiction." *ConL*, 13 (Fall 1972), 476-490.
    Glasgow is considered in this discussion of the differences in the relationship of heroines with nature and that of heroes.

Raper, J. R. "Glasgow's Psychology of Deceptions and *The Sheltered Life*." *So Lit Jour*, 8 (Fall 1975), 27-38.
    A more serious work than *Barren Ground*, *The Sheltered Life* is the most intense study Glasgow ever made of the themes she handled best throughout her career, those associated with evasive idealism.

_____. *Without Shelter: The Early Career of Ellen Glasgow*. Baton Rouge: Louisiana State Univ Press, 1971.
    A biographical-critical study of Miss Glasgow's fiction up to 1906 with emphases on conflicts in her personal life and her philosophic use of Darwinism as influences on her work.

Richards, Marion K. *Ellen Glasgow's Development as a Novelist*. The Hague: Mouton, 1971.
    Traces the development of Glasgow's craftsmanship from 1897 to 1927 and describes the nature of her accomplishments in style and technique.

Rouse, Blair. "Ellen Glasgow: Manners and Art." *Cabellian*, 4 (Spring 1972), 96-98.
    A brief reappraisal of Miss Glasgow's work that asserts that her reputation today suffers from fiction that offers mainly satire and tragedy to a confused age.

_____. "Ellen Glasgow: The Novelist in America." *Cabellian*, 4 (Autumn 1971), 25-35.
    Miss Glasgow's career illustrates "the problems of the novelist in America."

Scura, Dorothy. "One West Main." *Ellen Glasgow Newsletter*, 1, no. 1 (1974), 3-6.
    Deals with the house Ellen Glasgow lived in from 1887 to her death in 1945.

_____. See MISCELLANEOUS (Contemporary).

Spacks, Patricia M. "Taking Care: Some Women Novelists." *Novel*, 6 (Fall 1972), 36-51.
    Glasgow, among others, is discussed as being a woman novelist whose works reveal women taking care of others.

Steele, Oliver. "Ellen Glasgow's *Virginia*: Preliminary Notes." *SB*, 27 (1974), 265-289.
    These notes "represent a working method, by plot outlines, essentially different from that used in the composition of later novels."

Tutwiler, Carrington. *A Catalogue of the Library of Ellen Glasgow*. Charlottesville: Univ Press of Virginia, 1969.
    A much fuller list of Miss Glasgow's books than in Tutwiler's *Ellen Glasgow's Library*.

_____. *Ellen Glasgow's Library*. Charlottesville: Univ Press of Virginia, 1968.
    A descriptive list of books Miss Glasgow owned.

Woodress, James. See GENERAL--1st Woodress entry.

[HARBEN, WILL] Murphy, James K. "The Backwoods Characters of Will N. Harben." *SFQ*, 39 (September 1975), 291-296.
    A survey of the character traits of Harben's characters, who are infused with "vitality" instead of being stereotyped.

Roemer, Kenneth M. "1984 in 1894: Harben's *Land of the Changing Sun*." *Miss Quart*, 26 (Winter 1972-73), 29-42.

Half a century before Orwell, William N. Harben's utopian novel posed a challenge to nineteenth-century American faith in science and technology.

[HARRIS, CORRA] Simms, L. Moody, Jr. "Corra Harris on Patriotic Literary Criticism in the Post-Civil War South." *Miss Quart*, 25 (Fall 1972), 459-466.
  A reprint of the 1904 piece in *The Critic* in which Mrs. Harris, herself a successful Southern writer, blamed "patriotic criticism" for the "dearth of vital fiction" in the South.

_____. "Corra Harris on Northern and Southern Fiction." *Miss Quart*, 27 (Fall 1974), 475-481.
  Discusses and reprints Mrs. Harris' essay "Fiction, North and South," originally published in 1903, in which she asserted that Northern novelists far surpassed the Southern ones.

_____. See PAGE, THOMAS NELSON (Postbellum).

Talmadge, John E. *Corra Harris: Lady of Purpose*. Athens: Univ of Georgia Press, 1968.
  A biographical account of the author of *The Circuit Rider's Wife*.

[HARRIS, JOEL CHANDLER] Armistead, S. G. "Two Brer Rabbit Stories from the Eastern Shore of Maryland." *JAF*, 84 (October-December 1971), 442-444.
  Tales corresponding to "Mr. Rabbit Nibbles Up the Butter" and to the tar-baby story.

Brake, Robert. See GENERAL.

Burrison, John A. See CLEMENS, SAMUEL LANGHORNE (Postbellum).

Clark, William B. See GENERAL.

Cousins, Paul M. *Joel Chandler Harris: A Biography*. Baton Rouge: Louisiana State Univ Press, 1968.
  A biographical account of Harris' life and times based on much primary material originally gathered over forty years ago.

Crawford, John W. See GENERAL.

Dorson, Richard M. See GENERAL.

Flusche, Michael. "Joel Chandler Harris and the Folklore of Slavery." *Jour Am Stud*, 9 (December 1975), 347-363.
  Suggests that the study of folk songs and stories can give insights into slavery that more traditional sources cannot.

Glazier, Lyle. "The Uncle Remus Stories: Two Portraits of American Negroes." *Jour of Gen Ed*, 22 (April 1970), 71-79.
  Contrasts the black man as he is revealed in the white man's framework narrative in *Uncle Remus* and in the tales themselves.

Godbold, E. Stanly, Jr. See MISCELLANEOUS (Postbellum).

Harris, Joel Chandler. *Uncle Remus*. New York: Schocken Books, 1970.
  A facsimile reprint of the 1880 collection of tales, with an introduction by Stella B. Brookes, excerpted from her 1950 study, *J. C. Harris--Folklorist*.

Lamplugh, George R. See MISCELLANEOUS (Postbellum).

Light, Kathleen. "Uncle Remus and the Folklorists." *So Lit Jour*, 7 (Spring 1975), 88-104.
  Harris, who first introduced black folktales to both the general public and folklorists, did not initially hold the same attitude toward black folklorists as did the ethnologists.

Muffett, D. J. M. "Uncle Remus Was a Hausaman?" *SFQ*, 39 (June 1975), 151-166.
  A study of the origins of Harris' tales which urges further work to establish the links with Africa.

Mugleston, William F. "Julian Harris, the Georgia Press, and the Ku Klux Klan." *GHQ*, 59 (Fall 1975), 284-295.
  Includes discussion of the influence of Joel Chandler Harris' ideas on his son.

Rubin, Louis D., Jr. "Uncle Remus and the Ubiquitous Rabbit." *SouR*, 10 (Autumn 1974), 787-804.
  Presents, with attention to the historical perspective, the degree of Harris' espousal of his black characters' point of view.

_____. See MISCELLANEOUS (Postbellum).

_____. See GENERAL--6th Rubin entry.

Tumlin, John, ed. *Uncle Remus*, by Joel Chandler Harris. Savannah, Ga.: Beehive Press, 1975.
  A selection of sixty-four stories, with an introduction by the editor.

Turner, Arlin. "Joel Chandler Harris (1848-1908)." *Am Lit Realism*, 3 (Summer 1968), 18-23.
  A bibliographical essay.

_____. "Joel Chandler Harris in the Currents of Change." *So Lit Jour*, 1 (Autumn 1968), 105-111.
  An essay-review of *Joel Chandler Harris: A Biography* by Paul M. Cousins.

Turner, Darwin T. "Daddy Joel Harris and His Old-Time Darkies." *So Lit Jour*, 1 (Autumn 1968), 20-41.
  Harris not only introduced American readers to African myths about Brer Rabbit and the other animals, but also, at the same time, developed and popularized an Anglo-Saxon myth about "old-time" Negroes and their benevolent masters.

Voss, Arthur. See GENERAL.

[HARRIS, ROBERT HAMILTON] Willis, Katherine Jackson, and William Warren Rogers. "Robert Hamilton Harris: Georgia's Wiregrass Humorist." *GHQ*, 55 (Winter 1971), 492-500.
  Discusses Harris' contributions to the Thomasville *Weekly News* from 1876-1880.

III. Postbellum (1865-1920)

[HAYNE, PAUL HAMILTON] Ifkovic, Edward. "Two Poems for Paul Hamilton Hayne." *Am N&Q*, 6 (January 1968), 71-72.
    Catherine Poyas, a South Carolina poet, acknowledged her debt to Hayne in two poems composed after hearing him read "My Mother-Land," his first war poem.

Lanier, Doris. "The Death of Paul Hamilton Hayne." *GHQ*, 57 (Winter 1973), 579-584.
    Reprints an editorial Harry Stillwell Edwards wrote on Hayne for the *Macon Telegraph*, July 8, 1886.

Moore, Rayburn S. "Hayne the Poet: A New Look." *So Car Rev*, 2 (November 1969), 4-13.
    Despite significant weaknesses, Hayne deserves reconsideration on grounds of his scope, versatility, and sizable output of "passably good verse."

_____. "The Old South and the New: Paul Hamilton Hayne and Maurice Thompson." *So Lit Jour*, 5 (Fall 1972), 108-122.
    The Hayne-Thompson relationship reveals the influence of postbellum politics upon the friendship and the literary views of two writers of this era.

_____. "Paul Hamilton Hayne." *GaR*, 22 (Spring 1968), 106-124.
    A biographical summary.

_____. "Paul Hamilton Hayne as Editor, 1852-1860," in *South Carolina Journals and Journalists*. Columbia, S. C.: Southern Studies Program, 1975, pp. 91-108.
    Outlines Hayne's affiliation with and contributions to the *Southern Literary Gazette*, Charleston *Evening News*, *Russell's*, *Spectator*, and Charleston *Weekly News*.

_____. *Paul Hamilton Hayne*. Twayne's U. S. Authors Series, no. 202. New York: Twayne, 1972.
    A general critical estimate which pays particular attention to the poetry and re-evaluates it from a modern perspective.

Simms, L. Moody, Jr. "Paul Hamilton Hayne's Methods of Poetic Composition." *Miss Quart*, 24 (Winter 1970-71), 57-62.
    In an article in 1892, Hayne's son, William H. Hayne, described his father's working methods.

Young, Thomas Daniel. "How Time Has Served Two Southern Poets: Paul Hamilton Hayne and Sidney Lanier." *So Lit Jour*, 6 (Fall 1973), 101-110.
    A review-essay of Rayburn S. Moore's book on Hayne, which keeps the reader aware of the circumstances out of which the poetry came, and of Jack DeBellis' book on Lanier, which sees Lanier as an experimental poet, making significant contributions to modern symbolist techniques.

[HEARN, LAFCADIO] Kunst, Arthur E. *Lafcadio Hearn*. Twayne's U. S. Authors Series, no. 158. New York: Twayne, 1969.
    A biographical and critical analysis of Hearn's career, philosophical development, and experimentation in the short forms of English prose--the impressionistic essay, the atmospheric sketch, and the gothic tale.

Leary, Lewis. See GENERAL--1st Leary entry.

Libman, Valentina. See GENERAL.

Parsons, Coleman O. See MISCELLANEOUS (Postbellum).

Szwed, John F., and Carol Parssinen. "Lafcadio Hearn in Cincinnati." *New Rep*, 167 (October 7, 1972), 32-33.
    Deals with Hearn's work as a muckraking journalist in Cincinnati.

Turner, Arlin. "Introduction" to *Chita: A Memory of Last Island*. Chapel Hill: Univ of North Carolina Press, 1969.
    Summarizes biographical backgrounds of Hearn's first attempt at fiction and makes out a case for it as "a small masterpiece, a gem of impressionistic narration."

White, William. "Armand Hawkins: Bookseller to Lafcadio Hearn." *Am Bk Collector*, 21 (January 1971), 7-8.
    Chiefly a character sketch of the New Orleans book-seller in whose shop Hearn wrote articles for the *New Orleans Democrat* and conversed with friends.

_____. "On Lafcadio Hearn as a Book Reviewer." *PrS*, 45 (Spring 1971), 93.
    Brief quotations from a review and a notice appearing in the New Orleans *Item*, in the first of which Hearn blasted a novel he was reviewing; in the second, he stated that the *Item* would no longer review "fourth-rate" novels.

[HOPE, JAMES BARRON] Simms, L. Moody, Jr. "James Barron Hope: Virginia's Laureate." *Va Cavalcade*, 19 (Winter 1970), 22-29.
    A biographical sketch and comment on poems of the poet most often called on in Virginia for important occasions in the period following the Civil War.

[JOHNSTON, RICHARD MALCOLM] Polk, Noel E. See MISCELLANEOUS (Postbellum--1st Polk entry).

Simms, L. Moody, Jr. "Richard Malcolm Johnston on Rural Life in Middle Georgia." *GHQ*, 58 (Supplement 1974), 181-192.
    An edited reprinting of Johnston's "Middle Georgia Rural Life," first printed in 1892.

Voyles, Jimmy P. "Richard Malcolm Johnston's Literary Career: An Estimate." *MarkR*, 4 (February 1974), 29-34.
    Discusses the ways in which Johnston "bridges the gap between two schools of fiction, humor and local color."

[KING, GRACE] Bush, Robert. "Grace King (1852-1932)." *Am Lit Realism*, 8 (Winter 1975), 43-51.
    Bibliographical survey of secondary material, manuscripts, reprints, and editions.

_____, ed. *Grace King of New Orleans*. Baton Rouge: Louisiana State Univ Press, 1973.

A selection of Grace King's fiction, non-fiction, and letters, with a biographical introduction and notes by the editor.

_____. See CLEMENS, SAMUEL LANGHORNE.

_____. See GAYARRÉ, CHARLES (Postbellum).

Polk, Noel E. See MISCELLANEOUS (Postbellum--1st Polk entry).

Simpson, Claude M., Jr. "Grace King: The Historian as Apologist." *So Lit Jour*, 6 (Spring 1974), 130-138.
   A review of Robert Bush's *Grace King of New Orleans*, which points out that Bush's selections reflect the range of Grace King's work as fictionist and historian.

[LANIER, SIDNEY] Aaron, Daniel. See GENERAL.

Anderson, Charles R., ed. *Sidney Lanier: Poems and Letters*. Baltimore: Johns Hopkins Press, 1969.
   A selection of the best of Lanier's writing from the Centennial Edition (1945) for the general reader, with a critical introduction; includes twenty-five poems, seventy-four letters, notes, and a chronology.

Antippas, Andy P., and Carol A. Flake. "Sidney Lanier: Some Unpublished Early Manuscripts." *PBSA*, 68 (1974), 174-179.
   Title is descriptive.

_____, and _____, eds. "Sidney Lanier's Letters to Clare deGraffenreid." *AL*, 45 (May 1973), 182-205.
   Includes the edited correspondence, with an introduction by the editors.

DeBellis, Jack. *Sidney Lanier*. Twayne's U. S. Authors Series, no. 205. New York: Twayne, 1972.
   Evaluates Lanier's major poems against the artistic, historical, and philosophical contexts of the man and his times.

_____. "Sidney Lanier and German Romance: An Important Qualification." *CLS*, 5 (June 1968), 145-155.
   Tiger-Lilies owes less to German sources than has been claimed.

Edwards, C. H., Jr. "Bibliography of Sidney Lanier: 1942-1973." *BB*, 31 (January-March 1974), 29-31.
   Briefly annotated listing of primary and secondary materials, updating Vol. 6 of the Centennial edition of Lanier's works.

_____. "Lanier's 'The Symphony' 64-84." *Expl*, 31 (December 1972), Item 27.
   The musical effects of this portion of the poem are pointed out.

Edwards, J. S. "Sidney Lanier: Musical Pioneer." *GaR*, 22 (Winter 1968), 473-481.
   An assessment of Lanier as a flute virtuoso and his place in the history of American music.

Friedl, Herwig. See POE, EDGAR ALLAN (Antebellum--2nd Friedl entry).

Harwell, Richard. "Introduction" to *Tiger-Lilies: A Novel*. Chapel Hill: Univ of North Carolina Press, 1969.
   While admitting that Lanier's tale of Southern chivalry during the Civil War has little merit as a novel, Harwell explores the work's autobiographical and philosophical elements as, in Lanier's words, "the genuine and almost spontaneous utterance of a developing mind."

Havens, Elmer A. "Lanier's Critical Theory." *ESQ*, 55 (2nd Qtr., Part 3, 1969), 83-89.
   Suggests that Lanier's critical theory was too moralistic to be truly critical.

Inge, M. Thomas. See GENERAL.

Keller, Dean H. "Addendum to *BAL*: Sidney Lanier." *PBSA*, 67 (1973), 330.
   The additional item is a musical setting of "Evening Song."

Kimball, William J. "Realism in Sidney Lanier's 'Tiger-Lilies.'" *SAB*, 36 (March 1971), 17-20.
   Though imitative of German romance, this novel shows impressive realism in characters, combat scenes, and death in prison.

Leary, Lewis. See GENERAL--1st Leary entry.

Lease, Benjamin, ed. "Sidney Lanier and *Blackwood's Magazine*: An Unpublished Letter." *GHQ*, 53 (December 1969), 521-522.
   Lanier asked *Blackwood's* if it would be interested in an article or a series on conditions in the South during Reconstruction.

Libman, Valentina. See GENERAL.

Millgate, Michael. See FAULKNER, WILLIAM (Contemporary--1st Millgate entry).

Parks, Edd Winfield. *Sidney Lanier: The Man, The Poet, The Critic*. Athens: Univ of Georgia Press, 1968.
   A revaluation and critical appraisal of Lanier from three perspectives.

Reamer, Owen J. "Lanier's 'The Marshes of Glynn' Revisited." *Miss Quart*, 23 (Winter 1969-70), 57-63.
   Denies that the poem is a "mystic vision" and suggests instead that it reaffirms Lanier's belief that nature is symbolic of an ideal world.

Simms, L. Moody, Jr. "A Note on Sidney Lanier's Attitude Toward the Negro and Toward Populism." *GHQ*, 52 (September 1968), 305-307.
   Lanier's desired alliance between white and Negro farmers found brief fulfillment in the Populist movement.

Walcutt, Charles C., and J. E. Whitesell. See GENERAL.

Wright, Nathalia. "Edd Winfield Parks on Sidney Lanier." *So Lit Jour*, 2 (Fall 1969), 152-157.

III. POSTBELLUM (1865-1920)

An essay-review of *Sidney Lanier: The Man, The Poet, The Critic*, by the late Edd Winfield Parks, a book which represents his two chief scholarly interests: Southern poetry and criticism.

Young, Thomas Daniel. See HAYNE, PAUL HAMILTON (Postbellum).

[MALONE, WALTER] Rogers, Tommy W. "The DeSoto County Poet: Walter Malone." *Notes on Miss Writers*, 5 (Winter 1973), 84-97.
    An account of Malone's career.

[McCLELLAN, GEORGE MARION] Sherman, Joan R. "Tennessee's Black Poet: George Marion McClellan." *Tenn Stud in Lit*, 18 (1973), 147-162.
    McClellan's poetry "sensitively records the black artist's struggle to be both a Negro and an American."

[MURFREE, MARY NOAILLES] Carleton, Reese M. "Mary Noailles Murfree (1850-1922): An Annotated Bibliography." *Am Lit Realism*, 7 (Autumn 1974), 293-378.
    An extensive checklist of works by and about Murfree.

Durham, Frank. Untitled. *SHR*, 3 (Fall 1969), 400-401.
    An essay-review of Richard Cary's *Mary N. Murfree* (1967) and Perry D. Westbrook's *Mary Wilkins Freeman* (1967).

Lanier, Doris. "Mary Noailles Murfree: An Interview." *Tenn Hist Quart*, 31 (Fall 1972), 276-278.
    The reproduction of an article from the 15 November 1885 Macon (Georgia) *Telegraph* which "makes some interesting comments on Miss Murfree's personal characteristics, work habits, and methods of study."

Loyd, Dennis. "Tennessee's Mystery Woman Novelist." *Tenn Hist Quart*, 29 (Fall 1970), 272-277.
    A brief sketch of the career of Miss Murfree.

Murfree, Mary Noailles. *In the Tennessee Mountains*, ed. Nathalia Wright. Knoxville: Univ of Tennessee Press, 1970.
    Reprints the 1884 edition with an appreciation of Miss Murfree's achievements as a realistic portrayer of the character and language of East Tennesseans.

Nilles, Mary. "Craddock's Girls: A Look at Some Unliberated Women." *MarkR*, 3 (October 1972), 74-77.
    Most of Murfree's women characters are overly simple and not very believable.

Rhode, Robert D. See MISCELLANEOUS (Postbellum).

Parks, Edd Winfield. *Charles Egbert Craddock (Mary Noailles Murfree)*. Port Washington, N. Y.: Kennikat Press, 1972.
    A facsimile reprint of the 1941 critical biography.

Warfel, Harry R. "Local Color and Literary Artistry: Mary Noailles Murfree's *In the Tennessee Mountains*." *So Lit Jour*, 3 (Fall 1970), 154-163.
    Miss Murfree is memorable as a romantic artist transcending the immediate (local color) into the universal.

[PAGE, THOMAS NELSON] Bush, Robert. See MISCELLANEOUS (Postbellum).

Clark, Harry H. See GENERAL.

Godbold, E. Stanly, Jr. See MISCELLANEOUS (Postbellum).

Griffith, Benjamin W. See MISCELLANEOUS (Postbellum).

Gross, Theodore L. See GENERAL--1st Gross entry.

Holman, Harriet R. "Attempt and Failure: Thomas Nelson Page as Playwright." *So Lit Jour*, 3 (Fall 1970), 72-82.
    "...qualities in Page's character and in most of his fiction...suggest that drama was not his metier."

_____. "F. Marion Crawford and the Evil Eye." *Am N&Q*, 9 (March 1971), 103-104.
    Page ridicules superstitious Americans in Rome.

_____, ed. "*The Kentucky Journal of Thomas Nelson Page*." *KHSR*, 68 (January 1970), 1-16.
    In her introduction the editor traces the early career of Page in Kentucky.

_____, ed. "Thomas Nelson Page's Account of Tennessee Hospitality." *Tenn Hist Quart*, 28 (Fall 1969), 269-272.
    An editing of notes Page made of his favorable impressions of McMinnville, Tennessee, where he spoke on January 21, 1893. The notes are among Page's papers now housed at the University of Virginia.

_____. See FOX, JOHN, JR. (Postbellum--1st Holman entry.

King, Kimball. "Introduction" to *In Ole Virginia*. Chapel Hill: Univ of North Carolina Press, 1969.
    An analysis of Page's attitude towards the South as reflected in his collection of stories reprinted here in facsimile.

Lamplugh, George R. See MISCELLANEOUS (Postbellum).

Miller, Theodore C. See WASHINGTON, BOOKER T. (Postbellum).

Page, Rosewell. *When I Was a Little Boy*, with illustrations by Ellen Bruce. Miami, Fla.: Field Research Projects, 1970.
    Facsimile edition of an unpublished reminiscence by T. N. Page's brother, with a foreword and afterword by Harriet R. Holman.

Page, Thomas Nelson. *North African Journal, 1912, with Letters Along the Way*, ed. Harriet R. Holman. Miami, Fla.: Field Research Projects, 1970.

    The first publication of Page's journal with twenty-eight letters from Page and his wife about the journey; introduction, notes and index by the editor.

_____. *On the Nile in 1901*, ed. Henry Field. Miami, Fla.: Field Research Projects, 1969.

    The first publication of Page's diary of his journey on the Nile, January 9–March 8, 1901, by Page's grandson, Henry Field, with an introduction by Harriet R. Holman.

Polk, Noel E. See MISCELLANEOUS (Postbellum—1st Polk entry).

Rhode, Robert D. See MISCELLANEOUS (Postbellum).

Rubin, Louis D., Jr. "The Other Side of Slavery: Thomas Nelson Page's 'No Haid Pawn.'" *SLI*, 7 (Spring 1974), 95–99.

    Page, though he idealized plantation life, revealed in "No Haid Pawn" that he also felt the dark, threatening aspects of slavery.

_____. See MISCELLANEOUS (Postbellum).

_____. See GENERAL—6th Rubin entry.

Simms, L. Moody, Jr. "Corra Harris on the Declining Influence of Thomas Nelson Page." *Miss Quart*, 28 (Fall 1975), 505–509.

    Reprints portions of Mrs. Harris' 1907 "literary obituary" of Page.

Voss, Arthur. See GENERAL.

Woodress, James. See GENERAL—5th Woodress entry.

[PAGE, WALTER HINES] Gregory, Ross. *Walter Hines Page: Ambassador to the Court of St. James's*. Lexington: Univ Press of Kentucky, 1970.

    A historical study, based upon recently opened British documents, of Page's final years as ambassador to England (1915–1918) and his efforts to persuade President Wilson to intervene in World War I.

[PORTER, WILLIAM SYDNEY] Bungert, Hans. See GENERAL.

Echter, Reinhold. "O'Henry's 'Sound and Fury.'" *Neuren Sprachen*, 20 (July 1971), 370–379.

    Reprints the sketch and discusses it as parody.

E'jxenbaum, B. M. *O. Henry and the Theory of the Short Story*. Trans. I. R. Titunik. Ann Arbor, Mich.: Department of Slavic Languages and Literature, 1968.

    A translation from the Russian of an essay which first appeared in 1925.

Etulain, R. W. See GENERAL.

Libman, Valentina. See GENERAL.

Long, E. Hudson. *O. Henry: American Regionalist*. Southern Writers Series. Austin: Steck-Vaughn, 1969.

    Relates the fiction to Porter's early years in the South and in Texas, and affirms his importance as a regionalist.

Marks, Patricia. "O. Henry and Dickens: Elsie in the Bleak House of Moral Decay." *Eng Lang Notes*, 12 (September 1974), 35–37.

    O. Henry is indebted to *Bleak House* for the theme of "Elsie in New York"; the so-called "righteous" drive members of the lower class to their doom.

McLean, Malcolm D. "O. Henry in Honduras." *Am Lit Realism*, no. 3 (Summer 1968), 39–46.

    An account of O. Henry's six months in Honduras and location of spots described in his novel *Cabbages and Kings*.

Monteiro, George. "Hemingway, O. Henry, and the Surprise Ending." *PrS*, 47 (Winter 1973–74), 296–302.

    Despite his essential difference from O. Henry and "his public disclaimers notwithstanding, in practice Hemingway never did forsake the 'wow' or surprise ending."

O'Connor, Richard. *The Legendary Life of William S. Porter*. New York: Doubleday, 1970.

    Deals with Porter's "two lives," most of the book being devoted to the last eight years of his life.

Polk, Noel E. See MISCELLANEOUS (Postbellum—1st Polk entry).

Rea, John A. "The Idea for O. Henry's 'Gift of the Magi.'" *SHR*, 7 (Summer 1973), 311–314.

    Suggests that the "essential plot ingredients" along with "many of its circumstantial details" came from Emile Chevalet's "Dulvina."

Voss, Arthur. See GENERAL.

Weatherford, Richard M. "Stephen Crane and O. Henry: A Correction." *AL*, 44 (January 1973), 666.

    Paul M. Paine was the author of a parody of *The Red Badge of Courage*, not Porter.

Woodress, James. See GENERAL—1st Woodress entry.

[READ, OPIE] Baird, Reed A. "Opie Read: An American Traveler." *Tenn Hist Quart*, 33 (Winter 1974), 410–428.

    Read can be better appreciated "as a popular writer if we are aware that his life reflects an essential form of the American experience."

[RIVES, AMÉLIE] Moore, John H. "The Vagabond and the Lady: Letters from Richard Hovey to Amélie Rives." *Miss Quart*, 21 (Spring 1968), 131–143.

    Brief correspondence between a minor Northern poet and a minor Southern novelist in the late 1880's.

Taylor, Welford D. *Amélie Rives (Princess Troubetzkoy)*. Twayne U. S. Authors Series, no. 217. New York: Twayne, 1973.

A biographical and critical survey of the life and writings of a popular late nineteenth- and early twentieth-century novelist.

_____. "A 'Soul' Remembers Oscar Wilde." *Eng Lit in Transition*, 14, no. 1 (1970), 43-48.
Oswald Tyne, in Rives's autobiographical novel *Shadows of Flames*, is modeled on Oscar Wilde.

[RYAN, ABRAM JOSEPH] Boldrick, Msgr. C. C. "Father Abram J. Ryan: 'The Poet-Priest of the Confederacy.'" *FCHQ*, 46 (July 1972), 201-218.
A biographical sketch.

Lipscomb, Oscar H. "Some Unpublished Poems of Abram J. Ryan." *AlaR*, 25 (July 1972), 163-177.
A sketch of the "poet-priest of the South" precedes the poems.

Simms, L. Moody, Jr. "Father Abram Joseph Ryan: Poet of the Lost Cause." *Lincoln Herald*, 73 (Spring 1971), 3-7.
Traces Ryan's career as "the South's most beloved poet."

Weaver, Gordon, ed. *Selected Poems of Father Ryan*. Jackson: Univ and College Press of Mississippi, 1973.
A selection of sixty-three patriotic, religious, and personal poems by Ryan, with a brief introduction.

[SMITH, C. ALPHONSO] Braden, W. W. "C. Alphonso Smith on Southern Oratory Before the War." *So Speech Jour*, 36 (Winter 1970), 127-138.
Discusses the contribution of Smith to the emerging concept of Southern oratory.

[SMITH, CHARLES HENRY] Austin, James C. *Bill Arp*. Twayne's U. S. Authors Series, no. 162. New York: Twayne, 1969.
A study of the Bill Arp letters by Georgia humorist Charles Henry Smith, with emphasis on his thoughts on Southern history, his use of American English, and his recording of Georgia folklore.

Davis, Michael. See MISCELLANEOUS (Postbellum).

[TABB, JOHN BANNISTER] Miller, John C. See POE, EDGAR ALLAN (Antebellum--3rd Miller entry).

Polk, Noel E. See MISCELLANEOUS (Postbellum--1st Polk entry).

[TIMROD, HENRY] Barker, Addison. "Mr. Cannon's Unusual Schoolteacher." *Sandlapper*, 8 (May 1975), 17, 19.
A biographical account of Timrod's years of teaching.

Clark, Harry H. See GENERAL.

Green, Claud B. "Henry Timrod and the South." *So Car Rev*, 2 (May 1970), 27-33.
A revaluation.

[TOURGÉE, ALBION WINEGAR] Aaron, Daniel. See GENERAL.

Bowman, Sylvia E. "Judge Tourgée's Fictional Presentation of the Reconstruction." *Jour of Pop Culture*, 3 (Fall 1969), 307-323.
Title is descriptive.

Ealy, Marguerite, and Sanford Harovitz. "Albion Winegar Tourgée (1838-1905)." *Am Lit Realism*, 8 (Winter 1975), 53-80.
Bibliographical survey of primary and secondary material.

MacKaye, Steele, and Albion Tourgée. *A Fool's Errand*, ed. Dean H. Keller. Metuchen, N. J.: Scarecrow Press, 1969.
First printing of the dramatic version of the novel. The appendix contains a list of documents relating to the play and some of the reviews of it.

Magdol, Edward. "A Note of Authenticity: Eliab Hill and Nimbus Ware in *Bricks Without Straw*." *AQ*, 22 (Winter 1970), 907-911.
Discusses Hill as the fictional prototype for the fictional Ware.

Miller, Theodore C. See WASHINGTON, BOOKER T. (Postbellum).

Polk, Noel E. See MISCELLANEOUS (Postbellum--1st Polk entry).

White, Dana. "A Summons for the Kingdom of God on Earth: The Early Social Gospel Novel." *SAQ*, 63 (Summer 1968), 469-485.
Tourgée's *Murvale Eastman, Christian Socialist* is included as an example.

Yardley, Jonathan. "Friend of Freedom." *New Rep*, 162 (January 10, 1970), 30-32.
An essay-review of *Bricks Without Straw*, edited by Otto H. Olsen, which remarks that the author showed Southerners' responsibility for the failure of Reconstruction and recognized the South's vast possibilities for the literary imagination.

[TUGGLE, WILLIAM ORRIE] Current-Garcia, Eugene, and D. B. Hatfield, eds. *Shem, Ham & Japheth: The Papers of W. O. Tuggle*. Athens: Univ of Georgia Press, 1973.
An edition of the unpublished writings of Georgian Tuggle about life among Indians and whites between 1879-1882, with a biographical and historical introduction.

[TURNER, JOSEPH ADDISON] Huff, Lawrence. "Joseph Addison Turner and His Quarterly, the *Plantation*." *GHQ*, 54 (Winter 1970), 493-504.
Chronicles the founding and delineates the literary importance of the *Plantation*.

[WASHINGTON, BOOKER T.] Baker, Houston A., Jr. See GENERAL--1st, 3rd, and 4th Baker entries.

Bontemps, Arna. *Young Booker: The Story of Booker T. Washington's Younger Days*. New York: Dodd, Mead, 1972.
A biography for juveniles, covering Washington's life from his boyhood in Virginia to the Atlanta Exposition address in 1893.

Brown, Lloyd W. See GENERAL--2nd Brown entry.

Edmunds, P. W. See GENERAL.

Friedman, Lawrence J. "Life 'In the Lion's Mouth':
Another Look at Booker T. Washington." *JNH*, 59
(October 1974), 337-351.
    Washington paid a high price physically and
psychologically for his dedication to the cause
of "Tuskegee and Negro industrial training."

Grumbach, Doris. See GENERAL.

Harlan, J. C. "Booker T. Washington." *WVH*, 32
(January 1971), 121-123.
    A paper read at the annual meeting of the
West Virginia State Historical Society at
Charleston, October 3, 1970.

Harlan, Louis R. "Booker T. Washington and the
Kanawha Valley 1875-1879." *WVH*, 33
(January 1972), 124-141.
    An account of some of Washington's activities
as a teacher and helper of his people in Kanawha
Valley.

_____, ed. *The Booker T. Washington Papers*. Vol-
ume I: *The Autobiographical Writings*. Urbana:
Univ of Illinois Press, 1972.
    Newly edited texts of *Up from Slavery*, *Story
of My Life and Work*, and six shorter sketches,
with a historical introduction.

_____, ed. *The Booker T. Washington Papers*. Vol-
ume II: *1860-89*. Urbana: Univ of Illinois
Press, 1972.
    Annotated texts of over four hundred letters,
speeches, articles, and documents from Washington's birth through May 1889; thirteen volumes
are to follow.

_____, ed. *The Booker T. Washington Papers*. Vol.
III. Urbana: Univ of Illinois Press, 1974.
    Documents covering the period 1889-1895.

_____, ed. *The Booker T. Washington Papers*. Vol.
IV. Urbana: Univ of Illinois Press, 1975.
    Documents covering the period 1895-1898.

_____. "Booker T. Washington's West Virginia
Boyhood." *WVH*, 32 (January 1971), 63-85.
    Discusses the years from 1865-1872 when
Washington lived in the Kanawha Valley of West
Virginia.

_____. "The Secret Life of Booker T. Washington."
JSH, 37 (August 1971), 393-416.
    Discusses Washington's questionable motives
and activities which underlay his public role
as a black leader.

Harris, T. E., and P. C. Kennicott. "Booker T.
Washington: A Study of Conciliatory Rhetoric."
So Speech Jour, 37 (Fall 1971), 47.
    Washington's rhetoric was directed at appeas-
ing the blacks and pleasing the whites.

Huggins, Nathan I. "Making Visible and Invisible
Man." *Cweal*, 98 (May 18, 1973), 264-266.
    A review-essay of the first two volumes of a
projected thirteen-volume collection of the

papers of Booker T. Washington and of Louis R.
Harlan's *Booker T. Washington: The Making of a
Black Leader*.

Jones, Allen W. "The Role of Tuskegee Institute in
the Education of Black Farmers." *JNH*, 60
(April 1975), 252-267.
    A history and analysis of the role of
Booker T. Washington and Tuskegee in establishing
the Negro Farmers' Conference, the Tuskegee Experiment Station, and other organizations of concern to black farmers.

Miller, Theodore C. "The Booker T. Washington Dinner and Some American Writers." *Research Stud*,
39 (December 1971), 307-312.
    Deals with the generally antagonistic (Page,
for example) or unenthusiastic (Twain) reaction
to Theodore Roosevelt's inviting Washington to
dinner at the White House. Tourgée was the
only writer who praised Roosevelt's action.

Shaw, F. H. "Booker T. Washington and the Future of
Black Americans." *GHQ*, 56 (Summer 1972),
193-209.
    "When all the qualifications are made,
Washington was, in the language of the 1960's,
a 'black power' advocate."

Smith, Sidonie. See GENERAL.

Thornbrough, Emma Lou, ed. *Booker T. Washington*.
Great Lives Observed Series. Englewood Cliffs,
N. J.: Prentice-Hall, 1969.
    Structured according to Washington's views
of the world, the reactions of his contemporaries
to him, and his place in history.

Weisberger, B. A. *Booker T. Washington*. New York:
New American Library, 1972.
    Original paperback publication of a brief
survey biography of Washington.

White, Arthur O. "Booker T. Washington's Florida
Incident, 1903-1904." *FHQ*, 51 (January 1973),
227-249.
    Recounts problems when Washington was invited
to address a racially mixed group.

Woodward, C. Vann. "The Master of Tuskegee." *New
Rep*, 167 (November 11, 1972), 20-22.
    The Story of My Life and *Up From Slavery* were
largely written by ghost writers and do not present the complex man Booker T. Washington privately was.

[WHITMAN, ALBERY ALLSON] Isani, Mukhtar. See
GENERAL.

Marshall, Carl L. "Two Protest Poems by Albery A.
Whitman." *CLA Jour*, 19 (September 1975), 50-56.
    Two long narrative poems by Whitman, *Not a
Man and Yet a Man* and *The Rape of Florida*, emphasized the need for "full civil and political
rights for blacks."

Sherman, Joan R. "Albery Allson Whitman: Poet of
Beauty and Manliness." *CLA Jour*, 14
(December 1971), 126-143.
    A biographical and critical introduction to
the Reconstruction black poet (1851-1901). Includes bibliography.

III. Postbellum (1865-1920)

[WILLIAMS, ESPY W. H.] Talbot, Frances G. "Rediscovered--Espy W. H. Williams, Louisiana Playwright: A Checklist." *La Stud*, 9 (Summer 1970), 105-117.
    Williams (1852-1908), once called "the South's leading dramatist," wrote thirty-two plays.

[MISCELLANEOUS] Adams, Richard P. "Southern Literature in the 1890's." *Miss Quart*, 21 (Fall 1968), 277-281.
    In a "comparatively barren period," the writings of T. N. Page, G. W. Harris, J. L. Allen, Mark Twain, and Kate Chopin represent "a genuine proto-modern tradition in Southern literature."

Alexander, Nancy. "*Looking West from Comanche*: Robert T. Hill Comes to Texas." *SWR*, 59 (Winter 1974), 1-16.
    An account of geologist Hill's seven years in Texas, including information about his work on several Texas newspapers.

Bissell, Claude T. "Haliburton, Leacock, and the American Humorous Tradition." *Can Lit*, 39 (Winter 1969), 5-19.
    Mainly on Canadian writers but with some references to Twain and other American humorists.

Budd, Louis J. "Introduction" to "The Forgotten Decades of Southern Writing, 1890-1920" (A Symposium; see R. P. Adams, Paschal Reeves, and D. T. Turner under this Miscellaneous listing). *Miss Quart*, 21 (Fall 1968), 275-277.
    The purpose of this symposium is "to inquire if any of the literature published between 1890 and 1920 has intrinsic value or else had value for the major writers who grew up with it as their current models."

Burbank, Rex, and J. B. Moore, eds. *The Literature of the American Realistic Period*. Columbus, Ohio: Charles E. Merrill, 1970.
    An anthology arranged by genre with general introductions; Twain, Lanier, Toomer, J. W. Johnson, and Cable are represented.

Bush, Robert. "Dr. Alderman's Symposium on the South." *Miss Quart*, 27 (Winter 1973-74), 3-19.
    Contains previously unpublished letters of Woodrow Wilson, Frederick Jackson Turner, Thomas Nelson Page, Ellen Glasgow, W. P. Trent, Albert Shaw, Ashton Phelps, C. Alphonso Smith, G. P. Alexander, and Basil Gildersleeve, from which E. A. Alderman drew his material for his 1908 speech on the South's contribution to the nation.

Chametzky, Jules. "Our Decentralized Literature: A Consideration of Regional, Ethnic, Racial, and Sexual Factors." *Jahrbuch für Amerikastudien*, 17 (1972), 56-72.
    States that Cable, Chesnutt, and Chopin are more than just regional writers because of their concern with changes taking place in the nation as a whole.

Cohn, Jan. "The Civil War in Magazine Fiction of the 1860's." *Jour of Pop Culture*, 4 (Fall 1970), 355-382.
    An analysis of eighty-seven stories published in the 1860's shows most to be of mediocre quality, though sentimental treatment by female writers in the early years gives way to better work by more realistic male writers toward the end of the decade.

Davis, Michael. *The Image of Lincoln in the South*. Knoxville: Univ of Tennessee Press, 1971.
    Describes the change in the public image of Lincoln in the South from anathema to admiration, with full analyses of writings by Bledsoe, Mary B. Chesnut, Thomas Dixon, G. W. Harris, Charles H. Smith, Henry Watterson, and others.

Doughty, Nanelia S. "Realistic Negro Characterization in Post-bellum Fiction." *NALF*, 3 (1969), 57-62.
    Though the majority of nineteenth-century writers stereotyped blacks, exceptions can be found, including the work of Twain and Cable.

Eichelberger, Clayton L. *A Guide to Critical Reviews of U. S. Fiction, 1870-1910*. Metuchen, N. J.: Scarecrow Press, 1971.
    An index to critical comment on American fiction found in thirty periodicals of the late nineteenth century; entries for numerous major and minor Southerners are included.

Foster, Gaines M. "Mirage in the Sahara of the Bozart: *The Library of Southern Literature*." *Miss Quart*, 28 (Winter 1974-75), 3-19.
    Describes the compilation and reception of *The Library of Southern Literature*.

Friedlander, Mitzi. "History of a Theatre." *FCHQ*, 45 (July 1971), 305-314.
    History of the Grand Opera House, which opened in 1894, in Louisville, Kentucky.

Friedman, Lawrence J. *The White Savage: Racial Fantasies in the Postbellum South*. Englewood Cliffs, N. J.: Prentice-Hall, 1970.
    An analysis of the social and psychological roots of racial fantasies among white Southerners, based upon their factual and fictional writings.

Gaston, Paul M. *The New South Creed: A Study in Southern Mythmaking*. New York: Knopf, 1970.
    An intellectual history of the "New South" concept and period.

Godbold, E. Stanly, Jr. "A Battleground Revisited: Reconstruction in Southern Fiction, 1895-1905." *SAQ*, 73 (Winter 1974), 99-116.
    Deals with the differences in views of six Southern writers who wrote about Reconstruction: Glasgow, Page, Dixon, J. C. Harris, Cable, and John S. Wise.

Griffith, Benjamin W. "Csardas at Salt Springs: Southern Culture in 1888." *GaR*, 26 (Spring 1972), 53-59.
    In the summer of 1888 the Piedmont Chautauqua, organized by Henry W. Grady and others, presented a number of cultural attractions

including a Mexican band, a string quartet, and a reading by Thomas Nelson Page at Salt Springs, Georgia.

Herndon, Jane. "Henry McNeal Turner's African Dream: A Re-Evaluation." *Miss Quart*, 22 (Fall 1969), 327-336.
     Turner (1834-1915) was an advocate of African colonization and a precursor of recent leadership in the "Negro revolution" in the United States.

Heyl, Edgar G. "Plays by Marylanders, 1870-1916." *MHM*, 65 (Fall 1970), 301-303.
     A checklist of Maryland playwrights whose surnames begin with "R."

Hughes, Emmy. *Dissipations at Uffington House: The Letters of Emmy Hughes.* MVC Bulletin no. 8. Memphis, Tenn.: Memphis State Univ, 1975.
     A collection of thirty-five letters written in 1881-1887 to a British friend about the building of Uffington House in Rugby, Tennessee, and the lives of its occupants.

Jones, Lewis P. "The Second Epoch of *The State*, 1903-1913," in *South Carolina Journals and Journalists*. Columbia, S. C.: Southern Studies Program, 1975, pp. 17-39.
     A study of this important Columbia newspaper and the Gonzales family who edited it. Social and political history of the state are treated.

Lamplugh, George R. "The Image of the Negro in Popular Magazine Fiction, 1875-1900." *JNH*, 57 (April 1972), 177-189.
     Deals with Negro characters in the local-color fiction of Lizzie W. Shampney, Ruth McEnery Stuart, Joel Chandler Harris, Thomas Nelson Page, Harry Stillwell Edwards, Mollie Moore Davis, and others, as published in *Atlantic*, *Harper's*, *Scribner's*, and *Century*.

Mason, Julian. "Owen Wister and the South." (In "Four Authors View the South: A Symposium.") *SHR*, 6 (Winter 1972), 23-24.
     Although it does contain "intentional and strong negative social criticism," "the greater and more pervasive positive aspect" of *Lady Baltimore* is "the preservation of old Charleston through literature."

Moore, Rayburn S. *Southern Literary Magazines, II: 'A Distinctively Southern Magazine': The Southern Bivouac*." *So Lit Jour*, 2 (Spring 1970), 51-65.
     The poetry in the *Bivouac* is generally better than the fiction, and the literary criticism is primarily directed toward Southern writers but is not "blatantly parochial in tone."

Overstreet, Robert. "John T. Ford and the Savannah Theater." *So Speech Comm Jour*, 38 (Fall 1972), 51-60.
     "John T. Ford of Baltimore contributed richly to theater in Savannah."

Parsons, Coleman O. "Steamboating as Seen by Passengers and River Men: 1875-1884." *Miss Quart*, 24 (Winter 1970-71), 19-34.
     Descriptions of boats, scenery, Natchez, and Vicksburg by two cabin boys, a captain, and Lafcadio Hearn.

Polk, Noel E., comp. and ed. "Guide to Dissertations on American Literary Figures, 1870-1910: Part One." *Am Lit Realism*, 8 (Summer 1975), 177-280; Part Two, 8 (Autumn 1975), 291-340.
     Part I includes sections by individual compilers on Sherwood Bonner, Chesnutt, Chopin, John Fox, Jr., and Charles E. A. Gayarré; Part II contains sections on Richard Malcolm Johnston, Grace King, T. N. Page, W. S. Porter, Opie Read, John Bannister Tabb, and Albion Tourgée.

Polk, Noel E. "W. W. Hicks and *The XIX Century*, 1869-1871," in *South Carolina Journals and Journalists*. Columbia, S. C.: Southern Studies Program, 1975, pp. 121-131.
     A study of this Charleston periodical.

Reeves, Paschal. "From Halley's Comet to Prohibition." *Miss Quart*, 21 (Fall 1968), 285-290.
     Though "not all Southern writers [of this period] were oblivious to changing fashions in fiction," tradition generally held its grip; thus, "when we deduct Ellen Glasgow and James Branch Cabell, the remainder is negligible before the tidal wave to come."

Rhode, Robert D. *Setting in the American Short Story of Local Color: 1865-1900*. The Hague: Mouton, 1975.
     Reviews the fiction of ten local-color writers, including Clemens, Cable, Murfree, Page, and Allen, focusing on the element of setting and the increasing sophistication in the use of outdoor physical surroundings.

Rubin, Louis D., Jr. "Southern Local Color and the Black Man." *SouR*, 6 (Autumn 1970), 1011-1030.
     Traces the ways white Southern writers have depicted black characters, focusing on Simms, Page, J. C. Harris, Cable, and Clemens.

Simms, L. Moody, Jr. "Constance Fenimore Woolson on Southern Literary Taste." *Miss Quart*, 22 (Fall 1969), 362-366.
     A reprinting of an unsigned article published in 1878 in which Miss Woolson shows Southern preference for English and native writers rather than the recent Northern authors.

_____. "Josiah Royce and the Southern Race Question." *Miss Quart*, 22 (Winter 1968-69), 71-74.
     Philosopher of the Absolute, Royce suggested a long-range solution to the race problem in the United States in his *Race Questions, Provincialism and Other American Problems* (1908).

Sloane, Karen. "Plays about Louisiana, 1870-1915: A Checklist." *La Stud*, 8 (Spring 1969), 26-35.
     Title is descriptive.

Soderbergh, Peter A. "Florida's Image in Juvenile Fiction: 1909-1914." *FHQ*, 51 (October 1972), 153-165.
     Although dealing with non-Southern writers, the author centers his comments on Florida.

_____. "The South in Juvenile Series Books, 1907-1917." *Miss Quart*, 27 (Spring 1974), 131-140.
Juvenile series books of this era were a powerful force contributing "directly to the reinforcement of subjective misconceptions" about the South among the millions of young readers around the country.

Turner, Darwin T. "Southern Fiction, 1900-1910." *Miss Quart*, 21 (Fall 1968), 281-285.
The literature of this period at "its best" followed a tradition which "honored local color, sentimental romance, or a mixture"; at "its worst...Southern fiction suffered from melodrama, idealized characterization, provincial thought, and didactic moralizing."

Weaver, Richard M. *The Southern Tradition at Bay: A History of Postbellum Thought*, ed. George Core and M. E. Bradford. New Rochelle, N. Y.: Arlington House, 1968.
First completed in 1943 and now published posthumously, an evaluation of the Southern tradition through fictional and nonfictional materials, with commentary on such novelists as J. L. Allen, G. W. Cable, J. E. Cooke, J. C. Harris, T. N. Page, W. G. Simms, etc.

Willimon, W. H. "John William DeForest." *Sandlapper*, 5 (July 1972), 54-59.
A summary of DeForest's comments on postwar South Carolina while he was agent of the Freedman's Bureau.

Yoder, Edwin M., Jr. "Francis Warrington Dawson Revisited," in *South Carolina Journals and Journalists*. Columbia, S. C.: Southern Studies Program, 1975, pp. 1-15.
A study of this English-born editor's career with the Charleston *News and Courier* (1873-1889).

IV. Contemporary (1920–1975)

[ABBEY, EDWARD] Pilkington, Tom. "Edward Abbey: Western Philosopher, or How to be a 'Happy Hopi Hippie.'" *WAL*, 9 (Spring 1974), 17–31.
Sees in Abbey's writings a consistent statement that Western civilization is bankrupt because of its loss of contact with the finite realities of nature and body through over-reliance on abstract thought.

[AGEE, JAMES] Anon. "The Perpetual Promise of James Agee." *TLS*, no. 3,667 (June 9, 1972), 659–660.
This long review of *The Collected Poems of James Agee* and *The Collected Short Prose of James Agee* states that "with his entire creative life stretching ahead of him, he had almost nothing left to learn."

Agee, James. *Letters of James Agee to Father Flye*. Second Edition. Boston: Houghton Mifflin, 1971.
Contains a new preface and eleven previously unpublished letters by Father Flye, 1938-1950.

Barson, Alfred T. *A Way of Seeing: A Critical Study of James Agee*. Amherst: Univ of Massachusetts Press, 1972.
A study of Agee's vision.

Betts, Leonidas. "The 'Unfathomably Mysterious' *Let Us Now Praise Famous Men*." *EJ*, 59 (January 1970), 44-47, 51.
An unconventional book, *Let Us Now Praise Famous Men* presents an accurate picture of the life of Alabama tenant-farm families and a commentary on the human condition in general.

Broughton, George and Panthea. "Agee and Autonomy." *SHR*, 4 (Spring 1970), 101-111.
"Agee's entire literary output is...permeated with his commitment to the issue of personal autonomy."

Chesnick, Eugene. "The Plot Against Fiction: *Let Us Now Praise Famous Men*." *So Lit Jour*, 4 (Fall 1971), 48-67.
In *Let Us Now Praise Famous Men*, Agee, guilty of sacrificing life for art, "achieves only a kind of stasis because his identification with people is at once too near and too far to produce action."

Coles, Robert. *Irony in the Mind's Eye: Essays on Novels by James Agee, Elizabeth Bowen, and George Eliot*. Charlottesville: Univ Press of Virginia, 1974.
A child psychiatrist discusses *A Death in the Family*.

Condon, Judith. "James Agee in Paperback." *CamQ*, 5 (Autumn 1970), 200-207.
An essay-review of *Let Us Now Praise Famous Men*.

Cooper, Arthur. "Appreciating Agee." *Newsweek*, 73 (April 7, 1969), 86.
A laudatory review of Agee's *Collected Short Prose* and *Collected Poems*, both edited by Robert Fitzgerald.

Cowley, Malcolm. See MISCELLANEOUS (Contemporary-- 2nd Cowley entry).

Curry, Kenneth. "The Knoxville of James Agee's *A Death in the Family*." *Tenn Stud in Lit*, 14 (1969), 1-14.
Demonstrates the factual accuracy of the Knoxville scene of the novel and shows, among other things, Agee's use of the city as a device for "stressing conflicts within the family circle."

_____. "Notes on the Text of James Agee's *A Death in the Family*." *PBSA*, 64 (1st Qtr. 1970), 84-99.
A comparison of the first edition with the periodical appearances.

Dietrichson, Jan W. "Theme and Technique in James Agee's *A Death in the Family*." *Am Stud in Scand*, 6 (1974), 1-20.
Analyzes structure and themes.

Fitzgerald, Robert. "James Agee: A Memoir." *KR*, 30, no. 5 (1968), 587-624.
An abridged version of Fitzgerald's introduction to *The Collected Short Prose of James Agee*.

_____. "A Memoir," in *The Collected Short Prose of James Agee*. Boston: Houghton Mifflin, 1969, pp. 3-57.
A full biographical memoir of Agee from his days as a college student up to his early death, utilizing his letters and other personal

documents, and asserting his fulfillment as a writer of promise; prefaces Agee's uncollected prose, important to an understanding of his achievement.

Freeman, James A. "Agee's 'Sunday' Meditation." *Concerning Poetry*, 3 (Fall 1970), 37-39.
Irresponsible love begins in happiness but leads to desolation, which will be passed on to the next generation.

French, Warren. See MISCELLANEOUS (Contemporary-- 1st French entry).

Hiers, John T. See MISCELLANEOUS (Contemporary).

Howarth, W. L. "Some Principles of Autobiography." *New Lit Hist*, 5 (Winter 1974), 363-381.
Agee is one of a list of "poetic autobiographers" who "draw only tentative, experimental self-portraits."

Hynes, Samuel. "James Agee: *Let Us Now Praise Famous Men*," in *Landmarks of American Writing*, ed. Hennig Cohen. New York: Basic Books, 1969, pp. 328-340.
Agee's book about Southern sharecroppers in the thirties, fundamentally unclassifiable, "is a work of art concerned with the problems of creating a work of art."

Kramer, Victor A. "Agee and Plans for the Criticism of Popular Culture." *Jour of Pop Culture*, 5 (Spring 1972), 755-766.
Several times during the 1930's and 1940's Agee proposed one or more magazines or books for the serious analysis of advertisements, news stories, speeches, songs, and other products of America's popular culture. His movie criticism, which indicates that even mediocre films were of interest to him as anthropological data, suggests the direction these projects would have taken if they had materialized.

_____. "Agee in the Forties: The Struggle to Be a Writer." *Tex Quart*, 11 (Spring 1968), 9-17.
An introduction to several Agee manuscripts printed for the first time in this issue.

_____. "Agee's *Let Us Now Praise Famous Men*: Image of Tenant Life." *Miss Quart*, 25 (Fall 1972), 405-417.
Perhaps Agee's masterwork, this book is so complex that it has been called a failure, whereas what it accomplishes is a picture of a way of life.

_____. "Agee's Projected Screenplay for Chaplin: Scientists and Tramps." *SHR*, 7 (Fall 1973), 357-364.
Though only a beginning, the sketch for "Scientists and Tramps" shows important "insight into the difficulty of maintaining one's integrity in a society such as ours."

_____. "Agee's Use of Regional Material in *A Death in the Family*." *Appal Jour*, 1 (Autumn 1972), 72-80.
The novel reveals awareness of the values of a Tennessee mountain heritage.

_____. "The Complete 'Work' Chapter for James Agee's *Let Us Now Praise Famous Men*." *Tex Quart*, 15 (Summer 1972), 27-48.
Reproduces a part of a chapter omitted from the published work, apparently to save space; the omitted portion illustrates the "excruciating exactness" with which Agee "elaborated his vision of physical labor as the center of a way of life."

_____. "*A Death in the Family* and Agee's Projected Novel." *Proof*, 1 (1973), 139-154.
The editors of the uncompleted holograph of this work probably imposed a form that Agee did not intend.

_____. "James Agee's Unpublished Manuscript and His Emphasis on Religious Emotion in *The Morning Watch*." *Tenn Stud in Lit*, 17 (1972), 159-164.
"The unused manuscript consists of an alternate beginning and ending for the book and emphasizes the difficulty of an adult's sustaining his religious fervor."

_____. "The Manuscript and the Text of James Agee's *A Death in the Family*." *PBSA*, 65 (3rd Qtr. 1971), 257-266.
"The fundamental reason for the present article is to provide a listing of definite errors which have been incorporated into the text."

_____. "Premonition of Disaster: An Unpublished Section for Agee's *A Death in the Family*." *Costerus*, 1 (1974), 83-93.
An analytical and descriptive note on the manuscript accompanies publication of the complete text of "Premonition."

Larsen, Erling. *James Agee*. Minnesota Pamphlets on American Writers. Minneapolis: Univ of Minnesota Press, 1971.
A general critical introduction to Agee's poetry and prose.

Madden, David, ed. *Remembering James Agee*. Baton Rouge: Louisiana State Univ Press, 1974.
Reprints eleven essays on Agee by friends, associates, and fellow critics, and includes a new memoir by his wife and an introduction by the editor.

Magill, Frank. See MISCELLANEOUS (Contemporary).

Pells, R. H. See MISCELLANEOUS (Contemporary).

Perry, J. Douglas, Jr. "Thematic Counterpoint in *A Death in the Family*: The Function of the Six Extra Scenes." *Novel*, 5 (Spring 1972), 234-241.
The six extra scenes are essential to the novel in that they state both the basic family relationship and the basic issues.

Pratt, Linda Ray. "Imagining Existence: Form and History in Steinbeck and Agee." *SouR*, 11 (Winter 1975), 84-98.
Includes a study of how Agee gave artistic form to *Let Us Now Praise Famous Men*.

Ramsey, Roger. "The Double Structure of *The Morning Watch*." *Stud in the Novel*, 4 (Fall 1972), 494-503.
    A treatment of how Agee used the story of Christ's crucifixion as an underlying structure for the novella.

Rewak, William J. "James Agee's *The Morning Watch*: Through Darkness to Light." *Tex Quart*, 14 (Autumn 1973), 21-37.
    Discusses the progression in Agee's ideas.

Rupp, Richard. See MISCELLANEOUS (Contemporary).

Samway, Patrick. "James Agee: A Family Man." *Thought*, 47 (Spring 1972), 40-68.
    An examination of Agee's interest in family life and his "quest for an artistic form which would adequately express his vision of family life."

Seib, Kenneth. *James Agee: Promise and Fulfillment*. Pittsburgh: Univ of Pittsburgh Press, 1968.
    An introductory guide to Agee's published writings which attempts to rescue him from the graveyard of American authors of unfulfilled promise.

Sheed, Wilfrid. "All-American." *NYRB*, 12 (May 22, 1969), 36-38.
    An essay-review of *The Collected Short Prose of James Agee* in which the reviewer concludes that Agee "remained the quintessential promising young writer to the day of his death at forty-five."

_____. See MISCELLANEOUS (Contemporary).

Shepherd, Allen. "'A Sort of Monstrous Grinding Beauty': Reflections on Character and Theme in James Agee's *A Death in the Family*." *I Eng Yearbk*, 14 (Fall 1969), 17-24.
    Deals chiefly with methods of characterization, considered here to be the most significant feature of this novel.

Sosnoski, James J. "Craft and Intention in James Agee's *A Death in the Family*." *Jour of Gen Ed*, 20 (October 1968), 170-183.
    In this work death is treated as "simply an event"; the novel is an "intensely realistic examination of death and the human condition, masterfully disguised as domestic melodrama."

_____. "A Significant Failure." *Jour of Gen Ed*, 26 (April 1974), 69-76.
    A review of Alfred T. Barson's *A Way of Seeing: A Critical Study of James Agee*, which concludes that "Agee's vision is more significant than his art."

Stanford, Donald E. "The Poetry of James Agee: The Art of Recovery." *SouR*, 10 (Spring 1974), xvi-xix.
    An essay on Agee's relation to the poetry of the established literary tradition.

Stott, William M. See MISCELLANEOUS (Contemporary).

[AIKEN, CONRAD] Baldeshwiler, Eileen. See GENERAL.

Brown, Calvin S. "The Achievement of Conrad Aiken." *GaR*, 27 (Winter 1973), 477-488.
    A general survey of the literary career of Aiken, the "last survivor" of the "distinguished group" which produced "the revolution in American poetry about the time of the First World War."

Bungert, Hans. See GENERAL.

Carlile, Robert E. "*Great Circle*: Conrad Aiken's Musico-Literary Technique." *GaR*, 22 (Spring 1968), 27-36.
    Musical allusions to Mozart's *The Magic Flute* in Chapter 4 provide "a key to a greater understanding of the tone of the novel."

Costa, Richard. "Conrad Aiken (1889-1973): The Wages of Neglect." *Fiction Internat'le*, nos. 2/3 (1974), 76-80.
    In a 1967 interview Aiken discussed his relations with other writers and critics; neglect of him caused Aiken to become embittered.

Cowley, Malcolm. "Conrad Aiken: From Savannah to Emerson." *SouR*, 11 (Spring 1975), 245-259.
    Sees an underlying unity in Aiken's work, and two new developments in the later poems--an element of ancestral piety and a version of New England transcendentalism.

Crunden, Robert M. See MISCELLANEOUS (Contemporary).

DeMott, Benjamin. "Life Carved to a Pointed End." *SatR*, 54 (January 30, 1971), 23-25.
    Deals with Aiken's literary reputation.

Durrant, Geoffrey. "Aiken and Lowry." *Can Lit*, no. 64 (Spring 1975), 24-40.
    Compares and contrasts the use of Greek myth in Aiken's *Blue Voyage* and Lowry's *Ultramarine*, pointing out the influence of the former on the latter work.

Handa, Carolyn. "'Impulse': Calculated Artistry in Conrad Aiken." *Stud SF*, 12 (Fall 1975), 375-380.
    Aiken's short stories reveal a "wealth of artistry"; "Impulse" contains "clues to Aiken's intricate fictional and poetic styles."

Holloway, John. "Conrad Aiken, Folk-Poet." *Art Internat'l*, 15 (October 20, 1971), 80-84, 87.
    Discusses defects in Aiken's poetry and reasons for them.

Lawrence, Alexander A. "228 Habersham Street." *GaR*, 22 (Fall 1968), 317-334.
    A biographical account of Conrad Aiken's Savannah childhood and references to it in his works.

Lerner, Arthur. See POE, EDGAR ALLAN.

Magill, Frank N. See MISCELLANEOUS (Contemporary).

Mangione, Jerre. See MISCELLANEOUS (Contemporary).

McMichael, Charles T., and Ted R. Spivey. "'Chaos--hurray!--is come again': Heroism in James Joyce and Conrad Aiken." *SLI*, 3 (October 1970), 65-68.

Both *Finnegan's Wake* and Aiken's "The Coming Forth by Day of Osiris Jones" deal with the common man's potentiality for heroism.

Mellard, James M. See MISCELLANEOUS (Contemporary).

Ruffini, Rosalia, ed. "Due Lettere di Conrad Aiken." *SA*, 14 (1969), 451-454.
  Letters in which Aiken comments on his unorthodox religious views and his intentions in "The Crystal."

Sanders, Frederick K. "A Chronology of Awareness: A Poet's Vision." *SR*, 81 (Winter 1973), 172-184.
  A review-essay of Aiken's *Ushant* and *Collected Poems*, arguing that *Ushant* is Aiken's most important work, an incomparable autobiography, a twentieth-century pilgrim's progress, a poet's "Prelude" in prose.

Spivey, Ted R. "Conrad Aiken: Resident of Savannah." *SouR*, 8 (Autumn 1972), 792-804.
  These comments on Aiken's relations with Savannah include impressions from visits as well as some research in Aiken's work.

_____. "Conrad Aiken's *Ushant*: Record of a Contemporary Poet's Quest for Self-Knowledge." *SAB*, 36 (November 1971), 21-28.
  Ushant reveals that vision has enabled him to look calmly at the past.

Tabachnick, Stephen E. "The Great Circle Voyage of Conrad Aiken's *Mr. Arcularis*." *AL*, 45 (January 1974), 590-607.
  The "crucial element in Aiken's unified vision [is] the 'great circle' voyage"; traces Aiken's use of this image and interprets *Mr. Arcularis* in the light of it.

Waterman, Arthur E. "Conrad Aiken as Critic: The Consistent View." *Miss Quart*, 24 (Spring 1971), 91-110.
  Aiken's forty-four years of reviewing and commenting on twentieth-century literature reveal a carefully formulated theory.

_____. "The Evolution of Consciousness: Conrad Aiken's Novels and *Ushant*." *Critique*, 15, no. 2 (1973), 67-81.
  Sees consciousness as Aiken's answer to the breakdown between man and world in modern times.

[AMMONS, A. R.] Berry, Wendell. "A Secular Pilgrimage." *HudR*, 23 (Autumn 1970), 401-424.
  Ammons is discussed rather briefly as being one of three contemporary poets who has "turned to the natural world, not as a source of imagery, but as subject and inspiration."

Bloom, Harold. "Dark and Radiant Peripheries: Mark Strand and A. R. Ammons." *SouR*, 8 (Winter 1972), 133-149.
  Places Ammons in the Emersonian tradition and says that he and Strand are "miraculously strong poets."

_____. "Emerson and Ammons: A Coda." *Diacritics*, 3 (Winter 1973), 45-46.

Applying the terminology of Isaac Luria of Safed to Ammons' work, Bloom concludes that "in him the greatness and the desolating dangers of Emerson are renewed," that it is in his work that "we are compelled to find again the American sublime."

Carruth, Hayden. "Here Today: A Poetic Chronicle." *HudR*, 24 (Summer 1972), 320-336.
  This review-essay includes discussion of Ammons' *Briefings* and (brief) of Tate's *The Swimmers*.

Grossvogel, D. I. "Interview/A. R. Ammons." *Diacritics*, 3 (Winter 1973), 47-53.
  Contains typical questions and answers on typical interview topics.

Harmon, William. "'How Does One Come Home': A. R. Ammons's *Tape for the Turn of the Year*." *So Lit Jour*, 7 (Spring 1975), 3-32.
  Tape belongs in that select group of long poems "genuinely American and genuinely great."

Howard, Richard. See MISCELLANEOUS (Contemporary).

Jacobsen, Josephine. "The Talk of Giants." *Diacritics*, 3 (Winter 1973), 34-38.
  Ammons is a major American poet, concerned with choice, levels, and utility.

Kalstone, David. "Ammons' Radiant Toys." *Diacritics*, 3 (Winter 1973), 13-20.
  Discusses Ammons as a writer of pastoral poetry and defines his type of pastoral.

Mazzaro, Jerome. "Reconstruction in Art." *Diacritics*, 3 (Winter 1973), 39-44.
  Ammons has been influenced by a number of poets of the nineteenth century, especially Emerson.

Meredith, William. "I Will Tell You About It Because It is Interesting." *Parnassus*, 2 (Fall/Winter 1973), 175-185.
  A review of Ammons' *Collected Poems 1951-1971*.

Miles, Josephine. "Light, Wind, Motion." *Diacritics*, 3 (Winter 1973), 21-24.
  Ammons is concerned with finding illumination in the natural world and with balancing generality with motion.

Morgan, Robert. "The Compound Vision of A. R. Ammons's Early Poems." *Epoch*, 22 (Spring 1973), 343-363.
  Ammons is interested in finding unity in multiplicity.

Oberg, Arthur. "Frazzling Reality." *Ohio Rev*, 15 no. 3 (1974), 107-110.
  Believes that Ammons is "one of our most important poets."

Orr, Linda. "The Cosmic Backyard of A. R. Ammons." *Diacritics*, 3 (Winter 1973), 3-12.
  In his earlier work, Ammons was attempting poetry of transcendence; the earlier aim keeps interfering with his later aim to write poetry of motion.

Parker, Patricia A. "Configurations of Shape and Flow." *Diacritics*, 3 (Winter 1973), 25-33.
"Corsons Inlet" and "Saliences" are an important reflection of Ammons' seeking after a way to achieve shape without preventing flow.

Sheehan, Donald. "The Silver Sensibility: Five Recent Books of American Poetry." *ConL*, 12 (Winter 1971), 98-121.
Ammons' *Selected Poems* (1968) is among the works discussed in this review-essay.

Tarbet, Donald W. See MISCELLANEOUS (Contemporary).

Vendler, Helen. "Poetry: Ammons, Berryman, Cummings." *YR*, 62 (Spring 1973), 412-425.
Part of this review-essay concerns Ammons' *Collected Poems 1951-1971*, concluding that Ammons has the potential of writing "the first twentieth-century poetry wholly purged of the romantic."

Zweig, Paul. "The Raw and the Cooked." *PR*, 41 no. 4 (1974), 604-612.
Part of this review concerns Ammons' *Collected Poems 1951-1971*; Ammons' "real achievement" is "the lyrical articulation of small moments of experience."

[ANDERSON, SHERWOOD] McHaney, Thomas L. See FAULKNER, WILLIAM (1st McHaney entry).

Taylor, Welford D. "Sherwood Anderson." *Va Cavalcade*, 19 (Spring 1970), 42-47.
An account of Anderson's last years in Southwestern Virginia, where he used the name of "Buck Fever" as a journalistic mask to criticize bad local conditions.

[ANGELOU, MAYA] Kent, George E. "Maya Angelou's *I Know Why the Caged Bird Sings* and Black Autobiographical Tradition." *Kansas Quart*, 7 (Summer 1975), 72-78.
Discusses the "unique place" of this work in black autobiography.

_____. See MISCELLANEOUS (Contemporary).

Smith, Sidonie Ann. "The Song of a Caged Bird: Maya Angelou's Quest After Self-Acceptance." *SHR*, 7 (Fall 1973), 365-375.
"Maya Angelou's style testifies to her reaffirmation of self-acceptance, the self-acceptance she achieves within the pattern of the autobiography."

[ARMSTRONG, ANNE W.] Armstrong, Anne W. *This Day and Time*. Johnson City, Tenn.: Research Advisory Council of East Tennessee State Univ, 1970.
A reprint of the 1930 regional novel set in East Tennessee and Southwest Virginia with a personal reminiscence of the author by David McClellan and a biographical note.

Schrock, E. F. "An Examination of the Dialect in *This Day and Time*." *TFSB*, 37 (June 1971), 31-39.
Anne W. Armstrong's novel (1930, reprinted 1970) is a faithful representation of the dialect of the Big Creek section of Sullivan County, Tennessee, in the 1920's.

[ASWELL, JAMES] Bridges, Katherine. *A Writer's Library: A Catalog of the Library of James Aswell*. Natchitoches, La.: Russell Library, Northwestern State Univ, 1971.
Lists not only the library of Aswell but his manuscripts, tapes, movie films, letters, scrapbooks, and clippings. (Letters to him include ones from Fitzgerald, Hemingway, Witter Bynner, and Maugham.) The appendix is a biographical sketch by Aswell's wife.

[BARTH, JOHN] Aldridge, John W. See MISCELLANEOUS (Contemporary--both Aldridge entries).

Alter, Robert. See MISCELLANEOUS (Contemporary).

Altieri, Charles. "Organic and Humanist Models in Some English Bildungsroman." *Jour of Gen Ed*, 23 (October 1971), 220-240.
Barth's *Lost in the Funhouse* is among works discussed as showing twentieth-century changes in the English bildungsroman.

Bean, John C. "John Barth and the Festive Comedy: A Failure of Imagination in *The Sot-Weed Factor*." *XUS*, 10 (Spring 1971), 3-15.
Barth's novel is in the tradition of "festive comedy" typified by *The Taming of the Shrew* and *Tom Jones*. But unlike the earlier works, this novel fails because it "moves toward isolation and loneliness."

Bellamy, Joe David. See MISCELLANEOUS (Contemporary).

Bienstock, Beverly G. "Lingering on the Autognostic Verge: John Barth's *Lost in the Funhouse*." *MFS*, 19 (Spring 1973), 69-78.
All the stories "revolve around the search for one's identity amidst the tangled skeins of past, present, and future."

Boyd, G. N. and L. A. See MISCELLANEOUS (Contemporary).

Bradbury, John M. See MISCELLANEOUS (Contemporary).

Bryant, Jerry H. See MISCELLANEOUS (Contemporary--1st Bryant entry).

Conlee, John W. "John Barth's Version of *The Reeve's Tale*." *Am N&Q*, 12 (May-June 1974), 137-138.
Points out parallels between Chaucer's tale and Chapters 12-14, Part III, of *The Sot-Weed Factor*.

Dillard, R. H. W., et al. See MISCELLANEOUS (Contemporary).

Dippie, Brian W. "'His Visage Wild; His Form Exotick': Indian Themes and Cultural Guilt in John Barth's *The Sot-Weed Factor*." *AQ*, 21 (Spring 1969), 113-121.
In dealing with Indians and Marylanders, Barth "questions and rejects many conventional American myths" and "refrains from replacing them with new ones"; thus, he also "creates opportunities for fresh observation and appreciation of the limitless complexities which constitute an American."

IV. Contemporary (1920-1975)

Diser, Philip. See COOKE, EBENEZER.

Ewell, Barbara C. "John Barth: The Artist of History." *So Lit Jour*, 5 (Spring 1973), 32-46.
     The Sot-Weed Factor is a serious commentary on both the nature of history and the nature of the real.

Farwell, Harold. "John Barth's Tenuous Affirmation: 'The Absurd, Unending Possibility of Love.'" *GaR*, 28 (Summer 1974), 290-306.
     Barth tenuously affirms the value of "that kind of love which represents a creative attempt to be free from the prison of self."

Federman, Raymond, ed. *Surfiction: Fiction Now... and Tomorrow*. Chicago: Swallow Press, 1975.
     Reprints Barth's 1967 essay, "The Literature of Exhaustion."

Fiedler, Leslie. See GENERAL.

Gado, Frank. See MISCELLANEOUS (Contemporary).

Gillespie, Gerald. "Barth's 'Lost in the Funhouse': Short Story Text in Its Cyclic Context." *Stud SF*, 12 (Summer 1975), 223-230.
     The cycle *Lost in the Funhouse* "permits control over its implied infinity by a finite agent, the artist, who grasps for one last access to unending significance."

Gindin, James. See MISCELLANEOUS (Contemporary).

Glicksberg, Charles I. See MISCELLANEOUS (Contemporary).

Godshalk, William L. See CABELL, JAMES BRANCH (Postbellum).

Gresham, James T. "*Giles Goat-Boy*: Satyr, Satire, and Tragedy Twined." *Genre*, 7 (June 1974), 148-163.
     Views *Giles Goat-Boy* as a Menippean satire as described by Northrop Frye.

Gross, Beverly. "The Anti-Novels of John Barth." *ChiR*, 20 (November 1968), 95-109.
     An examination of the novels in an attempt to show that Barth "is not quite affirming art but he is negating silence."

Harper, Howard M., Jr. "Trends in Recent American Fiction." *ConL*, 12 (Spring 1971), 204-229.
     Barth is among the writers considered in this essay-review of books written between June 1968 and July 1970; the trend is toward emphasis on aesthetic form and "a rendering of subjective states."

Harris, Charles B. *Contemporary American Novelists of the Absurd*. New Haven, Conn.: College and Univ Press, 1971, pp. 100-120.
     The burlesque in Barth's works reflects his concern with a fragmented world.

Hassan, Ihab. See MISCELLANEOUS (Contemporary-- both Hassan entries).

Hauck, Richard B. See FAULKNER, WILLIAM (Contemporary--1st Hauck entry).

_____. See GENERAL.

Henkle, Roger. See ELLISON, RALPH (Contemporary).

Hicks, Granville. See MISCELLANEOUS (Contemporary).

Hinden, Michael. "*Lost in the Funhouse*: Barth's Use of the Recent Past." *TCL*, 19 (April 1973), 107-118.
     Lost in the Funhouse "reveals a dazzling display of modernist techniques even while it examines the depletion of certain forms of modernist expression and the unbearable self-consciousness of intellectual life."

Holder, Alan. "'What Marvelous Plot...Was Afoot?' History in Barth's *The Sot-Weed Factor*." *AQ*, 20 (Fall 1968), 596-604.
     In Barth's conception, the energy of the figures in his novel comes from their being "deeply and continuously immersed in *plots*"; the book "refuses to commit itself to a particular conception of the past, of historical truth" so that one wishes that it "conveyed more of a sense that Barth *had* to sculpt the past in the first place--that he did not stand outside it, but felt it impinge strongly on him."

Janoff, Bruce. "Black Humor: Beyond Satire." *Ohio Rev*, 14, no. 1 (1972), 5-20.
     Barth is referred to in this discussion of black humor as a type that goes beyond traditional satire in its view of the fusion of comedy and tragedy in man's absurdity.

_____. "Black Humor, Existentialism, and Absurdity: A Generic Confusion." *ArQ*, 30 (Winter 1974), 293-304.
     "In the end, black humor is aimed not so much at the affirmation of art and life as to the negation of silence and lifelessness." Barth is "convinced of the failure of words, of feeling, of art and of the efficacy of action in life or art" and "of the failure of failure."

Jones, D. Allan. "The Game of the Name in Barth's *The Sot-Weed Factor*." *Research Stud*, 40 (September 1972), 219-221.
     A discussion of denotations and connotations.

_____. "John Barth's 'Anonymiad.'" *Stud SF*, 11 (Fall 1974), 361-366.
     This tale "is at once a parodic epic, a pastoral romance, a history of literature, and a treatise on aesthetics."

Joseph, Gerhard. *John Barth*. Univ of Minnesota Pamphlets of American Writers, no. 91. Minneapolis: Univ of Minnesota Press, 1970.
     Biographical and critical examination.

Kattan, Naim. See MISCELLANEOUS (Contemporary).

Kennard, Jean E. "John Barth's Imitations of Imitations." *Mosaic*, 3 (Winter 1970), 116-131.
     Because Barth believes that all meaning is false, he writes novels that are imitations of novels.

Kiernan, Robert F. "John Barth's Artist in the Fun House." *Stud SF*, 10 (Fall 1973), 373-380.

"*Funhouse* is a story sequence that approaches the form of a *Künstlerroman*."

Klinkowitz, Jerome. "A Final Word for Black Humor." *ConL*, 15 (Spring 1974), 271-276.
  Barth is one of the few writers of black humor to become a major writer; he and the few others have done so because they broke away from the traditions of the type.

Knapp, Edgar H. "Found in the Barthouse: Novelist as Savior." *MFS*, 14 (Winter 1968-69), 446-451.
  An analysis of Barth's "Lost in the Funhouse" which finds that the story is a "mixture of myth, masque, cinema, and symposium."

Koelb, Clayton. "John Barth's 'Glossolalia.'" *CL*, 26 (Fall 1974), 334-345.
  "Glossolalia" in *Lost in the Funhouse* is a metrical composition that is not verse but is similar in form to Pindar's sixth Pythian ode, which is verse.

Kyle, Carol A. "The Unity of Anatomy: The Structure of Barth's *Lost in the Funhouse*." *Critique*, 13, no. 3 (1972), 31-43.
  The unity of this work rests in Frye's fourth classification of prose fiction as anatomy, the unity of which comes from multiplicity.

LeClair, Thomas. "John Barth's *The Floating Opera*: Death and the Craft of Fiction." *Tex Stud in Lit and Lang*, 14 (Winter 1972), 711-730.
  Barth's first novel foreshadows elements and thus clarifies his intentions in his later work.

_____. See MISCELLANEOUS (Contemporary).

Leff, Leonard J. "Utopia Reconstructed: Alienation in Vonnegut's *God Bless You, Mr. Rosewater*." *Critique*, 12, no. 3 (1971), 29-37.
  Barth's handling of the theme of alienation in *The Floating Opera* is briefly discussed in this article.

Lehan, Richard. See MISCELLANEOUS (Contemporary).

Le Rebellier, A. "A Spectatorial Skeptic: An Interview with John Barth." *Caliban*, 12 (1975).
  Includes questions and answers on typical interview topics.

Lutwack, Leonard. See MISCELLANEOUS (Contemporary).

Majdiak, Daniel. "Barth and the Representation of Life." *Criticism*, 12 (Winter 1970), 51-67.
  Examines the themes and techniques of *The End of the Road* in terms of Barth's own theory of the fictitious.

May, John R. See GENERAL.

McDonald, James L. "Barth's Syllabus: The Frame of *Giles Goat-Boy*." *Critique*, 13, no. 3 (1972), 5-10.
  The frame is the means by which Barth "surrounds an artifact (the *R. N. S.*) with a literary commentary and analysis of its composition and its effect on various readers."

Mercer, Peter. "The Rhetoric of *Giles Goat-Boy*." *Novel*, 4 (Winter 1971), 147-158.
  Discusses the rhetorical styles of the novel and their significance.

Morris, Christopher D. "Barth and Lacan: The World of the Moebius Strip." *Critique*, 17, no. 1 (1975), 69-77.
  The linguistic theories of Jacques Lacan will help clarify Barth's *Lost in the Funhouse* as a work which emphasizes the separation between the self and language.

Nevius, Blake. See MISCELLANEOUS (Contemporary).

Olderman, Raymond. *Beyond the Waste Land: A Study of the American Novel in the Nineteen-Sixties*. New Haven: Yale Univ Press, 1972, pp. 72-93.
  In *Giles Goat-Boy* George is in the waste land of the academic world and must seek the mythological and psychological forces that control his life.

Pinsker, Sanford. "John Barth: The Teller Who Swallowed His Tale." *Stud in the Twentieth Cent*, 10 (Fall 1972), 55-68.
  Barth is "the devourer of his own art."

Poirier, Richard. See MISCELLANEOUS (Contemporary).

Richardson, Jack. "Amusement and Revelation." *New Rep*, 159 (November 23, 1968), 30-35.
  An essay-review of *Lost in the Funhouse*.

Riche, James. See MISCELLANEOUS (Contemporary).

Rodrigues, Eusebio L. "The Living Sakhyan in Barth's *Giles Goat-Boy*." *NConL*, 2 (September 1972), 7-8.
  Giles learns through silence of the illusion of the self.

Rubin, Louis D., Jr. See GENERAL--1st and 3rd Rubin entries.

Russell, Charles. "The Vault of Language: Self-Reflective Artifice in Contemporary American Fiction." *MFS*, 20 (Autumn 1974), 349-359.
  Barth is among the writers included in this discussion of contemporary literature that "questions the nature of literary language and, in particular, metaphor."

Ryan, Marjorie. "Four Contemporary Satires and the Problem of Norms." *Satire Newsl*, 6 (Spring 1969), 40-46.
  Points out differences in modern and earlier, traditional satire; Barth's *The Floating Opera* is one of the examples of modern satire.

Scholes, Robert. "The Illiberal Imagination." *New Lit Hist*, 4 (Spring 1973), 521-540.
  Includes comments on Barth in a discussion of the "illiberal" nature of narrative.

_____. "Metafiction." *Iowa Rev*, 1 (Fall 1970), 100-115.
  Barth's *Lost in the Funhouse* is classified as a work of "metafiction."

Schulz, Max F. *Black Humor Fiction of the Sixties: A Pluralistic Definition of Man and His World.* Columbus: Ohio Univ Press, 1973.
One phase of Schulz's pluralistic definition is the "metaphysics of multiplicity," which is represented by Barth.

_____. "Toward a Definition of Black Humor." *SouR*, 9 (Winter 1973), 117-134.
The article contains several references to Barth's works as exemplifying specific characteristics of black humor.

Shimura, Masao. "John Barth, *The End of the Road*, and the Tradition of American Literature." *Stud in Eng Lit*, Eng. no. (1971), 73-87.
Suggests parallels in *The End of the Road* with *The Scarlet Letter* and *The Wild Palms*.

Slethaug, Gordon E. "Barth's Refutation of the Idea of Progress." *Critique*, 13, no. 3 (1972), 11-29.
In *The Sot-Weed Factor*, *Giles Goat-Boy*, and *Lost in the Funhouse*, Barth refutes the idea of progress, revealing a belief in cyclical "correspondence" which leads to a loss of faith in "the goodness of man, social institutions, and nature" and to the belief that man has both good and "savage" qualities.

Sommavilla, Guido. "Logica, tragica e mistero nell' epica di John Barth." *Letture*, 1 (1974), 3-26.
Deals with *Giles Goat-Boy*.

Stark, John O. *The Literature of Exhaustion: Borges, Nabokov, and Barth.* Durham, N. C.: Duke Univ Press, 1974.
A comparative analysis of these writers' assumptions about the nature of literature.

Sutton, Henry. "Notes toward the Destitution of Culture." *KR*, 30 (1968), 108-115.
Includes *Giles Goat-Boy* among novels of the sixties that are "paranoid simplifications of the world."

Tanner, Stephen. "John Barth's Hamlet." *SWR*, 56 (Autumn 1971), 347-354.
Deals with Todd Andrews of *The Floating Opera* as a twentieth-century Hamlet.

Tanner, Tony. See MISCELLANEOUS (Contemporary).

_____. "The American Novelist as Entropologist." *London Mag*, 10 (October 1970), 5-18.
Barth is among writers discussed as being concerned with entropology, the question of what, if anything, the released energies of the age are leading to.

Tatham, Campbell. "The Gilesian Monomyth: Some Remarks on the Structure of *Giles Goat-Boy*." *Genre*, 3 (December 1970), 364-375.
Deals with how this work reflects Joseph Campbell's discussion (in *The Hero with a Thousand Faces*) of the monomyth of heroic quest.

_____. "John Barth and the Aesthetics of Artifice." *ConL*, 12 (Winter 1971), 60-73.
An examination of Barth's aesthetics.

_____. "Message (Concerning the *Felt* Ultimacies of One John Barth)." *Boundary 2*, 3 (Winter 1975), 259-287.
Deals with the ways Barth "elaborately *manipulates* his fictions" in order to emphasize "the arbitrariness of existence."

Tharpe, Jac. *John Barth: The Comic Sublimity of Paradox.* Carbondale: Univ of Southern Illinois Press, 1974.
Attempts to provide a comprehensive study of Barth's entire philosophical, comic, and stylistic development.

_____. See MISCELLANEOUS (Contemporary).

Tilton, John W. "*Giles Goat-Boy*: An Interpretation." *BuR*, 18 (Spring 1970), 92-119.
Institutionalized creeds make it difficult for man to recognize his dual nature.

Trachtenberg, Stanley. "Counterhumor: Comedy in Contemporary American Fiction." *GaR*, 27 (Spring 1973), 33-48.
Barth's *End of the Road* and Ellison's *Invisible Man* provide evidence to support the idea that "the contemporary comic novel" rejects the assumptions upon which conventional comedy has been built.

Verzosa, Guillermina L. "The Unsayable and Its Expression in John Barth's *The End of the Road*." *St. Louis Univ Research Jour*, 5 (June 1974), 131-187.
Deals with the devices that Barth uses to express the unsayable.

Voelker, Joseph C. "The Drama of Digression: Narrative Technique in John Barth's *The Floating Opera*." *Cim Rev*, 29 (October 1974), 34-44.
Barth's use of eighteenth-century narrative modes in this novel goes back to the Sisyphean relationship between form and vision.

Walter, James F. "A Psychronology of Lust in the Menippean Tradition: *Giles Goat-Boy*." *TCL*, 21 (December 1975), 394-410.
We must place *Giles Goat-Boy* within the tradition of Menippean satire "in order to understand and evaluate it."

Wasson, Richard. "Notes on a New Sensibility." *PR*, 36, no. 3 (1969), 460-477.
Barth is among writers who "are skeptical of modernist notions of metaphor as a species of suprarational truth...and modernist conceptions of myth which make it a principle of order for art and of discipline for the subjective self."

Weixlmann, Joseph N. "John Barth: A Bibliography." *Critique*, 13, no. 3 (1972), 45-55.
Lists works by and about Barth, and other bibliographies.

_____. "The Use and Abuse of Smith's *Generall Historie* in Barth's *The Sot-Weed Factor*." *Stud in Am Humor*, 2 (October 1975), 105-115.
Barth uses Smith's work "to reduce to absurdity the sentimental myths" it gave birth to.

[BASSO, HAMILTON] Rocks, James E. "Hamilton Basso and the World View from Pompey's Head." *SAQ*, 71 (Summer 1972), 326-341.
A discussion of Basso's life and works.

[BENEFIELD, BARRY] Hatley, Donald W. "Folklore in the Fiction of Barry Benefield." *Miss Quart*, 21 (Winter 1967-68), 63-70.
During his fifty years as a reporter for the *New York Times*, Benefield wrote six novels and over one hundred short stories, in several of which he used characters and lore of his home town, Jefferson, Texas.

[BENNETT, HAL] Walcott, Ronald. "The Novels of Hal Bennett." *Black World*, 23 (June 1974), 36-48; (July 1974), 78-96.
A thorough analysis and assessment of the fiction of Virginia-born Bennett.

[BERRY, WENDELL] Berry, Wendell. "An Essay and a Meditation." *SouR*, 6 (Autumn 1970), 972-989.
Two works: the first an analysis of the "moral distortions of exploitative or sentimental regionalism," the second a meditation on Kentucky's Red River Gorge.

_____. "A Native Hill." *HudR*, 21 (Winter 1968), 601-634.
An autobiographical essay explaining why he left New York City to return to Port Royal, Kentucky.

_____. See AMMONS, A. R. (Contemporary).

_____. See GENERAL.

Ditsky, John. "Love as a Farm and a Forest." *Mod Poetry Stud*, 5 (Autumn 1974), 92-93.
Praises Berry's poetry for its emphasis on "the continuity of life in Nature."

Fields, Kenneth. "The Hunter's Trail: Poems by Wendell Berry." *Iowa Rev*, 1 (Winter 1970), 90-100.
Openings contains the best poetry Berry has written.

Fussell, Edwin. "Farm Poets and Garage Critics." *Parnassus*, 2 (1974), 25-32.
Classifies Berry as a "Farm Poet" and objects to his poetry and his way of life.

Morgan, Speer. "Wendell Berry: A Fatal Singing." *SouR*, 10 (Autumn 1974), 865-877.
Identifies Berry as America's first significant farmer-agrarian, surveys his prose and poetry, and assesses him as a "major voice in America."

Tarbet, Donald W. See MISCELLANEOUS (Contemporary).

[BETTS, DORIS] Betts, Doris. "Brief Prose, Long Subjects." *SAQ*, 72 (Winter 1973), 143-148.
In praise of brevity in short fiction.

_____. "Fiction, Induction and Deduction." *Arts in Soc*, 11 (Summer-Fall 1974), 276-284.
Presents her approach to the teaching of fiction-writing at the University of North Carolina.

_____. "The Literature of Laputa." *So Car Rev*, 5 (June 1973), 5-10.
Discusses the faults of contemporary British and American fiction and offers suggestions as to how it could be improved.

Carr, John. See MISCELLANEOUS (Contemporary).

Evans, Elizabeth. "Negro Characters in the Fiction of Doris Betts." *Critique*, 17, no. 2 (1975), 59-76.
The black characters are a "necessary part of the Southern place" of Betts's fiction, and though she is not emphasizing sociological concerns, she "does not choose to ignore the problems that surround daily living and social change."

Gaillard, Dawson. See MISCELLANEOUS (Contemporary).

Moose, Ruth. "Superstition in Doris Betts's New Novel." *NCarF*, 21 (May 1973), 61-62.
The use of folklore enhances the life-death theme in *The River to Pickle Beach*.

[BISHOP, JOHN PEALE] Coxe, Louis. "Romance of the Rose: John Peale Bishop and Phelps Putnam." *MQR*, 14 (Spring 1975), 150-158.
The Bishop portion of the essay evaluates him as a poet "who fought off a culture...in order to achieve [in Tate's words] 'the moment of aesthetic consciousness.'" Besides Tate, other Fugitives are briefly referred to.

Fleissner, Robert F. "Bishop's 'No More the Senator' Once More." *NConL*, 2 (January 1972), 11-14.
Points out similarities between this poem and Eliot's "The Love Song of J. Alfred Prufrock."

Hayhoe, George F. "John Peale Bishop's Theory of Poetry." *MarkR*, 4 (February 1974), 34-38.
Bishop believed that contemporary poets should "synthesize the apparent extremes of classicism and romanticism" and that "through diction and the discipline of verse, it was possible for the poet to create a world in time and space that men could enjoy and appreciate."

Kuehl, John and Jackson R. Bryer. See MISCELLANEOUS (Contemporary).

Vauthier, Simone. "The Meaning of Structure: Toward a New Reading of John Peale Bishop's *Act of Darkness*." *So Lit Jour*, 7 (Spring 1975), 50-76.
This work "weds the antithesis of violation and law, human cruelty and love, the vital animality of man and his struggling mind, the inherent ambivalence and endless transferability of desire itself."

[BLACKMAN, MARION CYRENUS] Blackman, Marion Cyrenus. *Look Away! Dixie Land Remembered*. New York: McCall Publishing Co., 1971.
A journalist recalls in this autobiographical memoir life in north-central Louisiana in the first part of this century.

[BODENHEIM, MAXWELL] Moore, Jack B. *Maxwell Bodenheim*. Twayne U. S. Authors Series, no. 156. New York: Twayne, 1970.

Focuses on reasons for Bodenheim's failure as a novelist.

Ravitz, Abe C. "Assault with Deadly Typewriter: The Hecht-Bodenheim Vendetta." *Cabellian*, 4 (Spring 1972), 104-111.
   One-time collaborators on plays, such as *The Master-Poisoner*, Hecht and Bodenheim later fell out, and Hecht continued to pillory the bizarre life of his former friend.

[BONTEMPS, ARNA] Anon. See MISCELLANEOUS (Contemporary--2nd Anon. entry).

Aptheker, Herbert. See GENERAL.

Baker, Houston A., Jr. "Arna Bontemps: A Memoir." *Black World*, 22 (September 1973), 4-9.
   A tribute occasioned by Bontemps' death.

Bone, Robert. See GENERAL.

Bridges, Katherine. See GENERAL.

Brown, Lloyd W. "The Expatriate Consciousness in Black American Literature." *SBL*, 3 (Summer 1972), 9-12.
   Deals with the black American's feeling that he is an alien in America seeking "to rediscover the more immediate Black American roots, in the ghetto or rural South, from which his middle-class status has cut him off." Bontemps is one of the writers discussed.

Brown, Sterling A. "Arna Bontemps: Co-Worker, Comrade." *Black World*, 22 (September 1973), 11, 91-97.
   A tribute occasioned by Bontemps' death.

Gayle, Addison, Jr. See GENERAL.

Grumbach, Doris. See GENERAL.

Hemenway, Robert. See GENERAL.

Isani, Mukhtar. See GENERAL.

Magill, Frank N. See MISCELLANEOUS (Contemporary).

Mangione, Jerre. See MISCELLANEOUS (Contemporary).

O'Brien, John. See MISCELLANEOUS (Contemporary--2nd O'Brien entry).

Rosenblatt, Roger. See MISCELLANEOUS (Contemporary--2nd Rosenblatt entry).

Spady, J. G. "In Memoriam: Memorial Services for Arna Bontemps." *CLA Jour*, 17 (September 1973), 117-119.
   Tributes to Bontemps.

Weil, Dorothy. "Folklore Motifs in Arna Bontemps' *Black Thunder*." *SFQ*, 35 (March 1971), 1-14.
   Lists folk motifs and argues that they are skillfully used to depict the slave community and to characterize individual personalities.

Young, James O. See MISCELLANEOUS (Contemporary).

[BROOKS, CLEANTH] Baym, Max I. See GENERAL.

Bromwich, David. See RANSOM, JOHN CROWE.

Brooks, Cleanth. "Telling It Like It Is in the Tower of Babel." *SR*, 79 (Winter 1971), 136-155.
   Attacks abuse of language in the church and in modern society.

_____. See GENERAL.

Core, George. See MISCELLANEOUS (Contemporary--1st Core entry).

Cowan, Louise. See MISCELLANEOUS (Contemporary).

Curnow, Wystan. See MISCELLANEOUS (Contemporary).

Drake, Robert. See MISCELLANEOUS (Contemporary).

Lentricchia, Frank. "The Place of Cleanth Brooks." *Jour of Aesthetics and Art Crit*, 29 (Winter 1970), 235-251.
   Brooks is the most contextual of all the New Critics; what seem to be inconsistencies in his theories are not inconsistent.

Littlejohn, David. See MISCELLANEOUS (Contemporary).

Montesi, Albert J. See MISCELLANEOUS (Contemporary).

Owen, Guy. See MISCELLANEOUS (Contemporary--1st Owen entry).

Payne, Michael. "La Critique Engagée: Literature and Politics." *CEA Critic*, 35 (January 1973), 4-8.
   Includes brief discussion of Brooks's "My Credo" (*Kenyon Review*, 13 [Winter 1951], 72-92) and of ways in which Brooks has departed from it in his criticism.

Shankar, D. A. "Cleanth Brooks and the 'Elegy Written in a Country Church-Yard.'" *Lit Criterion*, 9 (Winter 1970), 77-80.
   Discusses Brooks's use of Gray's poem to illustrate paradox as the language of poetry.

Strozier, Robert M. "Roger Ascham and Cleanth Brooks: Renaissance and Modern Critical Thought." *EIC*, 22 (October 1972), 396-407.
   "If we look closely at the standard humanistic criticism of the Renaissance we shall see that tendencies apparent there are repeated in much modern criticism, especially in the 'thematic' or New Critical approach to literature."

Wellek, René. "Cleanth Brooks, Critic of Critics." *SouR*, 10 (Winter 1974), 125-152.
   A survey and commentary on Brooks's views as critic of critics, mostly modern.

[CALDWELL, ERSKINE] Anon. "Midnight Assassins." *TLS*, May 23, 1968, p. 521.
   A review of Caldwell's *Miss Mamma Aimee*.

Anon. See MISCELLANEOUS (Contemporary--2nd Anon. entry).

Anderson, Thomas. See GENERAL.

Bungert, Hans. See GENERAL.

Caldwell, Erskine. *Deep South*. New York:
Weybright and Talley, 1968.
Autobiographical and historical material of
use to those concerned with Caldwell's fiction.

_____. *The Final Chapter of Tobacco Road*. Boston:
David Godine and Dartmouth Col Library, 1972.
A facsimile publication of the printer's-
copy typescript of the last chapter of *Tobacco
Road*, with an introduction by E. C. Lathem.

Coindreau, Maurice. See MISCELLANEOUS
(Contemporary--2nd Coindreau entry).

Goldstein, Malcolm. See MISCELLANEOUS
(Contemporary).

Gray, R. J. "Southwestern Humor, Erskine Caldwell,
and the Comedy of Frustration." *So Lit Jour*,
8 (Fall 1975), 3-26.
Caldwell owes a profound debt to the humorists of the Old Southwest in general, and to
George Washington Harris in particular.

Haight, A. L. See GENERAL.

Inge, M. Thomas. See MISCELLANEOUS (Contemporary--
1st Inge entry).

Korges, James. *Erskine Caldwell*. Minnesota Pamphlets on American Writers. Minneapolis:
Univ of Minnesota Press, 1969.
Attempts to offset critical condescensions
and neglect of Caldwell's work by affirming
that within the prolific corpus lies much good
writing which entitles him to respect as "one
of the important writers of our time."

Kuehl, John, and Jackson R. Bryer. See
MISCELLANEOUS (Contemporary).

Libman, Valentina. See GENERAL.

Ludington, Townsend. See MISCELLANEOUS
(Contemporary).

Maekawa Shunich . . . . See GENERAL.

Magny, Claude-Edmonde. See MISCELLANEOUS
(Contemporary).

Martin, Jay. See MISCELLANEOUS (Contemporary).

Nevius, Blake. See MISCELLANEOUS (Contemporary).

Pells, Richard H. See MISCELLANEOUS
(Contemporary).

Rubin, Louis D., Jr. See GENERAL--3rd Rubin
entry.

Sale, Richard B. "An Interview with Erskine
Caldwell." *Stud in the Novel*, 3 (Fall 1971),
316-331.
An interview with Caldwell in Dunedin,
Florida, on January 29, 1970.

Sutton, W. A. *Black Like It Is/Was: Erskine
Caldwell's Treatment of Racial Themes*.
Metuchen, N. J.: Scarecrow Press, 1974.
An analysis of the social and political
content of Caldwell's fiction.

Thompson, James J., Jr. "Erskine Caldwell and
Southern Religion." *SHR*, 5 (Winter 1971),
33-44.
"In an examination of religion as a theme in
Southern literature Caldwell rises to a position
of critical importance. Perhaps no other Southern author has dealt with the subject of religion as fully as Caldwell." His "portrayal of
Southern religion can be summed up...in the
three themes of fatalism, poverty of ethic, and
sexuality."

Voss, Arthur. See GENERAL.

Willingham, Calder. "True Myth-Maker of the Post-
Bellum South." *GHQ*, 59 (Summer 1975), 243-247.
Unlike Faulkner, who was a conscious literary
artist, Caldwell was a "true myth-maker or
creator of legend," and a precursor of "modern
black comedy."

Woodress, James. See GENERAL--1st Woodress entry.

[CAPOTE, TRUMAN] Anon. "People." *Time*, 97
(June 14, 1971), 44.
A report of comments between David Frost
and Capote.

Aldridge, John W. See MISCELLANEOUS (Contemporary--
both Aldridge entries).

Alter, Robert. See MISCELLANEOUS (Contemporary).

Bauerle, Richard F. "Stafford's 'Holcomb, Kansas.'"
Contemporary Poetry, 1 (Spring 1973), 27-30.
This poem deals with the reaction of the
people of Holcomb to Capote's visit there,
though Capote is not actually named in the poem.

Boyd, G. N. and L. A. See MISCELLANEOUS
(Contemporary).

Bridges, Katherine. See GENERAL.

Buchloh, Paul G. See GENERAL.

Bungert, Hans. See GENERAL.

Capote, Truman. "Portrait of Myself." *Cosmopol-
itan*, 173 (July 1972), 130-134.
Capote conducts a self-interview about his
life, loves, and art.

_____, Eleanor Perry, and Frank Perry. *Trilogy:
An Experiment in Multimedia*. New York:
Macmillan, 1969.
Deals with materials for a case study of the
process whereby three Capote stories were
adapted first for television, then for the
motion picture screen, with texts of stories
and scripts.

Christadler, Martin. See MISCELLANEOUS
(Contemporary).

Clarke, Girala. "Checking in with Truman Capote."
Esquire, 78 (November 1972), 136, 137, 187-188,
190.
An interview.

Coindreau, Maurice. See MISCELLANEOUS
(Contemporary).

Creeger, George R. "Animals in Exile: Criminal and Community in Capote's *In Cold Blood*." *Jahrbuch für Amerikastudien*, 14 (1969), 94-106.
     Deals with Capote's use of animal imagery in emphasizing the relationship between criminal and community.

Freese, Peter. "Das Motiv des Doppelgängers in Truman Capote's 'Shut a Final Door' und Edgar Allan Poes 'William Wilson.'" *LWU*, 1 (1968), 40-48.
     Deals with Gothic elements in Capote's story and points out similarities between it and Poe's "William Wilson."

French, Warren. See MISCELLANEOUS (Contemporary-- 2nd French entry).

Geduld, Harry M. See MISCELLANEOUS (Contemporary).

Gindin, James. See MISCELLANEOUS (Contemporary).

Haack, Dietmar. "Faction: Tendenzen zu einer kritischen Faktographie in den USA." *Amerikanische Lit im 20. Jahrhundert*, ed. Alfred Weber and Dietmar Haack. Göttingen: Vandenhoeck & Ruprecht, 1971, pp. 127-146.
     Suggests that the non-fiction novel be called the "faction" novel. Includes a discussion of *In Cold Blood*.

Hassan, Ihab. See MISCELLANEOUS (Contemporary-- both Hassan entries).

Hendin, Josephine. See O'CONNOR, FLANNERY (Contemporary--2nd Hendin entry).

Inge, M. Thomas. See MISCELLANEOUS (Contemporary-- 1st Inge entry).

Johnson, Michael L. See MISCELLANEOUS (Contemporary).

Kattan, Naïm. See MISCELLANEOUS (Contemporary).

Kazin, Alfred. "The World as a Novel: From Capote to Mailer." *NYRB*, 16 (April 8, 1971), 26-30.
     Deals with Capote's aims in *In Cold Blood* and Styron's in *The Confessions of Nat Turner*.

_____. See MISCELLANEOUS (Contemporary).

Kirby, David K. "The Princess and the Frog: The Modern Short Story as Fairy Tale." *Minn Rev*, 4 (Spring 1973), 145-149.
     Contains discussion of Capote's "Miriam."

Ludington, Townsend. See MISCELLANEOUS (Contemporary).

Malin, Irving, ed. *Truman Capote's "In Cold Blood": A Critical Handbook*. Belmont, Calif.: Wadsworth, 1968.
     A casebook collection of factual and critical material relating to the creation and reception of Capote's "non-fiction" novel, with a Capote bibliography by Jackson Bryer.

McAleer, John J. "*An American Tragedy* and *In Cold Blood*." *Thought*, 47 (Winter 1972), 569-586.

A record of the parallels between the two novels. The difference is that, while "Capote has reported on an event," Dreiser "has reported on the truth of human nature."

Murray, Edward. "*In Cold Blood*: The Filmic Novel and the Problem of Adaptation." *Lit/Film Quart*, 1 (April 1973), 132-137.
     Though Capote used the techniques of film in the novel, its film version is not successful.

Nance, William L. *The Worlds of Truman Capote*. New York: Stein and Day, 1970.
     A chronological critical analysis of Capote's fiction with specific attention to the influence of his personal life on his public work.

_____. See PORTER, KATHERINE ANNE (2nd Nance entry).

Nevius, Blake. See MISCELLANEOUS (Contemporary).

Perry, J. Douglas, Jr. See MISCELLANEOUS (Contemporary).

Pizer, Donald. "Documentary Narrative as Art: William Manchester and Truman Capote." *Jour of Mod Lit*, 2 (September 1971), 105-118.
     In Cold Blood is a successful documentary narrative because it gives meaning to actual events.

Schorer, Mark. See MISCELLANEOUS (Contemporary).

Stanzel, Franz. See MISCELLANEOUS (Contemporary).

Tanner, Tony, See MISCELLANEOUS (Contemporary).

Trimmier, Dianne B. "The Critical Reception of Capote's *Other Voices, Other Rooms*." *West Va Univ Bul: Phil Papers*, 17 (June 1970), 94-101.
     Early criticism was unfavorable, but since 1958 it has been generally favorable.

Trousdale, Marion. "Reality and Illusion in the Theatre." *Crit Quart*, 11 (Winter 1969), 347-359.
     The article alludes to *In Cold Blood*.

Vanderwerken, D. L. "Truman Capote: 1943-1968-- A Critical Bibliography." *BB*, 27 (July-September 1970), 57-60, 71.
     An unannotated listing of primary and secondary sources.

Weber, Alfred, and Dietmar Haack, eds. *Amerikanische Literature in 20. Jahrhundert*. Göttingen: Vandenhoeck & Ruprecht, 1971.
     Contains an essay by George R. Creeger on animal imagery in relation to theme in Capote's *In Cold Blood*.

Wickes, George. "A Natalie Barney Garland." *Paris Rev*, 61 (1975), 84-134.
     Recollection of Capote, Djuna Barnes, and others.

Zacharias, Lee. "Living the American Dream: 'Children on Their Birthdays.'" *Stud SF*, 12 (Fall 1975), 343-350.

This story is "a moving, affectionate comedy that is also brutal and shattering, a brilliant use of black humor that allows us to delight in that which should spin us into despair."

[CASH, WILBUR JOSEPH] Downs, R. B. *Books That Changed America.* New York: Macmillan, 1970.
    Among twenty-five books discussed is *The Mind of the South*, which Downs summarizes and affirms contributed to regional self-consciousness.

Morrison, Joseph L. "W. J. Cash: The Summing Up." *SAQ*, 70 (Autumn 1971), 477-486.
    Asserts that Cash's *The Mind of the South* should be regarded not as history but as a "work of social analysis," with important prophetic significance for the present day.

Pinkerton, Jan. See MISCELLANEOUS (Contemporary).

Simpson, Lewis P. See GENERAL--3rd Simpson entry.

Woodward, C. Vann. See MISCELLANEOUS (Contemporary).

[CHAPPELL, FRED] Carr, John. See MISCELLANEOUS (Contemporary).

Dillard, R. H. W. "Letters From a Distant Lover: The Novels of Fred Chappell." *Hollins Crit*, 10 (April 1973), 1-15.
    A survey of Chappell's work to date.

Graham, John, and George Garrett. See MISCELLANEOUS (Contemporary).

[CLAUDEL, ALICE MOSER] Fogle, Richard H. "Foreword" to *Southern Season*. Pikeville, Ky.: Appalachian Studies Center, 1972.
    An introductory appreciation to a collection of poems.

[COHN, DAVID] Howell, Elmo. See MISCELLANEOUS (Contemporary).

Simms, L. Moody, Jr. "David Lewis Cohn: An Annotated Bibliography." *Notes on Miss Writers*, 5 (Fall 1972), 65-68.
    A bibliography of "writer and social commentator" Cohn (1897-1960).

[CREEKMORE, HUBERT] Simms, L. Moody, Jr. "Hubert Creekmore: Mississippi Novelist and Poet." *Notes on Miss Writers*, 4 (Spring 1971), 15-21.
    An overview of Creekmore's literary career.

[CREWS, HARRY] Smith, David. "That Appetite for Life So Ravenous." *Shen*, 25 (Summer 1974), 49-55.
    Crews is like other young writers who are attracted to the "freakish" because of the "moral, social, political, and religious confusions of our time" but whose works carry the message *Don't be afraid!*

Watson, V. Sterling. "Arguments Over an Open Wound: An Interview with Harry Crews." *PrS*, 48 (Spring 1974), 60-74.
    Crews thinks of himself as a traditional story-teller who is interested in whatever new things may be happening in fiction.

[DALTON, HENRY] Howell, Elmo. "Henry Dalton: North Mississippi Poet." *Notes on Miss Writers*, 3 (Fall 1970), 81-86.
    An essay-review of Dalton's *Hill Born* (1954).

[DAVIDSON, DONALD] Allen, Ward. "Donald Davidson." *SR*, 78 (Spring 1970), 390-404.
    An appreciation of Davidson's poetry emphasizing the classical influence on him and the essentially religious character of his thought.

Bataille, Robert. See MISCELLANEOUS (Contemporary).

Brooks, Cleanth. "Agrarianism: 'A Very Great Success.'" *YR*, 64 (Spring 1975), 455-459.
    A review of *The Literary Correspondence of Davidson and Tate*.

Buffington, Robert. "Mr. Davidson in the Formal Garden." *GaR*, 24 (Summer 1970), 121-131.
    A portrait of Davidson as a college teacher with the aim of literary education rather than training.

Carter, T. H. See MISCELLANEOUS (Contemporary).

Cowan, Louise. "Portrait of a Tall Man." *So Lit Jour*, 7 (Fall 1974), 146-150.
    An essay-review of *The Literary Correspondence of Davidson and Tate*; Davidson believed in the "imperishability of poetry and the indestructibility of tradition" in an age that neglects poetry and tends to obliterate the past.

_____. See MISCELLANEOUS (Contemporary).

Dessommes, Larry. "The Antipodes of Modern Literature: A Discussion of Joyce and Davidson." *South-Central Bul*, 30 (Winter 1970), 179-181.
    Contrasts Davidson's treatment of the Ulysses story in "Old Sailor's Choice" with that of Joyce.

_____. "The Epistemological Implications in 'The Ninth Part of Speech.'" *Miss Quart*, 27 (Winter 1973-74), 21-32.
    The fundamental principle, Davidson's "Ninth Part of Speech," of education is "that man must wed thought to reality or must be assaulted by reality"; there is no middle ground.

Eaton, Charles E. "A Friendship of Poets: The Statesman and the Soldier." *GaR*, 28 (Winter 1974), 688-704.
    An essay-review of *The Literary Correspondence of Donald Davidson and Allen Tate.*

Fain, John T., and Thomas Daniel Young, eds. *The Literary Correspondence of Donald Davidson and Allen Tate.* Athens: Univ of Georgia Press, 1974.
    An edited and annotated selection of the correspondence from 1922 through 1966, with a complete register of the letters and chronologies, recording a long-standing literary friendship.

Hallman, David A. "Donald Davidson, Allen Tate and All Those Falling Leaves." *GaR*, 27 (Winter 1973), 550-559.

Davidson "was privately troubled by [Tate's] poetic technique and by his despairing resolution to the conflict of 'Ode to the Confederate Dead.'"

Hubbell, Jay B.   See GENERAL.

Inge, M. Thomas. "Donald Davidson Selects the Best Southern Novels." *Miss Quart*, 24 (Spring 1971), 155-158.
      A reprinting of Davidson's list in 1935 of the forty-three best Southern novels.

_____.   See CABELL, JAMES BRANCH.

Landess, Thomas. "The Art of Intimacy." *Univ Bookman*, 16 (Autumn 1975), 10-13.
      An essay-review of *The Literary Correspondence of Donald Davidson and Allen Tate*.

O'Brien, Michael, ed. "A Correspondence, 1923-1958: Edwin Mims and Donald Davidson." *SouR*, 10 (Autumn 1974), 904-922.
      The editor's introduction and the letters contain material on Tate, Ransom, and the Fugitive-Agrarian movements.

Shapiro, Edward S. "Donald Davidson and the Tennessee Valley Authority: The Response of a Southern Conservative." *Tenn Hist Quart*, 33 (Winter 1974), 436-451.
      "Davidson's attitude toward the TVA grew logically out of his interpretation of American history."

Simpson, Lewis P. "Introduction" to *Still Rebels, Still Yankees*, by Donald Davidson. Baton Rouge: Louisiana State Univ Press, 1972.
      Davidson adopted "the ancient vocation of the poet as the seer and prophet who speaks out of the whole and living tradition of his people."

Stewart, Randall. See GENERAL.

Stuart, Jesse. "America's Pindar Was My Guide." *Vanderbilt Alumnus*, 56 (March-April 1971), 16-19.
      A personal memoir and an appreciation of Davidson and his influence on Stuart's life and work.

Talmadge, John E., and William W. Davidson. "Growing Up in Georgia and Tennessee: The Letters of John E. Talmadge and William Wallace Davidson." *GaR*, 27 (Spring 1973), 5-32; (Summer 1973), 194-219.
      William Wallace Davidson mentions his brother Donald in passing.

Tate, Allen, and Donald Davidson. See TATE, ALLEN.

Weales, Gerald. See MISCELLANEOUS (Contemporary).

Wilson, James D. See MISCELLANEOUS (Contemporary).

Woodward, C. Vann. See MISCELLANEOUS (Contemporary).

Young, Thomas Daniel, and M. Thomas Inge. *Donald Davidson*, Twayne's U. S. Authors Series, no. 190. New York: Twayne, 1971.

An evaluation of Davidson's poetry and prose with emphasis upon his use of tradition and Southern history and his contribution to Agrarian thought.

_____.   See RANSOM, JOHN CROWE--1st Young entry.

[DAVIS, BURKE] Clark, Joseph D. "Burke Davis as Folklorist." *N Car F*, 19 (March 1971), 59-65.
      Details Davis' extensive use of folklore in *The Summer Land*.

[DEAL, BORDEN] Deal, Borden. "Storytelling as Symbolism." *SWR*, 53 (Summer 1968), 293-298.
      The critics must rediscover the meaning of storytelling as symbolism, since "narrative is the element in literature that is most ignored by modern criticism."

[DICKEY, JAMES] Anon. "Journey into Self." *Time*, 95 (April 20, 1970), 92-93.
      In part the impact of *Deliverance* comes from "a poetic empathy" the author feels for "the objects and forces that confront his men."

Adams, Percy. "The Epic Tradition and the Novel." *SouR*, 9 (January 1973), 300-310.
      Dickey's *Deliverance* is among the examples of the modern American novel in the epic tradition.

Arnett, David L. "An Interview with James Dickey." *ConL*, 16 (Summer 1975), 286-300.
      Questions and answers on typical interview topics.

Ashley, Franklin. *James Dickey: A Checklist*. Detroit: Gale Research Co., 1972.
      A descriptive bibliography of primary publications with an introduction by Dickey.

Beidler, Peter G. "The Pride of Thine Heart Hath Deceived Thee: Narrative Distortion in Dickey's *Deliverance*." *So Car Rev*, 5 (December 1972), 29-40.
      Points out that Ed Gentry, the narrator of *Deliverance*, is an unreliable narrator. Many of the unfavorable reviews were based on a misreading of Gentry's character.

Berry, David C. "Harmony with the Dead: James Dickey's Descent into the Underworld." *So Quart*, 12 (April 1974), 233-244.
      Dickey descends to his deceased family and rises nourished; but with more intensity of celebration in his war poems, the descent is employed to renew life and salute death.

Bleikasten, André. "Anatomie d'un bestseller: A propos de *Deliverance*." *RANAM*, 4 (1971), 116-129.
      Analyzes Dickey's *Deliverance* at length and finds it a work "cooked up according to the tested recipes for a bestseller," and a novel "too clever to be honest."

Borroff, Marie. "Creativity, Poetic Language, and the Computer." *YR*, 60 (June 1971), 481-513.
      Mentions James Dickey in a discussion of computer-produced poetry.

Calhoun, Richard J. "'His Reason Argues with His Invention': James Dickey's *Self-Interviews* and *The Eye-Beaters*." *So Car Rev*, 3 (June 1971), 9–16.
> Dickey's *Self-Interviews* and *The Eye-Beaters* show a falling-off of quality from previous work.

_____, ed. *James Dickey: The Expansive Imagination*. Deland, Fla.: Everett/Edwards, 1973.
> A collection of fourteen critical essays and an interview, ten of them reprinted, with a Dickey checklist.

_____. "Whatever Happened to the Poet-Critic?" *So Lit Jour*, 1 (Autumn 1968), 75–88.
> An essay-review of Dickey's *Babel to Byzantium: Poets and Poetry Now*.

Clemons, W. "James Dickey, Novelist." *NYTBR*, March 22, 1970, p. 22.
> An interview in which Dickey describes how he came to write *Deliverance* and how it feels to be a novelist.

Corrington, John W. "James Dickey's Poems: 1957–1967: A Personal Appraisal." *GaR*, 22 (Spring 1968), 12–23.
> An essay-review of *Poems: 1957-1967*.

DeMott, Benjamin. "The 'More Life' School and James Dickey." *SatR*, March 28, 1970, pp. 25ff.
> An essay-review of *Deliverance* and of *The Eye-Beaters, Blood, Victory, Madness, Buckhead and Mercy*.

Dickey, James. "The Greatest American Poet." *Atl*, 222 (November 1968), 53–62.
> A memoir-review in which Dickey deals with Allan Seager's biography of Theodore Roethke, *The Glass House*, and proclaims Roethke "the greatest poet this country has produced."

_____. *Sorties: Journals and New Essays*. Garden City, N. Y.: Doubleday, 1971.
> Dickey's working notes on his novel *Death's Baby Machine* and notes on various contemporary writers.

_____. See TATE, ALLEN (Contemporary).

Drake, Robert. See MISCELLANEOUS (Contemporary).

Edwards, C. Hines, Jr. "Dickey's *Deliverance*: The Owl and the Eye." *Critique*, 15, no. 2 (1973), 95–101.
> Believes that through the owl and eye imagery of *Deliverance*, Dickey attempts to make the reader face the darker aspects of human existence.

_____. "A Foggy Scene in *Deliverance*." *NConL*, 2 (November 1972), 7–9.
> Discusses the significance of fog as a symbol in Dickey's works, particularly in *Deliverance*.

Eyster, Warren. "Two Regional Novels." *SR*, 79 (Summer 1971), 469–474.
> A review of Dickey's *Deliverance* and of Guy Owen's *Journey for Joedel*, which finds the latter the better novel.

Fauchereau, Serge. "Entretien avec M. L. Rosenthal: 'Des figures intéressantes rien de plus.'" *Quinzaine Litt*, no. 126 (October 1-15, 1971), 9–11.
> Rosenthal believes that there are no real literary movements today but that there is an emphasis on violence in the work of a number of poets, including Dickey.

Garner, P. "The Deliverance Syndrome." *Atlanta Journal and Constitution Mag*, November 18, 1973, pp. 16–18, 23–34.
> Identifies the real-life prototypes for characters in *Deliverance*.

George, Sharon K. "James Dickey's 'Winter Trout.'" *Contemporary Poetry*, 1 (Spring 1973), 23–26.
> The theme of the poem is that winter is the source and "promise of regeneration."

Glancy, Eileen K. "James Dickey: A Bibliography." *TCL*, 15 (October 1969), 45–61.
> Includes works by and about Dickey.

_____. *James Dickey: The Critic as Poet, An Annotated Bibliography*. Troy, N. Y.: Whitston Publishing Co., 1971.
> Lists 229 items by Dickey and 167 about him, with a full critical introduction by the compiler.

Graham, John, and George Garrett. See MISCELLANEOUS (Contemporary).

Greiner, Donald J. "The Harmony of Bestiality in James Dickey's *Deliverance*." *So Car Rev*, 5 (December 1972), 43–49.
> In his fight for survival Ed Gentry not only acknowledges "his own bestiality" but encourages and cultivates it.

Guillory, Daniel. "Myth and Meaning in Dickey's *Deliverance*." *Coll Lit*, 3 (Winter 1975), 56–62.
> Deals chiefly with the significance of the river and Dickey's use of the hero myth in this novel.

_____. "Water Magic in the Poetry of James Dickey." *Eng Lang Notes*, 8 (December 1970), 131–137.
> The poet draws on and enlarges the traditional uses of water symbolism.

Gustafson, Richard. "The Peace of a Good Line." *Poet and Critic*, 6, no. 3 (1971), 29–33.
> Discusses Dickey's (and Stevens's) awareness of the differences between poetry and prose.

Howard, Richard. See MISCELLANEOUS (Contemporary).

Hughes, Richard. See MISCELLANEOUS (Contemporary).

Italia, Paul G. "Love and Lust in James Dickey's *Deliverance*." *MFS*, 21 (Summer 1975), 203–213.
> Discussion of patterning in scenes of sexual violence in the novel.

Jameson, Frederic. "The Great American Hunter, or, Ideological Content in the Novel." (Followed by comment by Sol Yurick.) *CE*, 34 (November 1972), 180–197.

Deliverance is a "myth incompletely realized" because the characters—and Dickey himself—cannot "shed their America for something radically different."

Landess, Thomas. "Traditionalist Criticism and the Poetry of James Dickey." *Occasional Rev*, 3 (Summer 1975), 5-26.
    Dickey's poetry is personal and local, therefore more positive than that of traditionalists like Eliot, Ransom, and Tate.

Libby, Anthony. "Fire and Light, Four Poets to the End and Beyond." *Iowa Rev*, 4 (Spring 1973), 111-126.
    Discusses the use of surrealist imagery by four poets, including Dickey.

Lieberman, Laurence, ed. *The Achievement of James Dickey*. Glenview, Ill.: Scott, Foresman, 1968.
    A collection of twenty-four poems, 1957-1967, with an introduction characterizing them as being animated by the "joy in the sheer pleasure of being."

_____. "The Expansional Poet: A Return to Personality." *YR*, 57 (Winter 1968), 258-271.
    Of the five volumes of poetry reviewed in this essay only one, *Poems: 1957-1967*, by James Dickey, is by a Southern poet. Lieberman discovers that the subject of Dickey's new poetry is "being in extremity stretched to the outer limits of joy and terror."

Lindborg, Henry J. "James Dickey's *Deliverance*: The Ritual of Art." *So Lit Jour*, 6 (Spring 1974), 83-90.
    More than an initiation into the art of killing, the novel is an exploration of the process of creation.

Love, Glen A. "Ecology in Arcadia." *ColQ*, 21 (Autumn 1972), 175-185.
    Deliverance illustrates the loss of the myth of the American landscape as Arcadia.

Markos, Donald W. "Art and Immediacy: James Dickey's *Deliverance*." *SouR*, 7 (Summer 1971), 947-953.
    An essay-review answering Benjamin DeMott's unfavorable assessment by maintaining that Dickey's novel is a serious and significant work of fiction.

Mills, Ralph, Jr. "The Poetry of James Dickey." *Tri-Quart*, 11 (Winter 1968), 231-242.
    A review-essay of *Poems 1957-1967* which speaks of Dickey's poetry as being a blend of the primitive and sophisticated; for full poetic maturity the "developments [of Dickey's poetry] need to derive from inner necessity and not in answer to the external demands of reputation or public role."

Morris, Harry. "A Formal View of the Poetry of Dickey, Garrigue, and Simpson." *SR*, 77 (1969), 318-325.
    Finds Dickey's poetry lacking.

Niflis, N. Michael. "A Special Kind of Fantasy: James Dickey on the Razor's Edge." *SWR*, 57 (Autumn 1972), 311-317.

Discusses characteristics of Dickey's poetry and expresses the belief that he is the greatest American poet.

Oates, Joyce Carol. "Out of Stone, into Flesh: The Imagination of James Dickey." *Mod Poetry Stud*, 5 (Autumn 1974), 97-144. Reprinted in Miss Oates's *New Heaven, New Earth*. New York: Vanguard, 1974.
    Discusses Whitmanesque qualities in Dickey's poetry, its masculinity and its personal element.

Owen, Guy. See MISCELLANEOUS (Contemporary—1st Owen entry).

Reiss, Barbara, and James, eds. *Self-Interviews: James Dickey*. Garden City, N. Y.: Doubleday, 1970.
    Transcripts of tape-recorded monologues by Dickey on topics established by the editors, including his life and career as a poet, his opinions of other Southern writers, and how he came to write several selected poems.

Robinson, James K. "Terror Lumped and Split: Contemporary British and American Poets." *SouR*, 6 (Winter 1970), 216-228.
    Dickey's *Buckdancer's Choice* is reviewed with a group of eighteen other works.

Samuels, C. T. "What Hath Dickey Delivered?" *New Rep*, 162 (April 18, 1970), 23-26.
    An essay-review of Dickey's *Deliverance* which finds improbabilities of plot but exciting reading in a puzzling story.

Shepherd, Allen. "Counter-Monster Comes Home: The Last Chapter of James Dickey's *Deliverance*." *NConL*, 3 (March 1973), 8-12.
    Discusses the changes in Ed Gentry revealed in the last chapter of the novel.

Silverstein, Norman. "James Dickey's Muscular Eschatology." *Salmagundi*, 22-23 (1973), 258-268.
    Sees Dickey as masculine and Southern.

Smith, Raymond. "The Poetic Faith of James Dickey." *Mod Poetry Stud*, 2 (1972), 259-272.
    Dickey's personal myth is based in nature.

Spears, Monroe K. *Dionysus and the City: Modernism in Twentieth Century Poetry*. New York: Oxford Univ Press, 1970.
    The section on Dickey places him in the category of those moving toward open poetry.

Stephenson, William. "*Deliverance* from What? *GaR*, 28 (Spring 1974), 114-120.
    A theme of Dickey's novel is that law and music, "not reckless freedom," keep men together; the freedom represented by Drew is real freedom.

Westendorp, T. A. See MISCELLANEOUS (Contemporary).

Willig, Charles L. "Ed's Transformation: A Note on *Deliverance*." *NConL*, 3 (March 1973), 4-5.
    Discusses the significance of a passage near the end of the novel in revealing Ed Gentry's changed attitude toward his life.

Yardley, Jonathan. "More of Superpoet." *New Rep*, 163 (December 5, 1970), 26-27.
  This review of Dickey's *Self-Interviews* states that Dickey is less candid here than in his poems and that he clings to his Southernness, e. g., the region's concept of family.

[DRAKE, ROBERT] Drake, Robert. "What I Write About: Death and Old Women." *CEA Critic*, 35 (November 1972), 10-15.
  An author's examination of his own "fictional subjects" and how he came by them.

[EAST, CHARLES] Simpson, Lewis P. See MISCELLANEOUS (Contemporary--1st Simpson entry).

Weaver, Gordon. "An Interview with Charles East." *Notes on Miss Writers*, 4 (Winter 1972), 87-108.
  An interview conducted in March 1971.

[ELLISON, RALPH] Anon. "An American, A Negro." *TLS*, January 18, 1968, pp. 49-50.
  An essay that concentrates on Ellison.

Baker, Houston A., Jr. See JOHNSON, JAMES WELDON (Contemporary--1st Baker entry).

_____. See GENERAL--4th Baker entry.

Bell, Bernard W. See MISCELLANEOUS (Contemporary--1st Bell entry).

Bell, James D. "Ellison's *Invisible Man*." *Expl*, 29 (November 1970), Item 19.
  Deals with a multiple pun in Ellison's use of words from the song "Ballin' the Jack" in the epilogue to the novel.

Bennett, Stephen B., and William W. Nichols. See MISCELLANEOUS (Contemporary).

Benoit, Bernard, and Michel Fabre. "A Bibliography of Ralph Ellison's Published Writings." *SBL*, 12 (Autumn 1971), 25-28.
  Covers 1937 through June 1971.

Bigsby, C. W. E. See MISCELLANEOUS (Contemporary).

Billingsley, R. G. See MISCELLANEOUS (Contemporary).

Boitani, Piero. See MISCELLANEOUS (Contemporary).

Boulger, J. D. "Puritan Allegory in Four Modern Novels." *Thought*, 44 (Autumn 1969), 413-432.
  Deals with *Invisible Man*, *The Last Hurrah*, *By Love Possessed*, and *Herzog*.

Brake, Robert. See GENERAL.

Brown, Lloyd W. "Ralph Ellison's Exhorters: The Role of Rhetoric in *Invisible Man*." *CLA Jour*, 13 (March 1970), 289-303.
  The role of rhetoric in *Invisible Man* is "to illuminate the conflict between opposing values and experiences."

_____. See GENERAL--2nd Brown entry.

Bryant, Jerry H. See MISCELLANEOUS (Contemporary--1st Bryant entry).

Bucco, Martin. "Ellison's Invisible West." *WAL*, 10 (Fall 1975), 237-238.
  Deals with the significance of the episode in which the narrator goes to see a Western movie.

Burrows, David J., et al. *Private Dealings: Modern American Writers in Search of Integrity*. Rockville, Md.: New Perspectives, 1974.
  Essays delivered in Stockholm by Fulbright scholars in 1965 and originally published in Sweden in 1969; one essay, by Grosvenor E. Powell, is on Ellison.

Carson, David K. "Ralph Ellison: Twenty Years After." *Stud in Am F*, 1 (Spring 1973), 1-23.
  Transcript of an interview with Ellison.

Cash, Earl A. "The Narrators in *Invisible Man* and *Notes From Underground*: Brothers in the Spirit." *CLA Jour*, 16 (June 1973), 505-507.
  The prologue and epilogue of *Invisible Man* and Part One of *Notes* reveal a surprising kinship.

Christadler, Martin. See MISCELLANEOUS (Contemporary).

Clarke, John H. "Ellison and His Novel: The Visible Dimensions of *Invisible Man*." *Black World*, 20 (December 1970), 27-30.
  An evaluation; faults Ellison for not using literature as an "instrument of liberation."

Clipper, Lawrence J. "Folkloric and Mythic Elements in *Invisible Man*." *CLA Jour*, 3 (March 1970), 229-241.
  Ellison superimposed a mythic pattern on the more obvious folkloric pattern of his novel.

Collier, Eugenia. "The Nightmare Truth of an Invisible Man." *Black World*, 20 (December 1970), 12-19.
  The dreams and semi-conscious states of the novel's protagonist contain the truth of his identity, which he seeks to find, and are thus the "crux" of the novel.

Cooke, Michael G. See MISCELLANEOUS (Contemporary--both Cooke entries).

Corrigan, Robert A. See GENERAL--1st Corrigan entry.

Corry, John. "Profile of an American Novelist: A White View of Ralph Ellison." *Black World*, 20 (December 1970), 116-125.
  Basically an interview in which Ellison discusses, among other things, himself and his views on writing and on being black.

Cosgrove, William. "Modern Black Writers: The Divided Self." *NALF*, 7 (Winter 1973), 120-122.
  The modern black writer is either an "invisible man" or a "native son." Ironically, Ellison's *Invisible Man* speaks for the native son and Wright's *Native Son* for the invisible man.

_____. "Strategies of Survival: The Gimmick Motif in Black Literature." *Stud in the Twentieth Cent*, no. 15 (Spring 1975), 109-127.

In black literature, before a search for
identity, there is the search for the "gimmick"
to survive.

Covo, Jacqueline. *The Blinking Eye: Ralph Waldo
Ellison*. Metuchen, N. J.: Scarecrow Press,
1974.
    Bibliographic essays and checklists on the
reception of Ellison's work in America, France,
Germany, and Italy from 1952 to 1971.

_____. "Ralph Ellison in France: Bibliographic
Essays and Checklist of French Criticism, 1954-
1971." *CLA Jour*, 16 (June 1973), 519-526.
    Ellison's status as a major Afro-American
writer has been recognized from the first.

_____. "Ralph Waldo Ellison: Bibliographic Essays
and Finding List of American Criticism." *CLA
Jour*, 15 (December 1971), 171-196.
    Title is descriptive.

Deutsch, Leonard J. "Ellison's Early Fiction."
NALF, 7 (Summer 1973), 53-59.
    Deals with the stories Ellison wrote between
1939 and 1945, and with misconceptions about
them.

_____. "Ralph Waldo Ellison and Ralph Waldo
Emerson: A Shared Moral Vision." *CLA Jour*, 16
(December 1972), 159-178.
    Ellison's protagonist in *Invisible Man*
finally learns the meaning and value of
self-reliance.

Doyle, Mary Ellen. "In Need of Folk: The Alienated Protagonists of Ralph Ellison's Short
Fiction." *CLA Jour*, 19 (December 1975),
165-172.
    The typical Ellison hero in the short fiction
is alienated "from himself, his own race, and
white-controlled society"; if there is hope for
escape from alienation, it lies in "his first
establishing or restoring a sense of cohesion
with his own race through some symbolic folk
member or custom."

Duff, Gerald. See REED, ISHMAEL (Contemporary).

Duffy, Martha. "Hustler and Fabulist." *Time*,
January 17, 1972, pp. 63-64.
    This review of *Gemini*, by Nikki Giovanni,
gives a brief biographical sketch of Nikki
Giovanni, comments on her feelings toward
whites, and points out her criticism of Ralph
Ellison.

Elkins, Stanley M. "The Slavery Debate." *Commentary*, 60 (December 1975), 40-54.
    Ellison is recognized as one who "gave the
search for black culture the authenticity and
legitimacy to which it was entitled."

Ellison, Ralph, and J. A. McPherson. "Indivisible
Man." *Atl*, 226 (December 1970), 45-60.
    Impressions of Ellison developed from con-
versations and correspondence.

Ellison, Ralph, et al. See MISCELLANEOUS
(Contemporary).

Emerson, O. B. See MISCELLANEOUS (Contemporary).

Everett, Chestyn. See GENERAL.

Fass, Barbara. "Rejection of Paternalism.
Hawthorne's 'My Kinsman, Major Molineaux' and
Ellison's *Invisible Man*." *CLA Jour*, 14
(Spring 1971), 317-323.
    Invisible Man may have its source in
Hawthorne, in an ironic sense, but it also owes
much to Emerson.

Fischer, Russell G. "*Invisible Man* as History."
CLA Jour, 17 (March 1974), 338-367.
    In his several roles Ellison's protagonist
experiences three major epochs of black American
history from Reconstruction to World War II.

Fontaine, William T. "The Negro Continuum from
Dominant Wish to Collective Act." *Af Forum*, 3,
no. 4/4, no. 1 (1968), 63-96.
    Part of the article deals with Ellison, ex-
pressing the belief that in certain episodes
Ellison is exposing Communism.

Ford, Nick A. "The Ambivalence of Ralph Ellison."
Black World, 20 (December 1970), 5-9.
    The reason why *Invisible Man* is considered
by many to be a good novel may be that its
ambivalence presents an intellectual challenge.

Foster, Frances. "The Black and White Masks of
Frantz Fanon and Ralph Ellison." *Black Acad
Rev*, 1 (Winter 1970), 46-58.
    The hero in *Invisible Man* reflects Fanon's
theory that blacks can regain their humanity
only by escaping alienation and analyzing
themselves.

Frohock, W. M. "The Edge of Laughter: Some Modern
Fiction and the Grotesque," in *Veins of Humor*,
ed. Harry Levin. Cambridge, Mass.: Harvard
Univ Press, 1972, pp. 243-254.
    Invisible Man is included among examples of
modern novels that "walk the tightrope" between
the grotesque and the ludicrous.

Fuller, Hoyt. "The Achievements of Ralph Ellison."
Black World, 20 (December 1970), 4.
    A listing of honors Ellison has received.

Gayle, Addison, Jr. See MISCELLANEOUS
(Contemporary--3rd Gayle entry).

_____. See GENERAL.

Gibson, Donald B. See MISCELLANEOUS
(Contemporary--1st Gibson entry).

Goede, William. See MISCELLANEOUS (Contemporary).

Gottesman, Ronald, ed. *Studies in Invisible Man*.
Columbus, Ohio: Charles E. Merrill, 1971.
    Reprints an early review, an interview with
Ellison, and six critical essays on the novel.

Graham, John, and George Garrett. See MISCELLANEOUS
(Contemporary).

Greene, Maxine. "Against Invisibility." *CE*, 30
(March 1969), 430-436.

Invisible Man can serve as a metaphor by which teachers can solve such current problems as that of relevance.

Griffin, Edward M. "Notes from a Clean, Well-Lighted Place: Ralph Ellison's *Invisible Man*." *TCL*, 15 (October 1969), 129-144.
   The style of the novel changes as the protagonist changes in place and thought.

Gross, Theodore L. See GENERAL--1st Gross entry.

_____. See MISCELLANEOUS (Contemporary--2nd Gross entry).

Grow, Lynn M. "The Dream Scenes of *Invisible Man*." *Wichita State Univ Bul*, 50 (August 1974), 1-13.
   Deals with the importance of the dream scenes in revealing Ellison's concept of the artist.

Gvereschi, Edward. "Anticipations of *Invisible Man*: Ralph Ellison's 'King of the Bingo Game.'" *NALF*, 6 (Winter 1972), 122-124.
   Like the novel, this short story is concerned with "identity, self-delusion, betrayal" and reveals "familiar techniques of sardonic humor, surrealism, and symbolic vision."

Harris, Trudier. "Ellison's 'Peter Wheatstraw': His Basis in Black Folk Tradition." *Miss FR*, 9 (Summer 1975), 117-126.
   Deals with the significance of the reaction of the protagonist in *Invisible Man* to Peter Wheatstraw.

Haslam, Gerald W. See MISCELLANEOUS (Contemporary--2nd Haslam entry).

Hays, Peter L. "The Incest Theme in *Invisible Man*." *WHR*, 23 (Autumn 1969), 335-339.
   The novel develops the theme that manipulation of blacks by whites is metaphorically incest.

Heller, Arno. "Ralph Ellisons *Invisible Man*: Das Rassenproblem als Analyse moderner Existenz." *Neueren Sprachen*, 21 (January 1972), 2-9.
   Deals with the consequences of the hero's race consciousness.

Hemenway, Robert. See GENERAL.

Henkle, Roger. "Symposium Highlights: Wrestling (American Style) with Proteus." *Novel*, 3 (1970), 197-207.
   This symposium on trends in the contemporary American novel included discussion of Ellison's address at the 1953 National Book Award ceremony. Barth was one of the panelists.

Hersey, John. *Ralph Ellison: A Collection of Critical Essays*. Twentieth Century Views. Englewood Cliffs, N. J.: Prentice-Hall, 1974.
   Collects fourteen previously published critical essays, with an original interview by the editor and a selected bibliography.

Horowitz, Floyd R. "An Experimental Confession from a Reader of *Invisible Man*." *CLA Jour*, 13 (March 1970), 304-314.

For Ellison experimental writing is "a struggle through illusion to reality," but Horowitz says there must be "a continuum of consciousness whereby the reader shares close with the hero the time-riddle of identity."

Howard, David C. "Points in Defense of Ellison's *Invisible Man*." *NConL*, 1 (January 1971), 13-14.
   Defends the theme and the techniques of the novel.

Howe, Irving. See GENERAL.

Inge, M. Thomas. See MISCELLANEOUS (Contemporary--1st Inge entry).

Johnson, Abby A. "Birds of Passage: Flight Imagery in *Invisible Man*. *Stud in the Twentieth Cent*, 14 (Fall 1974), 91-104.
   Deals with the significance of the various types of birds in the novel.

Kaiser, Ernest. "A Critical Look at Ellison's Fiction and at Social and Literary Criticism by and About the Author." *Black World*, 20 (December 1970), 53-59, 81-97.
   An attack on Ellison and his *Invisible Man* (and Richard Wright's *Black Boy*) for not being political, on the New Criticism, and on critics who have praised Ellison's novel.

Kattan, Naïm. See MISCELLANEOUS (Contemporary).

Kazin, Alfred. "Absurdity as Contemporary Style." *Medit Rev*, 1 (Spring 1971), 39-46.
   Ellison is among writers included in this discussion of works dealing with the "outsider" in an absurd world.

_____. See MISCELLANEOUS (Contemporary).

Kent, George E. "Ralph Ellison and Afro-American Folk and Cultural Tradition." *CLA Jour*, 13 (March 1970), 265-276.
   Ellison runs the whole gamut of black cultural and folk tradition in his novel.

Klotman, Phyllis R. "The Running Man as Metaphor in Ellison's *Invisible Man*." *CLA Jour*, 13 (March 1970), 277-288.
   Running has become a way of life for the narrator of *Invisible Man*, which is the culmination of the "Running Man metaphor" in American literature.

Kostelanetz, Richard. "Ralph Ellison: Novelist as Brown Skinned Aristocrat." *Shen*, 20 (Summer 1969), 56-77.
   A biographical and personality sketch.

Lane, James B. "Underground to Manhood: Ralph Ellison's *Invisible Man*." *NALF*, 7 (Summer 1973), 64-72.
   Deals with the aptness of New York as the setting for black dehumanization and with the invisible man as Everyman.

Lang, Hans J. See GENERAL.

Lasater, Alice. See MISCELLANEOUS (Contemporary).

IV. Contemporary (1920-1975)

LeClair, Thomas. See WRIGHT, RICHARD.

Lehan, Richard. See MISCELLANEOUS (Contemporary).

Levin, Harry. See GENERAL.

Lieber, Todd M. "Ralph Ellison and the Metaphor of Invisibility in Black Literary Tradition." *AQ*, 24 (March 1972), 86-100.
Discusses invisibility as a metaphor in use before Ellison's *Invisible Man.*

Lieberman, Marcia R. "Moral Innocents: Ellison's *Invisible Man* and *Candide*." *CLA Jour*, 14 (September 1971), 64-79.
Finds that *Invisible Man* has marked resemblance to *Candide*, and that *Invisible Man's* innocence is "moral rather than temporal or metaphysical...."

Liebman, Arthur. See MISCELLANEOUS (Contemporary).

Lillard, R. S. "A Ralph Waldo Ellison Bibliography (1914-1967)." *Am Bk Collector*, 19 (November 1968), 18-22.
Title is descriptive.

Lillard, Stewart. "Ellison's Ambitious Scope in *Invisible Man*." *EJ*, 58 (September 1969), 833-839.
Investigates the "epic qualities" in *Invisible Man* which he interprets as "social allegory" for a section of the United States and a major portion of the American Negroes' experience.

Lindberg, John. "'Black Aesthetic': Minority or Mainstream?" *North Am Rev*, 260 (Winter 1975), 48-52.
Expresses approval of Ellison's view of the black aesthetic.

Ludington, C. T., Jr. "Protest and Anti-Protest: Ralph Ellison." *SAB*, 34 (January 1969), 15-16.
According to the abstract of a paper read at the American Studies section of SAMLA (1968), Ellison argues against pure protest and for fiction that transcends racial boundaries.

_____. "Protest and Anti-Protest: Ralph Ellison." *SHR*, 4 (Winter 1970), 31-39.
Outlines Ellison's career, discusses his ideas about "Negro protest writing and artistic fiction," and gives primary consideration to *Invisible Man.*

Lutwack, Leonard. See MISCELLANEOUS (Contemporary).

Madden, David. See MISCELLANEOUS (Contemporary-- 1st Madden entry).

Mangione, Jerre. See MISCELLANEOUS (Contemporary).

Manucci, Loretta V. See MISCELLANEOUS (Contemporary).

Margolies, Edward. See MISCELLANEOUS (Contemporary--both Margolies entries).

Mason, Clifford. "Ralph Ellison and the Underground Man." *Black World*, 20 (December 1970), 20-26.

Invisible Man is structurally indebted to Wright's "The Man Who Lived Underground," though the goals of the protagonists of the two works are different.

May, John R. See MISCELLANEOUS (Contemporary).

_____. See GENERAL.

McDaniel, Barbara A. "John Steinbeck: Ralph Ellison's Invisible Source." *Pacific Coast Phil*, 8 (1973), 28-33.
Title is descriptive.

McDowell, Robert E., and George Fortenberry. See MISCELLANEOUS (Contemporary).

Mitchell, Louis D. "Invisibility--Permanent or Resurrective." *CLA Jour*, 17 (March 1974), 379-386.
Invisible Man is a "continual play on the western resurrective theme."

_____, and Henry J. Stauffenberg. "Ellison's B. P. Rinehart: 'Spiritual Technologist.'" *NALF*, 9 (Summer 1975), 51-52.
As pastor of the Holy Way Station, Rinehart, Ellison's "most effective minor character," is a "merchandising genius" who "emerges as a symbol of, a product of, and a palliative for communal frustration."

Moore, Robert H. "On Initiation Rites and Power: Ralph Ellison Speaks at West Point." *ConL*, 15 (Spring 1974), 163-186.
An interview of March 26, 1969.

Moorer, Frank E., and Lugene Baily. "A Selected Check List of Materials by and about Ralph Ellison." *Black World*, 20 (December 1970), 126-130.
Title is descriptive.

Mueller, William R. *Celebration of Life: Studies in Modern Fiction.* Mission, Kansas: Sheed and Ward, 1972.
A discussion of affirmation to be found in modern fiction. Ellison is considered under the heading "Man and Vocation."

Neal, Larry. "Ellison's Zoot Suit." *Black World*, 20 (December 1970), 31-52.
Left-wing attacks against Ellison for not being an active protester are unjustified because they fail to recognize that art is an aesthetic matter.

Nettelbeck, C. W. "From Inside Destitution: Celine's Barmadu and Ellison's Invisible Man." *Southern Rev* (Adelaide), 7 (November 1974), 246-253.
These writers are more effective than sociologists in allowing us "to identify with destitution."

Nevius, Blake. See MISCELLANEOUS (Contemporary).

Nichols, William W. "Ralph Ellison's Black American Scholar." *Phylon*, 31 (Spring 1970), 70-75.
Suggests many ironic parallels between Ellison's *Invisible Man* and Emerson's "American Scholar."

O'Brien, John. See MISCELLANEOUS (Contemporary--both O'Brien entries).

Omans, Stuart E. "The Variations on a Masked Leader: A Study on the Literary Relationship of Ralph Ellison and Herman Melville." *SAB*, 40 (May 1975), 15-23.
   Ellison draws on images, characters, and entire scenes in *Benito Cereno* to present his vision of the black in *Invisible Man*.

Panichas, George A. See MISCELLANEOUS (Contemporary).

Parrish, Paul A. "Writing as Celebration: The Epilogue of *Invisible Man*." *Renascence*, 26 (Spring 1974), 152-157.
   An examination of the narrator's readiness to return to the world in the epilogue of the novel.

Pearce, Richard. See MISCELLANEOUS (Contemporary).

Plante, P. R. See GENERAL.

Plessner, Monika. "Bildnis des Künstlers als Volksaufwiegler." *Merkur*, 24 (July 1970), 629-643.
   A review-essay of a German edition of *Invisible Man*; the reviewer defends Ellison's refusal to become a political activist.

Polsgrove, Carol. "Addenda to A Ralph Waldo Ellison Bibliography' (1914-1968)." *Am Bk Collector*, 20 (November-December 1969), 11-12.
   Addenda to a bibliography by R. S. Lillard, appearing in the *American Book Collector*, 19 (November 1968).

Powell, Grosvenor E. "Role and Identity in Ralph Ellison's 'Invisible Man,'" in David J. Burrows, et al., *Private Dealings: Eight Modern American Writers*. Stockholm: Almqvist & Witsell, 1969.
   Ellison "is more interested in describing an aspect of the universal human condition than he is in writing a 'negro' novel or even an American one."

Pryse, Marjorie. "Ralph Ellison's Heroic Fugitive." *AL*, 46 (March 1974), 1-15.
   Studies the relationship between the narrator of *Invisible Man* and the reader.

Radford, Frederick L. "The Journey Towards Castration: Interracial Sexual Stereotypes in Ellison's *Invisible Man*." *Jour Am Stud*, 4 (February 1971), 227-231.
   "All of the sexual encounters in Ellison's *Invisible Man* are linked in some measure to the theme of the imprisonment of the natural sexual individuality of the black male within the confines of white stereotype...."

Reilly, John M., ed. *Twentieth Century Interpretations of Invisible Man*. Englewood Cliffs, N. J.: Prentice-Hall, 1970.
   Reprints five full essays and nine excerpts and includes a chronology, selected bibliography, and introduction by the editor.

Riche, James. "The Politics of Black Modernism." *Lit and Ideology*, no. 8 (1971), 85-90.
   Ellison is among other black writers accused in this article of being racist.

Ridenour, Ronald. See WRIGHT, RICHARD.

Rodnon, Stewart. "Ralph Ellison's *Invisible Man*: Six Tentative Approaches." *CLA Jour*, 12 (March 1969), 244-256.
   Invisible Man can be approached by showing its relationship to classic and contemporary American literature and to the classics of western civilization. It can be dealt with purely on its own literary qualities or through an analysis of its themes; as an example of a novel of a special pattern; and finally by "pegging the novel directly" to the white-Negro experiences of the student.

_____. See CLEMENS, SAMUEL LANGHORNE.

Rollins, Ronald G. "Ellison's *Invisible Man*." *Expl*, 30 (November 1971), Item 22.
   A note on the character Lucius Brockway which discusses the meaning of his name and its significance in Chapter 10 of the novel.

Rosenblatt, Roger. See MISCELLANEOUS (Contemporary--both Rosenblatt entries).

Rubin, Louis D., Jr. See GENERAL--1st Rubin entry.

Ruotolo, Lucio P. See MISCELLANEOUS (Contemporary).

Rupp, Richard. See MISCELLANEOUS (Contemporary).

Sanders, Archie D. "Odysseus in Black: An Analysis of the Structure of *Invisible Man*." *CLA Jour*, 13 (March 1970), 217-228.
   Ellison chose the Homeric structure for his *Invisible Man* and used archetypes found in the *Odyssey*.

Savory, Jerold J. See MISCELLANEOUS (Contemporary).

Schafer, William J. "Irony from Underground--Satiric Elements in *Invisible Man*." *Satire Newsl*, 7 (Fall 1969), 22-29.
   Not strictly a satire, *Invisible Man* has a basis of bitter irony arising from an existential sense of the absurd expressed through use of folk humor and the white world seen through black eyes. The main feature of the satire is its subtlety and complexity.

_____. "Ralph Ellison and the Birth of the Anti-Hero." *Critique*, 10, no. 2 (1968), 82-93.
   A treatment of *Invisible Man* as a story which describes the birth of an anti-hero by creating a "fragment of an epic in form." The main character is a "no-man and everyman" on a modern epic quest.

Schmitz, Neil. See CLEMENS, SAMUEL LANGHORNE (2nd Schmitz entry).

Scholes, Robert. See MISCELLANEOUS (Contemporary).

Schraufnagel, Noel. See MISCELLANEOUS (Contemporary).

IV. CONTEMPORARY (1920-1975)

Scott, Nathan A. See MISCELLANEOUS (Contemporary).

Scruggs, Charles W. "Ralph Ellison's Use of the *Aeneid* in *Invisible Man*." *CLA Jour*, 17 (March 1974), 368-378.
    As Virgil before him had done, Ellison used myth to give a sense of cultural identity to his people and to dignify history.

Selke, Hartmut K. "An Allusion to Sartre's *The Flies* in Ralph Ellison's *Invisible Man*." *NConL*, 4 (May 1974), 3-4.
    Title is descriptive.

_____. "The Education at 'College of Fools': References to Emerson's 'Self-Reliance' in *Invisible Man*." *NConL*, 4 (January 1974), 13-15.
    Deals with the irony of the fact that Invisible Man is told to study Emerson's essay.

Sequira, Isaac. "The Uncompleted Initiation of the Invisible Man." *SBL*, 6 (Spring 1975), 9-13.
    Invisible Man crosses the "threshold of initiation" but it does not show him the direction to go.

Singh, Raman K. See MISCELLANEOUS (Contemporary-- 1st Singh entry).

Smith, Dwight L. See GENERAL.

Stark, John. "*Invisible Man*: Ellison's Black Odyssey." *NALF*, 7 (Summer 1973), 60-63.
    Points out similarities and differences in purpose and episodes in Ellison's novel and the *Odyssey*.

Stern, Frederick. See MISCELLANEOUS (Contemporary).

Sullivan, Philip E. "Buh Rabbit: Going through the Changes." *SBL*, 4 (Summer 1973), 28-32.
    Because he can adapt, Buh Rabbit represents both slave and militant black; thus he appears in *Invisible Man*.

Sylvander, Carolyn W. "Ralph Ellison's *Invisible Man* and Female Stereotypes." *NALF*, 9 (Fall 1975), 77-79.
    Concludes that Ellison's women characters lack humanity.

Tanner, Tony. See MISCELLANEOUS (Contemporary).

Tatham, Campbell. See GENERAL.

Tischler, Nancy M. See MISCELLANEOUS (Contemporary--3rd Tischler entry).

Trachtenberg, Stanley. See BARTH, JOHN (Contemporary).

Trimmer, Joseph F., ed. *A Casebook on Ralph Ellison's Invisible Man*. New York: Thomas Y. Crowell, 1972.
    Reprints historical and artistic background materials, eight critical essays, two statements by Ellison, with introductory notes, bibliography, and study questions by the editor.

_____. "Ralph Ellison's 'Flying Home.'" *Stud SF*, 9 (Spring 1972), 175-182.
    Symbolic patterns permeate this story by Ellison, who "is a master of the short story."

Turner, Darwin T. "Sight in *Invisible Man*." *CLA Jour*, 13 (March 1970), 258-264.
    Vision is the dominant image in the novel.

Vogler, Thomas A. "*Invisible Man*: Somebody's Protest Novel." *Iowa Rev*, 1 (Spring 1970), 64-82.
    Deals with the changes the invisible man undergoes in his search for his own identity; the black hero represents the writer, both facing the problem of finding a way "to *tell* it."

Wade, Melvin and Margaret. See GENERAL.

Walcott, Ronald. "Some Notes on the Blues Style and Space: Ellison, Gordone, and Tolson." *Black World*, 22 (December 1972), 4-29.
    Wright's "The Man Who Lived Underground" anticipates the "invisible man's plunge outside of history into space"; Ellison's novel is "informed by a sense of the blues."

Walling, William. "Ralph Ellison's *Invisible Man*: 'It Goes a Long Way Back, Some Twenty Years.'" *Phylon*, 34 (March 1973), 4-16.
    Outlines problems the novel presents and applies the traditional methods of literary criticism to its structure, symbolism, and imagery. Continued in the June 1973 issue of *Phylon*.

_____. "'Art' and 'Protest': Ralph Ellison's *Invisible Man* Twenty Years After." *Phylon*, 34 (June 1973), 120-134.
    Explores problems the novel raises of self-image for blacks, and sees it against the radical alteration in black consciousness which has occurred since its publication in 1952. See March issue of *Phylon*.

Waniek, Marilyn N. See MISCELLANEOUS (Contemporary).

Weinberg, Helen A. See MISCELLANEOUS (Contemporary).

Weinstein, Sharon R. "Comedy and the Absurd in Ellison's *Invisible Man*." *SBL*, 3 (Autumn 1972), 12-16.
    Explores humor in the novel as the ultimate means of appealing for brotherhood and love.

Williams, John A. "Ralph Ellison and *Invisible Man*: Their Place in American Letters." *Black World*, 20 (December 1970), 10-11.
    Praises *Invisible Man* but states that Ellison should make himself available to younger black writers.

Wilner, Eleanor R. "The Invisible Thread: Identity and Nonentity in *Invisible Man*." *CLA Jour*, 13 (March 1970), 242-257.
    "The invisible thread" of dignity and identity runs through the novel.

[FAULKNER, JOHN] Bradford, M. E. See FAULKNER, WILLIAM--6th Bradford entry.

Kent, George E. See MISCELLANEOUS (Contemporary).

Pruett, D. F. "Papers of John Faulkner." *MVC Bul*,
3 (Fall 1970), 81-84.
    The papers, including the manuscripts of John
Faulkner's published and unpublished works, are
now in the Mississippi Valley Collection of the
Brister Library at Memphis State University.

Sugg, Redding S., Jr. "Introduction" to *Cabin Road*.
Baton Rouge: Louisiana State Univ Press,
1969, pp. vii-xxv.
    Examines the form and content of John
Faulkner's fiction, takes note of his relationship to the tall-tale raconteurs and humorists
of the Old Southwest and to the local-colorists,
and finds his virtues to be "originality, dis-
tinctiveness, concentration" as a minor author.

_____. "John Faulkner's Vanishing South." *AH*, 22
(April 1971), 65-75.
    Centering on John Faulkner's paintings, the
article makes passing reference to his brother
William.

_____. "John's Yoknapatawpha." *SAQ*, 68
(Summer 1969), 343-362.
    John Faulkner's works show that he was in-
fluenced by the Southwest humorists and that
his skill in the genre should place him beside
Caldwell, Warren, and his brother William.

White, Helen, and Redding S. Sugg, Jr. "John
Faulkner: An Annotated Check List of His Pub-
lished Works and of His Papers." *SB*, 23
(1970), 217-229.
    A listing (with description) of the John
Faulkner papers now housed at Memphis State
University.

[FAULKNER, WILLIAM] Anon. See GENERAL--2nd and
6th Anon. entries.

Aaron, Daniel. See GENERAL--1st Faulkner entry.

Ackerman, R. D. "The Immolation of Isaac McCaslin."
Tex Stud in Lit and Lang, 16 (Fall 1974),
557-565.
    Sees Isaac's repudiation of his heritage as
self-immolation.

Adamowski, Thomas H. "Bayard Sartoris: Mourning
and Melancholia." *Lit and Psych*, 23 (1973),
149-158.
    Bayard suffers from melancholia and in his
death he unconsciously parodies Johnny's death
and "kills" the Sartoris myth.

_____. "Dombey and Son and Sutpen and Son." *Stud
in the Novel*, 4 (Fall 1972), 378-389.
    Offers parallels between these men "who
desire autonomy."

_____. "Joe Christmas: The Tyranny of Childhood."
Novel, 4 (Spring 1971), 240-251.
    Joe Christmas' choice of accepting his iden-
tity, defined by others in his childhood, makes
his life a ritual.

Adams, Richard P. "At Long Last, *Flags in the
Dust*." Review of the Random House edition.
SouR, 10 (Autumn 1974), 878-888.
    Outlines the editorial and textual short-
comings of this newly published novel, but finds
it, nevertheless, important in accounting for
Faulkner's development as a writer between 1926
and 1928.

_____. *Faulkner: Myth and Motion*. Princeton:
Princeton Univ Press, 1968.
    An analysis of Faulkner's technical devices
used in the major novels to fulfill his theory
that "The aim of every artist is to arrest motion, which is life, by artificial means...."

_____. "Some Key Words in Faulkner." *Tulane Stud
in Eng*, 16 (1968), 135-148.
    Faulkner's handling of such words as *doom*,
terrific, and *terrible* adds complexity and richness to his works.

_____. See GENERAL.

Ainsa, Fernando. "En el santuario de William
Faulkner." *Cuad Hisp*, 269 (November 1972),
232-243.
    An account of a visit to Oxford, Mississippi.

Aldridge, John W. See MISCELLANEOUS (Contemporary--
2nd Aldridge entry).

Alexandrescu, Sorin. "A Project in the Semantic
Analysis of the Characters in William Faulkner's
Work." *Semiotica*, 4 (1971), 37-51.
    A "typological analysis of Faulkner's
universe."

_____. "William Faulkner and the Greek Tragedy."
Romanian Rev, 24, no. 3 (1970), 102-110.
    Social hierarchy restricts individuals in
Faulkner's works in the same way that human
beings are restricted by the gods in Greek
tragedy.

_____. *William Faulkner*. Bucharest, Rumania:
Edituru pentre Literatura Universala, 1969.
    The first full-scale study of Faulkner in
Rumanian: "...not an attempt to explicate all
the Faulkner pieces but only to point to the
principles underlying the great number of
explications de textes which it still requires
in spite of the tremendous amount of existing
exegesis." Includes bibliographic footnotes;
numerous charts of characterization, plot, and
genealogy; appendices, and a descriptive index.

Alter, Robert. See MISCELLANEOUS (Contemporary).

Anderson, Hilton. "Two Possible Sources for
Faulkner's Drusilla Hawk." *Notes on Miss
Writers*, 3 (Winter 1971), 108-110.
    A suggestion that Faulkner may have patterned
one facet of Drusilla's career after Colonel
Falkner's characters, Ellen and Isabel, in
The Spanish Heroine and *The Siege of Monterrey*.
These girls dress as men and enter armies as
does Drusilla.

Angell, Leslie E. "The Umbilical Cord Symbol as
Unifying Theme and Pattern in *Absalom, Absalom!*"
Mass Stud in Eng, 1 (Fall 1968), 106-110.
    Symbolically the umbilical cord unites Rosa
and Clytie, Quentin and Shreve, the past and the
present.

Antoniadis, Roxandra V. "Faulkner and Balzac: The Poetic Web." *CLS*, 9 (September 1972), 303-325.
    Similarities in goals and narrative techniques mark both Balzac and Faulkner as creators of "the novel as poem."

Arnold, Edwin T. "Freedom and Stasis in Faulkner's *Mosquitoes*." *Miss Quart*, 28 (Summer 1975), 281-287.
    Besides the commonly mentioned themes of "sex, art, and the sterility of words," this novel also has an important fourth theme, "that of freedom and bondage," which must be taken into account for a full understanding of the novel's characters and meaning.

Arpad, Joseph. "William Faulkner's Legendary Novels: The Snopes Trilogy." *Miss Quart*, 22 (Summer 1969), 214-225.
    In its stress on a sense of life and a sense of legend, the trilogy may be "described as a *legendary novel*," the three novels being "unique fictional illustrations of how man seeks to understand the unknowable and enigmatic elements of his past, his people, and his place in terms of his own imagination."

Asals, Frederick. "Faulkner's *Light in August*." *Expl*, 26 (May 1968), Item 74.
    Discusses the parallel between Christ's temptation (Matt 4: 1-11) and Joe Christmas' affair with Joanna Burden.

Aswell, Duncan. "The Puzzling Design of *Absalom, Absalom!*" *KR*, 30, no. 1 (1968), 67-84.
    Maintains that the novel is the mind's search for purpose, meaning, and truth.

_____. "The Recollection and the Blood: Jason's Role in *The Sound and the Fury*." *Miss Quart*, 21 (Summer 1968), 211-218.
    Jason's monologues serve as ironic commentary on the major themes of the novel.

Atkins, Anselm. "The Matched Halves of *Absalom, Absalom!*" *MFS*, 15 (Summer 1969), 264-265.
    Chapters I-V and Chapters VI-IX show balance which reiterates, at structural level, "metaphorical identification" of Miss Rosa and Quentin, already indicated at thematic level.

Auer, Michael J. "Caddy, Benjy, and the Acts of the Apostles: A Note on *The Sound and the Fury*." *Stud in the Novel*, 6 (Winter 1974), 475-476.
    Acts 8: 26-40 provides a prototype of Benjy and of the name Candace.

Avni, Abraham. See GENERAL.

Banašević, Nikola, ed. *Actes du Ve Congres de l'Association Internationale de Littérature Comparée, Belgrade, 1967*. Belgrade: Univ de Belgrade; Amsterdam: Swets and Zeitlinger, 1969.
    Contains an essay by Calvin Brown on Faulkner's oral tradition and one by Jean Weisgerber on the similarities between certain Faulkner characters and Dostoyevsky's Raskalnikov.

Baquira, Josephina Q. "Themes, Styles, and Symbolism in *The Sound and the Fury*." *St. Louis Univ Research Jour*, 4 (December 1973), 658-672.
    Points out the importance of *Macbeth*, V, v, 16-28 in relation to the novel.

Barber, Marion. "The Two Emilys: A Ransom Suggestion to Faulkner?" *Notes on Miss Writers*, 5 (Winter 1973), 103-105.
    A note on the similarity between Faulkner's character and Ransom's "Emily Hardcastle, Spinster."

Barnes, Daniel R. "Faulkner's Miss Emily and Hawthorne's Old Maid." *Stud SF* 9 (Fall 1972), 373-377.
    "...there is ample evidence in plot, characterization and detail to indicate that Hawthorne's tale ["The White Old Maid"] may well have served as a major source for Faulkner's story ["A Rose for Emily"]."

Barrett, William. *Time of Need: Forms of the Imagination in the Twentieth Century*. New York: Harper and Row, 1972.
    Includes a lengthy discussion of Faulkner, with particular attention to *The Sound and the Fury*, "The Bear," and *Absalom, Absalom!*

Barth, J. Robert, S. J., ed. *Religious Perspectives in Faulkner's Fiction: Yoknapatawpha and Beyond*. Notre Dame: Univ of Notre Dame Press, 1972.
    Reprints ten essays on Faulkner's religious attitudes as reflected in his fiction, with introductory notes and commentary on each essay by the editor.

Bassett, John. *William Faulkner: An Annotated Checklist of Criticism*. New York: David Lewis, 1972.
    Criticism through 1971, designed as a continuation of Maurice Beebe's checklist in *MFS*, Spring 1967.

_____, ed. *William Faulkner: The Critical Heritage*. London and Boston: Routledge Kegan Paul, 1975.
    A selection of representative reviews and criticism outlining Faulkner's reputation from the twenties through the forties.

_____. "William Faulkner's *The Sound and the Fury*: An Annotated Checklist of Criticism." *RALS*, 1 (Autumn 1971), 217-246.
    "In the following checklist I try to provide a comprehensive record of the manifold published responses to the novel.... A series of asterisks marks the most useful general analyses."

Beards, Richard. "Parody as Tribute: William Melvin Kelley's *A Different Drummer* and Faulkner." *SBL*, 5 (Winter 1974), 25-28.
    Discusses Faulknerian echoes to be found in Kelley's *A Different Drummer* but emphasizes that Kelley has created a Southern world of his own.

Beauchamp, Gorman. "The Rite of Initiation in Faulkner's 'The Bear.'" *ArQ*, 28 (Winter 1972), 319-325.
    Traces Ike McCaslin's "ritualistic" experiences in the wilderness as they satisfy four

basic criteria for the (archetypal) initiation story.

———. *"The Unvanquished*: Faulkner's *Oresteia."* *Miss Quart*, 23 (Summer 1970), 273-277.
  The two works have thematic similarity in their concern with artistic moral vision.

Beaver, Harold. "The Count of Mississippi." *TLS*, no. 3,821 (May 30, 1975), 600-601.
  A long review of Blotner's *Faulkner: A Biography*.

Bedell, George C. *Kierkegaard and Faulkner: Modalities of Existence*. Baton Rouge: Louisiana State Univ Press, 1972.
  Kierkegaard's three basic modalities of existence--the aesthetical, the ethical, and the religious--are applied to Faulkner's novels to elucidate them and the nature of modern human existence.

Bedient, Calvin. "Pride and Nakedness: *As I Lay Dying."* *MLQ*, 29 (March 1968), 61-76.
  The polarity of nakedness and pride in the subject matter of the novel is supported by a nakedness of form and grotesqueness of style.

Behrens, Ralph. "Collapse of Dynasty: The Thematic Center of *Absalom, Absalom!"* *PMLA*, 89 (January 1974), 24-33.
  The most tenable theory for Sutpen's failure, which derives from II Samuel particularly, is that the very concept of dynasty is basically flawed.

Beidler, Peter G. "A Darwinian Source for Faulkner's Indians in 'Red Leaves.'" *Stud SF*, 10 (Fall 1973), 421-423.
  Suggests as this source Charles Darwin's journal of his voyage on the *Beagle*.

———. "Faulkner's Techniques of Characterization: Jewel in *As I Lay Dying."* *EA*, 21 (July-September 1968), 236-242.
  Concentrating on Jewel, the article discusses the importance of Faulkner's techniques of characterization.

Beja, Morris. See MISCELLANEOUS (Contemporary).

Bell, Haney H., Jr. "Sam Fathers and Ike McCaslin and the World in Which Ike Matures." *Costerus*, 7 (1973), 1-12.
  Discusses the relationship between Sam and Ike and the stages of Ike's maturing.

Bellman, Samuel I. See MISCELLANEOUS (Contemporary).

Benert, Annette. "The Four Fathers of Isaac McCaslin." *SHR*, 9 (Fall 1975), 423-433.
  Ike is dominated by his past because he cannot come to terms with the history dramatized through the active influence of four men: his father, his grandfather, his cousin, and Sam Fathers.

Benson, Jackson J. "Quentin Compson: Self-Portrait of a Young Artist's Emotions." *TCL*, 17 (July 1971), 143-159.

Quentin represents "both the modern artist in general and also, in many revealing ways, the agony of Faulkner in particular."

———. "Quentin's Responsibility for Caddy's Downfall." *Notes on Miss Writers*, 5 (Fall 1972), 63-64.
  Quentin is guiltless of Caddy's doom.

Berrone, Louis. "A Dickensian Echo in Faulkner." *Dickensian*, 71 (May 1975), 100-101.
  The episode in *A Fable* in which Corporal Brzewski and his men help a farmer prepare food echoes a scene in Chapter 2 of Dickens' *Somebody's Luggage*.

Bethea, Sally. "Further Thoughts on Racial Implications in Faulkner's 'That Evening Sun.'" *Notes on Miss Writers*, 6 (Winter 1974), 87-92.
  Develops the thesis that Nancy is not entirely responsible for her own misery; an answer to Scottie Davis' "Faulkner's Nancy: Racial Implications in 'That Evening Sun'" (*Notes on Miss Writers*, Spring 1972).

Bier, Jesse. "The Romantic Coordinates of American Literature." *BuR*, 18 (Fall 1970), 16-33.
  Uses Faulkner as one example of the small group of American writers who have a "sense of tragic realism," though noting that influences of earlier romantics may be seen in his work.

———. See GENERAL.

Blair, John G. "Camus' Faulkner: *Requiem for a Nun."* *BFLS*, 47 (1969), 249-257.
  Though Camus' adaptation is essentially faithful to the novel, his moral absolutism is apparent.

Blair, Walter. See GENERAL.

Blake, Nelson M. See MISCELLANEOUS (Contemporary).

Blanchard, Leonard A. "The Failure of the Natural Man: Faulkner's 'Pantaloon in Black.'" *Notes on Miss Writers*, 8 (Spring 1975), 28-32.
  Sees Rider of *Go Down, Moses* as not merely the portrait of a black, but as every man "stripped naked before the ultimate mysteries of life."

Blanchard, Margaret. "The Rhetoric of Communion: Voice in *The Sound and the Fury."* *AL*, 41 (January 1970), 555-565.
  A study of the narrator of the fourth section of this novel.

Bledsoe, A. S. "Colonel John Sartoris' Library." *Notes on Miss Writers*, 7 (Spring 1974), 26-29.
  Analyzes the contents of Sartoris' library as revealed in *The Unvanquished*.

Bleikasten, André. *Faulkner's As I Lay Dying*. Bloomington: Indiana Univ Press, 1973.
  A comprehensive analysis of genesis, language, technique, characterization, theme, and reception of the novel; translated from the 1970 French study.

_____. "Noces noires, noces blanches: Le jeu de désir et de la mort dans le monologue de Quentin Compson (*The Sound and the Fury*)." *RANAM*, 6 (1973), 142-169.
Focuses on the relationship between Quentin and Caddy.

_____, and François Pitavy. *William Faulkner: As I Lay Dying, Light in August*. Collection U/UZ. Serie "Études anglo-américaines. Dossiers littéraires." Paris: Librairie Armand Colin, 1970.
Critical analyses of the two novels by Bleikasten and Pitavy respectively, with specific chapters on technique, characterization, themes, style, reputation, etc., with a biographical-critical introduction and chronology by Michel Gresset and annotated bibliographies; in French.

Blotner, Joseph. "The Achievement of Maurice Edgar Coindreau." *So Lit Jour*, 4 (Fall 1971), 95-96.
An essay-review of *The Time of William Faulkner, A French View of Modern American Fiction: Essays by Maurice Edgar Coindreau*, edited and chiefly translated by George McMillan Reeves, foreword by Michel Gresset--consists of twenty-one essays collected over a thirty-year period, more than half of which focus on William Faulkner, which, according to Blotner, "is by itself worth the price of admission to the world of Maurice Edgar Coindreau."

_____. *Faulkner: A Biography*. New York: Random House, 1974.
A comprehensive account of Faulkner's life and career in two volumes.

_____. "Speaking of Books: Faulkner's *A Fable*." *NYTBR*, May 25, 1969, pp. 2, 34, 36, 38-39.
On the history of the composition of this novel.

_____. "William Faulkner: Committee Chairman," in R. B. Browne and Donald Pizer, eds. *Themes and Directions in American Literature*. Lafayette, Indiana: Purdue Univ Studies, 1969, pp. 200-219.
Recounts Faulkner's activities as chairman of a committee of writers related to Eisenhower's "People-to-People Program."

_____. "William Faulkner's Essay on the Composition of *Sartoris*." *YULG*, 47 (January 1973), 121-124.
Prints this previously unpublished piece which Faulkner wrote two years after the publication of *Sartoris* and in which he expresses his reaction to Boni and Liveright's rejection of the "Flags in the Dust" manuscript.

Boecker, Eberhard. *William Faulkner's Later Novels in German: A Study in the Theory and Practice of Translation*. Tübingen, Niemeyer, 1973.
Deals with the problems of translating Faulkner's works into German, focusing on *The Hamlet, Go Down, Moses, Intruder in the Dust, Requiem for a Nun, A Fable*, and *The Mansion*.

Boozer, William. *William Faulkner's First Book: The Marble Faun Fifty Years Later*. Memphis, Tenn.: Pigeon Roost Press, 1975.
Catalogues known copies of *The Marble Faun* and outlines the rare book's history at auction.

Borden, Caroline. "Characterization in Faulkner's *Light in August*." *Lit and Ideology*, no. 13 (1972), 41-50.
Treats the characters in the novel as grotesques.

Borgström, Greta I. "The Roaring Twenties and William Faulkner's *Sanctuary*." *Mod Språk*, 62 no. 3 (1968), 237-248.
The novel is a commentary on the Twenties and an attack on traditional values.

Boring, Phyllis Z. "Usmaíl: The Puerto Rican Joe Christmas." *CLA Jour*, 16 (1973), 324-333.
Points out parallels between *Light in August* and Pedro Juan Soto's novel; discusses Faulkner's influence on Latin American novelists.

Boswell, George W. "The Legendary Background in Faulkner's Works." *TFSB*, 36 (September 1970), 53-63.
Legends of the Old World and of American history that served as sources for Faulkner's legendary creations.

_____. "Notes on the Surnames of Faulkner's Characters." *TFSB*, 36 (September 1970), 64-66.
Faulkner chose family names from three sources--local names (folk etymologized), allegory, and sound.

_____. "Picturesque Faulknerisms." *Univ of Miss Stud in Eng*, 9 (1968), 47-56.
A tracing of Faulkner's mastery of language through such subjects as pronunciation, morphology, syntax, and proverbial expressions.

_____. "Superstition and Belief in Faulkner." *Costerus*, 6 (1972), 1-26.
Points out examples of Faulkner's use of folkloric superstitions and beliefs and concludes that Faulkner made use of folklore because it gave him "a view finder through which he could focus his lens sharply and unerringly on the human condition."

_____. "Traditional Verse and Music Influence in Faulkner." *Notes on Miss Writers*, 1 (Spring 1968), 23-30.
An attempt to trace and assess Faulkner's debt to traditional music and to relate it to the "recondite virtues" of his prose style.

Bowen, James K., and James A. Hamby. "Colonel Sartoris Snopes and Gabriel Marcel: Allegiance and Commitment." *Notes on Miss Writers*, 3 (Winter 1971), 101-107.
A discussion of Sarty's transformation from youthful allegiance to mature commitment in light of Marcel's existentialism.

Boyd, G. N. and L. A. See MISCELLANEOUS (Contemporary).

Bradford, M. E. "Addie Bundren and the Design of *As I Lay Dying*." *SouR*, 6 (Autumn 1970), 1093-1099.

A point-of-view study supporting the position that "Addie is the auditor of all the reveries in the novel."

_____. "An Aesthetic Parable: Faulkner's 'Artist at Home.'" *GaR*, 27 (Summer 1973), 175-181.

Faulkner's story which treats the conflict of "artist as artist, set over against artist as man" "has a real bearing on the theme of endurance and thus opens another way into the heart of Faulkner's vision."

_____. "All the Daughters of Eve: 'Was' and the Unity of *Go Down, Moses*." *ArlQ*, 1 (Autumn 1967), 28-37.

Faulkner shows that the consequences of trying to escape from the natural human condition or "fate" which includes women may be worse than fate itself.

_____. "Brother, Son, and Heir: The Structural Focus of Faulkner's *Absalom, Absalom!*" *SR*, 78 (Winter 1970), 76-98.

A study of Thomas Sutpen and Quentin Compson, who are paired horrors, and Faulkner's projection of what ails the postbellum South and the larger world it typifies.

_____. "Certain Ladies of Quality: Faulkner's View of Women and the Evidence of 'There Was a Queen.'" *ArlQ*, 1 (Winter 1967-68), 106-139.

Faulkner believed that women were the preservers and men the creators.

_____. "Faulkner's 'Elly': An Exposé." *Miss Quart*, 21 (Summer 1968), 179-187.

"Elly" is an exposé of the flapper and a study in the betrayal of "the old verities."

_____. "Faulkner's Last Words and 'The American Dilemma.'" *Mod Age*, 16 (Winter 1972), 77-82.

An analysis of Faulkner's "Gold Medal" speech of May 24, 1962, which attributes ideological confusion to "abuse of language."

_____. "'New Men' in Mississippi: *Absalom, Absalom!* and *Dollar Cotton*." *Notes on Miss Writers*, 2 (Fall 1969), 55-56.

Discusses parallels between Faulkner's *Absalom* and his brother's *Dollar Cotton*.

_____. "Spring Paradigm: Faulkner's Living Legacy." *Forum H*, 6 (Spring 1968), 4-7.

Discusses the implications of Faulkner's concept of "endurance."

_____. "That Other Patriarchy: Observations on Faulkner's 'A Justice.'" *Mod Age*, 18 (Summer 1974), 266-271.

"A Justice" provides "a ground for the proper interpretation of the other Indian material" and brings into perspective the excessive emphasis on the distinction between Faulkner's Indian Mississippi and his "civilized" Mississippi.

_____. "What Grandfather Said: The Social Testimony of Faulkner's *The Reivers*." *Occasional Rev*, 1 (February 1974), 5-15.

A study of the relationship of the form of this novel to its social implications.

Brogunier, Joseph. "A Housman Source in *The Sound and the Fury*." *MFS*, 18 (Summer 1972), 220-225.

"In characters and action, the scene between Caddy and Quentin at the branch (pp. 185-190) is remarkably like the situation in Poem LIII of *A Shropshire Lad*, 'The True Lover'; and even in the details of the setting, the poem and the scene in the novel are very similar."

_____. "A Source for the Commissary Entries in *Go Down, Moses*." *Tex Stud in Lit and Lang*, 14 (Fall 1972), 545-554.

Suggests a possible source in Dr. Martin Philips' diary.

Brooks, Cleanth. "Faulkner and History." *Miss Quart*, 25 (Spring 1972, Supplement), 3-14.

Faulkner's basically Christian view of man as fallible and yet capable of heroism causes him to present what may be called a providential view of history, rather than a millennial one.

_____. "Faulkner and the Muse of History." *Miss Quart*, 28 (Summer 1975), 265-279.

A study of how "the sense of history" Faulkner derived from Southern culture served him in his writings in dealing with the myth of the Old South and the American myth.

_____. "Faulkner as Poet." *So Lit Jour*, 1 (Autumn 1968), 5-19.

Early an admirer and imitator of Housman's poetry, Faulkner in his great prose works writes like the born poet that he was.

_____. "Faulkner's Criticism of Modern America." *VQR*, 51 (Spring 1975), 294-308.

Faulkner believed that "the American national idea" was inadequate because "it was not the product of history and lived experience" and thus resulted in a concentration on cash returns and a loss of community.

_____. "Faulkner's First Novel." *SouR*, 6 (Autumn 1970), 1056-1074.

A discussion of plot, theme, characterization, treatment of Negroes, elements of style, literary material, and "obsessive material" in *Soldiers' Pay*.

_____. "The Narrative Structure of *Absalom, Absalom!*" *GaR*, 29 (Summer 1975), 366-394.

The "final draft" of the novel, though it "needed better editing and proofreading" is "essentially coherent and in its parts self-consisting." Brooks argues that revisions in the manuscript have not destroyed the clarity of the book.

_____. "A Note on Faulkner's Early Attempts at the Short Story." *Stud SF*, 10 (Fall 1973), 381-388.

A look at some of the literary influences manifested by Faulkner's early sketches.

_____. "On *Absalom, Absalom!*" *Mosaic*, 7 (Fall 1973), 159-183.

A re-examination of the novel; Sutpen is an American type, not specifically a Southern plantation type.

_____. "The Poetry of Miss Rosa Canfield [sic]." *Shen*, 21 (Spring 1970), 199-206.

In the character of Miss Rosa Coldfield and in the "furious, exuberant rhetoric" of her talk to Quentin in *Absalom, Absalom!* Faulkner gave himself a "privileged means for indulging" a "hankering for the highfalutin and the grandiloquent, for a sonorous and bardic rhetoric" and "proved that it could be turned into a kind of poetry."

_____. "The Tradition of Romantic Love and *The Wild Palms*." *Miss Quart*, 25 (Summer 1972), 265-287.

Rougemont's *Love in the Western World* contends that romantic love must have obstacles in order to flourish: Faulkner's novels generally fit this pattern.

_____. "When Did Joanna Burden Die?: A Note." *So Lit Jour*, 6 (Fall 1973), 43-46.

Evidence points to August 6 as the date of Joanna's death.

_____. "William Faulkner: Vision of Good and Evil," in *Religion and Modern Literature*, ed. G. B. Tennyson and E. E. Ericson, Jr. Grand Rapids, Mich.: William B. Eerdmans, 1975, pp. 310-315.

Discusses Faulkner as a religious writer who is best understood in Christian context. Focuses on *Sanctuary* and "The Bear."

_____. See GENERAL--2nd Brooks entry.

Broughton, Panthea. "Masculinity and Menfolk in *The Hamlet*." *Miss Quart*, 22 (Summer 1969), 181-189.

The Hamlet is essentially a novel about men's lusts, intrigues, hoaxes, and other masculine concerns.

_____. "*Requiem for a Nun*: No Part in Rationality." *SouR*, 8 (Autumn 1972), 749-762.

A defense of the novel's unity of structure and meaning.

_____. *William Faulkner: The Abstract and the Actual*. Baton Rouge: Louisiana State Univ Press, 1974.

Examines the theme of evasion and distortion of existence through abstractions in seventeen novels and selected short stories.

Brown, Calvin S. "A Dim View of Faulkner's Country." *GaR*, 23 (Winter 1969), 501-511.

An essay-review of Elizabeth Kerr's *Yoknapatawpha: Faulkner's 'Little Postage Stamp of Native Soil'* as prejudiced, illogical scholarship.

_____. "Faulkner's Idiot Boy: The Source of the Simile in *Sartoris*." *AL*, 44 (November 1972), 474-476.

Argues that Harris Dickson's novel *The House of Luck* (1916) may have influenced Faulkner's attitudes toward the idiot in *Sartoris*.

_____. "Faulkner's Three-in-one Bridge in *The Reivers*." *NConL*, 1 (March 1971), 8-10.

Faulkner combined three actual bridges in the Iron Bridge in the novel.

_____. "Faulkner's Use of the Oral Tradition." *GaR*, 22 (Summer 1968), 160-169.

Discusses the conversion of oral techniques into written devices in some of Faulkner's novels.

_____. "*Sanctuary*: From Confrontation to Peaceful Void." *Mosaic*, 7 (Fall 1973), 75-95.

The novel divides itself into three parts-- the first in which differing individual characters confront each other; the second in which groups and attitudes confront each other; the third in which the confrontations fade away with no resolutions, leaving only apathy and indifference.

_____. See WEAVER, RICHARD.

Brumm, Anne-Marie. "Authoritarianism in William Faulkner's *Light in August* and Alberto Moravia's *Il Conformista*." *RLMC*, 26 (1973), 196-220.

Points out similarities in these two works, especially in Joe Christmas and Marcello Clerici.

Brumm, Ursula. "Forms and Functions of History in the Novels of William Faulkner." *Archiv*, 209 (1972), 43-56.

Ike and Quentin are the "historical consciousness" in the novels in which they appear.

_____. "Thoughts on History and the Novel." *CLS*, 6 (September 1969), 317-329.

Faulkner's work is discussed as an example of the use of history in the novel.

Brunauer, Dalma H. "Worshiping the Bear-God." *Chri and Lit*, 23 (Spring 1974), 7-35.

Discusses shamanism and bear-worship as elements in "The Bear."

Bryer, Jackson R. See MISCELLANEOUS (Contemporary-- both Bryer entries).

Brylowski, Walter. *Faulkner's Olympian Laugh: Myth in the Novels*. Detroit: Wayne State Univ Press, 1968.

An examination of Faulkner's use of myth in the novels in the light of the work of the Cambridge anthropologists.

Buchloh, Paul G. See GENERAL.

Bungert, Hans. *William Faulkner and die humoristische Tradition des amerikanischen Südens*. Heidelberg, Germany: Carl Winter, 1971.

Attempts "to evaluate William Faulkner as a humorist, to investigate the structural and thematic functions of the comic in his works, and to establish his position within the tradition of Southern literary humor."

_____. See GENERAL.

Burroughs, Franklin G., Jr. "God the Father and Motherless Children: *Light in August*." *TCL*, 19 (July 1973), 189-202.

Women "become the protagonists of the central thematic conflict of the novel."

Burton, Dolores M. "Intonation Patterns of Sermons in Seven Novels." *Lang and Style*, 3 (Summer 1970), 205-20.
    The Sound and the Fury was one of the novels from which sermons were read and recorded for the purpose of analyzing intonation patterns.

Butterworth, Keen. "A Census of Manuscripts and Typescripts of William Faulkner's Poetry." *Miss Quart*, 26 (Summer 1973), 333-359.
    Faulkner's poetry underwent more revision than he said it did.

Cabaniss, Allen. *Liturgy and Literature: Selected Essays*. University: Univ of Alabama Press, 1970.
    Examines the influence of Christian liturgical conventions in Western literature, with brief mention of *A Fable*.

_____. "To Scotch a Monumental Mystery." *Notes on Miss Writers*, 3 (Fall 1970), 79-80.
    Discusses an error in M. C. Falkner's *The Falkners of Mississippi* concerning the date of the erection of the Confederate monument in the Oxford Square.

Cady, Edwin H. See GENERAL.

Campbell, Harry M. "Faulkner's Philosophy Again: A Reply to Michel Gresset." *Miss Quart*, 23 (Winter 1969-70), 64-66.
    Campbell wishes to correct impressions given in a book review.

_____, and Ruel E. Foster. *William Faulkner: A Critical Appraisal*. New York: Cooper Square Publishers, 1970.
    A reprint of the first book-length study of Faulkner (1951).

Campbell, Jeff H. "Polarity and Paradox: Faulkner's *Light in August*." *CEA Critic*, 34 (January 1972), 26-31.
    Hightower's "paradoxical understanding of the nature of man's life" reconciles the polarities represented by the stories of Lena and Joe and thus provides a means to order the ambiguities of the novel.

Cantrell, Frank. "Faulkner's 'A Courtship.'" *Miss Quart*, 24 (Summer 1971), 289-295.
    This neglected short story shows Faulkner's use of source material and his skillful blending of the comic and the tragic.

_____. "An Unpublished Faulkner Short Story: 'Snow.'" *Miss Quart*, 26 (Summer 1973), 325-330.
    Related to "Mistral," this story of postponed revenge should have been published.

Capps, Jack L. "Three Faulkner Studies." *So Lit Jour*, 6 (Fall 1973), 117-121.
    An essay-review of *Faulkner's Revision of "Absalom, Absalom!"* and *Faulkner's Revision of "Sanctuary,"* both by Gerald Langford, and of *The Making of Go Down, Moses*, by James Early.

_____, ed. *The William Faulkner Collection at West Point and the Faulkner Concordances*. West Point, N. Y.: U. S. Military Academy, 1974.
    A pamphlet in an occasional-paper series with articles on the concordance by Robert H. Moore, on editing Faulkner by Albert Erskine, and a checklist of the Faulkner collection at the Academy.

Carey, Glenn O. "Faulkner and *Mosquitoes*: Writing Himself and His Age." *Research Stud*, 39 (December 1971), 271-283.
    Deals with the novel as it depicts the ways and attitudes of the time and relates it to some of Faulkner's non-fictional statements in the 1950's.

_____. "*Light in August* and Religious Fanaticism." *Stud in the Twentieth Century*, no. 10 (Fall 1972), 101-113.
    Light in August is Faulkner's strongest criticism of religious fanaticism and its evils of narrowness, harshness, and bigotry.

_____. "William Faulkner: Man's Fatal Vice." *ArQ*, 28 (Winter 1972), 293-300.
    War is Faulkner's symbol for the destructive and evil forces in life, for man's fatal vice. Faulkner stresses the fatal vice as reminder and encouragement that mankind's constructive forces must prevail.

_____. "William Faulkner on the Automobile as Socio-Sexual Symbol." *CEA Critic*, 36 (January 1974), 15-17.
    Quotes from several Faulkner works to support the conclusion that Faulkner considered the automobile to be "one of Western man's most important success and status symbols," a symbol "of sex and of man's spiritual deterioration."

_____. "William Faulkner: The Rise of the Snopeses." *Stud in the Twentieth Century*, no. 8 (Fall 1971), 27-64.
    A general discussion of Faulkner's treatment of the Snopeses in the trilogy and other writings.

Carter, T. H. See MISCELLANEOUS (Contemporary).

Castille, Philip. "'There Was a Queen' and Faulkner's Narcissa Sartoris." *Miss Quart*, 28 (Summer 1975), 307-315.
    Sees the story as "fundamentally affirmative" and "dominated not by Miss Jenny but by Narcissa," as an example of the practical, amoral women whom Faulkner admired for their proficiency "in getting things done" their own way.

Cecil, L. Moffitt. "A Rhetoric for Benjy." *So Lit Jour*, 3 (Fall 1970), 32-46.
    Two distinct levels of language are employed in Benjy's monologue, "Benjy's given rudimentary 'speech'" and the dialogue which "miraculously he recalls but cannot fully understand."

Chitragupta. "The World of Books: Multiple Focus on Faulkner." *Thought*, 26 (March 1974), 15-16.
    An account of a Faulkner seminar sponsored by USIS in Delhi in February 1974, in which American and Indian scholars participated.

Churchill, Allen. See MISCELLANEOUS (Contemporary).

Clark, Charles C. "'Mistral': A Study in Human Tempering." *Miss Quart*, 21 (Summer 1968), 195-204.
 This neglected short story, complex and carefully structured, contains some of Faulkner's major themes and anticipates the narrative form of *Absalom, Absalom!*

Clark, Eulalyn W. "Ironic Effects of Multiple Perspective in *As I Lay Dying*." *Notes on Miss Writers*, 5 (Spring 1972), 15-28.
 A detailing of the various discrepancies and misconceptions in the protagonists' viewpoints of each other and of how Faulkner reveals character thereby.

Clark, William B. See GENERAL.

Clark, William G. "Faulkner's *Light in August*." *Expl*, 26 (March 1968), Item 54.
 Joe Christmas' character is best understood as determined by his desire to know whether he is Negro or white.

_____. "Is King David a Racist?" *Univ Rev*, 34 (December 1967), 121-126.
 Maintains that Thomas Sutpen bars Negro blood from his line of descent for personal dynastic motives rather than through conformity to a stereotyped Southern character.

Clark, William J. "Faulkner's *Light in August*." *Expl*, 28 (November 1969), Item 19.
 An explanation of why Joe Christmas feels compelled to sleep in a stable on the night before Joanna is murdered.

Cobau, William W. "Jason Compson and the Cost of Speculation." *Miss Quart*, 22 (Summer 1969), 257-261.
 Faulkner's picture of trading in cotton is inaccurate but is used to characterize Jason.

Coindreau, Maurice. See MISCELLANEOUS (Contemporary--both Coindreau entries).

Collins, Carvel. "A Fourth Book Review by Faulkner." *Miss Quart*, 28 (Summer 1975), 339-346.
 Appearing with the text of Faulkner's review of John Cooper Powys's novel *Ducdame* is an introductory note describing John McClure's "contribution to Faulkner's literary development," the contents of the novel reviewed, the review itself and possible influence of the novel on Faulkner's later works.

_____, ed. *New Orleans Sketches*. New York: Random House, 1968.
 A new edition of the 1958 publication, with a new preface, a revised introduction, and Faulkner's 1925 essay on Sherwood Anderson.

_____, and Salvatore Quasimodo. *Faulkner: naturalismo y tragedia*. Colección Estar al día. Buenos Aires: Carlos Perez, 1968.
 Contains two brief essays on the naturalistic elements in Faulkner's work, especially *The Sound and the Fury* and *Soldiers' Pay*.

Collins, R. G. "The Game of Names: Characterization Device in *Light in August*." *Eng Rec*, 21 (October 1970), 82-87.
 Discusses the appropriateness of the characters' names.

_____. "*Light in August*: Faulkner's Stained Glass Triptych." *Mosaic*, 7 (Fall 1973), 97-157.
 The three story lines of the novel are interwoven to reveal Faulkner's view of the South in the 1930's.

Collmer, Robert G. See MISCELLANEOUS (Contemporary).

Commins, Dorothy B. "William Faulkner in Princeton." *Jour of Hist Stud*, 2 (1969), 179-185.
 An account by the widow of Saxe Commins.

Cook, Richard M. "Popeye, Flem and Sutpen: The Faulknerian Villain as Grotesque." *Stud in Am F*, 3 (Spring 1975), 3-14.
 Faulkner's treatment of his villains reveals that he knew that the "source of their strange power to fascinate and horrify" was "their profound and threatening incomprehensibility...their 'grotesqueness.'"

Cooley, Thomas W., Jr. "Faulkner Draws the Long Bow." *TCL*, 16 (October 1970), 268-277.
 The "broad pattern which marks the historical development of frontier humor is recapitulated in the sequence of Faulkner's own works."

Corrington, John W. "Escape into Myth: The Long Dying of Bayard Sartoris." *RANAM*, 4 (1971), 31-47.
 Bayard's death is an act of "desperation," born of his inability to find a compromise between the Sartoris myth and the world in which he lives, a world in which no new myth has replaced one which "may be obsolete."

Coughlan, Robert. *The Private World of William Faulkner*. New York: Cooper Square Publishers, 1972.
 A reprint of the 1954 biographical sketch.

Cowan, J. C. "Dream-Work in the Quentin Section of *The Sound and the Fury*." *Lit and Psych*, 24, no. 3 (1974), 91-98.
 Freudian definitions illumine the stylistic devices used to elaborate Quentin's character.

Cowan, Michael H., ed. *Twentieth Century Interpretations of The Sound and the Fury*. Englewood Cliffs, N. J.: Prentice-Hall, 1968.
 Reprints twelve essays on the novel, selected comments by Faulkner, and a chronology of the action and scene shifts.

Cowley, Malcolm. See MISCELLANEOUS (Contemporary--1st Cowley entry).

Crane, John K. "The Jefferson Courthouse: An *Axis Exsecrabilis Mundi*." *TCL*, 15 (April 1969), 19-23.
 The community is corrupted because slaves built the roof of the courthouse, a communal project.

Crawford, John W. See GENERAL.

Creighton, Joanne V. "The Dilemma of the Human
Heart in *The Mansion*." *Renascence*, 25
(Autumn 1972), 35-45.
　　The main characters of the novel are forced
to make a moral choice with regard to Flem's
murder. Faulkner shows that man does not live
in a fated world because his actions have "reverberations on a cosmic scale." In *The Mansion*
man can successfully fight evil.

_____. "Revision and Craftsmanship in Faulkner's
'The Fire and the Hearth.'" *Stud SF*, 11
(Spring 1974), 161-172.
　　An analysis of revisions demonstrates
"Faulkner's skillful 'composite' construction"
and shows him as a master craftsman.

_____. "Revision and Craftsmanship in the Hunting
Trilogy of *Go Down, Moses*." *Tex Stud in Lit
and Lang*, 15 (Fall 1973), 577-592.
　　A look at the four previously published
magazine stories that went into the novel.

_____. "Self-Destructive Evil in *Sanctuary*." *TCL*,
18 (October 1972), 259-270.
　　"The allegorical truth that *Sanctuary* con-
clusively demonstrates is...the inherent self-
destruction of evil," which is a central theme
in Faulkner's fiction.

_____. "Surratt to Ratliff: A Genetic Approach to
The Hamlet." *Mich Academician*, 6 (1973),
101-112.
　　Ratliff has more moral and intellectual
awareness than does Surratt.

Crunden, Robert M. See MISCELLANEOUS
(Contemporary).

Dabney, Lewis M. "Faulkner, the Red and the
Black." *Columbia Forum*, 1, n. 3.
(Spring 1972), 52-54.
　　Deals with the symbolism of the Indians in
relation to the blacks and the whites in "A
Justice," "The Bear," and "A Courtship."

_____. *The Indians of Yoknapatawpha*. Baton Rouge:
Louisiana State Univ Press, 1974.
　　A literary and historical study of the use
made of Indians in the short fiction of
Faulkner.

_____. "'Was': Faulkner's Classic Comedy of the
Frontier." *SouR*, 8 (Autumn 1972), 736-748.
　　This critical essay, which presents the
real life and artistic sources of the story
and Faulkner's comments on it, sees it in the
tradition of Southwestern humor.

Dahl, James. "A Faulkner Reminiscence: Conversations with Mrs. Maud Falkner." *Jour of Mod Lit*,
3 (April 1974), 1026-1030.
　　Personal impressions of Faulkner's mother
formed during a few conversations at her home
in Oxford.

Darnell, Donald G. "Cooper and Faulkner: Land,
Legacy and Tragic Vision." *SAB*, 34
(March 1969), 3-5.

Cooper and Faulkner share a tragic view of
America, seen notably through their recognition
of a missed second chance in the new world, in
Deerslayer and "The Bear."

D'Avanzo, Mario L. "Allusion in the Percy Grimm
Episode of *Light in August*." *Notes on Miss
Writers*, 8 (Fall 1975), 63-68.
　　Points out allusions to Shakespeare, Keats,
and E. A. Robinson and discusses how they func-
tion in the episode.

Davenport, F. Garvin. See MISCELLANEOUS
(Contemporary).

Davis, Scottie. "Faulkner's Nancy: Racial Implications in 'That Evening Sun.'" *Notes on Miss
Writers*, 5 (Spring 1972), 30-32.
　　Nancy's failure is a result of her own weak,
passive, masochistic nature, and is not the
fault of the Compsons.

Davis, William V. "Another Flower for Faulkner's
Bouquet: Theme and Structure in 'A Rose for
Emily.'" *Notes on Miss Writers*, 7 (Fall 1974),
34-38.
　　Analyzes the structure of the story in terms
of time.

_____. "Quentin's Death Ritual: Further Christian
Allusions in *The Sound and the Fury*." *Notes on
Miss Writers*, 6 (Spring 1973), 27-32.
　　Some additional notes to Carvel Collins'
treatment.

_____. "*The Sound and the Fury*: A Note on Benjy's
Name." *Stud in the Novel*, 4 (Spring 1972),
60-61.
　　More on the Biblical reference.

Degenfelder, E. Pauline. "The Film Adaptation of
Faulkner's *Intruder in the Dust*." *Lit/Film
Quart*, 1 (April 1973), 138-148.
　　Praises the film version, pointing out that
its success may be due to the fact that the
novel is not one of Faulkner's best works.

_____. "Yoknapatawphan Baroque: A Stylistic Anal-
ysis of *As I Lay Dying*." *Style*, 7 (Spring 1973),
121-156.
　　In this novel, "baroque style" is used "to
dramatize the individual's alienation from the
community"; colloquial style depicts "the solidarity of the community folk." Detailed analysis of the syntax and diction of the novel.

Delay, Florence, and Jacqueline de Labriolle.
"Márquez est-il le Faulkner colombien?" *Rev de
Litt Comparée*, 47 (January-March 1973), 88-123.
　　Deals with Faulknerian echoes in the works of
Márquez; Márquez, however, wants to speak in a
Latin American voice.

Detweiler, Robert. See MISCELLANEOUS (Contemporary).

DeVillier, Mary Anne G. "Faulkner's Young Man: As
Reflected in the Character of Charles Mallison."
Laurel Rev, 9, no. 2 (1969), 42-49.
　　Compares Mallison with other young men in
Faulkner's works.

Devlin, Albert J. "Faulknerian Chronology: Puzzles and Games." *Notes on Miss Writers*, 5 (Winter 1973), 98-101.
  A note on inconsistency between Section IV of "The Bear" and the rest of *Go Down, Moses*.

_____. "'How Much It Takes to Compound a Man': A Neglected Scene in *Go Down, Moses*." *Midwest Quart*, 14 (July 1973), 408-421.
  Deals with the importance, as far as the direction Ike's attitudes will take, of the scene in which Sophonsiba routs Hubert's mulatto mistress.

_____. "*The Reivers*: Readings in Social Psychology." *Miss Quart*, 25 (Summer 1972), 327-337.
  Social change is an obvious feature in this novel of initiation in which interrelationships of family and society enhance the meaning.

_____. "*Sartoris*: Rereading the MacCallum Episode." *TCL*, 17 (April 1971), 83-90.
  Maintains that "the MacCallums in no sense represent an unequivocal social and familial ideal....in no sense represent normality."

Dickerson, Mary Jane. "'The Magician's Wand': Faulkner's Compson Appendix." *Miss Quart*, 28 (Summer 1975), 317-337.
  Sees the Compson Appendix as "a new piece of writing which marks the culmination of a major phase in Faulkner's development as an artist and anticipates certain salient characteristics in the fiction of the final period of his career."

Dillon, Richard T. "Some Sources of Faulkner's Version of the First Air War." *AL*, 44 (January 1973), 629-637.
  Finds in writers Elliott White Springs and James Warner Bellah much of the material Faulkner used in writing about combat aviation.

Ditsky, John M. "'Dark, Darker than Fire': Thematic Parallels in Lawrence and Faulkner." *SHR*, 8 (Fall 1974), 497-505.
  Parallel themes in Faulkner and Lawrence "have found expression in remarkably similar language."

_____. "Faulkner's Carousel: Point of View in *As I Lay Dying*." *Laurel Rev*, 10, no. 1 (1970), 74-85.
  Addie is the "still point" in the circular motion of the multiple points of view in the novel.

_____. "From Oxford to Salinas: Comparing Faulkner and Steinbeck." *Steinbeck Quart*, 2 (Fall 1969), 51-55.
  In spite of their dissimilarities, Faulkner and Steinbeck are alike in some ways, especially in their attitudes toward nature.

_____. "Uprooted Trees: Dynasty and the Land in Faulkner's Novels." *Tenn Stud in Lit*, 17 (1972), 151-158.
  "A shift of emphasis from the propertied to the unpropertied occurs, and dynasty later becomes a spiritual heritage that is a metaphor for traditional values."

Doody, Terrence. "Shreve McCannon and the Confessions of *Absalom, Absalom!*" *Stud in the Novel*, 6 (Winter 1974), 454-469.
  Characters in the novel adopt the confessional style of either St. Augustine or Rousseau. By listening to Quentin, Shreve enables the reader to become involved as confessor.

Dove, George N. "Shadow and Paradox: Imagery in *The Sound and the Fury*," in *Essays in Memory of Christine Burleson*, ed. Thomas G. Burton. Johnson City: East Tenn State Univ, 1969.
  The consistency and complexity of the imagery and the development of the theme of degeneration and decay provide a remarkable unity in the novel.

Drake, Robert. See MISCELLANEOUS (Contemporary--1st Drake entry).

Duncan, Alastair B. "Claude Simon and William Faulkner." *Forum for Mod Lang Stud* (St. Andrews, Scotland), 9 (1973), 235-252.
  On Faulkner's influence on Simon.

Dunlap, Mary. "Sex and the Artist in *Mosquitoes*." *Miss Quart*, 22 (Summer 1969), 190-206.
  The intertwined themes of sex and art in the sterile world of the novel reveal the young Faulkner's indecision about their effects on each other.

_____. "William Faulkner's 'Knight's Gambit' and Gavin Stevens." *Miss Quart*, 23 (Summer 1970), 223-239.
  "Knight's Gambit" was written to give form and integration to five previously published short stories.

Durant, Will and Ariel. *Interpretations of Life: A Survey of Contemporary Literature*. New York: Simon and Schuster, 1970.
  A self-confessed "amateur" surveys the superficial aspects of Faulkner's work and its meaning.

Durham, Frank. See MISCELLANEOUS (Contemporary--3rd Durham entry).

Dussinger, Gloria. "Faulkner's Isaac McCaslin as Romantic Hero *Manqué*." *SAQ*, 68 (Summer 1969), 377-385.
  Faulkner characterizes Isaac McCaslin as modern man with his inescapable double consciousness.

Early, James. *The Making of Go Down, Moses*. Dallas: Southern Methodist Univ Press, 1972.
  A study of the genesis of *Go Down, Moses* from the hunting stories of 1934-35 to the publication of the book in 1942.

Edward, Sister Ann. See GENERAL.

Edwards, C. Hines, Jr. "A Hawthorne Echo in Faulkner's Nobel Prize Acceptance Speech." *NConL*, 1 (March 1971), 4-5.
  Certain statements in the speech strongly echo Hawthorne's comment on truth in literature in the Preface to *The House of Seven Gables*.

_____. "Three Literary Parallels to Faulkner's 'A Rose for Emily.'" *Notes on Miss Writers*, 7 (Spring 1974), 21-25.
Points to possible parallels in Dickens' *Great Expectations*, Browning's "Porphyria's Lover," and Poe's "To Helen."

Edwards, Duane. "Flem Snopes and Thomas Sutpen: Two Versions of Respectability." *Dal Rev*, 51 (Winter 1971-72), 559-570.
An analysis of *The Hamlet*, *Absalom, Absalom!*, *The Town*, and *The Mansion* reveals many parallels between the tragic figure of Thomas Sutpen and the comic figure of Flem Snopes.

Eigner, Edwin M. "Faulkner's Isaac and the American Ishmael." *Jahrbuch für Amerikastudien*, 14 (1969), 107-115.
Deals with characters in Faulkner who cannot accept responsibility; only in *The Reivers* are there those who are willing to do so.

Emerson, O. B. "Bill's Friend Phil." *JMiH*, 32 (May 1970), 135-145.
An examination of the assistance Faulkner received from his friend Phil Stone.

_____. "Faulkner and His Bibliographers." *BB*, 30 (April-June 1973), 90-92.
A brief review of the current state of Faulkner bibliographical study and a listing of the "most important Faulkner bibliographies."

_____. "Faulkner and His Friend: An Interview with Emily W. Stone." *Comment*, 10 (Spring 1971), 31-37.
A discussion of the relationship between Faulkner and Phil Stone.

_____. "Faulkner, the Mule, and the South." *Delta Rev*, 6 (November-December 1969), 108-110.
Faulkner's frequent use of the mule in his works suggests that he associates the mule with the Old South and its way of life which is passing away just as the mule is disappearing from the Southern scene.

_____. "William Faulkner's Nemesis--Major Frederick Sullens." *JMiH*, 36 (May 1974), 161-164.
A survey of Sullens' derogatory editorial publications on Faulkner in the *Jackson Daily News*.

Epstein, Seymour. See MISCELLANEOUS (Contemporary).

Eschliman, Herbert R. "Francis Christensen in Yoknapatawpha County." *Univ Rev*, 37 (March 1971), 232-239.
A statistical analysis of Faulkner's use of the cumulative sentence.

Esslinger, Pat M., et al. "No Spinach in *Sanctuary*." *MFS*, 18 (Winter 1972-73), 555-558.
Detailed examination of Faulkner's use of comic strip humor in the novel.

Everett, Walter K. *Faulkner's Art and Characters*. Woodbury, N. Y.: Barron's Educational Series, 1969.
Alphabetically arranged plot summaries of novels and of most of the short stories, a dictionary of 1,234 characters, and a selected bibliography.

Fadiman, Regina. *Faulkner's 'Light in August': Description and Interpretation of the Revisions*. Charlottesville: Univ Press of Virginia, 1975.
Title is descriptive.

Fairman, Marion A. See MISCELLANEOUS (Contemporary).

Farnham, James F. "A Note on One Aspect of Faulkner's Style." *Lang and Style*, 2 (Spring 1969), 190-192.
Suggests that Faulkner uses the correlatives "not only...but also" to indicate confusion or uncertainty.

Faulkner, Howard. "The Stricken World of 'Dry September.'" *Stud SF*, 10 (Winter 1973), 47-50.
In addition to the accuracy of the realism, "it is...the symbolic texture of the story that lifts it above cliché and furnishes its worth."

Faulkner, Jim. "Auntee Owned Two." *SouR*, 8 (Autumn 1972), 836-844.
A family memoir by a nephew of William Faulkner.

_____. "The Picture of John and Brother Will." *Delta Rev*, 7 (Fall 1970), 12-14.
John's son tells of the time he borrowed his famous uncle's red garden tractor to cut the grass at his own house and reveals how the only picture of the two most famous Faulkners came to be taken.

Faulkner, William. "And Now What's To Do," ed. James B. Meriwether. *Miss Quart*, 26 (Summer 1973), 399-402.
An undated Faulkner manuscript, but the tone is much like the later semi-fiction "Mississippi."

_____. "An Introduction for *The Sound and the Fury*," ed. James B. Meriwether. *SouR*, 8 (Autumn 1972), 705-710.
Faulkner presents his feelings about his favorite novel and comments on others of his works. The editor, James B. Meriwether, gives a history of the newly discovered manuscript, an assessment, and textual comments.

_____. "An Introduction to *The Sound and the Fury*." *Miss Quart*, 26 (Summer 1973), 410-415.
Written in 1933, this introduction by Faulkner is longer than the one printed with the book.

_____. "Mac Grider's Son," ed. James B. Meriwether. *Miss Quart*, 28 (Summer 1975), 347-351.
Faulkner's account (written for the Memphis *Commercial Appeal*) of his meeting with the younger son of John McGavock Grider, the erroneously assumed author of *War Birds: Diary of an Unknown Aviator*.

_____. *Marionettes*. Oxford, Miss.: Yoknapatawpha Press, 1975.
A limited facsimile edition of Faulkner's early play, issued in 500 copies, with Ben Wasson's essay "Memories of Marionettes."

_____. *The Marionettes: A Play in One Act*. Charlottesville: Bibliographical Society of the Univ of Virginia, 1975.
A limited facsimile edition of Faulkner's early play, issued in 126 copies, in memory of Linton Massey.

_____. "A Note on *A Fable*." *Miss Quart*, 26 (Summer 1973), 416-417.
Probably a note by Faulkner on advance publicity about the novel, one not used.

_____. "Nympholepsy," ed. James B. Meriwether. *Miss Quart*, 26 (Summer 1973), 403-409.
Faulkner's expansion of "The Hill," published in *The Mississippian*, undergraduate newspaper at the University of Mississippi.

Feibleman, James K. See MISCELLANEOUS (Contemporary).

Feild, Claire. "Defense Mechanisms Employed by the Faulkner White Racist and Their Effect on the Faulkner Negro." *RTE*, 4 (Spring 1970), 20-36.
Discusses these mechanisms and effects as revealed in six of Faulkner's novels.

Ferris, William R., Jr. "William Faulkner and Phil Stone: An Interview with Emily Stone." *SAQ*, 68 (Autumn 1969), 536-542.
An interview with Stone's widow, who discusses the influence of her husband and of authors like Joyce upon the early Faulkner.

Fetz, Howard W. "Of Time and the Novel." *XUS*, 8 (July 1969), 1-17.
The Sound and the Fury is one of the novels included in this discussion of the effects of the stream-of-consciousness technique.

Ficken, Carl. "The Christ Story in *A Fable*." *Miss Quart*, 23 (Summer 1970), 251-264.
An analysis of how Faulkner made obvious his use of Holy Week as a major structural device, though in his own individual manner, and why he uses the theme to show that man will prevail.

_____. "The Opening Scene in *Light in August*." *Proof*, 2 (1972), 175-184.
An early draft of the opening, in a salesman's dummy, at the University of Virginia, contains significant variations from other versions of the opening.

Fischel, Anne. "Student Views of Faulkner II." *Mod Occasions*, 1 (Winter 1971), 270-274.
Of all Faulkner's characters, only Lena White and Dilsey escape the restrictions of the past and are thus able to endure.

Flanagan, John T. "Folklore in Faulkner's Fiction." *Papers in Lang and Lit*, 5 (Summer 1969-- Supplement), 119-144.
Points out Faulkner's use of folklore in various works and discusses the significance of this use.

Flora, Joseph M. See CABELL, JAMES BRANCH (Postbellum--1st Flora entry).

Foster, Ruel E. "A Review of *William Faulkner: The Journey to Self-Discovery*, by H. Edward Richardson." *SAQ*, 69 (Summer 1970), 427-429.
A study of his early writings reveals Faulkner's attitude toward his Southern past and his struggle toward his true identity.

Franklin, Malcolm A. "A Christmas in Columbus." *Miss Quart*, 27 (Summer 1974), 319-322.
Franklin reminisces about a Christmas trip to Columbus, Mississippi, with his step-father, William Faulkner, and the rest of the family.

Franklin, Phyllis. "The Influence of Joseph Hergesheimer upon *Mosquitoes*." *Miss Quart*, 22 (Summer 1969), 207-213.
Technique, characterization, and satire may have been influenced by Hergesheimer's *The Bright Shawl* and *Linda Condon*.

_____. "Sarty Snopes and 'Barn Burning.'" *Miss Quart*, 21 (Summer 1968), 189-193.
A reading which makes Sarty Snopes, not Abner, the center of the story.

French, Warren. See MISCELLANEOUS (Contemporary-- 1st, 3rd, and 4th French entries).

Fridy, Will. "'Ichthus': An Exercise in Synthetic Suggestion." *SAB*, 39 (May 1974), 95-101.
Analysis of the fish symbol in the Quentin section of *The Sound and the Fury*.

Frohock, W. M. "Faulkner in France: The Final Stage." *Mosaic* (Univ of Manitoba), 4 (Spring 1971), 125-134.
Faulkner's influence has become so thoroughly absorbed in French fiction that "relationship" and "influence" are no longer meaningful words in that context.

Funk, Robert W. "Satire and Existentialism in Faulkner's 'Red Leaves.'" *Miss Quart*, 25 (Summer 1972), 339-348.
By satirizing the Indians' inability to adapt the white man's institution of slavery, Faulkner moves from satire to a universal comment on human mortality and the consequences of slavery.

Garmon, G. M. "Mirror Imagery in *The Sound and the Fury*." *Notes on Miss Writers*, 2 (Spring 1969), 13-24.
The mirror imagery in the Benjy section reinforces the section's dreamlike quality and the Quentin section "reinforces the memories which flash with almost irrational sequence through Quentin's frantic, suicide-bent mind."

Garrison, Joseph M., Jr. "Faulkner's 'The Brooch': A Story for Teaching." *CE*, 36 (September 1974), 51-57.
Offers suggestions for teaching "The Brooch" in an introductory course in literature.

Garzilli, Enrico. *Circles Without Center: Paths to Discovery and Creation of Self in Modern Literature*. Cambridge: Harvard Univ Press, 1972.
A philosophical, psychological study of modern literature with chapters on Faulkner's *Absalom, Absalom!* and *As I Lay Dying*.

Gates, Allen. "The Old Frenchman Place: Symbol of a Lost Civilization." *I Eng Yearbk*, no. 13 (Fall 1968), 44-50.
    Digging for treasure that is only an illusion in *The Hamlet* symbolizes the idea that it is "useless to try to dig among the ruins of the old in an effort to extract something of value, for nothing of value remains in the rubble of a former civilization."

Geduld, Harry M. See MISCELLANEOUS (Contemporary).

Geffen, Arthur. "Profane Time, Sacred Time, and Confederate Time in *The Sound and the Fury*." *Stud in Am F*, 2 (Autumn 1974), 175-197.
    On the importance of time in the novel.

Gelfant, Blanche H. "Faulkner and Keats: The Ideality of Art in 'The Bear.'" *So Lit Jour*, 2 (Fall 1969), 43-65.
    "The Bear," like Keats's "Ode on a Grecian Urn," has as its theme the conflict "between the reality of life and the ideality of art."

Gidley, Mark. "Elements of the Detective Story in William Faulkner's Fiction." *Jour of Pop Culture*, 7 (Summer 1973), 97-123.
    A detailed examination of Faulkner's reading of detective fiction, his interest in detective elements in works of authors such as Dostoyevsky and Balzac, and his use of detective story techniques in his own stories and novels.

Gidley, Mick. "Another Psychologist, a Physiologist and William Faulkner." *Ariel*, 2, no. 4 (1971), 78-86.
    Suggests the possibility of the influence of Havelock Ellis and Louis Berman on Faulkner.

_____. "One Continuous Force: Notes on Faulkner's Extra-Literary Reading." *Miss Quart*, 23 (Summer 1970), 299-314.
    To show that Faulkner was no "untutored genius," a survey of his reading in aesthetics, philosophy, criticism, and art history is made.

_____. "Some Notes on Faulkner's Reading." *Jour Am Stud*, 4 (July 1970), 91-102.
    Faulkner should be viewed "as a conscious intellect, transmitting the manifold sources of his knowledge into what he advocated: 'eternal verities.'"

Giermanski, James R. "William Faulkner's Use of the Confessional." *Renascence*, 21 (Spring 1969), 119-123, 166.
    The thesis is that *Requiem for a Nun* explores the method of "expiation through the suffering and penance of sin-telling."

Gindin, James. See MISCELLANEOUS (Contemporary).

Ginsberg, Elaine. See MISCELLANEOUS (Contemporary).

Giordano, Frank R., Jr. "*Absalom, Absalom!* as a Portrait of the Artist," in *From Irving to Steinbeck*, ed. Motley Deakin and Peter Lisca. Gainesville: Univ of Florida Press, 1972.
    Quentin Compson is Faulkner's portrait of a would-be artist as a confused young man, and the novel belongs in the artist-as-hero tradition.

Glicksberg, Charles I. See MISCELLANEOUS (Contemporary).

Gold, Joseph. "Dickens and Faulkner: The Uses of Influence." *Dal Rev*, 49 (Spring 1969), 69-79.
    Faulkner admired Dickens and was significantly influenced by him. General and specific parallels are cited.

_____. "The Faulkner Game; or, Find the Author." *So Lit Jour*, 1 (Spring 1969), 91-97.
    An essay-review of *Faulkner: Myth and Motion*, by Richard P. Adams, that finds it "a tantalizing and irritating collection of critical quotations, source references, critical insights and cursory interpretation."

_____. "'Sin, Salvation and Bananas': *As I Lay Dying*." *Mosaic*, 7 (Fall 1973), 55-73.
    The novel's theme concerns faith versus works, saying versus doing, life versus death; the "anti-life," represented by Addie, is overcome and life is celebrated.

Goldman, Arnold. "Faulkner and the Revision of Yoknapatawpha History," in *The American Novel and the Nineteen Twenties*, ed. Malcolm Bradbury and David Palmer. New York: Crane, Russak, 1971.
    Questions the assumption that Faulkner created a unified, coherent history in his Yoknapatawpha novels.

_____, ed. *Twentieth Century Interpretations of Absalom, Absalom!* Englewood Cliffs, N. J.: Prentice-Hall, 1971.
    Reprints four full essays, one excerpt, an index, and an outline of the novel with an original introduction and selected bibliography by the editor.

Golub, L. S. "Syntactic and Lexical Problems in Reading Faulkner." *EJ*, 59 (April 1970), 490-496.
    An understanding of the linguistic structures contributes to the meaning of a work as complex as Faulkner's *Light in August*.

Gotten, H. B. "Oxford." *Delta Rev*, 5 (December 1968), 14-16, 80-81.
    Around the town and in school Faulkner tended to be a "loner."

Graham, Don, and Barbara Shaw. "Faulkner's Small Debt to Dos Passos: A Source for the Percy Grimm Episode." *Miss Quart*, 27 (Summer 1974), 327-331.
    Finds the source of the episode in *Light in August* in the "Paul Bunyan" section of Dos Passos' *1919*, which had appeared separately in late 1931.

Grant, William E. "Benjy's Branch: Symbolic Method in Part I of *The Sound and the Fury*." *Tex Stud in Lit and Lang*, 13 (Winter 1972), 705-710.
    Stresses the importance of Christian baptismal symbolism in Benjy's section, and its connection to symbolism throughout the novel.

IV. Contemporary (1920-1975)

Gregory, Eileen. "Faulkner's Typescripts of *The Town*." *Miss Quart*, 26 (Summer 1973), 361-386.
Various versions of the manuscripts, including some letters on the integration problem.

Greiner, D. J. "Universal Snopesism: The Significance of 'Spotted Horses.'" *EJ*, 57 (November 1968), 1133-1137.
The desire for acquisition is a general human trait which needs only a Snopes to expose it.

Gresset, Michel. "Faulkner's 'The Hill.'" *So Lit Jour*, 6 (Spring 1974), 3-18.
One of Faulkner's first publications, this sketch was the germ of many of his stories.

_____. "Weekend, Lost and Revisited." *Miss Quart*, 21 (Summer 1968), 173-178.
Offers parallels between an uncollected Faulkner short story, "Mr. Acarius" (or "Weekend Revisited"), and Charles R. Jackson's popular novel, *The Lost Weekend*.

Gribbin, Daniel V. "Stories and Articles by William Faulkner in the Rare Book Collection of the University of North Carolina Library." *Bookman*, September 1972, pp. 23-27.
Title is descriptive.

Griffith, Benjamin W. "Faulkner's Archaic Titles and the *Second Shepherds' Play*." *Notes on Miss Writers*, 4 (Fall 1971), 62-63.
Forms of the archaic expressions "light in August" and "reivers" are found in the *Second Shepherds' Play*.

Groden, Michael. "Criticism in New Composition: *Ulysses* and *The Sound and the Fury*." *TCL*, 21 (October 1975), 265-277.
"...in *The Sound and the Fury*, especially in Quentin's section, Joyce is a major influence, and Faulkner's use of Joycean techniques contributes significantly to the novel's success."

Gross, Beverly. "Form and Fulfillment in *The Sound and the Fury*." *MLQ*, 19 (December 1968), 439-449.
Argues that the conclusion of the novel "is a final reflection of the disorder, the outrage, the meaninglessness to which the Compsons are reduced." Thus the conclusion "provides the novel's most intense depiction of sound and fury."

Gross, Theodore L. See GENERAL--1st Gross entry.

Grossman, Joel M. "The Source of Faulkner's 'Less Oft Is Peace.'" *AL*, 47 (November 1975), 436-438.
The source is Shelley's "To Jane."

Günter, Bernd. "William Faulkner's 'Dry September.'" *Neueren Sprachen*, 72 (November 1973), 607-616.
Discusses the ways Faulkner achieves unity in the "complex structure" of this story.

Gunter, Richard. "An Essay-Review." *Miss Quart*, 22 (Summer 1969), 264-279.
A detailed commentary on Irene Kaluza's *The Functioning of Sentence Structure in the Stream-of-consciousness Technique of William Faulkner's "The Sound and the Fury": A Study in Linguistic Stylistics* (1967).

Hagopian, John V. "*Absalom, Absalom!* and the Negro Question." *MFS*, 19 (Summer 1973), 207-211.
Concludes that "the novel as a whole clearly repudiates Southern racism."

_____. "The Biblical Background of Faulkner's *Absalom, Absalom!*" *CEA Critic*, 36 (January 1974), 22-24.
Recounts the similarity of Faulkner's novel to the narrative in II Samuel and shows that the main difference is David's love for his son as contrasted to Thomas Sutpen's lack of feeling.

Haight, A. L. See GENERAL.

Halsell, Willie D. See GENERAL.

Hamilton, Gary D. "The Past in the Present: A Reading of *Go Down, Moses*." *SHR*, 5 (Spring 1971), 171-181.
His handling of the time dimension gives unity to Faulkner's *Go Down, Moses*; "very much concerned with showing how that which was determines that which is," Faulkner continually juxtaposes past and present throughout the book.

Hancock, Maxine. "Fire: Symbolic Motif in Faulkner." *Eng Quart*, 3 (Fall 1970), 19-23.
Among other things, fire in Faulkner's works symbolizes sexuality and fertility.

Handy, William J. *Modern Fiction: A Formalist Approach*. Carbondale: Southern Illinois Univ Press, 1971.
Includes analysis of *As I Lay Dying*.

Harold, Brent. "The Value and Limitation of Faulkner's Fictional Method." *AL*, 47 (May 1975), 212-229.
Concludes that Faulkner, in spite of his historical orientation, is stylistically akin to Joyce, Henry Miller, Nabokov, and Hawkes.

Harris, Wendell V. "Of Time and the Novel." *BuR*, 16 (March 1968), 114-129.
Analyzes the rhetorical importance of the treatment of time in *David Copperfield*, *Nostromo*, and *The Sound and the Fury*, arguing of the last that Faulkner "in using the interior monologue to portray imperfect modes of apprehending time...made maximum use of that technique's tendency to emphasize the irrationality and imperfection of man's analytical thought."

Harter, Carol C. "Recent Faulkner Scholarship." *Jour of Mod Lit*, 4 (September 1974), 139-145.
An essay-review of 1972 books on Faulkner which concludes that "perhaps the opportunities for truly imaginative and generally illuminating studies of Faulkner's art are exhausted"; the reviewer finds only Sally Page's work on Faulkner's women really commendable.

_____. "The Winter of Isaac McCaslin: Revisions and Irony in Faulkner's 'Delta Autumn.'" *Jour of Mod Lit*, 1, no. 2 (1970/71), 209-225.

"Delta Autumn" is discussed as an example of how Faulkner revised the stories that became parts of *Go Down, Moses* so that in both theme and symbol they would make a unified novel.

Hartman, Geoffrey. "The Aesthetics of Complicity." *GaR*, 28 (Fall 1974), 384-403.
Faulkner is mentioned; *Absalom, Absalom!* is "the very granddaddy...of the American writer's concern with the technique of story-telling."

Harzic, Jean. *Faulkner: présence littéraire.* Paris, 1973.
Considers Faulkner as man and as writer.

Hauck, Richard B. "The Comic Christ and the Modern Reader." *CE*, 31 (February 1970), 498-506.
A general essay which includes analysis of *As I Lay Dying* and discussion of Joe Christmas; the article also concerns Barth's *Giles Goat-Boy*.

_____. See GENERAL.

Haury, Beth B. "The Influence of Robinson Jeffers' 'Tamar' on *Absalom, Absalom!*" *Miss Quart*, 25 (Summer 1972), 356-358.
The Jeffers poem appears to have influenced Faulkner more than the Biblical story.

Hayashi, Tetsumaro. See MISCELLANEOUS (Contemporary).

Hayhoe, George F. "William Faulkner's *Flags in the Dust.*" *Miss Quart*, 28 (Summer 1975), 370-386.
A review-essay which attempts "to gauge the shortcomings of the 1973 edition of *Flags*" by examining the history of the novel's composition, text, and publication.

Hays, Peter L. "More Light on *Light in August.*" *Papers on Lang and Lit*, 11 (Fall 1975), 417-419.
On transfiguration as an element in the novel.

_____. See MISCELLANEOUS (Contemporary).

Heimer, Jackson W. "Faulkner's Misogynous Novel: *Light in August.*" *BSUF*, 14 (1973), 11-15.
Argues that the novel shows that Faulkner himself was a misogynist.

Heller, Terry. "The Telltale Hair: A Critical Study of William Faulkner's 'A Rose for Emily.'" *ArQ*, 28 (Winter 1972), 301-318.
A quasi-syntactical approach to a character analysis of Emily.

Hemenway, Robert. "Enigmas of Being in *As I Lay Dying.*" *MFS*, 14 (Summer 1970), 133-146.
A detailed explication of Darl Bundren's reverie.

Henderson, Harry B., III. See GENERAL.

Hendin, Josephine. See O'CONNOR, FLANNERY (Contemporary--2nd Hendin entry).

Hepburn, Kenneth. "Faulkner's *Mosquitoes*: A Turning Point." *TCL*, 17 (January 1971), 19-28.
An attempt to demonstrate "that the pivotal point of Faulkner's career is not the somewhat acclaimed *Sartoris*, but the much disparaged *Mosquitoes*."

Hermann, John. "Faulkner's Heart's Darling in 'That Evening Sun.'" *Stud SF*, 7 (Spring 1970), 320-323.
"That Evening Sun" is primarily a story about Caddy.

Hess, Judith W. "Traditional Themes in Faulkner's 'The Bear.'" *TFSB*, 40 (June 1974), 57-64.
Discusses Faulkner's use of folklore in conjunction with "the themes of corruption and despair." The themes of folklore are "unambiguous," those of the "new industrial order" complex.

Hlavsa, Virginia V. "The Vision of the Advocate in *Absalom, Absalom!*" *Novel*, 8 (Fall 1974), 51-70.
Upon close analysis the nine chapters of the novel can be viewed as a nine-part trial.

Hoadley, Frank M. "The Theme of Atonement in the Novels of William Faulkner." *Northwest Rev*, 10 (Summer 1970), 30-43.
In earlier Faulkner works some characters suffer for no purpose, as opposed to characters in works beginning with *The Unvanquished* who do suffer for a purpose.

Hodgson, John A. "'Logical Sequence and Continuity': Some Observations on Typographical and Structural Consistency of *Absalom, Absalom!*" *AL*, 43 (March 1971), 97-107.
Argues that typography and "variform testimony" in the novel are more significant, and temporal sequence of narrative more complex, than has been formerly recognized.

Hoffman, Daniel. "William Faulkner: *The Bear*," in *Landmarks of American Writing*, ed. Hennig Cohen. New York: Basic Books, 1969, pp. 341-352.
Traces the themes of the Hunt, the Quest, and the Initiation in Faulkner's complex story; in his renunciation Isaac emerges as a spiritual but not a culture hero: "he can but show his heedless fellowman how difficult it is to live by the dictates of the soul."

Hoffman, Frederick J. "William Faulkner," in *American Winners of the Nobel Literary Prize*, ed. Warren G. French and Walter E. Kidd. Norman: Univ of Oklahoma Press, 1968, pp. 138-157.
A summary analysis of the fiction before and after the award of the Nobel Prize in 1950 and the influence it may have had on Faulkner's work.

Holland, Norman. "Fantasy and Defense in Faulkner's 'A Rose for Emily.'" *Hartford Stud in Lit*, 4 (1972), 1-31.
The reader of this story is able to participate "in an interplay of fantasy and defense reaching from the most infantile layers of the mind to the most adult."

Holman, C. Hugh. "*Absalom, Absalom!*: The Historian as Detective." *SR*, 79 (Autumn 1971), 542-553.
     The structure of the novel resembles that of the detective story, with the pieces being picked up from the past.

_____. See GENERAL.

Holmes, Edward M. "Requiem for a Scarlet Nun." *Costerus*, 5 (1972), 35-49.
     Points out similarities in concepts in *The Scarlet Letter* and *Requiem for a Nun*.

Houghton, Donald E. "Whores and Horses in Faulkner's 'Spotted Horses.'" *Midwest Quart*, 11 (Summer 1970), 361-369.
     The story represents a conflict between the men and their wives; by going after the horses, the men are rejecting "sexless wives."

Howard, A. B. "Huck Finn in the House of Usher: The Comic and Grotesque World of *The Hamlet*." *Southern Rev* (Adelaide), 5 (June 1972), 125-146.
     The unity of *The Hamlet* is discovered in the interplay of frontier humor and grotesque terror.

Howe, Irving. *William Faulkner: A Critical Study*. 3rd ed. Chicago: Univ of Chicago Press, 1975.
     The edition corrects earlier factual errors and has an additional chapter on *The Reivers*.

Howell, Elmo. "Faulkner and Scott and the Legacy of the Lost Cause." *GaR*, 26 (Fall 1972), 314-325.
     Compares Scott's interest in the Scottish past to Faulkner's interest in the Southern American past. Howell examines briefly Scott's *Waverley*, *Rob Roy*, and *Redgauntlet* and gives particular attention to Faulkner's *The Unvanquished*.

_____. "Faulkner's Country Church: A Note on 'Shingles for the Lord.'" *Miss Quart*, 21 (Summer 1968), 205-210.
     Since Faulkner distrusted formal religion, he was unable to portray country people in religious activities as skillfully as he showed them otherwise.

_____. "Faulkner's Elegy: An Approach to 'The Bear.'" *ArlQ*, 2 (Winter 1969-70), 122-132.
     The finest achievement in characterization in "The Bear" is not Sam Fathers or Ike McCaslin, but Boon Hogganbeck. In the story Faulkner is looking back to a more gracious time when men lived in harmony with nature and with one another.

_____. "Faulkner's Enveloping Sense of History: A Note on 'Tomorrow.'" *NConL*, 3 (March 1973), 5-6.
     Old Fentry is representative of Faulkner's conception of the South.

_____. "Mink Snopes and Faulkner's Moral Conclusions." *SAQ*, 67 (Winter 1968), 13-22.
     His characterization of Mink Snopes in *The Mansion* indicates that the South's "peculiar history" became less important to Faulkner as

he became a "contemporary in a nihilistic world."

_____. "A Name for Faulkner's City." *Names*, 16 (December 1968), 415-421.
     Discusses possible sources for Faulkner's naming of Jefferson.

_____. "William Faulkner, the Substance of Faith." *BYUS*, 9 (Summer 1969), 453-462.
     Discusses Faulkner's works as "one of the strongest affirmations of faith" in American literature.

_____. "William Faulkner's Chickasaw Legacy: A Note on 'Red Leaves.'" *ArQ*, 26 (Winter 1970), 293-303.
     Faulkner's aim in "Red Leaves" was to create a wilderness horror (Conrad's *Heart of Darkness*-- "The horror! The horror!") unsoftened by any recognized moral system yet to create a kind of joy in the sense that the *spectacle* of life is joyous.

_____. "William Faulkner's General Forrest and the Uses of History." *Tenn Hist Quart*, 29 (Fall 1970), 287-294.
     Deals with Faulkner's depiction of General Nathan Bedford Forrest in "My Grandmother Millard and General Bedford Forrest and the Battle of Harrykin Creek."

_____. "William Faulkner's Graveyard." *Notes on Miss Writers*, 4 (Winter 1972), 115-118.
     Presents some parallels between epitaphs on markers in St. Peter's Cemetery, Oxford, and those in Faulkner's fiction.

_____. "William Faulkner's Mule: A Symbol of the Post-War South." *Ky Folklore Record*, 15 (October-December 1969), 81-86.
     For Faulkner the mule is a symbol of endurance and of the linking of pride and humility.

_____. See MISCELLANEOUS (Contemporary).

Hubbell, Jay B. See GENERAL.

Hult, Sharon S. "William Faulkner's 'The Brooch': The Journey to the Riolama." *Miss Quart*, 27 (Summer 1974), 291-305.
     A reading of W. H. Hudson's *Green Mansions* is a key to the understanding of the central conflict of the story.

Hunt, Joel A. "William Faulkner and Rabelais: The Dog Story." *ConL*, 10 (Summer 1969), 383-388.
     Chapters 21 and 22 of *Pantagruel* are suggested as a probable source for Chapter 13 of *The Mansion*.

Hunter, Edwin R. *Faulkner: Narrative Practice and Prose Style*. Washington, D. C.: Windhover Press, 1973.
     A systematic explication of Faulkner's rhetorical and narrative techniques to prove the careful coherence of his art in fiction.

Hutchens, Eleanor N. "Towards a Poetics of Fiction: 5 'The Novel as Chronomorph.'" *Novel*, 5 (Spring 1972), 215-224.

Faulkner's "A Rose for Emily" and *The Sound and the Fury* are used in a discussion of the importance of time in shaping narratives.

Hutchinson, James D. "Time: The Fourth Dimension in Faulkner." *Sou Dak Rev*, 6 (Summer 1968), 91-103.
     Deals chiefly with concepts of time in Faulkner's works, especially in *The Sound and the Fury*.

Hutten, Robert W. "A Major Revision in Faulkner's *A Fable*." *AL*, 45 (May 1973), 297-299.
     Points out the way Faulkner transferred dialogue from one character to another when revising "Notes on a Horse Thief" into *A Fable*.

Inge, M. Thomas. "Faulknerian Light." *Notes on Miss Writers*, 5 (Spring 1972), 29.
     A short corrective note clearing up a common misconception about Faulkner's title *Light in August*.

_____, ed. *Studies in Light in August*. Columbus, Ohio: Charles E. Merrill, 1971.
     Reprints background materials by Faulkner and John Cullen, five contemporary reviews, six critical essays, and a plot outline of the novel.

_____. "The Virginia Face of Faulkner." *Va Cavalcade*, 24 (Summer 1974), 32-39.
     Information on Faulkner's residence in Charlottesville, including an analysis of the masks he assumed.

_____, ed. *William Faulkner: A Rose for Emily*. Columbus, Ohio: Charles E. Merrill, 1970.
     Reprints the story and twenty-nine critical excerpts and essays for a study of the origins, craft, and reputation of the story; includes an introduction, a bibliography, two stories by G. W. Cable and William Cobb for comparative study, and a reproduction of the first page of the original manuscript.

_____. "William Faulkner's *Light in August*: An Annotated Checklist of Criticism." *RALS*, 1 (Spring 1971), 30-57.
     Contains an annotated list of everything published on the novel through August 1970.

_____. See MISCELLANEOUS (Contemporary--1st Inge entry).

Ingram, F. L. *Representative Short Story Cycles in the Twentieth Century*. The Hague: Mouton, 1971.
     A study of cyclic or connected short stories as a genre, including a chapter on *The Unvanquished* which argues that it is not a novel.

Irvine, Peter L. "Faulkner and Hardy." *ArQ*, 26 (Winter 1970), 357-365.
     Although there is no overt evidence that Faulkner ever read Hardy, there are many internal similarities (World View, the moral universe, character typologies, attitudes toward nature and the land, etc.) between the two writers.

Irwin, John T. *Doubling and Incest/Repetition and Revenge: A Speculative Reading of Faulkner*. Baltimore: Johns Hopkins Univ Press, 1975.
     An examination of the structure underlying Faulkner's novels, drawing on structuralist and French psychoanalytic criticism with emphases on the themes mentioned in the title.

Iser, Wolfgang. *The Implied Reader: Patterns of Communication in Prose Fiction from Bunyan to Beckett*. Baltimore: Johns Hopkins Univ Press, 1974.
     This treatment of the reader's participation in the creative work includes discussion of Faulkner.

Israel, Calvin. "The Last Gentleman." *PR*, 35 (1968), 315-319.
     An account of a chance conversation with Faulkner in a New York park in 1956.

Izard, Barbara, and Clara Hieronymus. *Requiem for a Nun: On Stage and Off*. Nashville: Aurora Publishers, 1970.
     A study of the genesis of Faulkner's play, the author's intent, and its history during the following decades on stage and off in this country and abroad, with special attention to the Camus adaptation.

Jäger, Dietrich. "Der 'verheimlichte Raum' in Faulkners 'A Rose for Emily' und Brittings 'Der Schneckenweg.'" *LWU*, 1 (1968), 108-116.
     Deals with these two writers' use of the concealed room of the horror tale.

James, David L. "Hightower's Name: A Possible Source." *Am N&Q*, 13 (September 1974), 4-5.
     The name (from Psalms 18:2) points ironically to modern man's failure to reach God.

James, Stuart. "Faulkner's Shadowed Land." *Denver Quart*, 6 (Autumn 1971), 45-61.
     A study of point of view in Faulkner's works.

Jarrett, David W. "Eustacia Vye and Eula Varner, Olympians: The Worlds of Thomas Hardy and William Faulkner." *Novel*, 6 (Winter 1973), 163-174.
     Besides having a similar vision about "the working of time" on localities, Faulkner "repeats and adapts in detail from Hardy points of character, lines of imagery, narrative methods, and even individual names."

Jarrett-Kerr, Martin. *William Faulkner: A Critical Essay*. Contemporary Writers in Christian Perspective Series. Grand Rapids, Mich.: Eerdmans, 1970.
     A general assessment in terms of Faulkner's "implacability and outrage," his uses of comedy and tragedy, and his religious belief.

Johnston, Kenneth G. "Time of Decline: Pickett's Charge and the Broken Clock in Faulkner's 'Barn Burning.'" *Stud SF*, 11 (Fall 1974), 434-436.
     The time on the stopped clock in "Barn Burning" is the time of the beginning of Pickett's charge at Gettysburg, the crest of the cause of the South in the Civil War.

_____. "The Year of the Jubilee: Faulkner's 'That Evening Sun.'" *AL*, 46 (March 1974), 93–100.

"...the thematic center" of the story is the "historical fact" that "emancipation is a slow, complex psychological and social process." Faulkner is saying that by the time of the story "the movement toward social and legal equality and responsible freedom had been minimal."

Johnston, Walter E. "The Shepherdess in the City." *CL*, 26 (Spring 1974), 124–141.

Faulkner's *Light in August* is used as one example of a work in which a "pastoral" figure represents the failure of the modern mind to accept pastoral simplicity.

Justus, James H. See GENERAL.

Kaluza, Irena. *The Functioning of Sentence Structure in the Stream-of-Consciousness Technique of William Faulkner's "The Sound and the Fury": A Study in Linguistic Stylistics.* Krakow, Poland: Biblioteka Jagiellonska, 1967.

The main objective of this study is "to describe the linguistic structures of *The Sound and the Fury* in formal categories,...and then to find out whether they form a meaningful artistic system in the novel...."

Kane, Patricia. "Adaptable and Free: Faulkner's Ratliff." *NConL*, 1 (May 1971), 9–10.

Traces the Surratt-Ratliff characterization through various works.

_____. "The Narcissa Benbow of Faulkner's *Flags in the Dust*." *NConL*, 4 (September 1974), 2–3.

A comparison of Narcissa as she appears in *Sartoris* and in *Flags*.

Kartiganer, Donald M. "Process and Product: A Study of Modern Literary Form." *Mass Rev*, 12 (Autumn 1971), 789–816.

This second part of a two-part article focuses on a detailed comparison of Faulkner and Conrad.

_____. "*The Sound and the Fury* and Faulkner's Quest for Form." *ELH*, 37 (December 1970), 613–639.

Discusses the novel as the one which launched Faulkner on "The great decade of his career...." This novel represents the start of Faulkner's effort to cope with the problem of imposing order on a "fragmented" world.

Katz, Joseph. See GENERAL.

Kazin, Alfred. See MISCELLANEOUS (Contemporary).

Kearful, Frank J. "Tony Last and Ike McCaslin: The Loss of a Usable Past." *Univ of Windsor Rev*, 3 (Spring 1968), 45–52.

Ike McCaslin and Tony Last, from Waugh's *A Handful of Dust*, illustrate "the absurdity, nobility, and sinfulness of seeking in the ideal a better world than that which can be lived in."

Kearney, J. A. "Paradox in Faulkner's *Intruder in the Dust*." *Theoria*, 40 (1973), 55–67.

On Chick Mallison's relation to the community in which he lives.

Keech, James M. "The Survival of the Gothic Response." *Stud in the Novel*, 6 (Summer 1974), 130–144.

In this general discussion of the Gothic in modern fiction, Thomas Sutpen is referred to as a typical Gothic hero-villain.

Keefer, T. Frederick. "William Faulkner's *Sanctuary*: A Myth Examined." *TCL*, 15 (July 1969), 97–104.

Attacks the "myth" that *Sanctuary* is a potboiler.

Keith, D. L. "Faulkner in New Orleans." *Delta Rev*, 6 (May 1969), 46–49.

The French Quarter in New Orleans was to Faulkner what the Left Bank was to Hemingway, Stein, and their crowd.

Kellner, R. S. "A Reconsideration of Character: Relationships in *Absalom, Absalom!*" *Notes on Miss Writers*, 7 (Fall 1974), 39–43.

Analyzes relationships between Quentin, Shreve, Henry, and Charles.

Kent, George E. "The Black Woman in Faulkner's Works, with the Exclusion of Dilsey." *Phylon*, 35 (December 1974), 430–441; 36 (March 1975), 55–67.

Part I compares Faulkner's attitudes toward blacks with that of his brother John; Part II concludes that Faulkner had a tendency to sentimentalize and mythologize blacks instead of exploring complexities of character.

Kerr, Elizabeth. *Yoknapatawpha: Faulkner's "Little Postage Stamp of Native Soil."* New York: Fordham Univ Press, 1969.

A guide to Faulkner's fictional world correlated with the actual world of Lafayette County through footnote references to historical, sociological, and economic records.

Kibler, James E., Jr. "A Possible Source in Ariosto for Drusilla." *Miss Quart*, 23 (Summer 1970), 321–322.

Parallels are cited.

_____. "William Faulkner and Provincetown Drama, 1920–1922. *Miss Quart*, 22 (Summer 1969), 226–236.

Stark Young in his association with the Provincetown Theater may have first interested Faulkner in drama; further study is needed of the influence of drama on Faulkner's works.

King, F. H. "Benjamin Compson--Flower Child." *CEA Critic*, 31 (January 1969), 10.

A gimmick comparison of Benjy and flower children, ending with a comment on drug use.

Kinney, Arthur F. "Faulkner and the Possibilities for Heroism." *SouR*, 6 (Autumn 1970), 1110–1125.

A reading of "The Old People," "The Bear," and "Delta Autumn" as comprising a comprehensive statement of Faulkner's most significant ideas and attitudes.

Klinkowitz, Jerome F. "The Thematic Unity of *Knight's Gambit*." *Critique*, 11, no. 2 (1969), 81–100.

Stresses the community's reaction to various outsiders as Faulkner's means of achieving unity in the work.

Knieger, Bernard. "Faulkner's 'Mountain Victory,' 'Doctor Martino,' and 'There Was a Queen.'" *Expl*, 30 (February 1972), Item 45.
A disagreement with interpretations in *Crowell's Handbook of Faulkner*.

Knight, Karl F. "'Spintrius' in Faulkner's 'The Bear.'" *Stud SF*, 12 (Winter 1975), 31-32.
The "tragic and miscast" career of Percival Brownlee "supports the central theme of the relation between the races in 'The Bear' and *Go Down, Moses*."

Kobler, J. F. "Faulkner's 'A Rose for Emily.'" *Expl*, 32 (April 1974), Item 65.
On the significance of the handling of Emily's name in the title and in the story.

_____. "Lena Grove: Faulkner's 'Still Unravish'd Bride of Quietness.'" *ArQ*, 28 (Winter 1972), 339-354.
Lena Grove stands as Faulkner's example of "man's highest, most eternal, and most perfect accomplishment,...ART."

Kolodny, Annette. *The Lay of the Land. Metaphor as Experience and History in American Life and Letters*. Chapel Hill: Univ of North Carolina Press, 1975.
Briefly treats Faulkner's landscape in the last chapter.

Korenman, Joan S. "Faulkner's Grecian Urn." *So Lit Jour*, 7 (Fall 1974), 3-23.
Faulkner's attraction to "Keatsian stasis" is seen in Ike McCaslin as well as in a number of other Faulknerian characters "spanning almost the entire range of the author's long career."

Kostjakov, V. A. *Trilogija Uil'jama Folknera*. Saratov, Russia: Saratovskogo Universiteta, 1969.
A brief general critical study in Russian.

Krieger, Murray. See MISCELLANEOUS (Contemporary).

Kristensen, Sven M. See MISCELLANEOUS (Contemporary).

Kronenberger, Louis, and E. M. Beck. See GENERAL.

Kulin, Katalin. "Reasons and Characteristics of Faulkner's Influence on Modern Latin-American Fiction." *Acta Litt Acad Hungaricae*, 13 (1971), 349-363.
The two main influences come from Faulkner's representation of a reduced universe and of man's fight against inevitable destiny.

_____. "Razones y características de la influencia de Faulkner en la ficción latinoamericana moderna." *Sin Nombre*, 6, no. 1 (1975), 20-36.
A Spanish translation of the above.

Kulseth, Leonard I. "Cincinnatus among the Snopeses: The Role of Gavin Stevens." *BSUF*, 10 (Winter 1969), 28-34.
Emphasizes Stevens' resistance to Snopesism.

Kwiat, Joseph J., and Gerhard Weiss. See MISCELLANEOUS (Contemporary).

Lanati, Barbara. "Il primo Faulkner: *As I Lay Dying*." *Sigma*, 19 (1968), 83-119.
A general evaluation of the novel.

Landeira, Ricardo L. "*Aura, The Aspern Papers*, 'A Rose for Emily': A Literary Relationship." *Jour of Spanish Stud: Twentieth Cent*, 3 (Fall 1975), 125-143.
Points out similarities in Carlos Fuentes, James, and Faulkner.

Landor, Mikhail. "William Faulkner: New Translations and Studies." *Sov Lit*, 8 (1968), 180-185.
On translations and studies in Russia.

_____. See MISCELLANEOUS (Contemporary).

Lang, Béatrice. "An Unpublished Faulkner Story: 'The Big Shot.'" *Miss Quart*, 26 (Summer 1973), 312-324.
A story within a story, this work contains thematic possibilities Faulkner used in other works to follow.

Lang, Hans J. See GENERAL.

Langford, Beverly Y. "History and Legend in William Faulkner's 'Red Leaves.'" *Notes on Miss Writers*, 6 (Spring 1973), 19-24.
Historical evidence for the existence of Chief Tobba-tubby, possibly a partial model for Faulkner's Chickasaw chiefs.

Langford, Gerald. *Faulkner's Revision of Absalom, Absalom!: A Collation of the Manuscript and the Published Book*. Austin: Univ of Texas Library, 1971.
A collation of portions of the original handwritten version of the novel with corresponding sections of the published version, with an evaluation of the significance of Faulkner's changes.

_____. *Faulkner's Revision of Sanctuary*. Austin: Univ of Texas Press, 1972.
A collation of the unrevised galleys of the novel with the revised published version; the editor provides an assessment of this famous revision.

Lasater, Alice E. See MISCELLANEOUS (Contemporary).

Leary, Lewis. *William Faulkner of Yoknapatawpha County*. New York: Thomas Y. Crowell, 1973.
A general biographical and critical survey of Faulkner's life and career, with separate chapters devoted to *The Sound and the Fury*, *As I Lay Dying*, *Light in August*, and *Absalom, Absalom!*

_____. See GENERAL--1st Leary entry.

LeClair, Thomas. See MISCELLANEOUS (Contemporary).

Lehan, Richard. See MISCELLANEOUS (Contemporary).

Lensing, George S. "The Metaphor of Family in *Absalom, Absalom!*" *SouR*, 11 (Winter 1975), 99-117.
  Finds that the institution of the family is the basic metaphor and symbol on which Faulkner constructs his novel, and discusses the four versions of the family which Faulkner presents.

Levin, Harry. See GENERAL.

_____. See MISCELLANEOUS (Contemporary).

Levins, Lynn G. "The Four Narrative Perspectives in *Absalom, Absalom!*" *PMLA*, 85 (January 1970), 35-47.
  The narrative perspectives are differentiated by literary genres.

Levitt, Paul. "An Analogue for Faulkner's 'A Rose for Emily.'" *Papers on Lang and Lit*, 9 (Winter 1973), 91-94.
  Ransom's "Emily Hardcastle, Spinster" is the analogue.

Lewis, Clifford L. "William Faulkner: The Artist as Historian." *Midcontinent Am Stud Jour*, 10 (Fall 1969), 36-48.
  An analysis of the social and ethical ideas of *Intruder in the Dust* as they apply to race relations, with references to James W. Silver's *Mississippi: The Closed Society*.

Lhamon, W. T., Jr. "*Pylon*: The Ylimaf and New Valois." *WHR*, 24 (Summer 1970), 274-278.
  In the middle of the Yoknapatawpha works (which describe a sense of community), Faulkner wrote a significant statement about the nature of the city (New Orleans) and its lack of genuine family life ("ylimaf").

Libman, Valentina. See GENERAL.

Lilly, Paul R., Jr. "Caddy and Addie: Speakers of Faulkner's Impeccable Language." *Jour of Narrative Tech*, 3 (1973), 170-182.
  Neither character believes in the spoken word.

Linscott, Elisabeth. "Faulkner in Massachusetts." *New England Galaxy*, 10 (Winter 1969), 37-42.
  Reminiscences about Faulkner's weekend visits to the Massachusetts home of Random House editor Robert Linscott.

Little, Matthew. "*As I Lay Dying* and 'Dementia Praecox' Humor." *Stud in Am Humor*, 2 (April 1975), 61-70.
  Believes that the novel is a mixture of backwoods and sophisticated (highbrow) humor.

Littlejohn, David. "How Not to Write a Biography." *New Rep*, 170 (March 23, 1974), 25-27.
  An essay-review of Joseph Blotner's *Faulkner* objecting to the refusal to interpret biographical materials.

_____. See MISCELLANEOUS (Contemporary).

Litvin, Rina. "William Faulkner's *Light in August*." *Hasifrut*, 1 (1969), 589-598. (English summary).

The wagon wheel is a central image in this novel; concerns dynamic as opposed to static characters.

Lloyd, J. B. "An Annotated Bibliography of William Faulkner, 1967-1970." *Univ of Miss Stud in Eng*, 12 (1971), 1-57.
  This supplement to existing bibliographies contains long annotations and helpful subdivisions.

Lohner, Edgar. See GENERAL.

Longley, John L., Jr. "'Who Never Had a Sister': A Reading of *The Sound and the Fury*." *Mosaic*, 7 (Fall 1973), 35-53.
  Analyzes the main characters of the novel.

Longstreet, S. See GENERAL.

Lopez, Guido, "Letters and Comments: 'Faulkner and the Horses.'" Trans. Ruth Feldman. *YR*, 64 (Spring 1975), 468-476.
  An account of Faulkner's brief stay in Italy in September 1955.

Ludington, Townsend. See MISCELLANEOUS (Contemporary).

Luedtke, Carol. "*The Sound and the Fury* and *Lie Down in Darkness*." *LWU*, 4 (1971), 45-51.
  Deals with the ways these two novels portray the Old South.

MacMillan, Duane. "*Pylon*: From Short Stories to Major Work." *Mosaic*, 7 (Fall 1973), 185-212.
  Pylon is more readily seen as a unified whole if one recognizes that it develops themes and characters which had their germinal forms in "All the Dead Pilots," "Ad Astra," "Death Drag," and "Honor."

Madden, David. See MISCELLANEOUS (Contemporary-- 1st Madden entry).

Maekawa Shunichi . . . . See GENERAL.

Magny, Claude-Edmonde. See MISCELLANEOUS (Contemporary).

Malbone, Raymond G. "Promissory Poker in Faulkner's 'Was.'" *Eng Rec*, 22 (Fall 1971), 23-25.
  On harmony established by the bets.

Malraux, Andre. "*Preface to William Faulkner's Sanctuary*." *SouR*, 10 (Autumn 1974), 889-991.
  This 1933 essay, here translated by Violet M. Horvath, sees the irremediable as Faulkner's true subject, and hatred as the force that powers his work.

Manglaviti, Leo M. J. "Faulkner's 'That Evening Sun' and Mencken's 'Best Editorial Judgment.'" *AL*, 44 (January 1972), 649-654.
  Notes discovery of a heretofore unknown draft of "That Evening Sun" among Mencken's recently released papers at the New York Public Library.

Margolies, Edward. See MISCELLANEOUS (Contemporary-- 1st Margolies entry).

Martin, Carter W. "Faulkner's *Sartoris*: The Tailor Re-Tailored." *So Car Rev*, 6, no. 2 (1974), 56-59.
    Deals with clothing imagery in the novel; Bayard is unable to accept "The Everlasting Yea."

_____. See O'CONNOR, FLANNERY (Contemporary--1st Martin entry).

Martin, Jay. See MISCELLANEOUS (Contemporary).

Massey, Linton R. *William Faulkner, "Man Working," 1919-1962: A Catalogue of the William Faulkner Collections at the University of Virginia.* Charlottesville: Univ Press of Virginia, 1968.
    Shows extensive Faulkner material housed at the University of Virginia.

Materassi, Mario. "Faulkner Criticism in Italy." *ItQ*, 57 (1971), 47-85.
    English translation of an appendix to Materassi's *I romanzi di Faulkner*.

_____. *I romanzi di Faulkner*. Biblioteca di studi Americani, 17. Rome: Edizioni di Storia e Letteratura, 1968.
    A comprehensive study of all Faulkner's novels, divided into three creative phases, the works from *The Sound and the Fury* through *The Wild Palms* considered the major phase; in Italian.

Maud, Ralph. "Faulkner, Mailer, and Yogi Bear." *C Rev Am Stud*, 2 (Fall 1971), 69-75.
    A comparison of initiation in "The Bear" and *Why Are We in Vietnam*?

May, John R. See GENERAL.

McAlexander, Hubert, Jr. "William Faulkner--The Young Poet in Stark Young's *The Torches Flare*." *AL*, 43 (January 1972), 647-649.
    Sees Young's fictional character Eugene Oliver as modelled on Faulkner.

McCants, Maxine. "From Humanity to Abstraction: Negro Characterization in *Intruder in the Dust*." *Notes on Miss Writers*, 2 (Winter 1970), 91-104.
    Discusses Lucas as an abstract representative of his race and as an individual.

McCarthy, Mary. "One Touch of Nature." *New Yorker*, 45 (January 24, 1970), 39-57.
    Discusses the role of Nature in the works of various writers, including Faulkner, for whom Nature was a "force in human destiny."

McCormick, John. See MISCELLANEOUS (Contemporary).

McDonald, Walter R. "Coincidence in the Novel: A Necessary Technique." *CE*, 29 (February 1968), 373-388.
    Light in August is discussed in detail, and *Absalom, Absalom!* to a lesser extent, as examples of the use of coincidence in the novel.

_____. "Faulkner's 'The Bear': Part IV." *CEA Critic*, 34 (January 1972), 31-32.
    A note on this section taking at face value Ike's statement that "Sam Fathers set me free."

McElrath, Joseph R., Jr. "*Pylon*: The Portrait of a Lady." *Miss Quart*, 27 (Summer 1974), 277-290.
    Laverne Shuman, rather than the Reporter and the flyers, is the main subject of this novel.

McGlynn, Paul D. "The Chronology of 'A Rose for Emily.'" *Stud SF*, 6 (Summer 1969), 461-462.
    Understanding the chronology makes the plot more comprehensible and clarifies the function of time in the story.

McHaney, Thomas L. "Anderson, Hemingway, and Faulkner's *The Wild Palms*." *PMLA*, 87 (May 1972), 465-474.
    By allusions this novel sets Faulkner's gratitude to Anderson against Hemingway's behavior and makes plain the philosophical differences between the two younger writers.

_____. "A Deer Hunt in the Faulkner Country." *Miss Quart*, 23 (Summer 1970), 315-320.
    A journalistic account contemporaneous in time and place with Faulkner's first published hunting tale.

_____. "The Elmer Papers: Faulkner's Comic Portrait of the Artist." *Miss Quart*, 26 (Summer 1973), 281-311.
    The unfinished novel, not unlike *Mosquitoes*, seems to rate art and artist low, not because Faulkner held the highest standards for them.

_____. "The Falkners and the Origin of Yoknapatawpha County: Some Corrections." *Miss Quart*, 25 (Summer 1972), 249-264.
    Points out errors in previous accounts of the Falkner family and shows how certain facts about the family relate to Faulkner's mythical county.

_____. "Robinson Jeffers' 'Tamar' and *The Sound and the Fury*." *Miss Quart*, 22 (Summer 1969), 261-263.
    The incest theme in *The Sound and the Fury* and in *Absalom, Absalom!* has an analogue in Jeffers' long poem.

_____. "*Sanctuary* and Frazer's Slain Kings." *Miss Quart*, 24 (Summer 1971), 223-245.
    Successful adaptation of primitive myth and ritual, as reported by Frazer, makes the novel a significant work, rather than a pot-boiler, as it has been called.

_____. "The Text of *Flags in the Dust*." *Faulkner Concordance Newsl*, 2 (1973), 7-8.
    Criticism of the text used for the Random House edition.

_____. *William Faulkner's The Wild Palms: A Study*. Jackson: Univ Press of Mississippi, 1975.
    A comprehensive examination of the origins, composition, structure, and meaning of one of Faulkner's least appreciated experiments in the novel.

_____, and Albert Erskine. "Commentary on the Text of *Flags in the Dust*." *Faulkner Concordance Newsl*, 3 (May 1974), 2-4.

An exchange on the textual quality of the Random House edition of *Flags in the Dust*.

McWilliams, Dean. "William Faulkner and Michel Butor's Novel of Awareness." *Ky Romance Quart*, 19 (1972), 387-402.
Deals with the "creative use" that Butor has made of the Faulkner influence on him.

Meats, Stephen. "Who Killed Joanna Burden?" *Miss Quart*, 24 (Summer 1971), 271-277.
Questions the assumption that Joe Christmas killed Joanna Burden.

Meindl, Dieter. *Bewusstsein als Schicksal: Zu Struktur und Entwicklung von William Faulkners Generationenroman*. Stuttgart: Metzler, 1974.
A study of awareness of ancestors in *Sartoris*, *Absalom, Absalom!*, and *Go Down, Moses*.

Mellard, James M. "Caliban as Prospero: Benjy and *The Sound and the Fury*." *Novel*, 3 (Spring 1970), 233-248.
Benjy's Caliban-like features connect him with the literary tradition of the fool.

_____. "Faulkner's Jason and the Tradition of Oral Narrative." *Jour of Popular Culture*, 2 (Fall 1968), 195-210.
Jason's section in *The Sound and the Fury* follows the patterns of oral rather than of written narrative tradition.

_____. "Jason Compson: Humor, Hostility and the Rhetoric of Aggression." *SHR*, 3 (Summer 1969), 259-267.
Jason's rhetoric, a combination of humor and hostility, is essentially a rhetoric of agression. The rhetoric reveals Jason's world and judgment of it, and it allows Faulkner "to develop a character and to fulfill a narrative form."

_____. "*The Sound and the Fury*: Quentin Compson and Faulkner's 'Tragedy of Passion.'" *Stud in the Novel*, 2 (Spring 1970), 61-75.
Deals with Quentin's idealism.

_____. "Type and Archetype: Jason Compson as Satirist." *Genre*, 4 (June 1971), 173-188.
An analysis of Jason Compson.

Meriwether, James B. "A. E. Housman and Faulkner's Nobel Prize Speech: A Note." *Jour Am Stud*, 4 (February 1971), 247-248.
"Faulkner's image of griefs, grieving, is not only bolder than Housman's grieving flesh; he chose to leave it ambiguous."

_____. "Blotner's *Faulkner*." *Miss Quart*, 28 (Summer 1975), 353-369.
This review-essay of Blotner's two-volume biography indicates those areas in which the work is useful and reliable, and it also corrects errors and adds to the information supplied.

_____. *Checklist of William Faulkner*. Columbus, Ohio: Charles E. Merrill, 1970.
A selective checklist of primary and secondary materials.

_____, ed. *A Faulkner Miscellany*. Jackson: Univ Press of Mississippi, 1974.
A collection of texts, criticism, and bibliographical studies of unpublished writings by Faulkner.

_____, ed. "Faulkner's Correspondence with *Scribner's Magazine*." *Proof*, 3 (1973), 253-282.
First printing of correspondence from November 1928 through October 1935.

_____. "Faulkner's 'Mississippi.'" *Miss Quart*, 25 (Spring 1972, Supplement), 15-23.
Faulkner's long essay, published in 1954, mingles historical and geographical facts with autobiography and elements of his own fiction to produce a piece rich and complex in structure.

_____, ed. "Faulkner's 'Ode to the Louver.'" *Miss Quart*, 27 (Summer 1974), 333-335.
Explanatory note on and text of this previously unpublished Faulkner item.

_____, ed. "Faulkner's Speech at the Teatro Municipal, Caracas, in 1961." *Miss Quart*, 27 (Summer 1974), 337.
Explanatory note on and text of this previously unpublished item.

_____. *The Literary Career of William Faulkner: A Bibliographical Study*. Columbia: Univ of South Carolina Press, 1971.
An "authorized reissue" of the 1961 volume, with a new preface and a list of errata.

_____. "Notes on the Textual History of *The Sound and the Fury*," in *Art and Error: Modern Textual Editing*, ed. Ronald Gottesman and Scott Bennett. Bloomington: Indiana Univ Press, 1970.
Demonstrates the ways in which the history of composition and publication and other biographical data inform textual problems, with Faulkner's novel as the example.

_____. "The Novel Faulkner Never Wrote: His *Golden Book* or *Doomsday Book*." *AL*, 42 (March 1970), 93-96.
Speculates on what Faulkner probably had in mind when he spoke of his *Golden Book* or *Doomsday Book*, pointing out that it was not *The Reivers*.

_____. "A Prefatory Note by Faulkner for the Compson Appendix." *AL*, 43 (May 1971), 281-284.
Comments on and reproduces what appears to be a draft of Faulkner's prefatory note for the double-volume Modern Library *The Sound and the Fury* and *As I Lay Dying* of 1946.

_____. "A Proposal for a CEAA Edition of William Faulkner," in *Editing Twentieth Century Texts*, ed. Francess G. Halpenny. Toronto: Univ of Toronto Press, 1972.
While preparation of a definitive text is now impossible, scholars can begin to produce the textual apparatus for a collected edition of Faulkner's work.

_____. "The Short Fiction of William Faulkner: A Bibliography." *Proof*, 1 (1971), 293-329.

The bibliography lists Faulkner's published and unpublished stories, locates their manuscripts and typescripts, and describes the various forms of their texts. Sections are devoted to lost stories, excerpts from novels, and the contents of the several collected volumes of stories.

_____, ed. *Studies in The Sound and the Fury*. Columbus, Ohio: Charles E. Merrill, 1970.
Reprints nine critical essays on the novel.

_____. "Two Unknown Faulkner Short Stories." *RANAM*, 4 (1971), 23-30.
Deals with "Two Dollar Wife" and "Sepulture South," neither of which has been reprinted.

_____. "William Faulkner," in *Fifteen Modern American Authors*, ed. Jackson R. Bryer. Durham, N. C.: Duke Univ Press, 1969, pp. 175-210.
An essay-survey of scholarly research and criticism.

_____, and Michael Millgate, eds. *Lion in the Garden: Interviews with William Faulkner, 1926-1962*. New York: Random House, 1968.
Reprints all the known interviews from the beginning to the end of Faulkner's career, including the texts of the Nagano seminars published in Japan.

Messerli, Douglas. "The Problem of Time in *The Sound and the Fury*: A Critical Reassessment and Reinterpretation." *So Lit Jour*, 6 (Spring 1974), 19-41.
Surveys the extensive criticism on the subject of the phenomenon of time in Faulkner's novels and proceeds to show that *The Sound and the Fury* is a novel about time and the way four people experience it.

Michel, Laurence. *The Thing Contained: Theory of the Tragic*. Bloomington: Indiana Univ Press, 1970.
One chapter of this study, "Faulkner: Saying No to Death," analyzes Faulkner as a tragedian.

Middleton, John. "Shreve McCannon and Sutpen's Legacy." *SouR*, 10 (Winter 1974), 115-124.
After examining the comments of Hyatt Waggoner, Ruth Vande Kieft, and Cleanth Brooks, the author moves to his own interpretation of Shreve's function in *Absalom, Absalom!*

Miller, James E., Jr. "*Sanctuary*: Yoknapatawpha's Waste Land," in *Individual and Community: Variations on a Theme in American Fiction*, ed. K. H. Baldwin and D. K. Kirby. Durham, N. C.: Duke Univ Press, 1975, pp. 137-159.
Defends *Sanctuary* against adverse criticism; compares it, in character parallels and general tone, to Eliot's "Waste Land."

Millgate, Jane. "Quentin Compson as Poor Player: Verbal and Social Cliches in *The Sound and the Fury*." *RLV*, 34 (February 1968), 40-49.
The use of cliches by the novel's characters, especially Quentin, points up the barriers which exist between the characters and reality.

Millgate, Michael. "Faulkner and Lanier: A Note on the Name Jason." *Miss Quart*, 25 (Summer 1972), 349-350.
Suggests a possible parallel between Faulkner's Jason and lines in Lanier's poem "Corn."

_____. "Faulkner on the Literature of the First World War." *Miss Quart*, 26 (Summer 1973), 387-389.
Alludes to Siegfried Sassoon, Henri Barbusse, Rupert Brooke, and Stephen Crane.

_____. "Faulkner in Toronto: A Further Note." *UTQ*, 37 (January 1968), 197-202.
Correspondence between Millgate and J. M. Hinchley, a member of Faulkner's RCAF training squadron, confirms that Faulkner did not do any combat flying.

_____. "'The Firmament of Man's History': Faulkner's Treatment of the Past." *Miss Quart*, 25 (Spring 1972, Supplement), 25-35.
Though he was fascinated by the disturbed and recent past of his region, Faulkner did not write historical novels as such; rather, he was more intent on showing the way certain of his characters think about the past.

_____. "Starting Out in the Twenties: Reflections on *Soldiers' Pay*." *Mosaic*, 7 (Fall 1973), 1-14.
The novel is a self-conscious blending of the realities of the post-World War I era and "the abstract formalism of late romantic prose."

_____. *William Faulkner*. New York: Capricorn Books, 1971.
A reprint of the revised 1966 text of the critical study in the "Writers and Critics" series.

_____. *William Faulkner*. Barcelona: Barral Editores, 1972.
A Spanish translation of Millgate's *The Achievement of William Faulkner* (1966).

Milliner, Gladys. "The Third Eve: Caddy Compson." *Midwest Quart*, 16 (April 1975), 268-275.
Caddy is a "montage" of the first Eve and of the second, the Virgin Mary.

Milum, Richard A. "Faulkner and the Cavalier Tradition: The French Bequest." *AL*, 45 (January 1974), 580-589.
Studies the influence of the French Cavalier tradition on Faulkner.

_____. "'The Horns of Dawn': Faulkner and Metaphor." *Am N&Q*, 11 (May 1973), 134.
This metaphor of a cow, used for the paramour of Ike Snopes in *The Hamlet*, had been used previously in Faulkner's last published poem, "The Flowers That Died" (1933).

_____. "Ikkemotubbe and the Spanish Conspiracy." *AL*, 46 (November 1974), 381-391.
Finds the probable historical context for the relationship between Faulkner's Ikkemotubbe and DeVitry.

_____. "The Title of Faulkner's 'Red Leaves.'" *Am N&Q*, 13 (December 1974), 58-59.

A brief note concerning the significance of the red slippers in this story.

Minter, David. "Faulkner and the Uses of Biography." *GaR*, 28 (Fall 1974), 455-469.
An essay-review of Blotner's *Faulkner: A Biography*.

_____. *The Interpreted Design as a Structural Principle in American Prose.* New Haven: Yale Univ Press, 1969.
The concept of interpreted design--a man of design who dominates the action of his world, brought into contact with a man of interpretation through whose mind and voice his story is transmitted--is applied to seven works including *Absalom, Absalom!*

_____, ed. *Twentieth Century Interpretations of Light in August.* Englewood Cliffs, N. J.: Prentice-Hall, 1969.
Reprints three full critical essays, two condensations, and twenty excerpts, with a chronology of Faulkner's career, a brief selected bibliography, and an original introductory essay by the editor.

Momberger, Philip. "Faulkner's 'Country' as Ideal Community," in *Individual and Community: Variations on a Theme in American Fiction*, ed. K. H. Baldwin and D. K. Kirby. Durham, N. C.: Duke Univ Press, 1975, pp. 112-136.
Contends that Faulkner's master theme is man's need for communal ties and that in the first section, "The Country," of his collected stories, Faulkner presents a vision of communal health.

Monaghan, David M. "Faulkner's *Absalom, Absalom!*" *Expl*, 31 (December 1972), Item 28.
Points out parallels between p. 231 of *Absalom* and *Oedipus Rex*, 801-813.

_____. "Faulkner's Relationship to Gavin Stevens in *Intruder in the Dust*." *Dal Rev*, 52 (Autumn 1972), 449-457.
Summarizes the critical debate over whether Gavin Stevens is Faulkner's mouthpiece for the expression of racial views or is distinctly separated and ironically treated. Argues that while Stevens articulates many of Faulkner's own opinions and prejudices, he is presented as flawed by an excessive tendency to indulge in abstract thought rather than give primary attention to individuals and particular circumstances.

_____. "The Single Narrator of *As I Lay Dying*." *MFS*, 18 (Summer 1972), 213-220.
"The discrepancies [in the novel] previously ascribed to anachronism and clairvoyance can be accounted for quite readily if we accept that the whole action is a product of Addie's conscious stream, liberated as it must inevitably be, from the limitations of time and place. Even more important, the novel's themes acquire new dimensions and are enriched if it is approached in this manner."

Monteiro, George. "'Between Grief and Nothing': Hemingway and Faulkner." *Hemingway Notes*, 1 (Spring 1971), 13-15.

Robert Jordan and Wilbourne in *The Wild Palms* hold similar views.

_____. "Hemingway and Spain: A Response to Woodward." *Hemingway Notes*, 2 (Fall 1972), 16-17.
Re-states that the ending of *For Whom the Bell Tolls* was borrowed from the title portion of *The Wild Palms*.

_____. "The Limits of Professionalism: A Sociological Approach to Faulkner, Fitzgerald and Hemingway." *Criticism*, 15 (Spring 1973), 145-155.
Discusses critics who use a sociological approach to these writers.

Moore, Robert, ed. *The Faulkner Concordance Newsletter*, no. 3 (May 1974).
Reports on new fiscal support for the Concordance project and other matters.

Morell, Giliane. "The Last Scene of *Sanctuary*." *Miss Quart*, 25 (Summer 1972), 351-355.
Themes announced at the beginning of the novel are brought together in this last scene.

_____. "Prisoners of the Inner World: Mother and Daughter in *Miss Zilphia Gant*." *Miss Quart*, 28 (Summer 1975), 299-305.
Traces the relationship of this work to Faulkner's other writings of the same period and then gives a brief analysis of the story as "a tragedy in five acts."

Moses, Edwin. "Faulkner's *The Reivers*: The Art of Acceptance." *Miss Quart*, 27 (Summer 1974), 307-318.
This novel is "a worthy valediction" to Faulkner's work because it "embodies Faulkner's theme of acceptance artfully and realistically" and "comes fully to terms with the dark struggles and compulsions of the previous volumes...."

_____. "Faulkner's *The Hamlet*: The Passionate Humanity of V. K. Ratliff." *Notre Dame Eng Jour*, 8 (Spring 1973), 98-109.
Ratliff is a protagonist, and his struggle with Flem Snopes is "crucial to an understanding of the novel's world view."

Mottram, Eric. "Mississippi Faulkner's Glorious Mosaic of Impotence and Madness." *Jour Am Stud*, 2 (April 1968), 121-129.
An essay-review of several recent books, which maintains that Faulkner is a muddled thinker but a great story-teller.

_____. *William Faulkner.* The Profiles in Literature Series. London: Routledge & Kegan Paul, 1971.
Employs extracts from Faulkner's works to illustrate his general style and subject matter.

Muehl, Lois. "Form as Seen in Two Early Works by Faulkner." *Lib Chron*, 38 (1972), 147-157.
Analysis of the form in *Sartoris* and in *Light in August* reveals five devices that Faulkner used repeatedly.

Muhlenfeld, Elisabeth S. "Shadows with Substance and Ghosts Exhumed: The Women in *Absalom, Absalom!*" *Miss Quart*, 25 (Summer 1972), 289-304.
Though some critics have dismissed Faulkner's women characters as either sources of evil or flat stereotypes, detailed analysis of five women in this novel shows that they are carefully and fully developed.

Muir, Edward H. "A Footnote on *Sartoris* and Some Speculation." *Jour of Mod Lit*, 1 (March 1971), 389-393.
Bayard Sartoris' plane is like a real plane designed by W. W. Christmas and called the Christmas "Bullet."

Muller, Gilbert H. "The Descent of the Gods: Faulkner's 'Red Leaves' and the Garden of the South." *Stud SF*, 11 (Summer 1974), 243-249.
This story offers "a brilliant formulation of the South's failure to establish an Arcadian ideal--to resurrect an Eden on earth."

Mulqueen, James E. "Foreshadowing of Melville and Faulkner." *Am N&Q*, 6 (March 1968), 102.
A short story in the *Whig Review* (1845) brings to mind Melville's "Metaphysics of Indian Hating" and adumbrates Faulkner's *The Bear*.

_____. "*Light in August*: Motion, Eros, and Death." *Notes on Miss Writers*, 8 (Winter 1975), 91-98.
A study of the physical movement of characters in the novel.

Murphy, Denis M. "*The Sound and the Fury* and Dante's *Inferno*: Fire and Ice." *MarkR*, 4 (October 1974), 71-78.
Discusses "structural and philosophical" similarities between the two works.

Murray, D. M. "Faulkner, The Silent Comedies, and The Animated Cartoon." *SHR*, 9 (Summer 1975), 241-257.
"...there are particular conventions in Faulkner's humor that closely resemble particular conventions of the funny films."

Murray, Edward. See MISCELLANEOUS (Contemporary).

Myres, W. V. "Faulkner's Parable of Poetic Justice." *La Stud*, 8 (Fall 1969), 224-230.
Deals with "Shingles for the Lord."

Nadeau, Robert L. "The Morality of Act: A Study of Faulkner's *As I Lay Dying*." *Mosaic*, 6 (Spring 1973), 23-35.
Deals with Bergsonian echoes in Addie's conception of morality; the characters who react to Addie's death should be viewed as a part of the life process.

Nagel, James. See CLEMENS, SAMUEL LANGHORNE.

Naples, Diane C. "Eliot's 'Tradition' and *The Sound and the Fury*." *MFS*, 20 (Summer 1974), 214-217.
Relates Faulkner's novel to Eliot's "mythic" method.

Nash, Harry C. "Faulkner's 'Furniture Repairer and Dealer': Knitting Up *Light in August*." *MFS*, 16 (Winter 1970), 529-531.
Deals with the significance of the last chapter of the novel.

Nebeker, Helen E. "Chronology Revised." *Stud SF*, 8 (Summer 1971), 471-473.
A suggested chronology for "A Rose for Emily."

_____. "Emily's Rose of Love: Thematic Implications of Point of View in Faulkner's 'A Rose for Emily.'" *Rocky Mt MLA Bul*, 24 (March 1970), 3-13.
Suggests that the room was sealed by Emily's rejected lovers who wished to protect her image.

_____. "Emily's Rose of Love: A Postscript." *Rocky Mt MLA Bul*, 24 (December 1970), 190-191.
The date 1894 is not the date of Emily's father's death but of the remission of her taxes.

Nelson, Malcolm A. "'Yr Stars Fell' in *The Bear*." *Am N&Q*, 9 (March 1971), 102-103.
Suggests that the reference is to the great meteor shower in the constellation Leo which occurred in November 1833.

_____. "'Yr Stars Fell' in *The Bear*." *Am N&Q*, 12 (September 1973), 4-5.
Reference to the great Leonid shower of 1833 recorded by astronomers.

Nelson, Raymond S. "Apotheosis of the Bear." *Research Stud*, 41 (September 1973), 201-204.
Even after he is killed the bear remains immortal because he lives in legend.

Neufeldt, Leonard. "Time and Man's Possibilities in *Light in August*." *CaR*, 25 (June 1971), 27-40.
An examination of the "worlds of time" and the relationship of certain characters in the novel to these worlds.

Nevius, Blake. See MISCELLANEOUS (Contemporary).

Nicolet, William P. "Faulkner's 'Barn Burning.'" *Expl*, 34 (November 1975), Item 25.
Underwood deviled ham and sardines symbolize Sarty's moral choice.

Noble, David W. See GENERAL.

Nolte, William H. "Mencken, Faulkner and Southern Moralism." *So Car Rev*, 4 (December 1971), 45-61.
"Mencken and Faulkner were singularly alike in their assignment of the causes and effects of Southern moralism and the numerous paradoxes, ironies, and myths which that moralism fostered."

Norris, Nancy. "*The Hamlet*, *The Town*, and *The Mansion*: A Psychological Reading of the Snopes Trilogy." *Mosaic*, 7 (Fall 1973), 213-235.
The trilogy reveals not only that men "endure the sound of their own fury" but can "contribute toward making that endurance worth the agony and the sweat."

O'Brien, Matthew C. "Faulkner, General Chalmers, and the Burning of Oxford." *Am N&Q*, 12 (February 1974), 87-88.
    In a letter to the editor, Faulkner mistakenly blames Chalmers, whom he calls a Yankee; Chalmers was actually a Confederate general and an enemy of Colonel William C. Falkner.

_____. "A Note on Faulkner's Civil War Women." *Notes on Miss Writers*, 1 (Fall 1968), 56-63.
    A short treatment of the "duality" of both good and bad in Faulkner's Civil War women.

_____. "William Faulkner and the Civil War in Oxford, Miss." *JMiH*, 25 (May 1973), 167-174.
    Faulkner does not deal with the Civil War as fact, but rather as it emphasizes impressions on Jefferson.

O'Dea, Richard J. "Faulkner's Vestigial Christianity." *Renascence*, 21 (Autumn 1968), 44-54.
    Faulkner's Christianity resides in his emphasis on those virtues without which Christianity is impossible rather than in dogmatic statements or Christian symbols.

Olson, Ted. "Faulkner and the Colossus of Maroussi." *SAQ*, 71 (Spring 1972), 205-212.
    An account of Faulkner's trip to Athens, Greece, where he attended a dinner party with George Katsimbalis and tried to tell taller tales about his war adventures than Katsimbalis.

O'Nan, Martha. *The Role of Mind in Hugo, Faulkner, Beckett, and Grass*. New York: Philosophical Library, 1969.
    The theories of mind of Briquet, Janet, and Freud provide insights for understanding Faulkner's Benjy in *The Sound and the Fury*.

Otten, Terry. "Faulkner's Use of the Past: A Comment." *Renascence*, 20 (Summer 1968), 198-207, 214.
    Discusses history as myth, as legend, and as moral commentary in *Absalom, Absalom!*, "The Bear," *The Unvanquished* and *Requiem for a Nun*.

Page, Sally R. *Faulkner's Women: Characterization and Meaning*. Deland, Fla.: Everett/Edwards, 1972.
    A detailed analysis of women characters and the significance of femininity in Faulkner's fiction, with an introduction by Cleanth Brooks.

Palmer, William J. "Abelard's Fate: Sexual Politics in Stendhal, Faulkner, and Camus." *Mosaic*, 7 (Spring 1974), 29-41.
    Discusses Faulkner's use of the metaphor of castration in *Light in August*.

Panichas, George A. See MISCELLANEOUS (Contemporary).

Parker, Hershel. "What Quentin Saw 'Out There.'" *Miss Quart*, 27 (Summer 1974), 323-326.
    Quentin learned the secret of Bon's birth by seeing the "Sutpen faces" rather than by hearing of it from either Miss Rosa or Clytie or Henry.

Parsons, Thornton H. "Doing the Best They Can." *GaR*, 23 (Fall 1969), 292-306.
    In the implicit values of the Bundrens' often remarkable "familyness" is the profundity of *As I Lay Dying*.

Pate, Willard. "Benjy's Names in the Compson Household." *Furman Stud*, 15 (May 1968), 37-38.
    Characters in *The Sound and the Fury* reveal their attitudes toward the idiot by the appellations they use for him.

_____. "Pilgrimage to Yoknapatawpha." *Furman Mag*, Winter 1969, pp. 6-13.
    Reminiscence of a visit to Oxford in 1966.

Payne, Ladell. "The Trilogy: Faulkner's Comic Epic." *Stud in the Novel*, 1 (Spring 1969), 27-37.
    In the Snopes trilogy Faulkner used structural and stylistic devices established by Fielding as being characteristic of comic romance but differed from Fielding in blending the funny and the sad and in using a poetic style.

Pearce, Richard. "'Pylon,' 'Awake and Sing!' and the Apocalyptic Imagination of the 30's." *Criticism*, 13 (Spring 1971), 131-141.
    A study of the literature of the 30's which sees Faulkner's *Pylon* as a representative exploration of the apocalyptic vision.

_____. See MISCELLANEOUS (Contemporary).

Peavy, Charles D. *Go Slow Now: Faulkner and the Race Question*. Eugene: Univ of Oregon Books, 1971.
    A summary of Faulkner's attitudes on race as seen in his fiction and public statements which concludes that Faulkner held the contradictory position of believing in both civil rights and states' rights.

_____. "'If I Just Had a Mother': Faulkner's Quentin Compson." *Lit and Psych*, 23, no. 3 (1973), 114-121.
    An examination of the symptoms, causes, and effects of Quentin's neurosis.

_____. "Jason Compson's Paranoid Pseudo-Community." *Hartford Stud in Lit*, 2 (1970), 151-156.
    Jason has the symptoms of a paranoid; his "paranoid suspicions regarding his family have been gradually extended to the community at large."

_____. "A Note on the 'Suicide Pact' in *The Sound and the Fury*." *Eng Lang Notes*, 5 (March 1968), 207-209.
    The text of the novel and Faulkner's own comments show that Caddy never agreed to a suicide pact or to incest with Quentin.

Peckham, Morse. "The Place of Sex in the Work of William Faulkner." *Stud in the Twentieth Cent*, 14 (Fall 1974), 1-20.
    On the tension between Idealism and Biology in *A Fable*, *Requiem for a Nun*, and *The Wild Palms*.

Pells, Richard H. See MISCELLANEOUS (Contemporary).

Peraile, Esteban and Lorenzo. "Una lectura de *Los invictos*." *Cuad Hisp*, 291 (September 1974), 692-701.
    The theme of *The Unvanquished* is war, with the victory being death; the parts of the novel pair themselves into "attack" and "retreat."

Perkins, George. See GENERAL.

Perlis, Alan D. "*As I Lay Dying* as a Study of Time." *Sou Dakota Rev*, 10 (Spring 1972), 103-110.
    Deals with the reactions to and uses of time by various characters in the novel.

Perry, J. Douglas. See MISCELLANEOUS (Contemporary).

Peterson, Carl. *Each in Its Ordered Place: A Faulkner Collector's Notebook*. Ann Arbor, Mich.: Ardis Publishers, 1975.
    A bibliographic catalogue of primary and secondary materials in the author's personal collection of over 2,000 items listed.

Peterson, Richard F. "Faulkner's *Light in August*." *Expl*, 30 (December 1971), Item 35.
    Finds the original source of Joe Christmas' guilt-ridden feelings to be the toothpaste episode at the orphanage.

Pfeiffer, Andrew H. "Eye of the Storm: The Observers' Image of the Man Who Was Faulkner." *SouR*, 8 (Autumn 1972), 763-773.
    This essay gathers, compares, and comments on a large number of impressions of Faulkner the man.

_____. "'No Wiser Spot on Earth': Community and the Country Store in Faulkner's *The Hamlet*." *Notes on Miss Writers*, 6 (Fall 1973), 45-52.
    Deals with "Community" as theme, main character, and setting for the novel. Varner's store is the center of the community.

Phillips, Gene D. "Faulkner and the Film: The Two Versions of *Sanctuary*." *Lit/Film Quart*, 1 (July 1973), 263-273.
    Both film versions in different ways reflect the novel.

Pierle, Robert C. "Snopesism in Faulkner's *The Hamlet*." *Eng Stud*, 52 (1971), 246-252.
    A brief survey of the three stages of critical thought dealing with Snopesism, concluding with an analysis of the "essence of Snopesism and relationship to the fictional society in which it resides...."

Pinsker, Sanford. "An Ironic Reading of William Faulkner's 'The Bear.'" *Topic*, 12 (Spring 1972), 35-51.
    What Ike learned in the wilderness is of no practical value in a world from which the wilderness has disappeared.

Pitavy, François. *Faulkner's Light in August*. Rev. and trans. Gillian E. Cook, with the collaboration of the author. Bloomington: Indiana Univ Press, 1973.
    A comprehensive analysis of composition, structure, characterization, theme, style, and reception of the novel. Translated from the 1970 study.

_____. "A Forgotten Faulkner Story: 'Miss Zilphia Gant.'" *Stud SF*, 9 (Spring 1972), 131-142.
    A "remarkable treatment of a frustrated, sex-starved, and child-starved woman," "Miss Zilphia Gant" should be considered as an achievement in itself and "as a stage in an exploration that culminated in *Light in August*."

_____. "The Landscape in *Light in August*." *Miss Quart*, 23 (Summer 1970), 265-272.
    Setting and landscape are treated briefly in this novel and always in connection with characters so that the landscape is an image of a state of mind.

Plante, P. R. See GENERAL.

Pochmann, Henry A., and Joel A. Hunt. "Faulkner and His Sources." *ConL*, 11 (Spring 1970), 310-312.
    An exchange of letters regarding Hunt's essay "William Faulkner and Rabelais," *ConL* (Summer 1969). Pochmann claims that Hunt overlooked the importance of oral sources in Faulkner's fiction and Hunt denies doing so.

Polk, Noel. "Alec Holston's Lock and the Founding of Jefferson." *Miss Quart*, 24 (Summer 1971), 247-269.
    The treatment of the themes of freedom and responsibility in *Requiem for a Nun* makes it central to Faulkner's assessment of the human condition, and thus more than a technical experiment which failed.

_____. "The Critics and Faulkner's 'Little Postage Stamp of Native Soil.'" *Miss Quart*, 23 (Summer 1970), 323-335.
    An essay-review of Elizabeth Kerr's *Yoknapatawpha: Faulkner's "Little Postage Stamp of Native Soil"* (1969) which deplores the tendency of this author and similar critics who insist on paralleling actual places with Faulkner's settings and on interpreting his works as history and sociology.

_____. "Faulkner's 'The Jail' and the Meaning of Cecilia Farmer." *Miss Quart*, 25 (Summer 1972), 305-325.
    In this section of *Requiem for a Nun*, the jail, the structure of which is never changed, focuses on two views of life, the backward-looking and the forward-looking; and Cecilia Farmer is the symbol of man's sense of himself as a human being.

_____. "'Hong Li' and *Royal Street*: The New Orleans Sketches in Manuscript." *Miss Quart*, 26 (Summer 1973), 394-395.
    Reprints "Hong Li."

_____. "The Manuscript of *Absalom, Absalom!*" *Miss Quart*, 25 (Summer 1972), 359-367.
    An essay-review of Gerald Langford's 1971 book, *Faulkner's Revision of 'Absalom, Absalom!'*

_____. "The Staging of *Requiem for a Nun*." *Miss Quart*, 24 (Summer 1971), 299-314.
A review-essay of *Requiem for a Nun: Onstage and Off*, by Barbara Izard and Clara Hieronymus.

_____. "The Textual History of Faulkner's *Requiem for a Nun*." *Proof*, 4 (1975), 109-128.
Title is descriptive.

_____. Untitled. *Miss Quart*, 28 (Summer 1975), 387-392.
Review of *The Indians of Yoknapatawpha*, by Lewis M. Dabney, and of "Faulkner's Indians" by Marc A. Nigliazzo.

_____. "William Faulkner's *Marionettes*." *Miss Quart*, 26 (Summer 1973), 247-280.
A study of sources and literary qualities of *Marionettes*.

Porat, Tsfira. "Sawdust Dolls: Tragic Fate and Comic Freedom in Faulkner's *Light in August*." *Hasifrut*, 2 (1971), 767-782. (In Hebrew with English summary.)
Discusses the reasons Byron Bunch escapes Calvinistic domination and Joe Christmas does not.

Porter, Carolyn. "The Problem of Time in *Light in August*." *Rice Univ Stud (Stud in Eng)*, 61 (Winter 1975), 107-125.
On the roles structure and language play in Faulkner's handling of time in this novel.

Presley, Delma E. "Is Reverend Whitfield a Hypocrite?" *Research Stud*, 36 (March 1968), 57-61.
Whitfield does not sound or act like a hypocrite but is instead one of those who endure.

Price, Reynolds. "*Pylon*: The Posture of Worship." *Shen*, 30 (Spring 1968), 49-61.
A reading of the novel as the reporter's encounter with forces beyond his comprehension.

_____. See PRICE, REYNOLDS (Contemporary--4th Price entry).

Prince, John. "André Dhôtel, Steinbeck et Faulkner: quelques similitudes." *Caliban*, 6 (1969), 85-90.
Deals with reasons for Dhôtel's admiration of Faulkner and Steinbeck.

Prior, Linda. "Theme, Imagery, and Structure in *The Hamlet*." *Miss Quart*, 22 (Summer 1969), 237-256.
Imagery in the novel is molded into the basic theme of waste, both theme and imagery being supported by structure.

Pryse, Marjorie L. "Race: Faulkner's 'Red Leaves.'" *Stud SF*, 12 (Spring 1975), 133-138.
In this story, the "Negro body servant, archetypally marked by the Indians, transcends his social role as lower caste member and transforms his social exclusion into a metaphysical quest."

Putzel, Max. "Evolution of Two Characters in Faulkner's Early and Unpublished Fiction." *So Lit Jour*, 5 (Spring 1973), 47-63.
His drafts tell us much about Faulkner's apprenticeship and artistry, as in his early stories and sketches we can see the evolution of Bayard Sartoris and Caddy Compson.

_____. "What Is Gothic about *Absalom, Absalom!*" *So Lit Jour*, 4 (Fall 1971), 3-19.
What is Gothic in Faulkner is medieval chivalry.

Raisor, Philip. "Up from Adversity: William Faulkner's *A Fable*." *Sou Dakota Rev*, 11 (Summer 1973), 3-15.
In this novel Faulkner was attempting "to dramatize...his belief that slavery was the end result of a bad choice."

Ramsey, Roger. "Faulkner's *The Sound and the Fury*." *Expl*, 30 (April 1972), Item 70.
Discusses why Benjy is said to "smell" death.

Randel, Fred V. "Parentheses in Faulkner's *Absalom, Absalom!*" *Style*, 5 (Winter 1971), 70-87.
Parentheses in the novel represent the inner self and reveal the tension between the inner and outer worlds.

Raper, J. R. "Meaning Called to Life: Alogical Structure in *Absalom, Absalom!*" *SHR*, 5 (Winter 1971), 9-23.
"Using the alogical structure created through technical maneuvers similar to those employed by skilled cinematographers, Faulkner represents the major themes of the novel (the thwarted life), in key images (especially those of closed doors), and rather than stating the theme statically on the page, calls it to life in the reader."

Rea, J. "Faulkner's 'Spotted Horses.'" *Hartford Stud in Lit*, 2 (1970), 157-164.
In telling this story, Faulkner was more interested in the horses than in Flem Snopes; the horses are "poetry," are "Pegasus multiplied."

Reed, Joseph W., Jr. *Faulkner's Narrative*. New Haven, Conn.: Yale Univ Press, 1973.
Demonstrates the primacy of narrative in the stories and novels by applying principles derived from Faulkner's public interviews.

Reed, Richard. "The Role of Chronology in Faulkner's Yoknapatawpha Fiction." *So Lit Jour*, 7 (Fall 1974), 24-48.
The chronological mistakes in the fiction, when placed in proper perspective, emerge as minor flaws in such a major achievement.

Rhynsburger, Mark. "Student Views of William Faulkner I." *Mod Occasions*, 1 (Winter 1971), 264-269.
Deals with the significance of Darl in *As I Lay Dying*, Quentin in *The Sound and the Fury*, and Labove in *The Hamlet*.

Rice, Julian C. "Orpheus and the Hellish Unity in *Light in August*." *Centennial Rev*, 19 (Winter 1975), 380-396.
On Joe Christmas and Byron Bunch as characters with Orphean qualities.

Richards, Lewis. "Sex Under The Wild Palms--And a Moral Question." *ArQ*, 28 (Winter 1972), 326-332.
Work is "the supreme example" of Faulknerian (especially female) characters. "Absence of love and celebration of carnality and lechery."

Richardson, H. Edward. "The Decadence in Faulkner's First Novel: The Faun, the Worm, and the Tower." *EA*, 21 (July-September 1968), 225-235.
Deals with Faulkner's use of the themes and symbols of French Symbolism in *Soldiers' Pay*.

_____. *William Faulkner: The Journey to Self-Discovery*. Columbia: Univ of Missouri Press, 1969.
A critical-biographical study of Faulkner's literary apprenticeship through *Sartoris*.

Riche, James. See MISCELLANEOUS (Contemporary).

Riese, Utz. "The Dilemma of the Third Way (William Faulkner's Contradictory Humanism), I." *ZAA*, 16, no. 2 (1968), 138-155; Part II, 16, no. 3 (1968), 257-273.
Part I deals with Faulkner's treatment of the theme of alienation; Part II deals with Faulkner's "Southernness."

Righter, William. See GENERAL.

Rinaldi, Nicholas M. "Game Imagery in Faulkner's *Absalom, Absalom!*" *Conn Rev*, 4, no. 1 (1970), 73-79.
The imagery of games in the novels emphasizes the idea that for Sutpen everything is a game in which an opponent must be outwitted.

Robbins, J. Albert. See GENERAL.

Rogers, Douglas G. "Faulkner's Treatment of Negro Characters in *Sartoris* and *The Unvanquished*." *NDQ*, 43 (Spring 1975), 67-72.
In these novels (as well as in other works) Faulkner "asserts the definition of man as a moral being in upholding the moral integrity of the Negro."

Rome, Joy J. "Love and Wealth in *Absalom, Absalom!*" *Unisa Eng Stud*, 9, no. 1 (1971), 3-10.
Concentrates on the character of Sutpen.

Rosenberg, Bruce A. "The Oral Quality of Rev. Shegog's Sermon in William Faulkner's *The Sound and the Fury*." *LWU*, 2, no. 2 (1969), 73-88.
Comparing Shegog's sermon with transcriptions of live sermons reveals the orally realistic elements.

Rosenman, John. "Another *Othello* Echo in *As I Lay Dying*." *Notes on Miss Writers*, 8 (Spring 1975), 19-21.
Suggests that Darl's use of horse imagery may derive from Iago.

_____. "A Note on William Faulkner's *As I Lay Dying*." *Stud in Am F*, 1 (1973), 104-105.
Shakespeare's treatment of Macbeth is a possible influence on the characterization of Dewey Dell.

Ross, Stephen M. "Conrad's Influence in Faulkner's *Absalom, Absalom!*" *Stud in Am F*, 2 (Autumn 1974), 199-209.
Points out structural and psychological similarities between Faulkner's novel and Conrad's *Lord Jim* and "Heart of Darkness."

_____. "The 'Loud World' of Quentin Compson." *Stud in the Novel*, 7 (Summer 1975), 245-257.
For Quentin, talking is the "crucial mode" of confronting existence and he tries to experience life by putting it into words.

_____. "Shapes of Time and Consciousness in *As I Lay Dying*." *Texas Stud in Lit and Lang*, 16 (Winter 1975), 723-737.
Suggests that shifts in the tense of Faulkner's narration are a skillfully handled innovation rather than a flaw.

Rossky, William. "The Pattern of Nightmare in *Sanctuary*; or, Miss Reba's Dogs." *MFS*, 15 (Winter 1969-70), 503-515.
An examination of images of nightmare in the novel which depicts "the universal dream-horror of existence."

Rouberol, Jean. "Les Indiens dans l'oeuvre de Faulkner." *EA*, 26 (January-March 1973), 54-58.
Faulkner believed that the white man brought corruption to himself by corrupting the Indian and taking his land from him.

Rougé, Robert. See MISCELLANEOUS (Contemporary).

Rubens, Philip M. "St. Elmo and the Barn Burners." *Notes on Miss Writers*, 7 (Winter 1975), 86-90.
An explanation of St. Elmo Snopes's name in *The Hamlet*.

Rubin, Louis D., Jr. "Looking Backward." *New Rep*, 17 (October 19, 1974), 20-22.
An essay-review of *Versions of the Past: The Historical Imagination in American Fiction*, by Harry B. Henderson III, with comments on *Absalom, Absalom!*

_____. See GENERAL--3rd, 4th, and 9th entries.

Ruiz Ruiz, José M. "El sentido de la vida y de la muerte en *The Sound and the Fury*." *Filologia Mod*, 13 (1973), 117-138.
Deals with the symbols in the novel.

Ruotolo, Lucio P. See MISCELLANEOUS (Contemporary).

Sachs, Viola, ed. *Le Blanc et le Noir chez Melville et Faulkner*. Paris: Mouton, 1974.
An anthology of critical essays in French on the treatment of race in the two writers' fiction, with eleven essays on *Absalom, Absalom!* *Go Down, Moses* and *The Sound and the Fury*.

IV. Contemporary (1920-1975)

_____. _Le Sacre et le Profane: The Bear de William Faulkner_. Paris: Dept Anglo-Americain Université de Paris VIII, 1971.
   A collective explication of "The Bear" by twenty-eight French undergraduate students to demonstrate unity of structure; in English.

_____. _The Myths of America_. The Hague: Mouton, 1973.
   Studies in the symbolic structures of the American romance, with two chapters devoted to _Absalom, Absalom!_ and "The Bear."

Samway, Patrick J. "War: A Faulknerian Commentary." _ColQ_, 18 (Spring 1970), 370-378.
   Discusses _A Fable_ as it reveals Faulkner's ideas about war.

Sanderlin, Robert R. "_As I Lay Dying_: Christian Symbols and Thematic Implications." _So Quart_, 7 (January 1969), 155-166.
   Allusions and symbols from the Old and New Testaments enrich the account of a family's coming to terms with the realities of life and death.

Sanderson, J. L. "'Spotted Horses' and the Theme of Social Evil." _EJ_, 57 (May 1968), 700-704.
   In their destructiveness the horses may be seen as an element of social evil with Flem Snopes as exploiter.

Schlepper, Wolfgang. "Knowledge and Experience in Faulkner's _Light in August_." _Jahrbuch für Amerikastudien_, 18 (1973), 182-194.
   Deals with Faulkner's use of the verbs _know_, _believe_, and _remember_ in Chapter 6 of the novel.

Scholes, Robert. See MISCELLANEOUS (Contemporary).

Schmitter, Dean M., ed. _William Faulkner: A Collection of Criticism_. New York: McGraw-Hill, 1973.
   Reprints thirteen essays and excerpts with an introduction by the editor and a brief annotated bibliography.

Schmuhl, Robert. "Faulkner's _Sanctuary_: The Last Laugh of Innocence." _Notes on Miss Writers_, 6 (Winter 1974), 73-80.
   Analyzes Tommy's role in the novel.

Schrank, Bernice. "Patterns of Reversal in _Absalom, Absalom!_" _Dal Rev_, 54 (Winter 1974-75), 648-666.
   Attempts to connect Sutpen and the narrators in the novel by showing how the two are joined by "interlocking patterns of reversal."

Schrero, Elliot M. "_Another Country_ and the Sense of Self." _Black Acad Rev_, 2 (Spring-Summer 1971), 91-100.
   Compares Faulkner's _Absalom, Absalom!_ with Baldwin's _Another Country_.

Schwartz, Delmore. See MISCELLANEOUS (Contemporary).

Seltzer, Leon F. "Narrative Function Vs. Psychopathology: The Problem of Darl in _As I Lay Dying_." _Lit and Psych_, 25, no. 2 (1975), 49-64.
   A major flaw is the psychological inaccuracy of Darl's characterization since he does not fit the description of a schizoid.

Seyppel, Joachim. _William Faulkner_. Modern Literature Monograph. New York: Frederick Ungar, 1971.
   A brief introduction to Faulkner's work with emphasis on the theme of the _hermaphrodite_; translated from the German by the author.

Shepherd, Allen. "Code and Comedy in Faulkner's _The Reivers_." _LWU_, 6 (March 1973), 43-51.
   On comedy and ideas in the novel.

_____. "Hemingway's 'An Alpine Idyll' and Faulkner's 'Mistral.'" _Univ of Portland Rev_, 25 (Fall 1973), 63-68.
   Similarities between the two stories suggest that Faulkner was influenced by the Hemingway story.

Shimura, Masao. See BARTH, JOHN (Contemporary).

Showett, H. K. "Faulkner and Scott: Addendum." _Miss Quart_, 22 (Spring 1969), 152-153.
   Further clarification of a literary allusion in _The Hamlet_.

Simpson, H. A. "Yoknapatawpha: Faulkner's 'Little Postage Stamp of Native Soil.'" _Notes on Miss Writers_, 3 (Spring 1970), 43-47.
   An essay-review of Elizabeth M. Kerr's book of the same name (1969).

Simpson, Lewis P. "Faulkner and the Southern Symbolism of Pastoral." _Miss Quart_, 28 (Fall 1975), 401-415.
   Faulkner realized that "great art is not a counter to the ruthlessness of history but an expression of it," and he therefore "rejected the pastoral mode."

_____. "The Loneliness of William Faulkner." _So Lit Jour_, 8 (Fall 1975), 126-143.
   An essay-review of Blotner's _Faulkner: A Biography_, which finds the work a lengthy, highly detailed, and completely frank biography of Faulkner, written with an even hand and a sense of responsibility to the subject.

_____. See MISCELLANEOUS (Contemporary--1st Simpson entry).

Skaggs, Merrill M. See GENERAL.

Skerry, Philip J. See CLEMENS, SAMUEL LANGHORNE (Postbellum).

Smith, Beverly E. "A Note on Faulkner's 'Greenbury Hotel.'" _Miss Quart_, 24 (Summer 1971), 297-298.
   The Greenbury Hotel is modeled on the Peabody Hotel in Memphis.

Smith, Gerald J. "Medicine Made Palatable: An Aspect of Humor in _The Reivers_." _Notes on Miss Writers_, 8 (Fall 1975), 58-62.
   Points out similarities among Otis of _The Reivers_, Jason Compson, and Flem Snopes.

_____. "A Note on the Origin of Flem Snopes."
Notes on Miss Writers, 6 (Fall 1973), 56-57.
Finds a partial origin in John Scopes, syn-
onymous with the scientific method of proving
everything.

Smith, Julian. "A Source for Faulkner's *A Fable*."
AL, 40 (November 1968), 394-397.
Considers similarities of plot, some
important characters, and minor details of
Humphrey Cobb's *Paths of Glory* (1935) and
Faulkner's *A Fable*.

Smith, Raleigh W., Jr. "Faulkner's 'Victory': The
Plain People of Clydebank." *Miss Quart*, 23
(Summer 1970), 241-249.
Alec Gray of this story fails because of
pride that causes him to reject his family
ties.

Solomon, Eric. "From Christ in Flanders to
Catch-22: An Approach to War Fiction."
Texas Stud in Lit and Lang, 11 (Spring 1969),
851-866.
Includes a discussion of *A Fable*.

Sorenson, Dale A. "Structure in William Faulkner's
Sartoris: The Contrast Between Psychological
and Natural Time." *ArQ*, 24 (Autumn 1969),
263-270.
A structural analysis of *Sartoris* showing
Faulkner's manipulation of time images in
Bayard Sartoris' mind.

Spears, James E. "William Faulkner, Folklorist:
A Note." *TFSB*, 38 (December 1972), 95-96.
Deals with folklore in *Sartoris*.

Spilka, Mark. "Quentin Compson's Universal Grief."
ConL, 11 (Autumn 1970), 451-469.
A detailed examination of Quentin's role in
The Sound and the Fury. For him, unlike for
Jason, "there remains the possibility of
significant defeat, in which things of value
are lost...he grieves--and makes us grieve--
on universal bones...."

Spivey, Herman E. "Faulkner and the Adamic Myth:
Faulkner's Moral Vision." *MFS*, 19
(Winter 1973-74), 497-505.
Maintains that Faulkner did not subscribe to
the popular vision of the Adamic man but that
he did subscribe to an aspect of it--"lonely
man occasionally achieving strength and maturity
through contact with evil."

Stafford, T. J. "Tobe's Significance in 'A Rose
for Emily.'" *MFS*, 14 (Winter 1968-69), 451-453.
Stresses the contrast between Tobe and
Miss Emily.

Stafford, William T. "Hemingway/Faulkner: Marlin
and Catfish?" *SouR*, 6 (Autumn 1970), 1191-1200.
An essay-review of two Hemingway studies plus
Richard P. Adams' *Faulkner: Myth and Motion* and
Elizabeth M. Kerr's *Yoknapatawpha: Faulkner's
"Little Postage Stamp of Native Soil."*

_____. "'Some Homer of the Cotton Fields':
Faulkner's Use of the Mule Early and Late
(*Sartoris* and *The Reivers*)." *Papers on Lang
and Lit*, 5 (1969), 190-196.

Discusses the significance of Faulkner's
praise of the mule in relation to the central
themes of the novels.

Stanzel, Franz. See MISCELLANEOUS (Contemporary).

Stark, John. "The Implications for Stylistics of
Strawson's 'On Referring,' with *Absalom, Absalom!*
as an Example." *Lang and Style*, 6 (Fall 1973),
273-280.
Strawson's distinction between expressions
that describe and those that refer provide insight into this novel of Faulkner's.

Steinbeck, Elaine. See MISCELLANEOUS (Contemporary).

Stephens, Rosemary. "Ike's Gun and Too Many
Novembers." *Miss Quart*, 23 (Summer 1970),
279-287.
Confusing references to dates in "The Bear"
are clarified by a chronological table.

_____. "Mythical Elements of 'Pantaloon in Black.'"
Univ of Miss Stud in Eng, 11 (1970), 45-51.
Archetypes in this story point to deeper
meanings and a deliberate use of mythical
elements.

Sternberg, Meir. "The Compositional Principles of
Faulkner's *Light in August* and the Poetics of
the Modern Novel." *Hasifrut*, 2 (1970),
498-537. (In Hebrew, with English summary.)
A study of structure in relation to theme.

Stevens, Lauren R. "*Sartoris*: Germ of the
Apocalypse." *Dal Rev*, 49 (Spring 1969), 80-87.
Offers the belief that Faulkner saw in the
book the germ of his prophetic revelation.
Stevens thinks that Faulkner probably meant
apocalypse, not *apocrypha*, when talking about
Sartoris.

Stewart, Jack F. "Apotheosis and Apocalypse in
Faulkner's 'Wash.'" *Stud SF*, 6 (Fall 1969),
586-600.
Characterizing images establish the "contrasting social-psychic tensions that lead to
violence," and four "visionary scenes contrast
with the squalid background." Three of these
scenes concern the apotheosis of Sutpen; the
fourth involves Wash's transfiguration as
apocalyptic avenger.

Stewart, Randall. See GENERAL.

Stone, Edward. See GENERAL.

Stone, William B. "Ike McCaslin and the Grecian
Urn." *Stud SF*, 10 (Winter 1973), 93-94.
"Parallels and contrasts between the Keats
poem and the Faulkner stories support the view
that Ike was viewed ambivalently and somewhat
ironically by his author."

Stoneback, H. R. "Faulkner's Blues: 'Pantaloon in
Black.'" *MFS*, 21 (Summer 1975), 241-245.
Finds the source of the story in an "old
Southern black and white country blues song"--
"I Know You Rider" and "Easy Rider."

IV. Contemporary (1920-1975)

Strandberg, Victor. "Between Truth and Fact: Faulkner's Symbols of Identity." *MFS*, 21 (Autumn 1975), 445-457.
    The conflict between the truth and the facts is "typically the essence of the predicament of Faulkner's characters."

Straumann, Heinrich. *William Faulkner*. Frankfurt am Main/Bonn: Athenaum Verlag, 1968.
    The first full-length critical survey of Faulkner's life, works, and foreign reputation to appear in German.

Stronks, James. See POE, EDGAR ALLAN (Antebellum).

Sugg, Redding S., Jr. See FAULKNER, JOHN.

Sullivan, Ruth. "The Narrator in 'A Rose for Emily.'" *Jour of Narrative Tech*, 1 (September 1971), 159-178.
    The narrator is a voyeur who, after Emily's death, wishes to preserve her in story-form.

Sullivan, Walter. See MISCELLANEOUS (Contemporary--1st Sullivan entry).

Swanson, William J. See STYRON, WILLIAM (Contemporary--1st Swanson entry).

Swink, Helen. "William Faulkner: The Novelist as Oral Narrator." *GaR*, 26 (Summer 1972), 183-209.
    Faulkner's style "is basically rooted in the spoken word. He constantly attempts to recreate in the novelist-reader relationship the experience that exists between the storyteller and listener."

Tate, Allen. "Faulkner's *Sanctuary* and the Southern Myth." *VQR*, 44 (Summer 1968), 418-427.
    After a brief sketch of the rise of the Southern myth, Tate relates *Sanctuary* to certain aspects of the myth.

Taylor, Walter. "Faulkner: Social Commitment and Artistic Temperament." *SouR*, 6 (Autumn 1970), 1075-1092.
    A presentation and analysis of the various positions in Faulkner's public statements about Negroes.

_____. "Faulkner's Curse." *ArQ*, 28 (Winter 1972), 333-338.
    Examines the curse in *Absalom, Absalom!*, *Go Down, Moses*, *The Sound and the Fury*, and concludes that "the curse is slavery."

_____. "Faulkner's Pantaloon: The Negro Anomaly at the Heart of *Go Down, Moses*." *AL*, 44 (November 1972), 430-444.
    A study of Faulkner's treatment of blacks in *Go Down, Moses*.

_____. "Horror and Nostalgia: The Double Perspective of Faulkner's 'Was.'" *SHR*, 8 (Winter 1974), 74-84.
    "Was" evokes "the presentness of the past through the simultaneous application of the tragic and comic moods."

Terrier, Michel. See MISCELLANEOUS (Contemporary).

Thornton, Weldon. "A Note on the Source of Faulkner's Jason." *Stud in the Novel*, 1 (Fall 1969), 370-372.
    Suggests as a source the high priest Jason in the second book of *Maccabees* in the *Apocrypha*.

_____. "Structure and Theme in Faulkner's *Go Down, Moses*." *Costerus*, 3 (1975), 73-112.
    Sees the structure of the novel as primarily based upon "the complex thematic interrelationship of apparently separate stories...hinted by specific objects and events which recur in thematically related situations.

Tobin, Patricia. "The Time of Myth and History in *Absalom, Absalom!*" *AL*, 45 (May 1973), 252-270.
    Studies Faulkner's temporal, mythological and historical vision in the light of the synchronic and the diachronic.

Travis, Mildred K. "Echoes of *Pierre* in *The Reivers*." *NConL*, 3, no. 2 (1973), 11-13.
    Title is descriptive.

Trimmer, Joseph F. "*The Unvanquished*: The Teller and the Tale." *BSUF*, 10 (Winter 1969), 35-42.
    The limitations of Bayard's romantic outlook reveal "the human heart in conflict with itself."

_____. "V. K. Ratliff: A Portrait of the Artist in Motion." *MFS*, 20 (Winter 1974-1975), 451-467.
    Ratliff's "major contribution [in Faulkner's trilogy] is not heroic action but aesthetic creation"; his role is "symbolic of Faulkner's conception of the role of the artist."

Tucker, Edward L. "Faulkner's Drusilla and Ibsen's Hedda." *Mod Drama*, 16 (September 1973), 157-161.
    A comparison of Drusilla and Hedda finds many similarities between these two "complex" women.

Turner, Arlin. "William Faulkner and the Literary Flowering in the American South." *Durham Univ Jour*, 29 (March 1968), 109-118.
    Based upon a lecture given at the University of Durham, England, in January 1967. Deals with Faulkner's picture of the South.

_____. "William Faulkner: The Growth and Survival of a Legend--A Review Essay." *SHR*, 9 (Winter 1975), 91-97.
    Blotner's *Faulkner: A Biography* "amply justifies the scope, the plan, and the method of presentation chosen for it."

Tuso, Joseph F. "Faulkner's 'Wash.'" *Expl*, 27 (November 1968), Item 17.
    The mare Griselda's role as a foil for the young mother, Milly, is pointed up by the mare's name.

Tyner, Troi. "The Function of the Bear Ritual in Faulkner's *Go Down, Moses*." *Jour of the Ohio Folklore Soc*, 3 (1968), 19-40.
    Points out parallels with Thorpe's "Big Bear of Arkansas" and surmises that the novel emphasizes the white man's corruption of the black man.

Ulich, Michaela. *Perspektive und Erzählstruktur in William Faulkners Romanen von "The Sound and the Fury" bis "Intruder in the Dust." (Beihefte zum Jahrbuch für Amerika-Studien)*. Heidelberg: Carl Winter, 1972.
   Deals with point of view in the two novels mentioned in the title and in *As I Lay Dying, Absalom, Absalom!* and "The Bear."

Umphlett, Wiley Lee. See MISCELLANEOUS (Contemporary).

U. S. Military Academy Library Occasional Papers, no. 2 (1974).
   An issue devoted to Faulkner, including Albert Erskine on Faulkner and Random House, and "selective listing" of Faulkner materials at the Academy.

Utley, Francis L., Lynn Z. Bloom, and Arthur F. Kinney, eds. *Bear, Man, and God: Eight Approaches to William Faulkner's "The Bear."* New York: Random House, 1971.
   A revision of a casebook, with many deletions from the first edition and more than twenty-five added essays and excerpts.

Van Cromphout, Gustaav V. "Faulkner: Myth and Motion." *ES*, 53 (December 1972), 572-574.
   An essay-review of Richard P. Adams' *Faulkner: Myth and Motion*.

Vande Kieft, Ruth M. "Faulkner's Defeat of Time in *Absalom, Absalom!*" *SouR*, 6 (Autumn 1970), 1100-1109.
   A study of the theme of time and point of view in the novel.

Vickery, John B., and Olga W., eds. *Light in August and the Critical Spectrum*. Belmont, Calif.: Wadsworth Publishing, 1971.
   A casebook reprinting two background excerpts, fifteen critical essays, with a chronology, study questions, and a selective bibliography by the editors.

Vinson, Audrey L. "Miscegenation and Its Meaning in *Go Down, Moses*." *CLA Jour*, 14 (December 1970), 143-155.
   Faulkner created tableaux that "render meaning to his miscegenation theme," which was "too volatile, too close to ultimate truth about humanity" for him to approach directly.

Volpe, Edmond L. "Faulkner's 'Red Leaves': The Deciduation of Nature." *Stud in Am F*, 3 (Autumn 1975), 121-131.
   In this story, Faulkner presents "a vision of the inexorable brutal pattern of nature which decrees that every living thing...must die."

Vorpahl, Ben M. "Moonlight at Ballenbaugh's: Time and Imagination in *The Reivers*." *So Lit Jour*, 1 (Spring 1969), 3-26.
   The Reivers is important for its method, its framework, its fundamental incident, and its "implicit statement about the relationship between time and an individual consciousness."

Voss, Arthur. See GENERAL.

Waggoner, Hyatt H. "Faulkner's Critics." *Novel*, 3 (Fall 1969), 94-96.
   An essay-review of *Faulkner: Myth and Motion*, by Richard P. Adams, and of *Faulkner's Olympian Laugh: Myth in the Novels*, by Walter Brylowski, both of which Waggoner finds "well written, persuasive, with many fresh insights."

_____. "Hemingway and Faulkner: 'The End of Something.'" *SouR*, 4 (Spring 1968), 458-466.
   An essay-review of a large collection of volumes about Hemingway and Faulkner.

_____. "The Historical Novel and the Southern Past: The Case of *Absalom, Absalom!*" *So Lit Jour*, 2 (Spring 1970), 69-85.
   Although *Absalom, Absalom!* "upsets our received notions of both 'history' as an academic discipline and the 'historical novel' as a literary genre," it is "the product of an imagination profoundly aware of and concerned with the past."

Wagner, Linda W. "*As I Lay Dying*. Faulkner's All in the Family." *Coll Lit*, 1 (1974), 73-82.
   Deals with the ways character is revealed in the novel.

_____. "Faulkner's Fiction: Studies in Organic Form." *Jour of Narrative Tech*, 1 (January 1971), 1-14.
   Faulkner's novels are structured according to his belief that every novel has its own shape.

_____. *Hemingway and Faulkner: inventors/masters*. Metuchen, N. J.: Scarecrow Press, 1975.
   A comparative study of technique and theme in the two writers, with attention to their major novels and some short fiction.

_____. "Jason Compson: The Demands of Honor." *SR*, 79 (Autumn 1971), 554-575.
   Jason Compson IV is a tragic figure because "he is faced with tragedy which he can't beat and he still tries to do something with it."

_____, ed. *William Faulkner: Four Decades of Criticism*. East Lansing: Michigan State Univ Press, 1973.
   A revision of Hoffman and Vickery's *Three Decades of Criticism* (1960) which retains nine of the original twenty-two essays and adds sixteen new pieces and an index.

Walcutt, Charles C., and J. E. Whitesell. See GENERAL.

Walhout, Clarence P. "'The Earth is the Lord's': Religion in Faulkner." *Chri Schol Rev*, 4 (1974), 26-35.
   In Faulkner's works a relationship with God is a matter of one's relationship with nature and society.

Walker, Marshall. See WARREN, ROBERT PENN (Contemporary--1st Walker entry).

Walker, Ronald G. "Death in the Sound of Their Name: Character Motivation in Faulkner's *Sartoris*." *SHR*, 7 (Summer 1973), 271-278.
   Concerned with the "perils of mythologizing the Southern experience and the malaise and

sterility of Western man after the First World
War," *Sartoris* "is closer in tone and theme to
the great novels of the early 1930's" than to
Soldiers' Pay or *Mosquitoes*.

Wall, Carey. "Drama and Technique in Faulkner's
The Hamlet." *TCL*, 14 (April 1968), 17-23.
Thematic criticism can explain only the
realm of Faulkner's "public" vision; it is
another realm, that of his private vision,
that enables us fully to comprehend *The Hamlet*.

_____. "*The Sound and the Fury*: The Emotional
Center." *Midwest Quart*, 11 (Summer 1970),
371-387.
Deals with the significance of the style
of the monologues in the novel.

Walter, James. "Expiation and History: Ike
McCaslin and the Mystery of Providence." *La
Stud*, 10 (Winter 1971), 263-273.
Ike is one of Faulkner's characters whose
redemption grows out of his trust in his own
strength and in God's sustaining presence.

Walton, Gerald W. "Some Southern Farm Terms in
Faulkner's *Go Down, Moses*." *Pub of Am Dialect
Soc*, 47 (April 1967), 23-29.
Defines twenty-two farm terms found in *Go
Down, Moses* not listed in collegiate
dictionaries.

_____. "Tennie's Jim and Lucas Beauchamp." *Am N&Q*,
8 (October 1969), 23-24.
Lucas Beauchamp is the youngest brother of
Jim Beauchamp and not Jim's son, as incorrectly
stated in a footnote to "The Bear" in the latest
revised edition of *The American Tradition in
Literature*.

_____. "A Word List of Southern Farm Terms From
Faulkner's *The Hamlet*." *MFR*, 6 (1972), 60-75.
Lists and defines farm terms Faulkner used
in this novel and concludes that he used them
accurately.

Warren, Joyce W. "The Role of Lion in Faulkner's
'The Bear': Key to a Better Understanding."
ArQ, 24 (1968), 252-260.
Argues that only by seeing Lion as part of,
not in contradiction to, the awe-inspiring
spectacle of nature can one understand the
significance of the last bear hunt for Ike
McCaslin, who glimpses through the struggle of
Lion and Old Ben the eternal majesty of nature.

Watkins, Floyd C. "Faulkner and His Critics."
Tex Stud in Lit and Lang, 10 (Summer 1968),
317-329.
A survey of errors in Faulkner criticism.

_____. "Faulkner, Faulkner, Faulkner." *SR*, 82
(Summer 1974), 518-527.
A review of Blotner's *Faulkner: A Biography*
which finds it not an example of biography
as an art form but an exhaustive, encyclopedic
work which makes major contributions to the
understanding of the man and his writings.

_____. *The Flesh and the Word: Eliot, Hemingway,
Faulkner*. Nashville: Vanderbilt Univ Press,
1971.

Like Eliot and Hemingway, Faulkner moved
from objectiveness to abstraction, from image
and art to overt preachment, and thereby im-
paired the artistic quality of the later works.

_____. See MISCELLANEOUS (Contemporary).

Watson, James G. "'The Germ of My Apocrypha':
Sartoris and the Search for Form." *Mosaic*, 7
(Fall 1973), 15-33.
In this novel, it is not a post-war waste
land but the past that dominates and results in
stasis rather than motion for Bayard and Horace;
the birth of Benbow Sartoris may well represent
the rebirth of motion.

_____. *The Snopes Dilemma: Faulkner's Trilogy*.
Coral Gables, Fla.: Univ of Miami Press, 1970.
The recurring conflict between morality and
amorality in Faulkner's work provides a thematic
unity and structural cohesiveness to the triology.

Webb, James W. "A Review of *Yoknapatawpha:
Faulkner's 'Little Postage Stamp of Native Soil,'*
by Elizabeth M. Kerr." *SAQ*, 66 (Spring 1970),
300-301.
Webb says that Kerr gives signposts that will
enable Faulkner readers to make their way through
Yoknapatawpha County and gain greater insight
into Faulkner's writing.

Weber, Robert W. *Die Aussage der Form: Zur Textur
und Struktur des Bewusstseinsromans. Dargestellt
an W. Faulkners The Sound and the Fury*.
Heidelberg: Carl Winter, 1969.
Discusses the importance of form in *The Sound
and the Fury*.

Wegelin, Christof. "'Endure' and 'Prevail':
Faulkner's Modification of Conrad." *N&Q*, 21
(October 1974), 375-376.
Briefly discusses Faulkner's Nobel Prize
Speech and *A Fable* and contrasts the views of
Faulkner and Conrad on the question of whether
man will prevail.

Weinstein, Arnold L. *Vision and Response in Modern
Fiction*. Ithaca, New York: Cornell Univ Press,
1974.
Includes discussion of *The Sound and the Fury*
and *Absalom, Absalom!*

Weisgerber, Jean. *Faulkner et Dostoievski: Confluences et influences*. Travaux de la Faculté
de Philosophie et Lettres Tome XXXIX.
Bruxelles: Presses Universitaires de
Bruxelles, 1968.
A detailed analysis of the possible influences of Dostoievski on Faulkner and the confluences of their art and thought. (English
translation by Dean McWilliams. Athens: Ohio
Univ Press, 1974.)

_____. "Faulkner's Monomaniacs: Their Indebtedness
to Raskolnikov." *CLS*, 5 (June 1968), 181-193.
Some of Faulkner's characters are more
indebted to Dostoevsky than is readily apparent.

Weiss, Miriam. "Hell Creek Bottom Is: A Reminis-
cence." *JMiH*, 30 (August 1968), 196-201.
The Hell Creek Bottom that appears in
Faulkner's *The Reivers* is a real place.

West, Ray B., Jr. See MISCELLANEOUS
(Contemporary).

Wheeler, Sally P. "Chronology in *Light in August*."
So Lit Jour, 6 (Fall 1973), 20-42.
A complete chronology of the novel to help
order details and to provide insight and a
deeper understanding of the novel.

Wigley, Joseph A. "Imagery and the Interpreter,"
in *Studies in Interpretation*, ed. Esther M.
Doyle and Virginia Hastings Floyd. Amsterdam:
Rodopi NV, 1972.
A study of how Faulkner accomplishes his
purpose in *Absalom, Absalom!* "by painstaking
accumulation of images in several interwoven
patterns...."

Williams, John S. "The Final Copper Light of
Afternoon: Hightower's Redemption." *TCL*, 13
(January 1968), 205-215.
Hightower's redemption is "the movement
beyond despair and bondage to the past to joy
and openness to the future." His presence in
the novel adds depth and richness to several
layers of meaning.

Williams, Ora G. "The Theme of Endurance in *As I
Lay Dying*." *La Stud*, 9 (Summer 1970), 100-104.
The theme of endurance is one of the sig-
nificant themes in all of Faulkner's works.

Willingham, Calder. See CALDWELL, ERSKINE
(Contemporary).

Wilson, Gayle E. "'*Being Pulled Two Ways*': The
Nature of Sarty's Choice in 'Barn Burning.'"
Miss Quart, 24 (Summer 1971), 279-288.
The boy turns from the lawlessness of his
father to the law-abiding life of the
community.

Wilson, G. R., Jr. "The Chronology of Faulkner's
'A Rose for Emily' Again." *Notes on Miss
Writers*, 5 (Fall 1972), 44, 56, 58-62.
A postulation of a new chronology for the
story's events (1862-1936).

Wilson, Mary Ann. "Search for an Eternal Present:
Absalom, Absalom! and *All the King's Men*."
Conn Rev, 8 (October 1974), 95-100.
Compares Bergsonian concepts of time in the
two novels.

Wilson, Robert R. "The Pattern of Thought in
Light in August." *Rocky Mt MLA Bul*, 24
(December 1970), 155-161.
On the act of remembering in the novel.

Winn, James A. "Faulkner's Revisions: A Stylist
at Work." *AL*, 41 (May 1969), 231-250.
Discusses Faulkner's MS revisions.

Woodbery, Potter. "Faulkner's Numismatics: A Note
on *As I Lay Dying*." *Research Stud*, 39
(June 1971), 150-151.
Deals with the buffalo nickel to which Darl
refers.

Woodress, James. See GENERAL--1st three Woodress
entries.

Woodward, C. Vann. See MISCELLANEOUS (Contemporary).

Woodward, Robert H. "Robert Jordan's Wedding/
Funeral Sermon." *Hemingway Notes*, 2
(Spring 1972), 7-8.
Disputes George Monteiro's conclusion that
the ending of *For Whom the Bell Tolls* is bor-
rowed from the title portion of *The Wild Palms*.

Yonce, Margaret. "Faulkner's 'Atthis' and 'Attis':
Some Sources of Myth." *Miss Quart*, 23
(Summer 1970), 289-298.
Discusses the ways the myth of Attis, a
vegetation deity, is echoed in *The Hamlet* and
elsewhere in Faulkner.

Young, Glenn. "Struggle and Triumph in *Light in
August*." *Stud in the Twentieth Cent*, 15
(Spring 1975), 33-50.
The causes, effects, and organizing energies
of the fire of the Burdens' house are the sym-
bolic unifying element in this diverse book.

Young, Thomas Daniel, and Ronald E. Fine. See
MISCELLANEOUS (Contemporary).

Zellegrow, Ken. "Faulkner's Flying Tales--a View
of the Past." *Descant*, 16 (Summer 1972), 42-48.
Faulkner's war-time pilots are doomed,
courageous, and alienated.

Zender, Karl F. "A Hand of Poker: Game and Ritual
in Faulkner's 'Was.'" *Stud SF*, 11 (Winter 1974),
53-60.
The denouement of "Was," exhibiting "clearly
and compactly the dual formal requirements of
games and of rituals," is "tipped in favor of
ritual."

Zindel, Edith. *William Faulkner in den
deutschsprachigen Ländern Europas: Untersuchungen
zur Aufnahme seiner Werke nach 1945*. Hamburg:
Hartmut Lüdke, 1973.
The first full-length study of Faulkner's
reception in the German-speaking countries of
Europe.

Zyla, W. T., and W. M. Aycock, eds. *William
Faulkner: Prevailing Verities and World
Literature*. Proceedings of the Comparative
Literature Symposium, Vol. VI. Lubbock: Texas
Tech Univ, 1973.
Essays by Percy G. Adams on Faulkner and
French literature, Necla Aytür on the Turkish
response to Faulkner's writings, Cleanth Brooks
on the British reception of Faulkner's works,
Calvin S. Brown on Dilsey in comparison to other
servants in literature, Glauco Cambon on trans-
lating *Absalom, Absalom!*, Mary Sue Carlock on
Faulkner's view of motion, Gerald Langford on
Faulkner materials at the University of Texas,
and David H. Stewart on Faulkner, Sholokhov,
and regionalism.

_____, and _____, eds. See MISCELLANEOUS
(Contemporary).

[FITZGERALD, ZELDA SAYRE] Anon. "Putting Zelda
Back Centre of Stage." *TLS*, no. 3,592
(January 1, 1971), 8.

IV. Contemporary (1920-1975)

An essay-review of Nancy Milford's *Zelda: A Biography* that maintains that Zelda belonged centre of stage.

Bruccoli, Matthew J., et al. "Scott and Zelda: An Excerpt from a Pictorial Autobiography." *AH*, 25 (October 1974), 4-13.
> The article contains excerpts from the book published later.

_____, and Jennifer M. Atkinson, eds. *As Ever, Scott Fitz--Letters Between F. S. Fitzgerald and His Literary Agent Harold Ober, 1919-1940.* Philadelphia: Lippincott, 1972.
> Extensive references are made to the life and writings of Zelda Fitzgerald.

Going, William T. "Two Alabama Writers: Zelda Sayre Fitzgerald and Sara Haardt Mencken." *AlaR*, 23 (January 1970), 3-29.
> An extensive analysis of the writings and relationships of the wives of two famous husbands.

Hardwick, Elizabeth. *Seduction and Betrayal: Women and Literature*. New York: Random House, 1974.
> Zelda Fitzgerald is discussed in a chapter entitled "Victims."

Ludington, Townsend. See MISCELLANEOUS (Contemporary).

Milford, Nancy. *Zelda, A Biography*. New York: Harper and Row, 1970.
> A detailed biography.

Samuels, C. T. "A Woman's Place." *New Rep*, 162 (June 27, 1970), 24-27.
> An essay-review of *Zelda*, by Nancy Milford, which says that this book illuminates Zelda's fiction and points out that Fitzgerald's idea that women should know their place contradicts his apparent love for them.

[FLETCHER, JOHN GOULD] Behrens, Ralph. "John Gould Fletcher, Poet of Paradoxes." *Ark Lib*, 28 (Summer 1971), 9-13.
> Offers the author's personal recollections of Fletcher as well as an appreciation of his poetry.

Bridgewater, Patrick. *Nietzsche in Anglosaxony: A Study of Nietzsche's Impact on English and American Literature*. Leicester Univ Press, 1972. U. S. distribution Atlantic Highlands, N. J.: Humanities Press.
> The influence of Nietzsche's thought on Fletcher is discussed.

Carter, A. H. *Reading Recent American Literature*. Frankfurt am Main: Verlag Moritz Diesterweg, 1967.
> Includes a chapter explicating two poems by Fletcher, "The Skaters" and "Lincoln."

Lund, Mary G. "John Gould Fletcher, Geographer of the Uncharted Province of Beauty." *SR*, 76 (Winter 1968), 76-89.
> Fletcher's changing concepts of beauty, his concern with color, wind, and music are revealed in his *Selected Poems* (1938).

[FOOTE, SHELBY] Carr, John. See MISCELLANEOUS (Contemporary).

Garrett, George. "Foote's *The Civil War*: The Version for Posterity?" *Miss Quart*, 28 (Winter 1974-75), 83-92.
> An essay-review of *The Civil War: A Narrative*, Vol. III.

_____, ed. "Talking with Shelby Foote--June 1970." *Miss Quart*, 24 (Fall 1971), 405-427.
> A transcription of John Graham's interview with Foote at the Hollins College Conference on Creative Writing.

Graham, John, and George Garrett. See MISCELLANEOUS (Contemporary).

Harrington, Evans. "Interview with Shelby Foote." *Miss Quart*, 24 (Fall 1971), 349-377.
> Foote talks about influences on his work (Faulkner, Proust, James, Hemingway), his writing technique, and comments on contemporary American writers.

Howell, Elmo. See MISCELLANEOUS (Contemporary).

Kibler, James E., Jr. "Shelby Foote: A Bibliography." *Miss Quart*, 24 (Fall 1971), 437-465.
> Annotation of a list of Foote's works and a selective checklist of works about Foote.

Landess, Thomas H. "Southern History and Manhood: Major Themes in the Works of Shelby Foote." *Miss Quart*, 24 (Fall 1971), 321-347.
> Foote's work portrays the South's historical consciousness from the beginning of self-awareness to the flowering of self-analysis; his rebellion against the mythology of the region and his construction of his own "antimyth" create the tension necessary to the best literature.

Salzman, Jack. See GENERAL.

Shepherd, Allen. "Technique and Theme in Shelby Foote's *Shiloh*." *Notes on Miss Writers*, 5 (Spring 1972), 3-10.
> Shepherd admires the novel's authenticity and accurate military history but is even more impressed with Foote's insight into human nature.

Vauthier, Simone. "Fiction and Fictions in Shelby Foote's 'Rain Down Home.'" *Notes on Miss Writers*, 8 (Fall 1975), 35-50.
> Argues that the end of the short story causes the reader to reconsider the relationship of fiction to reality.

_____. "The Symmetrical Design: The Structural Patterns of *Love in a Dry Season*." *Miss Quart* 24 (Fall 1971), 379-403.
> The triadic structure is integral to the novel and enhances the theme and narrative method on several levels.

Williams, Wirt. "Shelby Foote's *Civil War*: The Novelist as Humanistic Historian." *Miss Quart*, 24 (Fall 1971), 429-436.
> Foote "has merged the methods of responsible historiography with the vivid resources of the

art of the novelist" to produce "one of our most literally pleasing histories."

[FORD, JESSE HILL] Carr, John. See MISCELLANEOUS (Contemporary).

Ford, Jesse Hill. "The Journal of the Plague Trip." *Delta Rev*, 7 (May/June 1970), 56, 58.
   A humorous account of Ford's trip to London during which he was plagued by the flu.

_____. "Let's Take an Old Fashioned Walk." *Delta Rev*, 7 (Fall 1970), 7-8.
   This is an anecdotal account of some of the problems, including the way the star walks, in making a movie and the experience of seeing oneself in the movies.

_____. "Slaving in California." *Delta Rev*, 5 (November 1968), 20.
   Ford relates his experiences in the West while working on the screenplay for *The Liberation of Lord Byron Jones*.

_____. "A Southern Notebook." *Delta Rev*, 5 (February 1968), 48-49.
   Ford's impressions of Southern farmers, "America in microcosm."

_____. "To a Young Southern Writer." *SouR*, 4 (Spring 1968), 291-298.
   Ford's comments about the contemporary Southern writer, and about the meaning of his past and present condition.

Landess, Thomas H. See MISCELLANEOUS (Contemporary).

Madden, David. See MISCELLANEOUS (Contemporary 2nd Madden entry).

Matthews, Jack. "What Are You Doing There? What Are You Doing Here? A View of the Jesse Hill Ford Case." *GaR*, 26 (Summer 1972), 121-144.
   Matthews finds a "principle of territoriality" motivating events surrounding the Ford case.

Magill, Frank N. See MISCELLANEOUS (Contemporary).

Watkins, Floyd C. See MISCELLANEOUS (Contemporary).

Weales, Gerald. See MISCELLANEOUS (Contemporary).

White, Helen. *Jesse Hill Ford: An Annotated Check List of Published Works and of His Papers*. Memphis, Tenn.: Memphis State Univ, 1974.
   Accounts for all published works and manuscripts deposited in the John Willard Brister Library at Memphis State; a special issue of the *Mississippi Valley Bul*, no. 7 (Spring 1974).

[GAINES, ERNEST J.] Billingsley, R. G. See MISCELLANEOUS (Contemporary).

Bryant, Jerry H. "Ernest J. Gaines: Change, Growth, and History." *SouR*, 10 (Autumn 1974), 851-864.
   Surveys Gaines's fiction, with the most space devoted to study of the character of Miss Jane Pittman.

_____. "*From Death to Life*: The Fiction of Ernest J. Gaines." *Iowa Rev*, 3, no. 1 (1972), 106-120.
   A general evaluation of Gaines's work, praising the "depth, humanity, and honesty."

Fenderson, Lewis H. See MISCELLANEOUS (Contemporary).

Hill, Mildred A. See GENERAL.

Ingram, Forrest, and Barbara Steinberg. "On the Verge: An Interview with Ernest J. Gaines." *New Orleans Rev*, 3, no. 4 (1973), 339-344.
   Questions and answers on typical interview subjects.

Jaskoski, Helen. See GENERAL.

Kent, George. "Struggle for the Image: Selected Books by or About Blacks During 1971." *Phylon*, 33 (Winter 1972), 304-323.
   An essay-review of a number of books, which calls Gaines's *Miss Jane Pittman* "outstanding."

Laney, Ruth. "A Conversation with Ernest Gaines." *SouR*, 10 (Winter 1974), 1-14.
   Questions and answers on typical interview topics.

McDonald, Walter R. "'You Not a Bum, You a Man': Ernest J. Gaines's *Bloodline*." *NALF*, 9 (Summer 1975), 47-49.
   On the unity of setting and theme in this work.

O'Brien, John. See MISCELLANEOUS (Contemporary--2nd O'Brien entry).

Peden, William. See MISCELLANEOUS (Contemporary--2nd Peden entry).

Petesch, Donald. See MISCELLANEOUS (Contemporary).

Rosenblatt, Roger. See MISCELLANEOUS (Contemporary--2nd Rosenblatt entry).

Schraufnagel, Noel. See MISCELLANEOUS (Contemporary).

Shelton, Frank W. "Ambiguous Manhood in Ernest J. Gaines's *Bloodline*." *CLA Jour*, 19 (December 1975), 200-209.
   Gaines's treatment of black manhood in the stories in this work "is frequently ambiguous, and he implies the danger of something important being lost through a single-minded concern with achieving it."

Stoelting, Winifred L. "Human Dignity and Pride in the Novels of Ernest J. Gaines." *CLA Jour*, 14 (March 1971), 340-358.
   Gaines's concern is not with the morality of a choice but with the dignity and pride of the character who makes the choice.

Williams, Sherley Anne. *Give Birth to Brightness: A Thematic Study of Neo-Black Literature*. New York: Dial Press, 1972.
   Gaines is one of the writers discussed in detail in this study of character types in black literature.

IV. Contemporary (1920-1975)

[GAITHER, FRANCES] Simms, L. Moody, Jr. "Frances Gaither: A Sketch." *Notes on Miss Writers*, 3 (Fall 1970), 73-78.

A short overview of the life and fiction of Mrs. Gaither, particularly her popular novels.

[GARRETT, GEORGE] Carr, John. See MISCELLANEOUS (Contemporary).

Burke, John, ed. *Regional Perspectives: An Examination of America's Literary Heritage*. American Library Association, 1973.

Five critics define the literary characteristics of their regions. Garrett speaks for the South.

"International Symposium on the Short Story." *KR*, 31, no. 4 (1969), 450-453.

Garrett is one of several whose views on the short story are presented here.

Israel, Charles. "Interview: George Garrett." *So Car Rev*, 6 (November 1973), 43-48.

Among other things, Garrett discusses what it means to be a "Southern writer."

Madden, David. See MISCELLANEOUS (Contemporary-- 2nd Madden entry).

Robinson, W. R. "Imagining the Individual: George Garrett's *Death of the Fox*." *Hollins Critic*, 8 (August 1971), 1-12.

An essay-review that says, "*Death of the Fox*, certainly Garrett's best novel, just could be a new standard by which we will measure the vitality and humanity of not only contemporary novels but of our own lives as well."

Slavitt, David R. "History--Fate and Freedom: A Look at George Garrett's New Novel." *SouR*, 7 (January 1971), 276-294.

An essay-review of *Death of the Fox*, written before its publication, which finds it to be "very probably one of the dozen best novels to have been written in my life-time."

[GIOVANNI, NIKKI] Bell, Bernard W. See MISCELLANEOUS (Contemporary).

Brooks, A. Russell. See MISCELLANEOUS (Contemporary).

Budd, Louis J. See MISCELLANEOUS (Contemporary).

Duffy, Martha. See ELLISON, RALPH (Contemporary).

Gibson, Donald B. See MISCELLANEOUS (Contemporary).

Giovanni, Nikki. *Gemini*. New York: Viking Press, 1971.

"An extended autobiographical statement on my first twenty-five years of being a black poet," by Knoxville native Giovanni.

_____, and James Baldwin. *A Dialogue*. Philadelphia: J. B. Lippincott, 1973.

A transcript of a 1971 television conversation between black writers of two different generations about race and literature.

_____, and Margaret Walker. *A Poetic Equation: Conversations Between Nikki Giovanni and Margaret Walker*. Washington, D. C.: Howard Univ, 1974.

Giovanni and Walker reveal different attitudes toward the black writer's purpose.

Palmer, R. Roderick. See MISCELLANEOUS (Contemporary).

Perloff, Marjorie. "Floral Decorations for Bananas." *Parnassus*, 2 (Fall/Winter 1973), 133-148.

Part of this review concerns Giovanni's *My House*.

Reeves, William J. See GENERAL.

Sheffey, Ruthe. See MISCELLANEOUS (Contemporary).

[GODSEY, EDWIN] Landess, Thomas H. "Edwin Godsey's *Cabin Fever* and the Aesthetics of Virtue." *GaR*, 23 (Fall 1969), 343-353.

A biographical reminiscence and critical explication showing Godsey's simultaneously moral and aesthetic maturation.

_____. See MISCELLANEOUS (Contemporary).

[GODWIN, GAIL] Gardiner, Judith K. "'A Sorrowful Woman': Gail Godwin's Feminist Parable." *Stud SF*, 12 (Summer 1975), 286-290.

This story "is a parable of negative ideology in which the traditional roles of wifehood and motherhood are seen as in themselves existentially dead and death-creating."

[GORDON, CAROLINE] Baker, Howard. "The Stratagems of Caroline Gordon: Or, the Art of the Novel and the Novelty of Myth." *SouR*, 9 (Summer 1973), 523-549.

Examines the use and meaning of myth in *The Glory of Hera*.

Baum, Catherine B., and Floyd C. Watkins. "Caroline Gordon and 'The Captive': An Interview." *SouR*, 7 (Spring 1971), 447-462.

Tape-recorded answers by Caroline Gordon to questions about the source, technique, and meanings of the short story "The Captive."

Boyd, G. N. and L. A. See MISCELLANEOUS (Contemporary).

Brown, Ashley. "The Achievement of Caroline Gordon." *SHR*, 2 (Summer 1968), 279-290.

Primarily from the influence of Ford Madox Ford, Miss Gordon developed as an impressionist with bold and far-reaching innovations.

_____. "Caroline Gordon's Short Fiction." *SR*, 81 (April-June 1973), 365-370.

An essay-review of *The Short Fiction of Caroline Gordon*, edited by Thomas H. Landess; emphasizes the anecdotal character of her fiction.

_____. "*None Shall Look Back*: The Novel as History." *SouR*, 7 (Spring 1971), 480-494.

Argues that Miss Gordon relates the two levels of action, public and private, in her novel through shift in point of view, "the technical feature peculiar to the novel."

Bungert, Hans. See GENERAL.

Cheney, Brainard. "Caroline Gordon's *The Malefactors*." *SR*, 79 (Summer 1971), 360-372.
    Asserts the excellence of *The Malefactors* and considers the reasons for its present low reputation.

Colquitt, Betsy F. See GENERAL.

Fletcher, Marie. "The Fate of Woman in a Changing South: A Persistent Theme in the Fiction of Caroline Gordon." *Miss Quart*, 21 (Winter 1967-68), 17-28.
    Asserts that Miss Gordon was concerned with the place of women in the post-Civil War South.

Gordon, Caroline. See CLEMENS, SAMUEL LANGHORNE (Postbellum).

_____, et al. See O'CONNOR, FLANNERY (Contemporary).

Landess, Thomas H. "The Function of Ritual in Caroline Gordon's *Green Centuries*." *SouR*, 7 (Spring 1971), 495-508.
    Develops the thesis that the rituals governing hunting and sexual conduct are used by Miss Gordon to define the characters and "provide a key to the moral meaning of the action."

_____, ed. *The Short Fiction of Caroline Gordon: A Critical Symposium*. Irving, Texas: Univ of Dallas Press, 1972.
    Collects six original essays, which systematically cover Miss Gordon's writings, by Louise Cowan, R. J. Dupree, Thomas H. Landess, J. C. Brown, J. E. Alvis, and M. E. Bradford.

Lewis, Janet. "*The Glory of Hera*." *SR*, 81 (Winter 1973), 185-194.
    A review which ultimately finds the novel "learned--and rather splendid--entertainment."

Madden, David. See MISCELLANEOUS (Contemporary--2nd Madden entry).

O'Connor, Mary. "On Caroline Gordon." *SouR*, 7 (Spring 1971), 463-466.
    Sympathetic personal comments on Miss Gordon's personality. Sees her project as that of creating her own myth of the South.

Rocks, James E. "The Christian Myth as Salvation: Caroline Gordon's *The Strange Children*." *Tulane Stud in Eng*, 16 (1968), 149-160.
    This novel reveals Miss Gordon's transition from the Agrarian to the Christian myth.

_____. "The Mind and Art of Caroline Gordon." *Miss Quart*, 21 (Winter 1967-68), 1-16.
    A critical assessment of Miss Gordon as an important fiction writer in the Southern Renaissance.

_____. "The Short Fiction of Caroline Gordon." *Tulane Stud in Eng*, 18 (1970), 115-135.
    Miss Gordon's short stories reveal her themes and techniques.

Rubin, Larry. "Christian Allegory in Caroline Gordon's 'The Captive.'" *Stud SF*, 5 (Spring 1968), 283-289.
    An analysis of "The Captive" on a "spiritual level" to show that Christian orientation appeared earlier in Miss Gordon's fiction than critics have heretofore acknowledged.

Squires, Radcliffe. "The Underground Stream: A Note on Caroline Gordon's Fiction." *SouR*, 7 (Spring 1971), 467-479.
    A study of the "metaphoric establishment" of Miss Gordon's later fiction, particularly the metaphors of stars and water.

Stanford, Donald E. "Caroline Gordon: From *Penhally* to *A Narrow Heart*." *SouR*, 7 (Spring 1971), xv-xx.
    A general survey of Miss Gordon's fiction with attention to its Southern qualities and its mythic method.

Stuckey, W. J. *Caroline Gordon*. Twayne's U. S. Authors Series, no. 200. New York: Twayne, 1972.
    An analytical appreciation of the novels and stories against the background of the fictional principles, her critical preoccupations, and the work of her contemporaries.

Toledano, Ben C. See MISCELLANEOUS (Contemporary).

Umphlett, Wiley Lee. See MISCELLANEOUS (Contemporary).

Woodress, James. See GENERAL--1st Woodress entry.

[GOYEN, WILLIAM] Coindreau, Maurice. See MISCELLANEOUS (Contemporary).

Madden, David. See MISCELLANEOUS (Contemporary--2nd Madden entry).

Phillips, Robert. "The Romance of Prophecy: Goyen's *In a Farther Country*." *SWR*, 56 (Summer 1971), 213-221.
    This out-of-print novel (1955) is an early ecological work.

_____. "Samuel and Samson: Theme and Legend in 'The White Rooster.'" *Stud SF*, 6 (Spring 1969), 331-333.
    Instead of being a realistic story, this is "a Western tall tale on one level and an allegory on another" dramatizing the battle of the sexes.

_____. "Secret and Symbol: Entrances to Goyen's *House of Breath*." *SWR*, 59 (Summer 1974), 248-253.
    A discussion of the importance of the secrets of individual characters and of the symbols in this novel.

[GRAHAM, ALICE WALWORTH] Simms, L. Moody, Jr. "Alice Walworth Graham: Popular Novelist." *Notes on Miss Writers*, 6 (Winter 1974), 63-68.
    A short summary of the writer's career.

[GRAU, SHIRLEY ANN] Grissom, Margaret S. "Shirley Ann Grau--A Checklist." *BB*, 28 (July-September 1971), 76-78.

IV. Contemporary (1920-1975)

An unannotated listing of works by Miss Grau.

Pearson, Ann. "Shirley Ann Grau: Nature is the Vision." *Critique*, 17, no. 2 (1975), 47-58.
A study of Grau's novels which sees nature as the focal point of her best fiction.

Watkins, Floyd C. See MISCELLANEOUS (Contemporary).

[GRAVES, JOHN] Bradford, M. E. "Arden Up the Brazos: John Graves and the Uses of the Pastoral." *SouR*, 9 (Autumn 1972), 949-955.
In *Goodbye to a River*, the narrator's return to the scenes of his boyhood, "Graves summarizes a dimension of human history as enacted in a Texas microcosm."

_____. "In Keeping with the Way: John Graves's *Hard Scrabble*." *SWR*, 60 (Spring 1975), 190-195.
A review of this 1974 work.

[GREEN, JULIAN HARTRIDGE] Thomas, H. F. "Parisian by Birth, Virginian at Heart: Southerner Makes French First." Richmond *Times-Dispatch*, June 13, 1971, Sect. F., pp. 1, 3.
Biographical data on French-born author Green's Southern family connections and his decision to remain an American Southerner, which the French Academy finally decided to overlook in electing him to membership.

[GREEN, PAUL] Clifford, John. "A True American Artist: Paul Green." *Players*, 48 (June-July, August-September 1973), 210-215.
Deals with the techniques of Green's outdoor dramas based on American history and folklore.

Goldstein, Malcolm. See MISCELLANEOUS (Contemporary).

Green, Paul. *Home to My Valley*. Chapel Hill: Univ of North Carolina Press, 1970.
Gathers twenty-three autobiographical sketches and folk tales based on experiences in Green's native Cape Fear River Valley, North Carolina.

Kenny, Vincent. *Paul Green*. Twayne's U. S. Authors Series, no. 186. New York: Twayne, 1971.
Focuses on Green's works rather than on the man and discusses his use of folk material and his democratic philosophy.

Lazenby, Walter S. *Paul Green*. Austin: Steck-Vaughn, 1970.
Deals with both lesser- and better-known plays by Green.

Long, E. Hudson. See GENERAL.

Pearce, Howard D. "From Folklore to Mythology: Paul Green's *Roll, Sweet Chariot*." *So Lit Jour*, 3 (Spring 1971), 62-78.
Although *Roll, Sweet Chariot* grows out of "a simple 'folk' impulse," it must be read "in terms of a ritualized action and a symbolic expression."

Spearman, Walter. See MISCELLANEOUS (Contemporary).

[GRIFFIN, JOHN HOWARD] Mansfield, Margaret. *Black Like Me Notes*. Lincoln, Nebraska: Cliff's Notes, 1971.
A study guide.

Rank, Hugh. "The Rhetorical Effectiveness of *Black Like Me*." *EJ*, 57 (September 1968), 813-817.
The major strength of this search for truth through a painful experiment is in the ethical appeal.

[HARRIS, JULIAN] Mugleston, William F. See HARRIS, JOEL CHANDLER (Postbellum).

Shankman, Arnold. "Julian Harris and the Ku Klux Klan." *Miss Quart*, 28 (Spring 1975), 147-169.
Discusses Harris' editorial career and his crusade against Klan bigotry.

[HARRISON, WILLIAM] Garrett, George P. "Ringing the Bell: William Harrison's 'In a Wild Sanctuary.'" *Hollins Critic*, 6 (October 1969), 1-11.
A review-essay on Harrison and his new novel.

[HAUN, MILDRED] Gower, Herschel. "Mildred Haun: The Persistence of the Supernatural." *La Stud*, 7 (Spring 1968), 65-71.
Discusses folk beliefs, particularly the supernatural, in the regional fiction of Mildred Haun.

Haun, Mildred. *The Hawk's Done Gone and Other Stories*, ed. Herschel Gower. Nashville: Vanderbilt Univ Press, 1968.
A collection of short stories with a critical introduction to the late Miss Haun's work by the editor.

[HELLMAN, LILLIAN] Adler, Jacob H. *Lillian Hellman*. Southern Writers Series. Austin: Steck-Vaughn, 1969.
Whether writing of the South or the world of diplomacy, Hellman's outlook is read as "liberal, intellectual, concerned with human problems on a grand scale."

_____. "Professor Moody's Miss Hellman." *So Lit Jour*, 5 (Spring 1973), 131-140.
An essay-review of *Lillian Hellman, Playwright*, by Richard Moody, which the reviewer says will be disappointing to the readers who wish to see Miss Hellman placed in the dramatic tradition and to literary critics of the drama since the author's approach is largely that of the theater.

Armato, Philip M. "'Good and Evil' in Lillian Hellman's *The Children's Hour*." *ETJ*, 25 (1973), 443-447.
The moral of the play is that justice without mercy is cruelty.

Bridges, Katherine. See GENERAL.

Eatman, James. "The Image of Destiny: *The Little Foxes*." *Players*, 48 (December-January 1973), 70-73.

The emphasis in the play is on the "detrimental effects of economic expansion."

Goldstein, Malcolm. See MISCELLANEOUS (Contemporary).

Heilman, Robert B. "Dramas of Money." *Shen*, 21 (Summer 1970), 20-33.
   The Little Foxes is described as over-simplified satire in this discussion of plays dealing with the theme of money.

Holmin, Lorena Ross. *The Dramatic Works of Lillian Hellman*. *Studia Anglistica Upsaliensia* (Uppsala Univ, Uppsala, Sweden), 10 (1973), 1-178.
   A monograph dealing with Hellman as an important American playwright.

Libman, Valentina--See GENERAL.

Long, E. Hudson. See GENERAL.

Moody, Richard. *Lillian Hellman: Playwright*. New York: Pegasus, 1972.
   A biography of Miss Hellman's public and private careers with attention to the impact of her moral and political convictions on her life and work.

Scheller, Bernhard. "Der paradoxe bürgerliche Held." *Weimarer Beiträge*, 21, no. 9 (1975), 116-137.
   Along with other writers, Hellman is discussed as a writer whose works reveal the alienated bourgeois writer.

Spacks, Patricia M. "Free Women." *HudR*, 24 (Winter 1971-72), 559-573.
   Includes a discussion of Hellman's memoir, *An Unfinished Woman*.

Weales, Gerald. See MISCELLANEOUS (Contemporary).

[HEYWARD, DUBOSE] Durham, Frank. "Porgy Comes Home--At Last!" *So Car Rev*, 2 (May 1970), 5-13.
   Relates the widespread acceptance and performance of Heyward's work.

_____. See MISCELLANEOUS (Contemporary--2nd Durham entry).

Goldstein, Malcolm. See MISCELLANEOUS (Contemporary).

Lucas, J. "'But Porgy Is Getting Awfully Close.'" *Carleton Misc*, 14 (Spring-Summer 1974), 67-72.
   Contends that the objection of certain influential black artists, notably Duke Ellington, to the Gershwin-Heyward *Porgy and Bess* should not blind us to its elements of authentic Gullah culture and to the quality of its music.

Malavelle, Maryse. "*Porgy*: du roman à l'opéra." *Caliban*, 9 (1972), 135-150.
   Deals with Samuel Smalls, a black beggar of South Carolina, as prototype of Porgy and with Porgy's progress, through novel, play, and opera, from non-hero to hero.

Shirley, Wayne D. "Porgy and Bess." *QJLC*, 31 (April 1974), 97-107.
   Deals with the evolution of the opera from Heyward's novel and with a first-draft libretto of the opera in the Library of Congress.

Slavick, William H. "Going to School to DuBose Heyward." *SLI*, 7 (Fall 1974), 105-129.
   Deals with Heyward's treatment of the black experience in *Porgy* and in *Mamba's Daughters*.

Williams, George. "Peregrinations of a Goat Cart." *Sandlapper*, 6 (October 1973), 41-49.
   An account of the remaking of Heyward's *Porgy* into Heyward's and Gershwin's opera *Porgy and Bess*.

[HIMES, CHESTER] Billingsley, R. G. See MISCELLANEOUS (Contemporary).

Bryant, Jerry H. See MISCELLANEOUS (Contemporary--2nd Bryant entry).

Hill, James Lee. "Bibliography of the Works of Chester Himes, Ann Petry and Frank Yerby." *Black Bks Bul*, 3 (Fall 1975), 60-72.
   Lists works by and about.

Himes, Chester. *The Quality of Hurt*. Vol. I. Garden City, N. Y.: Doubleday, 1972.
   An autobiography of the first forty-five years of Himes's life, 1909-1954, from his boyhood in Mississippi through his abandonment of the United States to live abroad.

Kane, Patricia, and Doris Y. Wilkinson. "Survival Strategies: Black Women in *Ollie Miss* and *Cotton Comes to Harlem*." *Critique*, 16, no. 1 (1974), 101-109.
   Iris in Himes's *Cotton Comes to Harlem* and Ollie in George Wylie's *Ollie Miss* survive instead of becoming victims, in spite of the fact that they are women, that they are black, and that they live in the city.

Manucci, Loretta V. See MISCELLANEOUS (Contemporary).

Margolies, Edward. "Experiences of the Black Expatriate Writer: Chester Himes." *CLA Jour*, 15 (1972), 421-427.
   A Case of Rage reveals that Himes has not fully assimilated his European experiences in his fiction.

_____. "The Thrillers of Chester Himes." *SBL*, 1 (Summer 1970), 1-11.
   Himes makes of the thriller a "moral, metaphysical and social comment" on the black experience.

Nelson, Raymond. "Domestic Harlem: The Detective Fiction of Chester Himes." *VQR*, 48 (Spring 1972), 260-276.
   Deals with the black experience as reflected in Himes's *Harlem Domestic* series.

Peden, William. See MISCELLANEOUS (Contemporary).

Schraufnagel, Noel. See MISCELLANEOUS (Contemporary).

Wade, Melvin and Margaret. See GENERAL.

[HURSTON, ZORA NEALE] Bone, Robert. See GENERAL.

Brake, Robert. See GENERAL.

Giles, James R. "The Significance of Time in Zora Neale Hurston's *Their Eyes Were Watching God*." *NALF*, 6 (Summer 1972), 52-53, 60.
    In this work the black view of time is emotional and hedonistic and triumphs over the rational and materialistic white view.

Hart, Robert C. See MISCELLANEOUS (Contemporary).

Hill, Mildred A. See GENERAL.

Huggins, Nathan. See MISCELLANEOUS (Contemporary).

Jordan, June. See WRIGHT, RICHARD (Contemporary).

Kilson, Marion. "The Transformation of Eatonville's Ethnographer." *Phylon*, 33 (Summer 1972), 112-119.
    Drawing on the experiences of her native Eatonville, Florida, and her education in anthropology under Franz Boas and Ruth Benedict, Zora Neale Hurston produced ethnographic fiction set in a self-contained black world from 1924-1942. Her later works (1943-1951) are primarily critical essays on the complexities of Southern society, especially race relations.

Petesch, Donald. See MISCELLANEOUS (Contemporary).

Rayson, Ann L. "*Dust Tracks on a Road*: Zora Neale Hurston and the Form of Black Autobiography." *NALF*, 7 (1973), 39-45.
    This work reflects the paradoxes of Hurston's personality.

_____. "The Novels of Zora Neale Hurston." *SBL*, 5 (Winter 1974), 1-10.
    Analyzes Hurston's four novels to support the thesis that they all have the same formula in theme and in characters; in their use of folklore, these works have many features of the ballad.

Southerland, Ellease. "Zora Neale Hurston: The Novelist-Anthropologist's Life/Works." *Black World*, 23 (August 1974), 20-30.
    Partly a biographical essay and partly brief individual surveys of Hurston's works.

Turner, Darwin T. See MISCELLANEOUS (Contemporary-- 2nd Turner entry).

Walker, S. Jay. "Zora Neale Hurston's *Their Eyes Were Watching God*: Black Novel of Sexism." *MFS*, 20 (Winter 1974-75), 519-527.
    This novel shows an "awareness of the stifling effects of sexism, but also indicates why the feminist movement has failed...to grasp the imaginations of black womanhood."

Washington, Mary Helen. "Zora Neale Hurston's Work: The Black Woman's Search for Identity." *Black World*, 21 (August 1972), 68-75.
    Deals with *Their Eyes Were Watching God* and the ways it accurately reflects black experience.

[HYMAN, MAC] Blackburn, William, ed. *Love, Boy: The Letters of Mac Hyman*. Baton Rouge: Louisiana State Univ Press, 1970.
    Contains 160 letters about the problems of a young writer addressed to Hyman's agent, publisher, family, and other writers.

[JARRELL, RANDALL] Adams, Charles M. "A Bibliographical Excursion with Some Biographical Footnotes on Randall Jarrell." *BB*, 28 (July-September 1971), 79-81.
    An account of a trip to Nashville to track down early Jarrell items, a list of which is appended to the essay.

Antin, David. "Modernism and Postmodernism: Approaching the Present in American Poetry." *Boundary 2*, 1 (Fall 1972), 98-133.
    Includes Jarrell among poets who should be represented more frequently in anthologies of modern poetry because their poetry reflects the structure of modern life.

Atlas, James. See GENERAL.

Boyers, Robert. "On Randall Jarrell." *Mod Occasions*, 2 (Spring 1972), 273-278.
    A review of *The Poetry of Randall Jarrell*, by Suzanne Ferguson.

Buchloh, Paul G. "Das Verhältnis des Amerikanischen Dichters zum Staat, dargestellt an Robert Frosts 'The Gift Outright' und Randall Jarrells 'The Death of the Ball Turret Gunner.'" *Jahrbuch für Amerikastudien*, 13 (1968), 205-214.
    Frost's poem emphasizes dedication to the state, whereas Jarrell's emphasizes the destruction of the individual by the state.

Dawson, Leven M. "Jarrell's 'The Death of the Ball Turret Gunner.'" *Expl*, 31 (December 1972), Item 29.
    An explication of the poem.

Donahue, Jane. "'Trading Another's Sorrows for Our Own': The Poetry of Randall Jarrell." *LWU*, 2, no. 4 (1969), 258-267.
    Jarrell was a poet "with too much negative capability"; his poetry concentrates on death and suffering.

Dunn, Douglas. "An Affable Misery: On Randall Jarrell." *Encounter*, 39 (October 1972), 42-48.
    Jarrell is in the tradition of Wordsworth, Frost, and Hardy; his poetry concentrates on human misery in contrast to past happiness.

Ferguson, Frances C. "Randall Jarrell and the Flotations of Voice." *GaR*, 28 (Fall 1974), 423-439.
    "Jarrell's celebrated 'authority' as a critic begins, in a close examination of 'Stories,' to participate in the same concern for 'voice' that his poems reveal."

Ferguson, Suzanne. *The Poetry of Randall Jarrell.* Baton Rouge: Louisiana State Univ Press, 1971.
An introduction to Jarrell's themes--loneliness, love, loss of youth, death, etc.--and an appreciation of his accomplishment from *Blood for a Stranger* (1942) to *Lost World* (1965).

Fowler, Russell. "Randall Jarrell's 'Eland': A Key to Motive and Technique in His Poetry." *Iowa Rev*, 5 (Spring 1974), 113-126.
Charts the development of Jarrell's technique and discusses the eland in "Seele im Raum" as the dramatic representation of "a subliminal awareness of human life that is both organic and mystical."

Gillikin, Dure Jo. "A Checklist of Criticism on Randall Jarrell 1941-1970--With an Introduction and a List of His Major Works." *BNYPL*, 75 (April 1971), 176-194.
Title is descriptive.

Hagenbüchle-Imfeld, Helen. *The Black Goddess: A Study of the Archetypal Feminine in the Poetry of Randall Jarrell. Swiss Studies in English*, Vol. 79, Zurich, Switzerland: Francke Verlag Bern, 1975.
A Freudian interpretation of Jarrell's poetry which treats feminine figures.

Hoffman, Frederick J., ed. *The Achievement of Randall Jarrell.* Glenview, Ill.: Scott, Foresman, 1970.
A selection of forty-one poems, 1942-1965, with an introduction to them as a "record of man's growing up into something puzzling, tawdry, and menacing."

Humphrey, Robert. "Randall Jarrell's Poetry," in R. B. Browne and Donald Pizer, eds., *Themes and Directions in American Literature.* Lafayette, Indiana: Purdue Univ Studies, 1969, pp. 220-233.
Attempts to identify the excellence of Jarrell's poetry generally unrecognized by literary historians.

Jarrell, Mary v. S. "*Faust* and Randall Jarrell: A Reminiscence." *Columbia Forum*, 2 (Summer 1973), 24-31.
Deals with Jarrell's reasons for translating *Faust*.

_____, ed. *Jerome: The Biography of a Poem.* New York: Grossman Publishers, 1971.
Publishes facsimiles of fifty worksheets for Jarrell's poem "Jerome," the seven engravings of Albrecht Dürer which inspired it, and Mrs. Jarrell's account of the creative process.

Jarrell, Randall. See MISCELLANEOUS (Contemporary).

Mazzaro, Jerome. "Arnoldian Echoes in the Poetry of Randall Jarrell." *WHR*, 23 (Autumn 1969), 314-318.
A comparison of Arnold and Jarrell (both poets of second rank whose work contains excellences) and comment on selected poems in Jarrell's *Collected Poems*.

_____. "Between Two Worlds: The Post-Modernism of Randall Jarrell." *Salmagundi*, 17 (1971), 92-113.
Discusses Jarrell's poetry and concludes that Jarrell held "a notable but not a paramount place" among poets of our time.

Nemerov, Howard. "Jarrell's *Complete Poems*." *KR*, 31, no. 4 (1969), 570-573.
An essay-review of Jarrell's poetry, a tribute to the late poet, and reminiscences of the reviewer.

Nitchie, George W. "Randall Jarrell: A Stand-in's View." *SouR*, 9 (Autumn 1973), 883-894.
An examination of World War II and of childhood in Jarrell's poetry.

Owen, Guy. See MISCELLANEOUS (Contemporary--1st Owen entry).

Quinn, Sister M. Bernetta. "Randall Jarrell: Landscapes of Life and LIFE." *Shen*, 20 (Winter 1969), 49-78.
Discusses Jarrell's use of dramatic landscapes to tell the story of life.

_____. "Thematic Imagery in the Poetry of Randall Jarrell." *SouR*, 5 (Autumn 1969), 1226-1235.
A study of five related images in Jarrell's *Complete Poems*: dream, wish, child, mirror, and star.

Richards, Bertrand F. "Jarrell's 'Seele in Raum.'" *Expl*, 33 (November 1974), Item 22.
The idea of the poem is that "if there is no meaning to existence, then existence itself is sinful--morally wrong."

Rosenthal, M. L. *Randall Jarrell.* Minnesota Pamphlets, no. 103. Minneapolis: Univ of Minnesota Press, 1972.
A general critical assessment with emphasis on the poetry and the philosophy Jarrell's poetry embodies.

Smith, Marcus. "Report to Randall Jarrell." *SHR*, 3 (Spring 1969), 124.
An original poem.

Staples, Hugh B. "Randall Jarrell." *ConL*, 15 (Summer 1974), 423-427.
A review of Suzanne Ferguson's *The Poetry of Randall Jarrell*, which concludes that Ferguson has "dispatched to rightful oblivion the false and Philistine image of Randall Jarrell 'the war-poet.'"

Weisberg, Robert. "Randall Jarrell: The Integrity of His Poetry." *Centennial Rev*, 17 (Summer 1973), 237-255.
Jarrell's best poems concern the child-adult relationship.

[JOHNSON, JAMES WELDON] Bacote, Clarence A. "James Weldon Johnson and Atlanta University." *Phylon*, 32 (Winter 1971), 333-343.
A detailed account of Johnson's university studies and extracurricular activities at Atlanta University, 1887-1894.

Baker, Houston A., Jr. "A Forgotten Prototype:
The Autobiography of an Ex-Colored Man and
Invisible Man." *VQR*, 49 (Summer 1973), 433-449.
   A comparison of these two works helps to
elucidate both as well as the works of later
black writers.

_____. See GENERAL--4th Baker entry.

Bell, Bernard W. "Folk Art and the Harlem
Renaissance." *Phylon*, 36 (June 1975), 155-163.
   Discusses the influence of Herder's folk
ideology on Johnson as well as other writers
of the Harlem Renaissance.

_____. See MISCELLANEOUS (Contemporary--1st Bell
entry).

Bontemps, Arna. See MISCELLANEOUS (Contemporary).

Brown, Lloyd W. "Black Biographies." *Can Rev Bks*,
2 (1974), 199-204.
   Includes a review of Eugene Levy's book on
Johnson.

Carroll, Richard A. "Black Racial Spirit: An
Analysis of James Weldon Johnson's Critical
Perspective." *Phylon*, 32 (Winter 1971),
344-364.
   Literary historians have generally ignored
or denigrated Johnson's literary criticism,
yet a careful study of his work reveals him
as an early and articulate exponent of a black
aesthetic.

Collier, Eugenia. "The Endless Journey of an
Ex-Coloured Man." *Phylon*, 32 (Winter 1971),
365-373.
   Johnson's novel *The Autobiography of an Ex-
Coloured Man* is structured upon a framework
of two journeys, a physical one and a psychological one, both moving between the black
world and the white, from both of which the
narrator is alienated.

Corrigan, Robert A. See GENERAL--1st Corrigan
entry.

Felton, H. W. *James Weldon Johnson*. New York:
Dodd, Mead, 1971.
   A biography for juveniles of the Florida-
born poet, teacher, editor, musician and founder
of the NAACP.

Fleming, Robert E. "Contemporary Themes in
Johnson's *Autobiography of an Ex-Coloured Man*."
NALF, 4 (1970), 120-124.
   Deals with the relevancy of this work.

_____. "Irony as a Key to Johnson's *The Autobiog-
raphy of an Ex-Coloured Man*." *AL*, 43
(March 1971), 83-96.
   Discusses the thesis that "*The Autobiography*...is a deeply ironic character study of
a marginal man" who narrates his life with
dramatic irony.

_____. See GENERAL.

Garrett, Marvin P. "Early Recollections on Structural Irony in *The Autobiography of an*

Ex-Coloured Man." *Critique*, 13, no. 2 (1971),
5-14.
   Maintains that the "narrator's recollections
represent the key to the novel's narrative
design...." and that the recollections are used
ironically "as a device which reveals the
fallibility of the narrator."

Gayle, Addison, Jr. See MISCELLANEOUS
(Contemporary--3rd Gayle entry).

_____. See GENERAL.

Grumbach, Doris. See GENERAL.

Hart, Robert C. See MISCELLANEOUS (Contemporary).

Haslam, Gerald W. See MISCELLANEOUS (Contemporary--
1st Haslam entry).

Huggins, Nathan. See MISCELLANEOUS (Contemporary).

Isani, Mukhtar. See GENERAL.

Jackson, M. M. "Letters to a Friend: Correspondence from James Weldon Johnson to George A.
Towns." *Phylon*, 29 (Summer 1968), 182-198.
   Twenty-two letters written between 1898 and
1934 to Johnson's former roommate at Atlanta
University and later professor of English there.
Johnson makes many references to his writings,
critical evaluations, and reports of financial
success.

Jackson, Miles, Jr. "James Weldon Johnson." *Black
World*, 19 (June 1970), 32-34.
   A brief survey of Johnson's career.

Jeffers, Lance. See MISCELLANEOUS (Contemporary).

Keller, Francis R. "The Harlem Literary Renaissance."
North Am Rev, 5 (May-June 1968), 29-34.
   This discussion of the aims of the Harlem
Renaissance includes references to Johnson.

Kostelanetz, Richard. "The Politics of Passing:
The Fiction of James Weldon Johnson." *NALF*, 3
(1969), 22-24, 29.
   The Autobiography of an Ex-Coloured Man emphasizes the alienated feeling of the black's
attempt to pass as white.

Levy, Eugene. *James Weldon Johnson: Black Leader,
Black Voice*. Negro American Biographies and
Autobiographies Series. Chicago: Univ of
Chicago Press, 1973.
   A full-length biography.

_____. "Ragtime and Race Pride: The Career of
James Weldon Johnson." *Jour of Popular Culture*,
1 (Spring 1968), 357-370.
   Represents Johnson's career as an embodiment
of the American Negro's dilemma: inability to
achieve popular success and still maintain racial
identity and racial pride.

Logan, Rayford W. "James Weldon Johnson and Haiti."
Phylon, 32 (Winter 1971), 396-402.
   In 1920 Johnson visited Haiti under U. S.
occupation and wrote two articles for the *Nation*
exposing abuses of U. S. imperialism.

Long, Richard A. "The Weapon of My Song: The Poetry of James Weldon Johnson." *Phylon*, 32 (Winter 1971), 374-382.
Johnson's earliest poems, dialect verse and lyrics in standard English, are marred by sentimentality and didacticism. A great step forward in his art is represented in *God's Trombones* (1927), cadenced free verse in which, without dialect, the speech of the black folk preacher is effectively suggested.

Margolies, Edward. See MISCELLANEOUS (Contemporary--2nd Margolies entry).

McDowell, Robert E. See MISCELLANEOUS (Contemporary).

_____, and George Fortenberry. See MISCELLANEOUS (Contemporary).

McGhee, Nancy B. See GENERAL.

Redding, Saunders. "James Weldon Johnson and the Pastoral Tradition." *Miss Quart*, 28 (Fall 1975), 417-421.
An analysis of the pastoral quality in Johnson's work helps the reader to appreciate his achievement outside the narrow limits of previous criticism.

Redmond, Eugene B. See GENERAL.

Rosenblatt, Roger. See MISCELLANEOUS (Contemporary--both Rosenblatt entries).

Ross, Stephen M. "Audience and Irony in Johnson's *The Autobiography of an Ex-Coloured Man*." *CLA Jour*, 18 (December 1974), 198-210.
Johnson's irony in the *Autobiography* is not directed at the protagonist, as some critics have argued, but at a hypothetical white audience whose value system the "ex-coloured man" cannot escape.

Tyms, James D. See MISCELLANEOUS (Contemporary).

Vauthier, Simone. "The Interplay of Narrative Modes in James Weldon Johnson's *The Autobiography of an Ex-Colored Man*." *Jahrbuch für Amerikastudien*, 18 (1973), 173-181.
This work is not the traditional black autobiography because its hero is "picaresque."

Wade, Melvin and Margaret. See GENERAL.

Waniek, Marilyn N. See MISCELLANEOUS (Contemporary).

Whalum, Wendell P. "James Weldon Johnson's Theories and Performance Practices of Afro-American Folksong." *Phylon*, 32 (Winter 1971), 383-395.
Johnson's discussions of Afro-American music in his autobiography, his novel *The Autobiography of an Ex-Coloured Man*, and the prefaces to his *Books of American Negro Spirituals* are the best guide to understanding this music, its history and cultural setting, available until Eileen Southern's *The Music of Black America* (1971).

Young, James O. See MISCELLANEOUS (Contemporary).

[JONES, MADISON] Hiers, John T. See WARREN, ROBERT PENN (Contemporary).

[KELLER, HELEN] Chambliss, Amy. See CLEMENS, SAMUEL LANGHORNE.

Vance, W. S. "The Teacher of Helen Keller." *AlaR*, 24 (January 1971), 51-52.
Examines some of the methods Miss Sullivan used in educating Helen Keller.

[KIMBROUGH, EDWARD] Simms, L. Moody, Jr. "Edward Kimbrough: Mississippi Novelist." *Notes on Miss Writers*, 4 (Winter 1972), 109-114.
A short overview of Kimbrough's career (1918-1965).

Stamper, Rexford. "A Critical Evaluation of the Novels of Edward Kimbrough." *Notes on Miss Writers*, 7 (Fall 1974), 54-62.
A short biographical sketch and summary of Kimbrough's literary career.

[LEE, DON] Bell, Bernard W. See MISCELLANEOUS (Contemporary).

Brooks, A. Russell. See MISCELLANEOUS (Contemporary).

Budd, Louis J. See MISCELLANEOUS (Contemporary).

Colley, Ann. "Don L. Lee's 'But He Was Cool Or: He Even Stopped for Green Lights': An Example of the New Black Aesthetic." *Concerning Poetry*, 4 (Fall 1971), 20-27.
Lee's techniques result from his desire to speak to only a black audience.

Gibson, Donald B. See MISCELLANEOUS (Contemporary).

Lee, Don L. "Directions for Black Writers." *Black Schol*, 12 (December 1969), 53-57.
Black writers must concentrate on their blackness.

Miller, Eugene E. "Some Black Thoughts on Don L. Lee's *Think Black!* Thunk by a Frustrated White Academic Thinker." *CE*, 34 (May 1973), 1094-1102.
Discusses the problems a white teacher faces in teaching the poetry of Don L. Lee and other black poets.

Mosher, Marlene. *New Directions from Don L. Lee*. Hicksville, N. Y.: Exposition Press, 1975.
A study of the various phases of Lee's writing.

Palmer, R. Roderick. See MISCELLANEOUS (Contemporary).

Shands, Annette O. "The Relevancy of Don L. Lee as a Contemporary Black Poet." *Black World*, 21 (June 1972), 35-48.
Discusses the ways in which Lee's language emphasizes the separateness of black culture.

Sheffey, Ruthe. See MISCELLANEOUS (Contemporary).

[LEE, HARPER] Erisman, Fred. "The Romantic Regionalism of Harper Lee." *AlaR*, 26 (April 1973), 122-136.

Harper Lee believes that the old ways of the South should be preserved if good and joined to Emerson's romanticism, which is reasonable and pragmatic.

McDonald, W. U., Jr. "Harper Lee's College Writings." *Am N&Q*, 6 (May 1968), 131-133.
    In campus publications while at the University of Alabama (1945-1949), Miss Lee showed an alertness to pretension and deception, for instance in a one-act play about a Southern politician.

[LONG, HUEY P.] Graham, H. D., ed. *Huey Long*. Great Lives Observed Series. Englewood Cliffs, N. J.: Prentice-Hall, 1970.
    A selection of excerpts arranged under three headings: Long Looks at the World (includes an abridgment of the autobiography, *Every Man a King*), Long Viewed by His Contemporaries, and Long in History, with an original introduction, chronology, afterword, and bibliographical notes by the editor.

[LYTLE, ANDREW NELSON] Avni, Abraham. See GENERAL.

Bataille, Robert. See MISCELLANEOUS (Contemporary).

Benson, Robert G. "The Progress of Hernando de Soto in Andrew Lytle's *At the Moon's Inn*." *GaR*, 27 (Summer 1973), 232-244.
    This novel depicts the "spiritual corruption" of De Soto, the main character, and the "corruption of Tovar, the center of consciousness through most of the action, whose sins are of the flesh rather than the spirit."

Bradford, M. E., ed. *The Form Discovered: Essays on the Achievement of Andrew Lytle*. Jackson, Miss.: Univ Press of Mississippi, 1973.
    A collection of ten previously published essays on Lytle's fiction with a checklist of publications by and about Lytle.

_____. "Toward a Dark Shape: Lytle's 'Alchemy' and the Conquest of the New World." *Miss Quart*, 23 (Fall 1970), 407-414.
    The novella "Alchemy," simpler and more straightforward than Lytle's other work, is nevertheless related to the thematic center of Lytle's career.

Carter, T. H. See MISCELLANEOUS (Contemporary).

Clark, Charles C. "The Fiction of Andrew Lytle." *Occasional Rev*, 1 (Fall 1974).
    An overview of the Lytle canon.

_____. "*A Name for Evil*: A Search for Order." *Miss Quart*, 23 (Fall 1970), 371-382.
    Views of Lytle's novel as an imitation of James's *The Turn of the Screw* have failed to see it as "the effects of a perverted view of tradition."

Core, George. "A Mirror for Fiction: The Criticism of Andrew Lytle." *GaR*, 22 (Summer 1968), 208-221.
    An essay-review of *The Hero with the Private Parts*.

Cowan, Louise. See MISCELLANEOUS (Contemporary).

DeBellis, Jack. See MISCELLANEOUS (Contemporary).

Fain, John T. "Segments of Southern Renaissance." *SAB*, 36 (May 1971), 23-31.
    A reconsideration of the writings of Lytle and John Donald Wade.

_____. See MISCELLANEOUS (Contemporary).

Jones, Madison. "A Look at 'Mister McGregor.'" *Miss Quart*, 23 (Fall 1970), 363-370.
    Andrew Lytle's first published story (1935) forecasts techniques and themes of his later novel, *The Velvet Horn*.

Joyner, Nancy. "The Myth of the Matriarch in Andrew Lytle's Fiction." *So Lit Jour*, 7 (Fall 1974), 67-77.
    The women in Lytle's fiction "do not fare well."

Krickel, Edward. "The Whole and the Parts: Initiation in 'The Mahogany Frame.'" *Miss Quart*, 23 (Fall 1970), 391-405.
    The boy of the story experiences with men on a duck hunt the archetypal patterns of initiation as they still exist in a society in which ritual is confused.

Landess, Thomas H. "Unity of Action in *The Velvet Horn*." *Miss Quart*, 23 (Fall 1970), 349-361.
    The unifying device in the novel is the archetypal experience of man's fall from innocence and the consequent suffering, redemption, and re-integration.

Landman, Sidney J. "The Walls of Mortality." *Miss Quart*, 23 (Fall 1970), 415-423.
    In "Jericho, Jericho, Jericho," the portrayal of Katharine McCowan in the throes of death is one of the finest pieces that has emerged from the Southern Renaissance and a parable of the fall of the South as well.

Lytle, Andrew. "The Old Neighborhood." *SouR*, 8 (Autumn 1972), 816-835.
    A family memoir, excerpted from *A Wake for the Living*.

_____. "The State of Letters in a Time of Disorder." *SR*, 79 (Autumn 1971), 477-497.
    Lytle expresses the view that a breakdown in form means a breakdown in meaning.

_____. *A Wake for the Living: A Family Chronicle*. New York: Crown Publishers, 1975.
    A personal chronicle of the history of Lytle's family in the South from pre-Revolutionary times to his generation.

Madden, David. See MISCELLANEOUS (Contemporary-- 2nd Madden entry).

Polk, Noel. "Andrew Nelson Lytle: A Bibliography of His Writings." *Miss Quart*, 23 (Fall 1970), 435-491.
    A descriptive listing of books, stories, essays, speeches with pertinent letters and a checklist of work about the author.

Toledano, Ben C. See MISCELLANEOUS (Contemporary).

Trowbridge, Clinton W. "The Word Made Flesh: Andrew Lytle's *The Velvet Horn*." *Critique*, 10, no. 2 (1968), 53-68.
   The book is treated as "deeply Christian"--about the paradox in fallen man who yearns to return to Eden while wanting "to forget that Eden ever existed." Also discussed is paganism versus Christianity.

Walcutt, Charles C., and J. E. Whitesell. See GENERAL.

Warren, Robert Penn. "Andrew Lytle's *The Long Night*: A Rediscovery." *SouR*, 7 (Winter 1971), 130-139. Reprinted from David Madden, ed., *Rediscoveries: Informal Essays in Which Well-Known Novelists Rediscover Neglected Works of Fiction by One of Their Favorite Authors*. New York: Crown Publishers, Inc., 1971, pp. 17-28.
   A presentation of the source of Lytle's novel and an examination of what Lytle did "to, for, with" the original oral narrative.

Weatherby, H. L. "The Quality of Richness: Observations on Andrew Lytle's *The Long Night*." *Miss Quart*, 23 (Fall 1970), 383-390.
   Memorable detail, not mere decoration, is as significant as theme and plot as the author allows "the real existence of things in all their immediacy, diversity, and locality to bring their life into his art."

Weston, Robert. "Toward a Total Reading of Fiction: The Essays of Andrew Lytle." *Miss Quart*, 23 (Fall 1970), 425-433.
   A discussion of Lytle's concept of the Controlling Image in fiction.

Yeh-Wei-Yu, Frederick. "Andrew Lytle's *A Name for Evil* as a Redaction of 'The Turn of the Screw.'" *Mich Quart Rev*, 11 (Summer 1972), 186-190.
   A treatment of this novella as an "analysis of the failures of the Agrarian movement."

Young, Thomas Daniel. See GENERAL--1st Young entry.

[MADDEN, DAVID] Laney, Ruth. "An Interview with David Madden." *SouR*, 11 (Winter 1975), 167-180.
   Most of the interview is devoted to Madden's comments on his novel *Bijou* and to a work in progress, *The Suicide's Wife*.

Pinsker, Sanford. "A Conversation with David Madden." *Critique*, 15, no. 2 (1973), 5-13.
   The interview focuses on *Cassandra Singing*.

_____. "The Mixed Cords of David Madden's *Cassandra Singing*." *Critique*, 15, no. 2 (1973), 15-26.
   "For all the loose threads and somewhat unconvincing resolution, there is a power in *Cassandra Singing*...."

[MARCH, WILLIAM] Bungert, Hans. See GENERAL.

Emerson, O. B. "William March and Southern Literature." *Carson-Newman Col Faculty Stud*, 1 (1968), 3-10.

An analysis of *The Looking Glass* and *99 Fables* that places March in the group of significant Southern authors and predicts that he may prove to be one of the great symbolic writers of his time.

Medlicott, Alexander J. "'Soldiers Are Citizens of Death's Gray Land': William March's *Company K*." *ArQ*, 28 (Autumn 1972), 209-224.
   In addition to being an anti-war novel, *Company K* reveals pre- and post-war American attitudes and thus can illuminate certain works of Fitzgerald and Hemingway.

Simmonds, Roy S. "A William March Checklist." *Miss Quart*, 28 (Fall 1975), 461-488.
   Title is descriptive.

_____. "William March's *Company K*: A Short Textual Study." *Stud in Am F*, 2 (1974), 105-113.
   Compares the magazine and the book versions and draws conclusions about March's methods of revision.

Walcutt, Charles C., and J. E. Whitesell. See GENERAL.

[McCULLERS, CARSON] Aldridge, John W. See MISCELLANEOUS (Contemporary--2nd Aldridge entry).

Austen, Roger. "But for fate and ban: Homosexual Villains and Victims in the Military." *CE*, 36 (November 1974), 352-359.
   In a discussion of literary works dealing with the relationship between an officer and an enlisted man, McCullers' *Reflections in a Golden Eye* is included.

Bigsby, C. W. E. "Edward Albee's Georgia Ballad." *TCL*, 13 (January 1968), 229-236.
   Considers Albee's dramatic version of Mrs. McCullers' *The Ballad of the Sad Café* as an attempt to formulate a hopeful response to man's dilemma.

Blöcker, Günter. "Erarbeitete Magie: Die Erzählerin Carson McCullers." *Merkur*, 29 (November 1974), 1079-1084.
   A survey of McCullers' work.

Bluefarb, Sam. See GENERAL.

Boyd, G. N. and L. A. See MISCELLANEOUS (Contemporary).

Broughton, Panthea R. "Rejection of the Feminine in Carson McCullers' *The Ballad of the Sad Cafe*." *TCL*, 20 (January 1974), 34-43.
   To read this work "is to experience the solitude of the heart and to understand how misconceptions of love only reinforce that solitude."

Bryant, Jerry H. See MISCELLANEOUS (Contemporary--1st Bryant entry).

Buchen, Irving H. "Carson McCullers: A Case of Convergence." *BuR*, 21 (Spring 1973), 15-28.
   Explores "the specific convergence of literature and psychology" in McCullers' work, particularly her interest in abnormal and adolescent psychology.

IV. Contemporary (1920-1975)

_____. "Divine Collusion: The Art of Carson McCullers." *Dal Rev*, 54 (Autumn 1974), 529-541.
The only ideal not shattered in McCullers' work is that of art. The mature artist is the only person to achieve any kind of wholeness.

Buchloh, Paul G. See GENERAL.

Bulgheroni, Marisa. See GENERAL.

Carr, Virginia Spencer. *The Lonely Hunter: A Biography of Carson McCullers*. Garden City, N. Y.: Doubleday, 1975.
A comprehensive account of the private and public lives of Carson McCullers.

Christadler, Martin. See MISCELLANEOUS (Contemporary).

Clark, Charlene K. "Pathos with a Chuckle: The Tragicomic Vision in the Novels of Carson McCullers." *Stud in Am Humor*, 1 (January 1975), 161-166.
Points to humor as an aspect of McCullers' novels most critics overlook; far from being "perverse and unnatural," the "juxtaposition of the tragic and the humorous" gives a realistic view of life.

Cook, Richard M. *Carson McCullers*. Mod Lit Monographs Series. New York: Frederick Ungar, 1975.
A critical summary of McCullers' life and work, focusing on her vision of isolation and loneliness and her use of the grotesque.

Cowley, Malcolm. See MISCELLANEOUS (Contemporary--2nd Cowley entry).

Dedmond, Francis B. "Doing Her Own Thing: Carson McCullers' Dramatization of 'The Member of the Wedding.'" *SAB*, 40 (May 1975), 47-52.
An account of how McCullers turned her novel into a successful play, with biographical information on the author.

Edmonds, Dale. *Carson McCullers*. Southern Writers Series. Austin: Steck-Vaughn, 1969.
A biographical-critical essay with special attention to thematic designs and use of regional materials in McCullers' work.

_____. "'Correspondence': A 'Forgotten' Carson McCullers Short Story." *Stud SF*, 9 (Winter 1972), 89-92.
"'Correspondence' is no stunning achievement, but it is a unified and effective minor work of short fiction."

Fletcher, Mary D. "Carson McCullers' 'Ancient Mariner.'" *Sou Central Bul*, 35 (Winter 1975), 123-125.
Points out parallels between Coleridge's poem and McCullers' "A Tree, A Rock, A Cloud."

French, Warren. See MISCELLANEOUS (Contemporary--2nd French entry).

Gaillard, Dawson F. "The Presence of the Narrator in Carson McCullers' *The Ballad of the Sad Café*." *Miss Quart*, 25 (Fall 1972), 419-427.

The narrator, who participates in the history of the town, is central to the power of the novel in that he moves the story out of history into tradition or myth.

Ginsberg, Elaine. See MISCELLANEOUS (Contemporary).

Gozzi, Francesco. "La narrativa di Carson McCullers." *SA*, 14 (1968), 339-376.
Deals with McCullers' treatment of her themes and concludes that she is only a novelist of the second rank.

Graver, Lawrence. *Carson McCullers*. University of Minnesota Pamphlets on American Writers, no. 84. Minneapolis: Univ of Minnesota Press, 1969.
A general introduction that finds that Mrs. McCullers' explorations of Southern grotesques are marked by "eccentric originality, artistic finish, and a bleak poetic effect."

Grinnell, James W. "Delving 'A Domestic Dilemma.'" *Stud SF*, 9 (Summer 1972), 270-271.
"The real irony of Martin and Emily's dilemma was that his concern for what others thought rendered him unable to show his love, the love which she needed in order to be well."

Hamilton, Alice. "Loneliness and Alienation: The Life and Work of Carson McCullers." *Dal Rev*, 50 (Summer 1970), 215-229.
Mrs. McCullers sees man as imperfect (symbolized by mutilations and deformities in her characters) and possibilities for human communication and happiness as severely limited. Detailed analysis of *The Heart Is a Lonely Hunter*, *Ballad of the Sad Café*, *Clock Without Hands*, and *Reflections in a Golden Eye*.

Hassan, Ihab. See MISCELLANEOUS (Contemporary--2nd Hassan entry).

Hendrick, George. "Almost Everyone Wants to Be the Lover: The Fiction of Carson McCullers." *BA*, 43 (Summer 1968), 389-391.
A brief summary of the major works and themes of Carson McCullers; calls for publication of a complete edition of the fiction and selections from the letters and notebooks.

Inge, M. Thomas. See MISCELLANEOUS (Contemporary--1st Inge entry).

Jaworski, Philippe. "La double quête de l'identite et de la réalité chez Carson McCullers." *NRF*, no. 199 (July 1969), 93-101.
Deals with the significance of *The Heart is a Lonely Hunter* in relation to McCullers' subsequent works.

Lasater, Alice. See MISCELLANEOUS (Contemporary).

Lawson, Lewis A. See MISCELLANEOUS (Contemporary).

LeClair, Thomas. See MISCELLANEOUS (Contemporary).

Longstreet, S. See GENERAL.

Madden, David. "Transfixed Among the Self-Inflicted Ruins: Carson McCullers's *The Mortgaged Heart*." *So Lit Jour*, 5 (Fall 1972), 137-162.

In *The Mortgaged Heart* Margarita G. Smith has given us a long look at "the mediocre side" of her sister.

Magny, Claude-Edmonde. See MISCELLANEOUS (Contemporary).

McNally, John. "The Introspective Narrator in 'The Ballad of the Sad Café.'" *SAB*, 38 (November 1973), 40-44.
    Through his internal monologue the narrator finds new meaning in his own existence.

Millichap, Joseph R. "Carson McCullers' Literary Ballad." *GaR*, 27 (Fall 1973), 329-339.
    "The use of the bizarre theory of love offered by the narrator of *Ballad* [*of the Sad Café*] as a formula for interpreting all of McCullers' fiction has hampered analysis not only of the *novella* itself but of her other works as well."

_____. "The Realistic Structure of *The Heart Is a Lonely Hunter*." *TCL*, 17 (January 1971), 11-17.
    A demonstration "through structural analysis" of "the psychological and social realism" of this work; "all elements of the novel--character, plot, style, setting, and symbol--are integrated in the larger purpose of presenting the failure of communication, the isolation, and the violence prevalent in modern society."

Missey, James. "A McCullers Influence on Albee's *The Zoo Story*." *Am N&Q*, 13 (April 1975), 121-124.
    Points out similarities between Albee's play and McCullers' "A Tree. A Rock. A Cloud."

Moers, Ellen. "Gotico femminile." *Comunità*, 29 (June 1975), 278-304.
    McCullers is included in this discussion of female writers of the Gothic form from Mary Shelley on.

Moore, Janice T. "McCullers' *The Ballad of the Sad Cafe*." *Expl*, 29 (November 1970), Item 27.
    Deals with the significance of the fowl imagery used in the portrayal of Cousin Lymon.

Nevius, Blake. See MISCELLANEOUS (Contemporary).

Pachmuss, Temira. "Dostoevsky, D. H. Lawrence, and Carson McCullers: Influences and Confluences." *Germano-Slavica*, 4 (1974), 59-63.
    The three writers are similar in their views of man and in their prose styles.

Perrine, Laurence. "Restoring 'A Domestic Dilemma.'" *Stud SF*, 11 (Winter 1974), 101-104.
    A note appearing in *Stud SF*, 9 (Summer 1972) "egregiously distorts the shape and meaning" of this work.

Presley, Delma Eugene. "Carson McCullers and the South." *GaR*, 28 (Spring 1974), 19-32.
    "If her early familiarity with the South bred contempt, then her exile's unfamiliarity with it bred something worse than contempt--vacuity."

_____. "Carson McCullers' Descent to Earth." *Descant*, 17 (Fall 1972), 54-60.
    McCullers' last work, *Clock Without Hands*, is a failure because McCullers could not find a proper form to present her new message of optimism.

_____. See O'CONNOR, FLANNERY (Contemporary--1st Presley entry).

_____. See MISCELLANEOUS (Contemporary).

Rechnitz, Robert M. "The Failure of Love: The Grotesque in Two Novels by Carson McCullers." *GaR*, 22 (Winter 1968), 454-463.
    Deals with the inability to love of characters in *Reflections in a Golden Eye* and *The Ballad of the Sad Café*.

Ríos Ruiz, Manuel. "Carson McCullers, la novelista del fatalismo." *Cuad Hisp*, no. 228 (December 1968), 763-771.
    McCullers, "in direct line with Faulkner," depicted the conflict between apparent reality and actual reality and "with a profound vision" pictured a "society in crisis."

Rivière, Yvette. "L'alienation dans les romans de Carson McCullers." *RANAM*, 4 (1971), 79-86.
    Every character in McCullers' novels, regardless of race or social or economic status, is shut up in himself, without hope of communication except through transient and illusory friendships.

Robinson, W. R. "The Life of Carson McCullers' Imagination." *SHR*, 2 (Summer 1968), 291-302.
    An instinct toward life, in which her imagination masters the dichotomies of man's own instincts toward life and toward death, is a major aspect of McCullers' fiction.

Schorer, Mark. See MISCELLANEOUS (Contemporary).

Skotnicki, Irene. "Die Darstellung der Entfremdung in den Romanen von Carson McCullers." *ZAA*, 20, no. 1 (1972), 24-45.
    McCullers' works, especially *The Heart is a Lonely Hunter* and *Clock Without Hands*, deal with alienation in a capitalistic society.

Smith, Margarita G., ed. *The Mortgaged Heart*. Boston: Houghton-Mifflin, 1971.
    A miscellany of McCullers' work edited, with an introduction, by her sister.

Stanley, William T. "Carson McCullers: 1965-1969, A Selected Checklist." *BB*, 27 (October-December 1970), 91-93.
    An unannotated listing of primary and secondary sources.

Taylor, William E. See MISCELLANEOUS (Contemporary).

Wikborg, Eleanor. *Carson McCullers' "The Member of the Wedding": Aspects of Structure and Style*. Gothenburg Studies in English, 31. Göteborg, Sweden: Acta Universitatis Gothoburgensis, 1975.
    A study of structure and style in relation to the themes of the work.

[McCURDY, HAROLD GRIER] Krickel, Edward. "Narcissus in North Carolina: Harold Grier McCurdy." *GaR*, 26 (Spring 1972), 71-77.
An essay-review of McCurdy's collection of poetry, *The Chastening of Narcissus*, that finds that in McCurdy's poetry "experience and perception are not transmitted to poetry in every case, that is, an objective correlative has not been found."

[McGILL, RALPH] Martin, H. H. *Ralph McGill, Reporter*. Boston: Atlantic-Little Brown, 1973.
A biographical account of the Tennessee-born editor of the Atlanta *Constitution* and an analysis of his journalism by a colleague of thirty years.

[MENCKEN, HENRY LOUIS] Anon. "Baltimore's Bad Boy: A Great and Beneficent Force." *TLS*, September 4, 1970, pp. 973-974.
An essay-review of *Mencken*, by Carl Bode.

Adler, Betty. "Bibliographic Check List." *Menckeniana*, nos. 37-44.
Title is descriptive.

_____, comp. *H. L. M. The Mencken Bibliography: A Ten Year Supplement, 1962-1971*. Baltimore, Md.: Enoch Pratt Free Library, 1971.
Supplements the bibliography published in 1961.

_____, comp. *Man of Letters: A Census of the Correspondence of H. L. Mencken*. Baltimore, Md.: Enoch Pratt Free Library, 1969.
Lists letters to and from Mencken; there is a separate section listing letters having to do with *The American Language*.

Anderson, Fenwick. "Mencken's Animadversions on Journalism." *Menckeniana*, no. 53 (Spring 1975), 6-8.
From 1924 to 1933 "Mencken regularly denounced the press in the pages of the *American Mercury*."

Babcock, C. Merton. See POE, EDGAR ALLAN.

Baer, John W. "H. L. Mencken: Exposer of Deceptions." *Menckeniana*, no. 48 (Winter 1973), 11-12.
Much of Mencken's writing is "descriptions of deception, the deceiver, and the deceived."

Bauer, Harry C. "The Glow and Gusto of H. L. Mencken's So and So's." *Menckeniana*, no. 47 (Fall 1973), 19-23.
Mencken showed remarkable virtuosity in his employment of the word *and*.

_____. "Iteration in HLM's Idiom Attic." *Menckeniana*, no. 55 (Fall 1975), 2-6.
When Mencken found "a perfect word or happy turn of phrase," he liked "to use the 'verbal delicacy' over and over again in telling ways."

Bode, Carl. *Mencken*. Carbondale: Southern Illinois Univ Press, 1969.
A full-length biography.

_____, ed. *The Young Mencken: The Best of His Work*. New York: Dial Press, 1973.
An anthology with an introduction by Bode.

Bonner, Thomas C. "Mencken as Whangdoodle: One Aspect of H. L. Mencken's Prose Style." *MarkR*, 3 (October 1971), 14-17.
Discusses the meanings of *Whangdoodle* that can be applied to Mencken's prose style.

Burr, John R. "H. L. Mencken: Scientific Skeptic." *Menckeniana*, no. 54 (Summer 1975), 1-8.
Mencken's philosophical position was "experimental or scientific skepticism, what HLM himself often called 'common sense.'"

Cairns, Huntington. "Mencken, Baltimore, and the Critics." *Menckeniana*, no. 45 (Spring 1973), 1-9.
A general review of reactions to Mencken, noting, however, that Mencken always enjoyed some critical support and that he has suffered no eclipse after his death.

_____. "The Quotable Mr. Mencken." *Menckeniana*, no. 54 (Summer 1975), 8-10.
Mencken is today "quoted more often than any other American writer including Mark Twain."

Chamberlain, John. "The Young Mencken." *Menckeniana*, no. 50 (Summer 1974), 6-8.
Title is descriptive.

Cheslock, Louis. "HLM Talks About Max Brodel." *Menckeniana*, no. 55 (Fall 1975), 6-8.
Reports Mencken's speech on "Max Brodel as Pianist" given on March 5, 1938.

_____. "Some Personal Memories of H. L. M." *Menckeniana*, no. 49 (Spring 1974), 3-11.
Memories of a Peabody Conservatory faculty member who "knew Henry Mencken as an intimate friend over a period of many years."

_____. See CABELL, JAMES BRANCH.

Christian, H. A. "'What Else Have You in Mind?': Louis Adamic and H. L. Mencken." *Menckeniana*, no. 47 (Fall 1973), 1-12.
A general historical look at the Adamic-Mencken relationship.

Cooney, C. F. "Mencken's Midwifery." *Menckeniana*, no. 43 (Fall 1972), 1-3.
Discusses Mencken's literary assistance of Walter White.

Dorsey, John, ed. *Mencken's Baltimore*. Magazine supplement to the Baltimore *Sun*, September 8, 1974.
A forty-page selection of writings by Mencken about the city of Baltimore, with illustrations and an introduction by Dorsey.

Douglas, George H. "Mencken's Critics in the Twenties." *Menckeniana*, no. 53 (September 1975), 1-5.
It is very important that we see Mencken "through the eyes of his contemporaries who often pierced through to the heart of his genius, and in ways that we cannot."

Eastman, John. "HLM's Voice for Posterity."
Menckeniana, no. 51 (Fall 1974), 9-11.
The only known transcription of Mencken's
voice is in the Caedmon album (TC 1082) "H. L.
Mencken Speaking."

Fullinwider, S. P. "Mencken's American Language."
Menckeniana, no. 40 (Winter 1971), 2-7.
Mencken's use of the American language suggests that there is an American tradition or
consciousness "which involves meeting the
changing and anxiety-provoking modern world
with humor and a degree of poise."

Geduld, Harry M. See MISCELLANEOUS (Contemporary).

Hart, Richard. "The Mencken Industry."
Menckeniana, no. 52 (Winter 1974), 3-14.
"The "pyramid" of publication on Mencken
"is firmly based and is rising at a steady
rate."

Hobson, Fred C., Jr. *Serpent in Eden: H. L.
Mencken and the South*. Chapel Hill: Univ of
North Carolina Press, 1974.
A full study of Mencken's attitudes toward
the South and his relations with Southern
writers through his published work and his
private correspondence.

Iversen, Anders. "Democratic Man, the Superior Man,
and the Forgotten Man in H. L. Mencken's *Notes
on Democracy*." *Eng Stud*, 50 (1969), 351-362.
As in *Notes on Democracy*, Mencken's "chief
ideas and concepts" were often irrelevant,
"which made it impossible for him to come to
grips with the real problems."

Jansen, K. Edward. "Mencken on Ibsen: Even Mencken
Nods." *Menckeniana*, no. 47 (Fall 1973), 13-18.
Mencken "praises Ibsen's lesser achievements
while rendering simple-minded his more important artistic accomplishments."

Jerome, W. P. "A Baltimore Episcopalian."
Menckeniana, no. 51 (Fall 1974), 7-9.
The "greatest of Mencken's hoaxes" is "his
long-trumpeted claim to be the arch-atheist of
his day."

Johnson, Gerald W. "Reconsideration: H. L.
Mencken." *New Rep*, 173 (December 27, 1975),
32-33.
Mencken was successful against mountebanks,
but his slapstick was not effective against
felons, nor would it be now.

_____. "Reconsideration: H. L. Mencken."
Menckeniana, no. 56 (Winter 1975), 1-3.
Reprinted from the *New Republic* (see
preceding entry).

Kellner, Bruce. "HLM and CVV: Friendship on
Paper." *Menckeniana*, no. 39 (Fall 1971), 2-9.
A look at "the warm friendship" and "curious
literary liaison" of Mencken and Carl Van
Vechten.

LaBelle, Maurice M. "H. L. Mencken's Comprehension
of Frederick Nietzsche." *CLS*, 7 (March 1970),
43-49.

Mencken's *The Philosophy of Frederick
Nietzsche* (1908) shows that he did not understand some of Nietzsche's most important concepts but was more interested in his iconoclasm.

Leary, Lewis. See GENERAL--1st Leary entry.

Levin, J. B. "National Convention Reporter."
Menckeniana, no. 41 (Spring 1972), 9-12.
In his convention reporting "HLM was much too
emotional not to take sides on current issues."

Libman, Valentina. See GENERAL.

Manchester, William. "The Last Years of H. L.
Mencken." *Atl*, 236 (October 1975), 82-90.
Memories of a seven-year friendship with
Mencken during the last years of his life.

Manglaviti, Leo M. J. "Markham and Mencken."
MarkR, 3 (February 1972), 38-39.
Points out a letter which Mencken wrote to
Markham, praising "The Man with the Hoe."

_____. See FAULKNER, WILLIAM (Contemporary).

Matheson, Terence J. "Mencken's Reviews of Sinclair
Lewis's Major Novels." *Menckeniana*, no. 51
(Fall 1974), 2-7.
"Mencken's personal biases as a social com-
mentator far too often stood in the way of his
properly evaluating Sinclair Lewis's novels."

Mayfield, Sara. *The Constant Circle: H. L.
Mencken and His Friends*. New York: Delacorte
Press, 1968.
A reminiscent biography.

McGrain, J. W., Jr. "Ayd and Criminal Aid."
Menckeniana, no. 45 (Spring 1973), 11-12.
A look at the relationship of Mencken and
Father Joseph J. Ayd, chaplain of the Maryland
Penitentiary.

Morrison, Joseph L. "Colonel H. L. Mencken,
C. S. A." *So Lit Jour*, 1 (Autumn 1968), 42-59.
Concludes that the Sage did not press his luck
as a social critic but contented himself with exploring the artful science of civilized life.

Motsch, Markus F. "H. L. Mencken and German Kultur."
Ger-Am Stud, 6 (1973), 21-42.
Discusses the influences of German culture on
Mencken, who followed the principles of late
eighteenth-century German criticism.

Nolte, William H. "Mencken on Art, Order, and the
Absurd." *Menckeniana*, no. 37 (Spring 1971),
1-7.
To Mencken, "life was a gift, not a burden";
his ideas on art, order and the absurd are not
what we might at first assume.

_____. See FAULKNER, WILLIAM (Contemporary).

_____. "*The Smart Set*: Mencken for the Defense."
Sou Dakota Rev, 6 (Autumn 1968), 3-11.
Focuses on the aim of Mencken and Nathan in
publishing works of new writers in *The Smart Set*.

Patterson, Maclean. "HLM's Credo." *Menckeniana*, 56 (Winter 1975), 10-11.
    Mencken's "Credo" is revealed in an exchange of letters between him and Dr. Donald F. Proctor.

_____. "Mencken-Pearl Letters." *Menckeniana*, no. 49 (Spring 1974), 12.
    Title is descriptive.

_____, et al. "Bibliographic Check List." *Menckeniana*, nos. 49-56 (1974-75).
    Title is descriptive.

Pentz, J. A. "Mencken at the Baltimore City College." *Menckeniana*, no. 38 (Summer 1971), 2-5.
    A remembrance of Mencken's annual appearance before the Current Events Club at the Baltimore City College.

Pons, Xavier. "H. L. Mencken et la biologie." *Caliban*, 9 (1972), 105-122.
    Mencken followed the principles of nineteenth-century biology, unaware that there were some differences between it and twentieth-century biology.

Powell, Arnold. "Mencken and the Absurdists." *Menckeniana*, no. 46 (Summer 1973), 3-8.
    A "comparative investigation," concluding that "Mencken would probably have found the modern absurdists unobjective and hopelessly sentimental."

Rasmussen, Frederick N. "Pen, Ink, and Mr. Mencken." *Menckeniana*, no. 48 (Winter 1973), 4-8.
    A study of McKee Barclay, who drew "The Subconscious Mencken" cartoon.

Reynolds, Robert D., Jr. "Robert Rives LaMonte: Mencken's 'Millionaire Socialist' Collaborator." *Menckeniana*, no. 48 (Winter 1973), 2-4.
    There was a "strange and enduring friendship" between Mencken and LaMonte, who had coauthored *Men Versus the Man* (1910).

Rosenshine, Annette. "Mr. Mencken Past Tense." *Menckeniana*, no. 37 (Spring 1971), 9-10.
    The history of Miss Rosenshine's bust of Mencken.

Rubin, Louis D., Jr. See GENERAL--1st Rubin entry.

Ruland, Richard. See CABELL, JAMES BRANCH (Postbellum).

Salzman, Jack. "Conroy, Mencken, and *The American Mercury*." *Jour of Pop Culture*, 7 (Winter 1973), 524-528.
    Describes Mencken's editorial relations with a few writers of the American Left, 1930-1933.

Scheideman, J. W. "H. L. Mencken and Willa Cather Compared in Louis Auchincloss' *Pioneers and Caretakers*." *Menckeniana*, no. 47 (Fall 1973), 24-25.
    "Less dramatic and more considered phrasing" by Auchincloss "would have aided the readers' comprehension."

Shapiro, Edward S. "The Southern Agrarians, H. L. Mencken, and the Quest for Southern Identity." *Am Stud*, 13 (Fall 1972), 75-92.
    A fully documented presentation of the quarrel between Mencken and the Agrarians about the nature of Southern culture, assessing particularly the significance for the Agrarians of the debate.

Shutt, James W. "H. L. Mencken and the Baltimore *Evening Sun* Freelance Column." *Menckeniana*, no. 48 (Winter 1973), 8-10.
    "...the essential Menckenian essay developed out of the daily experience of the Freelance work."

Shyre, Paul. "Mencken on Stage." *Menckeniana*, no. 56 (Winter 1975), 4-8.
    The producer/writer/star of *Blasts and Bravos--An Evening with H. L. Mencken* reflects on this production and its subject.

Stenerson, Douglas C. "Baltimore: Source and Sustainer of Mencken's Values." *Menckeniana*, no. 41 (Spring 1972), 1-9.
    The basic values to which Mencken was committed "developed within the atmosphere of thought and feeling available to him as he was growing up in the Baltimore of the 1880's and 1890's."

_____. *H. L. Mencken: Iconoclast from Baltimore*. Chicago: Univ of Chicago Press, 1971.
    Emphasizes Mencken's importance as a stylist.

_____. "Short-Story Writing: A Neglected Phase of Mencken's Literary Apprenticeship." *Menckeniana*, no. 30 (1969), 8-13.
    Mencken's short stories are flawed, but they provide insight into his early critical attitudes.

Sturm, D. N. "H. L. Mencken and the American Tradition of Anarchism." *Menckeniana*, no. 38 (Summer 1971), 6-7.
    "Mencken was the unsung and uncanonized ideologue for the modern-day radical."

Turaj, Frank. "H. L. Mencken's Philosophical Skepticism." *Menckeniana*, no. 48 (Winter 1973), 12-16.
    Mencken, greatly influenced by T. H. Huxley, almost always took a position of skepticism, one he "held seriously and philosophically."

Walt, James. "Conrad and Mencken. Pt. 2." *Conradiana*, 2 (Spring 1969-70), 100-110.
    Mencken's admiration for Conrad was based on Conrad's "tragic and sardonic view of man."

_____. "Conrad and Mencken, Pt. 3." *Conradiana*, 3, no. 1 (1970-71), 69-74.
    Deals with Mencken's Baltimore *Sun* articles and with Conrad's generally favorable reaction to what Mencken wrote about him.

_____. "Mencken and Conrad." *Conradiana*, 2 (Winter 1969-70), 9-21.
    Part 1 of Walt's article on Conrad and Mencken; discusses Mencken's admiration of Conrad's works.

Warren, George T. "The Mercury Idea."
Menckeniana, no. 47 (Fall 1973), 25-26.
"Henry Holt's *Unpopular Review* could have
started sowing the seed that later brought forth
the *American Mercury*."

West, James L. W. III. "Mencken's Review of *Tales
of the Jazz Age*." *Menckeniana*, no. 50
(Summer 1974), 2-4.
Mencken's unfavorable review "may well have
had some effect on Fitzgerald."

Williams, William H. A. "Realism and Iconoclasm:
H. L. Mencken as Drama Critic, 1904-1910."
Menckeniana, no. 46 (Summer 1973), 8-12.
Mencken as drama critic "posited a highly
optimistic view of the relationship between art
and human progress."

Williamson, Chilton, Jr. "Commonsense Politics."
Menckeniana, no. 43 (Fall 1972), 4-11.
Mencken "never got American politics out of
his system, but the New Deal helped to return
him to his earlier preoccupations."

Wilson, Edmund. "The Aftermath of Mencken." *New
Yorker*, 45 (May 31, 1969), 107-115.
Mencken is best understood in the light of
his German origins.

Wilson, Henry B. "Recalls HLM as Patient."
Menckeniana, no. 54 (Summer 1975), 10-11.
An opthalmologist recalls examining
Mencken, who, because of a cerebral accident,
had a reading difficulty.

Wingate, P. J. "H. L. Mencken on Watergate."
Menckeniana, no. 50 (Summer 1974), 4-5.
Mencken "would have been strangely mild--
even gentle and forgiving" in commenting on
Watergate after most of the facts were known.

_____. "The Making of a Menckenite."
Menckeniana, no. 56 (Winter 1975), 8-10.
An Eastern Shoreman became such a confirmed
Menckenite in 1933-34 that he never fails "to
greet with glee any new account of the Sage's
battles with the human race."

_____. "Mencken and Grasty." *Menckeniana*, no. 55
(Fall 1975), 8-9.
Charles Henry Grasty probably influenced
Mencken more than anyone else did.

Woodward, C. Vann. See MISCELLANEOUS
(Contemporary).

Wycherley, H. Alan. "'Americana': The Mencken-
Lorimer Feud." *Costerus*, 5 (1972), 227-236.
An account of the unsuccessful "counter-
attack" of the editor of the *Saturday Evening
Post* against Mencken's Americana feature in the
American Mercury.

_____. "H. L. Mencken vs. the Eastern Shore:
December 1931." *BNYPL*, 74 (June 1970), 381-390.
Deals with Mencken's reactions to two
lynchings in Maryland in 1931.

[MENCKEN, SARA HAARDT] Going, William T. See
FITZGERALD, ZELDA.

[MILLER, VASSAR] Owen, Guy. "Vassar Miller: A
Southern Metaphysical." *So Lit Jour*, 3
(Fall 1970), 83-87.
Miller is "one of the most powerful meta-
physical poets writing in America today."

[MIMS, EDWIN] O'Brien, Michael. "Edwin Mims: An
Aspect of the Mind of the South Considered: I."
SAQ, 73 (Spring 1974), 199-212.
Mims believed that the South's critics had a
vital role to play in its development.

_____. "Edwin Mims: An Aspect of the Mind of the
South Considered: II." *SAQ*, 73
(Summer 1974), 324-334.
Mims's *The Advancing South* was more than a
plea for the South's place in the nation; it
was a plea for the South's proper role among all
civilized and cultured nations.

_____. See DAVIDSON, DONALD (Contemporary).

[MITCHELL, MARGARET] Baker, Donald G. See GENERAL.

Draper, John W. "A Letter from Margaret Mitchell."
West Va Bul: Philological Papers, 17
(June 1970), 81-83.
Margaret Mitchell's response to Draper about
translating *Gone with the Wind* into French.

Gaillard, Dawson. "*Gone with the Wind* as
Bildungsroman or Why Did Rhett Butler Really
Leave Scarlett O'Hara?" *GaR*, 28 (Spring 1974),
9-18.
"Mitchell could endorse traditional values
while simultaneously undermining them in the
novel."

Groover, Robert L. "Margaret Mitchell: The Lady
from Atlanta." *GHQ*, 52 (March 1968), 53-69.
A journalistic synopsis of Margaret Mitchell's
life.

Libman, Valentina. See GENERAL.

Ludington, C. T., Jr. See MISCELLANEOUS
(Contemporary).

Shavin, Norman, and Martin Shartar. *The Million
Dollar Legends: Margaret Mitchell and "Gone
With The Wind."* Atlanta: Capricorn Corpora-
tion, 1974.
A heavily illustrated pamphlet, the text of
which traces the life and career of the author
and her famed novel on the twenty-fifty anniversary of her death.

Stern, Jerome. "*Gone with the Wind*: The South as
America" (in "Four Authors View the South: A
Symposium"). *SHR*, 6 (Winter 1972), 5-12.
So-called Southern myths, a staple of American popular literature, are actually American
myths localized in time and place; the popularity of *Gone with the Wind* is due to "its
accuracy as a dramatization of American
attitudes."

Watkins, Floyd C. "*Gone with the Wind* as Vulgar
Literature." *So Lit Jour*, 2 (Spring 1970),
86-103.

Gone with the Wind fails from an oversimpli-
fied regionalism, a too narrow patriotism,
prudishness, melodrama, and sentimentalism;
Margaret Mitchell, unlike Faulkner, fails to
present the great drama of the forces of
history.

[MONTGOMERY, MARION] Carr, John. See
MISCELLANEOUS (Contemporary).

Colvert, James B. "An Interview with Marion
Montgomery." *SouR*, 6 (Autumn 1970), 1041-1053.
Answers to questions mostly about
Montgomery's own fiction and poetry.

Landess, Thomas H. See MISCELLANEOUS
(Contemporary).

[MOORE, MERRILL] Basler, Roy P. *The Muse and the
Librarian*. Westport, Conn.: Greenwood Press,
1974.
Reprints an appreciative essay of 1958,
"Proteus and Apollo: The Poetry of Merrill
Moore."

[MORRIS, WILLIE] Carr, John. See MISCELLANEOUS
(Contemporary).

Kass, Carole. "Writer Says South Will Pioneer
Racial Harmony." Richmond *Times-Dispatch*,
May 19, 1971, p. B-6.
A report on an interview with Morris
regarding his book *Yazoo* and his departure
from the editorship of *Harper's*.

Madden, David. *The Poetic Image in Six Genres*.
Carbondale: Southern Illinois Univ Press,
1969.
Examines the concept of the poetic image
in the genres of poetry, fiction, films,
drama, and autobiography, using Morris' *North
Toward Home* as an example of the last.

Mitchell, Paul. "*North Toward Home*: The Quest for
an Intellectual Home." *Notes on Miss Writers*,
2 (Winter 1970), 105-109.
Morris' autobiography is the record of a
Southerner's successful search for intellectual
stimulation, found in New York City.

Moore, Robert H. "The Last Months at *Harper's*:
Willie Morris in Conversation." *Mississippi
Rev*, 3 (1974), 121-130.
Transcription of a 1971 interview.

Morris, Willie. *Yazoo: Integration in a Deep-
Southern Town*. New York: Harper's Magazine
Press, 1971.
In the autobiographical form of *North Toward
Home*, Morris narrates his discovery, on trips
home in 1969 and 1970 to observe accommodation
to desegregation, that the deep South offers
promise of a resolution to the racial conflict.

Pinkerton, Jan. See MISCELLANEOUS (Contemporary).

[MURRAY, ALBERT] McPherson, James A. "The View
from the Chinaberry Tree." *Atl*, 234
(December 1974), 118, 120-123.
Murray's *Train Whistle Guitar* "endeavors to
recreate a community of black people who have a

clear perspective on themselves and the world
about them."

[NOLAN, PAUL] Matherne, Beverly M. "Louisiana
Playwright: Paul T. Nolan; a Bibliographical
Essay." *La Stud*, 10 (Winter 1971), 244-256.
Nolan, who teaches English at the University
of Southwest Louisiana, is the author of many
one-act plays.

[O'CONNOR, FLANNERY] Anon. "Dust for Art's Sake."
Time, 93 (May 30, 1969), 70.
A review of Miss O'Connor's *Mystery and Manners* that says that while these essays do little
to enhance her considerable reputation, they do
throw light on its foundation and the problem of
being "a true Southerner, a devout Catholic and
a practicing creative artist at the same time."

Anon. "Long Day's Preaching." *TLS*, February 1,
1968, p. 101.
An essay-review of the Faber and Faber
reissued edition of *Wise Blood*.

Abbot, Louise H. "Remembering Flannery O'Connor."
So Lit Jour, 2 (Spring 1970), 3-25.
A moving and intimate account of the many
visits of the author of the article to Andalusia
and her impression of the funeral of Flannery
O'Connor.

Asals, Frederick. "Flannery O'Connor as Novelist:
A Defense." *Flannery O'Connor Bul*, 3
(Autumn 1974), 22-39.
O'Connor's novels are "largely successful and
impressive on their own terms."

_____. "Flannery O'Connor's 'The Lame Shall Enter
First.'" *Miss Quart*, 23 (Spring 1970), 103-120.
A reading of Miss O'Connor's longest short
story to illustrate the complexity of her art
and her "poetically" conceived fiction.

_____. "Flannery Row." *Novel*, 4 (Fall 1970), 92-96.
An essay-review of Carter W. Martin's *The
True Country: Themes in the Fiction of Flannery
O'Connor* and of Flannery O'Connor's *Mystery and
Manners*. Asals thinks that in her fiction "the
eye is O'Connor's pre-eminent sensory touchstone"
and that Martin's study is "not wholly without
insight, but its total effect is numbing."

_____. "The Mythic Dimensions of Flannery O'Connor's
'Greenleaf.'" *Stud SF* (Summer 1968), 317-330.
Traces out the various levels of non-
scriptural myth in the story.

_____. "The Road to *Wise Blood*." *Renascence*, 21
(Summer 1969), 181-194.
A scrutiny of O'Connor's first stories un-
covers "the kinds of motion which led both
toward and beyond" *Wise Blood*.

_____. "Hawthorne, Mary Ann, and 'The Lame Shall
Enter First.'" *Flannery O'Connor Bul*, 2
(Autumn 1973), 3-18.
Drawing comments from O'Connor's "introduc-
tion" to *A Memoir of Mary Ann* to establish
O'Connor's interest in Hawthorne, the article
explores the influence of "The Birthmark" on
"The Lame Shall Enter First."

Barcus, Nancy B. "Psychological Determinism and Freedom in Flannery O'Connor." *Cithara*, 12 (November 1972), 26-33.
> *The Violent Bear It Away* ultimately offers a "calculated rejection of psychological determinism as a final explanation of the nature of reality."

Bass, Eben. "Flannery O'Connor and Henry James: The Vision of Grace." *Stud in the Twentieth Cent*, no. 14 (Fall 1974), 43-68.
> O'Connor adapts James's restrictive point-of-view by using various kinds of narrators, observers, and sight symbols as both technique and theme.

Becham, Gerald. "Flannery O'Connor Collection." *Flannery O'Connor Bul*, 1 (1972), 66-71.
> Surveys the material in the O'Connor Collection in the Ina Dillard Russell Library at Georgia College.

Bergup, Sister Bernice. "Themes of Redemptive Grace in the Works of Flannery O'Connor." *Am Benedictine Rev*, 21 (June 1970), 169-191.
> Deals with the theology of O'Connor's work.

Blackwell, Louise. "Flannery O'Connor's Literary Style." *Antigonish Rev*, 10 (Summer 1972), 57-65.
> Discusses symbols, language, and theme in O'Connor's works.

_____. "Humor and Irony in the Works of Flannery O'Connor." *RANAM*, 4 (1971), 61-68.
> O'Connor is a traditional humorist and blends irony and humor in her works.

Borgman, Paul. "Three Wise Men: The Comedy of O'Connor's *Wise Blood*." *Chri and Lit*, 24 (Spring 1975), 36-48.
> The comedy comes from the conflict in the attitudes toward life of Mrs. Flood, Enoch Emery, and Hazel Motes.

Boyd, G. N. and L. A. See MISCELLANEOUS (Contemporary).

Brady, Charles. Untitled. *Cweal*, 97 (October 27, 1972), 93-94.
> An essay-review of Sister Kathleen Feeley's *Flannery O'Connor: Voice of the Peacock* and David Eggenschwiler's *The Christian Humanism of Flannery O'Connor*. Argues that these books are useful but not definitive because both authors err in accepting at face value Miss O'Connor's statements about her art.

Brittain, Joan T. "Flannery O'Connor--Addenda." *BB*, 25 (May-August 1968), 142.
> Corrects three errors in the bibliography published in *BB*, 25 (September-December 1967 and January-April 1968).

_____. "Flannery O'Connor, Part 2." *BB*, 25 (January-April 1968), 123-124.
> The final part of a bibliography of works by and about O'Connor, the first part of which appeared in *BB*, 25 (September-December 1967), 98-100.

_____, and Leon V. Driskell. "O'Connor and the Eternal Crossroads." *Renascence*, 22 (Autumn 1969), 49-55.
> A discussion of Andalusia, Georgia, as the location of "the crossroads where time and place and eternity somehow meet."

Brown, Ashley. "Grotesque Occasions." *Spec*, 221 (September 6, 1968), 330-332.
> An essay-review of the reissue of *A Good Man Is Hard to Find* by Faber and Faber.

Browning, Preston M., Jr. *Flannery O'Connor*. Carbondale: Southern Illinois Univ Press, 1974.
> The tensions between unbelief and the necessity of belief define the philosophic content and the religious motifs in O'Connor's fiction.

_____. "Flannery O'Connor." *ConL*, 16 (Spring 1975), 260-271.
> An essay-review of Gilbert Muller's *Nightmares and Visions*, Leon Driskell and Joan Brittain's *The Eternal Crossroads*, David Eggenschwiler's *The Christian Humanism of Flannery O'Connor*, Sister Kathleen Feeley's *Flannery O'Connor*, and Miles Orvell's *Invisible Parade*.

_____. "Flannery O'Connor and the Demonic." *MFS*, 19 (Spring 1973), 29-41.
> O'Connor "committed herself to a vision which places a positive valuation upon violence, upon 'spiritual crime'" in order to combat "the real enemy," which is "the heedless nihilism of the multitudes of faithless pilgrims."

_____. "Flannery O'Connor and the Grotesque Recovery of the Holy," in *Adversity and Grace: Studies in Recent American Literature*, ed. Nathan A. Scott, Jr. Chicago: Univ of Chicago Press, 1968.
> Deals with O'Connor's consideration of the problem of good and evil.

_____. "'Parker's Back': Flannery O'Connor's Iconography of Salvation by Profanity." *Stud SF*, 6 (Fall 1969), 525-535.
> In this story "the true secular and the true sacred interpenetrate and sustain one another."

Bryant, Jerry H. See MISCELLANEOUS (Contemporary--1st Bryant entry).

Buchloh, Paul G. See GENERAL.

Burns, Stuart L. "The Evolution of *Wise Blood*." *MFS*, 16 (Summer 1970), 147-162.
> An examination of five O'Connor short stories published between 1948 and 1952 which later became parts of *Wise Blood*, in an effort to define the function of the novel's pervasive sexuality.

_____. "Flannery O'Connor's Literary Apprenticeship." *Renascence*, 22 (Autumn 1969), 3-16.
> Provides a summary of "the ingredients" in O'Connor's apprenticeship writing "which contribute to the excellence of the later fiction."

_____. "Flannery O'Connor's *The Violent Bear It Away*: Apotheosis in Failure." *SR*, 76 (Spring 1968), 319-337.

Argues that the main thesis of the novel is that the man Tarwater has a truer vision of reality than does the so-called normal run of humanity.

_____. "Freaks in a Circus Tent: Flannery O'Connor's Christ-haunted Characters." *Flannery O'Connor Bul*, 1 (1972), 1-23.
O'Connor's "Christ-haunted" characters have "a sense of commitment."

_____. "How Wide Did 'The Heathen' Range." *Flannery O'Connor Bul*, 4 (1975), 25-41.
Although there is "no novel at all" in the manuscript fragment of "Why Do the Heathen Rage," the pieces do offer "insight into Flannery O'Connor's method of writing."

_____. "O'Connor and the Critics: An Overview." *Miss Quart*, 27 (Fall 1974), 483-495.
General reaction to O'Connor criticism with specific attention to six books published 1971-1974.

_____. "Structural Patterns in *Wise Blood*." *XUS*, 8 (July 1969), 32-43.
Discusses the symbolism of sex, water, and the coffin in this work.

Byrd, Turner F. "Ironic Dimensions in Flannery O'Connor's 'The Artificial Nigger.'" *Miss Quart*, 21 (Fall 1968), 243-251.
Artistic irony makes the meaning of the story not a true moment of revelation (grace) for the two main characters, but a confirmation of their prejudices.

Carlson, Thomas M. "Flannery O'Connor: The Manichaean Dilemma." *SR*, 77 (Spring 1969), 254-276.
Emphasizes the nature of the protagonist in O'Connor's works.

Carter, T. H. See MISCELLANEOUS (Contemporary).

Casper, Leonard. "The Unspeakable Peacock: Apocalypse in Flannery O'Connor," in *The Shaken Realist: Essays in Modern Literature in Honor of Frederick J. Hoffman*, ed. Melvin J. Friedman and John Vickery. Baton Rouge: Louisiana State Univ Press, 1970, pp. 287-299.
Views death as a constant provocation to Miss O'Connor's religious imagination and as her central theme.

Christadler, Martin. See MISCELLANEOUS (Contemporary).

Coindreau, Maurice. See MISCELLANEOUS (Contemporary--2nd Coindreau entry).

Cunningham, John. "Recent Works on Flannery O'Connor: A Review-Essay." *SHR*, 8 (Summer 1974), 375-388.
Reviews books on O'Connor by Miles Orvell, David Eggenschwiler, Gilbert Muller, Carter Martin, Sister Kathleen Feeley, and Josephine G. Hendin.

Davis, Jack and June. "Tarwater and Jonah: Two Reluctant Prophets." *XUS*, 9 (Spring 1970), 19-27.

Deals with O'Connor's use of the story of Jonah in *The Violent Bear It Away* to emphasize modern man's separation from God.

Denham, Robert D. "The World of Guilt and Sorrow: Flannery O'Connor's 'Everything That Rises Must Converge.'" *Flannery O'Connor Bul*, 4 (1975), 42-51.
The story is about the beginning of Julian's growth toward maturity.

Desmond, John F. "The Lessons of History: Flannery O'Connor's 'Everything That Rises Must Converge.'" *Flannery O'Connor Bul*, 1 (1972), 39-45.
Studies the doctrine of Convergence and the influence of Pierre Teilhard de Chardin in the O'Connor story.

_____. "The Mystery of the Word and the Act: *The Violent Bear It Away*." *Am Benedictine Rev*, 24 (1973), 342-347.
This work is concerned with the mystery of language and the mystery of silence, the latter suggesting both "Divine Presence and the void wherein spiritual choice must be struggled over and created."

_____. "The Shifting of Mr. Shiftlet: Flannery O'Connor's 'The Life You Save May Be Your Own.'" *Miss Quart*, 28 (Winter 1974-75), 55-59.
Discusses the development of Mr. Shiftlet in relation to "the unfolding action and the typological significance of the story."

Detweiler, Robert. See MISCELLANEOUS (Contemporary).

Dillard, R. H. W., et al. See MISCELLANEOUS (Contemporary).

Doxey, William S. "A Dissenting Opinion of Flannery O'Connor's 'A Good Man Is Hard to Find.'" *Stud SF*, 10 (Spring 1973), 199-204.
The structure of this short story is flawed; specifically, there is a shift in point-of-view.

Drake, Robert. "Flannery O'Connor," in *Religion and Modern Literature*, ed. G. B. Tennyson and E. E. Ericson, Jr. Grand Rapids, Mich.: William B. Eerdmans, 1975, pp. 393-406.
Describes O'Connor as an "uncompromising worker of Christian themes."

_____. "Flannery O'Connor and American Literature." *Flannery O'Connor Bul*, 3 (Autumn 1974), 1-22.
Examines the American qualities of O'Connor's fiction.

_____. "The Paradigm of Flannery O'Connor's True Country." *Stud SF*, 6 (Summer 1969), 433-442.
Examines implications of what O'Connor meant by "true country" and suggests that this meaning provides a "sobering *exemplum*" for all practicing writers.

Driskell, Leon V. "To Flannery O'Connor." *SHR*, 3 (Spring 1969), 145.
An original poem.

_____, and Joan T. Brittain. *The Eternal Crossroads: The Art of Flannery O'Connor*. Lexington: Univ Press of Kentucky, 1971.

In her total work, O'Connor sought to discover the eternal crossroads, "where time and place and eternity sometimes meet."

Dula, Martha A. "Evidences of the Prelapsarian in Flannery O'Connor's *Wise Blood*." *XUS*, 11 (Winter 1972), 1-12.
O'Connor portrays Hazel Motes, the unattractive hero of *Wise Blood*, a being initiated into the knowledge of good and evil, so as to suggest a symbolic re-enactment of the original.

Edelstein, Mark G. "Flannery O'Connor and the Problem of Modern Satire." *Stud SF*, 12 (Spring 1975), 139-144.
In O'Connor's satire of modern man "we see the startling similarities between ourselves and her grotesque atheists and hypocrites."

Eggenschwiler, David. *The Christian Humanism of Flannery O'Connor*. Detroit: Wayne State Univ Press, 1972.
Focuses on the thesis that O'Connor wrote consistently from the point of view of a Christian humanist and explored concerns of modern theologians and psychologists.

_____. "Flannery O'Connor's True and False Prophets." *Renascence*, 21 (Spring 1969), 151-161, 167.
The purpose "is to analyze conflicting forms of religious values" in *The Violent Bear It Away*, *Wise Blood*, and relevant short stories.

Esch, Robert M. "O'Connor's 'Everything That Rises Must Converge.'" *Expl*, 27 (April 1969), 58.
The condition of the eyes of Julian's mother at the end of the story "symbolize[s] the ultimate rejection of Julian."

Fahey, William A. "Flannery O'Connor's 'Parker's Back.'" *Renascence*, 20 (Spring 1968), 162-164, 166.
A reading of the story as Parker's "return" to ecstasy.

Farnham, James F. "Disintegration of Myth in the Writings of Flannery O'Connor." *Conn Rev*, 8 (October 1974), 11-19.
"...the essential experience of the Flannery O'Connor character is the disintegration of myth and the devastation which results from such disintegration."

Feeley, Sister Kathleen M. *Flannery O'Connor: Voice of the Peacock*. New Brunswick : Rutgers Univ Press, 1972.
Examines the fiction against O'Connor's Catholic and Southern background, with emphasis on her reading in and use of theology and philosophy.

_____. "Thematic Imagery in the Fiction of Flannery O'Connor." *SHR*, 3 (Winter 1969), 14-32.
The many forms of imagery in Miss O'Connor's fiction reveal her to be both poet and prophet. Her poetry makes the real world visible, and as a prophet she "cries out the existence of a spiritual world, no less real because invisible."

Flores-Del Prado, Wilma. "Flannery O'Connor's Gallery of Freaks." *St. Louis Univ Research Jour*, 2 (September-December 1971), 463-514.
On O'Connor's use of grotesque characters to show the need for spiritual faith.

French, Warren. See MISCELLANEOUS (Contemporary--1st French entry).

Friedman, Melvin J. "By and About Flannery O'Connor." *Jour of Mod Lit*, 1, no. 2 (1970-71), 288-292.
An essay-review of Carter W. Martin's *The True Country* and of O'Connor's *Mysteries and Manners*.

_____. "Flannery O'Connor: The Canon Completed, the Commentary Continuing." *So Lit Jour*, 5 (Spring 1973), 116-123.
An essay-review of *The Complete Stories of Flannery O'Connor* and of Josephine Hendin's *The World of Flannery O'Connor*.

_____. "Flannery O'Connor: The Tonal Dilemma." *So Lit Jour*, 6 (Spring 1974), 124-129.
An essay-review of Martha Stephens' *The Question of Flannery O'Connor*, which the reviewer calls "simply the best book we have" on O'Connor.

_____. "Flannery O'Connor's Sacred Objects," in *The Vision Obscured*, ed. Melvin J. Friedman. New York: Fordham Univ Press, 1970.
A revision of a 1966 essay on O'Connor's use of objects for thematic purposes.

_____. "John Hawkes and Flannery O'Connor: The French Background." *Boston Univ Jour*, 21, no. 3 (1973), 34-44.
On the influence of French poets and novelists on O'Connor and Hawkes.

Gafford, Charlotte K. "Chaucer's Pardoner and Haze Motes of Georgia," in *Essays in Honor of R. G. McWilliams*, ed. Howard Creed. Birmingham, Ala.: Birmingham-Southern College, 1970, pp. 9-12.
A comparison of the two characters on theological grounds.

Giroux, Robert. "Introduction" to *The Complete Stories of Flannery O'Connor*. New York: Farrar, Straus, and Giroux, 1971.
A memoir detailing O'Connor's relationships with publishers and with Thomas Merton.

Gordon, Caroline. "Heresy in Dixie." *SR*, 76 (Spring 1968), 263-298.
Compares and analogizes Flannery O'Connor to Gustave Flaubert in her religious and theological concern. Concludes with an explication of O'Connor's short story "Parker's Back."

_____. "Rebels and Revolutionaries: The New American Scene." *Flannery O'Connor Bul*, 3 (Autumn 1974), 40-56.
An examination of O'Connor's debt to Henry James.

Goss, James. "The Double Action of Mercy in 'The Artificial Nigger.'" *Chri and Lit*, 23 (1974), 36-45.
Deals with the justification and sanctification of Mr. Head and Nelson.

Gossett, Thomas F. "Flannery O'Connor on Her Fiction." *SWR*, 59 (Winter 1974), 34-42.
    Contains valuable information summarized and paraphrased from the 135 O'Connor letters in Mr. Gossett's possession.

_____. "Flannery O'Connor's Opinions of Other Writers: Some Unpublished Comments." *So Lit Jour*, 6 (Spring 1974), 70-82.
    Miss O'Connor's comments--from letters, meetings, and personal recollections of the author--on many writers, from Bernanos to Bourjaily.

_____. "No Vague Believer: Flannery O'Connor and Protestantism." *SWR*, 60 (Summer 1975), 256-263.
    Concerns O'Connor's religious opinions and her relationships and correspondence with a number of Protestant friends; based on several of O'Connor's unpublished letters.

Green, James L. "Enoch Emery and His Biblical Namesakes in 'Wise Blood.'" *Stud SF*, 10 (Fall 1973), 417-419.
    Enoch's "disappearance from the novella is consistent with O'Connor's biblical source."

Gregory, Donald. "Enoch Emery: Ironic Doubling in *Wise Blood*." *Flannery O'Connor Bul*, 4 (1975), 52-64.
    Enoch's presence in the novel gives it greater universality and a comic dimension that lends emphasis to the tragedy of Hazel Motes's "quest."

Gresset, Michel. "L'audace de Flannery O'Connor." *NRF*, 18 (December 1970), 61-71.
    O'Connor's works combine farce and drama.

Hamblen, Abigail A. "Flannery O'Connor's Study of Innocence and Evil." *Univ Rev*, 34 (June 1968), 295-297.
    On "A Good Man Is Hard to Find."

Harrison, Margaret. "Hazel Motes in Transit: A Comparison of Two Versions of Flannery O'Connor's 'The Train' with Chapter 1 of 'Wise Blood.'" *Stud SF*, 8 (Spring 1971), 287-293.
    O'Connor's short story "The Train," part of her M. F. A. thesis at the University of Iowa, "quite obviously formed the nucleus of the first chapter of 'Wise Blood'"; a comparison of the story and the chapter shows O'Connor's "growing awareness of her own peculiar thematic and technical aims."

Hassan, Ihab. See MISCELLANEOUS (Contemporary-- 2nd Hassan entry).

Hays, Peter L. "Dante, Tobit, and 'The Artificial Nigger.'" *Stud SF*, 5 (Spring 1968), 263-268.
    Parallels for Mr. Head's journey in "The Artificial Nigger" can be found in *The Divine Comedy* and in the Apocrypha's Book of Tobit.

_____. See MISCELLANEOUS (Contemporary).

Hegarty, Charles M., S. J. "A Man Though Not Yet a Whole One: Mr. Shiflet's Genesis." *Flannery O'Connor Bul*, 1 (1972), 24-38.
    Examines the meaning of "The Life You Save May Be Your Own" in light of O'Connor's three major revisions of the story.

_____. "A Note on Flannery O'Connor." *Stud SF*, 9 (Fall 1972), 409-410.
    A comparison and consideration of different versions of Miss O'Connor's essay, "The Church and the Fiction Writer," shows that "the studied logic of the original versions explodes with irony when seen in the light of the editorial re-writing as it appears in *America*."

Hendin, Josephine. "In Search of Flannery O'Connor." *Columbia Forum*, 13 (Spring 1970), 38-41.
    Deals with a visit to Milledgeville and an interview with O'Connor.

_____. *The World of Flannery O'Connor*. Bloomington, Indiana: Indiana Univ Press, 1970.
    Examines Miss O'Connor's fiction for the themes it suggests rather than the religious drama it illustrates, with a chapter comparing her work with that of Faulkner, Styron, and Capote.

Hicks, Granville. "Literary Horizons." *SatR*, May 10, 1969, p. 30.
    An appreciation of Miss O'Connor.

_____. See MISCELLANEOUS (Contemporary).

Hiers, John T. See MISCELLANEOUS (Contemporary).

Hivnor, Mary O. "Adaptations and Adaptors." *KR*, 30, no. 2 (1968), 265-273.
    Contains a full paragraph on an unsuccessful stage adaptation of "The Displaced Person."

Holman, C. Hugh. See GENERAL.

Howell, Elmo. "The Developing Art of Flannery O'Connor." *ArQ*, 29 (Autumn 1973), 266-276.
    Miss O'Connor's later fiction emphasizes the theme that the liberal mind, convinced of its own rationality and self-righteousness, cannot possibly comprehend the depths of human nature.

_____. "Flannery O'Connor and the Home Country." *Renascence*, 24 (Summer 1972), 171-176.
    Discusses religious and agrarian elements in O'Connor's works.

Hoyt, Charles A. See GENERAL.

Hughes, Richard. See MISCELLANEOUS (Contemporary).

Inge, M. Thomas. See MISCELLANEOUS (Contemporary-- 1st Inge entry).

Ingram, Forrest L. "O'Connor's Seven-Story Cycle." *Flannery O'Connor Bul*, 2 (Autumn 1973), 19-28.
    The first seven stories in *Everything That Rises Must Converge* constitute a cycle; the two stories added after O'Connor's death are not unified with the others.

Katz, Claire. "Flannery O'Connor's Rage of Vision." *AL*, 46 (March 1974), 54-67.
    Discusses the reasons for and the effects of O'Connor's use of violence in her works; her

works ultimately reflect "the central struggle between parent and child."

Kazin, Alfred. See MISCELLANEOUS (Contemporary).

Keller, Jane C. "The Figures of the Empiricist and the Rationalist in the Fiction of Flannery O'Connor." *ArQ*, 28 (Autumn 1972), 263-274.
Shows how O'Connor satirizes secular humanism in her novels and short stories by ridiculing the empiricist (Hazel Motes in *Wise Blood*) and the rationalist (George Rayber in *The Violent Bear It Away*).

Kellogg, Gene. "The Catholic Novel in Convergence." *Thought*, 45 (Summer 1970), 265-296.
O'Connor was among Catholic writers critical of both secularism and Catholics.

_____. *The Vital Tradition: The Catholic Novel in a Period of Convergence.* Chicago: Loyola Press, 1970.
Includes discussion of the significance of O'Connor's twentieth-century Catholic background.

Klevar, Harvey. "Image and Imagination: Flannery O'Connor's Front Page Fiction." *Jour of Mod Lit*, 4 (September 1974), 121-132.
Suggests the Milledgeville *Union Recorder* as a possible source of some of the realities of Miss O'Connor's fiction.

Kropf, Carl Ray. "Theme and Setting in 'A Good Man Is Hard to Find.'" *Renascence*, 24 (Summer 1972), 177-180, 206.
Emphasizes the setting as it relates to the story's theme: "One cannot separate the religious theme of her works from their Southern setting and its historical implications."

Lackey, Allen D. "Flannery O'Connor: A Supplemental Bibliography." *BB*, 30 (October-December 1973), 170-175.
An annotated supplement to earlier bibliographical listings on O'Connor in *BB*.

Littlefield, Daniel F. "Flannery O'Connor's *Wise Blood*: 'Unparalled Prosperity' and Spiritual Chaos." *Miss Quart*, 23 (Spring 1970), 121-133.
Miss O'Connor's belief that material prosperity has had a detrimental effect on man's spiritual well-being is the underlying theme of *Wise Blood*.

Lorch, Thomas M. "Flannery O'Connor: Christian Allegorist." *Critique*, 10, no. 2 (1968), 69-80.
An attempt to delineate the allegorical elements in Miss O'Connor's works while discussing the relationship between her religious beliefs and her art as shown in the allegory.

Lorentzen, Melvin E. "A Good Writer Is Hard to Find," in *Imagination and the Spirit: Essays in Literature and the Christian Faith Presented to Clyde S. Kilby*, ed. Charles A. Huttar. Grand Rapids, Mich.: Eerdmans, 1971.
O'Connor's grotesques embody "the mystery of iniquity and the mystery of redemption."

Maida, Patricia D. "'Convergence' in Flannery O'Connor's 'Everything That Rises Must Converge.'" *Stud SF*, 7 (Fall 1970), 549-555.
Examines the implications of the title in a story that describes essentially "an experience of a mother and son that changes the course of their lives." The mother-son relationship has both social and personal implications, but "on a larger scale, the story depicts the plight of all mankind."

Male, Roy R. "The Two Versions of 'The Displaced Person.'" *Stud SF*, 7 (Summer 1970), 450-457.
A comparison of the first version of "The Displaced Person," published in the *Sewanee Review* in 1954, and the later version, published in *A Good Man Is Hard to Find* in 1955, reveals much about Miss O'Connor's craft.

Martin, Carter W. "Comedy and Humor in Flannery O'Connor's Fiction." *Flannery O'Connor Bul*, 4 (1975), 1-12.
O'Connor's "comic-cosmic view of man" resembles that of Faulkner, and the view of both has "numberless" analogues in "classical and modern literature."

_____. "Flannery O'Connor and Fundamental Poverty." *EJ*, 60 (April 1971), 458-461.
On O'Connor's use of poverty as a symbol for fallen man.

_____. "Flannery O'Connor's Early Fiction." *SHR*, 7 (Spring 1973), 210-214.
O'Connor's "Iowa thesis stories taken together offer a valuable study of the apprenticeship of a great short-story writer."

_____. *The True Country: Themes in the Fiction of Flannery O'Connor.* Nashville: Vanderbilt Univ Press, 1969.
A critical explication of O'Connor's central themes of grace and redemption and of her narrative method which relies on symbolism, humor, irony, and satire.

May, John R. "Flannery O'Connor and the New Hermeneutic." *Flannery O'Connor Bul*, 2 (Autumn 1973), 29-42.
Discusses the variations from the traditional in the hermeneutical elements in O'Connor's fiction.

_____. "Flannery O'Connor: Critical Consensus and the 'Objective' Interpreters." *Renascence*, 27 (Summer 1975), 179-192.
O'Connor criticism is now in the stage of evaluating interpretations of her works. What is needed now is re-evaluation and interpretation of O'Connor's works themselves.

_____. "Of Huckleberry Bushes and the New Hermeneutic." *Renascence*, 14 (Winter 1972), 85-95.
O'Connor is seen as the best "illustration of the Old Criticism, which was often ultimately theological." Criticizes the New Critical approach.

_____. "Perspective: Art and Belief in Flannery O'Connor." *New Orleans Rev*, 4, no. 1 (1974), 86-91.

IV. CONTEMPORARY (1920-1975)

Review-essay of books on O'Connor by Eggenschwiler, Orvell, Walters, Driskell, and Brittain.

_____. "The Pruning Word: Flannery O'Connor's Judgment of Intellectuals." *SHR*, 4 (Fall 1970), 325-338.
Discusses "The Comforts of Home," "Good Country People," "Everything That Rises Must Converge," "The Partridge Festival," "The Enduring Chill," and "Revelation" as stories that deal "specifically with the troubled relationships of intellectuals to faith."

_____. "*The Violent Bear It Away*: The Meaning of the Title." *Flannery O'Connor Bul*, 2 (Autumn 1973), 83-86.
The title of O'Connor's novel should be read to mean the "kingdom of heaven manifests itself violently."

_____. See GENERAL.

Mayer, David R. "Apologia for the Imagination: Flannery O'Connor's 'A Temple of the Holy Ghost.'" *Stud SF*, 11 (Spring 1974), 147-152.
This story "shows the imaginative underpinnings of Flannery O'Connor's method of immanence," her incarnational art.

_____. "*The Violent Bear It Away*: Flannery O'Connor's Shaman." *So Lit Jour*, 4 (Spring 1972), 41-54.
Tarwater is possessed by a shaman spirit and thereby "can be seen in the context of a more widespread human search for the added dimension of life."

McCullagh, James C. "Aspects of Jansenism in Flannery O'Connor's *Wise Blood*." *Studies in the Humanities*, 3 (October 1972), 12-16.
Focuses on Jansenist influence on the treatment of sex in this novel.

_____. "Symbolism and the Religious Aesthetic: Flannery O'Connor's *Wise Blood*." *Flannery O'Connor Bul*, 2 (Autumn 1973), 43-58.
The "blending of psychological and theological concerns" in this work overcomes some of the surface distortion characteristic of most of O'Connor's fiction. Here the Oedipal theme is Christianized.

McDermott, John V. "Julian's Journey into Hell: Flannery O'Connor's Allegory of Pride." *Miss Quart*, 28 (Spring 1975), 171-179.
Rather than being a story of "transcendence," "Everything That Rises Must Converge" is "an allegory that reveals how man, through excessive pride, may lose all touch with reality and...destroy himself."

McDowell, Frederick P. W. "Toward the Luminous and the Numinous: The Art of Flannery O'Connor." *SouR*, 9 (Autumn 1973), 998-1013.
An essay-review of several works about O'Connor and of *The Complete Short Stories of Flannery O'Connor*.

McKenzie, Barbara. "Flannery O'Connor Country: A Photo Essay." *GaR*, 29 (Summer 1975), 328-362.
Title is descriptive.

Mellard, James M. "Violence and Belief in Mauriac and O'Connor." *Renascence*, 26 (Spring 1974), 158-168.
A study of the affinities of these two Roman Catholic writers.

Milder, Robert. "The Protestantism of Flannery O'Connor." *SouR*, 11 (Autumn 1975), 802-819.
Sees two religious ideas, the irremediable corruption of natural man and the exaltation of private religious experience, as the essential elements of the "Protestantism" of Flannery O'Connor's fiction.

Millichap, Joseph R. "The Pauline 'Old Man' in Flannery O'Connor's 'The Comforts of Home.'" *Stud SF*, 11 (Winter 1974), 96-99.
This story offers "a Calvinistic view of man constrained by his human heritage," which is "symbolized by the ghostly projection of the protagonist's dead father."

Montgomery, Marion. "Beyond Symbol and Surface: The Fiction of Flannery O'Connor." *GaR*, 22 (Summer 1968), 188-193.
An essay-review of *The Added Dimension: The Art and Mind of Flannery O'Connor*, edited by Melvin J. Friedman and Lewis A. Lawson, *Flannery O'Connor*, by Stanley Edgar Hyman, and of *Flannery O'Connor: A Critical Essay*, by Robert Drake, which finds Drake's the most satisfying work.

_____. "Flannery O'Connor's 'Leaden Tract Against Complacency and Conception.'" *ArQ*, 24 (Summer 1968), 133-147.
An explication of Flannery O'Connor's story "A Stroke of Good Fortune," showing its fundamental theme to be the loss of love and showing symbolism adapted from Dante and from Eliot's "Ash Wednesday."

_____. "Flannery O'Connor and the Natural Man." *Miss Quart*, 21 (Fall 1968), 235-242.
There is danger in insisting on symbolism in O'Connor's work; her major concern was "the modern heresy of the natural man with his fear of natural death rather than spiritual death."

_____. "Flannery O'Connor: Prophetic Poet." *Flannery O'Connor Bul*, 3 (Autumn 1974), 79-84.
The vivid surface of O'Connor's prose gives way to a "larger, transcendent world."

_____. "Flannery O'Connor: Realist of Distances." *RANAM*, 4 (1971), 69-78.
O'Connor's works reveal the "universality of the human condition."

_____. "Flannery O'Connor's Imitation of Significant Action." *Stud in the Twentieth Cent*, no. 3 (Spring 1969), 55-64.
Discusses metaphorical images in O'Connor's works and points out differences between O'Connor and the black humorists.

_____. "Flannery O'Connor's Territorial Center." *Critique*, 11, no. 3 (1969), 5-10.
Deals with the *Inferno* as the territorial center of O'Connor's fiction.

_____. "Flannery O'Connor's Transformation of the Sentimental." *Miss Quart*, 25 (Winter 1971), 1-18.

Miss O'Connor's use of the grotesque enables her to maintain her position as "realist of distances," and her use of violence underlines the preciousness of life.

_____. "In Defense of Flannery O'Connor's Dragon." *GaR*, 25 (Fall 1971), 302-316.

Discusses O'Connor's perception of evil in the world and her relationship to opponents of the consumer society.

_____. "Miss Flannery's 'Good Man.'" *Denver Quart*, 3 (Autumn 1968), 1-19.

In dealing with the good, O'Connor believed that the artist must start with the actual reality of the world, "in which the negative is more immediately arresting."

_____. "Miss O'Connor and the Christ-Haunted." *SouR*, 4 (Summer 1968), 665-672.

A polemical commentary on Miss O'Connor's work from a theologically conservative Christian perspective.

_____. "A Note on Flannery O'Connor's Terrible and Violent Prophecy of Mercy." *Forum H*, 7 (Summer 1969), 4-7.

In her works O'Connor makes diabolism literally present rather than allegorical, as in Hawthorne's works.

_____. "O'Connor and Teilhard de Chardin: The Problem of Evil." *Renascence*, 22 (Autumn 1969), 34-42.

O'Connor does not wholly subscribe to the theories of Chardin and at times is in direct opposition.

_____. "On Flannery O'Connor's 'Everything That Rises Must Converge.'" *Critique*, 13, no. 2 (1971), 15-29.

Julian, not his mother, is the story's protagonist. The convergence in the story is not of one person with another, but of Julian with the world of guilt and sorrow, achieved by realizing that he has spurned love.

_____, moderator. "Panel Discussion, Russell Auditorium, Georgia College, Sunday, April 7, 1974." *Flannery O'Connor Bul*, 3 (Autumn 1974), 57-78.

Transcripts of a panel discussion of O'Connor's works are printed. Panel members were Caroline Gordon, Robert Drake, Frederick Asals, and Rosa Lee Walston.

Mooney, Harry J., Jr. "Moments of Eternity: A Study in the Short Stories of Flannery O'Connor," in *The Shapeless God: Essays on Modern Fiction*, ed. Harry J. Mooney, Jr., and Thomas F. Staley. Pittsburgh: Univ of Pittsburgh Press, 1968, pp. 117-138.

A primary source of evil in O'Connor's stories "arises from persons so self-sufficient or...so limited, that they either reject or deny God because they cannot conceive the need of anything outside themselves."

Muller, Gilbert H. "The City of Woe: Flannery O'Connor's Dantean Vision." *GaR*, 23 (Summer 1969), 206-213.

Deals with "The Artificial Nigger" as an allegory based on the *Divine Comedy* with Head and Nelson taking "a modern journey to Hell [Atlanta] and back."

_____. *Nightmares and Visions: Flannery O'Connor and the Catholic Grotesque*. Athens: Univ of Georgia Press, 1972.

The fiction is examined within the context of O'Connor's orthodox Catholicism and her consistent use of the American grotesque tradition. This is the first Edd Winfield Parks Memorial Prize study.

_____. "*The Violent Bear It Away*: Moral and Dramatic Sense." *Renascence*, 22 (Autumn 1969), 17-25.

A study of the novel in terms of the Jamesian devices of the moral and dramatic senses.

Nance, William L. "Flannery O'Connor: The Trouble with Being a Prophet." *Univ Rev*, 36 (December 1969), 101-108.

Flannery O'Connor has made her role as social critic and truth-revealer the central dramatic concern of her fiction.

Nelson, G. B. *Ten Versions of America*. New York: Knopf, 1972.

An impressionistic interpretation of Hazel Motes as a character who reflects O'Connor's view of reality, included among chapters on ten literary characters.

Nevius, Blake. See MISCELLANEOUS (Contemporary).

Oates, Joyce Carol. "The Visionary Art of Flannery O'Connor." *SHR*, 7 (Summer 1973), 235-246.

Deals with *Everything That Rises Must Converge* as a "collection of revelations."

O'Brien, John T. "The Un-Christianity of Flannery O'Connor." *Listening*, 5 (Winter 1971), 71-82.

Suggests that it is best to forget O'Connor's Catholicism and Southern background because she was the follower of no particular creed.

O'Connor, Flannery. *Mystery and Manners: Occasional Prose*, ed. Sally and Robert Fitzgerald. New York: Farrar, Straus, and Giroux, 1969.

Collects eight published and seven unpublished prose essays and talks which provide a philosophical and aesthetic context for understanding O'Connor's fiction.

_____. "Novelist and Believer," in *Religion and Modern Literature*, ed. G. B. Tennyson and E. E. Ericson, Jr. Grand Rapids, Mich.: William B. Eerdmans, 1975.

O'Connor discusses the relationship of religious belief and novel-writing in relation to her own work, various literary trends, and in a very large and general context.

Oppegard, Susan H. "Flannery O'Connor and the Backwoods Prophets." *Americana-Norvegica*, 4 (1973), 305-325.

Points out similarities between Old
Old Testament prophets and O'Connor's "back
woods prophets"; interprets her Christian
theme.

Orvell, Miles D. "Flannery O'Connor." *SR*, 78
(Winter 1970), 184-192.
An assessment of Flannery O'Connor in the
light of some recent book-length studies of her
work, which, Orvell notes, is most frequently a
study of the operation of grace in human
relationships.

_____. *Invisible Parade: The Fiction of Flannery
O'Connor*. Philadelphia: Temple Univ Press,
1972.
Places O'Connor's fiction in the romance
tradition of Poe and Hawthorne, examines it in
terms of her religious views, and evaluates its
stylistic and structural patterns.

Pearce, Howard D. "Flannery O'Connor's Ineffable
'Recognitions.'" *Genre*, 6 (1973), 298-312.
On O'Connor's stories as morality plays.

Pearce, Richard. See MISCELLANEOUS (Contemporary).

Pinkerton, Jan. See MISCELLANEOUS (Contemporary).

Porter, Katherine Anne. See PORTER, KATHERINE ANNE.

Presley, Delma Eugene. "The Moral Function of Distortion in Southern Grotesque." *SAB*, 37
(May 1972), 37-46.
In works by Flannery O'Connor, Tennessee
Williams, and Carson McCullers, the grotesque
mode reminds us of what once was and what yet
might be.

_____. See MISCELLANEOUS (Contemporary).

Quinn, J. J. "A Reading of Flannery O'Connor."
Thought, 48 (1973), 520-531.
"A Good Man Is Hard to Find" is analyzed for
the purpose of discovering its three levels of
meaning.

Reiter, Robert, ed. *Flannery O'Connor*. The
Christian Critic Series. St. Louis, Missouri:
B. Herder Book Co., 1968.
Reprints ten selected essays with a
Christian perspective.

Rubin, Louis D., Jr. See GENERAL--3rd Rubin entry.

Rupp, Richard H. See MISCELLANEOUS (Contemporary).

Scouten, Kenneth. "The Mythological Dimensions of
Five of Flannery O'Connor's Works." *Flannery
O'Connor Bul*, 2 (Autumn 1973), 59-72.
The Oedipus myth is reflected in four of
these works and one of them "alludes to Greek
dramatic festivals."

Shear, Walter. "Flannery O'Connor: Character and
Characterization." *Renascence*, 20 (1968),
140-146.
Deals with the grotesque in O'Connor's
fiction.

Shinn, Thelma J. "Flannery O'Connor and the
Violence of Grace." *ConL*, 9 (Winter 1968),
58-73.
O'Connor joined together the traditions of
Roman Catholicism and Southern grotesque because she believed that "the violence of rejection in the modern world demands an equal
violence of redemption."

Simpson, Lewis P. See GENERAL--3rd Simpson entry.

Skaggs, Merrill M. See GENERAL.

Smith, Anneliese H. "O'Connor's 'Good Country
People.'" *Expl*, 33 (December 1974), Item 30.
By the end of the story Joy-Hulga is aware
that Vulcan is "but one of many gods," that "she
is dependent in both body and mind."

Smith, Francis J. "O'Connor's Religious Viewpoint
in *The Violent Bear It Away*." *Renascence*, 22
(Winter 1970), 108-112.
Considers allegorical implications in this
novel.

Solotaroff, Theodore. See MISCELLANEOUS
(Contemporary).

Sonnenfeld, Albert. "Flannery O'Connor: The
Catholic Writer as Baptist." *ConL*, 13
(Autumn 1972), 445-457.
"It is no accident that the Christian
denomination of the South is Baptist and that
religious extremists in that region are 'funda-
mentalists,' for Flannery O'Connor sees the
essential strategy of salvation as a return to
the stormy principles of the prophet in the
wilderness."

Spivey, Ted R. "Flannery's South: Don Quixote
Rides Again." *Flannery O'Connor Bul*, 1 (1972),
46-53.
Flannery's South has a noticeable Spanish
flavor.

_____. "Religion and the Reintegration of Man in
Flannery O'Connor and Walker Percy." *Spectrum*,
2 (1972), 67-179.
Discusses the need for the awareness of myth
and ritual in reading the works of both these
writers.

Stephens, Martha. "Flannery O'Connor and the
Sanctified-Sinner Tradition." *ArQ*, 24
(Autumn 1968), 223-239.
Miss O'Connor's work shows analogues to such
religious writers as Mauriac, Eliot, and Greene
in her treatment of the "Sanctified-Sinner" (one
who defies a God in whom he believes) and in her
attempt to communicate with a modern audience
hostile to the Christian view of life.

_____. *The Question of Flannery O'Connor*. Baton
Rouge: Louisiana State Univ Press, 1973.
A study focusing on the question of artistic
values and the tonal dimensions of O'Connor's
novels and stories.

Sullivan, Walter. "The Achievement of Flannery
O'Connor." *SHR*, 2 (Summer 1968), 303-309.

Miss O'Connor's achievement must be measured from the short stories, the two novels assuming only a supportive role. Contains analysis of the major short stories.

_____. See MISCELLANEOUS (Contemporary--1st Sullivan entry).

Tate, J. O. "The Uses of Banality." *Flannery O'Connor Bul*, 4 (1975), 13-24.
While banality is a matter of taste (for both reader and author) there "is no primary comedy unconnected with" banality in O'Connor's fiction, and the "vulgar is always set off by the sublime."

Taylor, Henry. "The Halt Shall Be Gathered To- gether: Physical Deformity in the Fiction of Flannery O'Connor." *WHR*, 22 (Autumn 1968), 325-338.
The deformed person may have a deeper realization of his spiritual condition, enabling him to bring others to some sort of spiritual redemption.

Trowbridge, Clinton W. "The Symbolic Vision of Flannery O'Connor: Patterns of Imagery in *The Violent Bear It Away*." *SR*, 76 (Spring 1968), 298-319.
An analysis of the religious symbolism of *The Violent Bear It Away* emphasizing the basic theme that only Christ can really satisfy man's spiritual hunger.

True, Michael D. "Flannery O'Connor: Backwoods Prophet in the Secular City." *Papers on Lang and Lit*, 5 (Spring 1969), 209-223.
A review-essay evaluating some critical works on O'Connor and some of her works themselves.

Vande Kieft, Ruth M. "Judgment in the Fiction of Flannery O'Connor." *SR*, 76 (Spring 1968), 337-356.
Miss O'Connor was a Christian writer whose work was apocalyptic and death-haunted, as most of her work indicates.

Voss, Arthur. See GENERAL.

Walston, Rosa Lee. "Flannery O'Connor as Seen by a Friend." *Carrell*, 14, nos. 1-2 (1974), 16-24.
A reminiscence.

_____. "Flannery: An Affectionate Recollection." *Flannery O'Connor Bul*, 1 (1972), 55-60.
A fond remembrance by Miss O'Connor's former teacher.

Walters, Dorothy. *Flannery O'Connor*. Twayne's U. S. Authors Series, no. 216. New York: Twayne, 1973.
Explores Miss O'Connor's fictional universe and finds in its theological dualities and seeming contradictions the primary source of her creative power.

Wilson, James D. "Luis Buñuel, Flannery O'Connor and the Failure of Charity." *Minn Rev*, 4 (Spring 1973), 158-162.
Both writers believe that charity cannot combat human depravity.

Wylder, Jean. "Flannery O'Connor: A Reminiscence and Some Letters." *North Am Rev*, 7 (Spring 1970), 58-65.
Concerns O'Connor's attendance at the Writer's Workshop at the University of Iowa and other matters.

Wynne, Judith F. "The Sacramental Irony of Flannery O'Connor." *So Lit Jour*, 7 (Spring 1975), 33-49.
In her narrative expressions of sacramental- ity, O'Connor has produced sophisticated irony, not transparent allegory.

Zyla and Aycock. See MISCELLANEOUS (Contemporary).

[O'DONNELL, GEORGE MARION] Simpson, Lewis P. "O'Donnell's Wall." *SouR*, 6 (Autumn 1970), xix-xxvii.
Beginning with personal recollections, this essay moves to speculation about the effect of the Southern past on O'Donnell's work as artist and as critic.

[OWEN, GUY] Carr, John. See MISCELLANEOUS (Contemporary).

Eyster, Warren. See DICKEY, JAMES (Contemporary).

French, Warren. See MISCELLANEOUS (Contemporary-- 3rd French entry).

Owen, Guy. "The Use of Folklore in Fiction." *N Car F*, 19 (March 1971), 73-79.
Discusses the adapting of folk motifs to fictional use in his four novels.

Simpson, Lewis P. See WELTY, EUDORA (Contemporary-- 1st Simpson entry).

White, Robert B., Jr. "The Imagery of Sexual Repres- sion in *Season of Fear*." *N Car F*, 19 (March 1971), 80-84.
The theme of the novel is brought out in its imagery, without which it "would lose its subtlety, its depth, its tone."

[PARKS, EDD WINFIELD] Moore, Rayburn S., Phinizy Spalding, John O. Eidson, and Hollis L. Cate. "Edd Winfield Parks: In Memoriam." *GaR*, 23 (Winter 1969), 512-518.
Brief remembrances of Parks as scholar, teacher, and friend.

Reeves, Paschal. "'On Banishing Nonsense: The Career of Edd Winfield Parks." *SHR*, 5 (Winter 1971), 72-75.
A memorial.

[PEERY, JAMES ROBERT] Simms, L. Moody, Jr. "James Robert Peery: Mississippi Journalist and Novelist." *Notes on Miss Writers*, 7 (Spring 1974), 30-32.
Short biographical sketch and synopsis of Peery's two novels.

[PERCY, WALKER] Abádi-Nagy, Zoltán. "A Talk with Walker Percy." *So Lit Jour*, 6 (Fall 1973), 3-19.
A Hungarian professor interviews Percy.

Atkins, Anselm. "Walker Percy and Post-Christian Search." *Centennial Rev*, 12 (Winter 1968), 73-95.
   Treats the philosophical and theological framework within which "Binx" Bolling's search is conceived and which makes the character intelligible.

Berrigan, J. R. "An Explosion of Utopias." *Moreana*, 38 (1973), 21-26.
   Love in the Ruins demonstrates the futility of Utopias based on such things as sex and science.

Boyd, G. N. and L. A. See MISCELLANEOUS (Contemporary).

Bradbury, John M. See MISCELLANEOUS (Contemporary).

Bradford, M. E. "Dr. Percy's Paradise Lost: Diagnostics in Louisiana." *SR*, 81 (Autumn 1973), 839-844.
   An essay-review of *Love in the Ruins* labelling it a distopia in the category of Menippean satire.

Bradley, Jared W. "Walker Percy and the Search for Wisdom." *La Stud*, 12 (Winter 1973), 579-590.
   Deals with Percy's theories about language.

Brooks, Cleanth. "The Current State of American Literature." *SouR*, 9 (Spring 1973), 273-287.
   After discussing views of current American literature by A. Alvarez, Alan Pryce-Jones, and William Jovanovich, Brooks offers some views of his own. He mentions several Southerners and uses Walker Percy as an example of a writer who makes effective use of his region.

Bryant, Jerry H. See MISCELLANEOUS (Contemporary--1st Bryant entry).

Buckley, William F., Jr. See WELTY, EUDORA (Contemporary) and MISCELLANEOUS (Contemporary).

Bunting, Charles T. "An Afternoon with Walker Percy." *Notes on Miss Writers*, 4 (Fall 1971), 43-61.
   An interview with Percy on May 27, 1971.

Byrd, Scott. "Mysteries and Movies: Walker Percy's College Articles and *The Moviegoer*." *Miss Quart*, 25 (Spring 1972), 165-181.
   Similarities are apparent between Percy's undergraduate essays and book reviews, published in the *Carolina Magazine* in 1935, and his references to murder mysteries and movies in his 1961 novel.

Carr, John. "An Interview with Walker Percy." *GaR*, 25 (Fall 1971), 317-332.
   Percy expresses his ideas about writing, the South, and his work.

_____. See MISCELLANEOUS (Contemporary).

Chesnick, Eugene. "Novel's Ending and World's End: The Fiction of Walker Percy." *Hollins Critic*, 10 (October 1973), 1-11.
   A general survey of Percy's work to date, with emphasis on his ideas and their origins.

Cremeens, Carlton. "Walker Percy, The Man and the Novelist: An Interview." *SouR*, 4 (Spring 1968), 271-290.
   A transcription of questions and comments about Eudora Welty, William Faulkner, James Baldwin, Ralph Ellison, Richard Wright, and Flannery O'Connor, with considerable space devoted to Percy's own novels, *The Moviegoer* and *The Last Gentleman*.

Dewey, Bradley R. "Walker Percy Talks about Kierkegaard: An Annotated Interview." *JR*, 54 (July 1974), 273-298.
   Title is descriptive.

Douglas, Ellen. *Walker Percy's The Last Gentleman*. Religious Dimensions in Literature, Seabury Reading Program. New York: Seabury Press, 1969.
   A critical introduction to and commentary on Percy's novel for the general reader and student interested in works which confront modern spiritual dilemmas.

Dowie, William, S. J. "Walker Percy: Sensualist Thinker." *Novel*, 6 (Fall 1972), 52-65.
   Discusses the blend of "experience and idea" in the novels of Percy.

Feibleman, James K. See MISCELLANEOUS (Contemporary).

Gaston, Paul. "The Revelation of Walker Percy." *ColQ*, 20 (Spring 1972), 459-470.
   Compares the treatment of the theme of malaise in *The Moviegoer* and *The Last Gentleman* with the treatment of the same theme in *Love in the Ruins*.

Godshalk, William L. "Walker Percy's Christian Vision." *La Stud*, 13 (Summer 1974), 130-141.
   Argues that Percy "is working not as an existentialist philosopher but as Christian commentator on the modern scene," that Thomas More is possessed of Faustian pride.

Henisey, Sarah. "Intersubjectivity in Symbolization." *Renascence*, 20 (Summer 1968), 208-214.
   A reading of *The Moviegoer* in relation to Percy's theory of symbolization.

Johnson, Mark. "The Search for Place in Walker Percy's Novels." *So Lit Jour*, 8 (Fall 1975), 55-81.
   With alienated homelessness as a controlling concept in his work, Percy uses the place in which his characters live to underline his themes and characterizations.

Kazin, Alfred. "The Pilgrimage of Walker Percy." *Harper's*, 242 (June 1971), 81-86.
   An overview of Percy's fiction.

_____. See MISCELLANEOUS (Contemporary).

Lauder, R. E. "The Catholic Novel and the 'Insider God.'" *Cweal*, 51 (October 25, 1974), 78-81.
   Compares Graham Greene and Percy as Catholic novelists; argues that Percy sees God's presence in all human life.

Lawson, Lewis A. "Walker Percy: The Physician as Novelist." *SAB*, 37 (May 1972), 58-63.
From disillusionment with science's silence on what it is like to be a man living in the world, Percy sees in *The Last Gentleman* a growing scientific willingness to consider the transempirical.

_____. "Walker Percy's Indirect Communications." *Tex Stud in Lit and Lang*, 11 (Spring 1969), 867-900.
Reasons that much of Percy's successful fiction "derives from two key strategies which resulted from his familiarity with Kierkegaard."

_____. "Walker Percy's Southern Stoic." *So Lit Jour*, 3 (Fall 1970), 5-31.
Percy admires the Stoic attitude "as it was embodied in William Alexander Percy and his class," but rejects it "as being irrelevant to the present generation."

_____. See MISCELLANEOUS (Contemporary).

LeClair, Thomas. "The Eschatological Vision of Walker Percy." *Renascence*, 26 (Spring 1974), 115-122.
A study of the three heroes in Percy's novels in terms of existentialism.

_____. See MISCELLANEOUS (Contemporary).

Lehan, Richard. "The Way Back: Redemption in the Novels of Walker Percy." *SouR*, 4 (Spring 1968), 306-319.
A summary of Percy's philosophical articles, particularly "The Man on the Train: Three Existential Modes," and an analysis of Percy's novels by the concepts outlined.

_____. See MISCELLANEOUS (Contemporary).

Luschei, Martin. *The Sovereign Wayfarer: Walker Percy's Diagnosis of the Malaise*. Baton Rouge: Louisiana State Univ Press, 1972.
An intellectual biography and analysis of Percy's philosophy which finds the roots of his novels in the existentialism of Kierkegaard and Marcel.

Madden, David. See MISCELLANEOUS (Contemporary--2nd Madden entry).

Percy, Walker. "New Orleans Mon Amour." *Harper's*, 237 (September 1968), 80-82, 86, 88, 90.
An article on New Orleans.

_____. See PERCY, WILLIAM ALEXANDER (Contemporary).

Pindell, Richard. "Basking in the Eye of the Storm: The Esthetics of Loss in Walker Percy's *The Moviegoer*." *Boundary 2*, 4 (Fall 1975), 219-230.
The novel reveals that the "danger of our modern loss" is that we will "beautify the loss and thereby repeat it."

Presley, Delma Eugene. "Walker Percy's 'Larroes.'" *NConL*, 3 (January 1973), 5-6.

Suggests that the statement "Larroes catch medloes" may be a corruption of the expression "Layovers to catch meddlers."

Rubin, Louis D., Jr. See GENERAL--3rd Rubin entry.

Sheed, Wilfrid. See MISCELLANEOUS (Contemporary).

Shepherd, Allen. "Percy's *The Moviegoer* and Warren's *All the King's Men*." *Notes on Miss Writers*, 4 (Spring 1971), 2-14.
Both novels dramatize in a Southern setting the search of the alienated young protagonist of aristocratic heritage for a stable identity in a fragmented world.

Simpson, Lewis P. See GENERAL--3rd Simpson entry.

Spivey, Ted R. See O'CONNOR, FLANNERY (Contemporary--2nd Spivey entry).

Tanner, Tony. See MISCELLANEOUS (Contemporary).

Taylor, Lewis J., Jr. "Walker Percy and the Self." *Cweal*, 50 (May 10, 1974), 233-236.
Examines Percy's ideas about the problems of the times and the failure of the individual.

Thale, Jerome. "Alienation on the American Plan." *Forum H*, 6 (Summer 1968), 36-40.
Percy's strength is the use of understatement and "fidelity" to avoid the potential melodramatics inherent in the theme of alienation.

Thale, Mary. "The Moviegoer of the 1950's." *TCL*, 14 (July 1968), 84-89.
Points out similarities between Percy's *The Moviegoer* and West's *Miss Lonelyhearts*.

Van Cleave, Jim. "Versions of Percy." *SouR*, 6 (Autumn 1970), 990-1010.
An examination of *The Moviegoer* in existential terms defined against William Alexander Percy's *Lanterns on the Levee*.

Vauthier, Simone. "Le temps et la mort dans *The Moviegoer*." *RANAM*, 4 (1971), 98-115.
Explicates Binx Bolling's grappling with the reality of time in relation to the reality of death.

Watkins, Floyd C. See MISCELLANEOUS (Contemporary).

Weinberg, Helen A. See MISCELLANEOUS (Contemporary).

Westendorp, T. A. See MISCELLANEOUS (Contemporary).

Whittington, M. J. "From the Delta." *Delta Rev*, 5 (February 1968), 30.
The author revisits Trail Lake and talks about the Percys.

Zeugner, John F. "Walker Percy and Gabriel Marcel: The Castaway and the Wayfarer." *Miss Quart*, 28 (Winter 1974-75), 21-53.
Discusses the existential influence of Marcel on Percy's work.

[PERCY, WILLIAM ALEXANDER] Holmes, William F. "William Alexander Percy and the Bourbon Era in the Yazoo-Mississippi Delta." *Miss Quart*, 26 (Winter 1972-73), 71-87.

The boyhood heroes that Percy describes in *Lanterns on the Levee* are part of the myth of the Old South.

Howell, Elmo. See MISCELLANEOUS (Contemporary).

Percy, Walker. "Introduction," *Lanterns on the Levee*, by W. A. Percy. Baton Rouge: Louisiana State Univ Press, 1973.

A reprint of the 1941 edition with a biographical introduction by Percy's nephew.

_____. "'Uncle Will' and His South." *SatR*, November 6, 1973, pp. 22-25.

Reminiscences about William Alexander Percy with comments on *Lanterns on the Levee*.

Van Cleave, Jim. See PERCY, WALKER.

Welsh, John R. "William Alexander Percy and His Writings: A Reassessment." *Notes on Miss Writers*, 1 (Winter 1969), 82-99.

A survey of Percy's life and thought.

[PETERKIN, JULIA] Cheney, Brainard. "Can Julia Peterkin's 'Genius' Be Revived for Today's Black Myth-Making?" *SR*, 80 (Winter 1972), 173-179.

An essay-review of *The Collected Short Stories of Julia Peterkin*, edited by Frank Durham (South Carolina Press, 1970). Cheney argues that Mrs. Peterkin's genius was best in the short story, not the novel, and that her fictional picture of the Negro is still relevant for today's society and will prove helpful to the black leadership's sense of reality and history.

Chewning, Harris. "A Secretary's Souvenir Now Rests in the Wofford Library." *Sandlapper*, 8 (April 1975), 47-50, 53.

Concerns the manuscript of *Scarlet Sister Mary*.

Durham, Frank, ed. *The Collected Stories of Julia Peterkin*. Columbia: Univ of South Carolina Press, 1970.

Collects thirty-three stories and sketches by Mrs. Peterkin which deal with the black experience in the South, with an extensive biographical and critical appreciation as an introduction by the editor.

_____. See MISCELLANEOUS (Contemporary--2nd Durham entry).

[PHARR, ROBERT DEANE] Epps, G. "The Art of Robert Deane Pharr." *The Richmond Mercury Book Review*, no. 1 (December 6, 1972), 1, 7.

Pharr writes carefully researched and intricate social novels about black life, drawing in part on his experience in Richmond, his birthplace.

O'Brien, John, and Raman K. Singh. "Interview with Robert Deane Pharr." *NALF*, 8 (Fall 1974), 244-246.

Questions and answers on typical interview topics.

[PHILLIPS, THOMAS HAL] Kelly, George M. "An Interview with Thomas Hal Phillips." *Notes on Miss Writers*, 6 (Spring 1973), 3-13.

An interview of November 1972.

[PIERCE, OVID WILLIAMS] McMillan, Douglas J. "Folkways in Ovid Pierce's 'The Wedding Guest.'" *N Car F*, 23 (November 1975), 125-218.

A catalogue of folk sayings, tales, beliefs, etc., in the novel.

West, Harry C. "Negro Folklore in Pierce's Novels." *N Car F*, 19 (March 1971), 66-72.

"Negro folklore contributes to the atmosphere of Pierce's three novels and counterpoints the agony of whites as they suffer rapid change in their values and beliefs."

[PORTER, KATHERINE ANNE] Anon. "Notes of a Survivor." *Time*, 95 (May 4, 1970), 99-100.

After a brief look at *Ship of Fools*, a "messy novel," the reviewer turns to Katherine Anne Porter's *The Collected Essays and Occasional Writings* and finds the dominant tone in it to be "that of a survivor, a woman who has gone it alone."

Aldridge, John W. See MISCELLANEOUS (Contemporary--2nd Aldridge entry).

Baker, Howard. "The Upward Path: Notes on the Work of Katherine Anne Porter." *SouR*, 4 (Winter 1968), 1-19.

A critical assessment of Miss Porter's work with analyses of a few short stories and *Ship of Fools*. (A revised version of this article appears in Brom Weber, ed., *Sense and Sensibility in Twentieth-Century Writing*. Carbondale & Edwardsville: Southern Illinois Univ Press, 1970.)

Baldeshwiler, Eileen. "Structural Patterns in Katherine Anne Porter's Fiction." *Sou Dakota Rev*, 11 (Summer 1973), 45-53.

Deals with three basic narrative patterns in Porter's work.

Barnes, Daniel R., and Madeline T. "The Secret Sin of Granny Weatherall." *Renascence*, 21 (Spring 1969), 162-165.

Makes a case for pregnancy as Granny's sin in "The Jilting of Granny Weatherall."

Beards, Richard D. "Stereotyping in Modern American Fiction: Some Solitary Swedish Madmen." *Mod Språk*, 63, no. 4 (1969), 329-337.

Porter's "Noon Wine" is one of four works discussed as including the stereotyped Swede.

Boyd, G. N. and L. A. See MISCELLANEOUS (Contemporary).

Buchloh, Paul G. See GENERAL.

Cheney, Brainard. Untitled. *SHR*, 4 (Fall 1970), 385-388.

An essay-review of *Katherine Anne Porter: A Critical Symposium* (1969), edited by Lodwick Hartley and George Core.

Cowley, Malcolm. See MISCELLANEOUS (Contemporary--2nd Cowley entry).

Detweiler, Robert. See MISCELLANEOUS (Contemporary).

Emmons, Winifred S. *Katherine Anne Porter: The Regional Stories*. Southwest Writers Series, no. 6. Austin: Steck-Vaughn, 1967.
    An analysis restricted to those short stories by Porter identifiably set in Texas.

Etulain, R. W. See GENERAL.

Givner, Joan. "Katherine Anne Porter and the Art of Caricature." *Genre*, 5 (March 1972), 51-60.
    Believes that Porter's use of caricature is a result of her acquaintance with Covarrubias, the Mexican artist, and her belief that caricature is something within people, not an exaggeration by the artist.

_____. "Katherine Anne Porter, Eudora Welty, and 'Ethan Brand.'" *Internat'l Fiction Rev*, 1, no. 1 (1974), 32-37.
    Compares the uses of the grotesque in Porter's "Theft" and Welty's "The Petrified Man" with Hawthorne's use of it in "Ethan Brand."

_____. "Porter's Subsidiary Art." *SWR*, 59 (Summer 1974), 265-276.
    An essay on the Porter letters recently donated to the McKeldin Library of the University of Maryland.

_____. "A Re-reading of Katherine Anne Porter's 'Theft.'" *Stud SF*, 6 (Summer 1969), 463-465.
    The meaning of the story is unambiguous. The theme is self-delusion in the face of evil.

Clicksberg, Charles I. See MISCELLANEOUS (Contemporary).

Gottfried, Leon. "Death's Other Kingdom: Dantesque and Theological Symbolism in 'Flowering Judas.'" *PMLA*, 84 (January 1969), 112-124.
    Behind Porter's parodic portrayal of hell lie Dante's *Inferno* and the poetry of T. S. Eliot.

Gross, Beverly. "The Poetic Narrative: A Reading of 'Flowering Judas.'" *Style*, 2 (Spring 1968), 129-139.
    Using "Flowering Judas" as an example, the article defines "poetic narrative" in terms of language and form.

Hardy, John E. *Katherine Anne Porter*. Modern Literature Monographs. New York: Frederick Ungar, 1973.
    Critical introduction and thematic analysis of the short fiction and *Ship of Fools*.

Hartley, Lodwick. "Katherine Anne Porter." *So Lit Jour*, 6 (Spring 1974), 139-150.
    An essay-review of *Katherine Anne Porter's Fiction*, by M. M. Liberman, and of *Katherine Anne Porter*, by John Hardy.

_____. "Stephen's Lost World: The Background of Katherine Anne Porter's 'The Downward Path to Wisdom.'" *Stud SF*, 6 (Fall 1969), 574-579.
    Philip Horton's biography *Hart Crane: The Life of an American Poet* (1937), particularly the first chapter, provides the best possible approach or gloss to "The Downward Path to Wisdom."

_____, and George Core, eds. *Katherine Anne Porter: A Critical Symposium*. Athens: Univ of Georgia Press, 1969.
    Reprints seventeen critical essays and personal memoirs, three by the editors; includes a selective bibliography of works by and about Porter.

Howell, Elmo. "Katherine Anne Porter and the Southern Myth: A Note on 'Noon Wine.'" *La Stud*, 11 (Fall 1972), 251-259.
    Porter's view of Southern life formed no basis for a larger view of Southern experience.

_____. "Katherine Anne Porter as a Southern Writer." *So Car Rev*, 4 (December 1971), 5-15.
    Miss Porter is broader in scope than many Southern writers. "She achieves her end not because of but in spite of her Southern background."

Kazin, Alfred. See MISCELLANEOUS (Contemporary).

Liberman, M. M. "Circe." *SR*, 78 (Fall 1970), 689-693.
    Review of *The Collected Essays and Occasional Writings of Katherine Anne Porter*.

_____. *Katherine Anne Porter's Fiction*. Detroit: Wayne State Univ Press, 1971.
    The exceptionally high quality of Miss Porter's fiction is to be accounted for largely "by its formal properties, verbal and rhetorical."

_____. "The Short Story as Chapter in *Ship of Fools*." *Criticism*, 10 (Winter 1968), 65-71.
    Rather than a novel, *Ship of Fools* is an apologue dramatizing the theme of helpless folly through a number of story-like chapters.

_____. "Some Observations on the Genesis of *Ship of Fools*: A Letter from Katherine Anne Porter." *PMLA*, 84 (January 1969), 136-137.
    An unpublished letter to Malcolm Cowley describing her voyage to Germany in 1931 supports an allegorical reading of *Ship of Fools*.

Madden, David. "The Charged Image in Katherine Anne Porter's 'Flowering Judas.'" *Stud SF*, 7 (Spring 1970), 277-289.
    Miss Porter's own experiences in Mexico provided the real-life image that led to "Flowering Judas." This became the "charged image" of her story. "As the elements of Laura's exterior and interior worlds intermingle, they cohere in a developing pattern of images which expands from the charged image...."

Magny, Claude-Edmonde. See MISCELLANEOUS (Contemporary).

IV. Contemporary (1920-1975)

Nance, William L. "Katherine Anne Porter and Mexico." *SWR*, 55 (Spring 1970), 143-153.
  Discusses the significance of Mexico in Miss Porter's life and work.

_____. "Variations on a Dream: Katherine Anne Porter and Truman Capote." *SHR*, 3 (Fall 1969), 338-345.
  Defines *dream* as "a vision of the ideal existence, precisely formulated and projected into an admittedly unattainable realm beyond time and place." Proposes that in this form the American dream has been essentially a Southern phenomenon, reflected in interesting and somewhat contrasting forms in the fiction of Katherine Anne Porter and Truman Capote.

Nevius, Blake. See MISCELLANEOUS (Contemporary).

Partridge, Colin. "'My Familiar Country': An Image of Mexico in the Work of Katherine Anne Porter." *Stud SF*, 7 (Fall 1970), 597-614.
  An "autobiographical reminiscence of her first attendance at a bullfight suggests that progression from 'adventure' into meaningful 'experience' that was to become a basis for many of her stories."

Pinkerton, Jan. "Katherine Anne Porter's Portrayal of Black Resentment." *Univ Rev*, 36 (Summer 1970), 315-317.
  A discussion of Porter's "portrayal of the relationship between blacks and whites in her Southern family" in "The Old Orders" stories.

Porter, Katherine Anne. *The Collected Essays and Occasional Writings of Katherine Anne Porter*. New York: Delacorte Press, 1970.
  Includes autobiographical essays and critiques of other Southern authors (Welty, Tate, and Flannery O'Connor).

Prater, William. "'The Grave': Form and Symbol." *Stud SF*, 6 (Spring 1969), 336-338.
  The form of the story leads to the revelation of the "grave" as a symbol of the "burial place" in Miranda's memory of an unpleasant but meaningful experience.

Redden, Dorothy S. "'Flowering Judas': Two Voices." *Stud SF*, 6 (Winter 1969), 194-204.
  Porter does not hold a strictly unitary view of life. Her view is essentially dual, and an examination of this duality makes many things fall into place, "including the basic role of tension in her work."

Samuels, C. T. "Placing Miss Porter." *New Rep*, 162 (March 7, 1970), 25-26.
  An essay-review of *The Collected Essays and Occasional Writings of Katherine Anne Porter* which welcomes only some of the new material, saying that Miss Porter is admirable only when her material pushes her beyond a lucid irony.

Schorer, Mark. See MISCELLANEOUS (Contemporary).

Solotaroff, Theodore. See MISCELLANEOUS (Contemporary).

Spence, Jon. "Looking-Glass Reflections: Satirical Elements in *Ship of Fools*." *SR*, 82 (Spring 1974), 316-330.
  If one reads the novel as satire, he will find "that Miss Porter's philosophic purpose is neither misanthropic nor pessimistic."

Sullivan, Walter. "Katherine Anne Porter: The Glories and Errors of Her Ways." *So Lit Jour*, 3 (Fall 1970), 111-121.
  "Again and again, reading *The Collected Essays*, one is struck by the narrowness of Miss Porter's view and her willingness to accept as final wisdom whatever cliche comes to hand."

_____. See MISCELLANEOUS (Contemporary--1st Sullivan entry).

Thomas, M. Wynn. "Strangers in a Strange Land: A Reading of 'Noon Wine.'" *AL*, 47 (May 1975), 230-246.
  Argues that a reading of the story indicates that it is about ordinary people who are "unaware that in their lives they act out the ceremony of fate."

Voss, Arthur. See GENERAL.

Waldrip, Louise, and Shirley Ann Bauer. *A Bibliography of the Works of Katherine Anne Porter* and *A Bibliography of the Criticism of the Works of Katherine Anne Porter*. Metuchen, N. J.: Scarecrow Press, 1969.
  A descriptive listing of primary and an annotated listing of secondary materials including dissertations and book reviews, through 1968.

Walsh, Thomas F. "The 'Noon Wine' Devils." *GaR*, 22 (Spring 1968), 90-95.
  A comparison of *Noon Wine* with Benét's *The Devil and Daniel Webster* emphasizing the Faustian pattern.

West, Ray B., Jr. See MISCELLANEOUS (Contemporary).

Wiesenfarth, Joseph. "Internal Opposition in Porter's 'Granny Weatherall.'" *Critique*, 11, no. 2 (1968-69), 47-55.
  Porter's earlier story "The Source" provides a "pattern" for the treatment of order and disorder in "The Jilting of Granny Weatherall"; Granny discovers that "to weather all is not necessarily to live...."

_____. "Negatives of Hope: A Reading of Katherine Anne Porter." *Renascence*, 25 (1973), 85-94.
  Ultimately, in spite of showing man in a negative way, Porter's works reveal that man "can be reborn and live again."

_____. "The Structure of Katherine Anne Porter's 'Theft.'" *Cithara*, 10 (May 1971), 65-71.
  The heroine of the story "begins a detective and ends a woman."

Wolff, Geoffrey. "Miss Porter." *Newsweek*, April 6, 1970, p. 91.
  This review of *The Collected Essays and Occasional Writings of Katherine Anne Porter* states that some pieces do not warrant printing, but some are very good, such as "Cotton Mather," which concerns Salem witchcraft.

Woodress, James. See GENERAL--1st Woodress entry.

Yannella, Philip R. "The Problems of Dislocation in 'Pale Horse, Pale Rider.'" *Stud SF*, 6 (Fall 1969), 637-642.
 Porter's fiction vitally involves issues which arise out of the transition from traditional to modern circumstances. In a story like "Pale Horse, Pale Rider" characters are spatially dislocated and, in addition, confront a new time, finding themselves almost totally unprepared for the modern world.

Zyla and Aycock. See MISCELLANEOUS (Contemporary).

[PRICE, REYNOLDS] Carr, John. See MISCELLANEOUS (Contemporary).

Drake, Robert. See MISCELLANEOUS (Contemporary).

Eichelberger, Clayton L. "Reynolds Price: 'A Banner in Defeat.'" *Jour of Pop Culture*, 1 (Spring 1968), 410-417.
 Many of Price's characters "live and move on a level considerably below their capabilities."

Hicks, Granville. See MISCELLANEOUS (Contemporary).

Price, Reynolds. "Dodging Apples." *SAQ*, 71 (Winter 1972), 1-15.
 Price expresses the opinion that it is more important to understand why a work is than to understand how. He explains why he believes all works of art have kinetic intent, discusses his own personal motives for writing, and makes specific reference to his reasons for composing *Michael Egerton*.

 ———. "News for the Mineshaft." *VQR*, 44 (Autumn 1968), 641-658.
 Price discusses *A Generous Man*.

 ———. *Things Themselves: Essays and Scenes*. New York: Atheneum, 1972.
 A selection of a third of Price's critical and personal essays, several relating to his own work and others on Faulkner and Welty.

"The Professional Viewpoint." *Twentieth Century Stud*, 1 (November 1969), 109-130.
 Price is one of a number of writers whose views on sexual themes in the modern novel are presented here.

Shepherd, Allen. "Love (and Marriage) in *A Long and Happy Life*." *TCL*, 17 (January 1971), 29-35.
 "Love, in its various manifestations, pervades...[Price's] stories and novels, which makes *A Long and Happy Life* both representative in a sense and indicative of Price's ability to make it new."

 ———. "*Love and Work* and the Unseen World." *Topic*, 12 (Spring 1972), 52-57.
 There is an element of an "unseen world" in this novel not to be found in Price's earlier works.

 ———. "Notes on Nature in the Fiction of Reynolds Price." *Critique*, 15, no. 2 (1973), 83-94.
 A study of natural signs and their origins in Price's fiction.

 ———. "Reynolds Price's *A Long and Happy Life*: The Epigraph." *NConL*, 2 (May 1972), 12-13.
 Presents three possible interpretations of the epigraph.

Skow, John. "Hag-Ridden." *Time*, 96 (October 12, 1970), 92-93.
 In Price's *Permanent Errors* themes appear like "sweaty dreams" and the stories are "ghosts."

Solotaroff, Theodore. "The Reynolds Price Who Outgrew the Southern Pastoral." *SatR*, September 26, 1970, pp. 27ff.
 An essay-review of *Permanent Errors*.

Vauthier, Simone. "The 'Circle in the Forest': Fictional Space in Reynolds Price's *A Long and Happy Life*." *Miss Quart*, 28 (Spring 1975), 123-146.
 An analysis of the various ways place functions in this novel.

Westendorp, T. A. See MISCELLANEOUS (Contemporary).

[RANSOM, JOHN CROWE] Aldridge, John W. See MISCELLANEOUS (Contemporary--2nd Aldridge entry).

Atlas, James. See GENERAL.

Barber, Marion. See FAULKNER, WILLIAM (Contemporary).

Bataille, Robert. See MISCELLANEOUS (Contemporary).

Baym, Max I. See GENERAL.

Berman, Ronald. "Confederates in the Backfield: Mr. Ransom and the Cleveland Browns." *New Rep*, 173 (October 4, 1975), 21-22.
 A former Kenyon student recalls Ransom's appreciation of football form on television.

Bradford, M. E. "A Modern Elegy: Ransom's 'Bells for John Whiteside's Daughter.'" *Miss Quart*, 21 (Winter 1967-68), 43-47.
 An analysis of the poem as a miniature but highly traditional elegy.

Bromwich, David. "Revisiting the New Critics." *Commentary*, 54 (November 1972), 79-82.
 In this essay-review of Ransom's *Beating the Bushes: Selected Essays 1941-1970* and of Cleanth Brooks's *A Shaping Joy: Studies in the Writer's Craft*, Bromwich briefly reviews the history of New Criticism. He concludes that it has "lost its influence."

Brown, Ashley. "Landscape into Art: Henry James and John Crowe Ransom." *SR*, 79 (Spring 1971), 206-212.
 Discusses Henry James's "The American Scene" as the source of Ransom's "Old Mansion."

Buffington, Robert. "The Poetry of the Master's Old Age." *GaR*, 25 (Spring 1971), 5-16.

An examination of some of Ransom's last poems and his revisions of earlier ones.

_____. "Ransom's Poetics: 'Only God, My Dear.'" *Mich Quart Rev*, 12 (Fall 1973), 353-360.
     A discussion of Ransom's theory of poetics as revealed in many of his statements.

Core, George. "Mr. Ransom and the House of Poetry." *SR*, 82 (Fall 1974), 619-639.
     A summary picture of Ransom's critical accomplishments, concluding that his performance as ontological critic powerfully influenced the Southern literary renascence and the whole course of contemporary criticism.

_____. "New Critic, Antique Poet." *SR*, 77 (1969), 508-516.
     Emphasizes classical qualities in Ransom's poetry.

_____. See MISCELLANEOUS (Contemporary--1st Core entry).

Cowan, Louise. See MISCELLANEOUS (Contemporary).

Crupi, Charles. "Ransom's 'Conrad in Twilight.'" *Expl*, 29 (November 1970), Item 20.
     Deals particularly with Ransom's use of the word *byre* in this poem.

Curnow, Wystan. See MISCELLANEOUS (Contemporary).

Curry, Gladys J. "Writers in Crisis." *Roots*, 1 (1970), 160-166.
     Discusses "Philomela" in relation to the theme of the absence of traditional values in modern America.

Durham, Frank. See TOOMER, JEAN--2nd Durham entry.

Elliot, Emory B., Jr. "Theology and Agrarian Ideology in the Critical Theory of John Crowe Ransom." *XUS*, 10 (Winter 1971), 1-7.
     "...Ransom's aesthetic theory is so closely interwoven with his theology and agrarian ideology that his critical theories have profound social and political implications, even if these implications are subtly, and perhaps unconsciously, expressed."

Hubbell, Jay B. See GENERAL.

Inge, M. Thomas. See MISCELLANEOUS (Contemporary-- 3rd Inge entry).

Jarrell, Randall. See MISCELLANEOUS (Contemporary).

Justus, James H. "A Note on John Crowe Ransom and Robert Penn Warren." *AL*, 41 (November 1969), 425-430.
     Discusses similarities in the two authors' approach to subject matter.

Kelly, Richard. "Captain Carpenter's Inverted Ancestor." *Am N&Q*, 7 (September 1968), 6-7.
     Ransom's "Captain Carpenter" may have been suggested by the sixteenth-century ballad "Captain Car."

Knight, Karl F. "Ransom's 'Conrad in Twilight.'" *Expl*, 30 (May 1972), Item 75.
     Offers identification of the "ribbon" mentioned in the poem.

Levitt, Paul. See FAULKNER, WILLIAM (Contemporary).

Magner, James E., Jr. *John Crowe Ransom: Critical Principles and Preoccupations*. The Hague: Mouton (New York: Humanities Press), 1971.
     An analysis of Ransom's literary criticism and its philosophical roots which finds Ransom an objective champion of the existent, things as they are, in the world and literature. Ransom, rather than Richards or Eliot, is the real father of New Criticism.

Mann, David, and Samuel H. Woods, Jr. "John Crowe Ransom's Poetic Revisions." *PMLA*, 83 (March 1968), 15-21.
     In Ransom's *Selected Poems* (1963) are both minor and major changes of the poems in the 1945 and 1955 collections.

McMillan, Samuel H. "John Crowe Ransom's 'Painted Head.'" *GaR*, 22 (Summer 1968), 194-197.
     Discusses the way the major irony of the poem is achieved.

Meyers, Walter E., Samuel H. Woods, Jr., and David Mann. "A Commentary on 'John Crowe Ransom's Poetic Revisions.'" *PMLA*, 85 (May 1970), 532-533.
     Meyers says that Woods and Mann, in a previous *PMLA* article (see above), handle denotation and connotation well, but not sound and syntax. Woods and Mann reply, item by item.

Owen, Guy. See MISCELLANEOUS (Contemporary--1st Owen entry).

Paluka, Frank. See GENERAL.

Parsons, Thornton H. *John Crowe Ransom*. Twayne's U. S. Authors Series, no. 150. New York: Twayne Publishers, 1969.
     A critical analysis, devoted exclusively to Ransom's poetry, which details the scrupulous techniques and sophisticated strategies by which he achieved an aesthetic detachment in the classical mode. Selected annotated bibliography.

Partridge, Colin. "Aesthetic Distance in John Crowe Ransom." *Southern Rev* (Adelaide), 3 (1968), 159-167.
     Aesthetic distance is carefully maintained by Ransom in his later work; it was not evident at the beginning of his career. It was consciously adopted to give form and complexity to poetic statement.

Pinsky, Robert. "Hardy, Ransom, Berryman: A 'Curious Air.'" *Agenda*, 10 (Spring-Summer 1972), 89-99.
     Discusses the stylistic devices of these three poets.

Pratt, William C. "Fugitive from the South: Ransom at Kenyon." *The Old Northwest*, June 1975.
     Title is descriptive.

Ransom, John Crowe. *Selected Poems*. New York: Alfred A. Knopf, 1969.
    This third edition of *Selected Poems* concludes with a section of eight "pairings"--original texts of poems side by side with later revisions, with commentary by the poet analyzing the creative process as it operated in each work.

Rubin, Louis D., Jr. "The Wary Fugitive John Crowe Ransom." *SR*, 82 (Fall 1974), 582-618.
    A lengthy analysis of Ransom's poetry praising it as some of the best of the twentieth century, a poetry which comes from a strongly rational intellect and a powerful emotional nature.

Schwartz, Delmore. See MISCELLANEOUS (Contemporary).

Shankar, D. A. "A Note on John Crowe Ransom." *Literary Criterion*, 9 (Summer 1971), 97-101.
    Deals with Ransom's poetic principles.

Simpson, Lewis P. See GENERAL--3rd Simpson entry.

Steinmann, Martin, Jr. "Cumulation, Revolution, and Progress." *New Lit Hist*, 5 (Spring 1974), 477-490.
    Ransom is mentioned as a representative New Critic.

Tate, Allen. "Gentleman in a Dustcoat." *SR*, 76 (Summer 1968), 375-382.
    A retrospective tribute to Ransom on the occasion of his eightieth birthday--delivered as an Honors Day address at Kenyon College.

_____. "Reflections on the Death of Ransom." *SR*, 82 (Fall 1974), 545-551.
    An appreciation of Ransom concluding with the statement that Ransom wrote "the most perspicuous, the most engaging, and the most elegant prose of all the poet-critics of our time."

Walker, Marshall. See WARREN, ROBERT PENN (Contemporary--1st Walker entry).

Warren, Robert Penn. "John Crowe Ransom (1888-1974)." *SouR*, 11 (Spring 1975), 243-244.
    A tribute delivered at the meeting of the American Academy of Arts and Letters, December 6, 1974.

_____. "Notes on the Poetry of John Crowe Ransom at His Eightieth Birthday." *KR*, 30, no. 3 (1968), 319-349.
    The theme central to Ransom's poetry is the haunting dualism in man's experience.

Weber, Robert. "Zur Genesis von J. C. Ransoms 'Master's in the Garden Again.'" *Jahrbuch für Amerikastudien*, 13 (1968), 196-204.
    Deals with the poem as being optimistic.

Whitman, A. Obituary. *NY Times*, July 4, 1974.
    A summary of Ransom's life and career.

Williams, Miller. "Color as Symbol and the Two-Way Metaphor in the Poetry of John Crowe Ransom." *Miss Quart*, 22 (Winter 1968-69), 29-37.
    Color is used in Ransom's poetry to emphasize polarity.

_____. *The Poetry of John Crowe Ransom*. New Brunswick, N. J.: Rutgers Univ Press, 1972.
    A general assessment of the works in the 1969 *Selected Poems* with explications of eleven additional specific poems.

Young, Thomas Daniel. "In His Own Country." *SouR*, 8 (Summer 1972), 572-593.
    A detailed history of John Crowe Ransom's move in the mid-1930's from Vanderbilt to Kenyon College, including the parts played by Allen Tate, Donald Davidson, and others.

_____. "John Crowe Ransom: A Major Minor Poet." *Spectrum*, 2 (1972), 37-46.
    Discusses "Necrological" as an example of Ransom's mastery of lyrical style.

_____. "John Crowe Ransom, 1888-1974." *Miss Quart*, 27 (Summer 1974), 275-276.
    A brief tribute to Ransom for his critical and poetical contributions to American literature.

_____. "A Kind of Centering." *GaR*, 28 (Spring 1974), 58-82.
    Treats Ransom's first years at Vanderbilt and his experience as an army officer in France during World War I.

_____. "Mostly Nurtured from England." *SR*, 82 (Fall 1974), 552-582.
    Ransom's years as a Rhodes Scholar induced in him the mature attitudes of his later credo: "In manners, aristocratic; in religion, ritualistic; in art, traditional."

_____. "A Slow Fire." *SR*, 81 (Autumn 1973), 667-690.
    A biographical essay taking Ransom from his final year in Oxford to his appointment in English at Vanderbilt University, where he remained for some twenty-odd years.

_____. *John Crowe Ransom*. Southern Writers Series, no. 12. Austin: Steck-Vaughn, 1970.
    A critical survey of Ransom's accomplishment as poet, critic, and "one of the most influential men of his generation."

_____, ed. *John Crowe Ransom: Critical Essays and a Bibliography*. Baton Rouge: Louisiana State Univ Press, 1968.
    A selection of criticism, an original memoir by *Kenyon Review* associate George Lanning, and a thorough bibliography of works by and about Ransom by Mildred B. Peters.

_____. Untitled. *GaR*, 27 (Summer 1973), 275-282.
    A review of two books on Ransom and of Ransom's *Beating the Bushes: Selected Essays, 1941-1970*.

_____. "Without Rank or Primacy." *Miss Quart*, 27 (Fall 1974), 435-445.
    An account of Ransom's first position as a teacher, in a high school in Taylorsville, Mississippi.

[RAVENEL, BEATRICE WITTE] Neuffer, C. H. "Historical Sensibility." *SAB*, 35 (March 1970), 62-65.
   This essay-review of *The Yemassee Lands: Poems of Beatrice Ravenel*, edited by Louis D. Rubin, Jr., commends the University of North Carolina Press for restoring a poet of such genuine merit.

Rubin, Louis D., Jr. "The Poetry of Beatrice Ravenel." *So Car Rev*, 1 (November 1968), 55-75.
   A biographical and critical discussion based on the contention that Beatrice Ravenel's poems were the best written in the South in the 1920's outside of Nashville, with eleven examples.

_____, ed. *The Yemassee Lands: Poems of Beatrice Ravenel*. Chapel Hill: Univ of North Carolina Press, 1969.
   A selection of published and unpublished verse by a little-known member of the Charleston circle of poets in the 1920's, with a biographical and critical introduction.

[REECE, BYRON HERBERT] Cook, Raymond A. "Byron Herbert Reece: Ten Years After." *GaR*, 22 (Spring 1968), 74-89.
   A biographical account of Reece's last years and his suicide.

[REED, ISHMAEL] Abel, Robert H. "Reed's 'I Am A Cowboy in the Boat of Ra.'" *Expl*, 30 (May 1972), Item 81.
   Ra is a black god whose rebirth promises the rebirth of the black people.

Ambler, Madge. "Ishmael Reed: Whose Radio Broke Down?" *NALF*, 6 (Winter 1972), 125-131.
   Discusses the ways the themes of Reed's "I Am a Cowboy in the Boat of Ra" are reflected in the novel *Yellow Back Radio Broke Down*.

Bellamy, Joe David. See MISCELLANEOUS (Contemporary).

Bryant, Jerry H. See MISCELLANEOUS (Contemporary--2nd Bryant entry).

Bush, Roland E. "Werewolf of the Wild West (On a novel by Ishmael Reed)." *BlackW*, 23 (January 1974), 51-52, 64-66.
   The novel discussed is *Yellow Back Radio Broke Down*.

Duff, Gerald. "Reed's *The Free-Lance Pallbearers*." *Expl*, 32 (May 1974), Item 69.
   The speech of his mother to Harry Sam in the opening pages of his novel is a parody of the deathbed scene in Ellison's *Invisible Man*.

Emerson, O. B. See MISCELLANEOUS (Contemporary--2nd Emerson entry).

Ford, Nick A. "A Note on Ishmael Reed: Revolutionary Novelist." *Stud in the Novel*, 3 (Summer 1971), 216-218.
   Reed is discussed as "the most revolutionary black novelist" now writing.

Kent, George. See MISCELLANEOUS (Contemporary).

Linebarger, J. M., and Monte Atkinson. "Getting to Whitey: Ishmael Reed's 'I Am a Cowboy.'" *Contemporary Poetry*, 2 (Spring 1975), 9-12.
   Discusses this poem as an "assault on white attitudes toward blacks."

O'Brien, John. "Ishmael Reed: An Interview." *Fiction Internat'le*, no. 1 (Fall 1973), 61-70.
   Questions and answers on typical interview topics.

Schmitz, Neil. "The Gumbo That Jes Grew." *PR*, 42 (1975), 311-316.
   A review of Reed's *The Last Days of Louisiana Red* which also evaluates earlier works by Reed and concludes that he "has yet to define himself as a writer."

_____. "Neo-Hoo Doo: The Experimental Fiction of Ishmael Reed." *TCL*, 20 (April 1974), 126-140.
   Investigates Reed's "considerable claim that he has found a way of writing fiction unlike those decreative and self-reflexive fictive modes in which his White contemporaries seem imprisoned."

Wade, Melvin and Margaret. See GENERAL.

[RICHARDSON, WILLIS] Peterson, Bernard L., Jr. "Willis Richardson: Pioneer Playwright." *Black World*, 26 (April 1975), 40-48, 86-88.
   A profile of North Carolina native Richardson, active during the 1920's, the first significantly productive modern Afro-American playwright.

[ROBERTS, ELIZABETH MADOX] Nevius, Blake. See MISCELLANEOUS (Contemporary).

Niles, Mary. "Social Development in the Poetry of Elizabeth Madox Roberts." *MarkR*, 2 (September 1969), 18-22.
   Roberts' belief that people should appreciate the physical world and other people influences the imagery in her poetry.

Smith, Jo R. "New Troy in the Bluegrass: Vergilian Metaphor and *The Great Meadow*." *Miss Quart*, 22 (Winter 1968-69), 39-46.
   Roberts uses the Aeneas myth in this historical novel about the transplanting of a woman and the establishing of her new life on the Kentucky frontier.

Woodress, James. See GENERAL--1st Woodress entry.

[RYLEE, ROBERT] Simms, L. Moody, Jr. "Robert Rylee, Mississippi Novelist." *Notes on Miss Writers*, 6 (Fall 1973), 41-44.
   A bibliographical note.

[SANCHEZ, SONIA] Bell, Bernard W. See MISCELLANEOUS (Contemporary).

Brooks, A. Russell. See MISCELLANEOUS (Contemporary).

Bullins, Ed., ed. *The New Lafayette Theater Presents*. Garden City, N. Y.: Anchor/Doubleday, 1974.

Six plays with critical comments by black
writers, including Sonia Sanchez.

Clarke, Sebastian. "Black Magic Woman: Sonia
Sanchez and Her Work." *Pres Af*, no. 78
(1971), 253-261.
Points out the chief subjects of Sanchez'
writings.

Gibson, Donald B. See MISCELLANEOUS
(Contemporary).

Kent, George. See MISCELLANEOUS (Contemporary).

Palmer, R. Roderick. See MISCELLANEOUS
(Contemporary).

[SCRUGGS, ANDERSON M.] Thurman, William R. "The
'Earth Day' of a Georgia Poet." *GHQ*, 55
(Summer 1971), 248-253.
Sees the poetry of Anderson M. Scruggs as
an account of the struggle between nature and
technological civilization.

[SEAY, JAMES] Carr, John. "An Interview with
James Seay." *Notes on Miss Writers*, 5
(Fall 1972), 35-57.
An interview with the Mississippi poet.

Graham, John, and George Garrett. See
MISCELLANEOUS (Contemporary).

[SETTLE, MARY LEE] Garrett, George. "Mary Lee
Settle's *Beulah Land Trilogy*," in *Rediscoveries*,
ed. David Madden (New York: Crown, 1971),
pp. 171-178.
An appreciative essay on Mary Lee Settle's
trilogy (published between 1956 and 1964)
dealing with the "history of the land and the
people of West Virginia."

[SHANDS, HUBERT A.] Durham, Frank. See
MISCELLANEOUS (Contemporary--2nd Durham entry).

Simms, L. Moody, Jr. "Hubert A. Shands' *White and
Black*: A Note." *Notes on Miss Writers*, 6
(Spring 1973), 25-26.
A brief comment.

[SMITH, LILLIAN] Baker, Donald G. See GENERAL.

Blackwell, Louise, and Frances Clay. *Lillian
Smith*. Twayne's U. S. Authors Series, no. 187.
New York: Twayne, 1971.
Assesses Smith's total work, on both racial
and other topics; her fiction, in the naturalistic tradition, is devoted to the removal of
barriers between people.

_____, and _____. "Lillian Smith, Novelist." *CLA
Jour*, 15 (June 1972), 452-458.
One Hour is almost completely lacking in the
objectivity of *Strange Fruit*, which, although
artistically superior, seems passé today in
comparison with the inferior novel, which remains more timely because of the problems it
poses.

Libman, Valentina. See GENERAL.

Sugg, Redding S., Jr. "Lillian Smith and the Condition of Woman." *SAQ*, 71 (Spring 1972), 155-164.
Deals with Lillian Smith's ideas about the
"responsibilities as well as the rights of
woman."

Sullivan, Margaret. "A Bibliography of Lillian
Smith & Paula Snelling." *MVC Bul* (Mississippi
Valley Collections, John Willard Brister Library,
Memphis State Univ), no. 4 (Spring 1971), 3-82.
A checklist of all significant writing by or
about Lillian Smith and her friend Paula
Snelling.

Thorburn, Neil. "*Strange Fruit* and Southern Tradition." *Midwest Quart*, 12 (January 1971),
157-171.
Examines both *Strange Fruit* and *Killers of
the Dream*, each "a model for the kind of understanding that must accompany any true conception
of segregationist thought in America."

White, Helen, and Redding S. Sugg, Jr. See
MISCELLANEOUS (Contemporary).

[SPENCER, ELIZABETH] Bunting, Charles T. "'In That
Time and at That Place': The Literary World of
Elizabeth Spencer." *Miss Quart*, 28 (Fall 1975),
435-460.
An interview of August 1972.

Cole, Hunter McK. "Elizabeth Spencer at Sycamore
Fair." *Notes on Miss Writers*, 6 (Winter 1974),
81-86.
A transcription of an April 1973 videotape
interview.

_____. "Windsor in Spencer and Welty: A Real and
an Imaginary Landscape." *Notes on Miss Writers*,
7 (Spring 1974), 2-11.
Explores Spencer's and Welty's uses of the
plantation Windsor, now in ruins, near Port
Gibson, Mississippi.

French, Warren. See MISCELLANEOUS (Contemporary--
1st French entry).

Haley, Josephine. "An Interview with Elizabeth
Spencer" and "A Biographical Note on Elizabeth
Spencer." *Notes on Miss Writers*, 1 (Fall 1968),
42-45.
A Mississippi writer, now living in Montreal,
discusses her novels.

Spencer, Elizabeth. "On Writing Fiction." *Notes on
Miss Writers*, 3 (Fall 1970), 71-72.
A short introduction to the reading of "First
Dark" at Gulf Park College.

Watkins, Floyd C. See MISCELLANEOUS (Contemporary).

[STEWART, RANDALL] Scott, Nathan A., Jr. See
MISCELLANEOUS (Contemporary).

Stevenson, John W. Untitled. *SHR*, 3 (Fall 1969),
404-405.
An essay-review of *Regionalism and Beyond:
Essays of Randall Stewart*, edited by George Core
(1968).

Stewart, Randall. See GENERAL.

[STRIBLING, THOMAS SIGISMUND] Durham, Frank. See MISCELLANEOUS (Contemporary--2nd Durham entry).

Eckley, Wilton. *T. S. Stribling*. Boston: Twayne Publishers, 1975.
An attempt to delineate the positive contributions made by Stribling to the Southern Renaissance, focusing primarily on the novels about Southern life and character.

Hilfer, Anthony C. See MISCELLANEOUS (Contemporary).

Libman, Valentina. See GENERAL.

Rocks, James E. "T. S. Stribling's Burden of Southern History: The Vaiden Trilogy." *SHR*, 6 (Summer 1972), 221-232.
"Stribling's picture of the South in his trilogy is so harsh and ruthless that it is perhaps overly partisan, but it deserves to be known primarily because it does chronicle Southern history in terms that are provocative and distressing."

[STUART, JESSE] Clarke, Mary. *Jesse Stuart's Kentucky*. New York: McGraw-Hill, 1968.
Deals with the life, folklore, and culture of Kentucky as reflected in the fiction and poetry of Stuart.

Foster, Ruel E. "Jesse Stuart's W-Hollow--Microcosm of the Appalachian." *Kansas Quart*, 2 (Spring 1970), 66-73.
Stuart's works reflect mountain life before the coming of twentieth-century technology.

Gibbs, Sylvia. "Jesse Stuart: The Dark Hills and Beyond." *Jack London Newsl*, 4 (January-April 1971), 56-69.
Deals with Stuart's writing as a reflection of his personal experiences.

_____. "Jesse Stuart's Cyclic Vision." *Jack London Newsl*, 3 (September-December 1970), 120-129.
Stuart's cyclic pattern is based chiefly on his personal experiences.

Huddleston, Eugene L. "Place Names in the Writings of Jesse Stuart." *WF*, 31 (1972), 169-177.
Deals with the significance of Stuart's use of the names of real places in his writing.

LeMaster, J. R. "Jesse Stuart: The Man and His Poetry." *Am Bk Collector*, 20 (Summer 1970), 13-19.
A treatment of Stuart's life as seen in his poetry.

_____. "Jesse Stuart's *Album of Destiny*--In Whitman's Eternal Flow." *Illinois Quart*, 36 (September 1973), 38-48.
Discusses Whitman's influence on the poems in this collection.

_____. "Jesse Stuart's Pictures in *Man with a Bull-Tongue Plow*." *MarkR*, 3 (1971), 17-20.
Discusses the devices that Stuart uses in creating images.

_____. "Jesse Stuart's Satirical Poems." *Am Bk Collector*, 23 (July-August 1973), 16-18.
A discussion of Stuart's satirical poems collected under the title *Birdland's Golden Age* and aimed at "social, political, and moral ineptitude."

_____. "The Poetry of Jesse Stuart: An Estimate for the Seventies." *SWR*, 56 (Summer 1971), 251-256.
Deals with the characteristics of Stuart's poetry and states the need for an edition of selected poems to aid in evaluating his work.

_____, ed. *The World of Jesse Stuart: Selected Poems*. New York: McGraw-Hill, 1975.
Title is descriptive.

Pennington, Lee. "Symbolism and Poetic Vision in Jesse Stuart." *Appal Jour*, 3 (Autumn 1975), 62-73.
Stuart's first collection of poetry, *Harvest of Youth*, was a basis for his subsequent work.

Perry, Dick. *Reflections of Jesse Stuart on a Land of Many Moods*. New York: McGraw-Hill, 1971.
Records within a narrative context interviews and conversations with Stuart about his land, life, and work.

Stuart, Jesse. "Introduction" to *Tennessee Hill Folk*, by Joe Clark. Nashville: Vanderbilt Univ Press, 1972.
A general autobiographical appreciation of the Appalachian life and culture captured in Clark's photographs.

_____. *My World*. Lexington: Univ Press of Kentucky, 1975.
Personal reminiscences about the author's Kentucky background and his travels in the states and abroad.

_____. "The Wonderful Bull-Tongue Plow." *Appalachian Rev*, 3 (Fall 1968), 9-14.
Stuart tells the story of the plow that gave its name to his most famous book of verse--*Man with the Bull-Tongue Plow*.

Woodbridge, Hensley C. "Jesse and Jane Stuart: A Bibliography." *Jack London Newsl*, 2 (September-December 1969) through 8 (January-April 1975).
Bibliographical supplements on the writing of Jesse and Jane Stuart have appeared in each issue of the volumes indicated.

Woodress, James. See GENERAL--1st Woodress entry.

[STYRON, WILLIAM] Anon. "Unslavish Fidelity: The Confessions of William Styron." *TLS*, May 9, 1968, p. 480.
A review of *The Confessions of Nat Turner*.

Akin, William E. "Toward an Impressionistic History: Pitfalls and Possibilities in William Styron's Meditation on History." *AQ*, 21 (Winter 1969), 805-812.
Though *The Confessions of Nat Turner* fails "to picture a creditable Nat Turner," it "may be the most profound treatment of slavery in

our literature because it portrays the black slavery experience in its essential schizophrenia and inhumanity in a fashion that no other study matches."

Aldridge, John W. See MISCELLANEOUS (Contemporary--2nd Aldridge entry).

Alter, Robert. See MISCELLANEOUS (Contemporary).

Anderson, Jervis. "Styron and His Black Critics." *Dissent*, 16 (March-April 1969), 157-166.
   Anderson disagrees with those critics who "demand that literature should serve the immediate ideological interests of the black community...," but feels that Styron should have shown "the need for moral change."

Aptheker, Herbert. See GENERAL.

Behar, Jack. "History and Fiction." *Novel*, 3 (Spring 1970), 260-265.
   An essay-review of Styron's *Nat Turner* and Mailer's *The Armies of the Night*, the former being condemned because Styron "tries to get too much mileage out of old mythologies."

Beja, Morris. See MISCELLANEOUS (Contemporary).

Bilotta, James D. "Critique of Styron's *Confessions of Nat Turner*." *Negro Hist Bul*, 38 (December 1974-January 1975), 326-327.
   Agrees with black writers who have accused Styron of creating "a pessimistically skewed image of the black personality."

Boyd, G. N. and L. A. See MISCELLANEOUS (Contemporary).

Browning, Preston M., Jr. "The Question for Being in Contemporary American Fiction." *Forum H*, 12, no. 1 (1974), 40-46.
   Includes a discussion of *Lie Down in Darkness*.

Brunauer, Dalma H. "Black and White: The Archetypal Myth and Its Development." *Barat Rev*, 6 (Summer 1971), 12-20.
   Deals with Styron's use of the traditional symbolism of black and white, dark and light.

Bryant, Jerry H. See MISCELLANEOUS (Contemporary--1st Bryant entry).

Bulgheroni, Marisa. "William Styron: il romanziere, il tempo e la storia." *SA*, 16 (1970), 407-428.
   A general assessment of Styron's novels and his use of history in the romance.

Burger, Nash K. "Truth or Consequences: Books and Book Reviewing." *SAQ*, 68 (1969), 152-166.
   Argues that Stark Young's *So Red the Rose* is a better novel than *The Confessions of Nat Turner* because Young never lost his "Southern-bred understanding."

Cannon, Patricia R. "Nat Turner: God, Man, or Beast?" *Barat Rev*, 6 (Summer 1971), 25-28.
   Argues that Styron's Nat Turner is a Christ-figure but an ambiguous one.

Clarke, John H., ed. *William Styron's Nat Turner: Ten Black Writers Respond*. Boston: Beacon Press, 1968.
   Ten black historians and writers, including novelists J. O. Killens and J. A. Williams, attack Styron's portrayal of Turner on literary, historical, and sociological grounds.

Cooke, Michael. "Nat Turner: Another Response." *YR*, 58 (Winter 1969), 295-301.
   An essay-review of *William Styron's Nat Turner: Ten Black Writers Respond* in which Cooke concludes that "the ten have elected a philosophical over a strictly literary criticism, legitimately subordinating formal technical points of analysis to a more ontological evaluation."

Core, George. "*The Confessions of Nat Turner* and the Burden of the Past." *So Lit Jour*, 2 (Spring 1970), 117-134.
   Styron's *Nat Turner* is a historical novel in which Nat is a sensitive man whose humanity and sacramental way of looking at the world lead to his undoing as a revolutionary leader and to his redemption as a man, a redemption which is also our own.

_____. "*Nat Turner* and the Final Reckoning of Things." *SouR*, 4 (Spring 1968), 745-751.
   An essay-review in praise of Styron's artistic achievement in *The Confessions of Nat Turner*.

Cunliffe, Marcus. "Black Culture and White America." *Encounter*, 34 (January 1970), 22-35.
   A detailed exploration of the implications of militant black consciousness for the American literary and academic communities, using the critical reception of Styron's *Nat Turner* to exemplify the complexity of interracial intellectual relations.

Curtis, Bruce. "Fiction, Myth and History in William Styron's *Nat Turner*." *Univ Col Quart*, 16 (January 1971), 27-32.
   Neither Styron nor his critics have honestly sought the real Nat Turner.

Delany, Lloyd T. "A Psychologist Looks at *The Confessions of Nat Turner*." *Psych Today*, 1 (January 1968), 11-14.
   Finds *The Confessions of Nat Turner* basically a failure because Styron has accepted ideas about blacks that are only myths.

Dillard, R. H. W. See MISCELLANEOUS (Contemporary).

Donno, Antonio. "I modi della violenza americana in alcuni romanzi dell' ultimo ventennio." *Antologia Vieussieux*, 35 (1974), 24-36.
   Styron is among the writers discussed as having written works in which violence reflects the repressions of capitalism.

Durden, Robert F. "William Styron and His Black Critics." *SAQ*, 68 (Spring 1969), 181-187.
   The main objection to Styron's controversial novel is his distortion of historical fact and his point of view, "daring to set down his own personal view of Nat's life as from inside Nat Turner in slavery."

IV. CONTEMPORARY (1920-1975)

Eggenschwiler, David. "Tragedy and Melodrama in *The Confessions of Nat Turner*." *TCL*, 20 (January 1974), 19-33.
    Styron's work reveals that the "creation [of melodramatic stereotypes], and the obscuring of the real humanity they mask, are destructive attempts to hide from a surmountable tragic vision of life."

Ellison, Ralph, et al. See MISCELLANEOUS (Contemporary).

Epstein, Seymour. See MISCELLANEOUS (Contemporary).

Forkner, Ben, and Gilbert Schricke. "An Interview with William Styron." *SouR*, 10 (Autumn 1974), 923-934.
    During a taped interview in France, Styron answers questions about *The Confessions of Nat Turner*, *Lie Down in Darkness*, and his work in progress.

Fossum, Robert H. *William Styron: A Critical Essay*. Contemporary Writers in Christian Perspective Series. Grand Rapids, Mich.: Eerdmans, 1968.
    Finds that Styron's four novels "depict the spiritual vacuity of our age and the desperate measures men adopt in an effort to fill it."

Franklin, Jimmie L. "Nat Turner and Black History." *Indian Jour of Am Stud*, 1, no. 4 (1971), 1-6.
    An account of the controversy over Styron's *Confessions of Nat Turner*.

Friedman, Melvin J. *William Styron*. Popular Writers Series, no. 3. Bowling Green, Ohio: Bowling Green Univ Popular Press, 1974.
    A pamphlet survey which places Styron's fiction in an international context and suggests that he is the least parochial of modern American writers.

_____, and Irving Malin, eds. *William Styron's The Confessions of Nat Turner: A Critical Handbook*. Wadsworth Guides to Literary Study. Belmont, Calif.: Wadsworth Publishing Company, 1970.
    A casebook containing materials for a study of the historical and aesthetic backgrounds of Styron's novel, with original essays by Roy A. Swanson and Karl Malkoff and a bibliography of primary and secondary materials on all Styron's work by Jackson Bryer and Marc Newman.

Galloway, David D. *The Absurd Hero in American Fiction: Updike, Styron, Bellow, Salinger*. Rev. ed. Austin: Univ of Texas Press, 1970.
    A revision of a 1966 work with an additional preface containing discussion of *The Confessions of Nat Turner*.

Genovese, Eugene D. See GENERAL.

Gilman, Richard. "Not Turner Revisited." *New Rep*, 158 (April 27, 1968), 23-32.
    An essay-review of *The Confessions of Nat Turner* that states that Styron's inability to imagine what it was like to be black, not his historical inaccuracy, produces a mediocre novel.

Gindin, James. See MISCELLANEOUS (Contemporary).

Glicksberg, Charles I. See MISCELLANEOUS (Contemporary).

Gresset, Michel. "William Styron." *NRF*, no. 204 (December 1968), 898-907.
    A review of *The Confessions of Nat Turner*.

Gross, Seymour L., and Eileen Bender. See TURNER, NAT.

Halpern, Daniel. "Checking in with William Styron." *Esquire*, 78 (August 1972), 142-143.
    A general report on a recent visit and interview with Styron, who comments on his current work, politics, Mailer, Tom Wolfe, and Clifford Irving.

Hassan, Ihab. See MISCELLANEOUS (Contemporary--both Hassan entries).

Hays, Peter L. See MISCELLANEOUS (Contemporary).

Hendin, Josephine. See O'CONNOR, FLANNERY (Contemporary--2nd Hendin entry).

Hiers, John T. See MISCELLANEOUS (Contemporary).

Hoffman, Frederick J. "The Cure of 'Nothing!': The Fiction of William Styron," in *Frontiers of American Culture*, ed. Ray B. Browne, et al. Lafayette, Indiana: Purdue Univ Studies, 1968, pp. 69-87.
    Treats the universal qualities in Styron's fiction.

Holder, Alan. "Styron's Slave: *The Confessions of Nat Turner*." *SAQ*, 68 (Spring 1969), 167-180.
    Expresses the belief that Styron's novel fails both as history and as literature.

Inge, M. Thomas. See MISCELLANEOUS (Contemporary--1st Inge entry).

Janeway, Elizabeth. See MISCELLANEOUS (Contemporary)

Kazin, Alfred. See CAPOTE, TRUMAN (Contemporary).

_____. See MISCELLANEOUS (Contemporary).

Kort, Wesley A. *Shriven Selves: Religious Problems in Recent American Fiction*. Philadelphia: Fortress Press, 1972.
    A chapter on *The Confessions of Nat Turner* and its religious implications finds that Styron moves in his work "from preoccupation with the rebel to celebration of the revolutionary."

Kretzoi, Charlotte. "William Styron: Heritage and Conscience." *Hungarian Stud in Eng*, 5 (1971), 121-136.
    Focuses on *Lie Down in Darkness*.

Lawson, Lewis A. See MISCELLANEOUS (Contemporary).

Luedtke, Carol L. See FAULKNER, WILLIAM (Contemporary).

Mackin, Cooper R. *William Styron*. Southern Writers Series, no. 7. Austin: Steck-Vaughn, 1969.

A critical assessment of Styron's fiction with emphasis on the social immediacy and the consummate artistry of *Nat Turner*.

Malin, Irving. "Styron's Play." *So Lit Jour*, 6 (Spring 1974), 151-157.
Styron's *In the Clap Shack* deals "with universal patterns of meaning--with the nature of freedom (rebellion against authority) and with the quality of language."

Markos, Donald W. "Margaret Whitehead in *The Confessions of Nat Turner*." *Studies in the Novel*, 4 (Spring 1972), 52-59.
Sexual frustration is an essential part of Turner's characterization.

Mellard, James M. See GENERAL.

Mellen, Joan. "William Styron: The Absence of Social Definition." *Novel*, 4 (Winter 1971), 159-170.
Faults Styron for lack of originality and for stating rather than dramatizing his social ideas.

Morris, Robert K., and Irving Malin, eds. *The Achievement of William Styron*. Athens: Univ of Georgia Press, 1975.
Contains seven new and three reprinted essays, an interview, and a secondary bibliography of criticism and reviews of Styron's works.

Morse, J. Mitchell. "Social Relevance, Literary Judgment, and the New Right; or, The Inadvertent Confessions of William Styron." *CE*, 30 (May 1969), 605-616.
Discusses *The Confessions of Nat Turner* as a sociological document but a poorly written one.

Mudrick, Marvin. *On Culture and Literature*. New York: Horizon Press, 1970.
Contains a comparative analysis of Mailer and Styron (pp. 176-199), both of whom, Mudrick says, have sold out in different ways to "the drawing-rooms of the Establishment."

Mullen, Jean S. "Styron's Nat Turner: A Search for Humanity." *Barat Rev*, 6 (Summer 1971), 6-11.
Styron's Nat is a universal figure, a tragic hero, and should not be judged as a racial figure.

Nevius, Blake. See MISCELLANEOUS (Contemporary).

Newcomb, Horace. "William Styron and the Act of Memory: *The Confessions of Nat Turner*." *ChiR*, 20, no. 1 (1968), 86-94.
A review which emphasizes the role of memory (those of both Styron and Nat Turner) in the search for identity in the novel.

Nolte, William H. "Styron's Meditation on Saviors." *SWR*, 58 (Autumn 1973), 338-348.
In *The Confessions of Nat Turner*, the savior is both victim and victimizer.

Normand, Jean. "L'homme mystifie: Les héros de Bellow, Albee, Styron et Mailer." *EA*, 22 (October-December 1969), 370-385.

Deals with Cass Kinsolving in *Set This House on Fire* and with Nat Turner.

_____. "'Un Lit de Tenebre' de W. Styron: Variations sur le Theme de Tristan." *EA*, 27 (January-March 1974), 64-71.
Title is descriptive.

Panichas, George A. See MISCELLANEOUS (Contemporary).

Pearce, Richard. *William Styron*. University of Minnesota Pamphlets on American Writers, no. 98. Minneapolis: Univ of Minnesota Press, 1971.
Finds irrational warfare to be Styron's central concern and locates him as a bridge between the humanistic and the absurd literary generations.

Perry, J. Douglas. See MISCELLANEOUS (Contemporary).

Pickens, Donald K. "Uncle Tom Becomes Nat Turner: A Commentary on Two American Heroes." *NALF*, 3 (1969), 45-48.
Both Uncle Tom and Nat Turner believe that one should live in the world but should keep his soul "apart and pure for the judgment day."

Pinsker, Sanford S. "Christ as Revolutionary/ Revolutionary as Christ: The Hero in Bernard Malamud's *The Fixer* and William Styron's *The Confessions of Nat Turner*." *Barat Rev*, 6 (Summer 1971), 29-37.
Yakob Bok in Malamud's novel moves from passive to active, whereas Nat Turner in Styron's novel moves from active to passive.

Platt, Gerald M. "A Sociologist Looks at *The Confessions of Nat Turner*." *Psych Today*, 1 (January 1968), 14-15.
Deals with historical shortcomings and faults in the characterization of Nat Turner.

Poirier, Richard. See MISCELLANEOUS (Contemporary).

Prasad, Thakur G. "*Lie Down in Darkness*: A Portrait of the Modern Phenomenon." *Indian Jour of Eng Stud*, 10 (1969), 71-80.
The novel reflects the modern age's concern with "solitary man, man alone and wrestling with himself."

Ratner, Marc L. "The Rebel Purged: Styron's *The Long March*." *ArlQ*, 2 (Autumn 1969), 27-42.
The Long March is a novel of rebellion that culminates in *The Confessions of Nat Turner*.

_____. "Rebellion of Wrath and Laughter: Styron's *Set This House on Fire*." *SouR*, 7 (Autumn 1971), 1007-1020.
A complex reading of the novel as social satire and personal tragi-comedy. Cass Kinsolving is seen as a comic-grotesque representative of romantic-puritan society who achieves his identity through rebellion.

_____. "Styron's Rebel." *AQ*, 21 (Fall 1969), 596-608.
Discusses Turner and other Styron characters as social rebels.

_____. *William Styron*. New York: Twayne Publishers, 1972.

Traces the development in the novels of Styron's treatment of the nature and psychological cause of rebellion in society; his main theme is the struggle toward self-realization.

Riese, Teut A. "Geschichtsverständnis und Geschichtsdichtung im Amerika des 20. Jahrhunderts," in *Amerikanischer Literatur im 20. Jahrhundert*, ed. Alfred Weber and Dieter Haack. Göttingen: Vanderhoeck & Ruprecht, 1971.

Includes *The Confessions of Nat Turner* in a discussion of works which indicate that the past is necessary for the understanding of the present.

Rocca, Luisa de Vecchi. "Nat Turner." *Nuova Antologia*, 510 (December 1970), 614-624.

A discussion of the facts of Nat Turner's life which should be taken into account in an evaluation of Styron's *The Confessions of Nat Turner*.

Sheed, Wilfrid. See MISCELLANEOUS (Contemporary).

Shepherd, Allen. "'Hopeless Paradox' and *The Confessions of Nat Turner*." *RANAM*, 4 (1971), 87-91.

Deals with paradoxes that cannot be resolved in Turner's concepts.

Simpson, Lewis P. See MISCELLANEOUS (Contemporary-- 1st Simpson entry).

Sitkoff, Harvard, and Michael Wreszin. "Whose Nat Turner?: William Styron vs. the Black Intellectuals." *Midstream*, 14 (November 1968), 10-20.

In spite of black objections to Styron's novel, historians have found it historically sound.

Stern, Frederick. See MISCELLANEOUS (Contemporary).

Sullivan, Walter. See MISCELLANEOUS (Contemporary--2nd Sullivan entry).

Suter, A. "Transcendence and Failure: William Styron's *Lie Down in Darkness*." *Caliban*, 12 (1975).

Deals with the characters' relationship with and attitudes toward death.

Swanson, William J. "Religious Implications in *The Confessions of Nat Turner*." *CimR*, 12 (July 1970), 57-66.

Margaret Whitehead becomes Nat's Beatrice.

_____. "William Faulkner and William Styron: Notes on Religion." *CimR*, 7 (March 1969), 45-52.

In response to critics who have found parallels in religious elements in *Lie Down in Darkness* and *The Sound and the Fury*, Swanson points out the differences in the two novels.

Thelwell, Mike. "Mr. William Styron and the Reverend Turner." *Mass Rev*, 9 (Winter 1968), 7-29.

An essay written in defense of Turner, concerned "with the future of his grandchildren-- to whom he used to be a hero." Thelwell finds Styron's character to be "a grotesque reduction" of the Turner "of historical record" and the novel to be important only as proof of the "truly astonishing persistence of white southern myths."

Tischler, Nancy M. See MISCELLANEOUS (Contemporary-- 3rd Tischler entry).

Tragle, Henry I. "Styron and His Sources." *Mass Rev*, 11 (Winter 1970), 134-153.

Finds a wealth of documents and living legends concerning Nat Turner in Southampton County, Virginia, a fact Styron had denied.

Urang, Gunnar. "The Voices of Tragedy in the Novels of William Styron," in *Adversity and Grace: Studies in Recent American Literature*, ed. Nathan A. Scott, Jr. Chicago: Univ of Chicago Press, 1968, pp. 183-209.

Styron has moved from a focus on the individual in *Lie Down in Darkness* to a wider focus on the social and the national in *Set This House on Fire*.

Via, Dan O., Jr. "Law as Grace in Styron's *Set This House on Fire*." *JR*, 51 (April 1971), 125-136.

Attributes "the new appreciation" of *Set This House on Fire* to "a recognition of its theological significance."

Watkins, Floyd C. See MISCELLANEOUS (Contemporary).

Weinberg, Helen A. See MISCELLANEOUS (Contemporary).

West, James L. W. III. "William Styron's Afterword to *The Long March*." *Miss Quart*, 28 (Spring 1975), 185-189.

Along with the text of the Afterword itself, which has never before appeared in English, the introductory note describes the publication history of the novel, its translation history, the importance of the Afterword, and the basis of this text of it.

White, John. "The Novelist as Historian: William Styron and American Negro Slavery." *Jour Am Stud*, 4 (February 1971), 233-245.

Argues that *The Confessions of Nat Turner* is essential reading for an overview of American slavery.

Whitney, Blair. "Nat Turner's Mysticism." *Barat Rev*, 6 (Summer 1971), 21-24.

Nat experiences epiphanies somewhat like those of Stephen Dedalus in *Ulysses*.

Wiemann, Renate. "William Styron: *Lie Down in Darkness*. Zum Problem der verlorenen und wiedergewonnen." *Neueren Sprachen*, 19 (July 1970), 321-332.

Deals with Styron's treatment of the theme of innocence.

Wilkerson, Margaret. "*The Iron Hand of Nat Turner*." *DramaR*, 16 (December 1972), 35-38.

Discusses Harry Dolan's drama based on Styron's *The Confessions of Nat Turner*.

[TATE, ALLEN] Anon. "Southern Gentleman of Letters." *TLS*, no. 3,603 (March 19 1971), 320.
An essay-review of Tate's *"The Swimmers" and Other Selected Poems* and *Essays of Four Decades*.

Aldridge, John W. See MISCELLANEOUS (Contemporary-- 2nd Aldridge entry).

Atlas, James. See GENERAL.

Bataille, Robert. See MISCELLANEOUS (Contemporary).

Bradford, M. E. "Angels at Forty Thousand Feet: 'Ode to Our Young Pro-Consuls of the Air' and the Practice of Poetic Responsibility." *GaR*, 22 (Spring 1968), 42-57.
A discussion of Tate's "Ode" as an ironic poem.

_____. *Rumors of Mortality: An Introduction to Allen Tate*. Dallas: Argus Academic Press, 1969.
A reading of Tate's poetry against the background of his diverse achievements as a "man of letters in the antique European sense."

Brooks, Cleanth. "On the Poetry of Allen Tate." *Mich Quart Rev*, 10 (Fall 1971), 225-228.
The themes and style of Tate's poems serve to "put in its most challenging form a fiercely dramatic speculation about man's ends and purposes."

_____. See DAVIDSON, DONALD (Contemporary).

Brown, Ashley. "Allen Tate as Satirist." *Shen*, 30 (Winter 1968), 44-54.
A brief sketch of American satirical writing and Tate's place in American satire, followed by an analysis of "Ode to Our Young Pro-Consuls of the Air."

Bruccoli, Matthew J., ed. *Fitzgerald/Hemingway Annual, 1974*. Englewood, Colorado: Microcard Editions Books.
Includes an interview with Tate.

Buffington, Robert. "The Directing Mind: Allen Tate and the Profession of Letters." *So Lit Jour*, 5 (Spring 1973), 102-115.
An essay-review of *Allen Tate*, by Ferman Bishop, *Allen Tate: A Literary Biography*, by Radcliffe Squires, and of *Allen Tate and His Works: Critical Evaluations*, also by Squires.

Carruth, Hayden. See AMMONS, A. R. (Contemporary).

Carter, T. H. See MISCELLANEOUS (Contemporary).

Core, George. "A Metaphysical Athlete: Allen Tate as Critic." *So Lit Jour*, 2 (Fall 1969), 138-147.
An essay-review of *Essays of Four Decades* that maintains that Tate's criticism has been "more consistent in the high level of its quality than has the criticism of any other critic of our time."

Cowan, Louise. "Allen Tate and the Garment of Dante." *SR*, 80 (1972), 377-382.
An essay-review of Radcliffe Squires's literary biography of Tate, which calls Tate "a poet who did not merely touch Dante's hem but put on his garment to cover the nakedness of the modern."

_____. See MISCELLANEOUS (Contemporary).

Cowley, Malcolm. See MISCELLANEOUS (Contemporary-- both Cowley entries).

Curnow, Wystan. See MISCELLANEOUS (Contemporary).

Davis, Joe Lee. "Allen Tate." *Mich Quart Rev*, 12 (Autumn 1973), 375-380.
An essay-review of Radcliffe Squires's biography of Tate, of his edition, *Allen Tate and His Work: Critical Evaluations*, and of Tate's *The Swimmers and Other Collected Poems*.

Davis, Robert Murray. "The Anthologist: Editor vs. Compiler." *PBSA*, 63 (4th Qtr. 1969), 321-323.
Points out that Lionel Trilling's anthology *The Experience of Literature* contains the second, not the final version of Tate's "Ode to the Confederate Dead."

Dickey, James. Untitled. *New Rep*, 173 (October 4, 1975), 22-24.
An essay-review of Tate's *Memoirs*, which finds the work to be the most pleasant book by one of the most powerful creative talents of "the *Old* South."

Donoghue, Denis. "Allen Tate's Seventy-Fifth Birthday." *TLS*, no. 3797 (December 13, 1974), 1414.
A report of, and a short biography prompted by, the celebration of Tate's birthday at Sewanee.

_____. "The American Style of Failure." *SR*, 82 (Summer 1974), 407-432.
Tate is one of several authors discussed as having "transform[ed] the mere state of failure into the artistic success of forms and pageants."

Dupree, Robert. "The Mirrors of Analogy: Three Poems of Allen Tate." *SouR*, 8 (Autumn 1972), 774-791.
Tate's analogical imagery is examined in "The Last Days of Alice," "The Cross," and "The Mediterranean," in order to present one of the poet's central themes: the contrast between modern man's view of the world as "dead" and manipulable and his ancestors' view of it as an organic whole.

Eaton, Charles E. See DAVIDSON, DONALD (Contemporary).

Edwards, Margaret F. "An Explication of Allen Tate's 'Ode to the Confederate Dead.'" *Contemporary Poetry*, 1 (Spring 1973), 31-34.
Interprets the poem as an exploration of the significance of death.

Fain, John Tyree, and Thomas Daniel Young, eds. "The Agrarian Symposium: Letters of Allen Tate and Donald Davidson, 1928-1930." *SouR*, 8 (Autumn 1972), 845-882.

    Prints letters of the period in which one can trace "the development of the Agrarian symposium *I'll Take My Stand*."

Fain, John Tyree, and Thomas Daniel Young. See DAVIDSON, DONALD (Contemporary).

Falwell, Marshall, and Thomas Daniel Young. *Allen Tate: A Bibliography*. New York: David Lewis, 1969.

    A checklist of works by and about Tate through 1967.

Fields, Kenneth. "Just and Unpredictable Proportions: Allen Tate's *Essays of Four Decades*." *SR*, 80 (Winter 1972), 180-196.

    An essay-review of *Essays of Four Decades*, emphasizing the difficulty of Tate's style but remarking that at least a dozen of his essays are indispensable for anyone engaged in the study of literature; Tate is better in his "literary" than in his "cultural" essays.

Ghiselin, Brewster. "A Dove." *Mich Quart Rev*, 10 (Autumn 1971), 229-230.

    Deals with the significance of Tate's statement that he gave up hunting after seeing a dove he had shot die.

Hallman, David A. See DAVIDSON, DONALD (Contemporary).

Helmick, E. T. "The Civil War Odes of Lowell and Tate." *GaR*, 25 (Spring 1971), 51-55.

    A comparison of the ideas and techniques of Tate and Robert Lowell.

Howard, Richard. See MISCELLANEOUS (Contemporary).

Hubbell, Jay B. See GENERAL.

Kane, Patricia. "An Irrepressible Conflict: Allen Tate's *The Fathers*." *Critique*, 10, no. 2 (1968), 9-16.

    The conflict of the novel is between "the ordered, ritualistic, family-centered old life and the destructive, disordered, personal new way" in the mid-nineteenth-century South. The article approaches this theme through the character of Lacy.

Korges, James. "Allen Tate: A Checklist Continued." *Critique*, 10, no. 2 (1968), 35-52.

    The first two pages are a reminiscence of Tate. Part I brings Thorp's list of Tate's books up to date. Also, periodical contributions since 1942 have been added.

Landess, Thomas H. See DAVIDSON, DONALD (Contemporary).

Lemon, L. T. "A Man of Letters." *PrS*, 44 (Winter 1969-70), 416-417.

    A brief review of Tate's *Essays of Four Decades* in which the reviewer says that Tate shows an abiding concern with human values and is occupied with a probing and detailed analysis of literature.

Newitz, Martin. "Tradition, Time, and Allen Tate." *Miss Quart*, 21 (Winter 1967-68), 37-42.

    A study of symbols for "tradition" and "time" in Tate's poetry and of its echoes of Eliot, Yeats, and Pope.

O'Dea, Richard J. "Allen Tate's Vestigial Morality." *Person*, 49 (Spring 1968), 256-262.

    Relates Tate's theory of knowledge to several poems--most importantly "The Wolves."

Porter, Katherine Anne. See PORTER, KATHERINE ANNE.

Sanders, Frederick K. "Theme and Structure in *The Fathers*." *ArlQ*, 1 (Winter 1967-68), 244-256.

    The theme is the "loss of the meaning of traditional forms, rituals, and patterns of behavior, and the change from a dominant concern for the public order to a dominant interest in the needs and impulses of the individual."

Schwartz, Delmore. See MISCELLANEOUS (Contemporary).

Simpson, Lewis P. See MISCELLANEOUS (Contemporary-- 1st Simpson entry).

Squires, Radcliffe. *Allen Tate: A Literary Biography*. New York: Pegasus, 1971.

    Deals with Tate's life and with Tate as a man of letters.

_____. "Allen Tate: A Season at Monteagle." *Mich Quart Rev*, 10 (Fall 1971), 57-65.

    A discussion of the poetry produced at Monteagle, Tennessee, in 1942.

_____, ed. *Allen Tate and His Work: Critical Evaluations*. Minneapolis: Univ of Minnesota Press, 1972.

    A collection of thirty-five previously published essays on Tate the man, the essayist, the novelist, and the poet, with an introduction and bibliography by the editor.

_____. "Allen Tate's *The Fathers*." *VQR*, 46 (Autumn 1970), 629-649.

    Cites Arthur Mizener's essay "*The Fathers* and Realistic Fiction" as a "clear and true" reading of the novel, but asserts that his discussion of the personal "foment of evolving obsessions" that possessed Tate will help in the understanding of the book.

_____. "Will and Vision: Allen Tate's Terza Rima Poems." *SR*, 78 (Autumn 1970), 543-562.

    An evaluation of three of Tate's poems--"The Maimed Man," "The Buried Lake," and "The Swimmers," the best of which is "The Swimmers."

Stanford, Donald E. "'Out of That Source of Time': The Poetry of Allen Tate." *SouR*, 7 (Summer 1971), xvii-xxiii.

    Brief comments on Tate's poetry as rooted in the South and in sensuous experience as opposed to abstraction.

Tate, Allen. "A Lost Traveller's Dream." *Mich Quart Rev*, 11 (Fall 1972), 225-236.

    The opening chapter of a memoir.

_____. *Memoirs and Opinions 1926-1974.* Chicago: Swallow Press, 1975.
Reprinted essays and recent reminiscences.

_____. "Poetry, Modern and Unmodern: A Personal Recollection." *HudR*, 21 (Summer 1968), 251-262.
Deals with contemporary poets who influenced him and those who did not. Included in *Essays of Four Decades*.

_____. "A Sequence of Stanzas: *Compiled and Read to a Group of Friends on His Seventy-Fifth Birthday, November 19, 1974.*" *VQR*, 51 (Winter 1975), 264-268.
Tate comments on some of his own stanzas and on stanzas by Landor, Edwin Muir, and George Seferis, and on death and love.

_____. *The Swimmers and Other Selected Poems.* New York: Scribner's, 1970.
The poet's selection of his best work of fifty years, several of the ninety-nine poems collected for the first time.

_____, and Donald Davidson. "The Agrarian Symposium: Letters of Allen Tate and Donald Davidson, 1928-1930." Ed. John T. Fain and Thomas Daniel Young. *SouR*, 8 (Autumn 1972), 845-882.
Selected from *The Literary Correspondence of Allen Tate and Donald Davidson*, these letters trace plans for the Agrarian symposium, *I'll Take My Stand*.

Thorp, Willard. "Allen Tate: A Checklist." *Critique*, 10, no. 2 (1968), 17-34.
This list is reprinted from Volume III of the *Princeton University Library Chronicle* of 1942, pp. 85-90.

Toledano, Ben C. See MISCELLANEOUS (Contemporary).

Uhlman, Thompson. "Tate's 'Death of Little Boys.'" *Expl*, 28 (March 1970), Item 58.
Deals with Tennyson allusions in the poem.

Warren, Austin. "Homage to Allen Tate." *SouR*, 9 (Autumn 1973), 753-777.
A review of Radcliffe Squires's literary biography of Tate, plus extended evaluations of *The Fathers* and others of Tate's works.

Webb, Max. See MISCELLANEOUS (Contemporary).

Wilson, James D. See MISCELLANOUS (Contemporary).

Woodward, C. Vann. See MISCELLANEOUS (Contemporary).

Young, Thomas Daniel. See RANSOM, JOHN CROWE--1st Young entry.

_____. See GENERAL.

[TAYLOR, PETER] Brooks, Cleanth. "The Southern Temper." *Archiv*, 206 (May 1969), 1-15.
Uses Taylor's "Miss Leonora When Seen Last" to exemplify the Southern spirit.

Goodwin, Stephen. "An Interview with Peter Taylor." *Shen*, 24 (Winter 1973), 3-20.

Elicits Taylor's responses about his attitudes toward his art.

Griffith, Albert J. *Peter Taylor*. Twayne's U. S. Authors Series, no. 168. New York: Twayne, 1970.
An assessment of Taylor's accomplishments with emphasis on his use of Southern locale and character and his place in the Southern Renaissance.

Howard, Richard. "Urgent Need and Unbearable Fear." *Shen*, 24 (Winter 1973), 44-47.
A review of Taylor's *Presences, Seven Dramatic Pieces*, which finds the work a "worthy experiment."

Peden, William A. "A Hard and Admirable Toughness: The Stories of Peter Taylor." *Hollins Critic*, 7 (February 1970), 1-9.
A review of Taylor's *Collected Stories* which concludes that Taylor's fiction "is no less accurate a reflection of some of the basic aspects of our times than the picture produced by the apostles of doom, destruction, and devastation."

Pinkerton, Jan. "A Critical Distortion of Peter Taylor's 'At the Drugstore.'" *NConL*, 1 (September 1971), 6-7.
Points out a misquotation from this story in another article, a distortion which results in misinterpretation of character.

_____. "The Non-Regionalism of Peter Taylor." *GaR*, 24 (Winter 1970), 432-440.
Discusses Taylor as an heretical Southern writer who propounds a "Yankee" theme of constant movement to new experience.

Raskin, Barbara. "Southern Fried." *New Rep*, 161 (October 18, 1969), 29-30.
An unfavorable review of *The Collected Stories of Peter Taylor*, followed by a correspondent's disagreement and rejoinder in the same journal (November 22, 1969), pp. 27-29.

Ricks, Christopher. "The Unignorable Real: A Review of *Collected Stories*, by Peter Taylor." *NYRB*, 14 (February 12, 1970), 22-24.
Taylor's stories are such "faithful renderings of small-town infidelities" that they seem almost like photographic realism.

Wolff, Geoffrey. "Master of Hidden Drama." *Newsweek*, 73 (October 20, 1969), 121-122.
A review of Taylor's *Collected Stories* in which Taylor is called the best man now writing the short story in English.

[TOOMER, JEAN] Ackley, Donald G. "Theme and Vision in Jean Toomer's *Cane*." *SBL*, 1 (Spring 1970), 45-65.
The theme concerns the black's passage from the world of slavery to the materialistic white world; the vision is the hope that one race will save the other through recognition of the differences between them.

Aptheker, Herbert. See GENERAL.

IV. Contemporary (1920-1975)

Baker, Houston A., Jr. See GENERAL--4th Baker entry.

Bell, Bernard W. "Jean Toomer's *Cane*." *Black World*, 23 (September 1974), 4-19, 92-97.
"When analyzed as a poetic novel, the disparate elements and illusive meanings of the book coalesce into an integral whole and provide a poignant insight into the dilemma of the modern black artist."

_____. "A Key to the Poems in *Cane*." *CLA Jour*, 14 (March 1971), 251-258.
On one level *Cane* is a deeply religious quest for the truth about man, God, and America. Incantational, progressing from a highly poetic to a heavily dramatic form, it is symbolic as well as metaphysical.

Blackwell, Louise. "Jean Toomer's *Cane* and Biblical Myth." *CLA Jour*, 17 (1974), 535-542.
Toomer uses biblical myth as a metaphor giving identity to black people.

Blake, Susan L. "The Spectatorial Artist and the Structure of *Cane*." *CLA Jour*, 17 (1974), 516-534.
In *Cane* there is a progression from "spectatorial detachment" to "personal involvement" to "artistic detachment."

Boitani, Piero. See MISCELLANEOUS (Contemporary).

Bone, Robert. See GENERAL.

Bontemps, Arna, ed. "Introduction," *Cane*, by Jean Toomer. New York: Harper & Row, 1969.
The introduction reviews Toomer's life and discusses the structure of *Cane*.

_____. See MISCELLANEOUS (Contemporary).

Cancel, Rafael A. "Male and Female Interrelationships in Toomer's *Cane*." *NALF*, 5 (1971), 25-31.
In this work the women, not the men, have "all the primitive instincts and lust for life."

Chase, Patricia. "The Women in *Cane*." *CLA Jour*, 14 (March 1971), 259-273.
The women characters are the threads which weave *Cane* together.

Christ, J. M. "Jean Toomer's 'Bona and Paul': The Innocence and Artifice of Words." *NALF*, 9 (Summer 1975), 44-46.
Argues that wordplay is a significant element in the story.

Cooke, Michael G. See MISCELLANEOUS (Contemporary--1st Cooke entry).

Corrigan, Robert A. See GENERAL--1st Corrigan entry.

Davis, Charles T. "Jean Toomer and the South: Region and Race as Elements within a Literary Imagination." *SLI*, 7 (Fall 1974), 23-37.
Deals with the significance of Toomer's realizations about race and home in relation to his development as an artist.

Dickerson, Mary Jane. "Sherwood Anderson and Jean Toomer: A Literary Relationship." *Stud in Am F*, 1 (Autumn 1973), 162-175.
Suggests that *Winesburg, Ohio* influenced both structure and theme in *Cane*.

Dillard, Mabel M. "Jean Toomer--The Veil Replaced." *CLA Jour*, 15 (June 1974), 468-473.
Deals with Toomer's concepts of race and prejudice.

Duncan, Bowie. "Jean Toomer's *Cane*: A Modern Black Oracle." *CLA Jour*, 15 (March 1972), 323-333.
The design and message of *Cane* can be understood if it is approached "through a discussion of the planes in the first study, a comparison of the first three pieces, and a comparison of the three sections of the book."

Durham, Frank. "Jean Toomer's Vision of the Southern Negro" (in "Four Authors View the South: A Symposium"). *SHR*, 6 (Winter 1972), 13-22.
In Toomer's "pioneering glimpse of the vitality of the Negro soul" in *Cane*, there is also "an anger at the injustice, bigotry, and cruelty to which the Negro was subjected."

_____. "The Poetry Society of South Carolina's Turbulent Year: Self-Interest, Atheism, and Jean Toomer." *SHR*, 5 (Winter 1971), 76-80.
A "recapturing" of the turbulence and outrage in the South Carolina Poetry Society in 1923 when Ransom's "atheistic" poem "Armageddon" won the Southern Prize and when there was discovered a Negro, Jean Toomer, on the Society's membership roll.

_____. *Studies in Cane*. Columbus, Ohio: Charles E. Merrill, 1971.
Reprints biographical background material, eight early reviews, and fourteen critical excerpts and essays on the novel.

Edward, Sister Ann. See GENERAL.

Elias, Robert H. *"Entangling Alliances with None": An Essay on the Individual in the American Twenties*. New York: W. W. Norton, 1973.
Toomer is one of the writers used to illustrate a sense of individual responsibility as one of the chief characteristics of the Twenties.

Farrison, W. Edward. "Jean Toomer's *Cane* Again." *CLA Jour*, 15 (March 1972), 295-302.
The many editions of *Cane* and the amount of criticism written on the work are a result of the book's portrayal of phases of black life not previously treated fully.

Fischer, William C. "The Aggregate Man in Jean Toomer's *Cane*." *Stud in the Novel*, 3 (Summer 1971), 190-215.
"Toomer's intentions come into clear focus when one responds to the book from the perspective of the extra-literary styles so crucial to the expressive modes of Afro-American culture."

Fisher, Alice P. "The Influence of Ouspensky's *Tertium Organum* upon Jean Toomer's *Cane*." *CLA Jour*, 17 (1974), 504-515.

Deals with the influence of Ouspensky on Toomer's experiments with language.

French, Warren. See MISCELLANEOUS (Contemporary--4th French entry).

Gayle, Addison, Jr. See GENERAL.

Gibson, Donald B. See MISCELLANEOUS (Contemporary).

Goede, William J. "Jean Toomer's Ralph Kabnis: Portrait of the Negro Artist." *Phylon*, 30 (Spring 1969), 73-85.
    Kabnis represents the artist moving "toward a commitment, through art, to the racial experience of Negroes."

Grant, Sister Mary Kathryn. "Images of Celebration in *Cane*." *NALF*, 5 (1971), 32-34, 36.
    The South is the source of identity and celebration for Ralph Kabnis.

Griffin, John C. "Jean Toomer: A Bibliography." *So Car Rev*, 7 (April 1975), 61-64.
    Lists works by Toomer and selected criticism.

_____. "A Chat with Marjory Content Toomer." *Pembroke Mag* (Pembroke, N. C.), 5 (1974), 15-27.
    A talk with Toomer's wife.

_____. "Two Poems by Jean Toomer." *Pembroke Mag*, 6 (1975), 67-88.
    Prints two previously unpublished poems that Waldo Frank suggested Toomer leave out of *Cane*.

Gross, Theodore L. See GENERAL--1st Gross entry.

Hart, Robert C. See MISCELLANOUS (Contemporary).

Heibling, Mark. "Sherwood Anderson and Jean Toomer." *NALF*, 9 (Summer 1975), 35-39.
    Though Anderson was "essentially indifferent" to those "who consciously sought to create or articulate a Black aesthetic," he and Toomer were friends for a time; the article offers possible reasons as to why Toomer and his work appealed to Anderson.

Huggins, Nathan. See MISCELLANEOUS (Contemporary).

Innes, Catherine L. "The Unity of Jean Toomer's *Cane*." *CLA Jour*, 15 (March 1972), 306-322.
    A study of the symbols, themes, images, and structure of *Cane*.

Jung, Udo. "Spirit-Torsos of Exquisite Strength: The Theme of Individual Weakness vs. Collective Strength in Two of Toomer's Poems." *CLA Jour*, 19 (December 1975), 261-267.
    "Cotton Song" and "Prayer" reveal how Toomer believed the problem of "inter-personal and intra-personal separation" might be solved.

Kesteloot, Lilyan. "Negritude and Its American Sources." *Boston Univ Jour*, 22 (Spring 1974), 54-64. Trans. from the French by Allen C. Kennedy.
    Deals with the influence of the writers of the Harlem Renaissance, including Toomer, on certain French writers.

Kopf, George. "The Tensions in Jean Toomer's 'Theatre.'" *CLA Jour*, 17 (1974), 498-503.
    Deals with the psychological tensions resulting from passivity versus action, freedom versus bondage.

Kraft, James. "Jean Toomer's *Cane*." *MarkR*, 2 (October 1970), 61-63.
    Deals with the symbolic significance of *Cane*.

Kramer, Victor A. "The 'Mid-Kingdom' of Crane's 'Black Tambourine' and Toomer's *Cane*." *CLA Jour*, 17 (1974), 486-497.
    Points out similarities in these two works.

Krasny, Michael J. "The Aesthetic Structure of Jean Toomer's *Cane*." *NALF*, 9 (Summer 1975), 42-43.
    Each of the three sections of *Cane* is an arc; all of the arcs ultimately "unite in a circle."

_____. "Design in Jean Toomer's *Balo*." *NALF*, 7 (Fall 1973), 103-104.
    This one-act sketch deals with the idea that black emotions have been restricted by white Christianity.

_____. "Jean Toomer's Life Prior to *Cane*: A Brief Sketch." *NALF*, 9 (Summer 1975), 40-41.
    Deals with Toomer's changing concepts towards his own role and that of the artist.

Lieber, Todd M. "Design and Movement in *Cane*." *CLA Jour*, 13 (September 1969), 35-50.
    Deals with the unity of this work relating art and experience.

Liebman, Arthur. See MISCELLANEOUS (Contemporary).

Ludington, C. T., Jr. See MISCELLANEOUS (Contemporary).

MacKethan, Lucinda H. "Jean Toomer's *Cane*: A Pastoral Problem" *Miss Quart*, 28 (Fall 1975), 423-434.
    This novel's "pastoral design...provides a certain measure of stability for the complex and often contradictory urges reflected in Toomer's work as he confronts the world that he, as both black man and modern man, must negotiate."

Margolies, Edward. See MISCELLANOUS--both Margolies entries.

Mason, Clifford. "Jean Toomer's Black Authenticity." *Black World*, 20 (November 1970), 70-76.
    Praises *Cane* as a work revealing that blacks must be aware of their blackness.

Matthews, George C. "Toomer's *Cane*: The Artist and His World." *CLA Jour*, 17 (1974), 543-559.
    Deals with aesthetic, regional, and spiritual elements in the novel.

McCarthy, Daniel P. "'Just Americans': A Note on Jean Toomer's Marriage to Margery Latimer." *CLA Jour*, 17 (1974), 474-479.
    Deals with reactions to Toomer's marriage and their effect on his career.

McDowell, Robert E., and George Fortenberry. See MISCELLANEOUS (Contemporary).

McKeever, Benjamin. "*Cane* as Blues." *NALF*, 4 (1970), 61-63.
  Deals with the theme of suffering in the novel.

Mellard, James M. See MISCELLANEOUS (Contemporary).

Nower, Joyce. See GENERAL--1st Nower entry.

O'Brien, John. See MISCELLANEOUS (Contemporary--1st O'Brien entry).

Reilly, John M. "Jean Toomer: An Annotated Checklist of Criticism." *RALS*, 4 (Spring 1974), 27-56.
  Lists, comments on, and indexes all Toomer criticism from 1923 to 1973.

_____. "The Search for Black Redemption: Jean Toomer's *Cane*." *Stud in the Novel*, 2 (Fall 1970), 312-324.
  Discusses the theme of the search for self-expression in relation to the form and settings of the novel.

Richmond, Merle. "Jean Toomer and Margery Latimer." *CLA Jour*, 18 (1974), 300.
  On Toomer and his wife.

Riley, Roberta. "Search for Identity and Artistry." *CLA Jour*, 17 (1974), 480-485.
  Deals with Toomer's concepts of the black experience revealed in *Cane*.

Rosenblatt, Roger. See MISCELLANEOUS (Contemporary--both Rosenblatt entries).

Scruggs, Charles. "Jean Toomer: Fugitive." *AL*, 47 (March 1975), 84-96.
  The author explores Toomer's ambivalent attitudes toward his racial heritage.

_____. "The Mark of Cain and the Redemption of Art: A Study in Theme and Structure of Jean Toomer's *Cane*." *AL*, 44 (May 1972), 276-291.
  Studies the theme of "Cane/Cain" and the relationship of the novel's episodes to its larger meaning.

Singh, Raman K. See MISCELLANEOUS (Contemporary--1st Singh entry).

Spofford, William K. "The Unity of Part One of Jean Toomer's *Cane*." *MarkR*, 3 (May 1972), 58-60.
  Recognizing the unity of Part One of the novel may provide help in the recognition of the unity of the whole work.

Stein, Marian L. "The Poet-Observer and 'Fern' in Jean Toomer's *Cane*." *MarkR*, 2 (October 1970), 64-65.
  The 'Fern' section is the pivot of the novel.

Taylor, Clyde. "The Second Coming of Jean Toomer." *Obsidian*, 1 (Winter 1975), 37-56.
  Deals with "the black messianic vision in *Cane*."

Thompson, Larry E. "Jean Toomer as Modern Man." *Ren 2*, 1 (1971), 7-10.
  On Toomer's search for "singularity."

Toomer, Jean. "Chapters from 'Earth-Being,' an Unpublished Autobiography." *Black Schol*, 2 (January 1971), 3-13.
  Toomer discusses the influence on him of his Uncle Bismarck.

Turner, Darwin T. "An Intersection of Paths: Correspondence Between Jean Toomer and Sherwood Anderson." *CLA Jour*, 17 (1974), 455-467.
  Deals with the importance of this correspondence.

_____. "Introduction," *Cane*, by Jean Toomer. New York: Liveright, 1975.
  Comments on Toomer's life, on *Cane*, and on the Harlem Renaissance.

_____. "Jean Toomer's *Cane*." *Negro Digest*, 18 (January 1970), 54-61.
  Discusses the revelation in the novel of the incompatibility between the search for identity and sexual fulfillment.

_____. See MISCELLANEOUS (Contemporary--2nd Turner entry).

Waldron, Edward E. "The Search for Identity in Jean Toomer's 'Esther.'" *CLA Jour*, 14 (March 1971), 277-280.
  Ultimately "Esther" is the interpretation of the light-skinned American Negro in the black community.

Watkins, Patricia. "Is There a Unifying Theme in *Cane*?" *CLA Jour*, 15 (March 1972), 303-305.
  "If there is a unifying theme..., it is the theme of man's inability to communicate and interact with fellow humans; the inability to understand and therefore to love; the inability to quicken another human soul."

Westerfield, Hargis. "Jean Toomer's 'Fern': A Mythical Dimension." *CLA Jour*, 14 (March 1971), 274-276.
  Fern Rosen is used to point up the Jewish and Christian myth. The poem is structured to suggest the incarnation of God, with a black Mary appearing as avatar in Georgia.

[WADE, JOHN DONALD] De Bellis, Jack. See MISCELLANEOUS (Contemporary).

Fain, John T. See LYTLE, ANDREW NELSON.

_____. See MISCELLANEOUS (Contemporary).

Inge, M. Thomas. "Introduction" to *Augustus Baldwin Longstreet*, by John Donald Wade, rev. ed. Athens: Univ of Georgia Press, 1969.
  Summarizes the importance of this biography and Wade's contribution to the biographical art; includes a bibliography of Wade's writings.

Maloney, Stephen R. See MISCELLANEOUS (Contemporary).

Smith, Gerald. See LONGSTREET, AUGUSTUS BALDWIN.

[WALKER, ALICE] Gaillard, Dawson. See MISCELLANEOUS (Contemporary).

Harris, Trudier. "Violence in *The Third Life of Grange Copeland*." *CLA Jour*, 19 (December 1975), 238-247.
 The novel develops the theme that violence and rejection of violence come from within the individual, that "powerlessness against whites is no excuse to destroy one's family or one's self."

O'Brien, John. See MISCELLANEOUS (Contemporary-- 2nd O'Brien entry).

Peden, William. See MISCELLANEOUS (Contemporary-- 2nd Peden entry).

[WALKER, MARGARET] Alexander, Margaret Walker. See WRIGHT, RICHARD (Contemporary).

Aptheker, Herbert. See GENERAL.

Giddings, Paula. "'A Shoulder Hunched Against a Sharp Concern': Some Themes in the Poetry of Margaret Walker." *Black World*, 21 (December 1971), 20-25.
 Deals principally with Walker's *Prophets for a New Day*.

Giovanni, Nikki. See GIOVANNI, NIKKI (Contemporary).

Grumback, Doris. See GENERAL.

Hull, Gloria T. "Black Women Poets from Wheatley to Walker." *NALF*, 9 (Fall 1975), 91-96.
 A survey including discussion of Walker's *For My People*.

Redmond, Eugene B. See GENERAL.

Rowell, Charles H. "An Interview with Margaret Walker." *Black World*, 25 (December 1975), 4-17.
 Includes questions and answers on typical interview topics.

Tyms, James D. See MISCELLANEOUS (Contemporary).

[WALSER, RICHARD] Anon. "A Bibliography of Richard Walser." *N Car F*, 19 (March 1971), 87-96.
 A complete list of Walser's writings to January 1, 1971.

[WARREN, ROBERT PENN] Aldridge, John W. "The Enormous Spider Web of Warren's World." *SatR*, October 9, 1971, pp. 31-37.
 An essay-review of Warren's *Meet Me in the Green Glen*.

  _____. See MISCELLANEOUS (Contemporary--2nd Aldridge entry).

Bataille, Robert. See MISCELLANEOUS (Contemporary).

Bauerle, Richard F. "The Emblematic Opening of Warren's *All the King's Men*." *Papers on Lang and Lit*, 8 (Summer 1972), 312-314.
 The first paragraph of the novel contains emblems indicating the three major themes of the novel.

Baym, Max I. See GENERAL.

Bergonzi, Bernard. "Nature, Mostly American." *SouR*, 6 (Winter 1970), 205-215.
 Warren's *Selected Poems: New and Old, 1923-1966* is reviewed with seven other contemporary works. The poet's common concern with nature and landscape is particularly noted.

Berthoff, Warner. "Dreiser Revisited." *Mod Occasions*, 2 (Winter 1972), 133-136.
 A review of Warren's *Homage to Theodore Dreiser* in which the reviewer points out some similarities between Warren and Dreiser.

Bisanz, Adam J. "Robert Penn Warren: The Ballad of Billie Potts: Ein amerikanisches 'Memorabile' auf dem Hintergrund europäischer Überlieferung." *Fabula*, 14 (1973), 71-90.
 On folk elements in this work.

Brooks, Cleanth. "Brooks on Warren." *Four Quarters*, 21 (May 1972), 19-22.
 An account of the Brooks-Warren relationship during their editorship of *The Southern Review*.

Bruffee, Kenneth A. "Elegiac Romance." *CE*, 32 (January 1971), 465-476.
 All the King's Men is one of the works designated an "elegiac romance," a type in which the hero is in quest of something and a narrator tells his story after his death.

Buchloh, Paul G. See GENERAL.

Bungert, Hans. See GENERAL.

Burt, David J. "A Folk Reference in Warren's *Flood*." *Miss Quart*, 22 (Winter 1968-69), 74-76.
 Discusses Warren's use of the folk ballad "Cotton-Eyed Joe" to reinforce thematic patterns.

  _____. "Robert Penn Warren's Debt to Homer in *Flood*." *NConL*, 3 (January 1973), 12-14.
 The prison sirens in the novel are remindful of the sirens in *The Odyssey*.

  _____, and Annette C. "Robert Penn Warren's Debt to Ibsen in *Night Rider*." *Miss Quart*, 22 (Fall 1969), 359-361.
 A metaphor used in the thematic development of the novel comes from Ibsen's *Peer Gynt*.

Cady, Edwin H. See GENERAL.

Casper, Leonard. "Ark, *Flood*, and Negotiated Covenant." *Four Quarters*, 21 (May 1972), 110-115.
 The novel centers on man's mortality and "intimations of a resurrection."

Cayton, Robert F. "The Fictional Voices of Robert Penn Warren." *Four Quarters*, 21 (May 1972), 45-52.
 A discussion of Warren's techniques for "the transformation of the voices of narrators into the voices of thematic agents."

Core, George. "In the Heart's Ambiguity: Robert Penn Warren as Poet." *Miss Quart*, 22 (Fall 1969), 313-326.

An evaluation of recent criticism of Warren's poetry and an assessment of Warren's present status as a poet.

Cowan, Louise. See MISCELLANEOUS (Contemporary).

Cowley, Malcolm. See MISCELLANEOUS (Contemporary—— 2nd Cowley entry).

Curnow, Wystan. See MISCELLANEOUS (Contemporary).

Davenport, F. Garvin, Jr. See MISCELLANEOUS (Contemporary).

Davison, Richard A. "Physical Imagery in Robert Penn Warren's 'Blackberry Winter.'" *GaR*, 22 (Winter 1968), 482-488.
    Discusses the responses of Seth's feet as indications of his changing awareness in his rite of passage.

Dooley, Dennis M. "The Persona RPW in Warren's *Brother to Dragons*." *Miss Quart*, 25 (Winter 1971), 19-30.
    RPW appears as a character in this dramatic poem, whose spiritual history is given in three long digressions parallel to that of Jefferson, the central concern of the poem.

Ellison, Ralph, et al. See MISCELLANEOUS (Contemporary).

Fairman, Marion A. See MISCELLANEOUS (Contemporary).

Ferguson, Suzanne. "'Something Which the Past Has Hid.'" *SR*, 80 (Summer 1972), 493-498.
    A review of Warren's *John Greenleaf Whittier's Poetry: An Appraisal and a Selection*.

Fisher, Ruth. "A Conversation with Robert Penn Warren." *Four Quarters*, 21 (May 1972), 3-17.
    A 1970 interview.

French, Warren. See MISCELLANEOUS (Contemporary—— 2nd French entry).

Gado, Frank. See MISCELLANEOUS (Contemporary).

Goldfarb, Russell M. "Robert P. Warren's Tollivers and George Eliot's Tullivers." *Univ Rev*, 36 (Spring 1970), 209-213.
    In *Flood*, Warren "looks back to *The Mill on the Floss* in order to suggest that the key to understanding the novel is understanding the incestuous attraction which patterns the lives of Maggie and Tom Tulliver."

_____. "Warren's Tollivers and Eliot's Tullivers II." *Univ Rev*, 36 (June 1970), 275-279.
    Although Warren does not rewrite *The Mill on the Floss*, certain parallels between it and *Flood* provide literary criticism a fresh approach to Eliot's well-discussed novel.

Goldstein, Laurence. "Audubon and R. P. Warren: To See and Record All Life." *Contemporary Poetry*, 1 (Winter 1973), 47-68.
    Deals with Warren's *Audubon*; Audubon is an authentic hero of American myth because his life reveals "the essential American soul."

Gray, Richard J. "The American Novelist and American History: A Revaluation of *All the King's Men*." *Jour of Am Stud*, 6 (1972), 297-307.
    Warren selects details to reveal the tragic pattern which history already contains within itself.

Grimshaw, James, Jr. "Robert Penn Warren's *Annus Mirabilis*." *SouR*, 10 (Spring 1974), 504-516.
    An essay-review of Warren's work produced between November 1970 and October 1971, with an extensive analysis of *Meet Me in the Green Glen*. The reviewer also discusses L. Hugh Moore's *Robert Penn Warren and History*, published during the same period.

Gross, Harvey. *The Contrived Corridor: History and Fatality in Modern Literature*. Ann Arbor: Univ of Michigan Press, 1971.
    Warren's concept of history as knowledge and process is discussed in the opening pages.

Guttenberg, Barnett. *Web of Being. The Novels of Robert Penn Warren*. Nashville, Tenn.: Vanderbilt Univ Press, 1975.
    Deals with Warren's theme of the individual's attainment of "the true being of selfhood through self-awareness and the realization" that he can ultimately create a "'new self.'"

Hayashi, Tetsumaro. See MISCELLANEOUS (Contemporary).

Herring, Henry D. "Madness in *At Heaven's Gate*: A Metaphor of the Self in Warren's Fiction." *Four Quarters*, 21 (May 1972), 56-66.
    Madness as a metaphor for disorder within the individual is central in this novel.

_____. "Politics in the Novels of Robert Penn Warren." *RANAM*, 4 (1971), 48-60.
    Politics plays an important part in all of Warren's novels except *The Cave* and his short stories.

Hiers, John T. "Buried Graveyards: Warren's *Flood* and Jones' *A Buried Land*." *Essays in Lit*, 2 (Spring 1975), 97-104.
    The graveyard episodes in both novels "represent the obliteration of a relatively homogeneous way of life, and epitomize the struggles of individuals and their isolated communities for integrity in the face of rapid urbanization and mechanization."

Howard, Richard. "Dreadful Alternatives: A Note on Robert Penn Warren." *GaR*, 29 (Spring 1975), 37-41.
    Deals with *Or Else——Poem/Poems, 1968-1974*, concluding that the "poem/poems" illustrate Warren's continuing "impulse" to be "against the stone, and toward the water, against what stands and toward what runs."

_____. See MISCELLANEOUS (Contemporary).

Hubbell, Jay B. See GENERAL.

Huff, Mary N., and Thomas Daniel Young. *Robert Penn Warren: A Bibliography*. New York: David Lewis, 1968.
    A checklist of works by and about Warren complete through 1967.

Irvine, Peter L. "The 'Witness' Point of View in Fiction." *SAQ*, 69 (Spring 1970), 217-225.
Warren is one of the writers discussed as having used a narrator who both observes and participates.

Janeway, Elizabeth. See MISCELLANEOUS (Contemporary).

Jarrell, Randall. See MISCELLANEOUS (Contemporary).

Justus, James H. "On the Politics of the Self-Created: *At Heaven's Gate*." *SR*, 82 (Spring 1974), 284-300.
This novel is a prelude to *All the King's Men* in its study of two things--the dehumanization caused by abstract power and the problem of self-definition.

_____. "Warren and the Doctrine of Complicity." *Four Quarters*, 21 (May 1972), 93-99.
Deals with the role of the doctrine of complicity in *All the King's Men* and *Brother to Dragons*.

_____. See RANSOM, JOHN CROWE.

Katope, Christopher G. "Robert Penn Warren's *All the King's Men*: A Novel of 'Pure Imagination.'" *Tex Stud in Lit and Lang*, 12 (Fall 1970), 493-510.
The novel's sun-moon imagery parallels that in Coleridge's *The Rime of the Ancient Mariner* and likewise suggests the importance of the imagination as a "value-creating capacity."

Kazin, Alfred. See MISCELLANEOUS (Contemporary).

Kehl, D. G. "Love's Definition: Dream as Reality in Robert Penn Warren's *Meet Me in the Green Glen*." *Four Quarters*, 21 (May 1972), 116-122.
The novel develops the theme that reality is self-identity and is brought about by love.

Keith, Philip. "Whittier and Warren." *Shen*, 23 (Summer 1972), 90-95.
A review of Warren's *Audubon: A Vision* and of his *John Greenleaf Whittier's Poetry: An Appraisal and a Selection*, which relates *Audubon* to the Whittier book and points out similarities between Warren and Whittier.

Köhring, Klaus H. "The American Epic." *SHR*, 5 (Summer 1971), 265-280.
A number of writers of the American epic are discussed, including Warren, who "asks the question of the mystery of human action" in *Brother to Dragons*.

Krieger, Murray. See MISCELLANEOUS (Contemporary).

Kronenberger, Louis, and E. M. Beck. See GENERAL.

Langman, F. H. "The Compelled Imagination: Robert Penn Warren's Conception of the Philosophical Novelist." *Southern Rev* (Adelaide), 4, no. 3 (1971), 192-202.
Deals with contradiction between Warren's definition of the philosophical novel and his actual practices in his own novels.

Light, J. F., ed. *Studies in All the King's Men*. Columbus, Ohio: Charles E. Merrill, 1971.
Reprints five background excerpts (including two essays by Warren), one early review, three source studies, and five critical essays, with an original essay by the editor.

Longley, John L., Jr. *Robert Penn Warren*. Southern Writers Series, no. 2. Austin: Steck-Vaughn, 1969.
A general critical introduction to Warren as a philosophical novelist concerned with the meaning of experience.

Madden, David. See MISCELLANEOUS (Contemporary--2nd Madden entry).

Martin, R. G. "Diction in Warren's *All the King's Men*." *EJ*, 58 (November 1969), 1169-1174.
The interaction of the plot with dialect reveals character through speech.

McCarron, William E. "Warren's *All the King's Men* and Arnold's 'To Marguerite--Continued.'" *AL*, 47 (March 1975), 115-116.
Warren made dramatic use of Arnold's poem in this novel.

McCarthy, Paul. "Sports and Recreation in *All the King's Men*." *Miss Quart*, 22 (Spring 1969), 113-130.
Jack Burden's references to swimming, football, and other activities serve as images to clarify themes connected with his struggle to find identity.

McClatchy, J. D. "Recent Poetry: Inventions and Obsessions." *YR*, 64 (Spring 1975), 427-430.
A review of Warren's *Or Else*, which compares the thematic element in this collection of poetry with that of Wordsworth's spots of time.

Meckier, Jerome. "Burden's Complaint: The Disintegrated Personality as Theme and Style in Robert Penn Warren's *All the King's Men*." *Stud in the Novel*, 2 (Spring 1970), 7-21.
Jack Burden is confronted with fragmented views of the world; the metaphor of the web, however, indicates the possibility of unification of the fragments.

Mellen, Joan. "Film and Style: The Fictional Documentary." *AR*, 32 (June 1973), 403-425.
All the King's Men is included in this discussion of film versions of "documentary" novels and the faults of American directors.

Montesi, Albert. See MISCELLANEOUS (Contemporary).

Moore, John Rees. "Robert Penn Warren: You Must Go Home Again." *SouR*, 4 (Spring 1968), 320-332.
An essay-review of John L. Longley's *Robert Penn Warren: A Collection of Critical Essays* and of Victor H. Strandberg's *A Colder Fire: The Poetry of Robert Penn Warren*, with assessments of Warren's poems.

Moore, L. Hugh, Jr. *Robert Penn Warren and History: The Big Myth We Live In*. New York: Humanities Press, 1970.

Suggests that for Warren the artist's highest function is to create for society from the past a usable historical myth embodying humane values.

_____. "Robert Penn Warren and the Terror of Answered Prayer." *Miss Quart*, 21 (Winter 1967-68), 29-36.
    A study of a theme from Dante in Warren's fiction.

Morris, Harry. "The Passions of Poets." *SR*, 79 (Spring 1971), 301-309.
    Warren's *Audubon* is one of the works discussed in this essay-review.

Murray, Edward. See MISCELLANEOUS (Contemporary).

Nakadate, Neil. "Robert Penn Warren and the Confessional Novel." *Genre*, 2 (1969), 326-340.
    Deals with *All the King's Men* and *World Enough and Time* as confessional novels.

Nevius, Blake. See MISCELLANEOUS (Contemporary).

Noble, David W. See GENERAL.

O'Brien, Joseph M. "Cultural History in *All the King's Men*." *NConL*, 2 (May 1972), 14-15.
    Because of the loss of myth and cultural ideals Jack Burden faces the "dilemma of man in mid-twentieth-century America."

Olson, David B. "Jack Burden and the Ending of *All the King's Men*." *Miss Quart*, 26 (Spring 1973), 165-176.
    The final twelve pages of the novel are in keeping with Jack's character; it is "in his nature" to pull back from any apex that would unequivocally conclude his story.

Payne, Ladell. "Willie Stark and Huey Long: Atmosphere, Myth, or Suggestion?" *AQ*, 20 (Fall 1968), 580-595.
    All the King's Men is much more directly based on the historical Long than is implied by such terms as "suggested," "atmosphere," "line of thinking and feeling," and "world of myth."

Perkins, George. See GENERAL.

Plante, P. R. See GENERAL.

Plumly, Stanley. "Robert Penn Warren's Vision." *SouR*, 6 (Autumn 1970), 1201-1208.
    An essay-review of Warren's *Incarnations, Poems 1966-68* and of *Audubon: A Vision*.

Quinn, Sister M. Bernetta. "Robert Penn Warren's Promised Land." *SouR*, 8 (Spring 1972), 329-358.
    Traces the development, and analyzes the meaning of landscape images in Warren's poetry.

Rougé, Robert. See MISCELLANEOUS (Contemporary).

Rubin, Louis D., Jr. "Dreiser and *Meet Me in the Green Glen*: A Vintage Year for Robert Penn Warren." *Hollins Critic*, 9 (April 1972), 1-10.

Warren's *Homage to Theodore Dreiser* and *Meet Me in the Green Glen* help to demonstrate that Warren "is a very important writer" and that his "high excellence as a writer comes not in spite of his great productivity, but because of it."

Sale, Richard B. "An Interview in New Haven with Robert Penn Warren." *Stud in the Novel*, 2 (Fall 1970), 325-354.
    Title is descriptive.

Scouten, Arthur H. "Warren, Huey Long, and *All the King's Men*." *Four Quarters*, 21 (May 1972), 23-26.
    Deals with Warren's purpose in writing this novel.

Shepherd, Allen. "Carrying Manty Home: Robert Penn Warren's *Band of Angels*." *Four Quarters*, 21 (May 1972), 101-109.
    Deals with the treatment of the theme of freedom and identity in this novel and in others of Warren's works.

_____. "The Case for Robert Penn Warren's Second Best Novel." *Cim Rev*, 20 (1972), 44-51.
    A discussion of *The Cave*.

_____. "The Poles of Fiction: Warren's *At Heaven's Gate*." *Tex Stud in Lit and Lang*, 12 (Winter 1971), 709-718.
    Warren's major characters are overshadowed by his minor characters because his major characters tend to stand for ideas while the minor ones possess "the vividness of the actual world."

_____. "Robert Penn Warren as Allegorist: The Example of *Wilderness*. *Rendezvous*, 6 (Spring 1971), 13-21.
    This novel combines "Bunyanesque allegory and conventional novelistic technique."

_____. "Robert Penn Warren's *Audubon: A Vision*: The Epigraph." *NConL*, 3 (January 1973), 8-11.
    The first epigraph indicates Audubon's inner state after he was almost killed; the second deals with Audubon's discovery of his real self.

_____. "Robert Penn Warren as a Philosophical Novelist." *WHR*, 24 (Spring 1970), 157-168.
    This designation of Warren as a "philosophical novelist" is appropriate since his most successful novels show the union of documentation and generalization about values.

_____. "Robert Penn Warren's 'Prime Leaf' as Prototype of *Night Rider*." *Stud SF*, 7 (Summer 1970), 469-471.
    The stories are similar in being founded on the same historical fact, in presenting the same sorts of characters, in focusing on comparable scenes, and in developing the same themes, though differing in degree of depth and explicitness.

_____. "Sugar-Boy as a Foil in *All the King's Men*." *NConL*, 1 (March 1971), 15.
    The character of Sugar-Boy is helpful in revealing that of Willie Stark.

_____. "Toward an Analysis of the Prose Style of Robert Penn Warren." *Stud in Am F*, 1 (Autumn 1973), 188-202.

A study of eight of Warren's novels reveals that in recent years he has moved toward an inorganic style.

_____. "Warren's *All the King's Men*: Using the Author's Guide to the Novel." *EJ*, 62 (May 1973), 704-708.

Warren's published comments about the novel are "cogent, substantial, and consistent."

_____. "Warren's Audubon: 'Issues in Purer Form' and 'The Ground Rules of Fact.'" *Miss Quart*, 24 (Winter 1970-71), 47-56.

Transmutation of one of Audubon's experiences into poetry reveals Warren's preference for historical events that present issues and his attempt to remain true to the "facts" of psychology.

_____. See PERCY, WALKER.

Simmons, James C. "Adam's Lobectomy Operation and the Meaning of *All the King's Men*." *PMLA*, 86 (January 1971), 84-89.

The scene in which Jack Burden watches Adam Stanton perform the operation brings all the main themes of the novel together.

Simpson, Lewis P. See MISCELLANEOUS (Contemporary--1st Simpson entry).

Slack, Robert C. "Willie Stark and William James," in *In Honor of Austin Wright*, ed. Joseph Baim, et al. (Carnegie Series in English). Pittsburgh: Carnegie-Mellon Univ, 1972.

Willie Stark echoes James's pragmatist philosophy.

Spears, Monroe K. "The Latest Poetry of Robert Penn Warren." *SR*, 78 (Spring 1970), 348-357.

A summation of the character of Warren's poetry written since 1954, a poetry more open and personal but guarded from sentimentality by its irony and detachment.

Spies, George H., III. "John Steinbeck's *In Dubious Battle* and Robert Penn Warren's *Night Rider*." *Steinbeck Quart*, 4 (Spring 1971), 48-55.

Night Rider contains many of the themes found in *In Dubious Battle*.

Stanzel, Franz. See MISCELLANEOUS (Contemporary).

Strandberg, Victor. "Robert Penn Warren: The Poetry of the Sixties." *Four Quarters*, 21 (May 1972), 27-44.

The major theme of Warren's poetry is the "osmosis of being."

_____. "Warren's Osmosis." *Criticism*, 10 (Winter 1968), 23-40.

Defines and traces through Warren's work a central theme: "the osmosis (interpenetration) of being."

Strout, Cushing. "*All the King's Men* and the Shadow of William James." *SouR*, 6 (Autumn 1970), 920-934.

An examination of the novel to support in detail Warren's assertion that the "scholarly and benign figure" of William James influenced the creation of Willie Stark.

Sullivan, Walter. "The Historical Novelist and the Existential Peril: Robert Penn Warren's *Band of Angels*." *So Lit Jour*, 2 (Spring 1970), 104-116.

Band of Angels fails because its characters lack credibility and because the author attempts to impose the errors of the present upon the past.

_____. See MISCELLANEOUS (Contemporary--1st Sullivan entry).

Sumner, D. Nathan. "The Function of Historical Sources in Hawthorne, Melville, and R. P. Warren." *Research Stud*, 40 (June 1972), 103-114.

There "is little major change in either style or use of history from the earlier works to *World Enough and Time*," but in *Brother to Dragons* Warren "forges a radical redefinition of the role of historical data."

Vauthier, Simone. "The Case of the Vanishing Narrator: An Inquiry into *All the King's Men*. *So Lit Jour*, 6 (Spring 1974), 42-69.

Traces the "precarious voyage" of the narrator-agent ("narratee") through the novel.

Walker, Marshall. "Making Dreams Work: The Achievement of Robert Penn Warren." *London Mag*, 15 (December 1975/January 1976), 33-46.

A general evaluation of Warren's work in all categories which concludes that "it is Warren's profound and realistic sense of the obligation upon us somehow to make our dreams work in a world of prose and imperfection that gives his writings their fundamental distinction." Includes some discussion of Faulkner and Ransom.

_____. "Robert Penn Warren: An Interview." *Jour Am Stud*, 8 (August 1974), 229-245.

What is happening to modern America is that human sensibility, human instinct for value, is changing.

Warren, Robert Penn. "Bearers of Bad Tidings: Writers and the American Dream." *NYRB*, 23 (March 20, 1975), 12-19.

Deals with the subversive theme of American literature.

_____. "A Dearth of Heroes." *AH*, 23 (October 1972), 4-7.

An introduction to a reissue of Dixon Wecter's *The Hero in America* is reprinted here.

_____. "Hawthorne Revisited: Some Remarks on Hellfiredness." *SR*, 81 (Winter 1973), 75-111.

Analyzes "My Kinsman, Major Molineux" and *The Scarlet Letter*, pointing out the ambiguities of good and evil in them.

_____. See CLEMENS, SAMUEL LANGHORNE.

_____. See LYTLE, ANDREW.

_____. See RANSOM, JOHN CROWE (Contemporary).

Watkins, Floyd D. See MISCELLANEOUS (Contemporary).

Whittington, Curtis, Jr. "The 'Burden' of Narration: Democratic Perspectives and First-Person

Point of View in the American Novel." *SHR*, 2 (Spring 1968), 236-245.
> Interprets Warren's *All the King's Men* and Cather's *My Ántonia* as "interesting examples of...interaction between America's society and its literature."

_____. "The Earned Vision: Robert Penn Warren's 'The Ballad of Billy Potts' and Albert Camus' *Le Malentendu*." *Four Quarters*, 21 (May 1972), 79-90.
> Discusses similarities in method and in theme in these two works.

Wilcox, Earl. "Right On! *All the King's Men* in the Classroom." *Four Quarters*, 21 (May 1972), 69-78.
> Examines the reasons why the novel is very teachable.

Wilson, James D. See MISCELLANEOUS (Contemporary).

Wilson, Mary Ann. See FAULKNER, WILLIAM (Contemporary).

Witt, R. W. "Robert Penn Warren and the 'Black Patch War.'" *KHSR*, 67 (October 1969), 301-316.
> Warren relies heavily on history (as is shown in detail in this essay) but he does not merely record the incidents of a brief era.

Witte, Flo. "Adam's Rebirth in Robert Penn Warren's *Wilderness*." *So Quart*, 12 (July 1974), 365-377.
> Adam's recognition of sin in others and finally and most importantly in himself brings about a rebirth which will enable him to "live at peace with himself and his brothers."

[WEAVER, RICHARD] Bradford, M. E. "The Agrarianism of Richard Weaver: An Appreciation." *Mod Age*, 14 (Summer-Fall 1970), 249-257.
> Shows the degree to which Weaver's ideas were stimulated by the Nashville Agrarianism of the 1920's and the vigor and originality of Weaver's thought.

Brown, Calvin S. "Southern Thought and National Materialism." *So Lit Jour*, 1 (Spring 1969), 98-106.
> An essay-review of *The Southern Tradition at Bay: A History of Postbellum Thought*, by Richard Weaver, in which Brown uses Faulkner's overall view of humanity to illustrate (as Weaver does not) Weaver's insistence that "the ideas found in the Southern tradition are basically valid and are relevant to the modern world."

Jones, Madison. Untitled. *SHR*, 4 (Winter 1970), 92-93.
> An essay-review of Richard M. Weaver's *The Southern Tradition at Bay: A History of Postbellum Thought* (1968).

Meyer, F. S. "Richard M. Weaver: An Appreciation." *Mod Age*, 14 (Summer-Fall 1970), 243-248.
> An analysis of Weaver's ability to combine the themes of tradition and individualism in his defense of conservatism.

Montgomery, Marion. "Richard Weaver Against the Establishment." *GaR*, 23 (Winter 1969), 433-459.
> An essay-review of Weaver's *The Southern Tradition at Bay* sees Weaver as "spokesman for human dignity within the necessities of human community."

Simpson, Lewis P. See GENERAL--3rd Simpson entry.

[WELTY, EUDORA] Anon., ed. *The Jackson Cookbook*. Jackson, Miss.: Symphony League, 1971.
> Contains an essay on "The Flavor of Jackson" by Miss Welty and a dedicatory recipe for "Squash Eudora."

Anon. "Shangri-La South." *Time*, 95 (May 4, 1970), 100.
> Jack in *Losing Battles* is really Eudora Welty's man. For him "life is a perpetual family reunion."

Anon. See GENERAL--2nd Anon. entry.

Aldridge, John W. "Eudora Welty: Metamorphosis of a Southern Lady Writer." *SatR*, April 11, 1970, pp. 21ff.
> An essay-review of *Losing Battles*.

_____. See MISCELLANEOUS (Contemporary--2nd Aldridge entry).

Allen, John A. "Eudora Welty: The Three Moments." *VQR*, 51 (Autumn 1975), 605-627.
> Deals with Welty's treatment of male and female in her works.

Baldeshwiler, Eileen. See GENERAL.

Blackwell, Louise. "Eudora Welty: Roots Versus Yellow Guitars." *RLA*, 15 (1973), 129-135.
> On family relationships in Welty's works.

Boatwright, James. "The Continuity of Love." *New Rep*, 167 (June 10, 1972), 24-25.
> On the evolution of *The Optimist's Daughter* from a story in the *New Yorker*.

_____. "Speech and Silence in *Losing Battles*." *Shen*, 25 (Spring 1974), 3-14.
> *Losing Battles* "not only *is* the voices, and the silences that sometimes lie between them... it is also *about* speech and silence."

Bolsterli, Margaret. "A Fertility Rite in Mississippi." *Notes on Miss Writers*, 8 (Fall 1975), 69-71.
> Sees the dragging of the river as a fertility rite to restore fecundity to the land by the recovery of the fertility goddess, Hazel Jamieson.

_____. "Mythic Elements in 'Ladies in Spring.'" *Notes on Miss Writers*, 6 (Winter 1974), 69-72.
> Points to the wasteland motif of Miss Welty's story.

Boyd, G. N. and L. A. See MISCELLANEOUS (Contemporary).

Bradford, M. E. "Looking Down from a High Place: The Serenity of Miss Welty's *Losing Battles*." *RANAM*, 4 (1971), 92-97.
Losing Battles is an elegiac novel of cultural survival.

_____. "Miss Eudora's Picture Book." *Miss Quart*, 26 (Fall 1973), 659-662.
A discussion of Welty's *One Time, One Place*.

Brooks, Cleanth. "The Past Reexamined: *The Optimist's Daughter*." *Miss Quart*, 26 (Fall 1973), 557-587.
The novel has the power of a small masterpiece; it is a tapestry of small-town life and dialogue in Southern idiom.

Brown, Ashley. "Eudora Welty and the Mythos of Summer." *Shen*, 20 (Spring 1969), 29-35.
The ironic romantic mode of *The Robber Bridegroom* results in the treating of "the doubleness of human nature as cogently as tragedy and comedy would have."

Bryant, J. A., Jr. *Eudora Welty*. Minnesota Pamphlets on American Writers, no. 66. Minneapolis: Univ of Minnesota Press, 1968.
A brief critical-analytical survey of Miss Welty's fiction.

_____. "Seeing Double in *The Golden Apples*." *SR*, 82 (Spring 1974), 300-316.
The Golden Apples, despite arguments to the contrary, does possess an aesthetic unity as it builds toward Virgie's climactic epiphany—of wandering forever on the earth again.

Buchloh, Paul G. See GENERAL.

Buckley, William F., Jr. "The Southern Imagination: An Interview with Eudora Welty and Walker Percy." *Miss Quart*, 26 (Fall 1973), 493-516.
A reprinting of the *Firing Line* television interview of 1972.

_____. See MISCELLANEOUS (Contemporary).

Bungert, Hans. See GENERAL.

Bunting, Charles T. "'The Interior World': An Interview with Eudora Welty." *SouR*, 8 (Autumn 1972), 711-735.
A wide-ranging interview, with extended passages on the author's practice of her art and on *Losing Battles*.

Burger, Nash K. "Eudora Welty's Jackson." *Shen*, 20 (Spring 1969), 8-15.
Burger reminisces about school days in Jackson with Miss Welty and provides a brief overview of her career.

Buswell, Mary Catherine. "The Mountain Figure in the Fiction of Eudora Welty." *West Va Univ Bul: Philological Papers*, 19 (July 1972), 50-63.
Finds Miss Welty's depiction of mountaineers to be accurate.

Carson, Franklin D. "The Passage of Time in Eudora Welty's 'Sir Rabbit.'" *Stud SF*, 12 (Summer 1975), 284-286.
Failure to observe indications of a passage of time has resulted in misreadings of this two-part story and of other sections of *The Golden Apples*.

_____. "'The Song of Wandering Aengus': Allusions in Eudora Welty's *The Golden Apples*." *Notes on Miss Writers*, 6 (Spring 1973), 14-18.
Deals with allusions to Yeats's poem in this work.

Carter, T. H. See MISCELLANEOUS (Contemporary).

Clark, Charles C. "*The Robber Bridegroom*: Realism and Fantasy on the Natchez Trace." *Miss Quart*, 26 (Fall 1973), 625-638.
This novella contains much irony in the form of history, folklore, and fairy tale in its statement of the dual nature of man.

Clemons, W. "Meeting Miss Welty." *NYTBR*, April 12, 1970, pp. 2, 46.
An interview in which Miss Welty talks about *Losing Battles*, the South, her writing habits, her interests, and her life.

Cochran, Robert W. "Welty's 'Petrified Man.'" *Expl*, 27 (December 1968), Item 25.
Deals with the appropriateness of Billy Boy's question at the end of the story.

Cole, Hunter McK. See SPENCER, ELIZABETH (CONTEMPORARY--2nd Cole entry).

Cooley, John R. "Blacks as Primitives in Eudora Welty's Fiction." *BSUF*, 14 (Summer 1973), 20-28.
For the most part, the blacks in Welty's works are primitivistic.

Coulthard, A. R. "Point of View in Eudora Welty's 'Old Mr. Marblehall.'" *Notes on Miss Writers*, 8 (Spring 1975), 22-27.
Believes the story is flawed by shifts in point of view between omniscient author and first-person.

Curley, Daniel. "Eudora Welty and the Quondam Obstruction." *Stud SF*, 5 (Spring 1968), 209-224.
An analysis of "A Still Moment."

_____. "A Time Exposure." *Notes on Miss Writers*, 5 (Spring 1972), 11-14.
Sees in Miss Welty's book of photographs (*One Time, One Place*) and its foreword much that is revelatory of her fiction.

Davis, Charles E. "The South in Eudora Welty's Fiction: A Changing World." *Stud in Am F*, 3 (Autumn 1975), 199-209.
Deals with the importance of place in Miss Welty's fiction.

_____. "Welty's 'Old Mr. Marblehall.'" *Expl*, 30 (January 1972), Item 40.
Suggests that the source is a romantic escape poem.

IV. Contemporary (1920-1975)

Detweiler, Robert. "Eudora Welty's Blazing Butterfly: The Dynamics of Response." *Lang and Style*, 6 (Winter 1973), 58-71.
Deals with "Old Mr. Marblehall."

Donlan, Dan. "'A Worn Path': Immortality of Stereotype." *EJ*, 62 (April 1973), 549-550.
On Welty's use of the phoenix myth.

East, Charles. "The Search for Eudora Welty." *Miss Quart*, 26 (Fall 1973), 477-482.
East discusses his own experience with Eudora Welty and her characters.

"Five Tributes." *Shen*, 20 (Spring 1969), 36-39.
Brief and very brief tributes to Miss Welty by Malcolm Cowley (her writing is "fastidious, scrupulous, marked by delicate discrimination, but never weak or paltering"), Martha Graham (Miss Welty's "novels and short stories are a national treasure"), Walker Percy ("Eudora Welty in Jackson"--points out the importance of place for a successful writer), Robert Penn Warren ("Out of the Strong"--what makes Miss Welty's work "hang together" is "a temperament so strongly and significantly itself that it can face the multiplicity of the world"), and Allen Tate ("a perfect case of art added to genius").

Fleischauer, John F. "The Focus of Mystery: Eudora Welty's Prose Style." *So Lit Jour*, 5 (Spring 1973), 64-79.
Ambiguity is a part of Eudora Welty's creative intellect which "shows shadows remotely, not things clearly."

French, Warren. See MISCELLANEOUS (Contemporary--2nd French entry).

Gingrich, Arnold. "Goosing a Gander." *Esquire*, 84 (December 1975), 14.
A description of how *Esquire* and Gingrich rejected a Welty short story; additional comment also on p. 161 of this issue.

Ginsberg, Elaine. See MISCELLANEOUS (Contemporary).

Givner, Joan. See PORTER, KATHERINE ANNE (Contemporary--2nd Givner entry).

Gossett, Louise Y. "Eudora Welty's New Novel: The Comedy of Loss." *So Lit Jour*, 3 (Fall 1970), 122-137.
Like Virginia Woolf, Eudora Welty in *Losing Battles* as well as in her other works "records the emergence of experience; the relationship of persons generates the fabric of life."

Graham, Kenneth. "La double vision d'Eudora Welty." *NRF*, no. 203 (November 1969), 744-753.
Welty blends the comic and the tragic.

Hardy, John E. "The Achievement of Eudora Welty." *SHR*, 2 (Summer 1968), 269-278.
The essential aspect of Miss Welty's fiction is the confrontation with the fundamental realities of her time, especially the reality of the absurd and the reality of the racial problem.

Harrell, Don. "Death in Eudora Welty's 'The Bride of the Innisfallen.'" *NConL*, 3 (September 1973), 2-7.
The story is concerned with the journey from life to death.

Hassan, Ihab. See MISCELLANEOUS (Contemporary--2nd Hassan entry).

Heilman, Robert B. "Salesmen's Deaths: Documentary and Myth." *Shen*, 20 (Spring 1969), 20-28.
Emphasizes the differences between Miss Welty's "The Death of a Traveling Salesman" and Arthur Miller's *Death of a Salesman*, the differences in setting being one of the main reasons for the dissimilarities between the themes and heroes of the two works; "Miller's drama of death drifts toward documentary, Miss Welty's toward myth."

Helterman, Jeffrey. "Gorgons in Mississippi: Eudora Welty's 'Petrified Man.'" *Notes on Miss Writers*, 7 (Spring 1974), 12-20.
Analyzes Miss Welty's use of the Perseus myth in this story.

Hiers, John T. See MISCELLANEOUS (Contemporary).

Hollenbaugh, Carol. "Ruby Fisher and Her Demon-Lover." *Notes on Miss Writers*, 7 (Fall 1974), 63-68.
An examination of Ruby Fisher's sensuality and imagination in "A Piece of News."

Howard, Zelma T. *The Rhetoric of Eudora Welty's Short Stories*. Jackson, Miss.: Univ and College Press of Mississippi, 1973.
An analytic critical assessment of the rhetorical strategies used in the short stories.

Howell, Elmo. "Eudora Welty and the Use of Place in Southern Fiction." *ArQ*, 28 (Autumn 1972), 248-256.
Argues that Miss Welty's fidelity to place adds an important dimension to her art as it does to Faulkner's and Flannery O'Connor's.

_____. "Eudora Welty's Civil War Story." *Notes on Miss Writers*, 2 (Spring 1969), 3-12.
An interpretation of "The Burning."

_____. "Eudora Welty's Comedy of Manners." *SAQ*, 69 (Autumn 1970), 469-479.
In analyzing *Delta Wedding*, Howell says that Miss Welty, like Jane Austen, does more than portray a provincial society, that she is concerned more with the values on which the civilized order is based.

_____. "Eudora Welty's Negroes: A Note on 'A Worn Path.'" *XUS*, 9 (Spring 1970), 28-32.
Offers the thesis that there is no racial conflict in this story.

Inge, M. Thomas. "Eudora Welty as Poet." *SHR*, 2 (Summer 1968), 310-311.
Considers Miss Welty's early experiments with poetry, and prints her poem "There."

Isaacs, Neil D. *Eudora Welty*. Southern Writers Series, no. 8. Austin: Steck-Vaughn, 1969.

An appreciation of the fiction with emphasis on myth, ritualism, speech patterns, and point of view.

_____. "Four Notes on Eudora Welty." *Notes on Miss Writers*, 2 (Fall 1969), 42-54.
Touches on *Delta Wedding*, *The Ponder Heart*, "Kin" in *The Bride of the Innisfallen*, and *The Golden Apples*.

Jones, Alun R. "A Frail Travelling Coincidence: Three Later Stories of Eudora Welty." *Shen*, 20 (Spring 1969), 40-53.
In "The Bride of the Innisfallen," "Going to Naples," and "No Place for You, My Love," the characters "journey into strange and unknown areas of being and bring back knowledge about themselves and the world in which they live"; in these stories "the world of love that she defines so precisely in her earlier stories is now the world of man...." in which "love and loneliness are basic to the human condition."

Justus, James H. See GENERAL.

Kirkpatrick, Smith. "The Anointed Powerhouse." *SR*, 77 (Winter 1969), 94-108.
As artist, Powerhouse is aware of the "chaos...both inside and outside" and longs "to escape from chaos into unity"; he realizes also that only love, the real "powerhouse," can bring about this unity.

Kloss, Robert J. "The Symbolic Structure of Eudora Welty's 'Livvie.'" *Notes on Miss Writers*, 7 (Winter 1975), 70-82.
A critical explication which finds the central conflict of the story to be of a sexual nature.

Kraus, W. Keith. "Welty's 'Petrified Man.'" *Expl*, 29 (April 1971), Item 63.
An explanation of the name Fletcher in the story as "an allusion to the practice of 'Fletcherism,' a nutritional health fad which had become popular at the beginning of the century."

Kreyling, Michael. "Myth and History: The Foes of *Losing Battles*." *Miss Quart*, 26 (Fall 1973), 639-649.
Implied in the novel are mythical and historical consciousness; Miss Welty's "feeling" for character makes this a novel true to the widest range of human life.

Kroll, Jack. "The Lesson of the Master." *Newsweek*, April 13, 1970, pp. 90-91.
This reviewer finds *Losing Battles* exhilarating but saddening because one is in the hands of a mastery that is disappearing from the world.

Kronenberger, Louis, and E. M. Beck. See GENERAL.

Kuehl, Linda. "The Art of Fiction XLVII: Eudora Welty." *Paris Rev*, no. 55 (1972), 72-97.
An interview with Miss Welty.

Landess, Thomas H. "The Function of Taste in the Fiction of Eudora Welty." *Miss Quart*, 26 (Fall 1973), 543-557.

Miss Welty does not avoid the "plain and unstylish" folk who seem all the more admirable in her fiction.

_____. "More Trouble in Mississippi: Family vs. Antifamily in Miss Welty's *Losing Battles*." *SR*, 79 (Fall 1971), 626-634.
An essay-review of the novel, which finds it to be "the highest comedy," offering "an optimistic vision of the future and hence of life itself" but lacking "a single significant action which embodies the entire meaning and central conflict."

Leonard, John. "I Care Who Killed Roger Ackroyd." *Esquire*, 84 (August 1975), 60-61, 120.
Two paragraphs on Miss Welty's association with mystery writer Ross MacDonald.

Manz-Kunz, Marie-Antoinette. *Eudora Welty: Aspects of Reality in Her Short Fiction*. Swiss Studies In English, Band 63. Bern, Switzerland: Francke Verlag, 1971.
A close critical reading of the short stories which attempts to characterize the attitudes toward reality held by Miss Welty's protagonists in their pursuit of experience.

Masserand, Anne. "Eudora Welty's Travellers." *So Lit Jour*, 3 (Spring 1971), 39-48.
The essential theme of Eudora Welty is symbolized in the contradictory attractions of the home and the journey and of commitment and non-commitment.

May, Charles E. "The Difficulty of Loving in 'A Visit of Charity.'" *Stud SF*, 6 (Spring 1969), 338-341.
One must understand the word "charity" in the title to mean "love," and thus Marian's visit to the Old Ladies' Home is her "first experience with the difficulty of loving."

_____. "*Le Roi Mehaigné* in Welty's 'Keela, The Outcast Indian Maiden." *MFS*, 18 (Winter 1972-73), 559-566.
The thesis is that Little Lee Roy is "the center of the reader's response to the story."

McDonald, W. U., Jr. "Eudora Welty Manuscripts: A Supplementary Annotated Finding List." *BB*, 31 (July-September 1974), 95-98, 126.
Updates 1963 listing.

_____. "Eudora Welty's Revisions of 'A Piece of News.'" *Stud SF*, 7 (Spring 1970), 232-247.
A study of the revisions of "A Piece of News" gives insight "into [Welty's] workmanship and...the workings of her imagination." This one story represents important characteristics of Miss Welty's writing both in the collection *A Curtain of Green* and in the works that followed.

_____. "Welty's 'Social Consciousness': Revisions of 'The Whistle.'" *MFS*, 16 (Summer 1970), 193-198.
A comparison of the two published versions of "The Whistle" "strengthens the case for 'social consciousness'" in the story.

McFarland, Ronald E. "Vision and Perception in the Works of Eudora Welty." *MarkR*, 2 (February 1971), 94-99.
Not all characters in Welty's fiction find the way to perception; however, those that do are able to lead meaningful lives.

McHaney, Thomas L. "Eudora Welty and the Multitudinous Golden Apples." *Miss Quart*, 26 (Fall 1973), 589-624.
Though not a novel, *The Golden Apples* parallels stories from Celtic and Graeco-Roman mythology to tales of rural Mississippi.

McMillen, William E. "Conflict and Resolution in Welty's *Losing Battles*." *Critique*, 15, no. 1 (1973), 110-124.
A study of character and meaning in the novel; Gloria is resisting both Granny and Julia Mortimer.

Moore, Carol A. "The Insulation of Illusion and *Losing Battles*." *Miss Quart*, 26 (Fall 1973), 651-658.
Illusions in this book help the close-knit family put off what Miss Welty has called the frustration of always losing "battles against everything."

Moss, Grant, Jr. "'A Worn Path' Retrod." *CLA Jour*, 14 (December 1971), 144-152.
Primarily a study of the characterization of Phoenix Jackson.

Myers, Susan L. "Dialogues in Eudora Welty's Short Stories." *Notes on Miss Writers*, 8 (Fall 1975), 51-57.
A study of how the speech patterns of Miss Welty's characters reflect their values and personalities.

Nevius, Blake. See MISCELLANEOUS (Contemporary).

Oates, Joyce Carol. "The Art of Eudora Welty." *Shen*, 20 (Spring 1969), 54-57.
"It is an outstanding characteristic of Miss Welty's genius that she can write a story that seems to me, in a way, about 'nothing'... and make it mean everything."

_____. "Eudora's Web." *Atl*, 225 (April 1970), 118-122.
A review of Miss Welty's *Losing Battles*.

Pawlowski, Robert S. "The Process of Observation: *Winesburg, Ohio* and *The Golden Apples*." *Univ Rev*, 37 (1971), 304, 393-398.
Both these works makes use of an objective point of view and reveal a sense of place.

Pickett, Nell Ann. "Colloquialism as a Style in the First-Person-Narrator Fiction of Eudora Welty." *Miss Quart*, 26 (Fall 1973), 559-576.
Miss Welty's view of the South is explained in her use of Southern Lowland dialect.

Polk, Noel E. "A Eudora Welty Checklist." *Miss Quart*, 26 (Fall 1973), 663-693.
Lists primary material and significant secondary sources.

Porter, Katherine Anne. See PORTER, KATHERINE ANNE.

Prenshaw, Peggy. "Cultural Patterns in Eudora Welty's *Delta Wedding* and 'The Demonstrators.'" *Notes on Miss Writers*, 3 (Fall 1970), 51-70.
Delta Wedding and "The Demonstrators" illustrate Miss Welty's skill in interpreting the cultural patterns that make up the complicated social structure in the modern South.

Price, Reynolds. "The Onlooker Smiling: An Early Reading of *The Optimist's Daughter*." *Shen*, 20 (Spring 1969), 58-73.
"Laurel has been both victim and judge--who goes beyond both into pure creation (only she has discovered the patterns of their lives--her parents', Fay's, the Chisoms', her friends', her own) and then comprehension, which is always comic."

_____. See PRICE, REYNOLDS.

Richmond, Lee J. "Symbol and Theme in Eudora Welty's 'Petrified Man.'" *EJ*, 60 (December 1971), 1201-1203.
The beauty parlor is the most significant of the three symbols in the story.

Ricks, Christopher. "Female and Other Impersonators." *New York Review of Books*, 15 (July 23, 1970), 8-13.
Maintains that *Losing Battles* is a meticulous work with innumerable felicities but a "gentle overkill" of similitudes.

Rubin, Louis D., Jr. "Everything Brought Out in the Open: Eudora Welty's *Losing Battles*." *Hollins Critic*, 7 (June 1970), 1-12.
A review article which concludes that the novel "demands that the reader invest time and attention without stint, for as long as it takes to read it through. What it requires is sentence-by-sentence participation. What it provides, for those willing to take part, is delight ending in wisdom."

_____. See GENERAL--3rd Rubin entry.

Rupp, Richard H. See MISCELLANEOUS (Contemporary).

Russell, Diarmid. "First Work." *Shen*, 20 (Spring 1969), 16-19.
Miss Welty's agent offers a brief survey of the publication history of her work.

Seidl, Frances. "Eudora Welty's Phoenix." *Notes on Miss Writers*, 6 (Fall 1973), 53-55.
Deals with the phoenix as symbol in "A Worn Path."

Semel, Jay M. "Eudora Welty's Freak Show: A Pattern in 'Why I Live at the P. O.'" *NConL*, 3 (May 1973), 2-3.
The things that concern her and the remarks she makes mark Sister as one who lives in a freak-world.

Shepherd, Allen. "Delayed Exposition in *The Optimist's Daughter*." *NConL*, 4 (September 1974), 10-14.
Deals with the structure of the novel.

Simpson, Lewis P. "The Chosen People." *SouR*, 6 (Summer 1970), xvii-xxiii.

    An essay-review of Guy Owen's *Journey for Joedel* and Eudora Welty's *Losing Battles*, with comments on the depression and the Agrarians.

_____. "An Introductory Note." *Miss Quart*, 26 (Fall 1973), 475-476.

    A tribute to Miss Welty and the introduction to the issue of the *Mississippi Quarterly* devoted to articles about Miss Welty.

Skaggs, Merrill M. See GENERAL.

Slethaug, Gordon E. "Initiation in Eudora Welty's *The Robber Bridegroom*." *SHR*, 7 (Winter 1973), 77-87.

    Suggests that the story is centered on characters' transition from a simplistic to a complex view of reality.

Smith, Carol P. "The Journey Motif in Eudora Welty's *The Robber Bridegroom*." *SSC Rev*, 1973, pp. 18-32.

    The various journeys of this work have both literal and figurative significance.

Stanford, Donald E. "Eudora Welty and the Pulitzer Prize." *SouR*, 9 (Autumn 1973), xx-xxiii.

    A brief critical survey of Miss Welty's fiction, with special attention to her prize-winning novel, *The Optimist's Daughter*, and to her relations with the *Southern Review*.

Stone, William B. "Eudora Welty's Hydrodynamic 'Powerhouse.'" *Stud SF*, 11 (Winter 1974), 93-96.

    "Powerhouse" draws much of its strength from water imagery.

Stuckey, William J. "The Use of Marriage in Welty's *The Optimist's Daughter*." *Critique*, 17, no. 2 (1975), 36-46.

    A study of the book as a novel of manners focusing particularly on the institution of marriage.

Tarbox, Raymond. "Eudora Welty's Fiction: The Salvation Theme." *AI*, 29 (Spring 1972), 70-91.

    Welty's alienated heroes often are susceptible to psychosexual fantasies.

Thompson, Victor H. "The Natchez Trace in Eudora Welty's 'A Still Moment.'" *So Lit Jour*, 6 (Fall 1973), 59-69.

    Welty recreates an accurate character type of the Natchez Trace.

Travis, Mildred K. "A Note on 'Wakefield' and 'Old Mr. Marblehall.'" *NConL*, 4 (May 1974), 9-10.

    On a possible Hawthorne influence on Welty.

Vande Kieft, Ruth M. "The Vision of Eudora Welty." *Miss Quart*, 26 (Fall 1973), 517-542.

    In addition to her "good ear," Miss Welty emphasizes vision in her fiction--consistent and varying--but faithful to the realities of life's contradictions.

Voss, Arthur. See GENERAL.

Walcutt, Charles C., and J. E. Whitesell. See GENERAL.

Welty, Eudora. "Artists on Criticism of Their Art: 'Is Phoenix Jackson's Grandson Really Dead?'" *Critical Inquiry*, 1 (September 1974), 219-221.

    Comments by Miss Welty on her story "A Worn Path."

_____. *Fairy Tale of the Natchez Trace*. Jackson: Mississippi Historical Society, 1975.

    The author examines her use of history, folklore, and Southern humor in *The Robber Bridegroom*.

_____. "The Feast Itself." *NY Times*, December 5, 1974. Reprinted in *Cultural Post*, newsletter for the NEA, March 1975.

    An essay on art and its dissemination.

_____. "From Where I Live." *Delta Rev*, 6 (November-December 1969), 69.

    Every Southern writer feels passionately about place. Any story, however, is good "only according to its faithfulness to the truths of the human heart."

_____. "A Note on Jane Austen." *Shen*, 20 (Spring 1969), 3-7.

    Jane Austen's novels live on because of their author's awareness of her own time and place, her knowledge "that the interesting situations of life can, and notably do, take place in the home."

_____. "Some Notes on Time in Fiction." *Miss Quart*, 26 (Fall 1973), 483-492.

    Without time and place the novelist could not come to grips with human experience.

West, Ray B., Jr. See MISCELLANEOUS (Contemporary).

[WHITEHEAD, JAMES] Burton, Marda. "An Interview with James Whitehead." *Notes on Miss Writers*, 5 (Winter 1973), 71-79.

    An interview of April 1972 before the publication of Whitehead's first novel.

Carr, John. See MISCELLANEOUS (Contemporary).

Graham, John, and George Garrett. See MISCELLANEOUS (Contemporary).

[WILKINSON, SYLVIA] Chappell, Fred. "Unpeaceable Kingdoms: The Novels of Sylvia Wilkinson." *Hollins Critic*, 8 (April 1971), 1-10.

    A review article which concludes that the "single most valuable quality of Miss Wilkinson's writing" is "the portrayal of the community of spirit between the natural world and those chosen few who know how to meet it."

Graham, John, and George Garrett. See MISCELLANEOUS (Contemporary).

[WILLIAMS, TENNESSEE] Anon. "One Heart Breaking." *Time*, 95 (January 19, 1970), 61.

    "The poignant internal music of *Camino Real* [is] the sound of one heart breaking."

Anon. "People." *Time*, 97 (January 11, 1971), 30.
Comments by Williams upon returning from a
Pacific cruise.

Anon. "People." *Time*, 98 (July 19, 1971), 28.
Comments on rewriting by the Russians of *A
Streetcar Named Desire*.

Anon. See GENERAL--2nd Anon. entry.

Adler, Jacob H. "Williams's Eight Ladies." *So Lit
Jour*, 8 (Fall 1975), 165-169.
An essay-review of *Eight Mortal Ladies Possessed*, by Tennessee Williams, a collection of
short stories.

Adler, Thomas P. "The Search for God in the Plays
of Tennessee Williams." *Renascence*, 26
(Autumn 1973), 48-56.
The view of God as threatening and vengeful
which many of Williams' characters share is not
Williams' own.

Berkowitz, Gerald. "The 'Other World' of *The Glass
Menagerie*." *Players*, 48 (April-May 1973),
150-153.
Deals with the significance of Williams' use
of physical settings that are "defined, theatri-
cally or symbolically, as being separate and
apart from the rest of the universe."

Blackwelder, James Ray. "The Human Extremities of
Emotion in *Cat on a Hot Tin Roof*." *Res Stud*, 38
(March 1970), 13-21.
The exploration of the extremes of the
animal and spiritual brings artistic unity to
this play, the theme of which is that "the mean
between the extremes is man's hope."

Blackwell, Louise. "Tennessee Williams and the
Predicament of Women." *SAB*, 35 (March 1970),
9-14.
Williams' women find meaning in life through
sexual relationships, but these characters vary
subtly as to the causes of frustration.

Blanke, Gustav H. "Das Bild des Menschen im
modernen amerikanischen Drama." *Neuren
Sprachen*, 18 (March 1969), 117-129.
Williams is among dramatists discussed as
making use of monstrosities in order to awaken
the audience to awareness.

Blitgen, Sister M. Carol. "Tennessee Williams:
Modern Idolater." *Renascence*, 22 (Summer 1970),
192-197.
Believes that Williams has an "Old-Testament
mind-set."

Browne, Ray B. See GENERAL.

Buckley, Tom. "Tennessee Williams Survives." *Atl*,
226 (November 1970), 98-106.
Impressions that develop from a visit with
Williams in Key West.

Campbell, Michael L. "The Theme of Persecution in
Tennessee Williams' *Camino Real*." *Notes on Miss
Writers*, 6 (Fall 1973), 35-40.
Persecution of the sensitive characters by
hardened "realists" is a major theme of
Williams' work.

Cate, Hollis L., and Delma E. Presley. "Beyond
Stereotype: Ambiguity in Amanda Wingfield."
Notes on Miss Writers, 3 (Winter 1971), 91-100.
Demonstrates how Williams avoids "typing"
Amanda Wingfield and attempts to establish her
role as the character who possesses a realistic
understanding of the Wingfield family's
problems.

Chesler, Stanley A. "*A Streetcar Named Desire*:
Twenty-five Years of Criticism." *Notes on Miss
Writers*, 7 (Fall 1974), 44-53.
A discussion of the criticism--the conflict
in views and the consent.

Cohn, Ruby. See MISCELLANEOUS (Contemporary).

Cole, Charles W., and Carol I. Franco. "Critical
Reaction to Tennessee Williams in the Mid-1960's."
Players, 49 (Fall/Winter 1974), 18-23.
Deals with *Slapstick Tragedy* (*The Mutilated*,
Gnadiges Fraulein) and *The Seven Descents of
Myrtle* and the reasons why these works were not
well received by critics.

Costello, Donald P. "Tennessee Williams' Fugitive
Kind." *Mod Drama*, 15 (May 1972), 26-43.
An examination of *Orpheus Descending* as a key
to an understanding and interpretation of the
whole body of Williams' work.

Davis, Ronald L. "All the New Vibrations:
Romanticism in 20th-Century America." *SWR*, 54
(Summer 1969), 256-270.
Two paragraphs deal with romantic qualities
in Williams' works.

Debusscher, Gilbert. "Tennessee Williams as
Hagiographer: An Aspect of Obliquity in Drama."
RLV, 40 (1974), 449-456.
Deals with *Suddenly Last Summer*, *Night of the
Iguana*, and *The Milktrain Doesn't Stop Here
Anymore*.

_____. "Tennessee Williams' Unicorn Broken Again."
Rev Belge de Philologie et d'Histoire, 49
(1971), 875-885.
Does not believe that *The Glass Menagerie* is
"social melodrama."

Dickinson, Hugh. *Myth on the Modern Stage*. Urbana:
Univ of Illinois Press, 1969.
Includes an essay on Williams' use of the
Eurydice story.

Drake, Constance. "Blanche Dubois: A Re-
evaluation." *Theatre Annual*, 24 (1969), 58-69.
Blanche is to be sympathized with, not
condemned.

Durham, Frank. "Tennessee Williams, Theatre Poet
in Prose." *SAB*, 36 (March 1971), 3-16.
American efforts at poetic drama have been
best realized not by verse but by poetic elements and vision in prose, as seen notably in
Williams' plays.

Engstrom, Alfred G. "The Man Who Thought Himself
Made of Glass and Certain Related Images." *SP*,
67 (July 1970), 390-405.

The broken unicorn in *The Glass Menagerie* is used as an example in this discussion of the metaphor of glass in literature.

Falb, Lewis W. "'Le naturalisme de 'papa': American Drama in France." *French Rev*, 45 (October 1971), 56-71.
    Williams is mentioned in this discussion of French rejection of American drama after World War II and through the Sixties.

French, Warren. See MISCELLANEOUS (Contemporary--1st and 2nd French entries).

Fritscher, John J. "Some Attitudes and a Posture: Religious Metaphor and Ritual in Tennessee Williams' Query of the American God." *Mod Drama*, 13 (September 1970), 201-215.
    A detailed examination of overt and implicit uses of religious images and metaphors in Williams' plays.

Gaines, Jim. "A Talk about Life and Style with Tennessee Williams." *SatR*, 55 (April 29, 1972), 25-29.
    Title is descriptive.

Goldstein, Malcolm. See MISCELLANEOUS (Contemporary).

Haight, A. L. See GENERAL.

Hainsworth, J. D. "Tennessee Williams: Playwright on a Hot Tin Roof?" *EA*, 20 (July-September 1967), 225-232.
    More than mere exercises in shock-therapy, *A Streetcar Named Desire* and *Cat on a Hot Tin Roof* transcend the psychological tensions embodied in the plays.

Harkness, J. D. "Thematic Integration in Tennessee Williams," in *Honors College Essays 1967-68*, ed. M. Thomas Inge, et al. East Lansing: Michigan State Univ Honors College, 1969, pp. 76-82.
    Williams' growth as a dramatist is best seen in his continuing exploration of the same basic qualities of human nature and its predilection for violence, sexuality, and love.

Hassan, Ihab. See MISCELLANEOUS (Contemporary--both Hassan entries).

Hays, Peter L. See MISCELLANEOUS (Contemporary).

Heilman, Robert B. *The Iceman, the Arsonist, and the Troubled Agent: Tragedy and Melodrama on the Modern Stage*. Seattle: Univ of Washington Press, 1973.
    Includes discussion of Williams' work as being representative of "cosmic despair" in modern drama.

Hilfer, Anthony C., and R. Vance Ramsey. "*Baby Doll*: A Study in Comedy and Critical Awareness." *Ohio Univ Rev*, 11 (1969), 75-88.
    Points out reasons for adverse criticism of this work.

Hill, F. A. "The Disaster of Ideals in *Camino Real* by Tennessee Williams." *Notes on Miss Writers*, 1 (Winter 1969), 100-109.

States that *Camino Real* dramatizes "the death of chivalric ideals."

Hirsch, Foster. "Sexual Imagery in Tennessee Williams' *Kingdom of Earth*." *NConL*, 1 (March 1971), 10-13.
    The house, the physical environment, and animals are used as sexual images in this work.

Howell, Elmo. "The Function of Gentlemen Callers: A Note on Tennessee Williams' *The Glass Menagerie*." *Notes on Miss Writers*, 2 (Winter 1970), 83-90.
    Amanda's tragedy is a parable of the inadequacy of modern life.

Inge, M. Thomas. See MISCELLANEOUS (Contemporary--1st Inge entry).

Kalem, T. E. "The Theater." *Time*, April 17, 1972, pp. 72-73.
    In a review of Williams' *Small Craft Warnings*, Kalem praises the play but rates it inferior to Williams' finest works.

Kalson, Albert E. "Tennessee Williams Enters *Dragon Country*." *Mod Drama*, 16 (June 1973), 61-67.
    An examination of the newest collection of Williams' works, which suggests his "continuing preoccupation with the relationship and interdependence of life and art."

_____. "Tennessee Williams' *Kingdom of Earth*: A Sterile Promontory." *Drama & Theatre*, 8 (Winter 1969-70), 90-93.
    Discusses the pessimistic view revealed in this play.

Kerr, Walter. *Thirty Plays Hath November*. New York: Simon & Schuster, 1969.
    Reprints reviews of *The Milk Train* and *The Seven Descents of Myrtle*.

King, Thomas L. "Irony and Distance in *The Glass Menagerie*." *ETJ*, 25 (1973), 207-214.
    Tom, not Amanda, is the center of the play.

Koepsel, Jürgen. *Der amerikanische Suden und seine Funktionen im dramatischen Werk von Tennessee Williams*. Mainzer, Studien zur Amerikanistik, 5. Bern & Frankfurt: Lang, 1974.
    Concludes that the South mainly provides scenery in Williams' works.

Kunkel, F. L. "Tennessee Williams and the Death of God." *Cweal*, 87 (February 23, 1968), 614-617.
    Williams' art is defined as decadent: his plays are populated with desperate, lonely people seeking salvation in sex, as the deity is represented as having lapsed into degeneracy and impotency, indifferent to human suffering, sometimes an object of derision.

Lenz, Harold. "At Sixes and Sevens--A Modern Theatrical Structure." *Forum H*, 11 (Summer-Fall 1973; Winter 1974), 73-79.
    Includes Williams' *Camino Real* in a discussion of plays that have six or seven characters.

Leon, Ferdinand. "Time, Fantasy, and Reality in *Night of the Iguana*." *Mod Drama*, 11 (May 1968), 87-96.
    A study of time and memory in the play.

Libman, Valentina. See GENERAL.

Link, Franz. *Tennessee Williams Dramen*. Darmstadt: Thesen Verlag, 1974.
    Focuses on themes in Williams' plays.

Long, E. Hudson. See GENERAL.

Macey, Samuel L. "Nonheroic Tragedy: A Pedigree for American Tragic Drama." *CLS*, 6 (March 1969), 1-19.
    Williams is one of the playwrights discussed as having written "nonheroic tragedy."

Miller, Jordan Y., ed. *Twentieth Century Interpretations of a Streetcar Named Desire*. Englewood Cliffs, N. J.: Prentice-Hall, 1971.
    Reprints three full essays, six excerpts, and ten reviews of the play with an original introduction and selected bibliography by the editor.

Mood, John J. "The Structure of *A Streetcar Named Desire*." *BSUF*, 14 (Summer 1973), 9-10.
    The structure and content of the play are foreshadowed by Blanche's first words.

Murray, Edward. See MISCELLANEOUS (Contemporary).

Nardin, James T. "What Tennessee Williams Didn't Write," in *Essays in Honor of Esmond Linworth Morilla*, ed. Thomas A. Kirby and William J. Olive. Baton Rouge: Louisiana State Univ Press, 1970, pp. 331-341.
    The effective use of offstage characters in Williams' plays is assessed.

Newlove, Donald. "A Dream of Tennessee Williams." *Esquire*, 72 (November 1969), 64, 173-178.
    Largely biographical.

Plante, P. R. See GENERAL.

Popkin, Henry. "Tennessee Williams Reexamined." *Arts in Virginia* (Virginia Museum), 2 (Spring 1971), 2-5.
    Traces the development of Williams' reputation and career.

Porter, Thomas E. *Myth and Modern American Drama*. Detroit: Wayne State Univ Press, 1969.
    Attempts to provide a sound theoretical and analytical foundation for dramatic criticism by examining nine plays as they relate to the American cultural milieu in which they were written; *A Streetcar Named Desire* is read as a play about the loss of the myth of a Southern tradition.

Presley, Delma Eugene. "The Search for Hope in the Plays of Tennessee Williams." *Miss Quart*, 25 (Winter 1971), 31-43.
    From *The Glass Menagerie* (1945) to *The Milk Train Doesn't Stop Here Anymore* (1964), Williams' heroes move from despair to hope, perhaps with debilitating effect on his later work.

_____. "Tennessee Williams: 25 Years of Criticism." *BB*, 30 (January-March 1973), 21-29.
    Unannotated listing of articles, books, and dissertations on Williams.

_____, and Hari Singh. "Epigraphs to the Plays of Tennessee Williams." *Notes on Miss Writers*, 3 (Spring 1970), 2-12.
    Deals with epigraphs as a clue to Williams' thematic development from 1945 to 1964, "the development of a hopefulness beyond despair."

_____. See MISCELLANEOUS (Contemporary).

_____. See O'CONNOR, FLANNERY.

Quirino, Leonard. "Tennessee Williams' Persistent *Battle of Angels*." *Mod Drama*, 11 (May 1968), 27-39.
    Battle of Angels provides a blueprint to Williams' more or less settled views on sex, society, religion, and the cosmos as well as a key to his dramatic metaphors.

Ramachandran, T. "Tennessee Williams and Feminine Misfits." *Mod Rev*, 124 (March 1969), 169-171.
    Deals with the preponderance of abnormal female heroines in Williams' plays.

Ramaswamy, S. "An Australian 'Doll's House': Ray Lawler's *Summer of the Seventeenth Doll*." *Indian Jour of Eng Stud*, 12 (December 1971), 115-122.
    Includes a comparison of this play with Williams' *Sweet Bird of Youth*.

Reck, Tom S. "The First *Cat on a Hot Tin Roof*: Williams' 'Three Players.'" *Univ Rev*, 34 (March 1968), 187-192.
    A study of the development of Williams' short story "Three Players of A Summer Game" into *Cat on a Hot Tin Roof*.

_____. "The Short Stories of Tennessee Williams: Nucleus for His Drama." *Tenn Stud in Lit*, 16 (1971), 141-154.
    "In addition to incidental themes, scenes, characterizations, and dialogue drawn from his fiction for use in the dramas, six of [Williams'] plays have grown rather specifically from early versions as short stories."

Reed, Rex. "Tennessee Williams Turns Sixty." *Esquire*, 76 (September 1971), 105-108, 216, 218, 220, 222-223.
    An interview.

Robey, Cora. "Chloroses--Pâles Roses and Pleurosis--Blue Roses." *Romance Notes*, 13 (Winter 1971), 250-251.
    The Gentleman Caller's hearing of "pleurosis" as "blue roses" could have its source in Baudelaire's rhyme "chloroses-pâles roses."

Rorem, Ned. "Tennessee Now and Then." *London Mag*, 15 (June/July 1975), 68-74.
    Williams' plays since 1960 are inferior to his earlier ones, but he still has "a trump card: his ability to write straight fiction."

Shuman, R. Baird. "Clifford Odets: A Playwright and His Jewish Background." *SAQ*, 71 (Spring 1972), 225-233.
Tennessee Williams is mentioned in this article as one of a few American playwrights to achieve the verisimilitude in dialect that Odets does.

Simon, John. "Theatre Chronicle." *HudR*, 21 (Summer 1968), 322-324.
The Seven Descents of Myrtle is a rehash of Williams' earlier and better plays.

Skloot, Robert. "Submitting Self to Flame: The Artist's Quest in Tennessee Williams, 1935-1954." *ETJ*, 25 (1973), 199-206.
Discusses Williams' views about the role of the artist.

Starnes, Leland. "The Grotesque Children of *The Rose Tattoo*." *Mod Drama*, 12 (February 1970), 357-369.
A study of the childlike qualities of the characters in the play, especially Serafina and Alvaro.

Steinbeck, Elaine. See MISCELLANEOUS (Contemporary).

Szeliski, John v. *Tragedy and Fear: Why Modern Tragic Drama Fails*. Chapel Hill: Univ of North Carolina Press, 1971.
Williams is among the dramatists whose works are used as examples in this discussion emphasizing the conflict between pessimism and optimism.

Taylor, William E. See MISCELLANEOUS (Contemporary).

The Theatre of Tennessee Williams, 4 vols. New York: New Directions, 1971-1972.
Thirteen of the earlier plays, with cast lists, production notes and Williams' essays that concern these plays.

Tischler, Nancy M. "The Distorted Mirror: Tennessee Williams' Self-Portraits." *Miss Quart*, 25 (Fall 1972), 389-403.
Though the most self-conscious self-portrait of Williams appears in various versions of *Battle of Angels*, *The Glass Menagerie* and *A Streetcar Named Desire* less pretentiously present aspects of Williams the "visceral" rather than the "cerebral" Romantic.

_____. *Tennessee Williams*. Southern Writers Series, no. 5. Austin: Steck-Vaughn, 1969.
Williams' vision is interpreted as essentially tragic and his greatest achievement found in his endowment of Southern experience with universal significance.

Vos, Nelvin. "The American Dream Turned to Nightmare: Recent American Drama." *Chri Schol Rev*, 1 (Spring 1971), 195-206.
Williams is among the modern playwrights discussed as having departed from the optimism which characterized the first three hundred years of American history.

Weales, Gerald. See MISCELLANEOUS (Contemporary).

Williams, Tennessee. *Memoirs*. New York: Doubleday & Co., 1975.
Autobiographical memoirs focusing on the personal experiences which have shaped the man and his plays.

_____. "Survival Notes: A Journal." *Esquire*, 78 (September 1972), 130-134, 166, 168.
Williams writes about his early career and about his reactions to interviewers.

_____. "What's Next on the Agenda, Mr. Williams?" *Medit Rev*, 1 (Winter 1971), 15-19.
A satirical account of a ward for the violent.

[WILLINGHAM, CALDER] Parr, J. L. "Calder Willingham: The Forgotten Novelist." *Critique*, 11, no. 3 (1969), 57-65.
Sees Willingham's major contribution as "redefining the nature of the American novel, and illustrating by stunning example exactly how the novel should be handled in light of current circumstances."

Willingham, Calder. See CALDWELL, ERSKINE (Contemporary).

[WINSLOW, ANNE GOODWIN] White, Helen, and Redding S. Sugg, Jr. "Lady into Artist: The Literary Achievement of Anne Goodwin Winslow." *Miss Quart*, 22 (Fall 1969), 289-302.
An evaluation of works by Mrs. Winslow (1875-1959), who published four novels after she was sixty-five, and whose life and works reveal important aspects of the concept of the Southern lady.

[WOLFE, THOMAS] Aldridge, John W. See MISCELLANEOUS (Contemporary--2nd Aldridge entry).

Austin, Neal F. *A Biography of Thomas Wolfe*. Austin: Roger Beacham, 1968.
A brief account of the exterior facts of Wolfe's life.

Baker, Christopher P., and Alan P. Clarke. "An Unpublished Thomas Wolfe Letter." *Miss Quart*, 25 (Fall 1972), 467-469.
A letter of appreciation for a favorable review of *Look Homeward, Angel* by Alan B. Clarke in the *Richmond Times-Dispatch* in 1929.

Beja, Morris. See MISCELLANEOUS (Contemporary).

Bellman, Samuel I. See MISCELLANEOUS (Contemporary).

Blake, Nelson M. See MISCELLANEOUS (Contemporary).

Boyle, Thomas E. "Frederick Jackson Turner and Thomas Wolfe: The Frontier as History and as Literature." *WAL*, 4 (Winter 1970), 273-285.
Compares the attitudes of Turner and Wolfe to traditional American myth.

Braswell, William. "An 'Interior Biography' of Thomas Wolfe." *So Lit Jour*, 3 (Fall 1970), 145-150.

With their carefully done notes and commentary, editors Richard S. Kennedy and Paschal Reeves succeed admirably in accomplishing their goal, which was "'to go back far enough with Wolfe's scattered jottings so that the edition [*The Notebooks of Thomas Wolfe*] would present a kind of interior biography of Wolfe.'"

Bredahl, A. Carl, Jr. "*Look Homeward, Angel*: Individuation and Articulation." *So Lit Jour*, 6 (Fall 1973), 47-58.
　　At Ben's death, the crucial moment in Eugene's life, Eugene is metamorphosed into "an artist who is able to see and articulate the formal coherence of life."

Bryer, Jackson. See MISCELLANEOUS (Contemporary-- both Bryer entries).

Bungert, Hans. See GENERAL.

Calhoun, Richard J., and Robert W. Hill. "'Tom, Are You Listening?' An Interview with Fred Wolfe." *So Car Rev*, 6, no. 2 (1974), 35-47.
　　Fred Wolfe is the sole surviving member of Thomas Wolfe's immediate family.

Cane, Melville. "Thomas Wolfe: A Memoir." *Am Schol*, 41 (Autumn 1972), 637-642.
　　Cane's recollections of his associations with Wolfe.

Capitanchick, Maurice. "Thomas Wolfe." *Bks and Bookmen*, 16 (July 1971), 24-28.
　　Deals with the relationship between Wolfe and Maxwell Perkins.

Carlile, Robert E. "Musical Analogues in Thomas Wolfe's *Look Homeward, Angel*." *MFS*, 14 (Summer 1968), 215-223.
　　A discussion of three musical analogues in the novel: leitmotif, modulation, and chromaticism.

Carlinsky, Daniel, ed. *A Century of College Humor*. New York: Random House, 1971.
　　Reprints Wolfe's satiric college drama "The Streets of Durham" from the *North Carolina Tarbaby*.

Churchill, Allen. See MISCELLANEOUS (Contemporary).

Cohn, Ruby. See MISCELLANEOUS (Contemporary).

Collmer, Robert G. See MISCELLANEOUS (Contemporary).

Corrington, John W. "Three Books About a Southern Romantic." *So Lit Jour*, 1 (Autumn 1968), 98-104.
　　An essay-review of *Thomas Wolfe: Three Decades of Criticism*, Turnbull's biography of Wolfe, and *The Letters of Thomas Wolfe to His Mother*.

Cowley, Malcolm. See MISCELLANEOUS (Contemporary-- 1st Cowley entry).

Cracroft, Richard H. "A Pebble in the Pool: Organic Theme and Structure in Thomas Wolfe's *You Can't Go Home Again*." *MFS*, 17 (Winter 1971), 533-553.

George Webber is the pebble in a "series of concentric circles."

_____. "Through Utah and the Western Parks: Thomas Wolfe's Farewell to America." *UHQ*, 37 (Summer 1969), 291-306.
　　On Wolfe's Western trip, just before his death.

Dessner, Lawrence Jay. "Thomas Wolfe's Mr. Katamoto." *MFS*, 17 (Winter 1971/72), 561-565.
　　Believes that Katamoto is a parody of the author and the hero.

Doten, Sharon. "Thomas Wolfe's 'No Door': Some Textual Questions." *PBSA*, 68 (1st Qtr. 1974), 45-52.
　　Discusses textual problems related to this short novel: the complications of manuscript materials.

Eichelberger, Clayton L. "Eliza Gant as Negative Symbol in *Look Homeward, Angel*." *ArlQ*, 1 (Winter 1967-68), 269-278.
　　Blames Eliza Gant's materialism for the collapse of the Gant family.

Etulain, R. W. See GENERAL.

Field, Leslie A. "Thomas Wolfe and the Kicking Season Again." *SAQ*, 69 (Summer 1970), 364-372.
　　A renewed interest in Wolfe, occasioned in part by Andrew Turnbull's biography and return to the fashion of yesteryear to debunk him, causes Field to focus on the misuse and abuse of Wolfe and to argue that he deserves to be reread and rediscovered.

_____. "Thomas Wolfe on the Couch and in Symposium." *So Lit Jour*, 5 (Fall 1972), 163-176.
　　An essay-review of *Thomas Wolfe: Ulysses and Narcissus*, by William V. Snyder, and *Thomas Wolfe and the Glass of Time*, edited by Paschal Reeves, in which the reviewer finds the latter book an antidote to the former one, in which Thomas Wolfe--Eugene Gant--George Webber is/are "placed on the couch and given over to 'professional' analysis."

_____, ed. *Thomas Wolfe: Three Decades of Criticism*. New York: New York Univ Press, 1968.
　　Reprints a wide selection of criticism published over the last thirty years.

Foster, Ruel E. "Thomas Wolfe's Mountain Gloom and Glory." *AL*, 44 (January 1973), 638-647.
　　Studies the influence of the mountains around Asheville, North Carolina, on Wolfe's works.

French, Warren. See MISCELLANEOUS (Contemporary-- 3rd French entry).

Gilman, Richard. "The Worship of Thomas Wolfe." *New Rep*, 158 (February 24, 1968), 31-34.
　　An essay-review of *Thomas Wolfe*, by Andrew Turnbull.

Gray, Richard. "Signs of Kinship: Thomas Wolfe and His Appalachian Background." *Appal Jour*, 1 (Spring 1974), 309-319.
　　Deals with Wolfe's use of his Appalachian background in *The Hills Beyond*.

Gurko, Leo. *Thomas Wolfe: Beyond the Romantic Ego*. New York: Thomas Y. Crowell Co., 1975. Emphasizes the need for a new approach to critical evaluation of Wolfe.

Harvey, Nancy L. "*Look Homeward, Angel*: An Elegiac Novel." *BSUF*, 13 (Winter 1972), 29-33. Compares this novel with Milton's "Lycidas."

Helmcke, Hans. See GENERAL.

Hiers, John T. See MISCELLANEOUS (Contemporary).

Hilfer, Anthony C. See MISCELLANEOUS (Contemporary).

Holman, C. Hugh. *The Loneliness at the Core: Studies in Thomas Wolfe*. Baton Rouge: Louisiana State Univ Press, 1975.
A collection of revised, previously published essays dealing, among other things, with Wolfe's tendency to rebel, the need to look beyond the autobiographical element in his work, and his success with the novella.

_____. See CENTRAL.

Hubbell, Jay B. See GENERAL.

Idol, John L., Jr. "The Plays of Thomas Wolfe and Their Links with His Novels." *Miss Quart*, 22 (Spring 1969), 95-112.
Wolfe's early plays contain symbols, ideas, and characters which are carried over into his novels.

_____. "Thomas Wolfe and Painting." *Re: A&L*, 2 (Spring 1969), 14-20.
Understanding Wolfe's knowledge of painting illuminates "his purposes and practices as a writer."

_____. "Thomas Wolfe's 'A Note on Experts.'" *Stud SF*, 11 (Fall 1974), 395-398.
This "curious piece of fiction" foreshadows "the satire to come in *The Web and the Rock*, *You Can't Go Home Again*, and *The Hills Beyond*.

Inge, M. Thomas. See MISCELLANEOUS (Contemporary-- 1st Inge entry).

Johnson, Elmer D. *Thomas Wolfe: A Checklist*. Kent, Ohio: Kent State Univ Press, 1970.
A descriptive bibliography of the books and a checklist of other primary and secondary materials, including theses and dissertations.

Justus, James H. See GENERAL.

Kennedy, Richard S., and Paschal Reeves, eds. *The Notebooks of Thomas Wolfe*. Chapel Hill: Univ of North Carolina Press, 1970.
An edited and annotated transcription in two volumes of nine-tenths of the total material in thirty-five pocket notebooks, carried intermittently by Wolfe from 1926 to 1938, designed to present "a kind of interior biography."

Knox, George. "The Great American Novel: Final Chapter." *AQ*, 21 (Winter 1969), 668-682.

In discussing the final debunking of the concept of the Great American Novel, Knox discusses Wolfe briefly.

Kristensen, Sven M. See MISCELLANEOUS (Contemporary).

Kronenberger, Louis, and E. M. Beck. See GENERAL.

Kuehl, John, and Jackson R. Bryer. See MISCELLANEOUS (Contemporary).

Kwiat, Joseph J., and Gerhard Weiss. See MISCELLANEOUS (Contemporary).

Landor, Mikhail. See MISCELLANEOUS (Contemporary).

LeClair, Thomas. See MISCELLANEOUS (Contemporary).

Lengeler, Rainer. "Thomas Wolfe and S. T. Coleridge." *N&Q*, 20 (September 1973), 332-333.
Points out similarities in the Cain passage in Wolfe's *Dark in the Forest, Strange as Time*, and Coleridge's "The Wanderings of Cain."

Libman, Valentina. See GENERAL.

Littlejohn, David. See MISCELLANEOUS (Contemporary).

Lohner, Edgar. See GENERAL.

Lyde, M. J. Untitled. *SHR*, 4 (Spring 1970), 181-183.
An essay-review of *The Letters of Thomas Wolfe to His Mother* (1968), edited by C. Hugh Holman and Sue Fields Ross, and of *Thomas Wolfe's Albatross: Race and Nationality in America* (1969), by Paschal Reeves.

Magny, Claude-Edmonde. See MISCELLANEOUS (Contemporary).

McElderry, B. R., Jr. "Thomas Wolfe's 'The Mountains.'" *So Lit Jour*, 3 (Fall 1970), 151-153.
Ryan's edition of Wolfe's play is useful for its numerous unpublished passages which throw light on Wolfe's efforts to become a dramatist.

Meehan, James. "Seed of Destruction: The Death of Thomas Wolfe." *SAQ*, 73 (Spring 1974), 173-183.
Wolfe's death was caused not by tuberculosis but by coccidioidal meningitis, a fungus disease also known as desert fever, contracted on a long trip to the West shortly before his death.

Meinke, Elke and Dieter. "Thomas Wolfe: Zum Tod in der Grossstadt." *Neuren Sprachen*, 18 (August 1969), 373-380.
Wolfe anticipates his own death in his description of death in the big city.

Millichap, Joseph R. "Narrative Structure and Symbolic Imagery in *Look Homeward, Angel*." *SHR*, 7 (Summer 1973), 295-303.
This study, "an analysis which emphasizes the structural form of the apprenticeship novel and the important symbolic imagery presented in the title and the prose poem, unifies the novel's complexities in the themes of self-discovery, self-realization, and self-expression."

Moore, Harry T. "Notes in the Eye of a Mountain-
ous Man." *SatR*, March 7, 1970, 23-24, 46.
An essay-review of *The Notebooks of Thomas
Wolfe*, ed. Richard S. Kennedy and Paschal
Reeves.

Murray, Edward. See MISCELLANEOUS (Contemporary).

Nevius, Blake. See MISCELLANEOUS (Contemporary).

O'Brien, Michael. "Thomas Wolfe and the Problem
of Southern Identity: An English Perspective."
SAQ, 70 (Winter 1971), 102-111.
Compares Wolfe's social alienation to that
of many Englishmen.

Payne, Ladell. *Thomas Wolfe*. Southern Writers
Series, no. 9. Austin: Steck-Vaughn, 1969.
Reads Wolfe's fiction and artistry against
his personal experience and aesthetic
convictions.

Perkins, George. See GENERAL.

Powell, W. Allen. "Thomas Wolfe's Phoenix Nest:
The Plays of Thomas Wolfe as Related to His
Fiction." *MarkR*, 2 (May 1971), 104-110.
Discusses Wolfe's plays as training for his
writing of his novels and foreshadowings of
various elements in them.

Reck, Rima Drell. "Céline and Wolfe: Toward a
Theory of the Autobiographical Novel." *Miss
Quart*, 22 (Winter 1968-69), 19-27.
A comparison of the technique of *Look
Homeward, Angel* and of *Death on the Installment
Plan*.

Reeves, Paschal. *Checklist of Thomas Wolfe*.
Columbus, Ohio: Charles E. Merrill, 1969.
A selective checklist of primary and
secondary materials.

_____. "Gleam from the Forge: Thomas Wolfe's
Emerging Idea of Brotherhood." *GaR*, 22
(Summer 1968), 247-253.
One of the most important differences between
the Gant and Webber cycles is the growing expression of the brotherhood of man in Wolfe's
late writing.

_____. "The Second Homeland of His Spirit:
Germany in the Fiction of Thomas Wolfe," in
Americana-Austriaca. Vol. II, ed. Klaus
Lanzinger. Stuttgart, Germany: Wilhelm
Braumüller, 1970.
Next to America, Wolfe liked Germany best
and all his life "displayed a marked affinity
for German culture."

_____, ed. *Studies in Look Homeward, Angel*.
Columbus, Ohio: Charles E. Merrill, 1970.
Reprints eleven selections reflecting contemporary response to Wolfe's novel and fifteen
critical statements on the author's intent, the
novel as a whole, and major themes, with a full
preface by the editor.

_____. "Thomas Wolfe and the Family of Man."
Spectrum, 2 (1972), 47-54.
Discusses reasons for the differing views of
George Webber and Eugene Gant.

_____, ed. *Thomas Wolfe and the Glass of Time*.
Athens: Univ of Georgia Press, 1971.
In effect the proceedings of a symposium
held at the University of Georgia on April 10-12,
1969, this book brings new information and new
light to the study of Thomas Wolfe. Major papers are by Richard S. Kennedy, Richard Walser,
and C. Hugh Holman, each accompanied by the
edited transcript of discussion that followed
the reading of the paper. An address by
Fred C. Wolfe, brother of the novelist, furnishes detailed, intimate recollections of the
Wolfe family. Two panel discussions are included in the edited transcriptions: "Thomas
Wolfe and the Theater," conducted by Ladell
Payne, and "New Directions in Wolfe Scholarship," by Paschal Reeves, organizer of the symposium and editor of this volume. An appendix
prints an unpublished letter from Wolfe to
Mrs. William E. Dodd, June 30, 1935.

_____. *Thomas Wolfe's Albatross: Race and National-
ity in America*. Athens: Univ of Georgia Press,
1969.
A study of Wolfe's fiction in the light of
his purpose of an epic portrayal of his native
land, his treatment of minority groups, and an
evaluation of his achievement as an artist.

Rubin, Larry. "An Echo of Poe in *Of Time and the
River*." *Poe Newsletter*, 3 (December 1970),
38-39.
A Wolfe passage depicting the "hypnotic
'clickety-clack'" of a train is compared to
Poe's use of rhythm and rhyme in "The Bells."

Rubin, Louis D., Jr., ed. *Thomas Wolfe*. Twentieth
Century Views. Englewood Cliffs, N. J.:
Prentice-Hall, 1973.
Reprints thirteen essays and reviews, and
two letters, with a chronology and bibliograph-
ical note by the editor.

_____. "Thomas Wolfe Once Again." *NCHR*, 50
(Spring 1973), 169-189.
Discusses Wolfe's fiction as a "dramatized
record of a writer's encounter with being an
artist in America."

Ryan, Pat M., ed. *The Mountains*, by Thomas Wolfe.
Chapel Hill: Univ of North Carolina Press,
1970.
First publication of the texts of Wolfe's
one-act and three-act versions of his early
attempt at drama with an introduction by the
editor evaluating Wolfe's work as a dramatist.

Ryssel, Fritz H. *Thomas Wolfe*. Modern Literature
Monographs. New York: Frederick Ungar, 1972.
A brief general survey which finds Wolfe's
work a lyrical celebration of America; translated from the German.

Scherting, Jack. "Echoes of *Look Homeward, Angel*
in Dylan Thomas's 'A Child's Christmas in
Wales.'" *Stud SF*, 9 (Fall 1972), 404-406.
Noting these echoes, "one wonders if the
American novelist's works had something more
than a casual influence on the development of
the Welshman's prose style."

Schmid, Hans. "A Note on Thomas Wolfe's Oktoberfest Letter." *Harvard Lib Bul*, 18 (October 1970), 367-370.
    A fist fight which Wolfe had in Munich and which he described in a letter to Aline Bernstein could have been the source for George Webber's fight in *The Web and the Rock*.

Schneider, Duane. "Thomas Wolfe and the Quest for Language." *Ohio Univ Rev*, 11 (1969), 5-18.
    Deals with Wolfe's theories of language as revealed in his letters and in *The Story of a Novel*.

Sheed, Wilfrid. See MISCELLANEOUS (Contemporary).

Simpson, Lewis P. "*The Notebooks of Thomas Wolfe*, edited by Richard S. Kennedy and Paschal Reeves." *SAQ*, 69 (Autumn 1970), 544-546.
    An essay-review of *The Notebooks*, which Simpson says shows evidence of meticulous scholarship and an imaginative grasp of Wolfe's life, and is an important source of studies of Wolfe's career in American letters.

_____. See GENERAL--3rd Simpson entry.

Singh, Hari. "Thomas Wolfe: The Idea of Eternity." *So Car Rev*, 1 (May 1969), 40-47.
    Wolfe's view of eternity evolves from grief in individual transience to hope in mankind's continual, painful progress.

Skipp, Francis E. "*Of Time and the River*: The Final Editing." *PBSA*, 64 (3rd Qtr. 1970), 313-322.
    Maxwell Perkins cut from the typescript of the novel passages which expressed Wolfe's "most deeply felt insights and certainties... what was closest to his heart."

Snyder, William U. *Thomas Wolfe: Ulysses and Narcissus*. Athens: Ohio Univ Press, 1971.
    A psychoanalytic study of Wolfe's career by a clinical psychologist who finds that Wolfe was deeply neurotic and bordered on manic-depressive psychosis and paranoia.

Spearman, Walter. See MISCELLANEOUS (Contemporary).

Styron, William. "The Shade of Thomas Wolfe." *Harper's*, 236 (April 1968), 96, 98-104.
    An essay-review of Andrew Turnbull's *Thomas Wolfe*.

Terrier, Michel. See MISCELLANEOUS (Contemporary).

Turnbull, Andrew. *Thomas Wolfe*. New York: Scribner's, 1968.
    A full-scale biography dealing, in some cases for the first time, with all aspects of Wolfe's private and public life.

Walther, John D. "'Luke' Looks Homeward: An Interview with Fred Wolfe." *Miss Quart*, 27 (Spring 1974), 141-163.
    A conversation with Wolfe's brother.

Wank, Martin. "Thomas Wolfe: Two More Decades of Criticism." *SAQ*, 69 (Spring 1970), 244-256.

Wank reviews the last two decades of Wolfe criticism, comments on the work of the leading Wolfe scholars, and concludes that the full wealth of Wolfe's thought has not yet been explored or conveyed.

Wolfe, Thomas. *The Letters of Thomas Wolfe to His Mother*, ed. C. Hugh Holman and Sue Fields Ross. Chapel Hill: Univ of North Carolina Press, 1968.
    A newly edited collection of some primary documents.

Woodress, James. See GENERAL--1st and 5th Woodress entries.

[WOLFE, TOM] Aldridge, John W. See MISCELLANEOUS (Contemporary--1st Aldridge entry).

Bellamy, Joe David. "A Quite Literary Conversation with Tom Wolfe." *In Touch*, 1 (June 1974), 60-61, 64, 72, 76, 79-80, 90, 106.
    An interview with the Virginia-born writer about his work and the contemporary literary scene.

_____. See MISCELLANEOUS (Contemporary).

Hagopian, John V. See MISCELLANEOUS (Contemporary).

Haynes, Dick. "A Conversation with Tom Wolfe." *New Dominion Life Style*, 2 (April 1975), 22-24.
    Wolfe discusses his attitudes towards the South and his home town of Richmond, Virginia.

Johnson, Michael L. See MISCELLANEOUS (Contemporary).

Krauss, Rosalind. "Café Criticism." *PR*, 42 (1975), 629-633.
    A review of *The Painted Word*, in which Wolfe "has given us the theater of his own rage at being excluded...from the work of art."

Meehan, Thomas. "The Time Renata Adler Didn't Dump Campbell's Soup on Tom Wolfe's Head." *SatR*, June 3, 1973, pp. 22-24.
    Recounts an incident concerning Wolfe at the First Annual A. J. Liebling Counter-Convention in New York in 1972.

Mok, M. "Tom Wolfe." *PW*, 203 (June 18, 1973), 34-35.
    An interview regarding *The New Journalism* and Wolfe's book in progress on the astronauts.

Phillips, William. "Conservative Chic: Tom Wolfe." *PR*, 42 (1975), 175-177.
    Accuses Wolfe of "peddling the most ignorant and backward prejudices" and of representing "conservative chic...taking potshots at radical chic."

Weber, Ronald. "Tom Wolfe's Happiness Explosion." *Jour of Pop Culture*, 8 (Summer 1974), 71-79.
    Wolfe's "vision of modern America...derives from a repeated mocking of the style and concerns of traditional culture and a celebration of the comic, pleasure-seeking, self-centered modes of the happiness explosion."

IV. Contemporary (1920-1975)

[WRIGHT, RICHARD] Anon. See GENERAL--2nd Anon. entry.

Aaron, Daniel. "Richard Wright and the Communist Party." *New Letters*, 38 (Winter 1971), 170-181.
   Deals with the reasons for Wright's acceptance and later rejection of the Communist Party.

Abcarian, Richard, ed. *Richard Wright's Native Son: A Critical Handbook.* Wadsworth Guides to Literary Study. Belmont, Calif.: Wadsworth Publishing Co., 1970.
   Reprints three essays by Wright, twenty-two reviews, eleven critical essays, six related essays, and three poems for controlled research on Wright's novel; includes a chronology and bibliography.

Alexander, Margaret Walker. "Richard Wright." *New Letters*, 38 (Winter 1971), 182-202.
   A reminiscence about her association with Wright.

Amis, Lola J. "Richard Wright's *Native Son*: Notes." *NALF*, 8 (Fall 1974), 240-243.
   Concludes that Book Three of the novel is anti-climactic.

Anderson, David D. "Chicago as Metaphor." *Great Lakes Rev*, 1 (Summer 1974), 3-15.
   Black Boy is included in a discussion of literary works dealing with Chicago.

Aptheker, Herbert. See GENERAL.

Baker, Houston A., Jr., ed. *Twentieth Century Interpretations of Native Son.* Englewood Cliffs, N. J.: Prentice-Hall, 1972.
   Reprints six full essays and excerpts with a lengthy introduction by the editor.

_____. See GENERAL--3rd Baker entry.

Bakish, David. *Richard Wright.* Modern Literature Monographs. New York: Frederick Ungar, 1973.
   A concise biographical-critical survey of Wright's life and career with emphasis on the social context of his writings.

_____. "Underground in an Ambiguous Dreamworld." *SBL*, 2 (Autumn 1971), 18-23.
   "The Man Who Lived Underground" develops the theme that life is an "ambiguous dreamworld."

Baldwin, Richard E. "The Creative Vision of *Native Son*." *Mass Rev*, 14 (Spring 1973), 378-390.
   A study of Bigger Thomas as a creative individual.

Bell, Bernard W. See MISCELLANEOUS (Contemporary--1st Bell entry).

Bennett, Stephen B., and William W. Nichols. See MISCELLANEOUS (Contemporary).

Berry, Faith. "On Richard Wright in Exile: Portrait of a Man as Outsider." *Negro Digest*, 18 (December 1968), 26-37.
   Deals with the effects of Wright's stay in Paris on his thinking and his writing.

Bigsby, C. W. E. See MISCELLANEOUS (Contemporary).

Billingsley, R. G. See MISCELLANEOUS (Contemporary).

Blake, Nelson M. See MISCELLANEOUS (Contemporary).

Bluefarb, Sam. See GENERAL.

Boitani, Piero. See MISCELLANEOUS (Contemporary).

Bolton, H. Philip. "The Role of Paranoia in Richard Wright's *Native Son*." *Kansas Quart*, 7 (Summer 1975), 111-124.
   Racism causes Bigger to be paranoid.

Bone, Robert. *Richard Wright.* Minnesota Pamphlets on American Writers, no. 74. Minneapolis: Univ of Minnesota Press, 1969.
   A biographical and critical appreciation of literary success against enormous odds on the part of Wright, who "created, out of his flight from nothingness and his compulsion to rebel, a memorable art."

Boyd, G. N. and L. A. See MISCELLANEOUS (Contemporary).

Brignano, Russell C. "Richard Wright: A Bibliography of Secondary Sources." *SBL*, 2 (Summer 1971), 19-25.
   Supplements previous bibliographies of secondary sources.

_____. *Richard Wright: An Introduction to the Man and His Works.* Pittsburgh: Univ of Pittsburgh Press, 1970.
   A study combining literary criticism, biography, and historical matter to elucidate the paramount public concerns of Wright: race relations in America, Marxism, contemporary international affairs, and his own changing philosophy.

Brivic, Sheldon. "Conflict of Values: Richard Wright's *Native Son*." *Novel*, 7 (Spring 1974), 231-245.
   "The ambivalence which critics have attacked in *Native Son* is really a complexity which adds to its validity, comprehension, and prophetic power...."

Brooks, Mary Ellen. "Behind Richard Wright's 'Artistic Conscience.'" *Lit and Ideology*, no. 13 (1972), 21-30.
   Heroes in Wright's works are those who have deliberately become outsiders.

Brown, Cecil. "Richard Wright's Complexes and Black Writing Today." *Negro Digest*, 18 (December 1968), 45-50, 78-82.
   Discusses reasons for Wright's exile.

Brown, Lloyd W. "Stereotypes in Black and White: The Nature of Perception in Wright's *Native Son*." *Black Acad Rev*, 1 (Fall 1970), 35-44.
   Bigger begins by trying to fit others into stereotypes and ends by examining himself.

_____. See GENERAL--2nd Brown entry.

Bruchac, Joseph. "Black Autobiography in Africa and America." *Black Acad Rev*, 2 (Spring-Summer 1971), 61-70.
    Black Boy is one of the works discussed as being in the tradition of black autobiography.

Bryant, Jerry H. See MISCELLANEOUS (Contemporary--2nd Bryant entry).

Cash, Earl J. See ELLISON, RALPH (Contemporary).

Cayton, Horace. "The Curtain: A Memoir." *Negro Digest*, 18 (December 1968), 11-15.
    An account of a train trip with Wright.

Cooke, Michael G. See MISCELLANEOUS (Contemporary--both Cooke entries).

Corrigan, Robert A. See GENERAL--1st Corrigan entry.

Cosgrove, William. "Strategies of Survival: The Gimmick Motif in Black Literature." *Stud in the Twentieth Cent*, no. 15 (Spring 1975), 109-217.
    In black literature, before a search for identity, there is the search for the "gimmick" to survive.

_____. See ELLISON, RALPH (Contemporary--1st Cosgrove entry).

Cowley, Malcolm. See MISCELLANEOUS (Contemporary--2nd Cowley entry).

Cripps, Thomas. "*Native Son*." *New Letters*, 38 (Winter 1971), 49-63.
    Deals with reasons for the failure of the movie version of the novel.

Crunden, Robert M. See MISCELLANEOUS (Contemporary).

Demarest, David P., Jr. "Richard Wright: The Meaning of Violence." *NALF*, 8 (Fall 1974), 236-239.
    Violence is a part of all the "memorable moments" in Wright's work; a reason perhaps is the "dual consciousness" of blacks brought about "by the violence of white America."

Dickstein, Morris. "The Black Aesthetic in White America." *PR*, 38 (Winter 1971-72), 376-395.
    Examines the characteristics of three generations of black writers, beginning with Wright's generation.

_____. "Wright, Baldwin, Cleaver." *New Letters*, 38 (Winter 1971), 117-124.
    Deals with Baldwin's attacks on Wright and with Cleaver's attacks on Baldwin.

Dixon, Melvin. "Richard Wright: Native Father and His Long Dream." *Black World*, 23 (March 1974), 91-95.
    A review-essay of Michel Fabre's *The Unfinished Quest of Richard Wright*.

Donlan, Dan M. "The White Trap: A Motif." *EJ*, 59 (October 1970), 943-944.
    In *Native Son* Bigger views the world as a "white blur."

Edward, Sister Ann. See GENERAL.

Emanuel, James A. "Fever and Feeling." *Negro Digest*, 18 (December 1968), 16-24.
    Deals with the images in *Native Son*.

Emerson, O. B. See MISCELLANEOUS (Contemporary--2nd Emerson entry).

Epstein, Seymour. See MISCELLANEOUS (Contemporary).

Everette, M. W. "The Death of Richard Wright's American Dream: 'The Man Who Lived Underground.'" *CLA Jour*, 17 (March 1974), 318-326.
    Completely pessimistic, "The Man Who Lived Underground" reveals "the extinction of the Black Boy's American dream."

Fabre, Michel. "Black Cat and White Cat: Richard Wright's Debt to Edgar Allan Poe." *Poe Stud*, 4 (June 1971), 17-19.
    Suggests that Poe's influence upon Wright was strong and extensive.

_____. "Impressions of Richard Wright: An Interview with Simone de Beauvoir." *SBL*, 1 (Autumn 1970), 3-5.
    A discussion of Wright's activities in France.

_____. "The Poetry of Richard Wright." *SBL*, 1 (Autumn 1970), 10-22.
    Deals with the themes of Wright's poems.

_____. "Richard Wright: The Man Who Lived Underground." *Studies in the Novel*, 3 (Summer 1971), 165-179.
    Finds that the source of Wright's 1944 story "The Man Who Lived Underground" is not Dostoevsky's *Notes from Underground* but an article from *True Detective Magazine*. The story is interpreted as a parable of literary creation and is said to represent Wright's most perfect short piece of fiction.

_____. "Richard Wright's First Hundred Books." *CLA Jour*, 16 (June 1973), 458-474.
    An outline of Wright's library and readings through 1940.

_____. *The Unfinished Quest of Richard Wright*. New York: William Morrow, 1973.
    A thorough, comprehensive biographical and intellectual history of Wright, translated from the French dissertation.

_____. "Wright's Exile." *New Letters*, 38 (Winter 1971), 136-154.
    Deals with Wright's reasons for exiling himself.

_____, and Edward Margolies. "A Bibliography of Richard Wright's Works." *New Letters*, 38 (Winter 1971), 159-169.
    Title is descriptive.

Felgar, Robert. "'The Kingdom of the Beast': The Landscape of *Native Son*." *CLA Jour*, 17 (March 1974), 333-337.
In this novel, Wright continually draws upon his "basic informing metaphor, 'the kingdom of the beast.'"

_____. "*Soul on Ice* and *Native Son*." *NALF*, 8 (Fall 1974), 235.
The sexual myth which Cleaver sets up in *Soul on Ice* can bring further insight into *Native Son*.

Fleming, Robert E. "Overshadowed by Richard Wright: Three Black Chicago Novelists." *NALF*, 7 (Summer 1973), 75-79.
Wright's portrayal of Chicago has overshadowed those by Waters E. Turpin, Alden Bland, and Frank London Brown.

_____. See GENERAL--2nd Fleming entry.

French, Warren. See MISCELLANEOUS (Contemporary--3rd French entry).

Gaskill, Gayle. "The Effect of Black/White Imagery in Richard Wright's *Black Boy*." *NALF*, 7 (Summer 1973), 46-48.
Wright reverses the symbolism which whites usually associate with black and white in order to suggest black's destruction of things white.

Gayle, Addison, Jr. "Richard Wright: Beyond Nihilism." *Negro Digest*, 18 (December 1968), 4-10.
Wright was the "last black writer to admonish men to listen" in order to avoid "a nihilistic attempt to negate the very structure of democracy itself" by those who had suffered from the failure of the American dream.

_____. See GENERAL.

Gibson, Donald B. "Richard Wright: A Bibliographical Essay." *CLA Jour*, 12 (June 1969), 360-365.
Focuses on the major critical materials available on the work of Richard Wright.

_____. "Richard Wright and the Tyranny of Convention." *CLA Jour*, 12 (June 1969), 344-357.
In nearly all his works, Wright is concerned with the individual in conflict with social convention.

_____. "Wright's Invisible Native Son." *AQ*, 21 (Winter 1969), 728-738.
Discusses Wright's character Bigger Thomas as one who is misinterpreted by most critics.

_____. See MISCELLANEOUS (Contemporary--1st Gibson entry).

Giles, J. R. "Richard Wright's Successful Failure: A New Look at *Uncle Tom's Children*." *Phylon*, 34 (September 1973), 256-266.
Maintains that the book is a unified work of art, making a realistic statement about the Southern blacks of its time and employing several of the same images and themes as *Native Son*.

Goede, William. See MISCELLANEOUS (Contemporary).

Goldstein, Malcolm. See MISCELLANEOUS (Contemporary).

Gounard, Jean-Francois. "Richard Wright as a Black American Writer in Exile." *CLA Jour*, 17 (March 1974), 307-317.
Influenced by the French existentialist philosophy, Wright wished to be accepted simply as a man, and not as a black man.

Graham, D. B. "*Lawd Today* and the Example of *The Waste Land*." *CLA Jour*, 17 (March 1974), 327-332.
Lawd Today makes use of the "imagery, motifs, and symbolism" of Eliot's poem.

Graham, Louis. "The White Self-Image Conflict in *Native Son*." *SBL*, 3 (Summer 1972), 19-21.
The white characters in the novel "have as much of an identity problem as Bigger."

Gross, Seymour L. "'Dalton' and Color-Blindness in *Native Son*." *Miss Quart*, 27 (Winter 1973-74), 75-77.
The source of the family name Dalton for Wright's central white characters is John Dalton's authorship of a 1794 treatise on colorblindness.

_____. See POE, EDGAR ALLAN (Antebellum).

Gross, Theodore L. See MISCELLANEOUS (Contemporary--2nd Gross entry).

_____. See GENERAL--1st and 3rd Gross entries.

Grumbach, Doris. See GENERAL.

Hajek, Friederike. "*American Tragedy*--Zwei Aspekte: Dargestellt in Richard Wrights *Native Son* und in Theodore Dreisers *An American Tragedy*." *ZAA*, 20 (1972), 262-279.
Dreiser's work represents an acceptance of capitalistic pressures, whereas Wright's is rebellious.

Haslam, Gerald W. See MISCELLANEOUS (Contemporary).

Hemenway, Robert. See GENERAL.

Hill, Mildred A. See GENERAL.

Houseman, John. "*Native Son* on Stage." *New Letters*, 38 (Winter 1971), 71-82.
Houseman worked with Wright on the stage version of the novel.

Howe, Irving. See GENERAL.

Hyman, S. E. "Richard Wright Reappraised." *Atl*, 225 (March 1970), 127-132.
A consideration of Wright's achievements in fiction.

Jackson, Blyden. "Richard Wright: Black Boy from America's Black Belt and Urban Ghettos." *CLA Jour*, 12 (June 1969), 287-309.
Emphasizes Wright's fellowship with his father in the world of the American Negro masses and suggests that Wright's real release came in that

fictional world which was closest to the actual world he had known in his youth.

_____. "Richard Wright in a Moment of Truth." *So Lit Jour*, 3 (Spring 1971), 3–17.
    That Wright's artistic imagination is most at home in the South can be seen in an early short story "Big Boy Leaves Home," which explicates the psychology and anthropology of American racism.

James, Charles L. "Bigger Thomas in the Seventies: A Twentieth-Century Search for Significance." *Eng Rec*, 22 (Fall 1971), 6–14.
    A consideration of Bigger Thomas' humane qualities.

Jeffers, Lance. See MISCELLANEOUS (Contemporary).

Jones, Lola. *Native Son Notes*. Lincoln, Neb.: Cliff's Notes, 1971.
    A study guide.

Jordan, June. "On Richard Wright and Zora Neale Hurston: Notes Toward a Balancing of Love and Hatred." *Black World*, 23 (August 1974), 4–8.
    Suggests reasons why Wright's novels were literary successes, whereas those of Hurston, who wrote during the same time, were not.

Kaiser, Ernest. See ELLISON, RALPH (Contemporary).

Kearns, Edward. "The 'Fate' Section of *Native Son*." *ConL*, 11 (Spring 1971), 146–155.
    While the "Fate" section may be "flawed," it is "far less so than critics have led us to believe. Its abstract and rhetorical qualities...are logical and necessary extensions of Wright's thematic strategy."

Kennedy, James G. "The Content and Form of *Native Son*." *CE*, 34 (November 1972), 269–286. (Followed by comment by Annette Conn.)
    Discusses content, plot and sub-plot of the novel.

Kent, George E. "On the Future Study of Richard Wright." *CLA Jour*, 12 (June 1969), 366–370.
    Kent lists the need of additional scholarship on Wright, including biography, bibliography, collected works, evaluative study of Wright's reading, Wright's relationship with the Communist Party, etc.

_____. "Richard Wright: Blackness and the Adventure of Western Culture." *CLA Jour*, 12 (June 1969), 322–343.
    Three sources of Wright's power are his double-consciousness, his personal tension, and his dramatic expression of black and white culture.

Killinger, John. *The Fragile Presence: Transcendence in Modern Literature*. Philadelphia: Fortress Press, 1973.
    Includes Wright in a discussion of religion in the works of black writers.

Kim, Kichung. "Wright, the Protest Novel, and Baldwin's Faith." *CLA Jour*, 17 (March 1974), 387–396.
    The debate between Baldwin and Wright goes beyond the question of "craftsmanship and provincialism."

Kinnamon, Keneth. *The Emergence of Richard Wright*. Urbana: Univ of Illinois Press, 1972.
    A study of the life, literary career, and social milieu of Wright from his birth through the publication of *Native Son* in 1940.

_____. "*Lawd Today*: Richard Wright's Apprentice Novel." *SBL*, 2 (Summer 1971), 16–18.
    The novel foreshadows elements that would be developed more fully in Wright's later works.

_____. "*Native Son*: The Personal, Social and Political Background." *Phylon*, 30 (Spring 1969), 66–72.
    Deals with Wright's personal experiences as they are revealed in the novel.

_____. "The Pastoral Impulse in Richard Wright." *Midcontinent Am Stud Jour*, 10 (Spring 1969), 41–47.
    A study of the retrospective rural nostalgia as a recurrent motif in Wright's work.

_____. "Richard Wright: Proletarian Poet." *Concerning Poetry*, 2 (Spring 1969), 39–50.
    Deals with Wright's early Marxist poems.

_____. "Richard Wright's Use of *Othello* in *Native Son*." *CLA Jour*, 12 (June 1969), 358–359.
    Bigger Thomas is Othello to Mary Dalton's Desdemona.

Klotman, Phyllis R. "Moral Distancing as a Rhetorical Technique in *Native Son*: A Note on 'Fate.'" *CLA Jour*, 18 (December 1974), 284–291.
    The shift in point of view from that of Bigger Thomas to that of Boris Max, in the third section of the novel, often criticized as a flaw in the novel, is instead a rhetorical device by which Wright achieves "moral distancing" and opens his reader's eyes to the deeper implications of the story.

_____, and Yancey Melville. "Gifts of Double Vision: Possible Political Implications of Richard Wright's 'Self-Consciousness' Thesis." *CLA Jour*, 16 (September 1972), 106–116.
    In *The Outsider*, Cross Damon and Ely Houston are both examples of the "outsider," who has achieved the objectivity of a "double consciousness" which can lead to knowledge and to communication.

Kostelanetz, Richard. "The Politics of Unresolved Quests in the Novels of Richard Wright." *XUS*, 8 (May 1969), 31–64.
    Deals with Wright's feelings of isolation in the South, in the Northern City, in the Communist Party, and in exile.

Larsen, R. B. V. "The Four Voices in Richard Wright's *Native Son*." *NALF*, 6 (Winter 1972), 105–109.
    A brief study of point of view in the novel.

Lawson, Lewis A. "Cross Damon: Kierkegaardian Man of Dread." *CLA Jour*, 14 (Spring 1971), 298–316.

In *The Outsider*, Wright offers "a Christian, rather than an atheistic existential view."

Leary, Lewis. "*Lawd Today*: Notes on Richard Wright's First/Last Novel." *CLA Jour*, 15 (June 1972), 411-420.
    Lawd Today stands on its own merits and in some ways surpasses the story of Bigger Thomas.

LeClair, Thomas. "The Blind Leading the Blind: Wright's *Native Son* and a Brief Reference to Ellison's *Invisible Man*." *CLA Jour*, 13 (March 1970), 315-320.
    In *Invisible Man* Ellison expands the sight-blindness pattern in *Native Son* to include symbolic images of light-dark, white-black, and visibility-invisibility.

Lehan, Richard. See MISCELLANEOUS (Contemporary).

Libman, Valentina. See GENERAL.

Liebman, Arthur. See MISCELLANEOUS (Contemporary).

Longstreet, S. See GENERAL.

Mangione, Jerre. See MISCELLANEOUS (Contemporary).

Mann, K. H. See GENERAL.

Manucci, Loretta V. See MISCELLANEOUS (Contemporary).

Margolies, Edward. *The Art of Richard Wright*. Carbondale: Southern Illinois Univ Press, 1969.
    Traces the development of Wright's principal themes--freedom, existential horror, and black nationalism--through his thirteen major works.

_____. See MISCELLANEOUS (Contemporary--both Margolies entries).

Mason, Clifford. See ELLISON, RALPH (Contemporary).

May, John R. See MISCELLANEOUS (Contemporary).

_____. See GENERAL.

McCall, Dan. *The Example of Richard Wright*. New York: Harcourt, Brace & World, 1969.
    Surveys Wright's work in terms of its relevant literary, moral, and political contexts.

McCarthy, Harold T. "Richard Wright: The Expatriate as Native Son." *AL*, 44 (March 1972), 97-117.
    Studies Wright's artistry against the background of his attitudes toward both American and European culture.

_____. See GENERAL.

McDowell, Robert E., and George Fortenberry. See MISCELLANEOUS (Contemporary).

Merkle, Donald R. "The Furnace and the Tower: A New Look at the Symbols of *Native Son*." *EJ*, 6 (September 1971), 735-739.
    The furnace symbolizes the blacks and the tower the whites.

Meyer, Shirley. "The Identity of 'The Man Who Lived Underground.'" *NALF*, 4 (1970), 52-55.
    Develops the thesis that "the acceptance of one's responsibility in an absurd world can result in self-realization."

Miller, Eugene E. "Voodoo Parallels in *Native Son*." *CLA Jour*, 16 (September 1972), 81-95.
    Points out elements of Haitian voodoo to be found in the scene in which Bigger kills Mary Dalton and explains the significance of Wright's use of these elements.

Mitchell, Louis D. "Richard Wright's Artistry." *Crisis*, 82 (February 1975), 62-66.
    Deals with *Native Son*, *Black Boy*, and *The Outsider*.

Nagel, James. "Images of 'Vision' in *Native Son*." *Univ Rev*, 36 (Winter 1969), 109-115.
    The images of vision in the novel "suggest this conclusion: blindness prompting isolation, impaired vision, alienation. Thus the imagery contributes to the central theme that the denial of personal identity is the worst form of oppression."

Neal, Larry. See ELLISON, RALPH (Contemporary).

Nevius, Blake. See MISCELLANEOUS (Contemporary).

O'Brien, John. See MISCELLANEOUS (Contemporary--1st O'Brien entry).

Oleson, Carole W. "The Symbolic Richness of Richard Wright's 'Bright and Morning Star.'" *NALF*, 6 (Winter 1972), 110-112.
    On the symbolism of rain and the flashing of the airplane.

Padmore, Dorothy. "A Letter from Dorothy Padmore." *SBL*, 1 (Autumn 1970), 5-9.
    In a letter to Michel Fabre, Mrs. Padmore's topics include Wright's continuing fight against racial inequality while he was in France.

Peden, William. See MISCELLANEOUS (Contemporary--2nd Peden entry).

Pells, R. H. See MISCELLANEOUS (Contemporary).

Perkins, George. See GENERAL.

Petesch, Donald. See MISCELLANEOUS (Contemporary).

Pitcole, Marcia. "*Black Boy* and Role Playing: A Scenario for Reading Success." *EJ*, 57 (November 1968), 1140-1142.
    A selection of twenty key scenes from the book, designed to encourage the student to read the entire book.

Plante, P. R. See GENERAL.

Primeau, Ronald. "Imagination as Moral Bulwark and Creative Energy in Richard Wright's *Black Boy* and Le Roi Jones' *Home*." *SBL*, 3 (Summer 1972), 12-18.
    Compares these two works as examples of modern romanticism.

_____. See GENERAL.

Prior, Linda. See POE, EDGAR ALLAN.

Pyros, John. "Richard Wright: A Black Novelist's
Experience in Film." *NALF*, 9 (Summer 1975),
53-54.
   Discusses the reasons why the film version
of *Native Son* was doomed to be a "filmic
fiasco."

Ray, David, and Robert M. Farnsworth, eds. *Richard
Wright: Impressions and Perspectives*. Ann
Arbor: Univ of Michigan, 1973.
   A reprint of the 1971 special issue of *New
Letters* devoted to personal reminiscences and
critical commentary on Wright, with a primary
bibliography.

Reed, Kenneth T. "*Native Son*: An American *Crime
and Punishment*." *SBL*, 1 (Summer 1970), 33-34.
   Believes that Wright used Dostoevsky's novel
as a model.

Reilly, John M. "*Lawd Today*: Richard Wright's
Experiment in Naturalism." *SBL*, 2
(Autumn 1971), 14-17.
   This is the only one of Wright's works in
which environment molds character.

_____. "Richard Wright: An Essay in Bibliography."
RALS, 1 (August 1971), 131-180.
   An essay-guide to primary and secondary
materials.

_____. "Richard Wright's Apprenticeship." *Jour of
Black Stud*, 2 (June 1972), 439-460.
   Deals with the significance of Wright's rela-
tionship with the Communist Party.

_____. "Self-Portraits by Richard Wright." *ColQ*,
20 (Summer 1971), 31-45.
   Examines Wright's "deliberate self-portraits"
in order to better comprehend his fiction.

Rickels, Milton and Patricia. *Richard Wright*.
Southern Writers Series, no. 11. Austin:
Steck-Vaughn, 1970.
   A chronologically arranged introduction to
Wright's career combining biography with de-
scriptive criticism of the works.

Ridenour, Ronald. "'The Man Who Lived Underground': A Critique." *Phylon*, 31
(Spring 1970), 54-57.
   Emphasizes universal and existential themes
in the story and asserts that it shows significant artistic growth from *Native Son* and is a
precursor of Ellison's *Invisible Man*.

Rosenblatt, Roger. See MISCELLANEOUS
(Contemporary--both Rosenblatt entries).

Sanders, Ronald. "Relevance for the Sixties:
Richard Wright Then & Now." *Negro Digest*, 18
(December 1968), 83-98.
   Deals with Wright's rejection of the senti-
mental in favor of "the primitive right of
anger."

_____. "Richard Wright and the Sixties." *Midstream*,
14 (August-September 1968), 28-40.
   Native Son and *Black Boy* foreshadow works
written in the Sixties by other black writers.

Savory, Jerold J. "Bigger Thomas and the Book of
Job: The Epigraph to *Native Son*." *NALF*, 9
(Summer 1975), 55-56.
   "Both Job and Bigger are rebels and both are
conscious that their revolts are against their
own attempts to remain silent, as well as against
others who try to offer them comforts which are
finally dissatisfying."

_____. See MISCELLANEOUS (Contemporary).

Schraufnagel, Noel. See MISCELLANEOUS
(Contemporary).

Scott, Nathan A., Jr. See MISCELLANEOUS
(Contemporary).

Senna, Carl. *Black Boy Notes*. Lincoln, Neb.:
Cliff's Notes, 1971.
   A study guide.

Sherr, Paul C. "Richard Wright: The Expatriate
Pattern." *Black Acad Rev*, 2 (Spring-Summer 1971),
81-90.
   Deals with the theme of expatriation in
Wright's works after 1947.

Siegel, Paul N. "The Conclusion of Richard Wright's
Native Son." *PMLA*, 89 (May 1974), 517-529.
   A re-interpretation of Max's courtroom speech
and his final scene with Bigger.

Simpson, Lewis P. See GENERAL--3rd Simpson entry.

Singh, Amritjit. "Misdirected Responses to Bigger
Thomas." *SBL*, 5 (Summer 1974), 5-8.
   Discusses Wright's use of Bigger Thomas in
Native Son "to carry home the message of the
book to its readers."

Singh, Raman K. "Christian Heroes and Anti-Heroes
in Richard Wright's Fiction." *NALF*, 6
(Winter 1972), 99-104, 131.
   Wright's heroes move from an acceptance of
Christianity in the earlier novels to a negation
of it in the later works.

_____. "Some Basic Ideas and Ideals in Richard
Wright's Fiction." *CLA Jour*, 13
(September 1969), 78-84.
   Bigger Thomas in *Native Son* is "an archetype
of the socially and psychologically oppressed
man."

_____. "Wright's Tragic Vision in *The Outsider*."
SBL, 1 (Autumn 1970), 23-27.
   Discusses Cross Damon as a tragic figure in
the Sophoclean manner.

_____. See MISCELLANEOUS (Contemporary--both Singh
entries).

Smith, Dwight L. See GENERAL.

Smith, Sidonie Ann. "Richard Wright's *Black Boy*:
The Creative Impulse of Rebellion." *So Lit
Jour*, 5 (Fall 1972), 123-136.

IV. Contemporary (1920-1975)

Wright's autobiography is a modern version of the slave narrative, describing the quest of the black soul for the "promised land" of a free identity.

Solotaroff, Theodore. See MISCELLANEOUS (Contemporary).

Sprandel, Katherine. *"The Long Dream."* *New Letters*, 38 (Winter 1971), 88-96.
    Deals with the theme of Wright's last novel.

Starr, Alvin. "The Concept of Fear in the Works of Stephen Crane and Richard Wright." *SBL*, 6 (Summer 1975), 6-9.
    Points out parallels in the type of fear depicted by these two writers.

Stephens, Martha. "Richard Wright's Fiction: A Reassessment." *GaR*, 25 (Winter 1971), 450-470.
    An answer to Ellison and Baldwin that "Wright could not write about real Negroes."

Tatham, Campbell. "Vision and Value in *Uncle Tom's Children*." *SBL*, 3 (Spring 1972), 14-23.
    Argues that the five stories that make up this work have the unity of a novel.

_____. See GENERAL.

Terrier, Michel. See MISCELLANEOUS (Contemporary).

Timmerman, John. "Symbolism as a Syndetic Device in Richard Wright's 'Long Black Song.'" *CLA Jour*, 14 (March 1971), 291-297.
    Sarah in Wright's story "is manipulated by external circumstances and fails to assert herself as a unique entity in confrontation with these circumstances." Her failure is that she does not develop her own version of external reality."

_____. "Trust and Mistrust: The Role of the Black Woman in Three Works by Richard Wright." *Stud in the Twentieth Century*, no. 10 (Fall 1972), 33-48.
    In "Long Black Song," "Bright and Morning Star," and *Lawd Today*, the women fail to face reality, forge their own reality, and provide possible salvation in relation to their men.

Turner, Darwin T. *"The Outsider*: Revision of an Idea." *CLA Jour*, 12 (June 1969), 310-321.
    In *The Outsider* Wright attempts to redefine the existential idea he had failed to clarify in *Native Son*.

_____. *"The Outsider*: Revision of an Idea." *SHR*, 4 (Winter 1970), 40-50.
    Reprinted from the *CLA Jour*, 12 (June 1969); the article was read by Professor Turner as part of a symposium, "Three Negro Novelists: Protest and Anti-Protest--A Symposium," at the meeting of SAMLA-SEASA in Jacksonville, Florida, November 15, 1968.

Wade, Melvin and Margaret. See GENERAL.

Walcott, Ronald. See ELLISON, RALPH (Contemporary).

Waniek, Marilyn N. See MISCELLANEOUS (Contemporary).

Watson, Edward A. "Bessie's Blues." *New Letters*, 38 (Winter 1971), 64-70.
    Deals with the character of Bessie Mears in *Native Son* and the style of her "blues."

Webb, Constance. "Richard Wright: A Bibliography." *Negro Digest*, 18 (January 1969), 86-92.
    A reprinting of the bibliography in Webb's biography of Wright.

_____. *Richard Wright: A Biography*. New York: Putnam's, 1968.
    The first thorough biographical account of Wright's life and career.

Weigel, Henrietta, et al. "Personal Impressions." *New Letters*, 38 (Winter 1971), 17-40.
    Impressions of Wright by a number of people who knew him.

Weiss, Adrian. "A Portrait of the Artist as a Black Boy." *Rocky Mt MLA Bul*, 28 (1974), 93-101.
    The imaginative experience is the important thing in the development of the artist.

Williams, John A. *The Most Native of Sons: A Biography of Richard Wright*. Garden City, N. Y.: Doubleday, 1970.
    Focuses on Wright's struggle for recognition.

Woodress, James. See GENERAL--1st Woodress entry.

Young, James O. See MISCELLANEOUS (Contemporary).

[YOUNG, STARK] Burger, Nash K. See STYRON, WILLIAM (Contemporary).

Kibler, James E., Jr. See FAULKNER, WILLIAM--2nd Kibler entry.

McAlexander, Hubert, Jr. See FAULKNER, WILLIAM.

Young, Thomas Daniel. "The Past in the Present: Another Look at *So Red the Rose*." *Notes on Miss Writers*, 1 (Spring 1968), 6-17.
    Discusses the Civil War as symbol in Young's novel, as well as in twentieth-century Southern literature.

[MISCELLANEOUS] Anon. "The Fugitive." *TLS*, April 25, 1968, p. 433.
    A brief history of *The Fugitive*.

Anon. *Manuscripts for Research*. Syracuse, N. Y. Five Associated Univ Libraries, 1969.
    Locates manuscript collections of Arna Bontemps and Erskine Caldwell at Syracuse University.

Abramson, Doris E. *Negro Playwrights in the American Theatre 1925-1959*. New York: Columbia Univ Press, 1969.
    An historical-critical examination of twenty plays by black dramatists from Garland Anderson's *Appearances* (1925) to Lorraine Hansberry's *Raisin in the Sun* (1959), with attention to Alice Childress (South Carolina), Hall Johnson (Georgia), Theodore Ward (Louisiana), and Richard Wright.

Aldridge, John W. "The American Novel at the Present Time." *RLV*, 40 (1974), 122-131.
Among others Capote and Tom Wolfe are discussed as writers of the new journalism and Barth as writer of black humor.

_____. *The Devil in the Fire: Retrospective Essays on American Literature and Culture.* New York: Harper's Magazine Press, 1972.
Reprints earlier reviews and criticism on Barth, Caldwell, Capote, Faulkner, McCullers, Katherine Anne Porter, Ransom, Styron, Tate, Warren, Welty, Wolfe, and other moderns.

Alter, Robert. "The New American Novel." *Commentary*, 60 (November 1975), 44-51.
Styron and Capote follow the Faulkner, Southern Gothic tradition, popular in the 1940's and 1950's, which has a sense of history altogether lacking in newer writers like Barth.

Anderson, Michael, and others. *Crowell's Handbook of Contemporary Drama.* New York: Thomas Y. Crowell, 1971.
A reference work including biographical and critical entries on Faulkner, Hellman, Williams and their major dramatic works.

Ayers, H. Brandt, and Thomas H. Naylor, eds. *You Can't Eat Magnolias.* New York: McGraw-Hill, 1972.
A symposium prepared by twenty-seven moderate, progressive Southerners, members of the L. Q. C. Lamar Society, addressed to the problems of the modern South partly in reply to *I'll Take My Stand*; contains three essays on culture by Reynolds Price, R. G. Holt, W. M. Alston, and William Flynt.

Bardolph, Richard. "Review of North Carolina Nonfiction, 1968-1969." *NCHR*, 47 (1970), 145-151.
Title is descriptive.

Bataille, Robert. "The Aesthetics and Ethics of Farming: The Southern Agrarian View." *Iowa State Jour of Research*, 49, no. 2, pt. 2 (1974), 189-193.
Includes views of Ransom, Tate, Davidson, Lytle, and Warren.

Beja, Morris. *Epiphany in the Modern Novel.* Seattle: Univ of Washington Press, 1971.
Discusses the presence of epiphanies, unifying moments of vision, in the works of Wolfe, Faulkner, and Styron.

Bell, Bernard W. "Contemporary Afro-American Poetry as Folk Art." *Black World*, 22 (March 1973), 16-26, 74-87.
Contemporary Afro-American poetry has its roots in Afro-American spirituals and folksongs; contains discussion of Wright, Ellison, Sonia Sanchez, J. W. Johnson, Nikki Giovanni, and Don L. Lee.

_____, ed. *Modern and Contemporary Afro-American Poetry.* Boston: Allyn and Bacon, 1971.
A number of Southern black poets are represented.

_____. "New Black Poetry: A Double-Edged Sword." *CLA Jour*, 15 (1971), 37-43.
Deals with the pull between love and hate in modern black poetry; references to Don L. Lee and Sonia Sanchez are included.

Bellamy, Joe David. *The New Fiction: Interviews with Innovative American Writers.* Urbana: Univ of Illinois Press, 1974.
Includes interviews with Barth, Tom Wolfe, and Ishmael Reed.

Bellman, Samuel I. "Hemingway, Faulkner and Wolfe...and the Common Reader." *SouR*, 4 (Summer 1968), 834-849.
An essay-review which argues that these writers' message and force as perceived by the general reader must first be taken into account before we can ask the right critical questions.

Bennett, Stephen B., and William W. Nichols. "Violence in Afro-American Fiction: An Hypothesis." *MFS*, 17 (Summer 1971), 221-228.
Finds that the kind of apocalyptic rage associated with contemporary black militants has been part of the imaginations of the best black writers, including Richard Wright and Ralph Ellison.

Bigsby, C. W. E., ed. *The Black American Writer.* 2 vols. Deland, Fla.: Everett/Edwards, 1969.
Contains general and specific essays on Southern black authors, such as Chesnutt, Wright, and Ellison.

Billingsley, R. G. "Forging New Definitions: The Burden of the Hero in Modern Afro-American Literature." *Obsidian*, 1 (Winter 1975), 5-21; *Black World*, 25 (December 1975), 38-45.
Deals with the question of why the hero of the modern Afro-American literary work is the way he is; includes discussion of Wright's *Native Son*, Himes's *If He Hollers Let Him Go*, Ellison's *Invisible Man* and "Flying Home," and Gaines's "Three Men" and *The Autobiography of Miss Jane Pittman*.

Billington, Monroe L. *The American South: A Brief History.* New York: Scribner's, 1971.
A survey-history of the South, from colonial times to the present, with attention to society, agriculture, education, literature, religion, race, politics, and economics; two chapters briefly review the antebellum, postbellum, and modern literature.

Black, Michael. "Black Literature: Three Critical Works." *GaR*, 24 (Spring 1970), 46-53.
A critical review of black literature with special attention to Edward Margolies, *Native Sons*; Robert Bone, *The Negro in America*; and David Littlejohn, *Black or White*.

Blake, Nelson M. *Novelists' America: Fiction as History, 1910-1940.* Syracuse: Syracuse Univ Press, 1969.
An historian attempts to discover historical truth in the work of eight major novelists who wrote about American life from 1910 through 1940, including Faulkner, Wolfe, and Wright.

IV. Contemporary (1920-1975)

Bliss, A., ed. *Sahara*, no. 4 (Summer 1974).
   A special "Atlanta Poets Number" with the work of twenty-one contemporary writers and a brief history of Atlanta poets.

Boitani, Piero. *Prosatori negri americani del Novecento*. Roma: Edizioni di Storia e Letteratura, 1973.
   Includes chapters on Toomer, Wright, and Ellison.

Boney, F. N. "Look Away, Look Away: A Distant View of Dixie." *GaR*, 23 (Fall 1969), 368-374.
   Stereotyped attitudes of Southern degeneracy held by other regions may motivate the South to a greater destiny of national leadership.

Bonner, John W., Jr. "Bibliography of Georgia Authors, 1967-1968." *GaR*, 22 (Winter 1968), 527-544.
   A checklist of books and pamphlets with descriptive annotation.

_____. "Bibliography of Georgia Authors, 1969." *GaR*, 24 (Spring 1970), 71-114.
   An annotated bibliography of 1969 Georgia authors.

Bontemps, Arna. *The Harlem Renaissance Remembered*. New York: Dodd, Mead, 1972.
   A collection of essays on aspects of and participants in the Harlem Renaissance, including comment on Toomer, DuBois, Johnson, and a memoir by Bontemps.

Borges, Jorge L., and Esther Zemborain de Torres. *An Introduction to American Literature*. Trans. L. C. Keating and R. O. Evans. Lexington: Univ Press of Kentucky, 1971.
   Capsule summaries on Poe, Twain, Lanier, W. S. Porter, Faulkner, Caldwell, Warren, Richard Wright, Capote, Williams, and W. H. Wright (S. S. Van Dine) are included.

Boswell, George. "The Mississippi Folklore Society." *JAF*, 82 (January-March 1969), 22.
   A brief history of the society.

Boyd, G. N. and L. A. *Religion in Contemporary Fiction: Criticism from 1945 to the Present*. San Antonio, Texas: Trinity Univ Press, 1973.
   A checklist of 1029 items, with entries on Barth, Capote, Faulkner, Caroline Gordon, McCullers, O'Connor, Percy, K. A. Porter, Styron, Welty, and Wright.

Bradbury, John M. "Absurd Insurrection: The Barth-Percy Affair." *SAQ*, 68 (Summer 1969), 319-329.
   The protagonists of the two most gifted of recent Southern writers inherit no moral or religious codes, only sensitivities.

Bradford, M. E. "The Agrarian Inheritance: An Affirmation." *Proc of the Gulf Coast Hist and Humanities Conf*, 4 (1973), 3-12.
   An address firmly asserting "that the Agrarians were on the right track."

_____. "Fire Bell in the Night: The Southern Conservative View." *Mod Age*, 17 (Winter 1973), 9-15.

An examination of *millennialism* in relation to the Southern conservative tradition.

Bradshaw, Herbert C. "Review of North Carolina Fiction, 1969-1970." *NCHR*, 48 (Spring 1971), 120-125.
   A summary of North Carolina fiction written during 1969-1970.

Brasner, William, and Dominick Consulo, eds. *Black Drama: An Anthology*. Columbus, Ohio: Charles E. Merrill, 1970.
   Includes Paul Green's revised script of his adaptation of Wright's *Native Son* (initially published here), Douglas Turner Ward's *Day of Absence* and *Happy Ending*, and Ossie Davis' *Purlie Victorious*, with a survey of Afro-American drama, 1858-1959, by Darwin T. Turner.

Breed, Paul F., and Florence M. Sniderman. *Dramatic Criticism Index: Bibliography of Commentaries on Playwrights from Ibsen to the Avant-Garde*. Detroit: Gale Research Co., 1972.
   Lists critical commentary on the dramatic work of Caldwell, Capote, Ossie Davis, Paul Green, Lillian Hellman, McCullers, Williams, Wolfe, Wright, and other Southerners.

Brooks, A. Russell. "The Motif of Dynamic Change in Black Revolutionary Poetry." *CLA Jour*, 15 (September 1971), 7-17.
   Black revolutionary poets are concerned with the change from what is to what will be; includes references to Don L. Lee, Nikki Giovanni, and Sonia Sanchez.

Brown, Calvin S. *Why Mississippi--of All Places?*
   An address at a Mississippi Writers' Conference, February 27, 1969. Long Beach, Miss.: Gulf Park College, 1969.
   Outlines cultural and historical reasons for the preeminence of Mississippi writers in modern American literature.

Bryant, Jerry H. *The Open Decision: The Contemporary American Novel and Its Background*. New York: Free Press, 1971.
   Examines the modern novel since World War II against the scientific, psychological, sociological, and philosophic currents of this century; comments on Barth, Ellison, McCullers, O'Connor, Walker Percy, and Styron.

_____. "Politics and the Black Novel." *Nation*, 213 (December 20, 1971), 660-662.
   Discusses violence in the works of black writers, including Wright, Chester Himes, and Ishmael Reed.

Bryer, Jackson R., ed. *Fifteen Modern American Authors: A Survey of Research and Criticism*. Durham, N. C.: Duke Univ Press, 1969.
   Includes essays on Faulkner and Wolfe.

_____, ed. *Sixteen Modern American Authors: A Survey of Research and Criticism*. New York: Norton, 1973.
   A new edition of *Fifteen Modern American Authors*, with essays on Faulkner and Wolfe.

Buckley, William F., Jr. *Firing Line: The Southern Imagination*. Columbia, S. C.: So Educational Communications Assn., 1972.
A pamphlet containing the transcript of an interview with Eudora Welty and Walker Percy taped in Jackson, Mississippi, on December 12, 1972, on the subject of Southern writing.

Budd, Louis, J. "The Not So Tender Trap: Some Dilemmas of Black American Poets." *Indian Jour of Am Stud*, 3, no. 1 (1973), 47-57.
Deals with the efforts of younger black poets, such as Don L. Lee and Nikki Giovanni, to write poetry completely free of white influence.

Buttita, Tony. *After the Good Gay Times*. New York: Viking Press, 1974.
Memoir by the owner of an Asheville, North Carolina, book store and editor of *Contempo*, with special attention to F. Scott Fitzgerald, whom he came to know in 1935.

Calhoun, Richard J. "Southern Voices: Past and Present." *SouR*, 4 (Spring 1968), 482-490.
An essay-review of six recent volumes of poetry by Southern writers and of one anthology representing the 1920's.

Carr, John, ed. *Kite-Flying and Other Irrational Acts: Conversations with Twelve Southern Writers*. Baton Rouge: Louisiana State Univ Press, 1972.
In-depth interviews with Doris Betts, Fred Chappell, Shelby Foote, Jesse Hill Ford, George Garrett, Larry L. King, Marion Montgomery, Willie Morris, Guy Owen, Walker Percy, Reynolds Price, and James Whitehead.

Carson, Betty F. "Richmond Renascence: The Virginia Writers' Club of the 1920's and *The Reviewer*." *Cabellian*, 2 (Spring 1970), 39-47.
Describes the activities of the club and the founding of the little magazine. Cabell was a member; Ellen Glasgow was not.

Carter, T. H. *Essays and Reviews*, ed. James Boatwright. Lexington, Va.: Shenandoah, 1968.
A collection of essays including eight on Southern letters devoted to such authors as Tate, Davidson, Faulkner, Welty, O'Connor, and Lytle.

Chapman, Abraham, ed. *New Black Voices: An Anthology of Contemporary Afro-American Literature*. New York: New American Library, 1972.
A number of Southern black writers are included.

Christadler, Martin, ed. *Amerikanische Literatur des Gegenwart*. Stuttgart: Alfred Kröner, 1973.
Includes essays on Flannery O'Connor, by André Bleikasten; John Barth, by Dieter Shulz; Truman Capote, by Hanspeter Dörfel; Ralph Ellison, by Brigitte Sheer-Schälzer; and Carson McCullers, by Klaus-Jürgen Popp.

Churchill, Allen. *The Literary Decade*. Englewood Cliffs, N. J.: Prentice-Hall, 1971.
A history of the publishing scene in mid-Manhattan in the 1920's with brief attention to Cabell, Wolfe, and Faulkner.

Clarke, John H., ed. *Harlem: Voices from the Soul of Black America*. New York: New American Library, 1970.
An anthology of stories with biographical notes; includes Southerners J. H. Clarke, J. O. Killens, and Loyle Hairston.

Cohn, Ruby. *Dialogue in American Drama*. Bloomington: Indiana Univ Press, 1971.
A study of the theatrical and artistic functions of dialogue in modern drama with a full chapter devoted to Williams and a brief discussion of plays by Wolfe.

Coindreau, Maurice. *Mémoires d'un traducteur*. Paris: Gallimard, 1974.
Includes comments about Southern literature and about conversations with Faulkner concerning Coindreau's translations of Faulkner's works.

_____. *The Time of William Faulkner: A French View of Modern American Fiction*. Columbia: Univ of South Carolina Press, 1971.
A collection of essays and prefaces, some newly translated, on Faulkner, Caldwell, Capote, Goyen, and O'Connor.

Collmer, Robert G. "The Displaced Person in the Novels of Gabriel Casaccia." *Re: A&L*, 3 (Spring 1970), 37-45.
This article about the Paraguayan novelist contains comments about why Faulkner's "A Rose for Emily" and the works of Thomas Wolfe appeal to Paraguayans.

Cook, Martha E., and Thomas Daniel Young. "Fugitive/Agrarian Materials at Vanderbilt University." *RALS*, 1 (Spring 1971), 113-120.
Title is descriptive.

Cook, Sylvia. "Gastonia: The Literary Reverberations of the Strike." *So Lit Jour*, 7 (Fall 1974), 49-66.
A discussion of the artistic use of the 1929 Gastonia, North Carolina, strike in the works of six novelists: Mary Heaton Vorse, Fielding Burke, Grace Lumpkin, Myra Page, Sherwood Anderson, and William Rollins.

Cooke, Michael G. "The Descent into the Underworld and Modern Black Fiction." *Iowa Rev*, 5 (1974), 72-90.
Includes commentary on Ellison and Toomer.

_____. *Modern Black Novelists*. Twentieth Century Views Series. Englewood Cliffs, N. J.: Prentice-Hall, 1971.
Reprints essays on American, African, and West Indian novelists, with two on Ellison and one on Richard Wright.

Core, George. "Ransom, Brooks, and the Idiom of Criticism." *So Lit Jour*, 5 (Fall 1972), 177-186.
The reviewer finds the two collections under his scrutiny (*Beating the Bushes: Selected Essays, 1941-1970*, by John Crowe Ransom, and

A Shaping Joy: Studies in the Writer's Craft, by Cleanth Brooks) almost antithetical, with each writer going too far in a given direction.

_____, ed. *Southern Fiction Today: Renascence and Beyond.* Athens: Univ of Georgia Press, 1969.
    A symposium containing three original essays on the Southern Renascence by Walter Sullivan, C. Hugh Holman, and Louis D. Rubin, Jr., to which the editor has added the transcript of a discussion between the critics and a critical afterword.

Couch, William, Jr., ed. *New Black Playwrights.* New York: Avon Books, 1970.
    Contains six plays by five authors, including Louisianians Douglas T. Ward and William W. Mackey, with an introduction by the editor.

Coursen, Herbert R., Jr., ed. *As Up They Grew: Autobiographical Essays.* Glenview, Ill.: Scott, Foresman, 1970.
    An anthology of autobiographical essays, including selections by Agee, W. A. Percy, Anne Moody, Lillian Smith, Capote, Jesse Stuart, and Willie Morris.

Cowan, Louise. *The Southern Critics.* Irving, Texas: Univ of Dallas Press, 1972.
    An introduction to the Fugitive-Agrarian writers who "made of criticism a moral and spiritual exercise"--Ransom, Tate, and Davidson--and their famous pupils--Warren, Brooks, and Lytle.

Cowley, Malcolm. *A Second Flowering: Works and Days of the Lost Generation.* New York: Viking Press, 1973.
    Reprints original and fuller texts of influential essays on Faulkner and Wolfe and mentions numerous other Southerners; the book is dedicated to Allen Tate.

_____. "What Books Survive from the 1930's?" *Jour Am Stud,* 7 (December 1973), 293-300.
    Aside from the obvious names of Faulkner, Mitchell, and Pearl Buck, Tate, K. A. Porter, Warren, McCullers, Wright, and Agee produced works that are significant.

Crunden, Robert M. *From Self to Society, 1919-1941.* Transitions in American Thought Series. Englewood Cliffs, N. J.: Prentice-Hall, 1972.
    Contains discussion of Aiken, Faulkner, and Wright.

Curnow, Wystan. "Romanticism and Modern American Criticism." *Stud in Romanticism,* 12 (Fall 1973), 777-799.
    Includes discussion of Brooks, Tate, Ransom, and, to a lesser extent, Warren.

Davenport, F. Garvin, Jr. *The Myth of Southern History: Historical Consciousness in Twentieth-Century Southern Literature.* Nashville: Vanderbilt Univ Press, 1970.
    Traces the patterns of thought which have led Southerners to consider their place in the nation and world as unique, as reflected in Southern writing; includes chapters on Thomas Dixon, the Agrarians, Faulkner, Warren, and Martin Luther King.

Day, Martin S. *History of American Literature: From 1910 to the Present.* Garden City, N. Y.: Doubleday, 1971.
    The second volume of a study guide with capsule summaries of all major and many minor Southern authors.

De Bellis, Jack. "The Southern Universe and the Counter-Renaissance." *SouR,* 4 (Spring 1968), 471-481.
    An essay-review of work by John Donald Wade and Andrew Lytle, and of two anthologies of the 1960's, one of poetry, one of fiction.

Dekle, Bernard. *Profiles of Modern American Authors.* Rutland, Vermont: Charles E. Tuttle, 1969.
    Brief biographical introductions for students to twenty-nine American writers, including Wolfe, Faulkner, Caldwell, and Tennessee Williams.

Dent, Thomas C., Richard Schechner, and Gilbert Moses, eds. *The Free Southern Theater by the Free Southern Theater: A Documentary of the South's Radical Black Theater, with Journals, Letters, Poetry, Essays and a Play Written by Those Who Built It.* Indianapolis: Bobbs-Merrill, 1969.
    A collection of essays, poetry, letters, and interviews, 1965-67, concerning the founding of the Free Southern Theater and its effectiveness as a voice for the Southern black experience.

Detweiler, Robert. "The Moment of Death in Modern Fiction." *ConL,* 13 (Summer 1972), 269-294.
    Deals with the importance of analysis of death scenes in stories by seven authors, including K. A. Porter, Faulkner, and O'Connor.

Dillard, R. H. W., George Garrett, and John Rees Moore, eds. *The Sounder Few: Essays from the Hollins Critic.* Athens: Univ of Georgia Press, 1971.
    Reprints essays on seventeen authors including O'Connor, Barth, Styron; contributors include Dillard, Garrett, Moore, Julia Randall, Louis D. Rubin, Jr., W. J. Smith, and Walter Sullivan.

Drake, Robert. "The Pieties of the Fiction Writer: The Writer and His Past." *CEA Critic,* 32 (October 1969), 3-4.
    Faulkner is used as "an example of a writer less concerned--or enmeshed--in a personal past than in the past of a region." The article also contains references to Katherine Anne Porter, Allen Tate, and other Southern writers.

_____, ed. *The Writer and His Tradition: Proceedings of the 1968 Southern Literary Festival.* Knoxville: Univ of Tennessee Department of English, 1969.
    Summary of an address by Cleanth Brooks and a transcript of a panel discussion between Brooks, James Dickey, Reynolds Price, and Drake on "The Writer and His Tradition."

Duke, Maurice. "*The Reviewer:* A Bibliographical Guide to a Little Magazine." *RALS,* 1 (Spring 1971), 58-103.
    Contains the history, complete annotated contents, and an index to *The Reviewer.*

_____. "Virginiana at the Cabell Library."
Cabellian, 2 (Spring 1970), 59.
Describes recent acquisitions.

Durham, Frank. "The First Nine Steck-Vaughn Pamphlets." *So Lit Jour*, 3 (Spring 1971), 109-119.
An essay-review which praises six of the
first nine pamphlets on Southern writers for
successfully giving overviews of their subjects
and fulfilling the aims of the series.

_____. "The Reputed Demises of Uncle Tom; or, The
Treatment of the Negro in Fiction by White
Southern Authors in the 1920's." *So Lit Jour*,
2 (Spring 1970), 26-50.
In examining *Birthright*, by T. S. Stribling,
White and Black, by H. A. Shands, *Porgy*, by
DuBose Heyward, and *Scarlet Sister Mary*, by
Julia Peterkin, Durham gives a "bird's-eye
view" of the fictional treatment of the Negro
by white Southerners in the 1920's, a treatment
in which new stereotypes replaced the older
ones.

_____. "The Southern Literary Tradition: Shadow
or Substance." *SAQ*, 67 (Summer 1968), 455-468.
The tension between hatred and love of the
South as expressed by Quentin in Faulkner's
Absalom, Absalom! has inspired the modern
writers of the South to create a body of
writing that is world literature.

_____. Untitled. *SHR*, 4 (Summer 1970), 279-280.
An essay-review of *Southern Fiction Today:
Renascence and Beyond* (1969), edited by George
Core.

Eddins, Dwight. "Wallace Stevens: America the
Primordial." *MLQ*, 32 (March 1971), 73-88.
A "Southern" portion to this article opens
with "The South, like the North, is a fairly
complex symbol in Stevens' work."

Ellison, Ralph, William Styron, Robert Penn Warren,
and C. Vann Woodward. "The Uses of History in
Fiction." *So Lit Jour*, 1 (Spring 1969), 57-90.
A transcription of a panel discussion at the
thirty-fourth annual meeting of the Southern
Historical Association in New Orleans, November
6, 1968, on writers' use of history in their
fiction, with emphasis on Styron's *The Confessions of Nat Turner*.

Emerson, O. B., ed. *Alabama Prize Stories--1970*.
Huntsville, Ala.: Strode Publishers, 1970.
An anthology of the twenty-nine best sub-
missions to a short-story contest for
Alabamians; the editor's introduction comments
on the themes and techniques employed in the
stories, and biographical notes are provided
on the contributors.

_____. "Cultural Nationalism in Afro-American
Literature," in *The Cry of Home: Cultural
Nationalism and the Modern Writer*, ed.
H. Ernest Lewald. Knoxville: Univ of
Tennessee Press, 1972.
Includes discussion of Wright, Ellison, and
Ishmael Reed.

Ensor, Allison. "'Tennessee' in Wallace Stevens'
'Anecdote of the Jar.'" *SHR*, 7 (Summer 1973),
315-321.
Stevens' choice of Tennessee was not a random
one; he "had visited Tennessee at least three
times prior to the writing of the poem."

Epstein, Seymour. "Politics and the Novelist."
Denver Quart, 4 (Winter 1970), 1-18.
Faulkner, Wright, and Styron are among those
writers whose works reveal a division between
politics and art.

Fain, John T. "Segments of Southern Renaissance."
SAB, 36 (May 1971), 23-31.
An essay-review of Andrew Lytle's *The Hero
with the Private Parts* and of *Selected Essays
and Other Writings of John Donald Wade*, edited
by Donald Davidson.

Fairman, Marion A. *Biblical Patterns in Modern
Literature*. Cleveland, Ohio: Dillon/Liederbach,
1972.
Examines the sources of Biblical patterns in
twentieth-century writing, with brief mentions
of Faulkner and Warren.

Farrison, W. Edward. "Much Ado about Negro Fiction:
A Review Essay." *CLA Jour*, 19 (September 1975),
90-100.
The book reviewed is Roger Rosenblatt's
Black Fiction.

Feibleman, James K. *The Way of Man: An Autobiog-
raphy*. New York: Horizon Press, 1969.
Includes a chapter on literary life in New
Orleans between the wars with memoirs of
Faulkner, W. A. Percy, and Roark Bradford.

Fenderson, Lewis H. "The New Breed of Black Writers
and Their Jaundiced View of Tradition." *CLA
Jour*, 15 (September 1971), 18-24.
Deals with a group of black writers who have
been accused of reverse-racism, including
Ernest J. Gaines.

Fleischmann, W. B., ed. *Encyclopedia of World
Literature in the 20th Century*. Vol. 1, A-F;
vol. 2, G-N; vol. 3 forthcoming. New York:
Frederick Ungar, 1967, 1969.
Contains biographical and bibliographical
entries on internationally known authors,
including many Southerners.

French, Warren, ed. *The Fifties: Fiction, Poetry,
Drama*. Deland, Fla.: Everett/Edwards, 1970.
Includes original essays on Faulkner by Mark
Leaf, Elizabeth Spencer by David Pugh, Flannery
O'Connor by Kenneth Frieling, James Agee by Gene
Ruoff, and Tennessee Williams by Jordan Miller;
contains a bibliography.

_____, ed. *The Forties: Fiction, Poetry, Drama*.
Deland, Fla.: Everett/Edwards, 1969.
Includes original essays on McCullers by
A. S. Knowles, Welty by R. J. Griffin, Warren
by J. H. Justus, Williams by C. W. E. Bigsby,
and Capote by G. W. Ruoff.

_____, ed. *The Thirties: Fiction, Poetry, Drama*.
Deland, Fla.: Everett/Edwards, 1967.

IV. CONTEMPORARY (1920-1975)

Includes original essays on Wolfe by Richard Walser, Faulkner by Warren French, Wright by Clifford Hand, and Southern poetry by Guy Owen.

_____, ed. *The Twenties: Fiction, Poetry, Drama.* Deland, Fla.: Everett/Edwards, 1975.
Thirty original essays, with subjects including Cabell, Faulkner, and Toomer.

Gado, Frank., ed. *First Person: Conversations on Writers & Writing.* Schenectady, N. Y.: Union College Press, 1973.
Six interviews, including ones with Warren and Barth.

Gaillard, Dawson. "Perspective: 'Then what...'?" *New Orleans Rev*, 4, no. 3 (1974), 276-282.
Review of David Madden's *The Shadow Knows*, Alice Walker's *In Love and Trouble*, and Doris Betts's *Beast of the Southern Wild and Other Stories.*

Gayle, Addison. "The Black Aesthetic: Defender." *Black World*, 24 (December 1974), 31-43.
Makes the charge that *I'll Take My Stand* was a "racist, fascist document bearing great similarities to *Mein Kampf.*"

_____. "The Black Aesthetic 10 Years Later." *Black World*, 23 (September 1974), 20-29.
Includes general comments on the relevance of Southern experience to modern black writers.

_____, ed. "The Harlem Renaissance: Towards a Black Aesthetic." *Midcontinent Am Stud Jour*, 11 (Fall 1970), 78-87.
Assuming that black men are culturally different from white, the author argues that critics should have provided, but failed to provide, the writers of the Harlem Renaissance with an aesthetic adequate for the creation of a black literature. James Weldon Johnson and Ralph Ellison are briefly discussed.

Geduld, Harry M. *Authors on Film.* Bloomington: Indiana Univ Press, 1972.
Reprints comments on films and film-making by thirty-five writers, including Capote, Faulkner, and Mencken.

Gibson, Donald B., ed. *Five Black Writers: Essays on Wright, Ellison, Baldwin, Hughes, and LeRoi Jones.* New York: New York Univ Press, 1970.
Reprinted essays, several on each writer.

_____, ed. *Modern Black Poets.* Twentieth Century Views. Englewood Cliffs, N. J.: Prentice-Hall, 1973.
Reprinted and original essays which comment on Toomer, Hayden, Lee, Sanchez, Giovanni, and other Southern poets.

Gindin, James. *Harvest of a Quiet Eye: The Novel of Compassion.* Bloomington: Indiana Univ Press, 1971.
In the final chapter of this study of "the tradition of compassion" in modern British and American fiction, brief attention is paid to Barth, Capote, Faulkner, and Styron.

Ginsberg, Elaine. "The Female Initiation Theme in American Fiction." *Stud in Am F*, 3 (Spring 1975), 27-37.
Includes discussion of Faulkner, Welty, and McCullers.

Glicksberg, Charles I. *The Sexual Revolution in Modern American Literature.* The Hague: Martinus Nijhoff (New York: Humanities Press), 1971.
A study of sexual themes and motifs in contemporary writings with discussions of Barth, Faulkner, K. A. Porter, and Styron, with references to others.

Godfrey, J. L. "Review of North Carolina Nonfiction, 1967-1968." *NCHR*, 46 (Spring 1969), 106-112.
A summary of North Carolina writings in nonfiction from 1967 to 1968.

Goede, William. "On Lower Frequencies: The Buried Men in Wright and Ellison." *MFS*, 15 (Winter 1969-70), 483-501.
In stressing the differences between the two authors, Goede argues that Ellison's *Invisible Man* "uses and transcends its 'source,' 'The Man Who Lived Underground'" because, since Wright does not make use of the "whole history of the Negro," his hero "fails to cross over to life"; Ellison, on the other hand, "projects the symbolic history and prophecy of the human race: a myth of man emerging from systems to assert his manhood."

Goldstein, Malcolm. *The Political Stage: American Drama and Theater of the Great Depression.* New York: Oxford Univ Press, 1974.
Contains discussion of Caldwell, Paul Green, Hellman, Heyward, Williams, and Wright.

Goodman, Paul, and Frank O. Gatell. *America in the Twenties.* New York: Holt, Rinehart and Winston, 1972.
A brief survey-history of the period with mention of the Scopes trial and racism in the South.

Graham, John, and George Garrett, eds. *The Writer's Voice: Conversations with Contemporary Writers.* New York: William Morrow, 1973.
Includes interviews with Fred Chappell, Shelby Foote, James Seay, James Whitehead, Sylvia Wilkinson, Ralph Ellison, and James Dickey.

Gross, Theodore L. "Black Culture in the Seventies." *Miss Quart*, 28 (Spring 1975), 191-203.
A review-essay on seven recent works concerning black artists.

_____. "The Idealism of Negro Literature in America." *Phylon*, 30 (Spring 1969), 5-10.
Wright and Ellison are among writers discussed as having been affected by nineteenth-century transcendentalism.

Hagopian, John V. "Mau-Mauing the Literary Establishment." *Stud in the Novel*, 3 (Summer 1971), 135-147.
Deals with militancy in modern black writing and with Tom Wolfe's reflection of black

militancy in *Radical Chic and Mau-Mauing the Flak Catchers*.

Hart, Robert C. "Black-White Literary Relations in the Harlem Renaissance." *AL*, 44 (January 1973), 612-628.
    Includes references to J. W. Johnson, Zora Neale Hurston, and Toomer.

Haslam, Gerald W., ed. *Forgotten Pages of American Literature*. Boston: Houghton Mifflin, 1970.
    An anthology of ethnic literature which includes selections from and critical headnotes on James Weldon Johnson and Richard Wright.

_____. "Two Traditions in Afro-American Literature." *Research Stud*, 37 (September 1969), 183-193.
    Deals with oral and written tradition in the works of various black writers, including Wright and Ellison.

Hassan, Ihab. "American Literature," in *World Literature Since 1945*, ed. Ivar Ivask and Gero von Wilpert. New York: Frederick Ungar, 1973, pp. 1-64.
    A survey of post-war American writing with commentary on Capote, Styron, Barth, Williams, and brief mentions of other Southerners.

_____. *Contemporary American Literature 1945-1972: An Introduction*. New York: Frederick Ungar, 1973.
    A broad introductory survey with special comment on Capote, Styron, Barth, Welty, McCullers, O'Connor, Williams, and numerous less significant Southerners.

Hayashi, Tetsumaro, ed. *Steinbeck's Literary Dimension: A Guide to Comparative Studies*. Metuchen, N. J.: Scarecrow Press, 1973.
    Includes comparative essays on Steinbeck and Faulkner and on Steinbeck and Warren.

Hays, Peter L. *The Limping Hero: Grotesques in Literature*. New York: New York Univ Press, 1971.
    Includes discussion of Faulkner, Williams, Styron, and O'Connor.

Heffernan, T. F. "Tactile Politics." *Cweal*, 96 (August 11, 1972), 431-433.
    This assessment of the Agrarian movement concludes that as a historical lesson it is still relevant.

Heiney, D., and L. H. Downs. *Contemporary Literature of the Western World*. 4 vols. Woodbury, N. Y.: Barron's Educational Series, 1974.
    Volumes 3 and 4 include study notes on many Southern authors.

Hemphill, Paul. *The Good Old Boys*. Garden City, N. Y.: Doubleday, 1974.
    Fifteen personal essays recounting a young Southerner's rediscovery of the sights, sounds, and moods of the contemporary South.

Hicks, Granville. *Literary Horizons: A Quarter Century of American Fiction*. New York: New York Univ Press, 1970.

Reprints reviews of books by fifteen modern authors, with new prefatory notes; includes comments on O'Connor, Price, and Barth.

Hiers, John T. "The Graveyard Epiphany in Modern Southern Fiction: Transcendence of Selfhood." *SHR*, 9 (Fall 1975), 389-403.
    As works by Agee, O'Connor, Wolfe, Welty, and Styron illustrate, "the tomb as *memento mori* may also become a window on eternity."

Hilfer, Anthony C. *The Revolt from the Village: 1915-1930*. Chapel Hill: Univ of North Carolina Press, 1969.
    A literary history and critical analysis of the organized attack on American provincialism, small-town mores, and the myth of the village as a rural paradise exempt from urban corruption, by a group of realistic writers from the Mid-West and South, including Twain, Stribling, and Wolfe.

Hoffman, Peggy. "Review of North Carolina Fiction, 1970-71." *NCHR*, 49 (Spring 1972), 121-126.
    Title is descriptive.

Holder, Elizabeth J. "Review of North Carolina Fiction, 1967-1968." *NCHR*, 46 (Spring 1969), 113-121.
    Title is descriptive.

Howard, Richard, ed. *Preferences*. New York: Viking Press, 1974.
    American poets select favorite poems from their own and others' work; includes Ammons, Dickey, Tate, and Warren.

Howell, Elmo. "The Greenville Writers and the Mississippi Country People." *La Stud*, 8 (Winter 1969), 348-360.
    Except for Faulkner, the chief writers of Mississippi have been Deltians--William Alexander Percy, David Cohn, Hodding Carter, Shelby Foote.

Hoyle, Bernadette W. "Review of North Carolina Nonfiction, 1970-1971." *NCHR*, 49 (1972), 146-151.
    Title is descriptive.

Huggins, Nathan. *Harlem Renaissance*. New York: Oxford Univ Press, 1971.
    An account of all phases of the Renaissance, with attention to such writers as Zora Neale Hurston, J. W. Johnson and Jean Toomer.

Hughes, Richard E. *The Lively Image: 4 Myths in Literature*. Cambridge, Mass.: Winthrop Publishers, 1975.
    A critical anthology designed to examine the Narcissus, Dionysus, Orpheus, and Christ myths, with commentary on the fiction of James Dickey and Flannery O'Connor.

Inge, M. Thomas. "Contemporary American Literature in Spain." *Tenn Stud in Lit*, 16 (1971), 155-167.
    Includes consideration of Faulkner, Wolfe, Caldwell, Williams, Capote, O'Connor, McCullers, Styron, and Ellison.

_____. "Recent Southern Literary Criticism: A Review Essay." *Appal Jour*, 2 (Autumn 1974), 46-61.
A general survey of recent criticism on Southern literature, which praises the lack of bias on the part of the critics.

_____. "Richmond's Great Debate: Agrarians Sought a Simpler Life." Richmond *Times-Dispatch*, December 6, 1970, p. F-1.
An account of the debate held in Richmond between John Crowe Ransom and Stringfellow Barr on the topic "Shall the South Go Industrial?" in November 1930.

Janeway, Elizabeth, ed. *The Writer's World.* New York: McGraw-Hill, 1969.
Contains the transcript of a panel discussion on "Violence in Literature" between Robert Penn Warren, William Styron, Robert Coles, and Theodore Solotaroff.

Janssens, G. A. *The American Literary Review: A Critical History, 1920-1950.* The Hague: Mouton, 1968.
A detailed literary history of the origins, editorial practices, and contents of the major literary reviews, including *The Southern Review*, *The Kenyon Review*, and *The Sewanee Review*, with numerous references to other Southern journals and to Southern authors.

Jarrell, Randall. *The Third Book of Criticism.* New York: Farrar, Straus, and Giroux, 1969.
Reprints "Fifty Years of American Poetry," which discusses the work of Ransom and Warren.

Jeffers, Lance. "Afro-American Literature: The Conscience of Man." *Black Schol*, 2 (January 1971), 47-53.
Includes discussion of Wright and J. W. Johnson.

Johnson, Michael L. *The New Journalism: The Underground Press, the Artists of Nonfiction and Changes in the Established Media.* Lawrence: Univ of Kansas Press, 1971.
A study of recent developments in journalism, non-fiction writing, and the underground press, with a chapter devoted to Capote and Tom Wolfe.

Kattan, Naïm. "L'éclatement du mythe." *Quinzaine Littéraire*, no. 126 (October 1-15, 1971), 12.
References to Ellison, Capote, and Barth are included in this discussion of the types of novels which have been successful in recent decades.

Kazin, Alfred. *Bright Book of Life: American Novelists & Storytellers from Hemingway to Mailer.* Boston: Atlantic Monthly/Little, Brown, 1973.
Collected essays and lectures, with commentary on Capote, Ellison, Faulkner, O'Connor, Walker Percy, K. A. Porter, Styron, and Warren, and mentions of many other Southern writers.

Kent, George. "Notes on the 1974 Black Literary Scene." *Phylon*, 36 (June 1975), 182-203.
A review-essay of the works of several authors, including Maya Angelou, Ishmael Reed, and Sonia Sanchez.

Keyssar-Franke, Helene. "Afro-American Drama and Its Criticism 1960-1972: An Annotated Check List with Appendices." *BNYPL*, 78 (Spring 1975), 276-346.
Title is descriptive.

King, Woodie, ed. *Black Short Story Anthology.* New York: Columbia Univ Press, 1972.
An anthology with biographical notes; includes writing by Killens, Giovanni, Alice Walker, Bennett, Fields, Gaines, and Ellison.

_____, ed. *Black Spirits: A Festival of New Black Poets in America.* New York: Vintage Books, 1972.
An anthology including poetry by Southerners Giovanni, Mae Jackson, Don Lee, Major Neal, "A Pfister," and Sanchez.

_____, and Ron Milner, eds. *Black Drama Anthology.* New York: Columbia Univ Press, 1972.
A collection of twenty-three contemporary plays by and about blacks including Elder and Mackey.

Krieger, Murray. *The Classic Vision: The Retreat from Extremity in Modern Literature.* Baltimore: Johns Hopkins Univ Press, 1971.
Includes discussion of Faulkner's *Light in August* and Warren's *All the King's Men*.

Kristensen, Sven M., ed. *Fremmede digtere i det 20 århundrede.* Vols. II and III. Copenhagen: G. E. C., 1968.
Contains essays on Faulkner and Wolfe.

Kuehl, John, and Jackson R. Bryer, eds. *Dear Scott/ Dear Max: The Fitzgerald-Perkins Correspondence.* New York: Scribner's, 1971.
The letters contain incidental commentary on John Peale Bishop, Caldwell, Rawlings, and Wolfe.

Kwiat, Joseph J., and Gerhard Weiss. "Responses of German Men of Letters to American Literature, 1945-1955." *Am-Austriaca*, 2 (1970), 30-44.
Wolfe and Faulkner are included among American writers considered important in post-war Germany.

Landess, Thomas H. "The Present Course of Southern Fiction: 'Every negro' and Other Alternatives." *ArlQ*, 1 (Winter 1967-68), 61-85.
Deals with the post-Southern Renaissance writer and includes discussion of works by Jesse Hill Ford, Marion Montgomery, and Edwin Godsey.

Landor, Mikhail. "Die Schule Sherwood Andersons." Trans. into German from the Russian of the original article (*Voprosy Literatury*, 13, no. 12 [1969]). *K&L*, 18 (1970), 841-855, 961-975.
Includes discussion of Anderson's influence on Faulkner and Wolfe.

LaPolla, Franco. *Struttura e mito nella narrativa americana del' 900.* Padova-Venezia: Marsilio, 1974.
Deals with adolescents in the works of a number of contemporary Southern writers.

Lasater, Alice E. "The Breakdown in Communication in the Twentieth-Century Novel." *So Quart*, 12 (October 1973), 1-14.

Discusses the relationship between the theme of alienation and technique. Includes discussion of Faulkner's *Absalom, Absalom!*, Ellison's *Invisible Man*, and a brief mention of McCullers' *The Heart Is a Lonely Hunter*.

Lawson, Lewis A. "Kierkegaard and the Modern American Novel," in *Essays in Memory of Christine Burleson*... Johnson City, Tenn.: Research Advisory Council, East Tennessee State Univ, 1969.
  Includes discussion of Styron, McCullers, and Walker Percy.

LeClair, Thomas. "Death and Black Humor." *Critique*, 17, no. 1 (1975), 5-40.
  Barth's *The Floating Opera* and Percy's *The Last Gentleman* are discussed as examples of "the consciousness of death as a source of motivation" in black humor, and Faulkner, Wolfe, and McCullers are briefly mentioned as "antecedents" in this concern with the consciousness rather than the event of death.

Lehan, Richard. *A Dangerous Crossing: French Literary Existentialism and the Modern American Novel*. Carbondale: Southern Illinois Univ Press, 1973.
  Includes discussion of Faulkner, Wright, Walker Percy, Ellison, and Barth.

Levin, Harry. "Literature and Cultural Identity." *CLS*, 10 (June 1973), 139-156.
  Includes comments on Faulkner's *A Fable* and on the Agrarians.

Liebman, Arthur. "Patterns and Themes in Afro-American Literature." *Eng Record*, 20, no. 3 (1970), 2-12.
  Wright, Ellison, and Toomer are among black writers used as examples in this discussion.

Lindberg-Seyersted, Brita. "American Fiction Since 1950." *Edda*, no. 4 (1971), 193-203.
  Southern writing is among the "schools" of writing discussed.

Littlejohn, David. *Interruptions*. New York: Grossman Publishers, 1970.
  Reprints reviews of Cleanth Brooks on Faulkner and Andrew Turnbull on Wolfe.

Ludington, Charles T., Jr. "Introduction to 'Four Authors View the South: A Symposium.'" *SHR*, 6 (Winter 1972), 1-4.
  Using literature to illumine culture, we can look at views of the South in works of Owen Wister, Jean Toomer, Karl Shapiro, and Margaret Mitchell, and "gain some sense of what its importance to the American mind was and still is."

Ludington, Townsend, ed. *The Fourteenth Chronicle: Letters and Diaries of John Dos Passos*. Boston: Gambit, 1973.
  Includes memoirs on and references to Caldwell, Capote, Faulkner, and Zelda Fitzgerald.

Lutwack, Leonard. *Heroic Fiction: The Epic Tradition and American Novels of the Twentieth Century*. Carbondale: Southern Illinois Univ Press, 1970.

Includes discussion of Ellison's *Invisible Man* and Barth's *The Sot-Weed Factor*.

Lytle, Andrew, ed. *The Best Fiction from the Sewanee Review*. New York: Delacorte, 1971.
  Includes works by Faulkner, Caroline Gordon, O'Connor, Peter Taylor, Warren, and Welty.

Madden, David, ed. *American Dreams, American Nightmares*. Carbondale: Southern Illinois Univ Press, 1970.
  Includes original essays on Faulkner's "The Bear" by C. Hugh Holman and on Ellison's *Invisible Man* by Allen Guttmann, with brief mention of other Southerners in general essays.

_____, ed. *Rediscoveries*. New York: Crown, 1971.
  Reevaluations of favorite novels; authors covered include Andrew Lytle, Harriette Arnow, Caroline Gordon, and William Goyen; contributors include Robert Penn Warren, Hollis Summers, Jesse Hill Ford, George Garrett, Brainard Cheney, Walker Percy, and Madden.

Magill, Frank N., ed. *The Contemporary Literary Scene 1973*. Englewood Cliffs, N. J.: Salem Press, 1974.
  Includes essays on Jesse Hill Ford, James Agee, Conrad Aiken, Arna Bontemps, and cultural activities in the South.

Magny, Claude-Edmonde. *The Age of the American Novel*. New York: Frederick Ungar, 1972.
  A translation from the French of a 1948 study of relations between American cinematographic and novelistic techniques, with a chapter on Faulkner and brief commentary on Caldwell, McCullers, K. A. Porter, and Wolfe.

Malkoff, Karl. *Crowell's Handbook of Contemporary American Poetry*. New York: Thomas Y. Crowell, 1973.
  A critical handbook of poetry since 1940, with entries on Ammons, Dickey, Giovanni, Jarrell, Don Lee, Sanchez, Margaret Walker, and the New Criticism.

Maloney, Stephen R. "Not for the 'Smart-Set in Omaha': The *Georgia Review* and Southern Literature." *New Orleans Rev*, 4 (1974), 197-202.
  An overview of the journal, which is praised for remaining constant to the character established for it by its founder, John Donald Wade.

Mangione, Jerre. *The Dream and the Deal: The Federal Writers Project, 1935-1943*. Boston: Little, Brown, 1972.
  Aiken, Wright, Ellison, and Bontemps were among those involved in the project.

Manucci, Loretta V. *I negri americana dalla Depressione al dopoguerra: Esperienzi sociali e documenti letterari*. Milano: Feltrinelli, 1974.
  The last chapter deals with black writers of the 1940's, including Wright, Himes, and Ellison.

Margolies, Edward. "The Image of the Primitive in Black Letters." *Midcontinent Am Stud Jour*, 11 (Fall 1970), 67-77.

Discusses the nature and function of the image of the primitive, and the persistence of the stereotype in the work of numerous contemporary authors, including Ellison, Faulkner, Toomer, Wright, and others.

_____. *Native Sons: A Critical Study of Twentieth-Century Negro American Authors*. Philadelphia: J. B. Lippincott, 1968.
Among writers considered are Chesnutt, Ellison, James Weldon Johnson, Toomer, and Wright.

Martin, Jay. *Nathanael West: The Art of His Life*. New York: Farrar, Straus, and Giroux, 1970.
Contains references to West's relations with several Southern authors, including Cabell, Caldwell, and Faulkner.

May, John R., S. J. "Images of Apocalypse in the Black Novel." *Renascence*, 23 (Autumn 1970), 31-45.
The apocalyptic tradition is discussed as having had a profound influence on the best of recent black literature, including Wright and Ellison.

McCormick, John. *The Middle Distance: A Comparative Literary History of American Imaginative Literature: 1919-1932*. New York: Free Press, 1971.
A critical history of literature written from 1919-1932 with emphasis on relations between U. S. and European writers; comments on Faulkner in full, with brief mention of other Southerners.

McDowell, Robert E. "Mothers and Sons: A View of Black Literature from South Africa, the West Indies, and America." *PrS*, 44 (Winter 1969-70), 356-368.
Discusses several writers and works, including *The Autobiography of an Ex-Coloured Man* by James Weldon Johnson.

_____, and George Fortenberry. "A Checklist of Books and Essays About American Negro Novelists." *Studies in the Novel*, 3 (Summer 1971), 219-236.
Includes checklists for Chesnutt, Ellison, Johnson, Toomer, and Wright.

Mellard, James M. "Solipsism, Symbolism, and Demonism: The Lyrical Mode in Fiction." *SHR*, 7 (Winter 1973), 37-52.
Aiken's "Silent Snow, Secret Snow" and Toomer's "Blood-Burning Moon" are discussed as differing examples of the lyrical mode.

Mirer, Martin, ed. *Modern Black Stories*. Woodbury, N. Y.: Barron's Educational Series, 1971.
An anthology with study aids and biographical notes, including works by Bennett, Yerby, Ellison, Poston, Bontemps, and Wright.

Montesi, Albert J. "Huey Long and *The Southern Review*." *Jour of Mod Lit*, 3 (February 1973), 63-74.
Long's relationship with the magazine was indirect (it was not a "kept" journal); it was able to publish works by many of the writers of the Southern Renaissance, and important works by Brooks and Warren came from their experience in Louisiana.

Morison, W. J. "Bryan and Darrow at Dayton: Issues or Personalities." *MVC Bul*, no. 5 (Fall 1972), 61-76.
A reconsideration of the Scopes case.

Murray, Albert. "Literary Implications of the Blues: The Hero as Improviser." *Quadrant*, 16 (November/December 1972), 34-38.
Title is explanatory.

Murray, Edward. *The Cinematic Imagination: Writers and the Motion Picture*. New York: Frederick Ungar, 1972.
Examines the impact of cinema on modern fiction and the problems of translating fiction into film, with chapters on Tennessee Williams, Faulkner, Wolfe, and Warren.

Neal, Larry. "Conquest of the South." *Drama Review*, 14 (1970), 169-174.
This essay-review of *The Free Southern Theater*, edited by Thomas C. Dent, Gil Moses, and Richard Schechner, praises the report on efforts to develop a socially committed black theater; some plays performed were *Purlie Victorious* and *Waiting for Godot*.

Nevius, Blake. *The American Novel: Sinclair Lewis to the Present*. Goldentree Bibliographies in Language and Literature. New York: Appleton-Century-Crofts, 1970.
A bibliographic guide to selected scholarship and criticism, with checklists on Barth, Cabell, Caldwell, Capote, Ellison, Faulkner, McCullers, O'Connor, K. A. Porter, Elizabeth Madox Roberts, Styron, Warren, Welty, Wolfe, and Wright.

"1968 Bibliography of Mississippi Writers." *Notes on Miss Writers*, 2 (Winter 1970), 115-125.
Contains listings for several Mississippi writers.

Oates, Joyce Carol, ed. *Scenes From American Life: Contemporary Short Fiction*. New York: Random House, 1973.
An anthology including stories by Ford, Taylor, Welty, O'Connor, Madden, and Barth.

O'Brien, John. "'Becoming' Heroes in Black Fiction: Sex, Iconoclasm, and the Immanence of Salvation." *SBL*, 2 (Autumn 1971), 1-5.
Heroes in works of Toomer, Wright, and Ellison, among others, undergo the kind of transformation that Cleaver describes in "On Becoming."

_____, ed. *Interviews with Black Writers*. New York: Liveright, 1973.
Among others, Bontemps, Ellison, Ernest J. Gaines, and Alice Walker are interviewed.

O'Neal, John. "Motion in the Ocean: Some Political Dimensions of the Free Southern Theatre." *Drama Review*, 12 (Summer 1968), 70-77.
Describes the efforts to bring drama to the black community in the South.

Owen, Guy, ed. *Modern American Poetry: Essays in Criticism*. Deland, Fla.: Everett/Edwards, 1972.
    An anthology of contemporary essays; topics include Ransom, Jarrell, and Dickey; contributors include Dickey, Brooks, Owen, and Richard J. Calhoun.

_____, and Mary C. Williams, eds. *New Southern Poets*. Chapel Hill: Univ of North Carolina Press, 1975.
    A selection of poetry from the first fifteen years of the *Southern Poetry Review*, with an introduction by Louis D. Rubin, Jr.

Owens, W. A. "The Golden Age of Texas Scholarship: Webb, Dobie, Bedichek, and Boatright." *SWR*, 60 (Winter 1975), 1-14.
    An essay on the lives, works, and critical perspectives of these four scholars.

Palmer, R. Roderick. "The Poetry of Three Revolutionists: Don L. Lee, Sonia Sanchez, and Nikki Giovanni." *CLA Jour*, 15 (September 1971), 25-36.
    Deals with the aims of these poets, their emphasis on black identity.

Panichas, George A., ed. *The Politics of Twentieth-Century Novelists*. New York: Hawthorne Books, 1971.
    Includes assessments of the political philosophies of Faulkner by Lewis A. Lawson, Ellison by Donald Gibson, and Styron by Melvin J. Friedman.

Pearce, Richard. *Stages of the Clown: Perspectives on Modern Fiction from Dostoyevsky to Beckett*. Carbondale: Southern Illinois Univ Press, 1970.
    Explores applications of the ancient clown tradition in the fiction of Ellison, Faulkner, and O'Connor.

Peden, William. "The American Short Story During the Twenties." *Stud SF*, 10 (Fall 1973), 367-371.
    The article contains brief references to several Southern writers.

_____. "The Black Explosion." *Stud SF*, 12 (Summer 1975), 231-241.
    This consideration of contemporary black American short-fiction writers includes discussion of, among others, Wright, Himes, Alice Walker, Ernest J. Gaines, and J. A. McPherson.

_____, and George Garrett, eds. *New Writing in South Carolina*. Columbia: Univ of South Carolina Press, 1971.
    An anthology of forty-seven contemporary stories and poems, with an appreciative introduction by the editors and biographical notes on contributors.

Pells, Richard H. *Radical Visions and American Dreams: Culture and Social Thought in the Depression Years*. New York: Harper and Row, 1973.
    An intellectual history of the 1930's, with attention to the Agrarians, Faulkner, Agee, Caldwell, Wright, and others.

Perry, J. Douglas, Jr. "Gothic as Vortex: The Form of Horror in Capote, Faulkner, and Styron." *MFS*, 19 (Summer 1973), 153-167.
    Discusses Gothic elements in the works of these three writers, who use the Gothic "to capture the irony of our twentieth-century existence."

Petesch, Donald. "The Role of Folklore in the Modern Black Novel." *Kansas Quart*, 7 (Summer 1975), 99-110.
    Includes discussion of Hurston, Wright, and Gaines.

Phillips, Elizabeth. "Review of North Carolina Fiction, Poetry, Juvenile Literature, 1973-74." *NCHR*, 52 (April 1975), 147-155.
    Title is descriptive.

Pinkerton, Jan. *Love, Capitalism, Violence, and Other Topics*. Boston: Allyn & Bacon, 1971.
    An anthology including a selection of readings on the South by Cash, Simkins, Willie Morris, O'Connor, and Woodward.

Poirier, Richard. *The Performing Self: Compositions and Decompositions in the Language of Contemporary Life*. New York: Oxford Univ Press, 1971.
    Includes discussion of Barth and Styron and very brief comment on Faulkner.

Powell, Eleanor B. "Review of North Carolina Fiction, 1968-1969." *NCHR*, 47 (April 1970), 131-137.
    A treatment of thirty-two recent works by North Carolinians.

Powell, William S. "North Carolina Bibliography, 1966-1967." *NCHR*, 45 (Spring 1968), 195-204.
    Title is descriptive.

_____. "North Carolina Bibliography, 1967-68." *NCHR*, 46 (Spring 1969), 171-177.
    Title is descriptive.

_____. "North Carolina Bibliography, 1968-69." *NCHR*, 47 (Spring 1970), 205-213.
    Title is descriptive.

_____. "North Carolina Bibliography, 1969-70." *NCHR*, 48 (Spring 1971), 186-193.
    A list of books dealing with North Carolina or by North Carolinians published during the year ending June 30, 1970.

_____. "North Carolina Bibliography, 1970-71." *NCHR*, 49 (Spring 1972), 195-203.
    A list of books dealing with North Carolina or by North Carolinians published during the year ending June 30, 1971.

_____. "North Carolina Bibliography, 1972-73." *NCHR*, 51 (Spring 1974), 215-223.
    Title is descriptive.

Presley, Delma Eugene. "The Moral Function of Distortion in Southern Grotesque." *SAB*, 37 (May 1972), 37-46.
    Includes discussion of the element of distortion in the use of the grotesque in works of O'Connor, McCullers, and Williams.

IV. Contemporary (1920-1975)

Proffer, C. R. *Soviet Criticism of American Literature in the Sixties*. Ann Arbor, Mich.: Ardis Publishers, 1972.
    Translations of thirteen essays and reprintings of six English-language pieces published in Moscow, including commentary on Caldwell, Capote, Ellison, Faulkner, McCullers, O'Connor, Styron, and other Southern writers.

Purcell, James. "Review of North Carolina Nonfiction, 1969-1970." *NCHR*, 48 (Spring 1971), 142-146.
    Title is descriptive.

Ragan, Sam. "North Carolina Writers and the Southern Tradition: Review of North Carolina Fiction, 1972-1973." *NCHR*, 51 (April 1974), 183-189.
    Title is descriptive.

Reid, Alfred S. "The Southern Exposure of Karl Shapiro" (in "Four Authors View the South: A Symposium"). *SHR*, 6 (Winter 1972), 35-44.
    "...for a while in the 1940's,...[Shapiro] responded freely to the Southern influences in the environment of his youth." Reid raises the question: If Mark Twain and Ralph Ellison are considered "Southern authors," why not Baltimore-born Karl Shapiro?

Reilly, John M. "Images of Gastonia: A Revolutionary Chapter in American Social Fiction." *GaR*, 28 (Fall 1974), 498-518.
    Examines six novels which dealt with the 1929 strike of textile workers in Gastonia, North Carolina.

Rexroth, Kenneth. *American Poetry in the Twentieth Century*. New York: Herder and Herder, 1971.
    A general survey of modern poetry with brief comments on many Southern poets, caustic criticism of the Agrarian poets, and a dismissal of the existence of any significant Southern poetry after them.

Richardson, Kenneth, ed. *Twentieth Century Writing: A Reader's Guide to Contemporary Literature*. London: Newnes Books, 1969.
    Entries on American writers include sixteen Southerners.

Riche, James. "Pragmatism: A National Fascist Mode of Thought." *Lit and Ideology*, no. 9 (1971), 37-44.
    Faulkner and Barth are included in a discussion of writers in whose works the heroes are "pragmatic" in one way or another.

Riley, Carolyn. *Contemporary Literary Criticism*. Vol. I. Detroit: Gale Research Co., 1973.
    A collection of brief excerpts from criticism of recent authors; includes both major and minor Southern writers, from Aiken to Wright.

_____, and B. Harte, eds. *Contemporary Literary Criticism*. Vol. II. Detroit: Gale Research Co., 1974.
    Continuing anthology of excerpts from criticism of contemporary writers, with major and minor Southern writers included.

Robinson, William R., ed. *Nommo: An Anthology of Modern Black African and Black American Literature*. New York: Macmillan, 1972.
    Includes poetry, fiction, and prose by Southerners H. "Rap" Brown, Cleaver, Cruse, Hayden, Killens, Knight, McPherson, Major, Neal, Reed, and Sanchez.

Roland, Charles P. *The Improbable Era: The South Since World War II*. Lexington: Univ Press of Kentucky, 1975.
    Has a chapter on literature.

Rosenberg, Bruce A. *The Art of the American Folk Preacher*. New York: Oxford Univ Press, 1970.
    An analytic study of the themes, formulas, structure, and making of the spontaneous chanted sermons of the fundamentalist evangelical preachers, black and white, in the South and Southwest, which finds in them compositional devices similar to those found in ancient and medieval epics; includes transcripts of twelve exemplary sermons.

Rosenblatt, Roger. "Black as the Color of Chaos." *Harvard Eng Stud*, 1 (1970), 249-261.
    Black fiction reflects tension between the ideas that black is beautiful and that it is not; includes references to Johnson, Toomer, Wright, and Ellison.

_____. *Black Fiction*. Cambridge, Mass.: Harvard Univ Press, 1974.
    Argues that black fiction has a unity derived from a conception of history in which the black protagonist struggles to achieve unattainable goals; comments on fiction by Bontemps, Ellison, Gaines, Johnson, Toomer, and Wright.

Rougé, Robert. *L'inquiétude religieuse dans le roman américain moderne*. Publications de l'université de Haute Bretagne 4. Paris: Librarie C. Klincksieck, 1973.
    Includes discussion of Faulkner and Warren.

Ruotolo, Lucio P. *Six Existentialist Heroes: The Politics of Faith*. Cambridge, Mass.: Harvard Univ Press, 1973.
    Contains discussion of Faulkner's *Go Down, Moses* and Ellison's *Invisible Man*.

Rupp, Richard H. *Celebration in Postwar American Fiction, 1945-1967*. Coral Gables, Fla.: Univ of Miami Press, 1970.
    A study of celebration--the acceptance and joyful approval of life--in ten writers, including Welty, O'Connor, Agee, and Ellison.

Savory, Jerold J. "Descent and Baptism in *Native Son, Invisible Man, Dutchman*." *Chri Schol Rev*, 3 (1973), 33-37.
    Discusses the result of the "descent into hell" and the "baptism by fire" of the main characters of each of these novels.

Saxon, John D. "Contemporary Southern Oratory: A Rhetoric of Hope, not Desperation." *So Speech Comm Jour*, 40 (Spring 1975), 262-274.
    Contemporary Southern oratory is "characterized by an aversion to the past rhetoric of

desperation and lost causes, by a spirit of renewal, and with a focus which is decidedly futuristic."

Scholes, Robert, ed. *Some Modern Writers: Essays and Fiction*. New York: Oxford Univ Press, 1970.
Reprints with critical introductions examples of prose and fiction by Faulkner and Ellison.

Schorer, Mark. *The World We Imagine: Selected Essays*. New York: Farrar, Straus and Giroux, 1968.
Reprints earlier published essays on Capote, McCullers, and K. A. Porter.

Schraufnagel, Noel. *From Apology to Protest: The Black American Novel*. Deland, Fla.: Everett/Edwards, 1973.
Deals with the black novel from 1940-1970 and includes discussion of Wright, Ellison, Himes, Gaines, and others.

Schwartz, Delmore. *Selected Essays of Delmore Schwartz*, ed. Donald A. Dike and David H. Zucker. Chicago: Univ of Chicago Press, 1970.
Includes essays on Faulkner, Ransom, and Tate.

Scott, Nathan A., Jr. "Judgment Marked by a Cellar: The American Negro Writer and the Dialectic of Despair," in *The Shapeless God: Essays on Modern Fiction*, ed. Harry J. Mooney, Jr., and Thomas F. Staley. Pittsburgh: Univ of Pittsburgh Press, 1969, pp. 139-169.
Examines the work of Wright, Ellison, and other black authors in the light of the traditions of the American novel, the symbol of the wounded Adam, and our religious inheritance of secularized Calvinism. Includes a critique of Randall Stewart's theological literary criticism.

Scura, Dorothy. "Glasgow and the Southern Renaissance: The Conference at Charlottesville." *Miss Quart*, 27 (Fall 1974), 415-434.
Gives an account of the literary conference held at Charlottesville, Virginia, in 1931, and emphasizes Ellen Glasgow's role in the meeting.

Seyersted, Per. "A Survey of Trends and Figures in Afro-American Fiction." *Am Stud in Scand*, 6 (1974), 67-86.
Focuses on black writers since Wright; several Southerners are included.

Shapiro, Edward S. "The Southern Agrarians and the Tennessee Valley Authority." *AQ*, 22 (Winter 1970), 791-806.
Drawing on original sources, the author presents the Agrarians' views on the Tennessee Valley Authority.

_____. (On the Agrarians). See MENCKEN, HENRY LOUIS.

Sheed, Wilfrid. *The Morning After: Selected Essays and Reviews*. New York: Farrar, Straus and Giroux, 1971.
Includes discussion of works by Agee, Walker Percy, Styron, and Williams.

Sheffey, Ruthe. "Wit and Irony in Militant Black Poetry." *Black World*, 22 (June 1973), 14-21.
Poems by Don L. Lee and Nikki Giovanni are used to illustrate irony in black militant poetry.

Shores, D. L. "Black English and Black Attitudes." *SAB*, 39 (November 1974), 104-112.
Views of black college educators at conferences organized by Norfolk State College, Virginia.

Shuptrine, Hubert, and James Dickey. *Jericho: The South Beheld*. Birmingham, Ala.: Oxmoor House, 1974.
A collaborative effort between a painter and a poet to capture the quality and character of the South.

Simpson, Lewis P. "The Southern Recovery of Memory and History." *SR*, 82 (Winter 1974), 1-32.
Includes comments on Faulkner, Tate, Warren, Charles East, and Styron.

_____. "Southern Spiritual Nationalism: Notes on the Background of Modern Southern Fiction," in *The Cry of Home: Cultural Nationalism and the Modern Writer*, ed. H. Ernest Lewald. Knoxville: Univ of Tennessee Press, 1972, pp. 189-210.
Slavery was a drawback to the development of the South as a "redemptive community"; the artist had to recognize himself as both Southerner and American before he could develop.

_____. "Walter Sullivan and the Southern Possibility." *So Lit Jour*, 5 (Spring 1973), 88-101.
An essay-review of Sullivan's *Death by Melancholy: Essays on Modern Southern Fiction*.

Singh, Raman K. "The Black Novel and Its Tradition." *ColQ*, 20 (Summer 1971), 23-29.
Includes discussion of Wright, Ellison, and Toomer.

_____, and Peter Fellowes, eds. *Black Literature in America: A Casebook*. New York: Thomas Y. Crowell, 1970.
Reprints selections by Julian Bond, Bontemps, Chesnutt, Don Johnson, James Weldon Johnson, Killens, Lucy Smith, Margaret Walker, Wright, and Yerby.

Smitherman, Geneva. "The Power of the Rap: The Black Idiom and the New Black Poetry." *TCL*, 19 (October 1973), 259-274.
Finds the power of the new black poetry comes from black oral tradition.

Solotaroff, Theodore. *The Red Hot Vacuum and Other Pieces on the Writing of the Sixties*. New York: Atheneum, 1970.
Reprints earlier published essays of the 1960's on Harry Golden, K. A. Porter, Wright, and O'Connor, with incidental commentary on other Southern writers.

Spearman, Walter, with Samuel Selden. *The Carolina Playmakers: The First Fifty Years*. Chapel Hill: Univ of North Carolina Press, 1970.
An informal history of the Carolina Players at U. N. C., 1918-1969, in whose productions

IV. CONTEMPORARY (1920-1975)

Thomas Wolfe and Paul Green played important parts.

Spiegel, Alan. "A Theory of the Grotesque in Southern Fiction." *GaR*, 26 (Winter 1972), 426-437.

The *grotesque* is a "type of character" which appears in a "special form" that distinguishes the contemporary Southern novel from its Northern counterpart.

Stanzel, Franz. *Narrative Situations in the Novel.* Translated from the German by James P. Pusack. Bloomington: Indiana Univ Press, 1971.

Examines techniques of narrative and point of view in fiction, using novels by Capote, Warren, and Faulkner as examples.

Steelman, Lala C. "Review of North Carolina Non-fiction 1971-1973." *NCHR*, 51 (April 1974), 161-169.

Title is descriptive.

Stein, A. F., and T. N. Walters, eds. *The Southern Experience in Short Fiction.* Glenview, Ill.: Scott, Foresman, 1971.

An anthology of nineteen stories by fifteen Southerners about the South, with an introduction, short commentaries on the stories, and study questions.

Steinbeck, Elaine, and Robert Wallsten, eds. *Steinbeck: A Life in Letters.* New York: Viking Press, 1975.

The letters include comments on Williams and Faulkner, and a letter from Faulkner is quoted.

Stern, Frederick. "Black Lit., White Crit?" *CE*, 35 (March 1974), 637-658.

The article contains several references to Ellison's critical and aesthetic principles and a brief reaction to two critical estimates of Styron's *The Confessions of Nat Turner*.

Stock, Irvin. "Black Literature, Relevance, and the New Irrationality." *Quadrant*, 16 (November/December 1972), 39-47.

A current appraisal.

Stott, William M. *Documentary Expressions and Thirties America.* New York: Oxford Univ Press, 1973.

A study of documentary media which created the images of Depression America; comments on several Southerners, culminating in a critique of Agee and Evans, *Let Us Now Praise Famous Men*, as a masterwork.

Struthers, J. R. "Alice Munroe and the American South." *CRev Am Stud*, 6 (Fall 1975), 196-204.

On the likenesses of the rural South and Southwestern Ontario.

Sullivan, Walter. *Death by Melancholy: Essays on Modern Southern Fiction.* Baton Rouge: Louisiana State Univ Press, 1972.

A collection of eight recently published essays reflecting the decline of Southern writing and culture: Faulkner, O'Connor, Warren, and K. A. Porter are treated at length.

_____. "In Time of the Breaking of Nations: The Decline of Southern Fiction." *SouR*, 4 (Spring 1968), 299-305.

An attempt to explain why recent Southern fiction (that of William Styron, Cormac McCarthy, etc.) is not as good as that of the generation just past.

_____. "Southern Writers in the Modern World: Death by Melancholy." *SouR*, 6 (Autumn 1970), 907-919.

Sees a decline in contemporary Southern writing caused by a draining away of metaphysical and religious concepts necessary to great writing.

Tanner, Tony. *City of Words: American Fiction, 1950-1970.* New York: Harper & Row, 1971.

A study of the evolving post-war American imagination, through the works of twenty-five novelists, including Barth, Capote, Ellison, and Percy.

Tarbet, Donald W. "Contemporary American Pastoral: A Poetic Faith." *Eng Record*, 23 (Winter 1972), 72-83.

Wendell Berry and Ammons, along with Gary Snyder, are poets who have urged a return to nature.

Taylor, Clyde. "Black Folk Spirit and the Shape of Black Literature." *Black World*, 21 (August 1972), 31-40.

Discusses the aims of black literature; several Southern writers are mentioned.

Taylor, W. D. "Creating by Established Literati Tends to Be Gregarious Activity." Richmond *Times-Dispatch*, August 19, 1973, p. F-1.

Describes both the conservative poetry-society school of poets and the avant-garde poets writing today in Virginia.

Taylor, William E., ed. *Modern American Drama: Essays in Criticism.* Deland, Fla.: Everett/Edwards, 1968.

Contains an essay on Williams; an essay on novelist-playwrights includes discussion of McCullers.

Terrier, Michel. *Individu et société dans le roman américain de 1900 à 1940: essai de poétique sociale.* (EA 52) Paris: Didier, 1973.

Includes analysis of works by Faulkner, Wright, and Wolfe.

Tharpe, Jac. "The Intellectual Scene Since World War II: Notes on Cultural History." *So Quart*, 12 (July 1974), 295-315.

A survey of American literary taste before and after 1945, with mention of several Southern writers and an extended discussion of Barth's "comic view of a dread world."

Thorp, Willard. "Setting the Record Straight." *KR*, 30, no. 4 (1968), 562-569.

An essay-review of *The Curious Death of the Novel* and of *The Teller in the Tale*, both by Louis D. Rubin, Jr.

Tischler, Nancy M. *Black Masks: Negro Characters in Modern Southern Fiction*. University Park: Pennsylvania State Univ Press, 1969.
A summary of types of Negro characters created by white and black authors of the Southern literary renaissance.

_____. "The Metamorphosis of the Brute Negro." *RANAM*, 4 (1971), 3-11.
Discusses concepts of the "brute Negro" in the works of a number of Southern writers, concluding that in recent times the Negro has become "the classic American hero."

_____. "Negro Literature and Classic Form." *ConL*, 10 (Summer 1969), 352-365.
Styron's *Nat Turner* and Ellison's *Invisible Man* are examined as two views of the experience of the Negro in America.

Toledano, Ben C. "Savannah Writers' Conference--1939." *GaR*, 22 (Summer 1968), 145-158.
An account of a conference whose lecturers were John Peale Bishop, Caroline Gordon, Andrew Lytle, George Stevens, Samuel Gaillard Stoney, and Allen Tate.

Towns, Stuart, and Churchill L. Roberts, eds. "A Bibliography of Speech and Theatre in the South for the Year 1972." *So Speech Comm Jour*, 39 (Fall 1973), 75-87.
Bibliography covers theses and dissertations as well as other published material.

_____, eds. "A Bibliography of Speech, Theatre, and Broadcasting in the South for the Year 1973." *So Speech Comm Jour*, 40 (Fall 1974), 81-93.
Title is descriptive.

_____, eds. "A Bibliography of Speech, Theatre, and Broadcasting in the South for the Year 1974." *So Speech Comm Jour*, 41 (Fall 1975), 89-92.
Title is descriptive.

Turner, Darwin T. *Black Drama in America: An Anthology*. Greenwich, Conn.: Fawcett, 1971.
Biographical notes on and plays by Willis Richardson, Theodore Ward, Randolph Edwards, and Ossie Davis are included.

_____. *In a Minor Chord: Three Afro-American Writers and Their Search for Identity*. Carbondale: Sou Illinois Univ Press, 1971.
Toomer and Hurston are two of the three authors treated in this work.

Tyms, James D. "The Black Poet and A Sense of Self--The Praise of Famous Men." *Jour of Religious Thought*, 32 (Spring-Summer 1975), 22-35.
Includes discussion of J. W. Johnson and Margaret Walker.

Umphlett, Wiley Lee. *The Sporting Myth and the American Experience*. Lewisburg, Pa.: Bucknell Univ Press, 1975.
A study of the sporting hero as an archetypal hero, with attention to Faulkner's Ike McCaslin and Caroline Gordon's Aleck Maury.

Verble, David. "'Martian Space' and the Spring Poetry Festival." *Tenn Poetry Jour*, 4 (Spring 1971), 40-41.
This festival at the University of Tennessee at Martin connected the Southern consciousness with that of the nation.

Vinson, James, ed. *Contemporary Poets*. 2nd ed. New York: St. Martin's Press, 1975.
Includes biographical, bibliographical, and critical entries on over eight hundred living poets writing in English, with many Southerners represented.

Waniek, Marilyn N. "The Space Where Sex Should Be: Toward a Definition of the Black American Literary Tradition." *SBL*, 6 (Fall 1975), 7-13.
Includes discussion of Johnson, Wright, and Ellison.

Ward, A. C., ed. *Longman Companion to Twentieth Century Literature*. 2nd ed. London: Longman, 1975.
Includes brief entries on the major Southern writers and critics.

Watkins, Floyd C. *The Death of Art: Black and White in the Recent Southern Novel*. Mercer Univ Lamar Memorial Lectures, no. 13. Athens: Univ of Georgia Press, 1970.
"Modern Southern novels which treat the relationship between the black man and the white man are highly prejudiced against the white. It may be possible to defend this bias as a historical, political, and social corrective; but as fiction the bias fails." Considers Faulkner, Warren, Styron, William Hoffman, Walker Percy, Feibleman, Grau, Elizabeth Spencer, and Jesse Hill Ford.

Weales, Gerald. *The Jumping Off Place: American Drama in the 1960's*. New York: Macmillan, 1969.
Contains discussion of Williams' work of the 1960's, Jesse Hill Ford's *The Conversion of Buster Drumwright* (and Donald Davidson's preface to it), brief discussion of Lillian Hellman, and brief mention of other Southerners.

Webb, Max. "Ford Madox Ford and the Baton Rouge Writers' Conference." *SouR*, 10 (Autumn 1974), 892-903.
Discusses Ford's impact on the 1935 conference and his attitudes toward the Agrarians; gives a sketch of his relations with Allen Tate.

Weber, Alfred, and Dietmar Haack, eds. *Amerikanische Literatur Im 20. Jahrhundert*. Göttingen: Vandenhoeck & Ruprecht, 1971.
Includes an essay on Capote's *In Cold Blood* and several general essays with brief discussions of many Southern writers; articles in German have English summaries.

Weinberg, Helen A. *The New Novel in America: The Kafkan Mode in Contemporary Fiction*. Ithaca: Cornell Univ Press, 1970.
Examines novels written against the New Critical aestheticism, in search of human value; comments on Ellison, Percy, and Styron briefly.

Welsh, John R. "Succinct Perspective." *SAB*, 35 (May 1970), 49-50.
A review of *Southern Fiction Today: Renascence and Beyond*, ed. George Core; this collection of lectures given at Davidson College in 1969 does not answer definitively the question of whether or not the Renascence is continuing, but it clearly frames the issues.

West, Ray B., Jr. *The Writer in the Room: Selected Essays*. East Lansing: Michigan State Univ Press, 1968.
Reprints earlier published essays on Faulkner, K. A. Porter, and Welty.

Westendorp, T. A. "Recent Southern Fiction: Percy, Price and Dickey." *Handelingen van het XXIXe Vlaams Filologencongres Antwerpen 16-18 april 1973*. Zellik, Belgium, 1973, pp. 188-198.
Deals with Price's *A Generous Man*, Dickey's *Deliverance*, and Percy's *Love in the Ruins*, and finds Percy's work the most promising.

Weygand, J. L. "News and Reviews of Private Presses." *Am Bk Collector*, 24 (July-August 1974) 40-42.
A short history of Storer's press of Starkville, Mississippi, begun in 1968.

Whisenhunt, D. W. "The Bard in the Depression: Texas Style." *Jour of Popular Culture*, 2 (Winter 1968), 370-386.
Discusses Texas amateur poetry of the 1930's as a folk expression of responses to the depression.

White, Helen, and Redding S. Sugg, Jr. *From the Mountain: Selections from Pseudopodia (1936), The North Georgia Review (1937-1941), and South Today*. Memphis, Tenn.: Memphis State Univ Press, 1972.
Reprints extensive selections from the writings of Lillian Smith and Paula Snelling, along with essays, reviews, poems, and stories by others, all about modern Southern literature and culture.

Whitlow, Roger. "The Harlem Renaissance and After: A Checklist of Black Literature of the Twenties and Thirties." *NALF*, 7 (Winter 1973), 143-146.
Some Southern black writers are listed.

Williams, M., ed. *Contemporary Poetry in America*. New York: Random House, 1973.
A broad spectrum of selections from over ninety poets, with many Southerners represented, from Warren to Jarrell to Ralph Adams and John Biguenet; many contribute autobiographical sketches.

Wilson, James D. "The Role of Slavery in the Agrarian Myth." *RANAM*, 4 (1971), 12-22.
Though the Agrarians did not want a return to slavery, they nevertheless were committing themselves to all the institutions of the antebellum order they admired and defended. U. B. Phillips, Frank Owsley, Davidson, Tate, and Warren are dealt with at length.

Woodward, C. Vann. "Why the Southern Renaissance?" *VQR*, 51 (Winter 1975), 222-239.
Woodward surveys the theories that have been offered as to the causes of the Southern Renaissance and concludes that it is not possible to pinpoint a cause. Davidson, Tate, Mencken, Cash, and Faulkner are referred to or dealt with in some detail, while there are short references to other Southerners.

Woolmer, J. H. *A Catalogue of the Fugitive Poets*. Andes, N. Y.: J. Howard Woolmer Books, 1972.
Lists 330 books and periodical contributions by the fifteen Fugitives with an introductory essay by Louis D. Rubin, Jr., "Fugitives as Agrarians: The Impulse Behind *I'll Take My Stand*."

Yardley, Jonathan. "The New Old Southern Novel." *PR*, 40 (1973), 286-293.
The evolution of the Southern novel from the 1920's to the present, with a look at the continuous themes of "place" and "family."

Yoder, E. M., Jr. "The Greening of the South." *Book World*, July 4, 1971, p. 7.
Notes the prophetic accuracy of the Southern Agrarians' *I'll Take My Stand* in predicting modern environmental and ecological problems.

Young, James O. *Black Writers of the Thirties*. Baton Rouge: Louisiana State Univ Press, 1973.
Includes discussion of Bontemps, Johnson, and Wright.

Young, Thomas Daniel, and Ronald E. Fine, eds. *American Literature: A Critical Survey*, Volume II. New York: American Book, 1968.
Reprints three essays on Faulkner by Cowley, Slatoff, and Backman.

Zug, Charles G., III. "Folklore and the Drama: The Carolina Playmakers and Their 'Folk Plays.'" *SFQ*, 32 (December 1968), 279-294.
A discussion of the Carolina Playmakers as part of the little theater movement and its relation to the American folk tradition.

Zyla, Wolodymur T., and Wendell M. Aycock, eds. *Proceedings of the Comparative Literature Symposium. Vol V: Modern American Fiction: Insights and Foreign Lights*. Lubbock: Texas Tech Univ, 1972.
Contains essays on Faulkner (Walter R. McDonald) and Katherine Anne Porter (Frances Hernández); discussion of O'Connor is included in an essay on short-story cycles by Forrest L. Ingram.

V. General

Anon. "Articles in American Studies, 1971." *AQ*, 24 (August 1972), 328-416.
This annual bibliography contains numerous entries centered on Southern belletristic writing.

Anon. "1966 Bibliography of Mississippi Writers." *Notes on Miss Writers*, 1 (Spring 1968), 32-39.
Includes Faulkner, Welty, Williams, and Wright.

Anon. *The Saturday Review of Literature Index: 1924-1944.* New York: R. R. Bowker, 1971.
A twenty-year guide to all articles, editorials, and reviews, containing references to much material by and about numerous Southern writers in the *Saturday Review*.

Anon. "Southern History in Periodicals, 1968: A Selected Bibliography." *JSH*, 35 (May 1969), 203-233.
The section "Social, Cultural, and Intellectual" has a number of entries relevant to literature.

Anon. "Southern History in Periodicals, 1971: A Selected Bibliography." *JSH*, 38 (May 1972), 241-272.
This annual bibliography contains numerous entries centered on Southern belletristic writing.

Anon. "Theses on American Topics in Progress and Completed at British Universities." *Jour Am Stud*, 4 (July 1970), 107-122.
Regular compilations of such material are promised. Work other than doctoral studies is included, and Faulkner appears often.

Aaron, Daniel. *The Unwritten War: American Writers and the Civil War.* New York: Alfred A. Knopf, 1973.
Includes discussion of Simms, Clemens, Tourgee, Lanier, Cable, and Faulkner.

Adams, Richard P. "Permutations of American Romanticism." *Stud in Romanticism*, 9 (Fall 1970), 249-268.
Includes discussion of Clemens and Faulkner.

Albrecht, Robert C., et al., eds. *Literature in America.* 3 vols. New York: Free Press, 1971.
An anthology of American literature, including selections by major Southern writers.

Anderson, D. D., et al., eds. *The Black Experience: Readings in Afro-American History and Culture from Colonial Times to the Nineteenth Century.* East Lansing: Michigan State Univ Press, 1969.
A collection of primary materials with introductory notes; includes Jefferson, Fitzhugh, David Walker, Nat Turner, and Chesnutt.

Anderson, John Q. "Popular Beliefs in Texas, Louisiana, and Arkansas." *SFQ*, 32 (December 1968), 304-319.
A summary of an extensive field collection.

_____. "Some Migratory Anecdotes in American Folk Humor." *Miss Quart*, 25 (Fall 1972), 447-457.
Humorous tales about bad roads, poor accommodations for travelers, rough practical jokes, and forcibly detained guests are examples of migratory anecdotes that passed back and forth between oral tradition and print in nineteenth-century America.

Anderson, Thomas. "'As Crazy as Two Waltzing Mice': About American Similes." *Mod Språk*, 65, no. 3 (1971), 223-226.
Mentions Twain and Caldwell as being among American writers who have made good use of American similes.

Appleby, Jane. "Is Southern English Good English?" *SAB*, 35 (March 1970), 15-19.
Yes, since the recent study in dialectology shows that diversity makes it impossible to declare one regional speech superior to another.

Aptheker, Herbert. "Afro-American Superiority: A Neglected Theme in the Literature." *Phylon*, 31 (Winter 1970), 336-343.
Contrary to assumptions by historians and critics, literature by black American writers generally rejects the concept of Afro-American inferiority. Racial pride, even black superiority, is a dominant theme at least by the 1920's. Southern writers discussed include Frederick Douglass, Jean Toomer, Arna Bontemps, Margaret Walker, Richard Wright, William Styron, Thomas Dixon, and Martin Luther King.

Atlas, James. "The Convicted Imagination: Notes on American Criticism." *London Mag*, 15 (October/November 1975), 39-52.

Traces the course of American literary criticism beginning with Howells. Includes detailed discussion of Ransom and Tate and brief discussion of Jarrell.

Austin, James C., and Donald A. Koch, eds. *Popular Literature in America*. Bowling Green, Ohio: Bowling Green Univ Popular Press, 1972.
Festschrift in honor of Professor L. N. Richardson; includes essays on Southern mountain fiction by Wilton Eckley, on G. W. Harris by Lewis Leary, on Post-Civil War writing by Arlin Turner, and other general essays touching on Southern literature.

Avni, Abraham. "The Influence of the Bible on American Literature: A Review of Research from 1955 to 1965." *BB*, 27 (October-December 1970), 101-106.
Includes references to research on Poe, Faulkner, and Lytle.

Bacot, Lucia, comp. "South Carolina Newspapers and Periodicals in the South Caroliniana Library," in *South Carolina Journals and Journalists*. Columbia, S. C.: Southern Studies Program, 1975, pp. 291-348.
A listing of the titles and dates of all South Carolina newspapers and periodicals in the library collection as of 1974; the listing includes microfilm holdings.

Baker, Donald G. "Black Images: The Afro-American in Popular Novels, 1900-1945." *Jour of Pop Culture*, 7 (Fall 1973), 327-346.
The image of the black has been generally negative and stereotyped. Includes comments on Lillian Smith's *Strange Fruit*, Dixon's *The Clansman*, and Mitchell's *Gone with the Wind*.

Baker, Houston A., Jr. "The Problem of Being: Some Reflections on Black Autobiography." *Obsidian*, 1 (Spring 1975), 18-30.
Contains analysis of Douglass' *Narrative*, Washington's *Up from Slavery*.

_____, ed. *Black Literature in America*. New York: McGraw-Hill, 1971.
An anthology with many Southern black authors represented; includes unit introductions, biographical notes, and bibliographies.

_____. *Long Black Song: Essays in Black American Literature and Culture*. Charlottesville: Univ Press of Virginia, 1972.
Attempts to distinguish black American culture from white culture, with full analyses of David Walker, Frederick Douglass, Booker T. Washington, W. E. B. Dubois, Richard Wright, and brief comments on other Southerners.

_____. *Singers of Daybreak: Studies in Black American Literature*. Washington, D. C.: Howard Univ Press, 1974.
Essays devoted to or including discussion of Douglass, B. T. Washington, Johnson, Ellison, and Toomer.

Baldeshwiler, Eileen. "The Lyric Short Story: The Sketch of a History." *Stud SF*, 6 (Summer 1969), 443-453.

Traces the development of the "lyric" short story from Turgenev and Chekhov through English and American short-story writers, including Aiken and Welty.

Barksdale, Richard, and Keneth Kinnamon, eds. *Black Writers of America: A Comprehensive Anthology*. New York: Macmillan, 1972.
Covers writers from 1760 to the present, with biographical and critical introductions; numerous Southerners.

Barnett, Louise K. *The Ignoble Savage: American Literary Racism, 1790-1890*. Westport, Conn.: Greenwood Press, 1975.
An analysis of Indian stereotypes in the frontier romance novels published between 1793 and 1868, with attention to John Esten Cooke, Simms, and some minor Southern writers.

Barr, S. "Verse in Virginia." Richmond *Times-Dispatch*, August 19, 1973, p. F-1.
A brief survey of poetry writing in Virginia from Richard Rich in the early 1600's to R. H. W. Dillard.

Bayliss, John F., ed. *Black Slave Narratives*. New York: Macmillan, 1970.
Reprints excerpts from narratives of several Southern blacks, with an introduction by the editor.

Baym, Max I. *A History of Literary Aesthetics in America*. New York: Frederick Ungar, 1973.
A survey of literary aesthetic theories with attention to Brooks, Poe, Ransom, Warren, and other Southern critics.

Berger, Arthur A. *Li'l Abner: A Study in American Satire*. New York: Twayne, 1970.
Finds satirical antecedents of Al Capp's "Li'l Abner" in the writings of William Byrd and the humorists of the Old Southwest.

Berry, Wendell. "An Essay and a Meditation." *SouR*, 6 (Autumn 1970), 972-989.
In the essay portion, "The Regional Motive," Berry rejects certain definitions of regionalism, including Southern regionalism. There are brief references to Faulkner and the Agrarians.

Besterman, Theodore. *Literature: English and American, A Bibliography of Bibliographies*. Totowa, N. J.: Rowman R. Littlefield, 1971.
A checklist of general and author bibliographies; most major Southern authors are included.

Bier, Jesse. *The Rise and Fall of American Humor*. New York: Holt, Rinehart and Winston, 1968.
A broad survey which includes discussions of the humorists of the Old Southwest, humor in Faulkner, and other Southern figures.

Blair, Walter. "'A Man's Voice, Speaking': A Continuum in American Humor," in *Veins of Humor*, ed. Harry Levin. Cambridge, Mass.: Harvard Univ Press, 1972, pp. 185-204.
Deals with the comic oral narrative and its effect on G. W. Harris, Mark Twain, and Faulkner.

Bluefarb, Sam. *The Escape Motif in the American Novel: Mark Twain to Richard Wright*. Columbus: Ohio State Univ Press, 1972.
   In addition to chapters on Huck Finn and Bigger Thomas, there is a chapter devoted to Jake Blount in McCullers' *The Heart is a Lonely Hunter*.

Bone, Robert. *Down Home: A History of Afro-American Short Fiction from Its Beginnings to the End of the Harlem Renaissance*. New York: G. P. Putnam's Sons, 1975.
   Examines the short stories of Chesnutt, Hurston, Toomer and Bontemps, as reflective of a struggle between pastoralists and anti-pastoralists.

Boney, F. N. "The Southern Aristocrat." *Midwest Quart*, 15 (April 1974), 215-230.
   A general survey of the concepts of Southern aristocracy, concluding that wealth is the main requirement for entry.

Bontemps, Arna. "The Slave Narrative: An American Genre," introduction to *Great Slave Narratives*, ed. Arna Bontemps. Boston: Beacon Press, 1969.
   Discusses the significance of the slave narrative as a means of self-expression and protest.

Brake, Robert. "The Lion Act Is Over: Passive/ Aggressive Patterns of Communication in American Negro Humor." *Jour of Pop Culture*, 9 (Winter 1975), 549-560.
   Used by a few writers such as J. C. Harris, Zora Neale Hurston, and Ellison, Negro humor has been little studied and its significance underestimated.

Brathwaite, Edward K. "The African Presence in Caribbean Literature." *Daedalus*, 103 (Spring 1974), 73-109.
   Although focusing on Caribbean literature, this essay refers briefly to the phenomenon of reconnection with African culture among black jazz musicians and poets of the United States. The whole Spring issue of this journal is devoted to slavery, colonialism, and racism.

Bridges, Katherine. "Some Representative Louisiana Writers." *Catholic Lib World*, 40 (February 1969), 352-355.
   Includes bibliographies for Cable, Capote, Hellman, and Bontemps.

Brignano, Russell C. *Black Americans in Autobiography*. Durham, N. C.: Duke Univ Press, 1974.
   An annotated checklist of 459 autobiographies by blacks written since the Civil War.

Broderick, John C., et al. "Recent Acquisitions of the Manuscript Division." *QJLC*, 30 (October 1973), 295-337.
   Includes listing of the Douglass papers and description of a Clemens manuscript in the Library of Congress.

Brooks, Cleanth. *The Relation of the Alabama-Georgia Dialect to the Provincial Dialects of Great Britain*. Port Washington, N. Y.: Kennikat Press, 1972.
   A facsimile reprint of Brooks's linguistic study of Southern dialects, his first book, issued originally in 1935.

_____. *A Shaping Joy: Studies in the Writer's Craft*. New York: Harcourt Brace Jovanovich, 1971.
   Reprints several essays on Faulkner, Poe, and Southern literature in general.

Brown, Lloyd W. "Beneath the North Star: The Canadian Image in Black Literature." *Dal Rev*, 50 (Autumn 1970), 317-329.
   Covers the West Indies as well as the United States.

_____. "Black Entitles: Names as Symbols in Afro-American Literature." *SBL*, 1 (Spring 1970), 16-44.
   Deals with the significance of the names given to characters in the works of black writers, including B. T. Washington, Wright, and Ellison.

Browne, Ray B., et al, eds. *Challenges in American Culture*. Bowling Green, Ohio: Bowling Green Univ Popular Press, 1970.
   Contains essays on Twain's *A Connecticut Yankee* (Tom H. Towers) and on Tennessee Williams and popular culture (John J. Fritscher).

Bruccoli, Matthew J., ed. *The Chief Glory of Every People: Essays on Classic American Writers*. Carbondale and Edwardsville: Southern Illinois Univ Press, 1973.
   Contains essays on Simms by Thomas L. McHaney and on Twain by James M. Cox.

Buchloh, Paul G., ed. *Amerikanische Erzählungen von Hawthorne bis Salinger: Interpretationen*. Neumünster: Karl Wachholtz Verlag, 1968.
   Includes an overview of American literature with specific commentary on Poe, Twain, Cable, Glasgow, Faulkner, K. A. Porter, Warren, Welty, McCullers, Capote, and O'Connor; an essay comparing Faulkner's fiction with that of Crane, Hemingway, and Britting; and a comparative analysis of Hemingway's "My Old Man" and Faulkner's "Barn Burning," all in German.

Bulgheroni, Marisa. *Il Demone del Luogo: Letture Americane*. Milan: Instituto Editoriale Cisalpino di Varese, 1968.
   Includes two essays on Poe and one on the American novel which includes discussion of McCullers.

Bungert, Hans, ed. *Die Amerikanische Short Story: Theorie und Entwicklung*. Darmstadt: Wissenschaftliche Buchgesellschaft, 1972.
   An anthology of essays, sixteen in English and seven in German, on the short story which comment critically on Aiken, Cabell, Cable, Caldwell, Capote, Faulkner, Gordon, March, Poe, Twain, Warren, Welty, Wolfe, and others.

Burke, W. J., et al. *American Authors and Books: 1640 to the Present Day*. New York: Crown, 1972.
   The third revised edition of a reference work, with brief entries on major and minor Southern writers.

V. General

Butterfield, S. *Black Autobiography in America*. Amherst, Mass.: Univ of Massachusetts Press, 1974.

A historical and critical account of the growth of black autobiography from the slave narratives through the 1970's, including attention to W. W. Brown, Douglass, J. W. Johnson, B. T. Washington, Wright, and other Southerners.

Cady, Edwin H. *The Light of Common Day: Realism in American Fiction*. Bloomington: Indiana Univ Press, 1971.

A definition and examination of "realism" in American literary history drawing on fiction and poetry by Twain, Faulkner, Poe, Warren, and the Southwest humorists, among others.

Calhoun, Richard J. "Southern Writing: The Unifying Strand." *Miss Quart*, 27 (Winter 1973-74), 101-108.

A review-essay of C. Hugh Holman's *The Roots of Southern Writing*.

_____, and John C. Guilds, eds. *A Tricentennial Anthology of South Carolina Literature, 1670-1970*. Columbia: Univ of South Carolina Press, 1971.

An anthology of selections from the work of forty authors from William Hilton (1664) to James Dickey, with a brief introduction by the editors, biographical headnotes, and a list of sources.

Chambers, Bradford, and Rebecca Moon, eds. *Right On! An Anthology of Black Literature*. New York: New American Library, 1970.

A thematic collection, with emphasis on modern writing; numerous Southerners are represented.

Chametzky, Jules. "Regional Literature and Ethnic Realities." *AR*, 31 (Fall 1971), 385-396.

Some writers usually categorized as regionalists (as Cable, Chesnutt, Chopin) have as their real subjects "the racial grounds of the southern tragedy...the assertion of a black ethos, and the terms of woman's entrapment within our cultural assumptions." Calling them regionalists and restricting critical attention to this aspect of their work misrepresents them and denies their significant concerns. Only Chesnutt's work is examined in detail.

Clark, Harry H. *American Literature: Poe Through Garland*. Goldentree Bibliographies. New York: Appleton-Century-Crofts, 1971.

Includes selective checklists of secondary comment on Twain, Poe, Cable, Page, Simms, and Timrod.

Clark, Thomas D. "The Impact of the Timber Industry on the South." *Miss Quart*, 25 (Spring 1972), 141-164.

In the early history of the South, for lack of transportation, technology, and skilled workmen, the timber industry was not developed; in recent decades scientific timber production has changed social and economic patterns and has replaced cotton in importance.

_____. "The Piedmont South in Historical Perspective." *Miss Quart*, 24 (Winter 1970-71), 1-17.

A good cross section, the Piedmont has reflected both positive and negative aspects of political, social, and religious characteristics of the South, and past experiences of the region may show the way to inevitable change in the future.

Clark, William B. "The Serpent of Lust in the Southern Garden." *SouR*, 10 (Autumn 1974), 805-822.

Studies the fascination with and the power of the myth of miscegenation in Southern writing.

Cobb, Buell. "The Sacred Harp of the South: A Study of the Origins, Practices, and Present Implications." *La Stud*, 7 (Summer 1968), 107-121.

Discusses the cultural and folk implications, past and present, of the Sacred Harp religious music.

Cohen, Hennig, ed. *Articles in American Studies: 1954-1968*. 2 vols. Ann Arbor: The Pierian Press, 1972.

This cumulative reprint of the annual bibliographies from the *American Quarterly* is made useful by complete indices; numerous Southerners are listed.

Cohen, Norm. "Robert W. Gordon and the Second Wreck of 'Old 97.'" *JAF*, 87 (January-March 1974), 12-38.

Presents the problem of a particular song and assesses the career of a significant collector of native American balladry, particularly of hillbilly songs.

Colquitt, Betsy F., ed. *Studies in Medieval, Renaissance, American Literature: A Festschrift*. Fort Worth, Texas: Texas Christian Univ Press, 1971.

Includes "E. A. Poe's Last Bid for Fame," by Haldeen Braddy, "Functional Imagery in Simms's *The Partisan*," by L. Moffitt Cecil, and "Nature and Grace in Caroline Gordon," by Louise Cowan.

Colvert, James B. "The Function of the Academic Critical Quarterly." *Miss Quart*, 23 (Spring 1970), 95-101.

Despite charges of sameness, such quarterlies remain committed to criticism, not to promoting literary movements and sociological commentary.

Combs, Richard E. *Authors: Critical and Biographical References*. Metuchen, N. J.: Scarecrow Press, 1971.

An index to references about 1,400 authors in 500 general critical studies of book length, including numerous Southerners.

Core, George. "Southern Letters and the New Criticism." *GaR*, 24 (Winter 1970), 413-431.

A modest defense of the New Criticism from a historical perspective.

Corrigan, Robert A. "Afro-American Fiction: A Checklist, 1853-1970." *Mid-Continent Am Stud Jour*, 11 (Fall 1970), 114-135.

Includes bibliographies of the fiction of Chesnutt, Ellison, James Weldon Johnson, Toomer, Wright, and others.

_____. "Afro-American Fiction Since 1970." *Am Stud*, 14 (Fall 1973), 85-90.
A second supplement to a bibliography which includes both major and minor black authors published since 1953.

Courtney, W. F., ed. *The Reader's Adviser: A Guide to the Best in Literature*. New York: R. R. Bowker, 1968.
Contains useful bibliographic data on works in print by and about the major Southern authors.

Cox, James M. "The South Once More." *SouR*, 82 (January-March 1974), 163-178.
An essay-review of C. Hugh Holman's *The Roots of Southern Writing*, Louis D. Rubin's *The Writer in the South*, Walter Sullivan's *Death by Melancholy*, Merrill M. Skaggs's *The Folk of Southern Fiction*, and Lewis P. Simpson's *The Man of Letters in New England and the South*.

Crawford, John W. "'Bred and Bawn in a Briar Patch'--Deception in the Making." *Sou Central Bul*, 34 (Winter 1974), 149-150.
Deals with deception as an archetypal motif in literature. Such literary figures as Harris' Brer Rabbit, Twain's Tom Sawyer, and Faulkner's Flem Snopes were all "'bred and bawn in a briar patch.'"

Dabbs, James M. *Haunted by God: The Cultural and Religious Experience of the South*. Richmond, Va.: John Knox Press, 1972.
A survey of the Southern character and culture and the place of religion in it from a personal point of view.

Dabney, Virginius. *Virginia: The New Dominion*. Garden City, N. Y.: Doubleday, 1971.
A survey-history of the state from 1607-1970 with brief attention to its literary and cultural life.

Davis, Arthur K., Jr. *Traditional Ballads of Virginia*. Charlottesville: Univ Press of Virginia, 1969.
A new printing of a 1929 publication.

Davis, A. P., and Saunders Redding, eds. *Cavalcade: Negro American Writing from 1760 to the Present*. Boston: Houghton Mifflin, 1971.
An anthology with section introduction and critical headnotes on the authors; includes over twenty-five Southerners.

Davis, C. T., and Daniel Walden, eds. *On Being Black: Writings by Afro-Americans from Frederick Douglass to the Present*. Greenwich, Conn.: Fawcett, 1970.
An anthology with critical introduction and headnotes, includes Chesnutt, Booker T. Washington, James Weldon Johnson, Toomer, Bontemps, Margaret Walker, Wright, and J. A. McPherson.

Davis, Richard B., C. Hugh Holman, and Louis D. Rubin, Jr., eds. *Southern Writing: 1585-1920*. New York: Odyssey, 1970.
An anthology of prose, poetry, and fiction divided into three units (1585-1800, 1800-1865, and 1865-1920), with unit introductions and critical headnotes; over 150 authors are represented.

Day, M. S. *History of American Literature: From the Beginning to 1910*. Volume I. New York: Doubleday, 1970.
A survey study guide; important Southern writers are covered.

Dennis, Frank A. "A Bibliography of Theses and Dissertations Relating to Mississippi, 1974." *JMiH*, 37 (May 1975), 209-215.
Title is descriptive.

DeVere, L. A. "Black English: Problematic but Systematic." *SAB*, 36 (May 1971), 38-46.
Black English raises social problems, but it is a logical language system. The article includes a selective bibliography on the subject.

Dobie, J. Frank. "The Writer and His Region." *SWR*, 59 (Autumn 1974), 423-431.
Proposes that it is now impossible to write a truly good book "that does not in outlook transcend the region on which it is focused."

Dorson, Richard M. "African and Afro-American Folklore: A Reply to Bascom and Other Misguided Critics." *JAF*, 88 (April-June 1975), 151-164.
Surveys the debate about and defends the thesis of multiple origins for folktales told by American blacks; brief reference to J. C. Harris' work.

Drake, Robert. "Rubin on Fiction and Other Matters." *SouR*, 6 (Summer 1970), 857-862.
An essay-review of *The Curious Death of the Novel: Essays in American Literature* and *The Teller in the Tale*.

Duke, Maurice. "Cabell's and Glasgow's Richmond: The Intellectual Background of the City." *Miss Quart*, 27 (Fall 1974), 375-391.
Briefly discusses the history of Richmond focussing on the cultural life at the time of Ellen Glasgow and James Branch Cabell.

Eaton, Clement. "Breaking a Path for the Liberation of Women in the South." *GaR*, 28 (Summer 1974), 187-199.
Eaton mentions several Southern writers, notably Ellen Glasgow, Kate Chopin, and James Lane Allen.

Edmunds, P. W. *Virginians Out Front*. Richmond, Va.: Whittet & Shepperson, 1972.
Biographical appreciations of Woodrow Wilson, Carter Glass, Booker T. Washington, Ellen Glasgow, Douglas S. Freeman, and six other distinguished Virginians.

Edward, Sister Ann. "Three Views on Blacks: The Black Woman in American Literature." *CEA Critic*, 37 (May 1975), 14-16.

Touches on characters in Faulkner, Toomer, Wright, and others.

Eisen, Jonathan. "Black Culture at Oberlin." *Cweal*, 87 (March 8, 1968), 676-677.
Reports on an Oberlin program in which Herbert Hill delivered an appreciation of black writers, and discussed the functions of American "Negritude" in literature to explain American blacks to white society and to themselves.

Ellis, L. Tuffly, and Barbara J. Stockley. "A Checklist of Theses and Dissertations in Texas Studies, 1964-1974." *SHQ*, 78 (October 1974), 183-198.
Grouped by school (Abilene Christian College and Baylor only) and arranged alphabetically by author within each grouping.

_____, and _____, comps. "A Checklist of Theses and Dissertations in Texas Studies, 1964-1974." *SHQ*, 79 (July 1975), 69-90; (October 1975), 205-219.
See above.

Emmerich, J. Oliver. *Two Faces of Janus: The Saga of Deep South Change*. Jackson: Univ and College Press of Mississippi, 1973.
Essays maintaining that the Old South is dead and has been replaced by a South of tolerance and honesty, by the editor of the McComb, Mississippi, *Enterprise-Journal*.

Etulain, R. W. *Western American Literature: A Bibliography*. Vermillion, S. D.: Dakota Press, 1972.
A checklist of books and articles with entries on Clemens, O. Henry, K. A. Porter, Wolfe, and others who are marginally Southerners.

Eubank, W. C. "Palmer's Century Sermon, New Orleans, January 1, 1901." *So Speech Jour*, 35 (Fall 1969), 28-39.
Discusses this sermon as an excellent example of ceremonial speech.

Evans, David. "Techniques of Blues Composition among Black Folksingers." *JAF*, 87 (July-September 1974), 240-249.
Contrasts the techniques of blues composition with those of white secular folksong, using many Southern examples.

Everett, Chestyn. "Tradition in Afro-American Literature." *Black World*, 25 (December 1975), 20-35.
Includes references to Chesnutt, Ellison, and others.

Everett, Robert B. "Georgiana Revisited: The Beehive Press in Perspective." *GaR*, 26 (Fall 1972), 347-349.
The Beehive Press of Savannah, Georgia, is reprinting valuable out-of-print books dealing with Georgia history and literature.

Ferris, William R., Jr. *Mississippi Black Folklore: A Research Bibliography and Discography*. Hattiesburg: Univ and College Press of Mississippi, 1971.
Unannotated bibliographical listings.

Fiedler, Leslie. *The Return of the Vanishing American*. New York: Stein and Day, 1968.
There are references to several Southerners, and Barth's *Sot-Weed Factor* is called the first example of the "New Western."

Fishwick, Marshall. "What Ever Happened to John Henry?" *SHR*, 5 (Summer 1971), 231-236.
A look at the history of black popular culture and a plea for black artists to "keep swinging and hammering."

Fleming, Robert E. "Humor in the Early Black Novel." *CLA Jour*, 17 (1973), 250-262.
W. W. Brown and Chesnutt are referred to in this discussion of the use of humor in black writing before 1910.

_____. "Roots of the White Liberal Stereotype in Black Fiction." *NALF*, 9 (Spring 1975), 17-19.
Includes discussion of W. W. Brown, Chesnutt, J. W. Johnson, and Wright, with brief mentions of Bontemps, Himes, and Reed.

Foerster, Norman, et al., eds. *American Poetry and Prose*. 5th ed. Boston: Houghton Mifflin, 1970.
An anthology with critical interchapters and headnotes; includes John Smith, Byrd, Jefferson, Poe, Timrod, Twain, Cable, Chesnutt, Lanier, Toomer, Wolfe, Faulkner, Wright, O'Connor, and Cleanth Brooks.

Ford, N. A., ed. *Black Insights: Significant Literature by Black Americans--1760 to the Present*. Waltham, Mass.: Ginn and Co., 1971.
An anthology with numerous Southerners represented.

Franklin, H. Bruce. "'A' is for Afro-American: A Primer on the Study of American Literature." *Minn Rev*, 5 (Fall 1975), 53-64.
New Left criticism. It was the slave who produced the significant literature of the South.

Frantz, Joe B. "Southwestern Collection." *SHQ*, 79 (July 1975), 91-106; (October 1975), 222-236.
Contains information of accessions to the University of Texas manuscripts collections and contains also a subject listing of recent historical publications relating to Texas.

Freedman, Alex S. "The Sociology of Country Music." *SHR*, 3 (Fall 1969), 358-362.
Describes and evaluates "several constituent elements concerning country music as an art form as well as an object of sociological analysis."

Freedman, F. S., ed. *The Black American Experience*. New York: Bantam Pathfinder Editions, 1970.
An anthology with introductory notes on Bennett, Hayden, Northup, Bontemps, Douglass, J. W. Johnson, Nat Turner, Washington, Holtzclaw, Cain, L. P. Hill, Holman, Bates, M. L. King, Ossie Davis, Margaret Walker, and Wright.

Gainer, Patrick W. *Folk Songs from the West Virginia Hills*. Grantsville, West Va.: Seneca Books, 1975.

Contains tunes, lyrics and background information on 108 of Child's ballads, folk songs, fiddle tunes, choral pieces, and Negro songs.

_____. *Witches, Ghosts, and Signs*. Grantsville, West Va.: Seneca Books, 1975.
A recounting of stories and tales which are a part of the oral tradition and folklore of the Southern Appalachians.

Garrett, George. "The South." *Am Libraries*, 3 (January 1972), 25-38.
Questions previous definitions of Southern literature and its characteristics and finds greater diversity and less unity than generally allowed.

Gayle, Addison, Jr., ed. *The Black Aesthetic*. New York: Doubleday, 1971.
A compilation of critical essays containing commentary on Bontemps, Chesnutt, Douglass, Ellison, Johnson, Killens, Toomer, Wright, and other Southern writers.

_____. *The Way of the World: The Black Novel in America*. Garden City, N. Y.: Anchor Press/ Doubleday, 1975.
Views the history of black fiction as a struggle for artistic freedom; extensive comment on all major and minor black Southern writers.

Genovese, Eugene D. *In Red and Black: Marxian Explorations in Southern and Afro-American History*. New York: Pantheon, 1971.
Collects nineteen essays, many of which deal with Southern slavery and modern attitudes toward the South, including Genovese's defense of Styron's *The Confessions of Nat Turner*.

Gérard, Albert. *Les Tambours du Néant: Le problème existentiel dans le roman américain*. Brussels: La Renaissance du Livre, 1969.
Includes discussion of Wright, Williams, and Faulkner.

Gerstenberger, Donna, and George Hendrick. *The American Novels: A Checklist of Twentieth Century Criticism on Novels Written Since 1789*. Vol. II: *Criticism Written 1960-1968*. Chicago: Swallow Press, 1970.
A supplement to the authors' 1960 checklist of criticism; over fifty-five Southern authors are represented.

_____. *Third Directory of Periodicals Publishing Articles on English and American Literature and Language*. Chicago: Swallow Press, 1970.
Information on 547 periodicals for contributors; lists seven journals with a specific interest in Southern literature and five devoted to Southern authors Cabell, Poe, and Twain.

Gohdes, Clarence. *Bibliographical Guide to the Study of Literature of the U. S. A.* Third edition, revised and enlarged. Durham, N. C.: Duke Univ Press, 1970.
Contains a section on "Selected Studies of Regional Literature."

Going, William T. "Alabama in the Short Story: Notes for an Anthology." *AlaR*, 22 (January 1969), 3-23.
Using the criterion of how well the author writes about the state, regardless of where he was born or lived, this collection would include stories by Johnson J. Hooper, Andrew Lytle, F. Scott Fitzgerald, and Truman Capote.

_____. *Essays on Alabama Literature*. University: Univ of Alabama Press, 1975.
A collection of nine previously published essays on facets of and figures in Alabama literature, mainly 20th century.

Grantham, Dewey W. "History, Mythology, and the Southern Lady." *So Lit Jour*, 3 (Spring 1971), 98-108.
An essay-review of three interpretations of the South which illustrate "the interplay between the depletion and renewal of research opportunities in the history of the South." The books discussed are *The American South: A Brief History*, by Monroe Lee Billington; *The Myth of Southern History: Historical Consciousness in Twentieth-Century Southern Literature*, by F. Garvin Davenport, Jr.; *The Southern Lady: From Pedestal to Politics, 1830-1930*, by Anne Firor Scott.

Greenspan, C. L., and L. M. Hirsch, eds. *All Those Voices: The Minority Experience*. New York: Macmillan, 1971.
An anthology of ethnic-oriented materials; Fitzhugh and Wright are represented.

Gross, Seymour L. "Literature and the Cultural History of the Negro." *So Lit Jour*, 2 (Spring 1970), 148-155.
An essay-review of Nancy M. Tischler's *Black Masks: Negro Characters in Modern Southern Fiction* which finds the book disappointing on a subject of such importance today.

Gross, Theodore L. *The Heroic Ideal in American Literature*. New York: The Free Press, 1971.
In a study of the tension between idealism and authority in archetypal figures of American literature, two chapters are devoted to "The Southern Hero" and "The Black Hero," with attention to numerous authors, including Simms, Page, Faulkner, Toomer, Wright, and Ellison.

_____. "The Idealism of Negro Literature in America." *Phylon*, 30 (Spring 1969), 5-10.
Seeks to explain the reasons for certain emphases in black writing. Includes references to a number of Southern writers, black and white.

_____. "Our Mutual Estate: The Literature of the American Negro." *AR*, 28 (Fall 1968), 293-303.
Criticizes previous scholarly and critical evaluations of black literature; uses Wright's *Native Son* as an example of a work that has been judged "parochially."

Grumbach, Doris. "Christianity and Black Writers." *Renascence*, 23 (Summer 1971), 198-212.
Traces the recorded criticism of black writers to the white Christian church, including

that of Douglass, B. T. Washington, J. W. Johnson, Margaret Walker, Arna Bontemps, and Richard Wright.

Guilds, John C., ed. *Nineteenth-Century Southern Fiction*. Columbus, Ohio: Charles E. Merrill, 1970.
    An anthology of eleven stories and tales with an introduction and critical headnotes.

Haight, A. L. *Banned Books*. New York: R. R. Bowker, 1970.
    Contains notes on the suppression of books by Cabell, Caldwell, Faulkner, Jefferson, Twain, and Tennessee Williams.

Halsell, Willie D. "A Bibliography of Theses and Dissertations Relating to Mississippi, 1970." *JMiH*, 33 (February 1971), 59-68.
    Includes works on literature and folklore, especially Faulkner.

_____. "A Bibliography of Theses and Dissertations Relating to Mississippi, 1973." *JMiH*, 36 (February 1974), 105-111.
    Title is descriptive.

_____. "Publications Relating to Mississippi." *JMiH*, 36 (May 1974), 205-209.
    Title is descriptive.

Hansen, Arlen J. "Entropy and Transformation: Two Types of American Humor." *Am Schol*, 43 (Summer 1974), 405-421.
    In a general discussion of visual and verbal humor, the article makes reference to G. W. Harris, A. B. Longstreet, Joseph Baldwin, and Mark Twain.

Harkness, D. J. "Louisiana: Leader in Literature." *Delta Rev*, 7 (May/June 1970), 20-21.
    A capsule history of Louisiana letters and a catalogue of contemporary writers associated with the state.

_____. *Tennessee and Alabama*. Knoxville: Univ of Tennessee Continuing Education Series, 1971.
    A sixteen-page pamphlet on miscellaneous cultural relations between the two states.

_____. *Tennessee and North Carolina: Land of Culture and Collards*. Knoxville: Univ of Tennessee Extension, 1969.
    Lists literature by and about natives of both states.

_____. *Tennessee and Virginia: The Mountain Empire*. Knoxville: Univ of Tennessee Extension, 1970.
    Lists literature by and about natives of both states.

_____. *Tennessee Heritage*. Knoxville: Univ of Tennessee Continuing Education Series, 1971.
    A twenty-page pamphlet summarizing miscellaneous cultural and literary data about Tennessee.

_____. *Tennessee: "The Most Interesting State,"* rev. ed. Knoxville: Univ of Tennessee Extension, 1968.
    Includes a list of Tennessee writers.

Harlow, Geoffrey, and James Redmond, eds. *The Year's Work in English Studies*. Volume 49. New York: Humanities Press for the English Association, 1970.
    Review-essays on scholarship for 1968; numerous Southern authors are mentioned.

Hauck, Richard B. *A Cheerful Nihilism: Confidence and "The Absurd" in American Humorous Fiction*. Bloomington: Indiana Univ Press, 1971.
    Studies the nihilistic but cheerful response of American humorists to the meaninglessness and absurdity in the universe, with full discussions of the Southwestern humorists, Twain, Faulkner, and Barth.

Havard, William C. "The New Mind of the South." *SouR*, 4 (Autumn 1968), 865-883.
    A study of the changing idea of the mind of the South, with brief references to several Southern writers.

_____. "Pride and Fall: A New Source for Interpreting Southern Experience." *SouR*, 10 (Autumn 1974), 823-839.
    This essay-review of R. M. Myers' *The Children of Pride* urges the literary importance of the letters and discusses their form and several leading themes of the collection.

_____. "Southwest Humor: Contemporary Style." *SouR*, 6 (Autumn 1970), 1185-1190.
    An essay-review of Brooks Hays's *Hotbed of Tranquility* which sees it as related to the tradition of Southwestern humor.

Havlice, Patricia P. *Index to American Author Bibliographies*. Metuchen, N. J.: Scarecrow Press, 1971.
    A listing, by subject, of author bibliographies found in periodicals from the late nineteenth century to 1970, with numerous Southerners included.

Helmcke, Hans, et al., eds. *Literatur und Sprache der Vereinigten Staaten: Aufsätze zu Ehren von Hans Galinsky*. Heidelberg: Winter, 1969.
    Contains essays on William Byrd and Thomas Wolfe.

Hemenway, Robert, ed. *The Black Novelist*. Columbus, Ohio: Charles E. Merrill, 1970.
    Reprints critical essays on Chesnutt, Yerby, Wright, and Ellison, and personal essays by Bontemps, Wright, and Ellison.

Henderson, Harry B., III. *Versions of the Past: The Historical Imagination in American Fiction*. New York: Oxford, 1974.
    Includes discussion of Twain's *A Connecticut Yankee* and of Faulkner's *Absalom, Absalom!*

Herron, Ima H. *The Small Town in American Drama*. Dallas: Southern Methodist Univ Press, 1969.
    An extensive, detailed history of portrayals of life and mores in small towns in more than 300 plays by American dramatists from Munford's *The Candidates* (1770) to Albee's *Virginia Woolf* (1962); includes commentary on most Southern playwrights and dramas set in the South. A companion study to Herron's *The Small Town in American Literature* (1939 and 1959).

Higgs, Robert J., and A. N. Manning, eds. *Voices from the Hills: Selected Readings of Southern Appalachia*. New York: Frederick Ungar, 1975.
A critical anthology of stories, poems, essays, and excerpts from Colonial times to the present delineating life in the Southern mountains.

Hill, Mildred A. "Common Folklore Features in African and African American Literature." *SFQ*, 39 (June 1975), 111-133.
Defends the importance of African influences by drawing parallels between works of African writers and those of American authors Charles W. Chesnutt, Zora Neale Hurston, Richard Wright, Ernest Gaines, and others.

Hill, Samuel S., Jr., and others. *Religion and the Solid South*. Nashville: Abingdon Press, 1972.
Six essays drawn from a 1969 symposium on "The Bible Belt in Continuity and Change" in which the authors examine the secular role of religion in Southern culture.

Holliday, Carl. *A History of Southern Literature*. Port Washington, N. Y.: Kennikat Press, 1969.
A new printing of a 1906 work.

Hollis, C. Carroll. "A Study of the Plain Folk." *So Lit Jour*, 6 (Spring 1974), 134-138.
An essay-review of *The Folk of Southern Fiction*, by Merrill Maguire Skaggs, which views the book as an important critical study of local-color writing in the South.

Holman, C. Hugh. *The Roots of Southern Writing: Essays on the Literature of the American South*. Athens: Univ of Georgia Press, 1972.
A collection of seventeen essays published over a twenty-five-year period which relate the work of the writers to their physical, social, and moral environment; Simms, Glasgow, Wolfe, Faulkner, and O'Connor are treated at length.

Holmes, William, and Edward Mitchell, eds. *Nineteenth-Century American Short Fiction*. Glenview, Ill.: Scott, Foresman, 1970.
An anthology with critical headnotes; includes Longstreet, Poe, G. W. Harris, Twain, Cable, Bonner, J. L. Allen, Chopin and T. N. Page.

Hoole, W. Stanley. *According to Hoole*. University: Univ of Alabama Press, 1973.
A collection of forty-six essays, articles and reviews on Southern literature and culture, including Hooper and Simms, with a brief autobiography by librarian, scholar, teacher Hoole.

Hough, R. L. "American Comedy." *PrS*, 48 (Fall 1974), 270-271.
A review of *The Comic Imagination in American Literature*, edited by Louis D. Rubin, Jr.

Howe, Irving. *Decline of the New*. New York: Harcourt, Brace and World, 1970.
Collects eighteen earlier published essays on modernist literature, several of which include brief discussions of Faulkner, Twain, Wright, and Ellison.

Howlett, William J. *Old St. Thomas' at Poplar Neck, Bardstown, Kentucky*. Cleveland, Ohio: Dillon/Liederbach, 1972.
A reprint of the 1906 history of St. Thomas' Seminary at Bardstown, Kentucky, where Jefferson Davis was educated and which figures in some Southern fiction.

Hoyt, Charles A., ed. *Minor American Novelists*. Carbondale: Southern Illinois Univ Press, 1970.
Includes original essays on Chesnutt by R. M. Farnsworth, Cabell by F. B. Millett, and Flannery O'Connor by Paul Levine.

Hubbell, Jay B. *Who Are the Major American Writers?* Durham, N. C.: Duke Univ Press, 1972.
A study of changes in literary judgments and critical standards in the reputations of American writers, with attention to Poe, Twain, Faulkner, Cabell, Davidson, Ransom, Tate, Warren, Wolfe, and numerous other Southerners.

Inge, M. Thomas, ed. *Agrarianism in American Literature*. New York: Odyssey Press, 1969.
An anthology including brief comment on and excerpts from William Byrd, Thomas Jefferson, John Taylor, Sidney Lanier, Henry Timrod, George Fitzhugh, G. W. Harris, Donald Davidson, Andrew Lytle, John Crowe Ransom, Robert Penn Warren, William Alexander Percy, James Agee, Elizabeth Madox Roberts, William Faulkner, among others.

_____. "Miguel Unamuno's *Canciones* on American Literature Translated with Commentary." *ArlQ*, 2 (Autumn 1969), 83-97.
Comments on Poe's influence on Unamuno and his fascination with Lanier.

_____. "William Dean Howells on Southern Literature." *Miss Quart*, 21 (Fall 1968), 291-304.
Reprints, with an introduction, Howells' "The Southern States in Recent American Literature" (1898), which discusses A. B. Longstreet, W. T. Thompson, J. G. Baldwin, G. W. Harris, G. W. Cable, J. C. Harris, Mary N. Murfree, John Fox, J. E. Cooke, T. N. Page, J. L. Allen, Paul Dunbar, Sidney Lanier, Henry Timrod, Paul H. Hayne, Opie Read, and Grace King along with less well-known writers.

Isani, Mukhtar A. "The Exotic and Protest in Earlier Black Literature: The Use of Alien Setting and Character." *SBL*, 5 (Summer 1974), 9-14.
Includes discussion of W. W. Brown and references to Albery Whitman, J. W. Johnson, and Arna Bontemps.

Jackson, Blyden, and Louis D. Rubin, Jr. *Black Poetry in America: Two Essays in Historical Interpretation*. Baton Rouge: Louisiana State Univ Press, 1974.
An interpretation of the principal directions of black poetry; includes discussion or mention of numerous Southerners.

Jacobs, Robert D. "Republics of Letters, North and South." *Miss Quart*, 28 (Winter 1974-75), 93-102.
A review-essay of Lewis P. Simpson's *The Man of Letters in New England and the South*.

Jaffe, Harry J. "American Negro Folklore: A Checklist of Scarce Items." *SFQ*, 37 (March 1972), 68-70.
    A list of early twentieth-century items not included in Melville Herskovits' *The Myth of the Negro Past*, Richard Dorson's *American Negro Folklore*, or Newbell Puckett's *Folk Beliefs of the Southern Negro*.

Jaskoski, Helen. "Power Unequal to Man: The Significance of Conjure in Works by Five Afro-American Authors." *SFQ*, 38 (June 1974), 91-108.
    Examines attitudes toward conjure in works by Chesnutt, Douglass, Gaines, George Marion McClellan, and Ann Petry.

Johnson, Lemuel A. *The Devil, the Gargoyle, and the Buffoon: The Negro as Metaphor in Western Literature*. Port Washington, N. Y.: Kennikat Press, 1971.
    A study of literary responses to the Negro and his blackness.

Jones, H. G. "Books About North Carolina, 1973-74." *Miss Quart*, 28 (Spring 1975), 205-213.
    An essay-review of a number of books on North Carolina history.

Jones, Lawrence W., comp. "Canadian Graduate Studies in American Literature: A Bibliography of Theses and Dissertations, 1921-1968." *C Rev Am Stud*, 1 (Fall 1970), 116-129.
    The *Canadian Review of American Studies* replaces the *CAAS Bulletin*. Over 250 items are listed, with Poe named in ten.

Justus, James H. "On the Restlessness of Southerners." *SouR*, 11 (Winter 1975), 65-83.
    This study of regional distinctiveness argues that restlessness is an American and Southern trait, and explores the theme in the work of Mark Twain, Wolfe, Faulkner, Welty, and others.

Kable, William S. "South Carolina District Copyrights: 1794-1820." *Proof*, 1 (1971), 180-198.
    A transcription of the significant data found in a ledger recently discovered at the University of South Carolina, containing a listing of South Carolina District Copyrights commencing with the year 1794.

Kaplan, Harold. *Democratic Humanism and American Literature*. Chicago: Univ of Chicago Press, 1972.
    Examines the responses of nineteenth-century American writers to the challenge of liberal democratic ideals, with chapters devoted to Poe and Twain.

Kartiganer, Donald M., and Malcolm A. Griffith, eds. *Theories of American Literature: The Critical Perspective*. New York: Macmillan, 1972.
    Reprints nineteen general essays; numerous Southerners are mentioned.

Katz, Joseph, ed. *Proof: The Yearbook of American Bibliographical and Textual Studies*. Volume 2. Columbia: Univ of South Carolina Press, 1972.
    Includes "The Colonial South Carolina Book Trade," by Calhoun Winton, "How Samuel Clemens Became Mark Twain's Publisher," by Frederick Anderson and Hamlin Hill, "The Expurgation of *Tom Sawyer Abroad*," by O. M. Brack, and "The Opening Scene of William Faulkner's *Light in August*," by Carl Ficken.

Kearns, F. E., ed. *The Black Experience: An Anthology of American Literature for the 1970's*. New York: Viking, 1970.
    An anthology, with critical headnotes, of writings by black and white authors about the experience of the Negro in America, including Poe, Simms, Kennedy, Cable, Twain, Russell, J. C. Harris, Dunbar, Chesnutt, Bontemps, Faulkner, Wright, Welty, Ellison, and O'Connor.

Ketterer, David. *New Worlds for Old: The Apocalyptic Imagination, Science Fiction, and American Literature*. Bloomington: Indiana Univ Press, 1974.
    Contains chapters on Poe and Twain, among others.

Kinnamon, Keneth. "The Political Dimension of Afro-American Literature." *Soundings*, 58 (Spring 1975), 130-144.
    Includes references to Douglass and Chesnutt.

Kozisek, J. L., comp. "Manuscript Acquisitions of the Department of Archives and History." *JMiH*, 37 (May 1975), 217-219.
    Title is descriptive.

Kronenberger, Louis, and Emily M. Beck, eds. *Atlantic Brief Lives: A Biographical Companion to the Arts*. Boston: Little, Brown, 1971.
    Contains brief biographies of numerous Southerners, including longer appreciative essays on Faulkner by Mark Schorer, Twain by Justin Kaplan, and Wolfe by Andrew Turnbull; also Robert Penn Warren writes on Cooper, and Eudora Welty on Jane Austen.

Kuhlmann, Susan. *Knave, Fool, and Genius: The Confidence Man as He Appears in Nineteenth-Century American Fiction*. Chapel Hill: Univ of North Carolina Press, 1973.
    Includes consideration of the humorists of the Old Southwest and of Mark Twain.

Lang, Hans Joachim, ed. *Der amerikanische Roman: Von den Anfängen bis zur Gegenwart*. Düsseldorf: August Bagel, 1972.
    Includes "Faulkner: *Absalom, Absalom!*" (Berndt Ostendorf, pp. 249-275), "Mark Twain: *Adventures of Huckleberry Finn*" (Douglas W. Jefferson, pp. 142-167), and "Ellison: *The Invisible Man*" (Martin Christadler, pp. 333-369).

Lass, A. H. *Plot Guide to 100 American and British Novels*. Boston: The Writer, 1971.
    Includes plots, critical summaries, and biographies for works by Twain, Cabell, Wolfe, Faulkner, Caldwell, McCullers, Warren, and Styron.

Leary, Lewis. *Southern Excursions: Essays on Mark Twain and Others*. Baton Rouge: Louisiana State Univ Press, 1971.

Collects eleven earlier essays, 1949-1970, on Twain, Lanier, Hearn, Chopin, Mencken, and Faulkner, and one new essay on G. W. Harris.

_____, with Carolyn Bartholet and Catharine Roth. *Articles in American Literature, 1950-1967.* Durham, N. C.: Duke Univ Press, 1970.
     Includes checklists of scholarship on over eighty Southern authors and a separate unit on "Regionalism."

Lemon, Lee T. *A Glossary for the Study of English.* New York: Oxford Univ Press, 1971.
     Brief mentions of the Fugitives, the Agrarians, and numerous Southern authors.

Levin, Harry, ed. *Veins of Humor.* Harvard English Studies 3. Cambridge, Mass.: Harvard Univ Press, 1972.
     Includes essays by Walter Blair and W. M. Frohock with commentary on Southern humorists, Faulkner, and Ellison.

Lewald, H. Ernest, ed. *The Cry of Home: Cultural Nationalism and the Modern Writer.* Knoxville: Univ of Tennessee Press, 1972.
     Includes essays on the background of modern Southern fiction by Lewis Simpson and on Afro-American writing by O. B. Emerson; an official project of the MLA "Literature and Society" session.

Libman, Valentina, comp. *Russian Studies of American Literature.* Trans. Robert V. Allen and ed. Clarence Gohdes. Chapel Hill: Univ of North Carolina Press, 1969.
     Bibliographical entries ranging from one to many items, on Cable, Caldwell, Faulkner, Lafcadio Hearn, Hellman, Thomas Jefferson, Lanier, Harper Lee, Mencken, Margaret Mitchell, Poe, O. Henry, Lillian Smith, T. S. Stribling, Williams, Wolfe, and Wright. There are more entries for Mark Twain than for any other writer included.

Lohner, Edgar, ed. *Der Amerikanische Roman im 19. und 20. Jahrhundert.* Berlin: Erich Schmidt Verlag, 1974.
     Includes essays on Mark Twain, Faulkner, and Wolfe.

Lomax, Alan, and Raoul Abdul, eds. *3000 Years of Black Poetry.* Greenwich, Conn.: Fawcett, 1971.
     Biographical notes on and excerpts from the work of numerous Southern blacks.

Long, E. Hudson. *American Drama from Its Beginnings to the Present.* Goldentree Bibliographies in Language and Literature. New York: Appleton-Century-Crofts, 1970.
     Selective checklists of secondary materials with a general entry on Southern drama and entries on several Southern dramatists, including Green, Hellman, and Williams.

Long, Richard A., and Eugenia W. Collier, eds. *Afro-American Writing: An Anthology of Prose and Poetry.* New York: New York Univ Press, 1972.
     A two-volume collection with selections and critical introductions; extensive Southern representation.

Longstreet, S. *We All Went to Paris.* New York: Macmillan, 1972.
     An informal history of Americans in France, 1776-1971, with discussions of Wright and McCullers, and an interview on Paris with Faulkner.

Ludwig, Richard M., ed. *Literary History of the United States: Bibliography Supplement II.* New York: Macmillan, 1972.
     Updates the earlier bibliographical supplements by covering 1958-1970; includes thirty-two additional author entries with numerous Southerners represented.

Luke, Myron H., ed. "Articles in American Studies, 1970." *AQ,* 23 (August 1971), 357-446.
     The folklore section, pp. 378-381, and the literature section, pp. 402-409, of this annual bibliography contain scattered annotated entries centering on Southern writers.

_____, ed. "Articles in American Studies, 1972." *AQ,* 25 (August 1973), 261-314.
     This annual bibliography contains numerous entries centering on Southern literature.

Maekawa Shunichi Kyōju Kanreki Kinen-ronbunshu [Essays and Studies in Commemoration of Professor Shunichi Maekawa's Sixty-First Birthday]. Tokyo: Eihōsha, 1968.
     Contains essays on Poe, Caldwell, and Faulkner.

Mann, K. H. *Anales del Departmento de Lenguas Modernas, Universidad de Costa Rica.* No. 1, August 1972. San Jose: Univ of Costa Rica, 1972.
     Contains essays on Poe and Wright.

Margolies, Edward. *A Native Sons Reader.* Philadelphia: Lippincott, 1970.
     A critical anthology including selections by William Attaway, Charles W. Chesnutt, Eldridge Cleaver, William Demby, Junius Edwards, Ellison, J. W. Johnson, Albert Murray, Diane Oliver, John Williams, and Wright.

Marks, Henry S. *Who Was Who in Alabama.* Huntsville, Ala.: Strode Publishers, 1972.
     Includes biographical notes on J. G. Baldwin, William March (Campbell), J. J. Hooper, Mary Johnston, T. S. Stribling, and other writers.

Marsh, John L. *A Student's Bibliography of American Literature.* Dubuque, Iowa: Kendall/Hunt Publishing Co., 1971.
     A selective checklist with author lists for major Southern writers of critical and biographical studies.

May, John R. *Toward a New Earth: Apocalypse in the American Novel.* Notre Dame: Univ of Notre Dame, 1972.
     Examines both the secular and religious versions of apocalypse in American fiction in Barth, Ellison, Faulkner, O'Connor, Twain, Wright, and others.

McCarthy, Harold T. *The Expatriate Perspective.* Cranbury, N. J.: Fairleigh Dickinson Univ Press, 1974.

A study of the idea of America as expressed in the works of the expatriate American novelists, including Mark Twain and Richard Wright.

McElroy, John. "The Hawthorne Style of American Fiction." *ESQ*, 19 (2nd Qtr. 1973), 117-123.
Includes discussion of Poe and of Clemens as one of Poe's followers in style; Faulkner is one of Hawthorne's followers.

McGhee, Nancy B. "The Folk Sermon: A Facet of the Black Literary Heritage." *CLA Jour*, 13 (September 1969), 51-61.
Discusses James Weldon Johnson's *God's Trombones* among many other works.

McMillan, James B. *Annotated Bibliography of Southern American English*. Coral Gables: Univ of Miami Press, 1971.
An annotated checklist of over 1100 studies of Southern speech and language with sections on literary dialect and figurative language.

McNamee, Lawrence F. *Dissertations in English and American Literature: Supplement One, 1964-1968*. New York: R. R. Bowker, 1969.
In addition to author entries, a separate section lists general dissertations on Southern literature.

McPherson, James M., et al. *Blacks in America: Bibliographical Essays*. New York: Doubleday, 1971.
Chronological surveys of primary and secondary material on the history and culture of Afro-Americans, with extensive references to the South and to Southern artists.

Mellard, James M. "Racism, Formula, and Popular Fiction." *Jour of Popular Culture*, 5 (Summer 1971), 10-37.
All writers of popular fiction employ formulaic elements in presenting black characters. These formulas rise out of the culture and are reinforced in it by the literature. Though racist propaganda-fiction employs such formulas heavily, the best authors use them originally and creatively to cut through racial stereotypes to human truth. Many Southern writers are treated, Dixon and Styron at length.

Miller, Ruth, and Paul J. Dolan, eds. *Race Awareness: The Nightmare and the Vision*. New York: Oxford Univ Press, 1971.
An anthology of readings on ethnic experiences, with selections by Southerners and about the South.

Miller, Wayne C. *An Armed America: Its Face in Fiction*. New York: New York Univ Press, 1970.
Includes discussion of Lanier's *Tiger-Lilies* and of Faulkner's *Soldiers' Pay*, *A Fable*, and World War I short stories; there are brief references to Simms and Mark Twain.

Morgan, L. C. "North Carolina Accents." *So Speech Jour*, 34 (Spring 1969), 174-182.
Examines remnants of colonial accents in North Carolina.

Morrison, Claudia B. *Freud and the Critic: The Early Use of Depth Psychology in Literary Criticism*. Chapel Hill: Univ of North Carolina Press, 1968.
Includes discussion of Poe, Twain, and Aiken.

Morrow, S. S. "A Brief History of Theatre in Nashville, 1807-1970." *Tenn Hist Quart*, 30 (Summer 1971), 178-189.
Title is descriptive.

Mukherjee, Sugit, and D. V. K. Raghavascharyulu, eds. *Indian Essays in Honour of Robert E. Spiller*. Bombay: Popular Prakashan, 1969.
Includes "Isabel Archer and Huck Finn: Two Responses to the Fruit of Knowledge" (Raj K. Kohli) and "The Pilgrim and the Picaro: A Study of Faulkner's *The Bear* and *The Reivers*" (V. R. N. Prasad).

Nagourney, Peter, and Susan Steiner, eds. *Growing Up American*. Belmont, Calif.: Wadsworth, 1972.
A collection of readings focused on the myth of equal opportunity in the United States, with selections from Frederick Douglass, M. C. Holman (Mississippi), Flannery O'Connor, and Booker T. Washington.

Nance, William L. "Eden, Oedipus, and Rebirth in American Fiction." *ArQ*, 31 (Winter 1975), 353-365.
Includes brief discussion of Faulkner's *The Sound and the Fury* and brief references to Clemens, Capote, Barth, and Southern fiction.

Nilon, Charles H. *Bibliography of Bibliographies in American Literature*. New York: R. R. Bowker, 1970.
Extensive coverage of bibliographical work on major and minor Southern authors, and general units on Regionalism.

Noble, David W. *The Eternal Adam and the New World Garden: The Central Myth in the American Novel Since 1830*. New York: George Braziller, 1968.
Discusses the American dream of the frontier as a new Eden as reflected in the works of eighteen novelists, including Faulkner and Warren.

Noble, Donald R. "Southern Writers in General Studies of American Literature." *Miss Quart*, 28 (Fall 1975), 521-530.
An omnibus review-essay of eleven books, which discovers that it is not the quality of the Southern writer or his Southernness which has interested contemporary commentators, but instead his existential qualities.

Nower, Joyce. "Foolin' Master." *Satire Newsletter*, 7 (Fall 1969), 5-10.
Discusses the satiric element in the "Fooling Master" folk tradition, and its modern forms in urban lore and in such writers as Langston Hughes, Jean Toomer, and Eldridge Cleaver.

_____. "The Tradition of Negro Literature in the United States." *NALF*, 3 (1969), 5-12.
Traces themes in black literature from 1760 to the present.

Paluka, Frank. "American Literary Manuscripts in the University of Iowa Libraries: A Checklist." *RALS*, 3 (Spring 1973), 100-120.
A listing, largely of letters, including such Southerners as Cabell, Cable, Glasgow, Ransom.

Parks, Edd Winfield. *Southern Poets*. New York: Phaeton Press, 1970.
A reprint of the 1936 critical introduction and anthology in the American Writers Series.

Partlow, Robert, ed. *Studies in American Literature in Honor of Robert Dunn Faner, 1906-1967*. Supplement to *Papers in Lang and Lit*, Summer 1969.
Includes essays on Poe and Faulkner.

Pavese, Cesare. *American Literature: Essays and Opinions*. Trans. Edwin Fussell. Berkeley: Univ of California Press, 1970.
Includes commentary on W. S. Porter, Faulkner, and Wright.

Perkins, George, ed. *The Theory of the American Novel*. New York: Holt, Rinehart, and Winston, 1970.
A collection of essays on the art of the novel by novelists, including Simms, Twain, Glasgow, Faulkner, Wolfe, Warren, and Wright.

Perrin, A. H. *924 Works of Fiction by Southern Appalachian Authors*. Berea, Ky.: Hutchins Library, Berea College, 1972.
A revised mimeographed checklist of books by and about Appalachians in the Weatherford-Hammond Mountain Collection at Berea College.

_____. *340 Books of Ballads and Songs in the Berea College Collection*. Berea, Ky.: Berea College Library, 1974.
A mimeographed checklist of books in the Berea collection, from Bishop Percy to John Jacob Niles.

_____. "The Weatherford-Hammond Mountain Collection of Berea College." *RALS*, 5 (Spring 1975), 98-100.
Title is descriptive.

Plaisance, E. C. "Cheniere: The Destruction of a Community." *La Hist*, 14 (Spring 1973), 179-193.
In addition to a history of the hurricane of October 1893, this article includes a poem, written in French, by a survivor, Jean Henriot, a translation, and comments on an earlier version presented by Ormonde Plater in the April 1971 issue of *Lousiana Folklore Miscellany*.

Plante, P. R. "American Courage." *Novel*, 5 (Winter 1972), 180-181.
In a glowing review of *Les Tambours du Neant* by Albert Gerard, the author observes that the work concentrates mainly on Melville, Hemingway, Faulkner, and, to a lesser degree, Robert Penn Warren, but also considers novels by Richard Wright, Ralph Ellison, and James Baldwin. He especially praises the first chapter which deals with the "international theme" in, among others, Tennessee Williams' *The Roman Spring of Mrs. Stone*.

Pochmann, Henry A., and Gay Wilson Allen. *Introduction to Masters of American Literature*. Carbondale: Southern Illinois Univ Press, 1969.
Includes introductory essays on Poe and Twain.

Pollard, Arthur, ed. *Webster's New World Companion to English and American Literature*. New York: World Publishing Co., 1973.
Includes entries on major and many minor Southern writers, with an appendix of secondary bibliography.

Post, L. C. "Joseph C. Falcon, Accordian Player and Singer: A Biographical Sketch." *La Hist*, 11 (Winter 1970), 63-79.
A biographical sketch, a recorded interview, and discography placing Falcon in the tradition of Louisiana Acadian folk music.

Primeau, Ronald. "Blake's Chimney Sweeper as Afro American Minstrel." *BNYPL*, 78 (Summer 1975), 418-430.
Some early Afro-American writers reflected the "heaven-as-reward-for-doing-one's-duty-now" philosophy of Blake's poems of "Innocence," whereas later writers, including Wright, reflect the attitudes of "Experience."

"Publications Relating to Mississippi." *JMiH*, 36 (November 1974), 393-934.
Title is descriptive.

Pudner, H. Peter. "People Not Pedagogy: Education in Old Virginia." *GaR*, 25 (Fall 1971), 263-285.
A survey of reading and educational tastes in early Virginia history.

Redmond, Eugene B. "The Black American Epic: Its Roots, Its Writers." *Black Schol*, 2 (January 1971), 15-22.
The roots of the black American heritage are in the African past--as, for example is reflected in Margaret Walker's *For My People*; James Weldon Johnson believed that this past was also reflected in the Uncle Remus stories.

Rees, Robert A., and Earl N. Harbert, eds. *Fifteen American Authors Before 1900*. Madison: Univ of Wisconsin Press, 1971.
Includes bibliographic essay-reviews of scholarship on "Literature of the Old South," by C. Hugh Holman, and "Literature of the New South," by Louis D. Rubin, Jr.

Reeves, William J. "The Significance of the Audience in Black Poetry." *NALF*, 9 (Spring 1975), 30-32.
Includes discussion of George Moses Horton and Nikki Giovanni.

Rickels, Milton. "The Louisiana Folklore Society." *JAF*, 82 (January-March 1969), 20-22.
A history of the state society, largely since 1956.

Righter, William. "Myth and Interpretation." *New Lit Hist*, 3 (Winter 1972), 319-344.
Twain and Faulkner are used as "cases in which myth is used as an interpretive means."

Robbins, J. Albert, ed. *American Literary Scholarship: An Annual, 1968*. Durham, N. C.: Duke Univ Press, 1970.

Contains essay-reviews of scholarship on numerous Southern authors, with specific chapters devoted to publications about Faulkner, by Olga Vickery, and Twain, by John C. Gerber.

_____, ed. *American Literary Scholarship: An Annual/1969*. Durham, N. C.: Duke Univ Press, 1971.
Includes bibliographical essays on Poe, Twain, and Faulkner; bibliographical references to criticism on numerous other Southerners is included in more general sections.

_____, ed. *American Literary Scholarship: An Annual, 1970*. Durham, N. C.: Duke Univ Press, 1972.
See above.

_____, ed. *American Literary Scholarship: An Annual/1971*. Durham, N. C.: Duke Univ Press, 1973.
See above.

_____, ed. *American Literary Scholarship: An Annual/1972*. Durham, N. C.: Duke Univ Press, 1974.
See above.

Robinson, Clayton. "Memphis in Fiction: Rural Values in an Urban Setting." *MVC Bul*, no. 5 (Fall 1972), 29-38.
A brief survey of writers who have used Memphis as a setting, from Faulkner's great-grandfather in 1880 to Eleanor Glaze in 1970.

Robinson, William H., ed. *Early Black American Poets*. Dubuque, Iowa: William C. Brown, 1969.
An anthology of poems, 1746-1890, with critical and biographical introductions; numerous Southern black authors are represented.

_____, ed. *Early Black American Prose*. Dubuque, Iowa: William C. Brown, 1970.
An anthology of letters, essays, narratives, stories, novel and drama excerpts, 1734-1913, with critical and biographical introductions; numerous Southern black authors are represented.

Rock, Virginia. "Agrarianism: Agrarian Themes and Ideas in Southern Writing." *Miss Quart*, 21 (Spring 1968), 145-156.
A selected bibliography.

Rubin, Louis D., Jr. "'The Barber Kept on Shaving': The Two Perspectives of American Humor." *SR*, 81 (Autumn 1973), 691-713.
Rubin comments on Simms, Twain, Barth, Mencken, and Ellison in developing his thesis that the vitality of American humor comes from the juxtaposition rather than the blending of two types of humor.

_____, ed. *A Bibliographical Guide to the Study of Southern Literature*. Baton Rouge: Louisiana State Univ Press, 1969.
Entries on twenty-three general topics and two hundred authors.

_____, ed. *The Comic Imagination in American Literature*. New Brunswick: Rutgers Univ Press, 1963.

A collection of thirty-two Voice of America papers, including general essays on Southern and old Southwestern humor and specific essays on humor in Poe, Twain, Caldwell, Cabell, Barth, Faulkner, Welty, O'Connor, and Percy.

_____. "The Great American Joke." *SAQ*, 72 (Winter 1973), 82-94.
Faulkner's comic masterpiece, *The Hamlet*, is an intensification of the same brand of humor as that of Byrd's *Dividing Line*, Baldwin's *Flush Times*, Longstreet's *Georgia Scenes*, Barth's *The Sot-Weed Factor*, and others.

_____. "Southern Literature: A Piedmont Art." *Miss Quart*, 23 (Winter 1969-70), 1-16.
Most twentieth-century Southern writers are from the Piedmont rather than the Tidewater area, mostly because social change has been greater in the Piedmont.

_____. "Southern Local Color and the Black Man." *SouR*, 6 (Autumn 1970), 1011-1030.
Discusses the literary results for certain writers depicting the black man of the conflict between the influence of the general thinking of their own time and the artist's ability to view all individuals as fully human. Simms, Page, J. C. Harris, Cable, and Mark Twain are used as examples.

_____. "A Study in Pastoral and History." *GHQ*, 59 (Winter 1975), 442-454.
An essay-review of Lewis P. Simpson's *The Dispossessed Garden: Pastoral and History in Southern Literature*.

_____. *William Elliott Shoots a Bear: Essays on the Southern Literary Imagination*. Baton Rouge: Louisiana State Univ Press, 1975.
A collection of previously published essays.

_____. *The Writer in the South: Studies in a Literary Community*. Athens: Univ of Georgia Press, 1972.
The 15th Mercer University Lamar Memorial Lectures, focusing on the hold of the Southern community on its writers from antebellum to modern times, with special attention to Twain, Faulkner, and the Fugitive-Agrarians.

_____, and C. Hugh Holman, eds. *Southern Literary Study: Problems and Possibilities*. Chapel Hill: Univ of North Carolina Press, 1975.
Four keynote papers and transcripts of five discussions by leading scholars on the present state of and new directions for Southern literary scholarship.

Sagendorph, Robb, ed. *America and Her Almanacs: Wit, Wisdom, and Weather, 1639-1970*. Boston: Little, Brown, 1970.
Brief history and illustrated anthology of almanac materials, some Southern.

Salzman, Jack, ed. *Prospects*. *Volume I*. New York: Burt Franklin, 1975.
An annual collection of American cultural essays, including articles on Twain, the Agrarians, and Shelby Foote, along with a portfolio of 1930 photographs of Southern people and places.

Schatz, Walter, ed. *Directory of Afro-American Resources.* New York: R. R. Bowker, 1970.
Locates by states organizations and institutions which hold materials documenting the history and culture of black Americans, with descriptions of the collections.

Schechter, William. *The History of Negro Humor in America.* New York: Fleet Press, 1970.
A survey of forms of Negro humor from colonial times to the present, with attention to its roles as a balm against oppression, as a force which perpetuated racism, and as a way of achieving understanding and compassion.

Schraufnagel, Nocl. "The Literary Image of the Negro." *PrS*, 44 (Fall 1970), 265-267.
Francis E. Kearns's anthology *The Black Experience*, while useful in describing the experience of blacks in this country in the last 150 years, includes more contemporary black writers.

Schulman, Steven A. "Howess Dewey Winfrey: The Rejected Songmaker." *JAF*, 87 (January-March 1974), 72-84.
Examines the lyrics of a south-central Kentucky songwriter, whose work has become part of the culture of his community, Irish Bottom.

Schulz, Max F., et al., eds. *Essays in American and English Literature Presented to Bruce Robert McElderry, Jr.* Athens: Ohio Univ Press, 1968.
Includes "Mark Twain's Search for Identity" (John C. Gerber, pp. 27-47) and "Europe as Catalyst for Thomas Wolfe" (C. Hugh Holman, pp. 122-137).

Scott, Anne Firor. *The Southern Lady: From Pedestal to Politics 1830-1930.* Chicago: Univ of Chicago Press, 1970.
A study of the process of women's emancipation in the South which contrasts the culturally defined image of the antebellum lady with the harsh reality of her life and describes the conditions which created new professional and political opportunities for the postbellum woman.

Simkins, Francis B., and Charles P. Roland. *A History of the South.* 4th ed. New York: Alfred A. Knopf, 1972.
A revision and an updating of the 1963 edition of Simkins' classic history, by his former student C. P. Roland, with emphasis on recent events.

Simms, L. Moody, Jr. "Aldine S. Kieffer and the *Musical Million*." *Jour of Popular Culture*, 3 (Fall 1969), 281-286.
The Virginia magazine *Musical Million* (1870-1915) had a great influence on musical and literary ideas in the rural South.

Simpson, Lewis P. *The Dispossessed Garden: Pastoral and History in Southern Literature.* Athens: Univ of Georgia Press, 1975.
Examines the relationship between pastoral and history as symbolic modes of the literary imagination in the South from the seventeenth century to the mid-twentieth century.

_____. *The Man of Letters in New England and the South.* Baton Rouge: Louisiana State Univ Press, 1973.
A collection of previously published essays; the second half includes discussions of Poe, Twain, Faulkner, George Marion O'Donnell, and the literary vocation in the South.

_____, ed. *The Poetry of Community: Essays on the Southern Sensibility of History and Literature.* Spectrum Monograph Series, Volume II. Atlanta: Georgia State Univ School of Arts and Sciences, 1972.
Essays, from MLA and NCTE conferences in 1970, on Richard Weaver, by George Core; W. J. Cash, by Joseph K. Davis; Simms, by John C. Guilds; Ransom, by Thomas Daniel Young; Wolfe, by Paschal Reeves; Wright, by Blyden Jackson; O'Connor and Percy, by Louise Cowan, with an introduction by the editor.

_____. "The Southern Writer and the Great Literary Secession." *GaR*, 24 (Winter 1970), 393-412.
Treats the Southern Renaissance as a late blooming of the mid-nineteenth century's literary alienation.

S[impson], L[ewis] P. "The Poetry of New Orleans." *SouR*, 4 (Summer 1968), xiii-xv.
A brief sketch of the city of New Orleans as a concept in the American literary imagination.

Sitterson, J. Carlyle. "New Light on Slavery and Racism in American History." *So Lit Jour*, 4 (Fall 1971), 87-94.
An essay-review of two volumes by two "able American historians" who bring together "in discriminating fashion the most recent historical scholarship on the Negro in American and Southern history." The two books are *American Counterpoint: Slavery and Racism in the North-South Dialogue*, by C. Vann Woodward, and *In Red and Black: Marxian Explorations in Southern and Afro-American History*, by Eugene D. Genovese.

Skaggs, Merrill M. *The Folk of Southern Fiction: A Study in Local Color Traditions.* Athens: Univ of Georgia Press, 1972.
A study of the plain-folk tradition in Southern local-color fiction and humor and its impact on the fiction of Faulkner, Welty, and O'Connor.

Smiley, David L. "The Quest for the Central Theme in Southern History." *SAQ*, 71 (Summer 1972), 307-325.
Fanny Kemble's *Georgia Journal* is mentioned in this article which discusses different ideas of the central theme in Southern history.

Smith, Dwight L. *Afro-American History: A Bibliography.* Santa Barbara, Calif.: Am Bibliographical Center, Clio Press, 1974.
Includes references to Ellison and Wright.

Smith, Sidonie Ann. *Where I'm Bound: Patterns of Slavery and Freedom in Black American Autobiography.* Westport, Conn.: Greenwood Press, 1974.
Includes detailed discussions of autobiographies by W. W. Brown, B. T. Washington, and Wright.

"Southern History in Periodicals, 1973: A Selected Bibliography." *JSH*, 40 (May 1974), 245-278.
    This annual bibliography, especially the "Social, Cultural, and Intellectual" section, contains references to literature.

"Southern History in Periodicals, 1974: A Selected Bibliography." *JSH*, 41 (May 1975), 225-232.
    The many entries provide information about literature and the arts, as well as history.

Spears, James E. "Notes on Negro Folk Speech." *N Car F*, 18 (November 1970), 154-157.
    A linguistic exploration of "salient aspects of the regional and social dialects of Southern Negro folk speech."

Spiller, Robert E., et al., eds. *Literary History of the United States*. 2 vols. New York: Macmillan, 1974.
    The fourth edition of a standard work, with one revised chapter, three new chapters on recent literature, and an updated bibliography through 1971.

St. Armand, Barton. "Two for the See-Saw: Criticism as Gesture." *Novel*, 5 (Winter 1972), 162-166.
    In an attack on John Lynen's *The Design of the Present: Essays on Time and Form in American Literature* and Jean Normand's *Nathaniel Hawthorne: An Approach to an Analysis of Artistic Creation*, the author uses Lynen's remarks on Poe as an example of the low level to which Lynen's techniques of criticism have sunk. In commenting on Normand's "French" attitude toward the "American soul," he points to Normand's fascination with primitivism and decadence and observes that "the French like Poe because he is decadent, Jerry Lewis because he is primitive, and Faulkner because he is both."

Starke, Catherine J. *Black Portraiture in American Fiction*. New York: Basic Books, 1971.
    A survey of the various stock and archetypal roles played by blacks in nineteenth- and twentieth-century fiction; the works of most major and minor Southern authors are examined.

Stern, Madeleine B. *Heads and Headlines: The Phrenological Fowlers*. Norman: Univ of Oklahoma Press, 1971.
    A biography of the Fowler family, 1830-1930, leading American exponents of phrenology, with commentary on their readings of Poe, Twain, and other authors.

Stewart, Randall. *Regionalism and Beyond*, ed. George Core. Nashville: Vanderbilt Univ Press, 1968.
    Reprints several of Stewart's essays on Southern literature: "Hawthorne and Faulkner," "Tidewater and Frontier," "Relation Between Fugitives and Agrarians," "Donald Davidson," and "Outlook for Southern Writing."

Stone, Edward. *A Certain Morbidness: A View of American Literature*. Carbondale: Southern Illinois Univ Press, 1969.

An analysis of the strain of morbidity and irrationality in American literature, with attention to Cable, Faulkner, and Poe.

Stuckey, Sterling. "Through the Prism of Folklore: The Black Ethos in Slavery." *Mass Rev*, 9 (Summer 1968), 417-437.
    An attempt to dispel many of the "stereotypical treatments of slave thought and behavior."

Szwed, John F. "Musical Adaptation among Afro-Americans." *JAF*, 82 (April-June 1969), 112-121.
    An analysis of the styles and performance roles of spirituals and blues.

Tarpley, Fred, ed. *Love and Wrestling, Butch and O. K.* Commerce, Tex.: Names Institute, 1973.
    Includes "Names Used for Humor in Poe's Fiction" (Burton R. Pollin, pp. 51-57), "Names in Eudora Welty's Fiction: An Onomatological Prolegomenon" (Jack D. Wages, pp. 67-72), "Eudora Welty and the Poetry of Names: A Note on *Delta Wedding*" (Elmo Howell, pp. 73-78), "Dubose Heyward's Names" (William Slavick pp. 85-90), and "Fictive Names in Mark Twain's *Pudd'nhead Wilson*" (Laura Smith, pp. 91-94).

Tate, Allen. *Essays of Four Decades*. Chicago: The Swallow Press, 1968.
    Dedicated to Ransom, Tate's anthology reprints several essays dealing with Southern letters and the work of Poe and John Peale Bishop.

Tatham, Campbell. "Double Order: The Spectrum of Black Aesthetics." *Midcontinent Am Stud Jour*, 11 (Fall 1970), 88-100.
    Argues that a double order of aesthetics is being applied to black literature: (1) primary concern with craftsmanship, or (2) concern with the magic of the creative process and the function of literature as a social and political force. Ellison and Wright are discussed.

Taylor, Welford D., ed. *Virginia Authors: Past and Present*. Richmond, Va.: Virginia Association of Teachers of English, 1972.
    A biographical and bibliographical guide to 152 authors who were born or lived in Virginia, from Sherwood Anderson to Willard H. Wright.

Tebbel, John. *The American Magazine: A Compact History*. New York: Hawthorn Books, 1969.
    A brief narrative history of American magazines, 1746 to the present, with mentions of major Southern periodicals.

Thompson, L. S. *The Southern Black: Slave and Free*. Troy, N. Y.: Whitston Publishing Co., 1970.
    A checklist of over 4,500 books and pamphlets relative to American slavery and the South from the beginnings to 1950, all available in Microform.

Tischler, Nancy M. "The Negro in Southern Fiction: Stereotype and Archetype." *NALF*, 2 (1968), 3-6.
    Deals with the stereotyping of the black man in both nineteenth- and twentieth-century fiction.

Towns, Stuart, and Norman DeMarco, eds. "A Bibliography of Speech and Theater in the South for the Year 1968." *So Speech Jour*, 35 (Fall 1969), 71-80.
A listing of significant titles on speech literature of the South, including some titles on theater.

_____, and Norman DeMarco, eds. "A Bibliography of Speech and Theater in the South for the Year 1969." *So Speech Jour*, 36 (Fall 1970), 71-78.
A continuation of the above.

_____, and Tice Miller, eds. "A Bibliography of Speech and Theatre in the South for the Year 1970." *So Speech Comm Jour*, 37 (Fall 1971), 84-91.
Covers theses and dissertations as well as other published material.

_____, and T. K. Wright, eds. "A Bibliography of Speech and Theatre in the South for the Year 1971." *So Speech Comm Jour*, 38 (Fall 1972), 91-108.
A continuation of the above.

Turner, Arlin. "Two Ways to Approach Southern Literature." *So Lit Jour*, 6 (Fall 1973), 111-116.
An essay-review of Richard Beale Davis' *Literature and Society in Early Virginia, 1608-1840* and of *The Man of Letters in New England and the South*, by Lewis P. Simpson.

Turner, Darwin T. "Afro-American Literary Critics." *Black World*, 19 (July 1970), 54-67.
White critics are incapable of judging black writing; a number of black Southern writers are mentioned.

_____. *Afro-American Writers*. Goldentree Bibliographies in Language and Literature. New York: Appleton-Century-Crofts, 1970.
Selective checklists of primary and secondary materials by and about over 135 black authors, including many Southerners such as Bontemps, Chesnutt, and Wright.

_____, ed. *Black American Literature*. Columbus, Ohio: Charles E. Merrill, 1970.
An anthology of essays, poetry, fiction, and drama with critical introductions and headnotes; numerous Southern black authors are represented.

Tuttle, William M., Jr., and Surendra Bhana. "New Resources in American Studies: Black Newspapers in Kansas." *Am Stud*, 13 (Fall 1972), 119-124.
A bibliography of black newspapers published in Kansas, plus an essay of brief commentary on black newspapers throughout the United States.

Twining, Mary A. "An Anthropological Look at Afro-American Folk Narrative." *CLA Jour*, 14 (September 1970), 57-61.
Points out that the folk tale or story is a vital tradition among Afro-Americans.

Van Doren, Charles L., and Robert McHenry, eds. *Webster's American Biographies*. Springfield, Mass.: G. C. Merriam Co., 1974.
Brief biographical entries on most major and minor authors and historical figures of the South.

Van Nostrand, A. D. *Everyman His Own Poet: Romantic Gospels in American Literature*. New York: McGraw-Hill, 1968.
Includes discussion of Poe, Wolfe, and Faulkner.

Voss, Arthur. *The American Short Story*. Norman: Univ of Oklahoma Press, 1973.
Critical survey of the development of short fiction with full chapters on Poe, Twain, O. Henry, Faulkner, Porter, and discussions of Cable, J. C. Harris, Page, Caldwell, Welty, and O'Connor.

Wade, Melvin and Margaret. "The Black Aesthetic in the Black Novel." *Jour of Black Stud*, 2 (June 1972), 391-408.
Includes discussion of Ellison, Chesnutt, Wright, Ishmael Reed, and Chester Himes.

Wager, Willis. *American Literature: A World View*. New York: New York Univ Press, 1968.
A general survey of American literature in its international context, with brief discussions of and references to numerous Southern authors.

Waggoner, Hyatt H. *American Poets from the Puritans to the Present*. Boston: Houghton Mifflin, 1968.
Contains discussion of the major Southern poets and some of the minor ones.

Wagner, J. *Black Poets of the United States: From Dunbar to Hughes*. Urbana: Univ of Illinois Press, 1973.
A comprehensive study of black poetry in the United States from slavery times to the Harlem Renaissance, with emphasis on the modern poets; translated from the 1962 French study.

Walcutt, Charles C., and J. E. Whitesell, eds. *The* Explicator *Cyclopedia*. Volume II: Traditional Poetry; Volume III: Prose. Chicago: Quadrangle Books, 1968.
Volume II reprints explications of poems by Lanier, Pinkney, and Poe; volume III reprints explications of fiction by Faulkner, Lytle, March, Poe, and Welty.

Walker, Hugh. *Tennessee Tales*. Nashville: Aurora Publishers, 1970.
A collection of sketches about Tennessee history, folklore, and culture.

Walser, Richard. *Literary North Carolina: A Brief Historical Survey*. Raleigh: State Department of Archives and History, 1970.
A survey of literary activity in the state from colonial times to 1970.

_____, ed. *Tar Heel Laughter*. Chapel Hill: Univ of North Carolina Press, 1974.
An anthology of folk and literary humor by native writers about North Carolina.

Watson, C. S. "A Denunciation on the Stage of Spanish Rule: James Workman's *Liberty in Louisiana* (1804)." *La Hist*, 11 (Summer 1970), 245–258.

An examination of the historical and political ideas of an anti-Spanish, pro-United States play first presented in the Charleston Theatre, 1804.

Weatherby, H. L. "Progress and Providence." *SouR*, 8 (Autumn 1972), 805–815.

This essay urges that the South might have, but failed to produce necessary metaphysical foundations for its culture. Some themes of Aquinas are offered to indicate the pattern such a *Summa* might have taken.

Whitlow, Roger. *Black American Literature: A Critical History*. Chicago: Nelson Hall, 1973.

A broad survey of the development of writing by blacks in the United States, with a checklist of 1500 books in the field; most major and minor Southerners are discussed.

_____. "Black Literature and American Innocence.": *SBL*, 5 (Summer 1974), 1–4.

Includes references to W. W. Brown, Chesnutt, Toomer, Hurston, Wright, Himes, and Ellison.

Wilgus, D. K., and Montell Lynwood. "Clure and Joe Williams: Legend and Blues Ballad." *JAF*, 81 (October–December 1968), 295–315.

A full account of a murder ballad current in portions of Kentucky and Tennessee; includes materials for the study of folk culture and local history.

Williams, Benjamin B. "Nineteenth Century Montgomery Authors." *AlaHQ*, 37 (Summer 1975), 136–145.

A brief survey of Montgomery authors of the nineteenth century, including Hooper.

Williams, Kenny J. *They Also Spoke: An Essay on Negro Literature in America 1787–1930*. Nashville: Townsend Press, 1970.

Assesses literature by blacks, from Jupiter Hammon to the Harlem Renaissance as an integral part of American literature; comments on much Southern literature.

Williams, Ora. "A Bibliography of Works Written by American Black Women." *CLA Jour*, 15 (March 1972), 354–377.

Several Southern writers are mentioned: Faulkner, Lillian Smith, Kate Chopin, etc. The main part is, as the title indicates, a bibliography of works written by American black women.

Woodress, James. *American Fiction, 1900–1950: A Guide to Information Sources*. Detroit: Gale Research Co., 1974.

Includes bibliographical essays on Cabell, Caldwell, Faulkner, Glasgow, Gordon, K. A. Porter, W. S. Porter, E. M. Roberts, Stuart, Wolfe, and Wright.

_____, ed. *American Literary Scholarship: An Annual/1966*. Durham, N. C.: Duke Univ Press, 1968.

Includes essays on scholarship on Twain and Faulkner; other Southerners are included in more general sections.

_____, ed. *American Literary Scholarship: An Annual, 1967*. Durham, N. C.: Duke Univ Press, 1969.

Essay-reviews of 1967 scholarship on Twain, Faulkner, Poe, and numerous Southern authors.

_____, ed. *Eight American Authors: A Review of Research and Criticism*. Revised Edition. New York: Norton, 1971.

Revised bibliographical essays on Poe by Jay B. Hubbell and on Twain by Harry Hayden Clark.

_____, et al., eds. *Essays Mostly on Periodical Publishing in America: A Collection in Honor of Clarence Gohdes*, Durham, N. C.: Duke Univ Press, 1973.

Includes essays on local color and on Page and Wolfe.

Young, Thomas Daniel. "The Literary Vocation in the South." *SR*, 83 (Fall 1975), 730–736.

An essay-review of three books on the writer in the South in the twentieth century: Andrew Lytle, *A Wake for the Living: A Family Chronicle*; Lewis P. Simpson, *The Dispossessed Garden*; and Allen Tate, *Memoirs and Opinions 1926–1974*.

_____, Floyd C. Watkins, and Richmond Croom Beatty, eds. *The Literature of the South*. Glenview, Illinois: Scott, Foresman, 1968.

A revised edition of the anthology with updated critical commentaries, a reduction of some of the early historical material, and the addition of new fiction by Capote, Grau, McCullers, O'Connor, Porter, Warren, Welty, and Wolfe.

Index

In the Index, figures in parentheses indicate the number of subject-headings under which entries by a given author are to be found if that author's name appears under more than one subject-heading on a particular page.

Aaron, Daniel, 216, 239
Abádi-Nagy, Zoltán, 175
Abbot, Louise H., 166
Abcarian, Richard, 216
Abdul, Raoul, 249
Abel, Robert H., 184
Abramson, Doris M., 9, 222
Ackerman, R. D., 113
Ackley, Donald G., 193
Adair, Douglass, 6
Adamowski, Thomas H., 113
Adams, Charles M., 154
Adams, John F., 14
Adams, Percy, 104
Adams, Richard P., 88, 113, 239
Aderman, Ralph M., 14
Adler, Betty, 162
Adler, Jacob H., 152, 208
Adler, Thomas P., 208
Agrawal, I. N., 57
Ainsa, Fernando, 113
Akin, William E., 186
Albrecht, Robert C., 239
Aldridge, John W., 197, 202, 223
Alexander, Jean, 14
Alexander, Margaret Walker, 216
Alexander, Nancy, 88
Alexandrescu, Sorin, 113
Alford, Terry L., 42
Allen, Bruce A., 14
Allen, Gay Wilson, 251
Allen, John A., 202
Allen, John D., 10
Allen, Michael, 14
Allen, Ward, 103
Alsen, Eberhard, 14, 57
Alter, Robert, 223
Altieri, Charles, 95
Ambler, Madge, 184
Amis, Lola J., 216
Amur, G. S., 14
Amyot, Gerald F., 14
Anderson, Carl L., 14, 57
Anderson, Charles R., 11, 83
Anderson, D. D., 239
Anderson, D. M., 57
Anderson, David D., 216
Anderson, Fenwick, 162
Anderson, Frederick, 57
Anderson, Hilton, 12, 113
Anderson, Imbert E., 14
Anderson, Jervis, 187

Anderson, John Q., 78, 239
Anderson, Michael, 223
Anderson, Poul, 49
Anderson, Thomas, 239
Andrews, J. C., 42
Andrews, William L., 54, 55, 57
Angell, Leslie E., 113
Antin, David, 154
Antippas, Andy P., 83
Antoniadis, Roxandra V., 114
Appleby, Jane, 239
Aptheker, Herbert, 11, 239
Arikawa, Shoji, 57
Armato, Philip M., 152
Armistead, J. M., 14
Armistead, S. G., 80
Arner, Robert D., 1, 2, 3, 5 (2), 55, 57
Arnett, David L, 104
Arnold, Edwin T., 114
Arpad, Joseph J., 10, 114
Asals, Frederick, 114, 166
Ashley, Franklin, 104
Asociación Argentina de Estudios Americanos, 14
Aspiz, Harold, 58
Asselineau, Roger, 14
Aswell, Duncan, 114
Atkins, Anselm, 114, 176
Atkinson, Monte, 184
Atlas, James, 239
Auer, Michael, 114
Austen, Roger, 159
Austin, Bliss, 49
Austin, James C., 58, 86, 240
Austin, Neal F., 211
Avni, Abraham, 240
Aycock, W. M., 147, 238
Ayers, H. Brandt, 223

Babcock, C. Merton, 15, 58
Bacot, Lucia, 240
Bacote, Clarence A., 155
Baender, Paul, 58, 73
Baer, John W., 162
Baetzhold, Howard G., 58
Baily, Lugene, 110
Bain, Robert, 1, 6
Baird, Reed A., 85
Baker, Christopher P., 211
Baker, Donald G., 240
Baker, Houston A., Jr., 100, 156, 216, 240

Baker, Howard, 150, 178
Bakish, David, 216
Baldeshwiler, Eileen, 178, 240
Baldwin, Richard E., 54, 216
Bales, Kent, 15
Banašević, Nikola, 114
Bandy, W. T., 15
Banta, Martha, 15, 58
Baquira, Josephina Q., 114
Barber, Marion, 114
Barbour, Philip L., 5 (2)
Barcus, Nancy B., 167
Bardolph, Richard, 223
Barker, Addison, 86
Barksdale, Richard, 240
Barnes, Daniel R., 114, 178
Barnes, Madeline T., 178
Barnett, Louise K., 240
Barr, S., 240
Barrett, William, 114
Barsness, John A., 58
Barson, Alfred T., 91
Barth, J. Robert, 114
Barthes, Roland, 15
Barton, Marion, 58
Barzun, Jacques, 15
Baskett, Sam S., 5
Basler, Roy P., 166
Bass, Eben, 167
Bassett, John, 114
Bataille, Robert, 223
Battilana, Marilla, 15
Bauer, Harry C., 162
Bauer, Shirley Ann, 180
Bauerle, Richard F., 101, 197
Baum, Catherine, 150
Baum, Joan, 58
Bayliss, John F., 240
Baym, Max I., 240
Bean, John C., 95
Beards, Richard D., 114, 178
Beatty, Richmond C., 1
Beauchamp, Gorman, 114-115
Beaver, Harold, 15, 58, 115
Becham, Gerald, 167
Beck, Emily M., 248
Bedell, George C., 115
Bedient, Calvin, 115
Beebe, Maurice, 58
Behar, Jack, 187
Behrens, Ralph, 115, 148
Beidler, Peter, 58, 104, 115
Beja, Morris, 223

Bell, Bernard W., 156, 194, 223
Bell, H. H., Jr., 15
Bell, Haney H., Jr., 115
Bell, James D., 107
Bellamy, Joe David, 58, 215, 223
Bellman, Samuel I., 223
Beloff, Max, 3
Belson, Joel J., 58
Benardete, Jane J., 59
Bender, Bert, 55
Bender, Eileen, 42
Benert, Annette, 115
Bennett, Stephen B., 223
Benoit, Bernard, 107
Benson, Jackson J., 115
Benson, Randolph, 3
Benson, Robert G., 158
Benton, Richard P., 15-16
Bercovitch, Sacvan, 59
Berger, Arthur A., 240
Berger, Sidney, 59
Bergeron, Jeannette, 42
Bergholz, Harry, 59
Bergmann, Frank, 59
Bergonzi, Bernard, 197
Bergup, Sister Bernice, 167
Berke, Richard, 16
Berkhofer, Robert F., Jr., 3
Berkove, Lawrence I., 59
Berkowitz, Gerald, 208
Berman, Ronald, 181
Berrigan, J. R., 176
Berrone, Louis, 115
Berry, David C., 104
Berry, Faith, 216
Berry, Wendell, 94, 240
Berthoff, Warner, 42, 197
Bertolotti, D. S., 59
Besterman, Theodore, 240
Bethea, Sally, 115
Betts, Leonidas, 91
Bhana, Surendra, 255
Bickley, R. Bruce, Jr., 59
Bickman, Martin, 16
Bie, Wendy A., 59
Bienstock, Beverly G., 95
Bier, Jesse, 115, 240
Biglane, Jean, 49
Bigsby, C. W. E., 159, 223
Billingsley, R. G., 223
Billington, Monroe L., 223
Bilotta, James D., 187
Binger, Carl, 3
Birchfield, James, 59
Bisanz, Adam J., 197
Bissell, Claude T., 88
Black, Michael, 223
Blackburn, William, 154
Blackwelder, James Ray, 208
Blackwell, Louise, 167, 185, 194,
    202, 208
Blair, John G., 115
Blair, Walter, 59, 240
Blake, Nelson, 223
Blake, Susan L., 194
Blanchard, Leonard A., 115
Blanchard, Margaret, 115
Blanck, Jacob, 13, 59
Blanke, Gustav H., 208
Blasingame, John W., 42
Bledsoe, A. S., 115

Bleikasten, André, 104, 115-116
Blish, James, 16, 49
Bliss, A., 224
Blitgen, James, Sister M. Carol, 208
Blöcker, Günter, 159
Bloom, Harold, 94
Bloom, Lynn Z., 145
Blotner, Joseph, 116
Bluefarb, Sam, 241
Blues, Thomas, 59
Boardman, John, 49
Boatwright, James, 202
Bode, Carl, 162
Boecker, Eberhard, 116
Boitani, Piero, 224
Boldrick, C. C., 86
Bolsterli, Margaret, 202
Bolton, H. Philip, 216
Bone, Robert, 216, 241
Boney, F. N., 224, 241
Bonner, John W., Jr., 224
Bonner, Thomas, Jr., 55
Bonner, Thomas C., 162
Bontemps, Arna, 11, 86, 194, 224,
    241
Boos, Florence, 16
Boos, William, 16
Boozer, William, 116
Borden, Caroline, 116
Borges, Jorge L., 224
Borgman, Paul, 167
Borgström, Greta I., 116
Boring, Phyllis Z., 116
Borowitz, Helen O., 16
Borroff, Marie, 104
Boswell, George W., 116, 224
Bottorff, William K., 49
Boulger, J. D., 107
Bowen, James K., 59, 116
Bowman, Sylvia E., 86
Boyd, G. N., 224
Boyd, Julian P., 3
Boyd, L. A., 224
Boyers, Robert, 154
Boyle, Thomas E., 211
Brack, O. M., Jr., 59
Bradbury, John M., 224
Bradbury, Malcolm, 59-60
Braddy, Haldeen, 16
Braden, W. W., 42, 86
Bradford, M. E., 117, 152, 158,
    176, 181, 191, 202, 203, 224
Bradley, Jared W., 176
Bradshaw, Herbert C., 224
Brady, Charles, 167
Brake, Robert, 241
Bramsbäck, Birgit, 16
Branch, Edgar M., 60
Brand, John M., 60
Brant, Irving, 4
Brasner, William, 224
Braswell, William, 211
Brathwaite, Edward K., 241
Bray, Robert, 60
Bredahl, A. Carl, Jr., 212
Breed, Paul F., 224
Brent, Robert, 3
Breslaw, Elaine G., 6
Briceland, A. V., 42
Briden, E. F., 60
Bridges, Katherine, 42, 95, 241

Bridgewater, Patrick, 148
Brie, Hartmut, 16
Brignano, Russell C., 216, 241
Britt, David D., 54
Brittain, Joan T., 167
Brivic, Sheldon, 216
Brodie, Fawn M., 3
Broderick, John C., 241
Brodwin, Stanley, 60
Brogan, Howard O., 60
Brogunier, Joseph, 60, 117
Bromwich, David, 181
Bronzwaer, W., 16
Brooks, A. Russell, 224
Brooks, Cleanth, 16, 103, 117-118,
    176, 191, 193, 197, 203, 241
Brooks, Curtis M., 16
Brooks, Mary Ellen, 216
Broughton, George, 91
Broughton, Panthea, 91, 118, 159
Broussard, Louis, 16
Brown, Ashley, 150, 167, 181,
    191, 203
Brown, Calvin S., 93, 118, 202,
    224
Brown, Cecil, 216
Brown, Lloyd W., 100, 107, 156,
    216-217, 242
Brown, Sterling A., 100
Browne, R. B., 60
Browne, Ray B., 242
Browning, Preston M., Jr., 167,
    187
Bruccoli, Matthew J., 148, 191,
    242
Bruchac, Joseph, 217
Bruffee, Kenneth A., 197
Brumm, Anne-Marie, 118
Brumm, Ursula, 118
Brunauer, Dalma H., 118, 187
Bruns, Gerald L., 16
Brussell, I. R., 49
Bryant, J. A., Jr., 203
Bryant, Jerry H., 149, 224
Bryer, Jackson R., 224, 230
Brylowski, Walter, 118
Bucco, Martin, 107
Buchen, Irving H., 159-160
Buchloh, Paul G., 154, 242
Buckley, Tom, 208
Buckley, William F., Jr., 203,
    225
Budd, Louis J., 60, 88, 225
Buffington, Robert, 103, 181-182,
    191
Buford, R., 49
Bugliari, Jeanne, 60
Bulgheroni, Marisa, 187, 242
Bullins, Ed, 184
Bungert, Hans, 118, 242
Bunting, Charles T., 176, 185,
    203
Burbank, Rex, 88
Burg, David F., 60
Burger, Nash K., 187, 203
Burke, John, 150
Burke, W. J., 242
Burns, Graham, 61
Burns, Shannon, 16
Burns, Stuart, 61, 167-168
Burr, John R., 162

Burrison, John A., 61
Burroughs, Franklin G., Jr., 118
Burrows, David J., 107
Burt, Annette C., 197
Burt, David J., 197
Burt, Donald C., 16
Burton, Dolores M., 119
Burton, Marda, 207
Bush, Lewis M., 38
Bush, Robert, 38, 61, 79, 82-83, 88
Bush, Roland E., 184
Buswell, Mary Catherine, 203
Butcher, Philip, 52-53, 61
Butler, M. D., 61
Butterfield, R. W., 16
Butterfield, S., 242
Butterfield, Stephen T., 9
Butterworth, Keen, 119
Buttita, Tony, 225
Byers, John R., Jr., 61
Byrd, Scott, 176
Byrd, Turner F., 168

Cabaniss, Allen, 119
Cady, Edwin, 61, 242
Cairns, Huntington, 162
Calhoun, Richard J., 42, 105, 212, 225, 242
Cameron, Kenneth W., 16-17
Camp, James, 42
Campbell, Felicia F., 17
Campbell, Frank, 61
Campbell, Harry M., 119
Campbell, Ina, 61
Campbell, J. P., 17
Campbell, Jeff H., 119
Campbell, Michael L., 53, 208
Campos, Haraldo, 17
Canario, John W., 17
Canary, Robert H., 50
Cancel, Rafael A., 194
Candelaria, Cordelia, 17
Cane, Melville, 212
Cannon, Patricia R., 187
Cantrell, Frank, 119
Capitanchick, Maurice, 212
Capps, Jack L., 119
Cardwell, Guy A., 42, 61
Carey, Glenn O., 119
Carleton, Reese M., 84
Carlile, Robert E., 93, 212
Carlinsky, Daniel, 212
Carlson, Eric W., 17
Carlson, Thomas M., 168
Carlton, Holt, 79
Carr, John, 176, 185, 225
Carr, Virginia S., 160
Carringer, Robert L., 17
Carrington, George C., Jr., 61
Carroll, Richard A., 156
Carruth, Hayden, 94
Carson, Betty F., 225
Carson, David K., 107
Carson, Franklin D., 203
Carson, Herbert L., 61
Carter, A. H., 148
Carter, Lin, 50
Carter, T. H., 225
Cary, Richard, 61
Casale, Ottavio M., 17

Casey, Daniel J., 61
Cash, Earl A., 107
Casper, Leonard, 168, 197
Castille, Philip, 119
Cate, Hollis L., 61, 208
Cauthen, I. B., Jr., 17, 18
Cayton, Horace, 217
Cayton, Robert F., 197
Cecil, L. Moffitt, 17, 62, 119
Cevasco, G. A., 17
Chamberlain, John, 162
Chambers, Bradford, 242
Chambliss, Amy, 62
Chametzky, Jules, 88, 242
Chancellor, Ann, 50
Chandler, Alice, 17
Chapman, Abraham, 225
Chappell, Fred, 207
Chase, Patricia, 194
Chellis, Barbara A., 62
Cheney, Brainard, 151, 178 (2)
Chesler, Stanley A., 208
Cheslock, Louis, 50, 162
Chesnick, Eugene, 91, 176
Chewning, Harris, 178
Chitragupta, 119
Christ, J. M., 194
Christadler, Martin, 6, 225
Christian, H. A., 162
Christopher, J. R., 62
Christopherson, Merrill, 39
Churchill, Allen, 225
Cirlot, Juan-Eduardo, 17
Cixous, Hélène, 17
Clark, C. E. Frazer, Jr., 17
Clark, Charlene K., 160
Clark, Charles C., 120, 158, 203
Clark, Eulalyn W., 120
Clark, George P., 17
Clark, Harry H., 242
Clark, James W., Jr., 43
Clark, Joseph D., 104
Clark, Thomas D., 242
Clark, William B., 242
Clark, William G., 120
Clark, William J., 120
Clarke, Alan P., 211
Clarke, Girala, 101
Clarke, John H., 107, 187, 225
Clarke, Mary, 186
Clarke, Sebastian, 185
Clasby, Nancy T., 11
Claudel, Alice M., 17-18
Clay, Frances, 185
Cleman, John, 53
Clemons, W., 105, 203
Clerc, Charles, 62
Clifford, John, 152
Clifton, James M., 43
Clipper, Lawrence J., 107
Cloutier, Arthur C., 62
Clymer, Kenneth J., 62
Coard, Robert L., 62
Cobau, William W., 120
Cobb, Buell, 242
Coburn, Mark D., 62
Cochran, Robert W., 203
Cohen, Edward H., 2, 62
Cohen, Hennig, 43, 242
Cohen, Norm, 242
Cohen, William, 3

Cohn, Jan, 88
Cohn, Ruby, 225
Coindreau, Maurice, 225
Cole, Charles W., 208
Cole, Hunter McK., 185
Coles, Robert, 91
Colley, Ann, 157
Collier, Eugenia, 107, 156, 249
Collins, Carvel, 120
Collins, R. G., 120
Collmer, Robert G., 225
Colquitt, Betsy F., 242
Colvert, James B., 166, 242
Colwell, James L., 18, 62
Combs, Richard E., 242
Commins, Dorothy B., 120
Condon, Judith, 91
Conlee, John W., 95
Connelly, Thomas L., 43
Consulo, Dominick, 224
Cook, Martha E., 225
Cook, Raymond A., 78, 184
Cook, Richard M., 120, 160
Cook, Sylvia, 225
Cooke, J. W., 3, 9
Cooke, Michael G., 187, 225
Cooley, John R., 203
Cooley, Thomas W., Jr., 120
Cooney, C. F., 162
Cooney, James F., 18
Cooper, Arthur, 91
Coplin, Keith, 62
Core, George, 1, 158, 182, 187, 191, 197, 225-226, 242
Corrigan, Robert A., 242-243
Corrington, John W., 105, 120, 212
Corry, John, 107
Cosgrove, William, 107, 217
Costa, Richard, 93
Costello, Donald P., 208
Couch, William, Jr., 226
Coughlan, Robert, 120
Coulter, E. Merton, 43
Coulthard, A. R., 203
Coursen, Herbert R., Jr., 226
Courtney, W. F., 243
Cousins, Paul M., 81
Cover, James P., 50 (2)
Covici, Pascal, Jr., 18
Covo, Jacqueline, 108
Cowan, James C., 120
Cowan, Louise, 103, 191, 226
Cowan, Michael H., 120
Cowley, Malcolm, 93, 226
Cox, James M., 18, 62, 243
Cox, Leland, 43
Cox, R. Merritt, 3
Coxe, Louis, 99
Cracroft, Richard H., 62, 212
Crane, John K., 120
Cranwell, John P., 50
Craven, Wesley F., 5
Crawford, John W., 243
Creeger, George R., 102
Cremeens, Carlton, 176
Creighton, Joanne V., 121
Cripps, Thomas, 217
Cronin, Frank C., 62
Crowley, John W., 62-63
Crowson, E. T., 10, 12

Crunden, Robert M., 226
Crupi, Charles, 182
Cunliffe, Marcus, 187
Cunningham, Joan, 54
Cunningham, John, 168
Curley, Daniel, 203
Curnow, Wystan, 226
Current-Garcia, Eugene, 12, 86
Curry, Gladys J., 182
Curry, Kenneth, 91
Curtis, Bruce, 187
Curtis, M. J., 6
Cutting, Rose Marie, 1

Dabbs, James M., 243
Dabney, Lewis M., 121
Dabney, Virginius, 243
Dahl, Curtis, 63
Dahl, James, 121
Dameron, J. Lasley, 18
Dameron, Penn, 50
Daniel, W. Harrison, 43
Darnell, Donald G., 121
D'Avanzo, Mario L., 18, 63, 121
Davenport, F. Garvin, Jr., 226
David, Beverly R., 63
Davidson, Donald, 39
Davidson, Gustav, 18
Davidson, Loren K., 63
Davidson, William W., 104
Davis, A. P., 243
Davis, Arthur K., Jr., 243
Davis, C. T., 243
Davis, Charles E., 43, 203
Davis, Charles T., 194
Davis, Curtis C., 10, 13
Davis, Jack L., 18, 168
Davis, Joe Lee, 50, 191
Davis, June H., 18, 168
Davis, Michael, 88
Davis, Richard B., 2 (2), 3, 5,
    6, 18, 43, 243
Davis, Robert M., 191
Davis, Ronald L., 208
Davis, Scottie, 121
Davis, William V., 6, 121
Davison, Ned J., 18
Davison, Richard A., 198
Dawson, Leven M., 154
Day, M. S., 243
Day, Martin S., 226
DeBellis, Jack, 83, 226
Debouzy, Marianne, 63
Debusscher, Gilbert, 208
Dedmond, Francis B., 160
DeFalco, Joseph M., 18
Degenfelder, E. Pauline, 121
Degler, Carl N., 43
DeGrazia, Emilio, 19
Dekle, Bernard, 226
Delaney, Joan, 19
Delaney, Paul, 63
Delany, Lloyd T., 187
Delay, Florence, 121
Delesalle, Jean-François, 19
DeMarco, Norman, 255
Demarest, David P., Jr., 217
DeMott, Benjamin, 63, 93, 105
Dendinger, Lloyd N., 19
Denham, Robert D., 168
Dennis, Frank A., 243

Dent, Thomas C., 226
Denton, Lynn W., 63
Desmond, John F., 168
Dessner, Lawrence J., 212
Dessommes, Larry, 103
Detweiler, Robert, 204, 226
Deutsch, Leonard J., 108
DeVere, L. A., 243
DeVillier, Mary Anne G., 121
Devlin, Albert J., 122
Dewey, Bradley R., 176
Dickerson, Mary Jane, 122, 194
Dickey, James, 191, 235
Dickinson, Hugh, 208
Dickson, Bruce D., Jr., 43
Dickstein, Morris, 217
Dietrichson, Jan W., 91
Dillard, Mabel M., 194
Dillard, R. H. W., 103, 226
Dillingham, William B., 43 (2)
Dillon, Richard T., 122
Dinan, John S., 63
Dippie, Brian W., 95
Diser, Philip E., 2
Ditsky, John M., 63, 99, 122
Dixon, Melvin, 54, 217
Dobie, J. Frank, 243
Dolan, Paul J., 250
Dolmetsch, Carl R., 2
Donahue, Jane, 154
Donaldson, Scott, 63
Donlan, Dan M., 204, 217
Donno, Antonio, 187
Donoghue, Denis, 191
Doody, Terrence, 122
Dooley, Dennis M., 198
Dorsey, John, 162
Dorson, Richard M., 243
Doten, Sharon, 212
Doughty, Nanelia S., 88
Douglas, Ellen, 176
Douglas, George H., 162
Dove, George N., 122
Dowell, Richard W., 19
Dowie, William, 176
Downing, Gloria, 24
Downs, L. H., 229
Downs, R. B., 103
Doxey, William S., 39, 168
Doyle, Charles C., 19
Doyle, Mary Ellen, 108
Doyle, Paul A., 63
Doyno, Victor A., 63
Drabeck, Bernard A., 19
Drake, Constance, 208
Drake, Robert, 168, 226, 243
Drake, William, 19
Draper, John W., 165
Driskell, Daniel, 19
Driskell, Leon V., 167, 168
Duff, Gerald, 184
Duffy, Martha, 108
Duke, Maurice, 41, 50, 79, 226-
    227, 243
Dula, Martha A., 169
Duncan, Alastair B., 122
Duncan, Bowie, 194
Dunlap, Mary 122
Dunn, Douglas, 154
Dupree, Robert, 191
Duram, James C., 63

Durant, Ariel, 122
Durant, Will, 122
Durden, Robert F., 187
Durham, Frank, 84, 153, 178, 194,
    208, 227
Durrant, Geoffrey, 93
Durzak, Manfred, 19
Dussinger, Gloria, 122

Eakin, Paul J., 19
Ealy, Marguerite, 86
Early, James, 122
East, Charles, 204
Eastman, John, 163
Eatman, James, 152
Eaton, Charles E., 103
Eaton, Clement, 243
Eaton, Richard B., 53
Echter, Reinhold, 85
Eckley, Wilton, 186
Eddings, Dennis W., 19
Eddins, Dwight, 227
Edelstein, Mark G., 169
Edgar, W. B., 6
Edmonds, Dale, 160
Edmunds, P. W., 243
Edward, Sister Ann, 243
Edwards, C. H., Jr., 83, 105,
    122-123
Edwards, Duane, 123
Edwards, J. S., 83
Edwards, Margaret F., 191
Egan, Joseph J., 53
Eggenschwiler, David, 169, 188
Ehrlich, Heyward, 19
Eichelberger, Clayton L., 88,
    181, 212
Eigner, Edwin M., 123
Eisen, Jonathan, 244
E'jxenbaum, B. M., 85
Elagin, Ivan, 19
Elias, Robert H., 2, 194
Elkins, Stanley M., 108
Elkins, William R., 19
Elliot, Emory B., Jr., 182
Elliott, Michael, 64
Ellis, Helen E., 63
Ellis, L. Tuffly, 244
Ellison, George R., 41
Ellison, Ralph, 227
Ellyson, Louise, 19
Elsbree, Langdon, 63
Emanuel, James A., 217
Emblen, D. L., 63
Emerson, Everett H., 5
Emerson, O. B., 123, 159, 227
Emmerich, J. Oliver, 244
Emmons, Winifred S., 179
Empiric, Julienne H., 19
Englekirk, John E., 19
Engstrom, Alfred G., 208
Ensor, Allison, 63-64, 227
Epps, G., 178
Epstein, Seymour, 227
Erickson, John D., 20
Erisman, Fred, 157
Erskine, Albert, 133
Esch, Robert M., 169
Eschholz, Paul A., 64
Eschliman, Herbert R., 123
Espy, John, 56

Esslinger, Pat M., 123
Etulain, R. W., 244
Eubank, W. C. 244
Evans, David, 244
Evans, Elizabeth, 13, 99
Evans, Walter, 20
Evans, William, 53
Everett, Chestyn, 244
Everett, Robert B., 244
Everett, Walter K., 123
Everette, M. W., 217
Ewell, Barbara C., 96
Eyster, Warren, 105

Fabre, Michel, 107, 217
Fadiman, Regina, 123
Fahey, William A., 169
Fain, John T., 103, 158, 191-192, 227
Fairman, Marion A., 227
Falb, Lewis W., 209
Falk, Doris V., 20
Falwell, Marshall, 192
Farber, J. Z., 3
Farnham, James F., 123, 169
Farnsworth, Robert M., 54, 221
Farrison, W. Edward, 9, 13, 194, 227
Farwell, Harold, 96
Fass, Barbara, 108
Fauchereau, Serge, 105
Faulkner, Howard, 123
Faulkner, Jim, 123
Feaster, John, 58
Federman, Raymond, 96
Feeley, Sister Kathleen M., 169
Feibleman, James K., 227
Feild, Claire, 124
Felgar, Robert, 218
Felton, H. W., 156
Fenderson, Lewis H., 227
Ferguson, Frances C., 154
Ferguson, Suzanne, 155, 198
Ferris, William R., Jr., 124, 244
Fetterley, Judith, 64
Fetz, Howard W., 124
Ficken, Carl, 124
Fiedler, Leslie, 244
Field, Leslie A., 212
Fields, Kenneth, 99, 192
Fine, Ronald E., 238
Finger, Hans, 20
Finholt, Richard D., 20
Fischel, Anne, 124
Fischer, Russell G., 108
Fischer, William C., 194
Fisher, Alice P., 194
Fisher, Benjamin F., IV, 20
Fisher, Marvin, 64
Fisher, Ruth, 198
Fishwick, Marshall, 244
Fite, Montgomery, 64
Fitzgerald, Robert, 91
Flake, Carol A., 83
Flanagan, John T., 124
Fleck, Richard F., 64
Fleischauer, John F., 204
Fleischmann, W. B., 227
Fleissner, Robert F., 99
Fleming, Robert E., 156, 218, 244
Fletcher, Marie, 151

Fletcher, Mary D., 160
Fletcher, Richard M., 20
Flexner, James T., 5-6
Flora, Joseph M., 50
Flores-Del Prado, Wilma, 169
Flory, Wendy S., 20
Flusche, Michael, 81
Foerster, Norman, 244
Fogle, Richard H., 103
Folmsbee, Stanley J., 10
Foner, Eric, 42
Fontaine, William T., 108
Forclaz, Roger, 20
Ford, Nick A., 108, 184, 244
Forkner, Ben, 188
Fortenberry, George, 64, 232
Fossum, Robert H., 188
Foster, Edward F., 64
Foster, Frances, 108
Foster, Gaines M., 88
Foster, Ruel E., 124, 186, 212
Fowler, Russell, 155
Fraiberg, Louis, 20
Franco, Carol I., 208
Frank, William L., 49
Franklin, H. Bruce, 244
Franklin, Jimmie L., 188
Franklin, Malcolm A., 124
Franklin, Phyllis, 124
Frantz, Joe B., 244
Frederick, John T., 64
Freedman, Alex S., 244
Freedman, F. S., 244
Freehafer, John, 20
Freeman, Fred B., Jr., 20-21
Freeman, James A., 92
Freese, Peter, 102
Freimarck, John, 64
French, Bryant M., 65
French, Warren, 227-228
Fridy, Will, 124
Friedl, Herwig, 21
Friedlander, Mitzi, 88
Friedman, Lawrence J., 87, 88
Friedman, Melvin J., 169, 188
Fritscher, John J., 209
Frohock, W. M., 108, 124
Frushell, Richard C., 21
Fucilla, Joseph G., 43
Fulkerson, Gerald, 11
Fuller, Daniel J., 65
Fuller, Hoyt, 108
Fullinwider, S. P., 163
Funk, Robert W., 124
Furrow, Sharon, 21
Fussell, Edwin, 99

Gabbard, G. H., 50
Gado, Frank, 228
Gafford, Charlotte K., 169
Gaillard, Dawson, 21, 160, 165, 228
Gainer, Patrick W., 244-245
Gaines, Jim, 209
Gale, Robert L., 21, 65
Galloway, David D., 188
Ganzel, Dewey, 65
Gardiner, Judith K., 150
Gardner, Joseph H., 65
Gargano, James W., 21, 65
Garmon, Gerald M., 21, 124

Garner, P., 105
Garrett, George, 148, 152, 185, 226, 228, 233, 245
Garrett, Marvin P., 156
Garrett, Walter, 21
Garrison, Joseph M., Jr., 21, 124
Gartner, Carol B., 54
Garzilli, Enrico, 124
Gaskill, Gayle, 218
Gaston, Georg M., 65
Gaston, Paul L., 176
Gaston, Paul M., 88
Gatell, Frank O., 228
Gates, Allen, 125
Gay, Sydney H., 4
Gayle, Addison, Jr., 228, 245
Geduld, Harry M., 228
Geffen, Arthur, 125
Geismar, Maxwell, 65
Gelfant, Blanche H., 125
Gendre, André, 21
Genovese, Eugene D., 245
George, Sharon K., 105
Gérard, Albert, 245
Gerber, Gerald E., 21
Gerber, John C., 65
Gerstenberger, Donna, 245
Gervais, Ronald J., 65
Ghiselin, Brewster, 192
Gibbs, Sylvia, 186
Gibson, Donald B., 65, 218, 228
Gibson, William M., 65
Giddings, Paula, 197
Gidley, Mark, 125
Gidley, Mick, 125
Giermanski, James R., 125
Giles, James R., 54, 154, 218
Gilkes, Lillian, 39
Gillespie, Gerald, 96
Gillespie, N. C., 12
Gillikin, Dure Jo, 155
Gilman, Richard, 188, 212
Gindin, James, 228
Gingrich, Arnold, 204
Ginsberg, Elaine, 228
Giordano, Frank R., Jr., 125
Giroux, Robert, 169
Gittleman, Edwin, 3
Givner, Joan, 179
Glancy, Eileen K., 105
Glazier, Lyle, 81
Glick, Wendell, 65
Glicksberg, Charles I., 228
Goad, Mary Ellen, 66
Godbold, E. Stanly, Jr., 79, 88
Godfrey, J. L., 228
Godshalk, William L., 50, 79, 176
Goede, William J., 195, 228
Goetz, Thomas H., 21
Goff, Frederick, 3
Gogol, John M., 22, 66
Gohdes, Clarence, 245
Going, William T., 148, 245
Gold, Joseph, 125
Goldfarb, Russell M., 198
Goldhurst, William, 22
Goldman, Arnold, 125
Goldstein, Laurence, 198
Goldstein, Malcolm, 228
Goldstien, Neal L., 66
Golub, L. S., 125

Goodman, Paul, 228
Goodwin, Stephen, 193
Goodyear, Russell H., 66
Gordon, Caroline, 66, 169
Goss, James, 169
Gossett, Louise Y., 204
Gossett, Thomas F., 170
Gotten, H. B., 125
Gottesman, Ronald, 108
Gottfried, Leon, 66, 179
Goudie, Andrea, 66
Gounard, Jean-François, 218
Gower, Herschel, 152
Gozzi, Francesco, 160
Graham, D. B., 22
Graham, Don B., 125, 218
Graham, H. D., 158
Graham, John, 228
Graham, Kenneth, 204
Graham, Louis, 218
Granger, Byrd H., 22
Grant, Sister Mary Kathryn, 195
Grant, William A., 43
Grant, William E., 125
Grantham, Dewey W., 245
Gravely, William H., Jr., 22
Graver, Lawrence, 160
Graves, Wallace, 66
Gray, R. J., 101
Gray, Richard J., 198, 212
Green, Alan W. C., 43
Green, Claud B., 86
Green, James L., 170
Greene, Maxine, 108
Greenspan, C. L., 245
Greer, H. Allan, 22
Gregory, Donald, 170
Gregory, Eileen, 126
Gregory, Ralph, 66
Gregory, Ross, 85
Greiner, Donald J., 105, 126
Grenander, M. E., 66
Gresham, James T., 96
Gresset, Michel, 126, 170, 188
Gribben, Alan, 66
Gribbin, Daniel V., 126
Grieve, A. I., 22
Griffin, Edward M., 109
Griffin, John C., 195
Griffin, Marjorie, 40, 45
Griffith, Albert J., 193
Griffith, Benjamin W., 88, 126
Griffith, Clark, 66
Griffith, Lucille, 43
Griffith, Malcolm A., 248
Grimshaw, James, Jr., 198
Grinnell, James W., 160
Grissom, Margaret S., 151
Groden, Michael, 126
Groover, Robert L., 165
Gross, Beverly, 96, 126, 179
Gross, Harvey, 198
Gross, Seymour, 22, 42, 218, 245
Gross, Theodore, 228, 245
Grossman, Joan D., 22
Grossman, Joel M., 126
Grossvogel, D. I., 94
Grow, Lynn M., 109
Grumbach, Doris, 245
Guidacci, Margherita, 22
Guilds, John C., 39, 246

Guillory, Daniel, 105
Gundersen, Joan R., 3
Günter, Bernd, 126
Gunter, Richard, 126
Gurko, Leo, 213
Gustafson, Richard, 105
Gutman, Herbert G., 43
Guttenberg, Barnett, 198
Gvereschi, Edward, 109

Haack, Dietmar, 102 (2), 237
Haberland, Paul M., 43
Hagenbüchle-Imfeld, Helen, 155
Hagopian, John V., 126, 228
Haight, A. L., 246
Hainsworth, J. D., 209
Hajek, Friederike, 218
Hakac, John, 66
Haley, Josephine, 185
Halliburton, David, 22
Hallman, David A., 103
Halper, Nathan, 50
Halpern, Daniel, 188
Halsell, Willie D., 246
Hamblen, Abigail A., 170
Hamby, James A., 116
Hamilton, Alice, 160
Hamilton, Gary D., 126
Hammond, Alexander, 22
Hancock, Maxine, 126
Handa, Carolyn, 93
Handy, William J., 126
Hansen, Arlen J., 246
Hansen, Chadwick, 66
Hanson, R. Galen, 66
Harap, Louis, 22
Harbert, Earl N., 251
Hardwick, Elizabeth, 148
Hardy, John E., 179, 204
Harkey, Joseph H., 22, 66
Harkness, D. J., 246
Harkness, J. D., 209
Harlan, J. C., 87
Harlan, Louis R., 87
Harlow, Geoffrey, 246
Harmon, William, 94
Harold, Brent, 126
Harovitz, Sanford, 86
Harp, Richard L., 22
Harper, Howard M., Jr., 96
Harrell, Don W., 66, 204
Harrell, Laura D. S., 44
Harrington, Evans, 148
Harris, Charles B., 96
Harris, Helen L., 66
Harris, Kathryn M., 22
Harris, T. E., 87
Harris, Trudier, 109, 197
Harris, Wendell V., 126
Harrison, Margaret, 170
Harrison, Stanley R., 66
Hart, John E., 66
Hart, Richard, 163
Hart, Robert C., 229
Harter, Carol C., 126
Hartley, Lodwick, 179
Hartman, Geoffrey, 127
Hartman, Harry, 50
Harvey, Nancy L., 213
Harwell, Richard, 13, 44, 83
Harzic, Jean, 127

Haskell, John D., 23
Haslam, Gerald W., 229
Hasley, Louis, 67
Hassan, Ihab, 229
Haswell, Henry, 23
Hatch, Alden, 2
Hatfield, D. B., 86
Hatley, Donald W., 99
Hattaway, Herman, 11
Hatvary, George E., 23
Hauck, Richard B., 44, 127, 246
Haury, Beth B., 127
Havard, William C., 246
Havens, Elmer A., 83
Havlice, Patricia P., 246
Hawke, David F., 1, 5
Hay, Robert P., 3, 5
Hayashi, Tetsumaro, 229
Hayhoe, George, 99, 127
Hayne, Barrie, 41
Haynes, Dick, 215
Hays, Peter L., 109, 127, 170, 229
Hayter, Alethea, 23
Heaney, Howell J., 23
Heermance, J. Noel, 9, 54
Heffernan, T. F., 229
Hegarty, Charles M., 170
Heibling, Mark, 195
Heilman, Robert B., 153, 204, 209
Heimer, Jackson W., 127
Heiney, D., 229
Heller, Arno, 109
Heller, Terry, 127
Helmcke, Hans, 246
Helmick, E. T., 192
Helms, Randel, 23
Helterman, Jeffrey, 204
Hemenway, Robert, 54, 127, 246
Hemphill, Paul, 229
Henderson, Harry B., III, 246
Hendin, Josephine, 170
Hendrick, George, 160, 245
Henisey, Sarah, 176
Henkle, Roger, 109
Henninger, Francis J., 23
Hepburn, Kenneth, 127
Herbst, Jurgen, 5
Hermann, John, 127
Herndon, Jane, 89
Herrick, Thomas C., 51
Herring, Henry D., 198
Herron, Ima H., 246
Hersey, John, 109
Hess, Jeffrey A., 23
Hess, Judith W., 127
Heyl, Edgar G., 89
Hicks, Granville, 170, 229
Hieronymus, Clara, 129
Hiers, John T., 198, 229
Higgs, Robert J., 247
Hilfer, Anthony C., 209, 229
Hill, F. A., 209
Hill, Hamlin, 67
Hill, James Lee, 153
Hill, Mildred A., 247
Hill, Robert W., 212
Hill, Samuel S., Jr., 247
Hill, West T., Jr., 44
Hinden, Michael, 23, 96
Hinz, Evelyn J., 23, 36

Hirsch, David H., 23
Hirsch, Foster, 209
Hirsh, L. M., 245
Hivnor, Mary O., 170
Hlavsa, Virginia V., 127
Hoadley, Frank M., 127
Hoberg, Perry F., 23
Hobson, Fred C., Jr., 163
Hodgson, John A., 127
Hoffman, Daniel, 23, 127
Hoffman, Frederick J., 127, 155, 188
Hoffman, Gerhard, 23
Hoffman, Michael J., 67
Hoffman, Peggy, 229
Hoffmeister, Charles C., 23
Hoge, James O., 39
Hogue, L. Lynn, 23
Holder, Alan, 96, 188
Holder, Elizabeth J., 229
Holland, Norman, 127
Hollander, John, 23
Hollenbaugh, Carol, 204
Holliday, Carl, 247
Hollis, C. Carroll, 247
Holloway, John, 93
Holman, C. Hugh, 79, 128, 213, 247, 251
Holman, Harriet R., 23-24, 79, 84
Holmes, Edward M., 128
Holmes, William, 247
Holmes, William F., 177
Holmin, Lorena R., 153
Holoquist, Michael, 24
Hook, Andrew, 67
Hoole, W. Stanley, 247
Horowitz, Floyd R., 109
Hough, Robert L., 67, 247
Houghton, Donald E., 128
Houseman, John, 218
Hovet, Theodore R., 54
Howard, A. B., 128
Howard, David C., 109
Howard, E. G., 7
Howard, Richard, 193, 198, 229
Howard, Zelma T., 204
Howarth, William L., 24, 92
Howe, Irving, 128, 247
Howell, Elmo, 12, 14, 39, 53, 67, 103, 128, 170, 179, 204, 229
Howlett, William J., 247
Hoyle, Bernadette W., 229
Hoyt, Charles A., 247
Hubbell, Jay B., 24, 247
Hubert, Thomas, 39
Huddleston, Eugene L., 186
Hudson, Martha B., 43
Huff, Lawrence, 86
Huff, Mary N., 198
Huggins, Nathan I., 87
Hughes, Emmy, 89
Hughes, Richard E., 229
Hull, Gloria T., 197
Hult, Sharon S., 128
Humma, John B., 24
Hummel, Ray O., Jr., 44
Humphrey, Robert, 155
Hunchett, William, 11
Hunt, Joel A., 128, 139
Hunter, Edwin R., 128
Hussey, John P., 24

Hutchens, Eleanor N., 128
Hutchinson, James D., 129
Hutten, Robert W., 129
Hyman, S. E., 218
Hyneman, Esther F., 24
Hynes, Samuel, 92

Idol, John L., Jr., 24, 213
Ifkovic, Edward, 82
Illiano, Antonio, 67
Inge, M. Thomas, 12, 24, 44, 51, 79, 104 (2), 129, 196, 204, 229, 247
Ingram, Forrest L., 129, 149, 170
Ingrasci, Hugh J., 51
Innes, Catherine L., 195
Irvine, Peter L., 129, 199
Irwin, John T., 129
Isaacs, Neil D., 204-205
Isani, Mukhtar A., 24, 247
Iser, Wolfgang, 129
Israel, Calvin, 129
Israel, Charles, 13, 150
Italia, Paul G., 105
Iverson, Anders, 163
Izard, Barbara, 129

Jackson, Blyden, 218-219, 247
Jackson, David K., 10, 24
Jackson, M. M., 156
Jackson, Miles, Jr., 156
Jacobs, Robert D., 13, 24, 44, 247
Jacobs, William Jay, 25
Jacobsen, Josephine, 94
Jaffe, Harry J., 248
Jäger, Dietrich, 129
Jager, Ronald B., 67
James, Charles L., 219
James, David L., 129
James, Stuart B., 67, 129
Jameson, Frederic, 105
Janeway, Elizabeth, 230
Jannaccone, Pasquale, 25
Janoff, Bruce, 96
Jansen, K. Edward, 163
Janssens, G. A., 230
Jarrell, Mary, 155
Jarrell, Randall, 230
Jarrett, David W., 129
Jarrett-Kerr, Martin, 129
Jaskoski, Helen, 248
Jaworski, Philippe, 160
Jeffers, Lance, 230
Jeffrey, David K., 25
Jenkins, William D., 51
Jerome, W. P., 163
Johannsen, Kris, 51
Johnson, Abby A., 109
Johnson, Ellwood, 67
Johnson, Elmer D., 213
Johnson, Gerald W., 163
Johnson, Lemuel A., 248
Johnson, Mark, 176
Johnson, Michael L., 230
Johnson, Paul D., 11
Johnston, Kenneth G., 129-130
Johnston, Walter E., 130
Jones, Allen W., 87
Jones, Alun R., 205
Jones, D. Allan, 96

Jones, H. G., 248
Jones, Howard M., 7
Jones, Joseph, 67
Jones, Lawrence W., 248
Jones, Lewis P., 88
Jones, Lola, 219
Jones, Madison, 158, 202
Jordan, June, 219
Joseph, Gerhard J., 25, 96
Joyner, Nancy, 158
Jung, Udo, 195
Justus, James H., 182, 199, 248

Kable, William S., 1, 248
Kahn, Sholom, Jr., 67
Kaiser, Ernest, 109
Kalem, T. E., 209
Kalson, Albert E., 209
Kalstone, David, 94
Kaluza, Irena, 130
Kane, Patricia, 130, 153, 192
Kaplan, Harold, 248
Kaplan, Justin, 68
Kapoor, S. D., 68
Karatson, André, 25
Karpowitz, Steven, 68
Karras, Bill, 38
Kartiganer, Donald M., 130, 248
Kass, Carole, 166
Katope, Christopher G., 199
Kattan, Naïm, 230
Katz, Claire, 170
Katz, Joseph, 248
Kazin, Alfred, 102, 109, 176, 230
Kearful, Frank J., 130
Kearney, J. A., 130
Kearns, Edward, 219
Kearns, F. E., 248
Keech, James M., 130
Keefer, T. Frederick, 130
Kegel, Paul L., 68
Kehl, D. G., 199
Kehler, Joel R., 25
Keith, D. L., 130
Keith, Philip, 199
Keller, Dean H., 55, 83
Keller, Francis R., 156
Keller, Jane C., 171
Kelley, David J., 25
Kellner, Bruce, 163
Kellner, R. S., 130
Kellogg, Gene, 171
Kelly, George M., 178
Kelly, Richard, 182
Kennard, Jean E., 96
Kennedy, J. Gerald, 25, 44
Kennedy, James G., 219
Kennedy, Richard S., 213
Kennedy, X. J., 42
Kennicott, P. C., 87
Kenny, Vincent, 152
Kent, George E., 95, 109, 130, 149, 219, 230
Kerr, Elizabeth, 130
Kerr, Howard, 68
Kerr, Walter, 209
Kesteloot, Lilyan, 195
Kesterson, David B., 25, 68
Ketcham, Ralph, 4
Ketterer, David, 25, 68, 248
Keyssar-Franke, Helene, 230

Kibler, James E., 13, 39-40, 130, 148
Kiernan, Robert F., 96
Kilburn, Patrick E., 25
Killinger, John, 219
Killion, R. G., 44
Kilson, Marion, 154
Kim, Kichung, 219
Kimball, William J., 25, 44, 68, 83
Kime, Wayne R., 25
King, F. H., 130
King, Kimball, 84
King, Thomas L., 209
King, Woodie, 230
Kinghorn, Norton D., 68
Kinnamon, Keneth, 219, 248
Kinney, Arthur, 130, 145
Kiralis, Karl, 68
Kirby, David K., 102
Kirkham, Bruce, 68
Kirkpatrick, Smith, 205
Klass, Philip, 68
Klevar, Harvey, 171
Klinkowitz, Jerome, 97, 130
Kloss, Robert J., 205
Klotman, Phyllis R., 109, 219
Knapp, Edgar H., 97
Knieger, Bernard, 131
Knight, Karl F., 131, 182
Knowlton, Edgar C., Jr., 25
Knox, George, 213
Kobler, J. F., 131
Koch, Donald A., 240
Koelb, Clayton, 97
Koepsel, Jürgen, 209
Köhring, Klaus H., 199
Kolb, Harold H., Jr., 68
Kolin, Philip C., 68
Kolodny, Annette, 40, 131
Koloski, Bernard J., 56
Kopf, George, 195
Korenman, Joan S., 131
Korges, James, 101, 192
Korn, B. W., 44
Kort, Wesley A., 188
Kostelanetz, Richard, 109, 156, 219
Koster, Donald N., 25
Kostjakov, V. A., 131
Kozisek, J. L., 248
Kraft, James, 195
Kramer, Victor, 92, 195
Krasny, Michael J., 195
Kraus, W. Keith, 68, 205
Krause, Sydney J., 68
Krauss, Rosalind, 215
Krauth, Leland, 69
Kretzoi, Charlotte, 188
Kreyling, Michael, 205
Krickel, Edward, 158, 162
Krieger, Murray, 230
Kristensen, Sven M., 230
Kroll, Jack, 205
Kronenberger, Louis, 248
Kropf, Carl R., 171
Krumpelmann, John T., 44
Kuehl, John, 230
Kuehl, Linda, 205
Kuhlmann, Susan, 248
Kulin, Katalin, 131

Kulseth, Leonard I., 131
Kunkel, F. L., 209
Kunst, Arthur E., 82
Kwiat, Joseph J., 230
Kyle, Carol A., 97

LaBelle, Maurice M., 163
Labriolle, Jacqueline de, 121
Lackey, Allen D., 171
LaGuardia, David M., 25
Lamplugh, George R., 89
Lanati, Barbara, 131
Landeira, Ricardo L., 131
Landess, Thomas H., 104, 106, 148, 150, 151, 158, 205, 230
Landman, Sidney J., 158
Landor, Mikhail, 131, 230
Lane, James B., 109
Laney, Ruth, 149, 159
Lang, Béatrice, 131
Lang, Hans J., 248
Lange, Victor, 25
Langford, Beverly Y., 131
Langford, Gerald, 131
Langman, F. H., 199
Lanier, Doris, 79, 82, 84
Lapides, Frederick R., 13
Lapidus, Deborah, 75
LaPolla, Franco, 230
Larsen, Erling, 92
Larsen, R. B. V., 219
Larson, Barbara A., 2
Lasater, Alice E., 230
Lashley, Dolores, 11
Lass, A. H., 248
Lauder, R. E., 176
Lawrence, Alexander A., 93
Lawson, Lewis, 26, 177, 219, 231
Lazenby, Walter S., 152
Leary, Lewis, 26, 56, 69, 131, 220, 248-249
Lease, Benjamin, 26, 40, 83
LeClair, Thomas, 26, 97, 177, 220, 231
Lee, Grace F., 26
Lee, L. L., 69
Lees, Daniel E., 26
Leff, Leonard J., 97
Lehan, Richard, 69, 177, 231
Leibman, Mary C., 26
LeMaster, J. R., 186
Lemay, J. A. Leo, 4, 7, 41
Lemon, L. T., 192, 249
Lengeler, Rainer, 213
Lensing, George S., 132
Lentricchia, Frank, 26, 100
Lenz, Harold, 209
Leon, Ferdinand, 210
Leonard, John, 205
LeRebellier, A., 97
Lerner, Arthur, 26
Levin, Harry, 231, 249
Levin, J. B., 163
Levine, Richard A., 26
Levine, Stuart, 26
Levine, Susan, 26
Levins, Lynn G., 132
Levitt, Paul, 132
Levy, Eugene, 156
Lévy, Maurice, 26
Lewald, H. Ernest, 249

Lewis, Clifford, 132
Lewis, Janet, 151
Lewis, Stuart A., 69
Lhamon, W. T., Jr., 132
Libby, Anthony, 106
Liberman, M. M., 179
Libman, Valentina, 249
Lieber, Todd M., 26, 44, 110, 195
Lieberman, Laurence, 106
Lieberman, Marcia, 110
Liebman, Arthur, 231
Liebman, Sheldon, 26
Light, J. F., 199
Light, Kathleen, 81
Light, Martin, 69
Lillard, R. S., 110
Lillard, Stewart, 110
Lilly, Paul R., Jr., 132
Lima, Robert, 26
Lindberg, John, 110
Lindberg-Seyersted, Brita, 231
Lindborg, Henry J., 69, 106
Lindgren, W. H., III, 7
Linebarger, J. M., 184
Link, Franz H., 27, 210
Linscott, Elisabeth, 132
Lipscomb, Oscar H., 86
Little, Matthew, 132
Littlefield, Daniel F., 171
Littlejohn, David, 132, 231
Litvin, Rina, 132
Livingston, James L., 69
Ljungquist, Kent, 27
Lloyd, James B., 69, 132
Loberger, Gordon J., 27
Lodge, Henry C., 6
Logan, Rayford W., 156
Lohner, Edgar, 249
Lomax, Alan, 249
Lombard, Charles, 27
Long, E. Hudson, 85, 249
Long, Richard A., 157, 249
Long, Timothy, 69
Longley, John L., Jr., 132, 199
Longstreet, S., 249
Lopez, Guido, 132
Lorch, Fred W., 69
Lorch, Thomas M., 171
Lord, John B., 27
Lorentzen, Melvin E., 171
Love, Glen A., 106
Lowery, Robert E., 69
Loyd, Dennis, 84
Lucas, J., 153
Ludington, Charles T., Jr., 110, 231
Ludington, Townsend, 231
Ludwig, Richard M., 249
Luedtke, Carol L., 132
Luke, Myron H., 249
Lund, Mary G., 148
Lundquist, James, 27
Luschei, Martin, 177
Lutwack, Leonard, 231
Lycette, Ronald, 69
Lyde, M. J., 213
Lynd, Staughton, 4
Lynen, John F., 27
Lynwood, Montell, 256
Lytle, Andrew, 231

Mabbott, Thomas O., 27
MacDonald, Edgar E., 51, 79-80
Macey, Samuel L., 210
MacKethan, Lucinda H., 195
Mackin, Cooper R., 188
MacMillan, Duane, 132
Madden, David, 92, 160, 166, 179, 231
Magdol, Edward, 86
Magill, Frank N., 231
Magner, James E., Jr., 182
Magny, Claude-Edmonde, 231
Maida, Patricia D., 171
Majdiak, Daniel, 97
Malavelle, Maryse, 153
Malbone, Raymond G., 132
Male, Roy R., 171
Malin, Irving, 102, 189 (2)
Malkoff, Karl, 231
Malone, Dumas, 4
Maloney, Stephen R., 231
Malraux, André, 132
Manchester, William, 163
Mangione, Jerre, 231
Manglaviti, Leo M. J., 132, 163
Manierre, William R., 70
Mann, Carolyn, 70
Mann, David, 182
Mann, K. H., 249
Manning, A. N., 247
Mansfield, Margaret, 152
Manucci, Loretta V., 231
Manz-Kunz, Marie-Antoinette, 205
Marambaud, Pierre, 1, 2
Marcadé, Bernard, 27
Marder, Daniel, 27
Margolies, Edward, 44, 153, 217, 220, 231-232, 249
Markos, Donald W., 106, 189
Marks, Henry S., 249
Marks, Patricia, 85
Marler, Robert F., 27
Marovitz, Sanford E., 27, 86
Marrs, Robert L., 27
Marsh, John L., 27, 249
Marshall, Carl L., 87
Martin, Bruce K., 27
Martin, Carter W., 133, 171
Martin, H. H., 162
Martin, Jay, 70, 232
Martin, John S., 4
Martin, R. G., 199
Martindale, Colin, 27
Marx, Leo, 70
Mason, Clifford, 110, 195
Mason, Julian, 4, 5, 55, 89
Mason, Melvin R., 10
Masserand, Anne, 205
Massey, Linton R., 133
Materassi, Mario, 133
Matherne, Beverly M., 166
Matheson, Terence J., 163
Matthews, George C., 195
Matthews, Jack, 149
Mattson, J. Stanley, 70
Maud, Ralph, 133
Mauranges, J.-P., 70
May, Charles E., 205
May, John R., 56, 70, 171-172, 232, 249
Mayberry, George, 70

Mayer, David R., 172
Mayfield, Sara, 163
Maynard, Reid, 70
Mazow, Julia, 27
Mazzaro, Jerome, 94, 155
McAleer, John J., 102
McAlexander, Hubert, Jr., 133
McCall, Dan, 220
McCants, Maxine, 133
McCarron, William E., 199
McCarthy, Daniel P., 195
McCarthy, Harold T., 70, 220, 249
McCarthy, Kevin M., 28
McCarthy, Mary, 133
McCarthy, Paul, 199
McClatchey, J. D., 199
McColley, Robert, 7
McCormick, John, 232
McCullagh, James C., 172
McCullough, Joseph B., 70
McDaniel, Barbara A., 110
McDermott, John F., 70
McDermott, John V., 172
McDonald, James L., 97
McDonald, W. U., Jr., 158, 205
McDonald, Walter R., 133, 149
McDowell, Frederick P. W., 172
McDowell, Robert E., 232
McElderry, B. R., Jr., 28, 213
McElrath, Joseph R., 28, 70, 133
McElroy, John, 250
McElroy, M. D., 28
McFarland, Ronald E., 206
McFaul, John M., 44
McGhee, Nancy B., 250
McGlynn, Paul D., 133
McGrain, J. W., Jr., 163
McHaney, Thomas L., 40, 133, 206
McHenry, Robert, 255
McIntyre, James P., 70
McKee, John D., 70
McKeever, Benjamin, 196
McKeithan, D. M., 28
McKenzie, Barbara, 172
McLean, Malcolm D., 85
McLean, Robert C., 28
McLoughlin, William G., 4
McMahan, Elizabeth E., 71
McMichael, Charles T., 93
McMillan, Douglas J., 178
McMillan, James B., 250
McMillan, Samuel H., 182
McMillan, William E., 206
McNair, Donald, 44
McNally, John, 161
McNamee, Lawrence F., 250
McNeill, Warren, 51
McPherson, J. A., 108, 166
McPherson, James M., 250
McWilliams, Dean, 134
Meats, Stephen E., 40, 134
Meckier, Jerome, 199
Medlicott, Alexander J., 159
Meehan, James, 213
Meehan, Thomas, 215
Meindl, Dieter, 134
Meinke, Dieter, 213
Meinke, Elke, 213
Mellard, James M., 134, 172, 232, 250
Mellen, Joan, 189, 199

Mendelsohn, Edward, 71
Mercer, Peter, 97
Meredith, William, 94
Meriwether, James B., 40, 134-135
Merivale, Patricia, 28
Merkle, Donald R., 220
Merrens, H. R., 7
Messerli, Douglas, 135
Metcalf, Patricia, 38
Mews, Siegfried, 71
Meyer, F. S., 202
Meyer, Gerard P., 51
Meyer, Horst E., 71
Meyer, Shirley, 220
Meyers, Walter E., 182
Michel, Laurence, 135
Middleton, John, 135
Milder, Robert, 172
Miles, Edwin A., 44
Miles, Elton, 44
Miles, Josephine, 94
Milford, Nancy, 148
Miller, Bruce E., 71
Miller, Eugene E., 157, 220
Miller, J. Hillis, 71
Miller, James E., Jr., 135
Miller, John C., 28
Miller, Jordan Y., 210
Miller, Leo, 71
Miller, Ruth, 71, 250
Miller, Theodore C., 87
Miller, Tice, 255
Miller, Wayne C., 250
Miller, William C., 71
Millgate, Jane, 135
Millgate, Michael, 135 (2)
Millichap, Joseph R., 71, 161, 172, 213
Milliner, Gladys W., 56, 135
Mills, Nicolaus, 71
Mills, Ralph, Jr., 106
Milum, Richard A., 135
Minter, David, 11, 136
Mintz, Max M., 4
Miranda, J. E., 28
Mirer, Martin, 232
Mirkin, Harris G., 4
Missey, James, 161
Mitchell, Edward, 247
Mitchell, Louis D., 110, 220
Mitchell, Paul, 166
Mixon, Wayne, 71
Mize, George E., 28
Moers, Ellen, 161
Mohr, Clarence L., 10, 44
Mok, M., 215
Mokashi-Punekar, S., 28
Moldenhauer, Joseph J., 28
Momberger, Philip, 136
Monaghan, David M., 136
Monteiro, George, 28, 71, 85, 136
Montesi, Albert J., 232
Montgomery, Henry C., 4
Montgomery, Marion, 172-173, 202
Mood, John J., 210
Moody, Richard, 153
Moon, Rebecca, 242
Mooney, Harry J., Jr., 173
Moore, Carol A., 206
Moore, Harry T., 214

Moore, J. B., 88
Moore, Jack B., 7, 99
Moore, Janice T., 161
Moore, John H., 85
Moore, John R., 199
Moore, L. Hugh, Jr., 200
Moore, Rayburn S., 28, 45, 49, 82, 89, 175
Moore, Robert H., 110, 136, 166
Moorer, Frank E., 110
Moose, Ruth, 99
Morell, Giliane, 136
Morgan, D. T., Jr., 6
Morgan, L. C., 250
Morgan, Robert, 94
Morgan, Speer, 99
Morison, W. J., 232
Morley-Mower, Geoffrey, 51
Morris, Christopher, 97
Morris, Harry, 106, 200
Morris, Robert K., 189
Morrison, Claudia B., 250
Morrison, Joseph L., 103, 163
Morrow, S. S., 250
Morsberger, Robert E., 71
Morse, J. Mitchell, 189
Morse, John T., Jr., 4
Moses, Edwin, 136
Moses, Gilbert, 226
Mosher, Marlene, 157
Moskowitz, Sam, 29
Moss, Grant, Jr., 206
Moss, Sidney P., 29
Motsch, Markus F., 163
Mott, Bertram, Jr., 71
Mottram, Eric, 136
Mower, George R., 45
Moyne, Ernest J., 71
Mudrick, Marvin, 189
Muehl, Lois, 136
Mueller, William R., 110
Muffett, D. J. M., 81
Mugleston, William F., 81
Muhlenfeld, Elisabeth S., 137
Muir, Edward H., 137
Mukherjee, Sugit, 250
Muldowny, John, 11
Mullen, Jean S., 189
Muller, Gilbert H., 137, 173
Mulqueen, James E., 29, 71, 137
Murphy, Christina J., 29
Murphy, Denis M., 137
Murphy, James K., 80
Murr, Judy S., 80
Murray, Albert, 232
Murray, D. M., 137
Murray, Edward, 102, 232
Murtuza, Athar, 29
Musgrave, Marian E., 45
Myers, Margaret, 72
Myers, Robert M., 45
Myers, Susan L., 206
Myres, W. V., 137

Nadeau, Robert L., 137
Nagel, James, 72, 220
Nagourney, Peter, 250
Nakadate, Neil, 200
Nance, William L., 102, 173, 180, 250
Naples, Diane C., 137

Nardin, James T., 210
Nash, Harry C., 137
Naylor, Thomas H., 223
Neal, Larry, 110, 232
Nebeker, Helen E., 72, 137
Nelson, G. B., 173
Nelson, Malcolm A., 137
Nelson, Raymond, 153
Nelson, Raymond S., 137
Nemerov, Howard, 155
Nethery, Wallace, 29
Nettelbeck, C. W., 110
Nettesheim, Josefine, 29
Neufeldt, Leonard, 137
Neuffer, C. H., 184
Nevius, Blake, 232
Newcomb, Horace, 189
Newitz, Martin, 192
Newlin, Paul A., 29
Newlove, Donald, 210
Nibbelink, Herman, 72
Nichols, Charles H., 45
Nichols, William W., 11, 110, 223
Nicolet, William P., 137
Niflis, N. Michael, 106
Niles, Mary, 184
Nilles, Mary, 84
Nilon, Charles H., 250
Nitchie, George W., 155
Noble, David W., 250
Noble, Donald R., Jr., 41, 250
Nolte, William H., 137, 163, 189
Normand, Jean, 189
Norris, Nancy, 137
Norse, Clifford C., 45
Norton, Wesley, 45
Nower, Joyce, 250

Oates, Joyce Carol, 106, 173, 206, 232
Oates, Stephen B., 42, 45
Oberg, Arthur, 94
O'Brien, John, 178, 184, 232
O'Brien, John T., 173
O'Brien, Joseph M., 200
O'Brien, Matthew C., 138
O'Brien, Michael, 104, 165, 214
Obuchowski, Peter, 29
Ocano, Armando, 29
O'Connell, N. J., 6
O'Connor, Mary, 151
O'Connor, Richard, 85
O'Connor, Roger, 29
O'Dea, Richard J., 138, 192
Odessky, Marjory H., 72
Oelke, Karl E., 29
Olderman, Raymond, 97
Oleson, Carole W., 220
Oliphant, Mary C. Simms, 39
Olson, David B., 200
Olson, Ted, 138
Omans, Stuart E., 111
O'Nan, Martha, 138
O'Neal, John, 232
Oppegard, Susan H., 174
Orr, Linda, 94
Orth, Michael, 72
Orvell, Miles, 29, 174
Osofsky, Gilbert, 45
Osowski, Judy, 29
Ostrom, Alan, 72

Ostrom, John, 29
Otten, Terry, 138
Ousby, Ian V. K., 30
Overstreet, Robert, 89
Owen, Guy, 165, 175, 233
Owens, W. A., 233

Pachmuss, Temira, 161
Padmore, Dorothy, 220
Page, Rosewell, 84
Page, Sally R., 138
Palmer, R. Roderick, 233
Palmer, William J., 138
Paluka, Frank, 251
Panichas, George A., 233
Park, Martha M., 72
Parker, Hershel, 72, 138
Parker, Patricia A., 95
Parks, Edd Winfield, 83, 84, 251
Parr, J. L., 211
Parramore, T. C., 7
Parrish, Paul A., 111
Parsons, Coleman O., 72, 89
Parsons, Thornton H., 138, 182
Parssinen, Carol, 82
Partlow, Robert, 251
Partridge, Colin, 180, 182
Pate, Willard, 138
Patrick, Walton R., 72
Patterson, Maclean, 164
Paul, Raymond, 30
Pauly, Thomas H., 30, 72
Pavese, Cesare, 251
Pavnaskar, Sadanand R., 30
Pawley, Thomas D., 9
Pawlowski, Robert S., 206
Payne, Ladell, 80, 138, 200, 214
Payne, Michael, 100
Pearce, Howard D., 152, 174
Pearce, Richard, 138, 189, 233
Pearce, Roy H., 72
Pearson, Ann, 152
Pease, Jane H., 42
Pease, William H., 42
Peavy, Charles D., 138
Peckham, Morse, 138
Peden, William, 233
Peden, William A., 193
Pells, Richard H., 233
Pemberton, J. M., 30
Pennington, Lee, 186
Pentz, J. A., 164
Peraile, Esteban, 139
Peraile, Lorenzo, 139
Percy, Walker, 178
Perkins, George, 251
Perlis, Alan D., 139
Perloff, Marjorie, 150
Perret, Joseph J., 53
Perrin, A. H., 251
Perrine, Laurence, 161
Perry, Dick, 186
Perry, Eleanor, 101
Perry, Frank, 101
Perry, J. Douglas, Jr., 92, 233
Perry, Patsy B., 11
Peter, Emmett, Jr., 51
Peterson, Bernard L., Jr., 184
Peterson, Carl, 139
Peterson, Merrill D., 4
Peterson, Richard F., 139

Petesch, Donald, 233
Pettit, Arthur, 72
Pfeiffer, Andrew H., 139
Phillips, Elizabeth, 233
Phillips, Gene D., 139
Phillips, H. Wells, 30
Phillips, Robert, 151
Phillips, William, 215
Pickens, Donald K., 189
Pickering, Sam, Jr., 7
Pickett, Nell Ann, 206
Pierle, Robert C., 49, 139
Pilcher, George W., 2
Pilkington, Tom, 91
Pinckney, Elise, 5
Pindell, Richard, 177
Pinkerton, Jan, 180, 193, 233
Pinsker, Sanford S., 97, 139,
    159, 189
Pinsky, Robert, 182
Pitavy, François, 116, 139
Pitcher, Edward W., 30
Pitcole, Marcia, 220
Pizer, Donald, 102
Plaisance, E. C., 251
Plante, P. R., 251
Plater, Ormonde, 12
Platt, Gerald M., 189
Plessner, Monika, 111
Plumly, Stanley, 200
Pochmann, Henry A., 139, 251
Poirier, Richard, 233
Polk, Noel E., 89, 139-140, 158,
    206
Pollard, Arthur, 251
Pollin, Burton, R., 30-32
Polsgrove, Carol, 111
Pons, Xavier, 164
Popkin, Henry, 210
Porat, Tsfira, 140
Porte, Joel, 32
Porter, Carolyn, 140
Porter, Dorothy, 7
Porter, Thomas E., 210
Post, L. C., 251
Potter, Richard H., 56
Powell, Arnold, 164
Powell, Eleanor B., 233
Powell, Grosvenor E., 111
Powell, W. Allen, 214
Powell, William E., 40
Powell, William S., 233
Powers, Lyall, 72
Prasad, Thakur G., 189
Prater, William, 180
Pratt, Annis, 80
Pratt, Linda Ray, 92
Pratt, William C., 92, 182
Prenshaw, Peggy, 206
Presley, Delma E., 140, 161, 174,
    177, 208, 210, 233
Price, Reynolds, 140, 206
Primeau, Ronald, 220, 251
Prince, Gilbert, 72
Prince, John, 140
Prior, Linda T., 32, 140
Proffer, C. R., 234
Pruett, D. F., 113
Pry, Elmer R., 32
Pryse, Marjorie L., 111, 140
Pudner, H. Peter, 251

Purcell, James, 234
Putzel, Max, 140
Pyros, John, 221

Quarles, Benjamin, 11
Quasimodo, Salvatore, 120
Quinn, David B., 7
Quinn, J. J., 174
Quinn, Sister M. Bernetta, 155,
    200
Quinn, Patrick F., 32
Quirino, Leonard, 210

Rachal, John, 72-73
Rackham, Jeff, 73
Radford, Frederick L., 111
Ragan, Sam, 234
Raghavascharyulu, D. V. K., 250
Raisor, Philip, 140
Ramachandran, T., 210
Ramaswamy, S., 210
Ramsey, R. Vance, 209
Ramsey, Roger, 93, 140
Randel, Fred V., 140
Randel, William, 53
Rank, Hugh, 152
Raper, J. R., 80, 140
Raskin, Barbara, 193
Rasmussen, Frederick N., 164
Ratner, Marc L., 189-190
Ravitz, Abe C., 100
Rawick, George P., 45
Ray, David, 221
Rayan, Krishna, 32
Rayson, Ann L., 154
Rea, J., 140
Rea, John A., 85
Reamer, Owen J., 83
Rechnitz, Robert M., 161
Reck, Rima Drell, 214
Reck, Tom S., 210
Redden, Dorothy S., 180
Redding, Saunders, 157, 243
Redmond, Eugene B., 251
Redmond, James, 246
Reece, James B., 32
Reed, Joseph W., Jr., 140
Reed, Kenneth T., 32, 73, 221
Reed, Rex, 210
Reed, Richard, 140
Reeder, Roberta, 32
Rees, Robert A., 40, 45, 73, 226,
    251
Rees, Thomas R., 32
Reeves, Paschal, 89, 175, 213,
    214
Reeves, William J., 251
Regan, Robert, 32
Reid, Alfred S., 234
Reilly, John E., 32-33
Reilly, John M., 55, 111, 196,
    221, 234
Rein, David M., 33
Reiss, Barbara, 106
Reiss, James, 106
Reiss, T. J., 33
Reiter, Robert, 174
Render, Sylvia L., 55
Renwick, John, 7
Requa, Kenneth A., 73
Rexroth, Kenneth, 234
Rewak, William J., 93

Reynolds, Albert E., II, 73
Reynolds, Robert D., Jr., 164
Rhode, Robert D., 89
Rhynsburger, Mark, 140
Ricardou, Jean, 33
Rice, Julian C., 141
Richard, Claude, 33
Richards, Bertrand F., 155
Richards, Lewis, 141
Richards, Marion K., 80
Richardson, H. Edward, 141
Richardson, Jack, 97
Richardson, Kenneth, 234
Riche, James, 111, 234
Richmond, Lee J., 33, 206
Richmond, Merle J., 196
Rickels, Milton, 73, 221, 251
Rickels, Patricia, 221
Ricks, Christopher, 193, 206
Ridenour, Ronald, 221
Ridgely, J. V., 33, 40
Riemer, Neal, 5
Riese, Teut A., 190
Riese, Utz, 141
Righter, William, 251
Riley, Carolyn, 234
Riley, Roberta, 196
Rinaldi, Nicholas M., 141
Ringe, Donald A., 9, 53, 56
Ríos Ruiz, Manuel, 161
Ritchey, David, 7, 45
Ritunnano, Jeanne, 73
Rivière, Yvette, 161
Roaten, Darnell, 7
Robbins, J. Albert, 33, 251-252
Robbins, W. L., 7
Robert, Joseph C., 42
Roberts, Churchill L., 237
Roberts, Leonard, 45
Robey, Cora, 210
Robinson, Clayton, 251
Robinson, David, 33
Robinson, E. Arthur, 33-34
Robinson, Fred C., 73
Robinson, James K., 106
Robinson, S. C., 7
Robinson, W. R., 150, 161
Robinson, William H., 251
Robinson, William R., 234
Rocca, Luisa deV., 190
Roche, A. John, 34
Rock, Virginia, 251
Rocks, James E., 34, 99, 151, 186
Rodgers, Paul C., Jr., 73
Rodnon, Stewart, 73, 111
Rodrigues, Eusebio L., 97
Roemer, Kenneth M., 73, 80
Rogers, Douglas G., 141
Rogers, Franklin R., 73
Rogers, George C., Jr., 45
Rogers, Rodney O., 73
Rogers, Tommy W., 10, 13, 45, 84
Rogers, William W., 81
Roland, Charles P., 234
Rollins, Ronald G., 111
Roloff, Hans-Gert, 25
Rome, Joy J., 141
Rorem, Ned, 210
Rose, Alan H., 13 (2)
Rose, Marilyn G., 34
Rosen, Kenneth M., 56

Rosenberg, Bruce A., 141, 234
Rosenblatt, Roger, 234
Rosenfeld, Alvin H., 34
Rosenman, John, 141
Rosenshine, Annette, 164
Rosenthal, Bernard, 34
Rosenthal, M. L., 155
Ross, Michael L., 73
Ross, Stephen M., 141, 157
Rossky, William, 141
Rothman, Julius, 51-52
Rouberol, Jean, 141
Rougé, Robert, 234
Rountree, Thomas J., 34
Rouse, Blair, 80
Rouse, Parke, Jr., 1, 7
Rowell, Charles H., 197
Rowlette, Robert, 73-74
Rubens, Philip M., 141
Rubin, Larry, 151, 214
Rubin, Louis D., Jr., 53, 74, 81,
    85, 89, 141, 183, 184, 200,
    206, 214, 247, 251
Ruffini, Rosalia, 94
Ruiz Ruiz, José M., 141
Ruland, Richard, 52
Rule, Henry B., 74
Rulon, Curt M., 74
Ruoff, John C., 45
Ruotolo, Lucio P., 234
Rupp, Richard H., 234
Russ, Joanna, 34
Russell, Charles, 97
Russell, Diarmid, 206
Russell, J. Thomas, 34
Rust, Richard, 45, 74
Ryan, Marjorie, 97
Ryan, Pat M., 214
Ryssel, Fritz H., 214

Sachs, Viola, 141-142
Sagendorph, Robb, 252
Sale, Richard B., 101, 200
Salzberg, Joel, 34
Salzman, Jack, 164, 252
Samuels, C. T., 106, 148, 180
Samway, Patrick, 93, 142
Sanderlin, Robert R., 142
Sanders, Archie D., 111
Sanders, Frederick K., 94, 192
Sanders, Ronald, 221
Sanderson, J. L., 142
Sands, Kathleen, 34
Sanford, Charles L., 34
Santraud, J. M., 34
Sapper, Neil, 74
Savory, Jerold J., 221, 234
Saxon, John D., 234
Scafidel, Beverly, 12
Scafidel, James R., 14
Schaefer, Charles W., 34
Schäfer, Jürgen, 74
Schafer, William J., 111
Schatz, Walter, 253
Schechner, Richard, 226
Schechter, William, 253
Scheick, William J., 74
Scheideman, J. W., 164
Scheller, Bernhard, 153
Scherting, Jack, 74, 214
Schilmeister, Deborah, 52

Schinto, Jeanne, 74
Schlegel, Dorothy B., 52
Schlepper, Wolfgang, 142
Schley, Margaret A., 52
Schmid, Hans, 215
Schmitter, Dean M., 74, 142
Schmitz, Neil, 74, 184
Schmuhl, Robert, 142
Schneider, Duane, 215
Scholes, Robert, 97, 235
Schonhorn, Manuel, 74
Schorer, Mark, 235
Schrank, Bernice, 142
Schraufnagel, Noel, 235, 253
Schrero, Elliot M., 142
Schricke, Gilbert, 188
Schrock, E. F., 95
Schulman, Steven A., 253
Schulz, Max F., 98, 253
Schuster, Richard, 34
Schwaab, Eugene L., 45
Schwaber, Paul, 34
Schwartz, Arthur, 34
Schwartz, Delmore, 235
Schweninger, Loren, 46
Scott, Anne F., 253
Scott, Arthur L., 74
Scott, John A., 46
Scott, Nathan A., Jr., 235
Scouten, Arthur H., 200
Scouten, Kenneth, 174
Scrivner, Buford, Jr., 75
Scruggs, Charles W., 112, 196
Scura, Dorothy, 80, 235
Sears, Robert R., 74
Sederberg, Nancy B., 46
Sedlack, Robert P., 55
Seelye, John, 34, 75
Seib, Kenneth, 93
Seidl, Frances, 206
Selden, Samuel, 235
Selke, Hartmut K., 112
Seltzer, Leon F., 142
Semel, Jay M., 206
Senelick, Laurence, 34
Senna, Carl, 221
Sequira, Isaac, 112
Serio, John N., 34
Serrano-Plaja, Arturo, 75
Seyersted, Per, 56, 235
Seyppel, Joachim, 142
Shackford, James A., 10
Shands, Annette O., 157
Shankar, D. A., 100, 183
Shankman, Arnold, 152
Shapiro, Edward S., 104, 164, 235
Sharma, Mohan Lal, 75
Shartar, Martin, 165
Shavin, Norman, 165
Shaw, Barbara, 125
Shaw, F. H., 87
Shear, Walter, 174
Sheed, Wilfrid, 93, 235
Sheehan, Bernard W., 4
Sheehan, Donald W., 95
Sheehan, Peter J., 35
Sheffey, Ruthe, 235
Shelton, Frank W., 149
Shepherd, Allen, 93, 106, 142,
    148, 177, 181, 190, 200-
    201, 206

Sherman, Joan R., 84, 87
Sherr, Paul C., 221
Shillingsburg, Miriam J., 7, 40
Shimura, Masao, 98
Shingleton, Royce G., 46
Shinn, Thelma J., 174
Shirley, Wayne D., 153
Shockley, Ann A., 46
Shores, D. L., 235
Showett, H. K., 142
Shrell, Darwin H., 46, 75
Shulman, Robert, 35
Shuman, R. Baird, 211
Shuptrine, Hubert, 235
Shutt, James W., 164
Shyre, Paul, 164
Siegel, Paul N., 221
Siegle, Lin C., 52
Silva, Fred, 78
Silverman, Kenneth, 8
Silverstein, Norman, 106
Simkins, Francis B., 253
Simmonds, Roy S., 159
Simmons, James C., 201
Simms, L. Moody, Jr., 10, 38,
    49, 78, 81, 82 (3), 83, 85,
    86, 89, 103 (2), 150, 151,
    157, 175, 184, 185, 253
Simon, John, 211
Simonson, Harold P., 75
Simpson, Claude M., 75, 83
Simpson, H. A., 142
Simpson, Lewis P., 2, 46, 75,
    104, 142, 175, 207, 215, 235,
    253
Sims, James H., 35
Singh, Amritjit, 221
Singh, Hari, 215
Singh, Raman K., 178, 221, 235
Sippel, Erich W., 35
Sitkoff, Harvard, 190
Sitterson, J. Carlyle, 253
Skaggs, David C., 7
Skaggs, Merrill M., 253
Skaggs, Peggy, 56
Skallerup, Harry R., 4
Skeen, C. E., 8
Skerry, Philip J., 75
Skipp, Francis E., 215
Skloot, Robert, 211
Skotnicki, Irene, 161
Skow, John, 75, 181
Slack, Robert C., 201
Slavick, William H., 153
Slavitt, David R., 150
Slethaug, Gordon E., 98, 207
Sloane, David E. E., 35
Sloane, Karen, 89
Slotkin, Richard, 8
Smiley, David L., 11, 253
Smith, Allan, 35
Smith, Anneliese H., 174
Smith, Beverly E., 142
Smith, Carol P., 207
Smith, David, 103
Smith, Dorothy J., 75
Smith, Dwight L., 253
Smith, Francis J., 174
Smith, Gerald J., 14, 142-143
Smith, Herbert F., 35
Smith, Jo R., 184

Smith, Julian, 143
Smith, Lucian R., 75
Smith, Marcus, 155
Smith, Margarita G., 161
Smith, Patricia, 35
Smith, Raleigh W., Jr., 143
Smith, Raymond, 106
Smith, Robert A., 55
Smith, Sidonie Ann, 95, 221, 253
Smith, Stewart, 57
Smith, Winston, 12
Smitherman, Geneva, 235
Smuda, Manfred, 35
Sniderman, Florence M., 224
Snyder, William U., 215
Soderbergh, Peter A., 89-90
Solomon, Andrew, 75
Solomon, Eric, 143
Solomon, Jack, 75
Solotaroff, Theodore, 181, 235
Sommavilla, Guido, 98
Sonnenfeld, Albert, 174
Sorenson, Dale A., 143
Sosnoski, James J., 93
Soule, George H., Jr., 35
Southerland, Ellease, 154
Spacks, Patricia M., 80, 153
Spady, J. G., 100
Spangler, George M., 56, 75
Spearman, Walter, 235
Spears, James E., 143, 254
Spears, Monroe K., 106, 201
Spence, Jon, 180
Spencer, Paul, 52
Spiegel, Alan, 236
Spies, George H., III, 201
Spilka, Mark, 143
Spiller, Robert E., 254
Spitzer, Gary, 18
Spivey, Herman E., 143
Spivey, Ted R., 93, 94, 174
Spofford, William K., 75, 196
Sprandel, Katherine, 222
Squires, Radcliffe, 151, 192
Stafford, John S., 4
Stafford, T. J., 143
Stafford, William T., 143
Stamper, Rexford, 157
Standart, Phoebe, 75
Stanford, Donald E., 93, 151, 192, 207
Stanley, William T., 161
Stanton, Michael N., 2
Stanzel, Franz, 236
Staples, Hugh B., 155
Stark, John, 112, 143
Stark, John O., 98
Starke, Catherine J., 254
St. Armand, Barton L., 35, 254
Starnes, Leland, 211
Starobin, R. S., 46
Starr, Alvin, 222
Stauffer, Donald B., 35
Steele, Oliver, 80
Steelman, Lala C., 236
Steen, Ivan D., 46
Stein, A. F., 236
Stein, A. M., 35
Stein, Allen F., 35, 75
Stein, Marian L., 196
Steinbeck, Elaine, 236

Steinberg, Barbara, 149
Steiner, Susan, 250
Steinmann, Martin, Jr., 183
Stenerson, Douglas C., 164
Stephens, Martha, 174, 222
Stephens, Rosemary, 143
Stephenson, William, 106
Stern, Frederick, 236
Stern, Jerome, 165
Stern, Madeleine B., 35, 76, 254
Sternberg, Meir, 143
Stessin, Lawrence, 76
Stevens, Lauren R., 143
Stevenson, John W., 185
Stewart, Jack F., 143
Stewart, Randall, 254
Stock, Irvin, 236
Stockley, Barbara J., 244
Stoelting, Winifred L., 149
Stokes, Durward T., 12
Stone, Albert E., 11
Stone, Edward, 254
Stone, William B., 143, 207
Stoneback, H. R., 143
Stott, William M., 236
Stovall, Floyd, 35
Stowell, Robert, 76
Strandberg, Victor, 35, 144, 201
Straumann, Heinrich, 144
Strickland, Edward, 35
Stromberg, Jean S., 36
Stronks, James, 36
Strout, Cushing, 201
Strozier, Robert M., 100
Struthers, J. R., 236
Stuart, Jesse, 104
Stuckey, Sterling, 254
Stuckey, W. J., 151
Stuckey, William J., 207
Sturdevant, James R., 76
Sturm, D. N., 164
Styron, William, 215, 227
Sugg, Redding S., 113, 185, 211, 238
Sullivan, Margaret, 185
Sullivan, Philip E., 112
Sullivan, Ruth, 57, 144
Sullivan, Walter, 174-175, 180, 201, 236
Sumner, D. Nathan, 201
Suter, A., 190
Sutton, Henry, 98
Sutton, Robert P., 46
Sutton, W. A., 101
Swanson, William J., 190
Sweeney, Gerard M., 36
Sweet, Charles A., Jr., 36
Swink, Helen, 144
Sykes, Robert H., 76
Sylvander, Carolyn W., 112
Szeliski, John v., 211
Szwed, John F., 82, 254

Tabachnick, Stephen E., 94
Talbot, Frances G., 88
Talbott, Linda H., 76
Talmadge, John E., 81, 104
Tanner, Stephen, 98
Tanner, Tony, 98, 236
Tanselle, G. Thomas, 36
Tarbet, Donald W., 236

Tarbox, Raymond, 207
Tarpley, Fred, 254
Tarrant, Desmond, 52
Tate, Allen, 36, 144, 183, 254
Tate, J. O., 175
Tatham, Campbell, 76, 98, 222, 254
Taxel, Joel, 55
Taylor, Clyde, 196, 236
Taylor, Henry, 175
Taylor, Lewis J., Jr., 177
Taylor, Robert, Jr., 76
Taylor, W. D., 236
Taylor, Walter, 144
Taylor, Welford D., 85-86, 95, 254
Taylor, William E., 236
Tebbel, John, 254
Teller, Walter, 55
Terrier, Michel, 236
Teunissen, John J., 36
Thale, Jerome, 177
Thale, Mary, 177
Tharpe, Jac, 98, 236
Thelwell, Mike, 190
Thomas, C. E., 40
Thomas, Charles E., 46
Thomas, Dwight, 36
Thomas, H. F., 152
Thomas, M. Wynn, 180
Thompson, G. R., 36
Thompson, James J., Jr., 101
Thompson, L. S., 254
Thompson, Larry E., 196
Thompson, Victor H., 207
Thorburn, Neil, 185
Thornbrough, Emma Lou, 87
Thornton, Weldon, 144
Thorp, Willard, 192, 236
Thurman, William R., 185
Tilton, John W., 98
Timmerman, John, 36, 222
Tischler, Nancy M., 211, 237, 254
Titus, Warren I., 79
Tobin, Patricia, 144
Todd, W. B., 76
Toledano, Ben C., 237
Tomlinson, David, 40
Torres, Esther Z., 224
Towers, Tom H., 76
Towery, Patricia, 46
Towns, Stuart, 237, 255
Trachtenberg, Alan, 76
Trachtenberg, Stanley, 98
Tracy, Robert, 76
Tragle, Henry I., 42, 190
Travis, Mildred K., 37, 144, 207
Trensky, Anne, 76
Trieber, J. Marshall, 37
Trimmer, Joseph F., 112, 144
Trimmier, Dianne B., 102
Troubetzkoy, Ulrich, 37
Trousdale, Marion, 102
Trowbridge, Clinton W., 159, 175
True, Michael D., 175
Tucker, Edward L., 10 (2), 46, 79, 144
Tuckey, John S., 76
Tuerk, Richard, 37
Tumlin, John, 81
Turaj, Frank, 164

Turnbull, Andrew, 215
Turner, Arlin, 53-54, 76, 81, 82, 144, 255
Turner, D. R., 76
Turner, Darwin T., 81, 90, 112, 196, 222, 237, 255
Tuso, Joseph F., 144
Tuttle, William M., Jr., 255
Tutwiler, Carrington, 80
Twining, Mary A., 255
Tyms, James D., 237
Tynan, Daniel J., 37
Tyner, Troi, 144

Uhlman, Thompson, 192
Ulich, Michaela, 145
Umphlett, Wiley Lee, 237
Underhill, Irving S., 77
Untermeyer, Louis, 52, 77
Urang, Gunnar, 190
Utley, Francis L., 145

Vance, W. S., 157
Van Cleave, Jim, 177
Van Cromphout, Gustaav V., 145
Vande Kieft, Ruth, 145, 175, 207
Van Der Beets, Richard, 59
Vanderbilt, Kermit, 37, 77
Vandersee, Charles, 77
Vanderwerken, D. L., 102
Van Doren, Charles L., 255
Van Nostrand, A. D., 255
van Pelt, C. B., 4
Varnado, S. L., 37
Vauthier, Simone, 41, 99, 148, 157, 177, 181, 201
Veler, Richard P., 37
Vendler, Helen, 95
Verble, David, 237
Verzosa, Guillermina L., 98
Via, Dan O., Jr., 190
Vickery, John B., 145
Vickery, Olga W., 145
Vinson, Audrey L., 145
Vinson, James, 237
Virtanen, Reino, 37
Vitanza, Victor J., 37
Vitt-Maucher, Gisela, 37
Voelker, Joseph C., 98
Vogler, Thomas A., 112
Volpe, Edmond L., 145
Vorpahl, Ben M., 77, 145
Vos, Nelvin, 211
Voss, Arthur, 255
Voyles, Jimmy P., 82

Wade, Margaret, 255
Wade, Melvin, 255
Wagenknecht, Edward, 52, 77
Wager, Willis, 255
Wages, Jack D., 8, 37
Waggoner, Hyatt A., 145, 255
Wagner, J., 255
Wagner, Linda W., 145
Wagner, Paul R., 6
Wakelyn, Jon L., 41
Walcott, Ronald, 99, 112
Walcutt, Charles C., 255
Walden, Daniel, 243
Waldrip, Louise, 180
Waldron, Edward E., 196

Waldrop, Keith, 42
Walhout, Clarence P., 145
Walker, Franklin, 77
Walker, Hugh, 255
Walker, I. M., 77
Walker, Marshall, 201
Walker, Ronald G., 55, 145
Walker, S. Jay, 154
Wall, Carey, 146
Wallace, Alfred R., 37
Walling, William, 112
Wallsten, Robert, 236
Walne, Peter, 6
Walser, Richard, 5, 13, 255
Walsh, John, 37
Walsh, Thomas F., 37, 180
Walston, Rosa Lee, 175
Walt, James, 164
Walter, James F., 98, 146
Walters, Dorothy, 175
Walters, T. N., 236
Walters, Thomas N., 77
Walther, John D., 215
Walton, Gerald W., 146
Wander, P. C., 46
Waniek, Marilyn N., 237
Wank, Martin, 215
Ward, A. C., 237
Wardenaar, Leslie A., 1
Warfel, Harry R., 84
Waring, Joseph I., 46
Warner, Richard, 52
Warnken, William P., 57
Warren, Austin, 192
Warren, George T., 165
Warren, Joyce W., 146
Warren, Robert Penn, 77, 159, 183, 227
Washington, Mary Helen, 154
Wasson, Richard, 98
Waterman, Arthur E., 94
Watkins, Floyd C., 146, 150, 165, 237
Watkins, Patricia, 196
Watkins, T. H., 77
Watson, Charles N., Jr., 37, 46
Watson, Charles S., 41, 256
Watson, Edward A., 222
Watson, H. R., 8
Watson, James G., 146
Watson, V. Sterling, 103
Weales, Gerald, 237
Weatherby, H. L., 159, 256
Weatherford, Richard M., 85
Weathersby, Robert W., II, 13
Weaver, Gordon, 86, 107
Weaver, Richard M., 90
Weaver, William, 77
Webb, Constance, 222
Webb, Max, 237
Webb, James W., 146
Weber, Alfred, 102, 237
Weber, Robert, 183
Weber, Robert W., 146
Weber, Ronald, 215
Weeks, Lewis E., Jr., 77
Wegelin, Christof, 146
Weidman, Bette S., 37, 41
Weigel, Henrietta, 222
Weil, Dorothy, 100
Weiner, Bruce I., 38

Weinberg, Helen A., 237
Weinstein, Arnold L., 146
Weinstein, Sharon R., 112
Weintraub, Rodelle, 77
Weisberg, Robert, 155
Weisberger, B. A., 87
Weisgerber, Jean, 146
Weiss, Adrian, 222
Weiss, Gerhard, 230
Weiss, Miriam, 146
Weixlmann, Joseph W., 98
Welch, Emmons, 52
Welland, Dennis, 77
Wellek, René, 100
Wellman, Manly W., 12
Wells, Daniel A., 38
Wells, David M., 77
Welsh, John R., 9, 10, 46, 178, 238
Werge, Thomas, 77
Wertz, Linda L., 38
Wertz, S. K., 38
West, Harry C., 12, 178
West, James L. W. III, 46, 165, 190
West, Ray B., Jr., 238
Westburg, Barry, 38
Westendorp, T. A., 238
Westerfield, Hargis, 196
Weston, Robert, 159
Wexman, Virginia, 77
Weygand, J. L., 238
Whalum, Wendell P., 157
Wheeler, Otis B., 57
Wheeler, Sally P., 147
Wheelock, C. Webster, 77
Whisenhunt, D. W., 238
White, Arthur O., 87
White, Dana, 86
White, Helen, 113, 149, 211, 238
White, John, 190
White, Robert B., Jr., 175
White, William, 82
Whitesell, J. E., 255
Whitla, William, 38
Whitlow, Roger, 238, 256
Whitman, A., 183
Whitman, Sarah Helen, 38
Whitney, Blair, 190
Whittington, Curtis, Jr., 201-202
Whittington, M. J., 177
Wickes, George, 102
Wideman, John, 55
Wiemann, Renate, 190
Wiesenfarth, Joseph, 180
Wigley, Joseph A., 147
Wikborg, Eleanor, 161
Wilbur, Richard, 38
Wilcox, Earl, 202
Wilgus, D. K., 256
Wilkerson, Margaret, 190
Wilkinson, Doris Y., 153
Williams, Benjamin B., 256
Williams, George, 153
Williams, H. G., 8
Williams, John A., 112, 222
Williams, John S., 147
Williams, Kenny J., 256
Williams, Leonard, 14
Williams, M., 238
Williams, Miller, 183

Williams, Ora G., 147, 256
Williams, Sherley Anne, 149
Williams, William H. A., 165
Williams, Wirt, 148
Williamson, Chilton, Jr., 165
Willig, Charles L., 106
Willimon, W. H., 90
Willingham, Calder, 101
Willis, Katherine J., 81
Wilner, Eleanor R., 112
Wilson, Edmund, 78, 165
Wilson, Gayle E., 147
Wilson, G. R., Jr., 147
Wilson, Henry B., 165
Wilson, James D., 38, 78, 175, 238
Wilson, Major L., 46
Wilson, Mark K., 78
Wilson, Mary Ann, 147
Wilson, Robert R., 147
Wilt, Napier, 47
Wimsatt, Mary Ann, 41
Wingate, P. J., 165
Winn, James A., 147
Winton, Calhoun, 8

Wintz, Cary D., 55
Witt, R. W., 202
Witte, Flo, 202
Wolff, Cynthia G., 57
Wolff, Geoffrey, 180, 193
Woodberry, George E., 38
Woodbery, Potter, 147
Woodbridge, Hensley C., 38, 186
Woodress, James, 256
Woods, Samuel H., Jr., 182
Woodson, Thomas, 38
Woodward, C. Vann, 87, 238
Woodward, Robert H., 147
Woolmer, J. H., 238
Wreszin, Michael, 190
Wright, Nathalia, 83
Wright, T. K., 255
Wrobel, Arthur, 42
Wycherley, H. Alan, 165
Wylder, Jean, 175
Wynne, Judith F., 175
Wysong, Jack P., 78

Yanella, Philip R., 181

Yardley, Jonathan, 86, 107, 238
Yeh-Wei-Yu, Frederick, 159
Yellin, Jean F., 47
Yoder, Edwin M., Jr., 90, 238
Yonce, Margaret, 38, 147
Young, Glenn, 147
Young, James O., 238
Young, Thomas Daniel, 82, 103, 104, 183, 191–192, 192, 198, 222, 225, 238, 256
Yu, Beongcheon, 78

Zacharias, Lee, 102
Zaraspe, Raquel S., 78
Zellegrow, Ken, 147
Zender, Karl F., 147
Zeugner, John F., 177
Zimmerman, Melvin, 38
Zindel, Edith, 147
Zlotnick, Joan, 57
Zug, Charles G., III, 238
Zwahlen, Christine, 78
Zweig, Paul, 95
Zyla, W. T., 147, 238